COLLINS
COBUILD

POCKET IDIOMS
DICTIONARY

**THE UNIVERSITY
OF BIRMINGHAM**

**COLLINS
COBUILD**

HarperCollins*Publishers*

HarperCollins Publishers
77-85 Fulham Palace Road
London   W6 8JB

COBUILD is a trademark of William Collins Sons & Co Ltd

© HarperCollins Publishers Ltd 1996
First published in Great Britain 1996

2 4 6 8 1 0 9 7 5 3 1

ISBN 0 00 375095 7

Computer typeset by Jeremy Clear.

Printed and bound in Great Britain by
Caledonian International Book Manufacturing Ltd, Glasgow, G64.

Corpus Acknowledgements

We would like to acknowledge the assistance of the many hundreds of
individuals and companies who have kindly given permission for
copyright material to be used in The Bank of English. The written
sources include many national and regional newspapers in Britain and
overseas; magazine and periodical publishers; and book publishers in
Britain, the United States, and Australia. Extensive spoken data has
been provided by radio and television broadcasting companies; research
workers at many universities and other institutions; and numerous
individual contributors. We are grateful to them all.

Note

Entered words that we have reason to believe constitute trademarks
have been designated as such. However, neither the presence nor absence
of such designation should be regarded as affecting the
legal status of any trademark.

Editorial Team

Founding Editor in Chief
John Sinclair

Editorial Director
Gwyneth Fox

Editorial Manager
Rosamund Moon

Editors

David Morrow   Elizabeth Potter   Miranda Timewell

Computer Staff
Tim Lane
Mike Ashton

The Bank of English
Jeremy Clear
Ramesh Krishnamurthy

Secretarial Staff
Sue Crawley
Michelle Devereux

Design and Production
Ray Barnett
Jill McNair

Managing Director, Collins Dictionaries
Robin Wood

Acknowledgements

We would like to thank Jenny Watson for her invaluable assistance during the final stages of this dictionary. We would also like to thank and acknowledge all those who worked on the COBUILD Dictionary of Idioms, on which this dictionary is based: in particular, Jane Bradbury, Michael Lax, and John Todd.

Introduction

The **COBUILD Pocket Dictionary of Idioms** is the second title in the new
COBUILD series of small format dictionaries. It has been specially adapted
from the COBUILD Dictionary of Idioms.

An idiom is a special kind of phrase. It is a group of words which have a
different meaning when used together from the one it would have if the
meaning of each word were taken individually. For example, *bite someone's
head off* means to speak to them in an unpleasant, angry way: it has nothing
to do with causing them physical harm.

In the COBUILD Pocket Dictionary of Idioms, we deal with over 3000 idioms
in current British and American English. We illustrate them with over 3000
examples, taken from The Bank of English. These examples show how
idioms are used in real English.

The COBUILD Pocket Dictionary of Idioms pays special attention to the
ways in which idioms vary. Our explanations of idioms, written in full
sentences, give the meanings of idioms and the contexts in which they are
typically used. They also show clearly the pragmatic functions of idioms: the
ways in which they are used to express evaluations or show approval or
disapproval. This is a very important part of idiom use in English. More
detailed information about idiom variations, idiom frequencies, and
pragmatics can be found in the bigger COBUILD Dictionary of Idioms.

A new feature in the COBUILD Pocket Dictionary of Idioms is that we have
included accounts of the origins of idioms, to try to show how these
expressions have developed their current idiomatic meanings. It is important to remember that there are only a few idioms whose histories and
origins we can be certain about. In many cases, there is a lot of argument
about their origins. Although scholars have suggested explanations which
are possible or likely, nobody really knows for sure.

There is a workbook on idioms, the **COBUILD Idioms Workbook**, which
can be used with the COBUILD Pocket Dictionary of Idioms. This workbook
was written by Malcolm Goodale, and it concentrates on 250 of the idioms in
the dictionary.

We hope that you find the COBUILD Pocket Dictionary of Idioms useful,
easy to use, and interesting. If you have any comments or suggestions, we
would be delighted to hear from you. You can e-mail us at
editors@cobuild.collins.co.uk.

Rosamund Moon, Editorial Manager

Guide to the Dictionary Entries

How to find the idiom you are looking for

In the main dictionary text, idioms are grouped under headwords, which are arranged alphabetically. Use the index, which is at the back of the dictionary, to find out which headword the idiom you are looking for is under. You will see that one of the words in each idiom is highlighted: this is the headword in the main text where you will find the idiom. Note that idioms are placed under a headword which corresponds exactly to one of the words in the idiom. For example, *spill the beans* is under **beans** rather than **bean**. However, if the idiom is a variant form, it may be dealt with under a headword which is not one of the words in the form of the idiom that you are looking for. In these cases, there is a cross-reference in the index to the right headword.

Generally, the word we choose as headword is a noun. If there are two nouns, then the headword is the first noun. If the idiom contains no nouns, then an adjective is chosen. If the idiom contains no nouns or adjectives, then the headword will be either a verb or an adverb.

There are four main exceptions to this general rule:

1. The word chosen as headword is normally a fixed word in the idiom: that is, it never varies. If there is only one noun in the idiom and it varies, we have chosen to put the idiom under another word which is fixed. For example, *beat your breast* has a common variation *beat your chest*, and so you will find the idiom under the verb **beat**.

2. Occasionally, our rule for choosing headwords would mean that two idioms which contain similar words would end up in very different parts of the dictionary. In this case, we put them under the same headword. For example, we put both a *fair crack of the whip* and *crack the whip* under the headword **whip**.

3. If an idiom contains two nouns, but the first noun is a very general word such as 'end' or 'top', then the idiom will be found at the second noun.

4. Finally, similes such as *white as a sheet* are always dealt with under their adjectives rather than under their nouns.

Order of idioms

Under each headword, idioms are arranged in alphabetical order. Note, however, that if the first word in an idiom is 'a' or 'the', it is not taken into account in the alphabetical ordering. Major variant forms are given underneath the main form, but do not affect the alphabetical ordering of the main forms.

Explanations of meanings, pragmatics, and usage

The explanations in this dictionary, as in other COBUILD dictionaries, are written in full sentences using language which is as simple as possible. Where idioms have two or more different meanings, these are dealt with in separate numbered paragraphs.

The dictionary explanations show where idioms have some special pragmatic function such as conveying an opinion, emphasizing, or criticizing. For example, the formula 'If you say that... you mean that...' shows that an idiom is used to convey an opinion or evaluation.

The explanations also give information about the likely contexts in which idioms are used, in particular where there are restrictions. If an idiom is used only or mainly in one geographical variety of English, we show this at the beginning of the explanation, for example by putting 'British' or 'mainly American'. Idioms that are considered dated are labelled 'old-fashioned'. If an idiom may cause offence, we say so at the end of the explanation.

Extra information

Two symbols are used in this dictionary, □ and ♦. Both indicate that we have included extra information about the idiom. The paragraphs marked □ contain information about variations which need special comment. They are also used to give the full forms of proverbs and sayings which are used in shortened forms as other kinds of idiom.

The symbol ♦ indicates information about the origins of idioms. When it comes directly under the headword, the information that it gives applies to all the idioms under that headword. When it comes at the bottom of an idiom entry, the information that it gives applies only to the idiom in that entry. ♦ is also occasionally used to give information about variant spellings of one of the words in the idiom.

Cross-references

There are three types of cross-reference. The first type comes at the end of the explanation and begins with the word 'Compare'. This refers you to another idiom which has a similar form to the one you are looking at, or which may be confused with it. The second type also comes at the end of the explanation and is used where idioms are restricted to British (or American) English and have close counterparts in American (or British) English. The third type of cross-reference comes in the explanations of idiom origins and tells you that there is another idiom whose origin is related in some way to the one you are looking at.

A

ace

◆ In many card games, the ace is the card with the highest score.

the ace in your hand

British If you have **the ace in** your **hand**, you have something which you can use to gain an advantage when you need it. *You have to convince your opponent that you have the ace in your hand. Especially in politics. Everyone bluffs in politics.*

have an ace in the hole

American If you **have an ace in the hole**, you have something which you can use to gain an advantage when you need it. *He doesn't usually risk that much unless he thinks he has an ace in the hole.*

◆ In 'stud' poker, you have an ace in the hole when you have an ace as your 'hole' card: see 'hole card' at **hole**.

play your ace

If someone **plays** their **ace**, they do something clever and unexpected which gives them an advantage over other people. *She went on to say that he was also a very important criminal lawyer who had defended men on heavy charges. And then she played her ace. He also had a number of clients who were involved in the gold business.*

within an ace of something

Mainly British If you say that someone comes **within an ace of** something, you mean that they very nearly succeed in doing it. *She had just watched her hero come within an ace of a place in the Wimbledon quarter finals, only to lose his grip on the game.*

◆ In this expression, 'ace' refers to a score of one on a dice, rather than a playing card.

aces

◆ In many card games, the ace is the card with the highest score.

hold all the aces

If you say that someone **holds all the aces**, you mean that they are in a very strong position because they have more advantages and more power than anyone else. *They hold all the aces and are not going to make changes voluntarily because it wouldn't be in their own interests.*

acid

the acid test

If you refer to something as **the acid test**, you mean that it will show or prove how effective or useful something is. *The acid test for the vaccine will be its performance in African countries where malaria is raging more fiercely than in Colombia.*

◆ Nitric acid can be used to test whether a metal is pure gold because it corrodes most metals but does not affect gold.

act

◆ The metaphors in these expressions relate to performers entertaining audiences.

a balancing act

If you say that someone is performing **a balancing act**, you mean that they are trying to please two or more people or groups or to follow two or more sets of ideals that are in opposition to each other. *Mr Alia is performing a delicate balancing act. He talks of reform, but clings to old certainties.*

a class act

If you say that someone, for example a sports player or a performer, is **a class act**, you mean that they are very good at what they do. *Koeman is a class act. He's got great control and can hit passes from one side of the pitch to the other with amazing accuracy.*

clean up your act

If a person or organization **cleans up** their **act**, they stop behaving badly or irresponsibly, and begin to act in a more socially acceptable way. *The Minister warned the press two years ago that privacy laws would be implemented unless newspapers cleaned up their act.*

get in on the act

If you **get in on the act**, you start doing something which was first done by someone else, usually so that you can have the same success as them, or get some advantage for yourself. *It is rather like the Greens in Britain in the eighties: everyone wants to get in on the act.*

get your act together

If you say that someone needs to **get their act together**, you mean that they need to take control of themselves and to organize their affairs more effectively so that they can deal successfully with things and can avoid failure. *The State Opposition is beginning to get its act together after a long period of muddling through.*

a hard act to follow

If you say that someone is **a hard act to follow**, you mean that they are so impressive or so effective that it will be difficult for anyone else to be as good or as successful. *He had a hard act to follow. His predecessor was a brilliant intellectual who also drew, as Chancellor, on long practical experience as an observer of the economic scene.*

actions

actions speak louder than words

If you say that **actions speak louder than words**, you mean that people show what they really think and feel by what they do, rather than by what they say. People sometimes use this expression when they want to criticize someone who says one thing but does something else. *Codes of Discipline should encompass procedure for dealing with harassment. However, actions speak louder than words. Elaborate policies and procedures in themselves would not achieve much without commitment to change from the top.*

Adam

not know someone from Adam

If you say that you **don't know** someone **from Adam**, you mean that you do not know them at all, and would not recognize them if you saw them. *We'll have one contact, who is simply a voice on the phone to us. I don't know him from Adam.*

◆ According to the Bible, Adam was the first human being.

ado

much ado about nothing

If you say that people are making **much ado about nothing**, you mean that they are making a lot of fuss about something which is not as important or significant as they think it is. *After one year, I dropped out of the course because it was much ado about nothing really. It was all about style, not about content.*

◆ 'Much Ado About Nothing' is the title of a play by Shakespeare.

air

clear the air

If you do something to **clear the air**, you deal openly with misunderstandings, problems, or jealousy, and try to get rid of them. *Some groups in our community seem to suffer from discrimination. An independent enquiry could clear the air and sort out the problem.*

hot air

If you describe what someone says or writes as **hot air**, you are criticizing it for being full of false claims and promises. *In a sense, all the rhetoric about heightened co-operation can be seen as just so much hot air. There are still endless disputes.*

in the air

If something such as a change, idea, or feeling is **in the air**, people are aware of it or think it is going to happen even though it is not talked about directly. *Great excitement was in the air that week in London and, as the newspapers reported, in Paris, Berlin and St Petersburg as well.*

into thin air
out of thin air

If someone or something vanishes **into thin air**, they disappear completely and nobody knows where they have gone. If something appears **out of thin air**, it appears suddenly and unexpectedly. *Her husband snatched their two children and disappeared into thin air for years... A crisis had materialised out of thin air.*

up in the air

If an important decision or plan is **up in the air**, it has not been decided or settled yet. *At the moment, the fate of the Hungarian people is still up in the air.*

walk on air
float on air

If you say that you **are walking on air** or **floating on air**, you mean that you feel very happy or excited because of something nice that has happened to you. *As soon as I know I'm in the team it's like walking on air... I can't believe that I've won. I'm floating on air.*

airs

airs and graces
put on airs and graces
put on airs

If you say that someone has **airs and graces**, you disapprove of them for behaving in a way which shows that they think they are more important than other people. You can also say that someone **puts on airs and graces** or **puts on airs**. The form 'airs and graces' is used only in British English. *Ian is such a nice bloke. He has no airs and graces... He put on no airs, but his charisma was enormous.*

aisles

roll in the aisles

If you say that people in an audience or group **are rolling in the aisles**, you mean that they are laughing so much at something that they find it hard to stop. Verbs such as 'rock', 'reel', and 'laugh' are sometimes used instead of 'roll'. *It's all good knockabout stuff that has them rolling in the aisles... On the evidence so far, it's unlikely that the story-lines will have us reeling in the aisles.*

♦ The aisles in a theatre or cinema are the gaps between the blocks of seats.

alec

a smart alec
a smart aleck

If you describe someone as **a smart alec**, you dislike the fact that they think they are very clever and they always have an answer for everything. The spelling **a smart aleck** is also used, especially in American English. *They've got some smart alec of a lawyer from London to oppose bail, and by God they're not going to get away with it... I hate smart-aleck kids who talk like dictionaries.*

alley

a blind alley

If you refer to a way of working or thinking as **a blind alley**, you mean that it is useless or is not leading to anything worthwhile. *Did she regard teaching as a blind alley?*

♦ A blind alley is a street which is closed at one end.

right up your alley

If you say that something is **right up** your **alley**, you mean that it is the kind of thing you like or know about. *I thought this little problem would be right up your alley.*

☐ You can also say that something is **right down** your **alley**. *I'll need* *whatever information you can turn up within the week. I have other people looking into this from other angles. But this case seems right down your alley.*

all-singing

all-singing, all-dancing

If you describe something new as **all-singing, all-dancing**, you mean that it is very modern and advanced, with a lot of additional facilities. This expression is used more commonly in British English than American. *As long as you don't expect the latest all-singing, all-dancing Japanese marvel, the camera represents an excellent buy – and one that I can recommend.*

altar

sacrificed on the altar of something

You say that someone or something **is being sacrificed on the altar of** a particular ideology or activity when they suffer unfairly and are harmed because of it. *The European Community remains adamant that the interests of its twelve million farmers can't be sacrificed on the altar of free trade.*

American

American as apple pie

If you say that something or someone is as **American as apple pie**, you mean that they are typical of American culture or an American way of life. *Zurmo's family has been in the gun business for 60 years. To him, guns are as American as apple pie.*

◆ Apple pie is a traditional dessert that is thought of as typically American.

ante

◆ In card games such as poker, the ante is the amount of money which each player must place on the table before the game begins.

up the ante: 1
raise the ante

In a dispute or contest, if you **up the ante** or **raise the ante**, you increase the demands that you are making or the risks that you are taking, which means that your eventual losses or gains will be greater. *Whenever they reached their goal, they upped the ante, setting increasingly* *complex challenges for themselves.*

up the ante: 2
raise the ante

If you are investing money in something and you **up the ante** or **raise the ante**, you increase the value of the investment you are offering. *Its network television division upped the ante by paying an estimated $2 million a year for an overall deal.*

ape

go ape
go ape crazy

If someone **goes ape** or **goes ape crazy**, they start to behave in an uncontrolled or irrational way, for example because they are very excited or very angry about something. *The guitar player is a hairy heavy metal fan who runs home from rehearsals to go ape to the sound of Slayer, Rush, Megadeth and Metallica.*

appetite

whet someone's appetite

If something **whets** your **appetite** for a particular thing, it increases your desire for that thing or other similar things. *Winning the World Championship should have whetted his appetite for more success.*

◆ To whet a knife means to sharpen it.

apple

the apple of your eye

If you say that someone is **the apple of** your **eye**, you mean that you are very fond of them. *I was the apple of my father's eye.*

◆ In the past, the pupil in the eye was sometimes called the apple.

a bad apple
a rotten apple
a bad apple spoils the barrel

If you refer to someone as **a bad apple** or as **a rotten apple**, you mean that they are very dishonest, immoral, or unpleasant, and that they have a bad influence on the people around them. *It's an opportunity for them to make clear that they are not going to tolerate a bad apple in the United States Senate.*

☐ People talk about **a bad apple** or **a rotten apple spoiling the barrel** when they are talking particularly about the bad influence which the person has. *Let's be positive, not negative. One bad apple doesn't spoil the barrel... He says there are some rotten apples in our security barrel.*

◆ If a rotten apple is stored with good apples, it causes the good ones to rot.

applecart

upset the applecart
overturn the applecart

If someone or something **upsets the applecart** or **overturns the applecart**, they do something which causes trouble or which spoils a satisfactory situation. *Their acquisition of nuclear arms could upset the whole Asian applecart.*

apple-pie

in apple-pie order

Fairly old-fashioned If someone says that everything is **in apple-pie order**, they mean that everything in a place is very neat, tidy, and well-organized. *On the upper deck everything was very much in apple pie order.*

apples

apples and oranges

Mainly American If you say that two things are **apples and oranges** or that comparing them is like comparing **apples with oranges**, you are pointing out that these things are completely different in every respect. *We really can't compare the data any more, it's not the same, it's just apples and oranges.*

apron

apron strings: 1

If you say that one person is tied to another's **apron strings**, you are criticizing the first person for remaining dependent at an age when they should be independent. If someone cuts the **apron strings**, they become independent from the other person. *At 21, I was still living the life I'd been living when I was 15. I just had to get away from that, to cut those apron strings.*

apron strings: 2

If you say that a country or institution is tied to another's **apron strings**, you mean that the first country or institution is controlled by the second when you think it should be independent. If they cut the **apron strings**, they become independent from the other country or institution. *Today few big pension funds remain tied by company apron-strings.*

◆ This expression was originally used to refer to a child, particularly a boy, who remained too much under the influence of his mother at an age when he should have become independent.

area

a grey area

If you refer to something as **a grey area**, you mean that it is unclear, or that it does not fall into a specific category of things, so that nobody knows how to deal with it properly. *The court action to decide ownership of Moon Shadow has highlighted the many grey areas in the law affecting stolen animals.*

◆ 'Grey' is also spelled 'gray', especially in American English.

ark

out of the ark
go out with the ark

British If you say that something is **out of the ark**, you are complaining in a light-hearted way that it is very old-fashioned and outdated. You can also say that something **went out with the ark** when you want to say that it is completely outdated. *Its steering was simply dreadful and its cramped-up short-arm driving position was straight out of the ark... You know tyres are made from oil, they're not made from rubber any more; that went out with the ark.*

◆ According to the Bible, the ark was the boat in which Noah and his family survived the flood.

arm

at arm's length: 1

If you keep someone **at arm's length**, you avoid being friendly with them or getting emotionally involved with them. *Brian felt more guilt than grief. He'd tried to get close, but his father had kept him at arm's length.*

at arm's length: 2

You can say that one person or organization is **at arm's length** from another when they are not closely connected, for example because it would be improper for them to influence one another. *The prison service is moving towards becoming a self-regulating agency at arm's length from government.*

chance your arm

British If you **chance** your **arm**, you do something risky or daring in order to get something you want. *Sport is about going out and giving it your best shot, chancing your arm for glory. What is there to be frightened about?*

cost an arm and a leg

If you say that something **costs an arm and a leg**, you are emphasizing that it costs a lot of money. *It cost us an arm and a leg to get here. But it has been worth every penny and more.*

give your right arm

If you say that you would **give** your **right arm** for something or to do something, you are emphasizing that you want it a lot, and you would do almost anything to get it. *I can do nothing but think about my ex-husband. I would give my right arm to be able to start again.*

◆ Most people are right-handed, and so consider their right arm as more important than their left.

put the arm on someone

American If you **put the arm on** someone, you try to force them to do what you want. *Women like you are not only writing checks, but you're putting the arm on other people to give as well.*

twist someone's arm

If you say that someone **is twisting** your **arm** to make you do something, you mean that they are trying hard to persuade you to do it. *I didn't twist your arm to make you come. You wanted to because you sensed a story.*

□ You can also talk about **arm-twisting**. *He borrowed 70 per cent of the dividend-money from his banks, after some arm-twisting.*

arms

up in arms

If someone is **up in arms** about something, they are very angry about it and are protesting strongly. *More than one million shopkeepers are up in arms against the new minimum tax. They are threatening a day's closure in protest.*

♦ 'Arms' in this expression means weapons.

arrow

a straight arrow

Mainly American If you describe someone as **a straight arrow**, you mean that they are very conventional, honest, and moral. *I was very much a product of my environment. I was very traditional, a real straight arrow in lots of ways… It was impossible to imagine such a well-scrubbed, straight-arrow group of young people rioting over anything – except perhaps the number of chocolate chips in the dining hall cookies.*

axe (*American* ax)

an axe hanging over something

If you say that there is **an axe hanging over** something, you mean that it is likely to be destroyed soon. If you say that there is **an axe hanging over** someone, you mean that they are likely to lose their job soon. *The axe was hanging over 600 jobs at oil giant BP last night.*

get the axe: 1

If someone **gets the axe**, they lose their job. *During the 1981 recession, most layoffs hurt factory or construction workers. But this time, business managers, executives and technical staff are getting the axe.*

get the axe: 2

If something such as a project or part of a business **gets the axe**, it is cancelled or ended suddenly. *There will be cuts of $170 billion in defense, and almost $120 billion in domestic spending. Any idea what specific programs will get the ax?*

have an axe to grind

If you say that someone **has an axe to grind**, you mean that they have particular attitudes and prejudices about something, often because they think they have been treated badly or because they want to get a personal advantage. *Lord Gifford believed cases should be referred by an independent agency which, as he put it, doesn't have an axe to grind.*

♦ There are several explanations for the origin of this expression. One is a story told by Benjamin Franklin about a man who managed to get his own axe sharpened by asking a boy to show him how his father's grindstone worked.

B

babes

babes in the wood

You refer to people as **babes in the wood** when they are naive, innocent, and inexperienced, and they are involved in a complex situation where they are likely to be exploited or have problems. *They come from a country that is monolingual and monocultural and has been for thousands of years. They're like babes in the woods when it comes to trying to deal with this multi-ethnic society that we all just take for granted.*

◆ An old story tells of two young orphans who were left in the care of their uncle. If the children died, the uncle would inherit the family fortune. The uncle ordered a servant to take them into a wood where they died and their bodies were covered with leaves by the birds. There is a pantomime based on this story.

baby

leave someone holding the baby

British If you **are left holding the baby**, you are made responsible for a problem that nobody else wants to deal with. *If anything goes wrong on this, Agnes, it's you and I who'll be left holding the baby, not our clever friend.*

throw the baby out with the bath water

If you warn someone not to **throw the baby out with the bath water**, you are warning them not to reject something completely just because parts of it are bad, as you think that other parts of it are good. *By excluding the only member of the squad with any real experience of Olympic tensions and strains, the selection committee have thrown the baby out with the bath water.*

back

behind your back

If someone says something about you **behind** your **back**, they say unkind and unpleasant things about you to other people. If someone does something **behind** your **back**, they do it secretly in order to harm you. *I knew behind his back his friends were saying, 'How can he possibly put up with that awful woman?'... He had discovered that it was safer to have the Press on his side than to have correspondents sneaking around behind his* *back asking embarrassing questions.*

break the back of something: 1

If you **break the back of** a task, you deal with the most difficult parts of it or the main part of it. *The new government hopes to have broken the back of the economic crisis by the middle of this year. If it fails in this task, then the political consequences could be disastrous.*

break the back of something: 2

To **break the back of** something means to do something which will weaken it and lead to its eventual destruction. *Arms cuts should not be implemented too quickly or they'll break the back of his country's armed forces.*

get someone's back up

If you say that someone or something **gets** your **back up**, you mean that they annoy you. *I thought before I spoke again. The wrong question was going to get her back up.*

◆ This expression may refer to cats arching their backs when they are angry.

get your own back

British If someone **gets** their **own back** on you, they take revenge on you because of something that you have done to them. *A disgruntled worker got his own back after rowing with his boss by locking the whole firm out of the computer system.*

have your back to the wall

If you say that someone **has** their **back to the wall**, you mean that they have very serious problems or are in a very difficult situation, which will be hard to deal with. *Battered by the economic situation and unable to provide any long-term answer to the terrorism, the fledgling Labour government had its back to the wall.*

off the back of a lorry

British If someone says that something has fallen **off the back of a lorry**, or that they got something **off the back of a lorry**, they mean that they have bought something that was stolen. *The only evidence of any criminal tendencies is that Pete once bought the boys a bicycle cheap off the back of a lorry.*

on someone's back
get off someone's back

If you say that someone is **on** your **back**, you are complaining that they are annoying you by criticizing you and putting a lot of pressure on you. If you tell someone to **get off** your **back**, you are telling them angrily to stop criticizing you and leave you alone. *The crowd aren't forgiving, they can be a bit fickle, and as soon as you make a mistake they are on your back... For once in their money-grabbing little lives, why don't they get off our backs?*

stab someone in the back
If you say that someone that you trusted **has stabbed** you **in the back**, you mean that they have done something which hurts and betrays you. *She seemed to be incredibly disloyal. She would be your friend to your face, and then stab you in the back.*

☐ **A stab in the back** is an action which hurts and betrays someone. *Hard-liners are reportedly calling the plan for a joint delegation to the talks 'a stab in the back'.*

☐ **Back-stabbing** is talk or gossip which is intended to harm someone. *People begin to avoid one another, take sides, be drawn into gossip and back-stabbing.*

you scratch my back and I'll scratch yours
People say **'you scratch my back and I'll scratch yours'** to mean that one person helps another on condition that the second person helps them in return. *For men, commitments are based on common interest: I'll scratch your back if you'll scratch mine.*

☐ **Back-scratching** is helping someone so that they will help you in return. *And they know that a bit of helpful back-scratching when the state needs their services can be amply repaid one day.*

backwards

bend over backwards
lean over backward
If you **bend over backwards** or **lean over backward** to do something, you try very hard to do it and to help or please someone, even if it causes you trouble or difficulties. *We are bending over backwards to ensure that the safeguards are kept in place.*

bacon

save someone's bacon
British If someone or something **saves** your **bacon**, they get you out of a dangerous or difficult situation. *Your mother once saved my bacon, did you*

know that. She lent me money when I needed it.

◆ One explanation for this expression is that 'bacon' is related to an old word for 'back', so to save your bacon meant to save your back from a beating. Another is that in the past, bacon stored during the winter had to be guarded from hungry dogs. A third explanation is that the expression was formerly thieves' slang meaning 'to escape'.

bag

be someone's bag

If you say that something **is** not your **bag**, you mean that you are not very interested in it or are not very good at it. *'Being an umpire is not my bag,' Mr. Anders says. 'I'd rather be a player.'*

◆ This expression may have originated in the slang spoken by American jazz musicians. They sometimes referred to the type of jazz they played, or to their own distinctive style of jazz, as their 'bag'.

in the bag

If you say that something is **in the bag**, you mean that you feel certain that you will get it or achieve it. *Between you and me, laddie, it's in the bag. Unofficially, the job's yours.*

◆ The bag referred to here is a hunting bag, in which hunters carry home the animals and birds they have shot.

leave someone holding the bag

If you **are left holding the bag**, you are made responsible for a problem that nobody else wants to deal with. This expression is used more commonly in American English than British. *If a project goes bust, investors are left holding the bag.*

a mixed bag

If you describe something as **a mixed bag**, you mean that it contains things that are of very different kinds or qualities. *The papers carry a mixed bag of stories on their front pages.*

◆ The bag referred to here is a hunting bag containing different kinds of animals and birds.

someone's bag of tricks

If you refer to someone's **bag of tricks**, you mean that they have a set of special techniques or methods to use in their work. *Audiences seemed disconcerted by Welles' unconventional camera techniques, the jarring cuts between scenes, the shock effects that Welles pulled out of his bag of tricks.*

◆ This expression refers to the bag in which conjurers carry the equipment they need for their performances.

bait

fish or cut bait

American You can tell someone to **fish or cut bait** when you want them to stop wasting time and make a decision to do something. *Morale and stamina were said to be low after seven weeks of stalemate – the time had come to fish or cut bait.*

◆ The literal meaning behind this expression seems to be that it is time for someone to make a definite decision either to start fishing, or else to prepare the bait so that other people can fish.

take the bait
rise to the bait

If you **take the bait** or **rise to the bait**, you react to something that someone has said or done in exactly the way that they wanted you to react. *When the talk turned to horses, she told him how she had fallen off as a child and lost her nerve. He immediately took the bait, offering to teach her to ride... It's important not to rise to the bait and get cross.*

◆ In fly-fishing, the fish rise to the surface of the water to take the bait, and so they get caught.

baker

a baker's dozen

Old-fashioned If you have **a baker's dozen** of things, you have thirteen of them. *It's the idea of Alan Else, series co-ordinator, who has picked out a baker's dozen of top events between April and September.*

◆ Medieval bakers in England had a bad reputation for cheating their customers by selling underweight loaves. After regulations were introduced to fix the standard weight of loaves, bakers began to add a thirteenth loaf to each dozen to make sure they were not breaking the law.

balance

in the balance

If you say that a situation is **in the balance**, you mean that it is not clear what is going to happen. *I heard that one of the judges had died unexpectedly and that the choice of his successor was in the balance, with*

Holroyd and a couple of others as the most likely candidates.

♦ A balance is a set of scales which consists of two dishes suspended from a horizontal bar.

ball

a ball and chain

If you describe someone or something as **a ball and chain**, you mean that they restrict your freedom to do what you want. *Our national debt is an economic ball and chain dragging us down, keeping longer term interest rates high.*

♦ In the past, prisoners were sometimes chained by the leg to a heavy metal ball to prevent them from escaping.

the ball is in your court

If you tell someone that **the ball is in** their **court**, you are pointing out that it is their responsibility to decide what to do next in a particular situation. *The ball is now in his court. I, and indeed others, have told him quite clearly what we think. He has to decide.*

behind the eight ball

Mainly American If you say that someone or something is **behind the eight ball**, you mean that they are in trouble or in a difficult position. *For one thing, you don't need a secondary school education to work out that if a child doesn't get the basics in primary school they are way behind the eight ball.*

♦ In the game of pool, the 'eight ball' is a ball with a number 8 on it, which players have to pot last. If the eight ball is between the cue ball and the ball which the player is trying to hit, the player is likely to hit the eight ball first, which is a foul shot.

a crystal ball

If you say that someone is looking into **a crystal ball**, you mean that they are trying to predict the future. *What you really need to help you select your new car is a crystal ball to tell you how much it will be worth two, three or four years down the road.*

♦ A crystal ball is a glass ball used by some fortune-tellers to predict the future. They say that they can see visions of future events within the ball.

drop the ball

Mainly American If you say that someone **has dropped the ball**, you are criticizing them for something foolish or incompetent that they have done. *Lafferty, instead of really being helpful, had tried to pass off the new arrival's sponsorship duties to his staff, and the staff dropped the ball.*

have a ball

If you **have a ball**, you enjoy yourself and have a really good time. *I've enjoyed every minute of politics. I've had a ball.*

◆ In this expression, a 'ball' is a formal dance.

a new ball game
a different ball game

If you describe a situation as **a new ball game** or **a different ball game**, you mean that it has changed so much that people will have to change the way they deal with it or consider it. *From Monday to Thursday Gary turns up for work in a sober grey pinstripe suit with a white shirt and plain navy tie. But Fridays are a whole new ball game when it comes to dressing for the office. The suit is gone and Gary arrives in designer jeans... If military force were to be used, then that could be a completely different ball game.*

◆ 'Ball game' is often used in American English to refer to a game of baseball.

on the ball: 1

If you describe someone as **on the ball**, you mean that they are alert and deal with things in an intelligent way. *Some clubs struggle in their attempts to raise money. A few are on the ball and make a thoroughly professional job of it.*

on the ball: 2

If you describe someone as **on the ball**, you mean that they have the necessary qualities to achieve success. *The big Spaniard made no bones of the fact that he is still afraid of Chiappucci: 'Chiappucci is still on the ball. He's stronger than last year and being Italian he won't just be looking for a placing.'*

◆ In football, the player who is on the ball has the ball at their feet and is in control of it.

play ball: 2

If you agree to **play ball** with someone, you agree to do what they have asked you to do, or you agree to work with them in order to achieve something that you both want. Compare **play hardball**; see **hardball**. *The Association of British Insurers has threatened to withdraw its support if the banks and building societies refuse to play ball.*

set the ball rolling

If you **set the ball rolling**, you start an activity or you do something which other people will join in with later. *A fierce price war is now underway with all the big supermarket rivals cutting prices. Sainsbury set the ball rolling last week with 30 per cent discounts on a wide range of brands.*

take the ball and run with it

If you **take the ball and run with it**, you take an idea or plan that someone else has started and you develop it in order to see if it will be successful or useful. *Whatever he does in that hour is up to him. If he studies, fine. If he stares at the walls, well there's nothing we can do. He's the one who has to take the ball and run with it.*

□ Other nouns and pronouns are often used instead of 'ball'. *Any competent programmer could do it on a home computer and I'm hoping that someone else will take this and run with it because I haven't had the time.*

◆ The game referred to here is American football.

the whole ball of wax

Mainly American If you refer to **the whole ball of wax**, you are referring to the whole of something or to a number of different things which form a whole. *Perry wanted it all, the whole ball of wax. He wanted the Society for himself.*

ballistic

go ballistic

If someone **goes ballistic**, they get extremely angry and start behaving in a very forceful or irrational way as a result. *They claim the singer went ballistic after one member of his band allegedly failed to show for a sound check on the recent American tour.*

◆ This expression uses the image of a ballistic missile, and the powerful explosion which it causes.

balloon

the balloon goes up

Mainly British If you say that **the balloon has gone up**, you mean that a situation has become very serious or something bad has just happened. *On the Saturday the balloon went up. Henry said he would be going out to a conference and not returning until the Sunday afternoon. Sara told him to* *take all his things and not to return at all.*

◆ In the First World War, balloons were used both to protect targets from air raids and to observe the enemy. The fact that a balloon had gone up therefore indicated that trouble was coming.

ballpark

◆ A ballpark is a park or stadium where baseball is played.

a ballpark figure
a ballpark estimate

Mainly American **A ballpark figure** or **a ballpark estimate** is an approximate figure or quantity. *But what are we talking about here – a few thousand, millions, two bucks? Give me a ballpark figure.*

in the ballpark

Mainly American If you say that someone or something is **in the ballpark**, you mean that their ideas, actions, or estimates are approximately right, although they may not be exactly right. *Doctor Adams pointed out that as a piece of subtle surgical equipment it cost about £5 – an underestimate, maybe, but in the right ballpark.*

in the same ballpark

Mainly American If you say that one person or thing is **in the same ballpark** as another, you mean that the first person or thing is comparable to the second, or is as good or important as the second. *As a general investigative agency, they're not in the same ballpark as the FBI.*

balls

break someone's balls

If you say that someone **breaks** your **balls**, you mean that they seem to take pleasure in creating a great deal of unnecessary trouble for you. This expression is often used to refer critically to women who seem to enjoy destroying the sexual confidence of men. Many people find this expression offensive. *Men prefer a twitchy little eye-flutterer even if she is breaking their balls behind the scenes.*

☐ You can refer to someone who behaves in this way as **a ball-breaker**, and describe their behaviour as **ball-breaking**. *Another professor raised a great laugh by characterizing Jane Eyre as a novel written by one sex-starved ball-breaker about another.*

keep balls in the air

If you have to **keep** a lot of **balls in the air**, you have to deal with many different things at the same time. *They had trouble keeping all their balls in the air. In management terms, they were trying to do too much and things were starting to break down.*

banana

slip on a banana skin
slip on a banana peel

If someone **slips on a banana skin** or **slips on a banana peel**, they say or do something that makes them look stupid and causes them problems. *You can be walking across Westminster Bridge full of noble thoughts at one moment and slipping on a banana peel the next.*

◆ Comedies and cartoons often use the device or image of a character slipping on a banana skin, falling over, and looking foolish: the origin of this is unknown.

band

a one-man band
a one-woman band

If you describe someone as **a one-man band**, you mean that they carry out every part of an activity themselves, without any help from anyone else. A woman who is like this is sometimes described as **a one-woman band**. *I'm a one-man band, Mr Herold. At present I haven't even got a secretary.*

◆ A one-man band is a street entertainer who plays several different instruments at the same time.

bandwagon

jump on the bandwagon

If you say that someone, especially a politician, **has jumped on the bandwagon**, you disapprove of their involvement in an activity or movement, because you think that they are not sincerely interested in it, but are involved in it because it is likely to succeed or it is fashionable. 'Climb on', 'get on', and 'join' can be used instead of 'jump on'. *One of the dangers of following fads is that there are always bound to be inexperienced people ready to jump on the bandwagon and start classes in whatever is fashionable, with little or no training or qualifications of their own.*

☐ 'Bandwagon' is also used in many other expressions such as someone's **bandwagon is rolling**, to mean that an activity or movement is getting increasing support. *The Government's determination to push ahead with the sell-off of British Rail underlines its desire to keep the privatisation bandwagon rolling.*

◆ In American elections in the past, political rallies were often publicized by a band playing on a horse-drawn wagon which was driven through the streets. Politicians sat on the wagon and those who wished to show their support climbed on board.

bang

more bang for the buck
more bangs for your bucks

Mainly American If you get **more bang for the buck** or **more bangs for your bucks**, you get a bigger quantity or better quality of something than you would expect to get for the amount that you spend. *With this program you get more bang for the buck you've spent on computers.*

☐ You can also say that someone gets **little bang for the buck**, when they get less than they expected for the amount of money they spent.

not with a bang but a whimper

If you say that something happens **not with a bang but a whimper**, you mean that it is less effective or exciting than people expected or intended. *The Cannes film festival approached its climax yesterday not with a bang but a whimper, as thousands of disappointed festival-goers left early.*

☐ You can also say that something happened **with a bang and not a whimper**, or **with neither a bang nor a whimper**. *Should the monarchy go, it would be with a memorable bang and not a whimper... The last Hampshire match at Dean Park ended not with a bang, not even with a whimper; just an old-fashioned draw.*

◆ This is the last line of T. S. Eliot's poem 'The Hollow Men' (1925): 'This is the way the world ends Not with a bang but a whimper.'

bank

break the bank

If you say that something will not **break the bank**, you mean that it will not cost a lot of money or will not cost more than you can easily afford. *Porto Cervo is expensive, but there are restaurants and bars that* *won't break the bank.*

◆ If one gambler wins all the money that a casino has set aside to pay all the winning bets, they are said to have broken the bank.

baptism

a baptism of fire

If your first experience of a new situation is very difficult or unpleasant, you can describe it as **a baptism of fire**. *They have given themselves a baptism of fire by playing what many would consider the four best teams in the world.*

◆ This expression originally referred to the deaths of martyrs by burning. It was later used by the French Emperors Napoleon Bonaparte and Napoleon III to refer to someone's first experience of battle.

bark

your bark is worse than your bite

If you say that someone's **bark is worse than** their **bite**, you mean that they seem to be much more severe or unfriendly than they really are. *My bark is definitely worse than my bite. When people get to know me, they'll tell you I'm just a big softy really.*

☐ People often vary this expression. For example, you can suggest that someone is as severe or unfriendly as they seem by saying that their **bite is as bad as** their **bark**. *Wales' team will discover today that England's bite is as vicious as their bark.*

barrel

have someone over a barrel

If you are having discussions or negotiations with someone and you say that they **have** you **over a barrel**, you mean that they have put you in a position where you cannot possibly win. *The unions wish they had more options. Jobs are tight, they know that, and they feel management has them over a barrel.*

◆ This expression may refer to a method used in the past to save someone who had almost drowned. The person was placed face down over a barrel, which was then rocked gently backwards and forwards until all the water had drained from their lungs.

scrape the bottom of the barrel
scrape the barrel

If you say that someone **is scraping the bottom of the barrel** or is **scraping the barrel**, you mean that they are using something or doing something that is not very good, because they cannot think of anything better to use or do. *The game designers were scraping the bottom of the barrel for ideas when they came up with this one.*

barrelhead

on the barrelhead
on the barrel

American If you pay cash **on the barrelhead** or **on the barrel** for something, you pay for it immediately and in cash. The British expression is **on the nail**. *Customers usually pay cash on the barrelhead, so bad debts aren't much of a problem.*

◆ The most likely explanation for this expression comes from the days when settlers first started living in the American West. Saloons often consisted of just a room with a barrel of drink in it, and customers who wanted to drink had to put their money on the top of the barrel before being served, as credit was not given.

barrels

give someone both barrels

If you **give** someone **both barrels**, you attack them fiercely, aggressively, and forcefully. *Greenwood took this up with Butler and gave him both barrels.*

◆ This expression refers to the firing of both barrels of a double-barrelled gun.

base

◆ In baseball, players have to hit the ball and then run round all four corners or bases to score a run.

get to first base: 1

If you cannot **get to first base**, you cannot begin to make progress with your plans. *We couldn't get to first base with any U.S. banks. They didn't want to take the risk.*

get to first base: 2
get to second base

Mainly American People use expressions such as **get to first base** and **get to second base** to refer to the degree of sexual intimacy they have achieved with their girlfriend or boyfriend. *On a date, would it be easier to get to second base with Laverne or Shirley?*

off base

American If you say that someone's judgement or opinion is **off base**, you mean that it is mistaken or wrong. *I don't think the church is off base at all in taking a moral stand on this.*

♦ In baseball, if a player is caught off base, a member of the opposite team gets them out while they are between bases.

touch base

If you **touch base** with someone, you contact them, often when you have not spoken to them or seen them for a long time. *Afterward Forstmann had touched base with his partners and found that they, too, harbored a vague distaste for the tobacco business.*

♦ In baseball, batters have to touch the first, second, and third bases to score a run.

bases

touch all the bases
cover all the bases

Mainly American If you say that someone **touches all the bases**, you mean that they deal with or take care of all the different things that they should. You can also say that they **cover all the bases**. *This is an exceptionally good contract. It touches all of the bases of what the people said were the problems... The boss covers all bases when he sets up a job.*

♦ In baseball, batters have to touch the first, second, and third bases to score a run.

basket

a basket case: 1

If you describe a country or organization as **a basket case**, you mean that its economy or finances are in a very bad state. *The popular image about Latin America a few years ago was that it was a basket case.*

a basket case: 2

If you say that someone is **a basket case**, you mean that they are crazy or insane. *Mary comes to work in tears every day, and you wouldn't believe the bags under her eyes. She's gained fifteen pounds, as well. I tell you, she's turning into a basket case.*

◆ This expression was originally used to describe someone, especially a soldier, who had lost all four limbs. It may have come about because some of these people had to be carried around in baskets.

bat

go to bat for someone

Mainly American If you say that someone **goes to bat for** you, you mean that they give you their support or help. *She was just fabulous in going to bat for me, in not being judgmental, in seeing me through and helping me work it out.*

◆ This expression refers to a baseball player who comes off the bench and takes the place of another batter.

like a bat out of hell

If you go somewhere **like a bat out of hell**, you go there very quickly. *I didn't see her face, but I knew it was a woman. She tore across the highway like a bat out of hell. I damn nearly ploughed right into her.*

off your own bat

British If you do something **off** your **own bat**, you choose to do it or decide to do it rather than being told to do it. *'Who's put you up to this call? Someone's told you to talk to me.' 'I'm doing it off my own bat, John.'*

◆ In cricket, players can score runs either by hitting the ball themselves, or when their partner hits it, or when the ball is not hit at all but goes beyond the wicket.

play a straight bat: 1

British If you say that someone **plays a straight bat**, you mean that they try to avoid answering difficult questions. *But last Saturday her interviewee played a straight bat, referring all inquiries to his solicitors before driving off.*

play a straight bat: 2

Old-fashioned, British If someone **plays a straight bat**, they do things in an honest and simple way because they have traditional ideas and values. *Amit, then 14, was very surprised to find that 'playing a straight bat' was* *not considered all that important in his new school.*

◆ In cricket, to play a straight bat means to play very correctly and cautiously, in order not to risk being out.

right off the bat

Mainly American If something happens **right off the bat**, it happens immediately or at the very beginning of a process or event. *It was just as well that he learned right off the bat that you can't count on anything in this business.*

◆ The image here is of a ball bouncing quickly off a baseball bat.

bath

an early bath

British If you are involved in an activity and you take **an early bath**, you stop doing it and leave before you have finished. Compare **send** someone **to the showers**; see **showers**. *At test screenings of Platoon, The War of the Roses and Goodfellas at least a quarter of the audience had opted for an early bath.*

◆ In football and other sports, players who are sent off cannot return to the field and so can take a bath before the game is finished.

take a bath

If a person or a company **takes a bath**, they lose a lot of money on an investment. *Investors in the company took a 35 million dollar bath on the company, which entered bankruptcy proceedings 18 months ago.*

baton

pass the baton
pick up the baton

If someone **passes the baton** to you, they pass responsibility for something to you. *Does this mean that the baton of leadership is going to be passed to other nations?*

☐ If you **pick up the baton**, you take over responsibility for something. *The heyday for conservationists was the mid and late 1980s when councils really picked up the baton of public concern and became the standard bearers in the quality of life versus nature debate.*

◆ In a relay race, team members pass on the baton as they finish running their stage of the race.

bats

have bats in your belfry

If you say that someone **has bats in** their **belfry**, you mean that they have peculiar ideas or are crazy.

batteries

recharge your batteries

If you **recharge** your **batteries**, you take a break from activities which are tiring or stressful so that you can relax and will feel refreshed when you return to those activities. *After playing in the Divisional Championship, I took a long break from the game to recharge my batteries.*

◆ When people recharge batteries, they put an electrical charge back into the batteries by connecting them to a machine that draws power from another source of electricity, such as the mains.

battle

the battle lines are drawn

If you say that **the battle lines are drawn** between opposing groups or people, you mean that a fight or argument is about to start, and that it has become clear what the main points of conflict or disagreement will be. *The battle lines were drawn yesterday for the fiercest contest in the history of local radio. Forty-eight applicants submitted their proposals in the chase for eight London broadcasting licences.*

fight a losing battle

If you **are fighting a losing battle**, you are trying to achieve something, but you are very unlikely to succeed. *The producer says the theaters have been fighting a losing battle with television, movies, and video cassettes.*

join battle

If you **join battle** with someone, you decide that you are going to try and beat them in an argument or contest. *This new company intends to join battle with Cellnet and Vodafone in the mobile telecoms market.*

a running battle

If you have **a running battle** with someone, you argue with them or fight with them over a long period of time. *Police have been engaged in running battles with people protesting against the sharp increase in the price of the country's staple food, maize meal.*

win the battle, lose the war
lose the battle, win the war

If you say that someone **has won the battle, but lost the war**, you mean that, although they have won a minor conflict, they have been defeated in a larger, more important one, of which it was a part. *We will get our justice. They have won the battle but they haven't won the war. We will have our day in court.*

□ You can also say that someone **has lost the battle** but intends to **win the war**, to mean that they have lost a small conflict but still think they can win the larger one. *If you do start smoking again it does not mean you are a failure. Learn from what went wrong and pick another day to stop again. You may have lost the battle, but you can still win the war.*

bay

keep something at bay

If you **keep** something or someone **at bay**, you keep it from attacking you or affecting you in some other way. *Tooth decay can be held at bay by fluoride toothpaste and good dentistry.*

◆ When a hunted animal is at bay, it is trapped by the hounds and forced to turn and face them to defend itself. However, if the animal is successfully defending itself in this position, you can say that it is holding the hounds at bay. This second use seems the most likely origin of the expression.

bead

draw a bead on
take a bead on

Mainly American If you **draw a bead on** a target or **take a bead on** it, you aim your weapon at it. *There was only one spot where the light through the trees would have enabled him to draw a bead on his target.*

◆ The bead is the small marker on top of the end of the barrel on some guns, which is used to aim at the target.

beam

be way off beam

British If you say that something **is way off beam**, you mean that it is completely wrong or mistaken. *The writer was so hilariously way off-beam in his criticism of soccer that every single reader will want to see the article* *for themselves.*

◆ This refers to the use of a radio signal or beam to direct aircraft which were coming in to land. A radio transmitter on one side of the runway transmitted dots, or short tones, while one on the other side transmitted dashes, or long tones. If pilots were coming in on the right course, the dots and dashes merged and the pilots heard a continuous tone.

bean

◆ There are several slang meanings for 'bean'. In the following expressions, it means money.

a bean counter
count the beans

If you refer to someone as **a bean counter**, you mean that they are only interested in narrow questions such as how much money a business makes and spends, without caring about wider issues, for example, people's welfare. You usually use this expression when you disagree with this approach. *The reason for America's failure is that we have bean-counters running our companies. The Japanese have engineering and manufacturing people.*

□ You can refer to this type of approach as **bean counting**, or you can say that someone **is counting the beans**. *He is as prone as he ever was to sudden outbursts against the Hollywood establishment – the bean-counting producers, the idiot studio heads, the lawyers, the grandiose agents... I'm not trivializing this, but no funds were lost and no customers were affected. We should count the beans better, that's all.*

not have a bean

Fairly old-fashioned, British If you say that someone **hasn't got a bean**, you mean that they have very little money. *When we married we hadn't a bean so we bought all our furniture second-hand.*

beans

full of beans

If you say that someone is **full of beans**, you mean that they are happy, excited, and full of energy. *Jem was among them, pink-cheeked and full of beans after a far longer sleep than anybody else had got.*

◆ This originally referred to a horse that was well-fed and therefore full of energy.

know how many beans make five

    Old-fashioned, British If you say that someone **knows how many beans make five**, you mean that they are intelligent and sensible. *The major concern of most parents is that the children are taught the basics, so that when they graduate they can talk nicely, spell properly and know how many beans make five.*

◆ This is a very old expression which used by the Spanish writer Cervantes in his novel 'Don Quixote' (1605). It may be based on a riddle.

not amount to a hill of beans
not worth a row of beans

    If you say that something **doesn't amount to a hill of beans** or **isn't worth a hill of beans**, you mean that it is completely worthless and insignificant. You can also say that something is **not worth a row of beans**. *In this world the problems of people like us do not amount to a hill of beans.*

◆ Beans are sometimes planted in groups in a little mound of earth, although they are usually grown in rows.

spill the beans

    If you **spill the beans**, you reveal the truth about something secret or private. *He always seemed scared to death I was going to spill the beans to the cops.*

bear

like a bear with a sore head

    Mainly British If you say that someone is behaving **like a bear with a sore head**, you are criticizing them for behaving in a very bad-tempered and irritable way. *I mean, it was quite obvious, wasn't it, that she really didn't want to go, but there you were, like a bear with a sore head, tantrums all the time, little legs drumming on the floor.*

loaded for bear

    American If you say that someone **is loaded for bear**, you mean that they are ready and eager to do something. *A young squadron commander named Joshua Painter led the briefing. He had eight aircraft loaded for bear.*

◆ Someone who is loaded for bear has ammunition which is powerful enough to kill a bear, even though they may be hunting smaller animals.

beast

no use to man or beast
no good to man or beast

If you say that someone or something is **no use to man or beast** or **no good to man or beast**, you are emphasizing that they are completely useless. *Circumstances had compelled him, much against his will, to take no less than six beginners, some of them first-voyagers, of no use to man or beast.*

◆ This is part of the old saying, 'When the wind is in the east, 'tis neither good for man nor beast.'

beat

beat your breast
beat your chest

If you say that someone **is beating** their **breast** or **is beating** their **chest**, you mean that they are very publicly showing regret or anger about something that has gone wrong. You usually use these expressions to suggest that the person is not being sincere but is trying to draw attention to himself or herself. *He is very thoughtful with the players. He doesn't go around beating his chest all the time. He knows when a quiet chat is what's needed.*

□ You can describe the action of doing this as **breast-beating** or **chest-beating**. *His pious breast-beating on behalf of the working classes was transparently bogus, but it was a clever public relations job.*

miss a beat: 1

If someone says or does something without **missing a beat**, they continue to speak or they do it without pausing, even though you might have expected them to hesitate. *'Are you jealous?' 'Only when I'm not in control,' he says, not missing a beat.*

miss a beat: 2

If you say that someone does not **miss a beat**, you mean that they always know what is going on and so they are able to take advantage of every situation. *This time we played like machines. The longer the game went the stronger we got, and we never missed a beat.*

◆ The 'beat' referred to here is probably a heartbeat, although it may refer to a beat in music.

beaver

an eager beaver

If you describe someone as **an eager beaver**, you mean that they are very enthusiastic about work or very anxious to please other people. You usually use this expression to show that you find their behaviour foolish or annoying. *George was like a sneaky kid. He lied, boasted, was an eager beaver without the ability to live up to his promises.*

◆ Beavers are often associated with hard work, as they spend a lot of time building shelters and dams out of mud and wood.

beck

at someone's beck and call

If you say that someone is **at** another person's **beck and call**, you mean that they are always ready to carry out that person's orders or wishes, even when these orders or wishes are unreasonable. *You're a person in your own right, not just a mum or a partner, and your child must understand that you can't always be at his beck and call for every little thing.*

◆ 'Beck' is an old word meaning a gesture, for example a nod or a movement of the hand or forefinger, which represents a command such as 'Come here.'

bed

get into bed with someone

If you say that one person or group **is getting into bed with** another, you mean that they have made an agreement and are intending to work together. You usually use this expression to show disapproval. *The BBC might have been criticised for getting into bed with Sky TV last summer, but it's easy to see now why they did.*

get out of bed the wrong side

If you say that someone **got out of bed the wrong side**, you mean that they are in a very bad mood without there seeming to be any obvious reason for it. *Sorry I was so unpleasant when I arrived this morning. I must have got out of bed the wrong side.*

◆ This relates to the old superstition that it was unlucky to put the left foot on the ground first when getting out of bed. 'Get off on the wrong foot' is based on a similar belief.

put something to bed

If you **put** a plan or task **to bed**, you achieve it or complete it
successfully. *Before putting the agreement to bed, we still had to satisfy
Fran Murray.*

♦ On an old-style printing press, the bed is the flat part that holds the
type. If journalists talk about putting a newspaper or magazine to bed,
they are talking about making the final changes before printing.

you have made your bed and will have to lie on it

If someone tells you '**you have made your bed and will have to lie on
it**', they are telling you in an unsympathetic way that you have to accept
the unpleasant consequences of a decision which you made at an earlier
time. 'In' is often used instead of 'on'. *Curiously it never occurred to her
even to consider leaving Barry. Her strict religious upbringing had
convinced her that marriage was for life – in her eyes she had made her bed
and would have to lie in it.*

☐ This expression is very variable. For example, you can say to someone,
'**you've made your bed, now lie on it**' or just '**you've made your bed**'.
*You wouldn't expect us to turn around and say 'Oh well, you know you've
made your bed – you're the one that caused the problem.'*

bee

the bee's knees

British If you say that something or someone is **the bee's knees**, you are
saying in a light-hearted way that you like them a great deal. *I bought this
white sweatshirt – I thought I looked the bee's knees.*

♦ Some people believe that this expression refers to the way in which
bees transfer pollen from their bodies to pollen sacs on their back legs.
However, it seems more likely that it dates from the 1920s, when other
similar expressions such as 'the cat's pyjamas' began to be used.

have a bee in your bonnet

If you say that someone **has a bee in** their **bonnet** about something,
you mean that they feel very strongly about it and keep talking or
thinking about it. This is often something that you think is unimportant.
This expression is considered old-fashioned in American English. *I've got
a bee in my bonnet about the confusion between education and training.*

♦ Two images are suggested by this expression. The first is of thoughts
buzzing inside someone's head like bees. The second is of someone who

has a bee trapped in their hat and is anxious to get it out before they are stung.

beeline

make a beeline for something

If you **make a beeline for** something, you go straight to it without any hesitation or delay. *The boys head for computer games while the girls make a beeline for the dolls.*

◆ It used to be believed that bees, having collected the pollen, flew back to the hive in a straight line. In fact, this belief has been proved to be incorrect. 'As the crow flies' is based on a similar idea.

beer

not all beer and skittles

British If you say that something **isn't all beer and skittles**, you mean that it is not always as enjoyable or as easy as other people think it is. *Living on your own isn't all beer and skittles. It can be lonely too.*

◆ The game of skittles is associated with beer because it is traditionally played in pubs.

small beer

British If you say that something is **small beer**, you mean that it is insignificant compared with another thing. *The present series of royal scandals makes the 1936 abdication look like pretty small beer.*

◆ 'Small beer' originally meant weak beer.

beggars

beggars can't be choosers

If someone says to you **'beggars can't be choosers'**, they mean that you should not reject an offer or a particular course of action, because it is the only one which is available to you. *'So would you be happy to work wherever you got a job?' 'Initially, yeah. I mean, I think initially you've got to take anything that comes around because beggars can't be choosers.'*

bell

ring a bell

If something **rings a bell**, it is slightly familiar to you and you are aware that you have heard it before, although you may not remember it *fully. The sergeant made notes while she talked. 'I'll check and see if we've anything on him,' he said. 'It doesn't ring a bell at the moment.'*

ring someone's bell

American If someone or something **rings** your **bell**, you find them very attractive, exciting, or satisfying. *Well, truthfully, after a couple of comedies that didn't exactly ring my bell, I thought I'd like to do something that is very unusual, that hadn't been seen before.*

saved by the bell

People say **'saved by the bell'** when they are in a difficult situation and at the last possible moment something happens which allows them to escape from it. *There was another period of silence. It was broken by the sound of Eleanor's car pulling up outside the front door. 'Saved by the bell,' I said.*

♦ This expression refers to the bell which signals the end of a round in a boxing match.

bells

alarm bells ring
warning bells ring

If something sets **alarm bells ringing**, people begin to be aware of a problem in a situation. You can also talk about **warning bells ringing**. *The islanders' fight for compensation has set alarm bells ringing round the world... He didn't understand the half of it but warning bells were beginning to ring in the back of his mind.*

bells and whistles

If you refer to **bells and whistles**, you are referring to special features or other things which are not essential parts of something, but which are added to make it more attractive or interesting. *People also crave anxiety-free products – simple items without lots of fancy bells and whistles and complex instructions.*

♦ In the past, organs were used in cinemas to accompany silent films. Some of these organs had devices attached to them which produced sound effects such as bells and whistles.

belly-up

go belly-up

If a company **goes belly-up**, it fails and does not have enough money to pay its debts. *Factories and farms went belly up because of the debt crisis.*

◆ This expression may refer to dead fish floating upside down near the surface of the water.

belt

below the belt

If you describe what someone has done as **below the belt**, you mean that it is unfair or cruel. *Highly-sensitive information about another person can often be used as a weapon against them, and these kinds of blows below the belt are the surest way to destroy a friendship or love affair.*

◆ In boxing, it is against the rules to hit an opponent below the level of the belt.

belt and braces

British If you say that someone has a **belt and braces** approach to doing something, you mean that they take extra precautions to make sure that it will work properly. *He described airport security as an overly belt and braces approach, at huge cost to industry.*

tighten your belt

If you have to **tighten** your **belt**, you have to spend less and live more carefully because you have less money than you used to have. *Clearly, if you are spending more than your income, you'll need to tighten your belt.*

☐ You can also talk about **belt-tightening**. *The nation's second largest bank announced a series of layoffs and other belt-tightening measures today to counteract heavy losses.*

under your belt

If you have something **under** your **belt**, you have already achieved it or done it. *He'll need a few more games under his belt before he's ready for international football.*

bend

round the bend

If you say that someone is **round the bend**, you think that their ideas or behaviour are very strange or foolish. This expression is used more commonly in British English than American. *If anyone told me a few months ago that I'd meet a marvellous person like you I'd have said they were round the bend.*

berth

give someone a wide berth

If you **give** someone or something **a wide berth**, you deliberately avoid them. *I wouldn't mess with people like that, not me. I give them a wide berth.*

◆ A berth is the amount of space which a sailing ship needs to manoeuvre safely.

bets

hedge your bets

If you say that someone **is hedging** their **bets**, you mean that they are avoiding making decisions, or are committing themselves to more than one thing, so that they will not make a mistake whichever way the situation develops. *Political forecasters are hedging their bets about the likely outcome of this Saturday's Louisiana governor's race.*

◆ When bookmakers accept a large bet, they often try to protect themselves against heavy losses by laying bets with other bookmakers. This practice is called 'hedging'.

bib

your best bib and tucker

Old-fashioned If you are wearing your **best bib and tucker**, you are wearing your best clothes, for example because you are going to a very important or formal event. *The Middle East peace conference kicks off on October 30th in Madrid with all the guests on the invitation list promising to turn up on time in best bib and tucker.*

◆ In the past, a 'bib' was the part of an apron which covered the chest. A 'tucker' was an ornamental frill of lace or muslin which women wore round the top of their dresses to cover their necks and shoulders.

big

get too big for your boots
get too big for your britches

In British English, if you say that someone **is getting too big for** their **boots**, you are criticizing them for behaving as if they are much more important or clever than they really are. *Get too big for their boots, kids these days. Think the whole universe should revolve round them.*

☐ In American English, you say that someone **is getting too big for** their **britches**.

◆ 'Britches' is also spelled 'breeches'. Britches are trousers which reach as far as your knees.

bike

on your bike

British People say **'on your bike'** when they are telling someone to go away or stop behaving in a foolish way. *It was a heated game, and when I got Alec I just said something like 'You're out mate, on your bike.'*

☐ This expression is often used to say that someone has been sacked from their job. *By the end of the week Neilsen had been told to get on his bike by new boss Jim Duffy.*

bill

bill and coo

Old-fashioned If you say that two lovers **are billing and cooing**, you mean that they are talking together in an intimate and loving way. *Jenny decided to end their marriage when she caught Paolo billing and cooing down the phone to an ex-girlfriend.*

◆ In this expression, lovers are being compared to a pair of doves touching their beaks or bills together and cooing.

a clean bill of health: 1

If someone is given **a clean bill of health**, they are told that they are completely fit and healthy. *He had a full medical late last year and was given a clean bill of health.*

a clean bill of health: 2

If something is given **a clean bill of health**, it is examined or considered and then judged to be in a satisfactory condition. *Fourteen seaside resorts failed to meet the environmental and safety standards, while 43 were given a clean bill of health.*

◆ A bill of health was a certificate which was given to a ship's master to present at the next port the ship arrived at. It stated whether or not there was an infectious disease aboard the ship or in the port it was departing from.

fit the bill
fill the bill

If someone or something **fits the bill**, they are exactly the right person or thing that is needed in a particular situation. You can also say that someone or something **fills the bill**. *I wanted someone who really knew their way around film-making and I knew that Richard would fit the bill.*

◆ The 'bill' in this expression is a public notice advertising something such as a show or a play.

foot the bill

If you have to **foot the bill** for something, you have to pay for it. *Police will have to foot the bill for the slight damage to both cars.*

◆ This expression may come from the practice of someone paying a bill and signing it at the bottom, or 'foot'.

sell someone a bill of goods

American If you **have been sold a bill of goods**, you have been deceived or told something that is not true. *I began to realize that I'd been sold a bill of goods, that I wasn't in any way incompetent or slothful.*

◆ This expression may refer to someone buying a batch of goods when they have only seen a list of what it contains and not the goods themselves.

bind

a double bind

If you are in **a double bind**, you are in a very difficult situation, because you have problems that cannot be solved easily or without causing more problems. *He was in a classic double bind, with the Chinese suspecting him and his Cabinet of supporting the guerrillas, while the guerrillas considered them mere tools of the Chinese.*

◆ 'Bind' is a slang word meaning a difficult situation or predicament.

bird

the bird has flown

If you are looking for someone and you say that **the bird has flown**, you mean that they have escaped or disappeared. *He'd been told to follow the woman to work and sit outside the Health Centre till she came out again. Instead he'd wandered off God knows where, come back at her normal leaving time and found the bird had flown.*

a bird in the hand
a bird in the hand is worth two in the bush

If you refer to something that you have as **a bird in the hand**, you mean that it is better to keep it than to try to get something better and risk having nothing at all. *Another temporary discount may not be what you want, but at least it is a bird in the hand.*

☐ This expression comes from the proverb **a bird in the hand is worth two in the bush**.

a bird of passage

If you describe someone as **a bird of passage**, you mean that they never stay in one place for long. *Most of these emigrants were birds of passage who returned to Spain after a relatively short stay.*

◆ Birds that migrate are sometimes referred to as 'birds of passage'.

the early bird catches the worm
an early bird

If you tell someone that **the early bird catches the worm**, you are advising them that if they want to do something successfully then they should start as soon as they can. *If you're going to make it to the Senate, you need to start right now. The early bird catches the worm.*

☐ You can refer to someone who gets up early in the morning or who does something before other people as **an early bird**. *We've always been early birds, up at 5.30 or 6am.*

eat like a bird

If you say that someone **eats like a bird**, you mean that they do not eat very much. *She ate like a bird, was inclined to refuse a glass of wine, and was only interested in talking about her work.*

give someone the bird: 1

British, old-fashioned If an audience shouts at an entertainer or sports player to show their disapproval, you can say that the audience **gives** them **the bird**. *He made a couple of mistakes and the crowd immediately gave him the bird.*

give someone the bird: 2

Mainly American If someone **gives** you **the bird**, they make a rude and offensive gesture with one hand, with their middle finger pointing up and their other fingers bent over in a fist, in order to show their contempt, anger, or defiance of you. *Chip took a break from telling sundry adoring females how beautiful their eyes were to surreptitiously give Alex the bird.*

a little bird told me

If you say that **a little bird told** you a piece of information, you mean that you are not going to say how you found out about it or who told it to you. *Incidentally, a little bird tells me that your birthday's coming up.*

a rare bird

If you describe someone or something as **a rare bird**, you mean that there are not many people or things like them. *Diane Johnson's book is that rare bird, an American novel of manners.*

◆ 'A rare bird' is a translation of the Latin expression 'rara avis', which was used by the Roman writer Juvenal in the 2nd century AD to describe a black swan. At the time, black swans were unknown, although they were later discovered in Australia.

birds

the birds and the bees

People sometimes describe sex and sexual reproduction as **the birds and the bees**, usually because they find it embarrassing to talk about these things openly, or because they are trying to be humorous to hide the fact that they find it embarrassing. *At the age of 16 I remember having yet another discussion about the birds and the bees with my father.*

◆ People sometimes explain sex and sexual reproduction to children by telling them how animals reproduce.

birds of a feather
birds of a feather flock together

If you describe two or more people as **birds of a feather**, you mean that they are very similar in many ways. *She and my mother were birds of a feather. You felt something special between them that left you out.*

□ This expression comes from the proverb **birds of a feather flock together**, which means that people from the same group or with the same interests like to be with each other.

for the birds

If you say that something is **for the birds**, you think that it is stupid, boring, or worthless. *This journal business is for the birds. It's a waste of time.*

kill two birds with one stone

If you **kill two birds with one stone**, you manage to achieve two things at the same time. *We can talk about Union Hill while I get this business over with. Kill two birds with one stone, so to speak.*

biscuit

take the biscuit

British If you say that someone or something **takes the biscuit**, you are expressing surprise or anger at their extreme behaviour or qualities. *I've heard some odd things in my day but that took the biscuit.*

♦ This is similar to 'take the cake', which refers to the practice in the past of awarding cakes as prizes in competitions: see **cake**.

bit

♦ A bit is a piece of metal which is held in a horse's mouth by the bridle and reins.

champ at the bit
chomp at the bit

If you **are champing at the bit** or **are chomping at the bit**, you are impatient to do something, but are prevented from doing it, usually by circumstances that you have no control over. *Foremen had been champing at the bit to strike before next week's meeting.*

get the bit between your teeth

If you **get the bit between** your **teeth**, you become very enthusiastic and determined about doing a particular job or task. *You're persistent when you get the bit between your teeth, I'll say that for you.*

♦ The bit should be positioned at the back of a horse's mouth, behind its back teeth. When a horse bolts, it sometimes takes the bit between its teeth, which makes it very difficult for a rider or driver to use the reins to control it.

bite

bite off more than you can chew

If you say that someone **has bitten off more than** they **can chew**, you mean that they are trying to do something that is far too difficult for them to manage. *Don't bite off more than you can chew simply because everything is going so well.*

a second bite at the cherry
two bites of the cherry

British If you get **a second bite at the cherry** or have **two bites of the cherry**, you have a second chance to do something, especially something that you failed at the first time. *We might, if we push hard enough, get a second bite at the cherry in two years' time... I've had two bites of the cherry. Which was rather nice because all the mistakes I made with the first one, I hope I haven't repeated.*

biter

the biter gets bit

British You can say that **the biter gets bit** when someone suffers as a result of their own actions, especially when they were intending to hurt someone else. *Sympathy seldom abounds when the biter gets bit.*

◆ 'Biter' is an old word meaning a swindler or con man.

bitten

once bitten, twice shy
once bitten

People say **'once bitten, twice shy'** when they are explaining that a recent and unpleasant personal experience has made them very cautious about getting involved in similar situations in the future. Sometimes people just say **'once bitten'**. *I'm certainly not looking for new boyfriends or thinking of having any more kids. Once bitten, twice shy... Do not expect Tokyo's punters, once bitten, to come rushing back for more.*

black

black and white

If someone sees things in **black and white**, they see complex issues in simple terms of right and wrong. If a situation appears **black and white**, it seems to be a simple question of right and wrong, although it may in fact be very complex. These expressions are often used to criticize people who treat complex things in a very simple way. *The thing is not as black and white as the media have said.*

□ You can also talk about a **black and white** question or issue, or about seeing things in **black and white** terms. *People think this is a sort of black and white issue that's very simple and that you can just make a decision.*

in black and white

If you say that something is **in black and white**, you mean that you have written proof of it. *You know, we've seen it. It's written right here in black and white.*

in the black

If a person or organization is **in the black**, they do not owe anyone any money. Compare **in the red**; see **red**. *Last year, the company was back in the black, showing a modest pre-tax surplus of £4.6 million.*

◆ This expression comes from the practice in the past of using black ink to fill in entries on the credit side of a book of accounts.

not as black as you are painted

If you say that someone is **not as black as** they **are painted**, you mean that they are not as bad as other people say they are. *They had a strong mutual dislike of each other. I once said to Hilda, 'She's not as black as you paint her.'*

□ This expression comes from the proverb **the devil is not as black as he is painted**.

blank

draw a blank: 1

If you are trying to find someone or something and you **draw a blank**, you cannot find them. If you are trying to find out about something and you **draw a blank**, you fail to find out about it. *I searched among the bottles and under and behind and inside everything I could think of and drew a blank.*

draw a blank: 2

Mainly American If you **draw a blank**, you are unable to remember something or to answer a question you are asked. *Why do we recognise a face, but sometimes draw a blank when it comes to the name?*

draw a blank: 3

Mainly British In a sporting contest, if a team or competitor **draws a blank**, they do not score any goals or points, or win any races. *Rangers drew a blank at Hibernian – the champions were held nil-nil.*

◆ Originally, to draw a blank meant to be given a losing ticket in a lottery.

blanket

a wet blanket: 1

If you say that someone is **a wet blanket**, you mean that they spoil other people's fun because they are boring or miserable. *'Hey', said Thack, looking at Michael. 'Stop being such a wet blanket.'*

a wet blanket: 2

If something throws **a wet blanket** over an event or situation, it makes it less successful or enjoyable than it would otherwise have been. *Barre is worried that the Clinton economic plan will throw a wet blanket over the recovery.*

blanks

fire blanks

British If you say that someone **is firing blanks**, you mean that although they are trying very hard, they are failing to achieve anything. *Dalian and his fellow attackers continued to fire blanks against Norwich and it was left to full-back Steve Staunton to provide Villa's first goal.*

♦ Blanks are gun cartridges which contain explosive but do not contain a bullet, so that they do not cause any injuries or damage when the gun is fired.

bleed

bleed someone dry
bleed someone white

If a person, organization, or country **is bled dry**, they are made weak, for example by being forced to use up all their money or resources. You can also say that someone **is bled white**. *He extorted money from me on a regular basis for five years. But he was careful not to bleed me dry.*

♦ In the past, doctors often treated patients by bleeding them, which involved extracting some of their blood.

blind

blind as a bat

If you say that someone is as **blind as a bat**, you mean that they cannot see very well. *Without my glasses I was blind as a bat.*

♦ Most bats are active only at night and find their way by sending out sounds and sensing objects from the echoes, rather than by using their eyesight.

the blind leading the blind

You can describe a situation as **the blind leading the blind** when the person in charge is just as incapable of doing the task as the person who they are meant to be helping or guiding. *Their attempts to help the Third World poor were rather like the blind leading the blind.*

□ This expression is sometimes varied by replacing 'blind' with another adjective appropriate to the subject that is being talked about. *His work certainly shocked the critics at his 1976 exhibition at New York's Museum of Modern Art. One damned it as an example of 'the banal leading the banal'.*

◆ This expression comes from one of the stories told by Jesus in the Bible: 'Let them alone: they be blind leaders of the blind. And if the blind lead the blind, both shall fall into the ditch.' (Matthew 15:14)

fly blind

If someone **is flying blind** in a situation, they do not have anything to help or guide them. *With billions of dollars at stake, the two presidents weren't willing to boost their offer while they were flying blind.*

◆ A pilot is flying blind when they are piloting an aircraft without using visual navigation, but relying solely on their instruments.

swear blind

British If someone **swears blind** that something is true, they insist that they are telling you the truth, even though you are not sure whether or not to believe them. The American expression is **swear up and down**. *He had a reputation for being a bit of a philanderer but he swore blind that he had met the right girl in me and said he wanted to settle down.*

blink

on the blink

A piece of machinery that is **on the blink** is not working properly. *We had to have the washing done at the laundry because our machine was on the blink.*

block

on the block

American If something is put **on the block**, it is offered for sale at auction. The British expression is **under the hammer**. *The team's money worries had forced them to put the club on the block.*

put your head on the block
put your neck on the block

If you **put** your **head on the block** or **put** your **neck on the block**, you risk your reputation or position by taking a particular course of action. *When the Prime Minister called a by-election in his own constituency, he put his head on the block... He really put his neck on the block there and it's great to see his bravery being rewarded.*

◆ The 'block' here is a special piece of wood on which a prisoner was made to place his or her head before being beheaded.

a stumbling block

    A stumbling block is a problem which stops you from achieving something. *Your inability to choose between material security and emotional needs is a major stumbling block to your happiness.*

    ◆ This expression comes from the Bible: '...that no man put a stumbling block or an occasion to fall in his brother's way.' (Romans 14:13)

blocks

off the blocks: 1
out of the blocks
off the starting blocks

    Off the blocks, **out of the blocks**, and **off the starting blocks** are used in expressions which tell you how quickly someone starts to do something. For example, if someone is 'first out of the blocks', they start to do something before everyone else. *Ontario was not fast off the starting blocks in developing any systematic intervention aimed at land conservation.*

off the starting blocks: 2
off the blocks
out of the blocks

    If someone gets **off the starting blocks**, **off the blocks**, or **out of the blocks**, they succeed in starting to do something, often despite difficulties. *People thought I was totally mad and, if they think that, then you just can't get off the starting block.*

    ◆ These expressions come from athletics, where sprinters put their feet against pieces of equipment called starting blocks to help them start quickly when the race begins.

blood

after your blood

    If someone is **after** your **blood**, they want to harm or punish you, because you have harmed them or made them angry. *The entire street-gang network of New York is after their blood.*

bad blood

    If there is **bad blood** between two people or groups, they have hostile feelings towards each other because of the arguments or quarrels they have had in the past. *Ever since the days of the Revolution there had always been bad blood between the two arms of the Soviet security forces.*

    ◆ People used to think that feelings such as anger and resentment were carried in the blood.

bay for blood

British If you say that people **are baying for blood**, you mean that they are demanding that a particular person should be hurt or punished, because of something that person has done. *A large number of shareholders are now baying for his blood and although he owns a massive 15 percent of his company, he will be lucky to survive.*

♦ This expression compares the people's demands to the sounds that hounds make on a hunt.

blood and thunder

British If you describe a speech or performance as **blood and thunder**, you mean that it is full of exaggerated feelings or behaviour. *In a blood-and-thunder speech, he called for sacrifice from everyone.*

blood is thicker than water

When people say **'blood is thicker than water'**, they mean that someone's loyalty to their family is greater than their loyalty to anyone else. *Families have their problems and jealousies, but blood is thicker than water.*

blood, sweat, and tears

If you say that a task or project involves **blood, sweat, and tears**, you mean that it is very hard to carry out and needs a lot of effort or suffering. *It's almost as if the end product – the songs themselves – are less important than the blood, sweat and tears that went into them.*

☐ People sometimes vary this expression by replacing one of the nouns with a noun relevant to the subject they are talking about. *It seemed absurd to be told to sum up a story that has taken years of blood, sweat and creativity in '25 words or less'.*

have blood on your hands

If you say that someone **has blood on** their **hands**, you are accusing them of being responsible for a death, or for the deaths of several people. *I want him to know he has my son's blood on his hands.*

in cold blood

If you say that one person killed another **in cold blood**, you mean that they did it in a calm and deliberate way, rather than in anger or self-defence. People often use this expression to express shock or horror at a killing. *They murdered my brother. They shot him down in cold blood.*

☐ You can describe a killing as **cold-blooded** or say that the person who did it is **cold-blooded**. *The argument is self-defence, but it is clear to Blackburn that she is a cold-blooded killer.*

♦ In medieval times, people believed that certain emotions changed the temperature of the blood.

in your blood

If you say that something is **in** your **blood**, you mean that it is a very important part of you and seems natural to you, for example because it is traditional in your family or culture. *Trilok has music in his blood. 'I was born into a family of musicians.'*

like getting blood out of a stone
like getting blood out of a turnip

If you have difficulty persuading someone to give you money or information, you can say that it is **like getting blood out of a stone**. In American English, you can also say that it is **like getting blood out of a turnip**. *The goods have to be returned to their rightful owner and getting money back from the seller is like getting blood from a stone.*

make your blood boil

If you say that something **makes** your **blood boil**, you mean that it makes you very angry. *It makes my blood boil. He doesn't like the players yet he's always trying to interfere.*

♦ See the explanation at 'in cold blood'.

make your blood run cold
make your blood freeze

If you say that something **makes** your **blood run cold** or **makes** your **blood freeze**, you mean that it frightens or shocks you a great deal. *The rage in his eyes made her blood run cold... It's a blood-freezing image of corrupted innocence.*

♦ See the explanation at 'in cold blood'.

new blood
fresh blood

If you talk about **new blood** or **fresh blood**, you are referring to new people who are brought into a company or organization to make it more efficient, exciting, or innovative. Compare **young blood**. *The July Ministerial reshuffle is a chance to freshen up the government and make way for new blood.*

out for blood

If people are **out for blood**, they intend to attack someone, or to make them suffer in some other way. *They seem to be out for blood, and they're attacking everywhere where their enemy is.*

scent blood
taste blood

In a competitive situation, if you **scent blood**, you sense a weakness in your opponent and take advantage of it. If you **taste blood**, you have a small victory and this encourages you to think that you can defeat your opponent completely. *Right wing parties, scenting blood, have been holding talks aimed at building an alternative coalition... The real opposition to the Government continues to be its own backbenchers who have now tasted blood for the first time.*

◻ You can also say that someone gets **a scent of blood** or **a taste of blood**. *The market has got the scent of blood and, having sniffed it, they are going for it.*

sweat blood

You can say that you **are sweating blood** to emphasize that you are working very hard to achieve something. *I sweat blood to write songs with tunes that you can remember.*

young blood

If you talk about **young blood**, you are referring to young people who are brought into a company or organization in order to provide new ideas or new talent. Compare **new blood**. *The selectors have at last shown some bravery and forward thinking and gone for some young blood, fielding a side whose average age is just 26.*

◻ You can refer to young people who are full of enthusiasm and fresh ideas as **young bloods**. *Ray Floyd proved he can still compete with the young bloods when he became the oldest winner of the US Open at 43.*

blot

a blot on your escutcheon

British, old-fashioned If there is **a blot on** your **escutcheon**, you have damaged your reputation by doing something wrong. *For the leaders, this is probably a blip rather than a blot on the escutcheon.*

◆ An escutcheon is a shield, especially a heraldic shield displaying a coat of arms.

blow

strike a blow for something
strike a blow against something

If you **strike a blow for** something such as a cause or principle, you do something which supports it or makes it more likely to succeed. If you **strike a blow against** something, you succeed in weakening its harmful effect. *Johan has struck a blow for equality against an obvious and intolerable anomaly in the law... We have struck a major blow against drug dealing and crack manufacture in London.*

blows

come to blows

If two people **come to blows**, they disagree so much about something that they start to fight. *Some residents nearly came to blows over the proposal.*

blue

out of the blue

If something happens **out of the blue**, it happens unexpectedly. *Then, out of the blue, a solicitor's letter arrived.*

◆ This expression compares an unexpected event to a bolt of lightning from a blue sky. The expressions 'out of a clear blue sky' and 'a bolt from the blue' are based on a similar idea.

bluff

call someone's bluff

If someone has made a threat and you **call** their **bluff**, you put them in a position in which they would be forced to do what they have been threatening. You do this because you do not really believe that they will carry out their threat. *At a meeting with student representatives on October 12, Mr Lukanov warned that he would deal severely with any protest actions in the universities. Now that the students have called his bluff, it remains to be seen what Mr Lukanov can do.*

◆ In poker, a player who is bluffing is playing as though they have a strong hand when in fact they have a weak one. If another player calls the first player's bluff, they increase their stake to the required amount and ask the first player to show their cards.

board

above board

If you describe a situation or business as **above board**, you mean that it is honest and legal. *If you are caught out in anything not strictly above* *board, you may find yourself having to provide the taxman with old bank statements and proofs of income going back years.*

◆ This expression comes from card games in which players place their bets on a board or table. Anything that takes place under the table is likely to be against the rules, whereas actions above the table, where other players can see them, are probably fair.

across the board

If a policy or development applies **across the board**, it applies equally to all the people or areas of business connected with it. *It seems that across the board all shops have cut back on staff.*

□ You can also talk about an **across-the-board** policy or development.*All the environmental groups deplored across-the-board cuts announced by the government last October.*

◆ This was originally an American expression which was used in horse racing. If someone bet across the board, they bet on a horse to win or to come second, third, or fourth.

back to the drawing board

If you say that you will have to go **back to the drawing board**, you mean that something which you have done has not been successful and you will have to start again or try another idea. *Failing to win means going back to the drawing board, identifying shortcomings and attempting to improve on them.*

◆ Drawing boards are large flat boards, on which designers or architects place their paper when drawing plans or designs.

go by the board
go by the boards

If a plan or activity **goes by the board** or **goes by the boards**, it is abandoned and forgotten, because it is no longer possible to carry it out. 'Go by the board' is used in British English and 'go by the boards' is used in American English. *Although you may have managed to persuade him, while he was at school, to do some constructive revision before examinations, you may find that all your efforts go by the board when he is at university.*

◆ To go by the board originally meant to fall or be thrown over the side of a ship.

sweep the board

British If someone **sweeps the board** in a competition or election, they win all the prizes or seats. *The opposition has swept the board in Sofia,* *where the renamed Communists have failed to win a single seat.*

♦ This expression comes from card games where players place the money they are betting on a board or table. The image is of the winner sweeping his or her arm across the table to collect all the money.

take something on board: 1

British If you **take** an idea, suggestion, or fact **on board**, you understand it or accept it. *I listened to them, took their comments on board and then made the decision.*

take something on board: 2

British If you **take a** task or problem **on board**, you accept responsibility for it and start dealing with it. *All you have to do is phone, telex or fax us. Our co-ordinator will take your problem on board and solve it.*

♦ The literal meaning of this expression is to take something onto a boat or ship.

boat

float someone's boat

If something **floats** your **boat**, you find it exciting, attractive, or interesting. *I can see its appeal. But it doesn't float my boat.*

in the same boat

If you say that two or more people are **in the same boat**, you mean that they are in the same unpleasant or difficult situation. *If baldness is creeping up on you, take heart – 40 per cent of men under 35 are in the same boat.*

push the boat out

British If you **push the boat out**, you spend a lot of money in order to have a very enjoyable time or to celebrate in a lavish way. *I earn enough to push the boat out now and again.*

♦ This expression may come from people having a farewell party before setting sail on a voyage.

rock the boat

If someone tells you not to **rock the boat**, they are telling you not to do anything which might cause trouble or upset a stable situation. *Diplomats are expecting so much instability in a power struggle after his death that they argue it's unwise to rock the boat now… I'm outspoken, sometimes critical of the organization, which is seen as boat-rocking, upsetting a comfortable arrangement.*

Bob

Bob's your uncle

British When you are describing a process or series of events, you can say **'Bob's your uncle'** to indicate that it ends exactly as expected or in exactly the right way. *See this safety valve here? Well, if the boiler should ever get too hot, the safety valve releases all the excess steam, and Bob's your uncle. No problem.*

◆ This expression dates back to a political scandal of 1886. The Prime Minister Robert Cecil gave his nephew the position of Chief Secretary for Ireland, and many people criticized him for this. The name 'Bob' is short for 'Robert'.

body

a body blow

Mainly British If you receive **a body blow**, something happens which causes you great disappointment or difficulty. *The result will deliver a body blow to Conservative party confidence.*

◆ In boxing, a body blow is a punch between the breast-bone and the navel.

keep body and soul together
hold body and soul together

If you do something to **keep body and soul together**, you do it because it is the only way you can earn enough money to buy the basic things that you need to live. *For a while he held body and soul together by working as a laborer.*

over my dead body

If you reply **'over my dead body'** when a plan or action has been suggested, you are saying emphatically that you dislike it, and will do everything you can to prevent it. *They will get Penbrook Farm only over my dead body.*

boil

come to the boil
bring something to a boil

If a situation or feeling **comes to the boil** or **comes to a boil**, it reaches a climax or becomes very active and intense. 'Come to the boil' is used in British English and 'come to a boil' is used in American English. *Their anger with France came to the boil last week when they officially protested*

at what they saw as a French media campaign against them... The
opposition is sure to bring the dispute back to the boil in any election
campaign.

off the boil: 1

British In sport, if someone goes **off the boil**, they are less successful
than they were in the past. *I concede that I went slightly off the boil last*
season.

off the boil: 2

British If a feeling or situation goes **off the boil**, it becomes less intense
or urgent. *If a relationship seems to be going off the boil, it is a good idea to*
appraise the situation.

on the boil: 1

British If a situation or feeling is **on the boil**, it is at its point of greatest
activity or intensity. *Across the border in Sweden, a similar debate is on the*
boil.

on the boil: 2

British In sport, if a person is **on the boil**, they are performing very
successfully. *All three players are obviously on the boil at the moment in the*
Italian league.

bold

bold as brass

If you say that someone does something **bold as brass**, you mean that
they do it without being ashamed or embarrassed, although their
behaviour is shocking or annoying to other people. *Barry has come into*
the game bold as brass, brash and businesslike.

◆ This expression may be based on an incident that occurred in 1770,
when the London Evening Post illegally published a report of
Parliamentary proceedings. As a result, the printer was put in prison. The
Lord Mayor, Brass Crosby, released him and was punished by being
imprisoned himself. There were public protests and Crosby was soon
released.

bolt

a bolt from the blue

If you say that an event or piece of news was like **a bolt from the blue**,
you mean that it surprised you because it was completely unexpected.
You use this expression mainly when talking about unpleasant things. *A*

Foreign Office spokesman had described the coup as 'a bolt from the blue'.

◆ This expression compares an unexpected event to a bolt of lightning from a blue sky. The expressions 'out of a clear blue sky' and 'out of the blue' are based on a similar idea.

shoot your bolt

British If you say that someone **has shot** their **bolt**, you mean that they have done everything they can to achieve something but have failed, and now can do nothing else to achieve their aims. *The opposition have really shot their bolt; they'll never ever get any more votes than this.*

◆ This expression uses the idea of an archer who has only one arrow or 'bolt' and is defenceless once he has fired it.

bone

a bone of contention

A **bone of contention** is an issue or point that people have been arguing about for a long time. *Pay, of course, is not the only bone of contention.*

◆ The image here is of two dogs fighting over a bone.

close to the bone
near to the bone

If you say that a remark or piece of writing is **close to the bone** or **near to the bone**, you mean that it makes people uncomfortable, because it deals with things which they prefer not to be discussed. *This isn't strictly satire, it's far too close to the bone to be funny.*

cut to the bone

If resources or costs **are cut to the bone**, they are reduced as much as they possibly can be. *We managed to break even by cutting costs to the bone.*

have a bone to pick with someone

If you say that you **have a bone to pick with** someone, you mean that you are annoyed with them about something, and you want to talk to them about it. *'I have a bone to pick with you.'* *She felt justified in bringing up a matter that she had been afraid to discuss before.*

◆ This expression may refer to the fact that dogs often fight over bones.

bones

the bare bones

If you refer to **the bare bones** of something, you are referring to its most basic parts or details. *We worked out the bare bones of a deal.*

feel something in your bones

If you say that you can **feel** something **in** your **bones**, you mean that you feel very strongly that you are right about something, although you cannot explain why. *Joe, I have a hunch you're going to lose tonight. I just feel it in my bones.*

make no bones about something

If you **make no bones about** something, you do not hesitate to express your thoughts or feelings about it, even though other people may find what you say unacceptable or embarrassing. *There will be changes in this Welsh team until we get it right. I make no bones about that.*

◆ This expression may refer to a bowl of soup being easy to eat because there are no bones in it. Alternatively, it may refer to gambling. 'Bones' is an old word for dice, so a gambler who 'makes no bones' throws the dice after just one shake, rather than performing an elaborate ritual.

book

bring someone to book

British If someone **is brought to book**, they are punished officially for something that they have done wrong. *No-one has yet been brought to book for a crime which outraged Italy.*

◆ Originally if someone was brought to book, they were ordered to prove that something they had said or done was in keeping with a written rule or agreement.

by the book

If you do something **by the book**, you do it correctly and strictly according to the rules. *Although the manager of the shop wasn't aggressive, he played things by the book and was completely unforgiving. So I was taken down to the police station and charged with theft.*

close the book on something

If you **close the book on** something, you bring it to a definite end. You often use this expression to talk about a difficult or unpleasant situation being brought to an end. *Lawyers say they are happy to close the book on one of the most frustrating chapters of the company's history.*

in your book

You can say **'in** my **book'** when you are stating your own belief or opinion, especially when it is different from the beliefs or opinions of other people. *People can say what they like, but in my book he's not at all a* *bad chap.*

an open book
a closed book

If you say that a person's life or character is **an open book**, you mean that you can find out everything about it, because nothing is kept secret. *Her long life is not a completely open book, but it is full of anecdotes and insights into her part in Hollywood history.*

☐ If you say that something or someone is **a closed book** to you, you mean that you know or understand very little about them. *Economics were a closed book to him. It constituted a strange, illogical territory where two and two didn't always make four.*

throw the book at someone

If a person in authority **throws the book at** someone who has committed an offence, they give them the greatest punishment that is possible for the offence that they have committed. *The prosecutor is urging the judge to throw the book at Blumberg.*

◆ This expression refers to a book in which laws are written down.

you can't judge a book by its cover

If someone says '**you can't judge a book by its cover**', they mean that you should wait until you know someone or something better before deciding whether you like them, because your first impressions may be wrong. *We may say that we don't believe in judging a book by the cover, but research has shown that we do, over and over again.*

books

cook the books

If someone **cooks the books**, they dishonestly change the figures in their financial accounts or change other kinds of written evidence in order to deceive people or steal money. *Four years ago, he vowed to strike back after discovering that a promoter was cooking the books.*

◆ The 'books' in this expression are books of accounts.

in someone's good books
in someone's bad books

British If you are **in** someone's **good books**, you have done something that has pleased them. *While Becky was out, Jamie made an attempt to get back in her good books by doing all the housework.*

☐ If you are **in** someone's **bad books**, you have done something that has annoyed them. *Sir John was definitely in the Treasury's bad books for incorrect thinking on economic prospects.*

boot

get the boot

If someone **gets the boot**, they lose their job. *The chief reason he got the boot was because the Chancellor didn't trust him any more.*

☐ You can also use these expressions to talk about someone whose partner has ended their relationship, often in a sudden or unkind way. *Sean has been given the boot by his girlfriend after admitting he'd been unfaithful to her.*

put the boot into someone: 1
put the boot in

British If someone **puts the boot into** a person or thing, especially a very weak person or thing, they criticize them very severely or are very unkind about them. You can also say that they **put the boot in**. *There's no one quite like an unpublished novelist for putting the boot into established reputations.*

put the boot in: 2

British If someone **puts the boot in**, they attack another person by kicking or hitting them. *Policemen who are tempted to put the boot in occasionally will have to tread more carefully in future.*

boots

die with your boots on

If you say that someone **died with** their **boots on**, you mean that they died while they were still actively involved in their work. *Unlike most Asian businesspeople, who die with their boots on, he has very sensibly left the entire running of Seamark to his son, apart from the occasional word of advice.*

☐ People sometimes replace 'boots' with another word which relates to a person's job or life. *His career lasted longer than his looks. Wrinkles and all, he died with his greasepaint on.*

◆ This expression was originally used to refer to a soldier who died in battle.

fill your boots

British If you **fill** your **boots** with something valuable or desirable, you get as much of it as you can. *Not everything in Japan looks bleak: having filled their boots with cheap capital in 1987–89, many companies remain liquid enough to do without bank loans.*

lick someone's boots
lick someone's shoes

If you say that one person **licks** another person's **boots** or **licks** their **shoes**, you are critical of them because they will do anything at all to please the second person, often because the second person is powerful or influential and the first person wants something from them. *Even if you didn't have an official position you'd still be a big shot locally, everybody'd be licking your boots.*

☐ You can call someone who does this a **bootlicker**.

step into someone's boots
fill someone's boots

Mainly British In sport, if you take over from another person who has been injured or who has given up their position, you can say that you **step into** their **boots**. If you are as successful as them, you can say that you **fill** their **boots**. Compare **step into** someone's **shoes**; see **shoes**. *Michael Kinane, the leading Irish jockey, has turned down the chance to step into Steve Cauthen's boots and ride for Sheikh Mohammed next season... It is sad that he's gone, but if ever there was a man to fill his boots, it's Kevin Keegan.*

bootstraps

pull yourself up by your bootstraps

If you say that someone **has pulled** themselves **up by** their **bootstraps**, you are showing admiration for them because they have improved their situation by their own efforts, without help from anyone else. *It was his ability to pull himself up by his bootstraps which appealed to Mrs Thatcher. She defied those with misgivings by making him deputy chairman.*

◆ Bootstraps are straps attached to a boot which you use for pulling it on.

bottom

the bottom falls out of something

If **the bottom falls out of** a market or industry, people stop buying its products in as large quantities as before. *But just as quickly, the bottom fell out of the American home video game market.*

bow

bow and scrape

If you accuse someone of **bowing and scraping**, you mean that they are behaving towards a powerful or famous person in a way that you consider too respectful. *I'm hoping my hereditary title will not put off prospective customers. It can be a drawback because some people feel they have to bow and scrape.*

◆ If you bow, you bend your body towards someone as a formal way of greeting them or showing respect. In the past, 'scraping' was a form of bowing which involved drawing back one leg and bending the other.

box

a black box

You can refer to a process or system as **a black box** when you know that it produces a particular result but you do not understand how it works. *Only a decade ago cancer was a black box about which we knew nothing at the molecular level.*

◆ In an electronic or computer system, a black box is a self-contained part. You can understand its function without knowing anything about how it works.

out of the box

Mainly American If you come **out of the box** in a particular way, you begin an activity in that way. If you are first **out of the box**, you are the first person to do something. *Are you anticipating that Clinton is going to come right out of the box with a whole series of fairly substantial decisions?... Arco is definitely first out of the box with an alternative gas for cars without catalytic converters.*

◆ This refers to a player running out of the box, which is the marked area where the batter stands, towards first base after hitting the ball in baseball.

out of your box

British If you say that someone is **out of** their **box**, you mean that they are drunk or affected by drugs, or that they are very foolish. *The guy must have been seriously out of his box!*

boy

a whipping boy

If you refer to someone or something as **a whipping boy**, you mean that people blame them when things go wrong, even though they may not be responsible for what has happened. *Honecker may have become a convenient whipping boy for the failures of the communist regime.*

◆ A whipping boy was a boy who was educated with a prince and was punished for the prince's mistakes because tutors were not allowed to hit the prince.

your blue-eyed boy
your fair-haired boy

If you say that a man is someone's **blue-eyed boy** or **fair-haired boy**, you mean that the person has a very high opinion of the man and gives him special treatment. You usually use these expressions to indicate that you think the person is wrong to have this opinion or to treat the man so favourably. 'Blue-eyed boy' is used mainly in British English and 'fair-haired boy' is used mainly in American English. *He'd lost interest in Willy by that time – I was the blue-eyed boy... Okay, okay. I won't do anything to hurt your fair-haired boy. And business is business. We'll work together as we always have.*

brains

pick someone's brains

If you **pick** someone's **brains**, you ask them for advice or information, because they know more about a subject than you do. *She, in turn, picked my brains about London – as she'd never been outside of the US and was thinking about a trip to England.*

rack your brains

If you **rack** your **brains**, you think very hard about something or try very hard to remember it. *They asked me for fresh ideas, but I had none. I racked my brain, but couldn't come up with anything.*

☐ You can refer to this activity as **brain-racking**.

◆ The old-fashioned spelling 'wrack' is occasionally used instead of 'rack' in this expression. An old meaning of 'to rack' was to stretch severely. This meaning has been retained in this expression and in 'the rack', an instrument of torture that stretched the body of the victim.

brass

the brass ring

American If someone is reaching for **the brass ring** in a competitive situation, they are trying to gain success or a big reward or profit. *There* *are good and bad features to living among people who are all young, on the make and going for the brass ring professionally.*

◆ On some merry-go-rounds, a brass ring was placed just out of the reach of the riders. If a rider managed to grab it, they won a free ride.

cold enough to freeze the balls off a brass monkey

British People sometimes say **'it's cold enough to freeze the balls off a brass monkey'** to emphasize that the weather is extremely cold. This expression is often varied. People often refer to this expression indirectly, for example by saying that it's 'brass monkey weather'. *It was a cold snap in the middle of spring with winds bitter enough to freeze a brass monkey.*

◆ A brass monkey was a plate on a warship's deck on which cannon balls were stacked. In very cold weather the metal contracted, causing the stack to fall down.

get down to brass tacks

If people **get down to brass tacks**, they begin to discuss the basic, most important aspects of a situation. *The third congress of Angola's ruling party was due to get down to brass tacks today with a debate on the party's performance during the last five years.*

◆ The usual explanation for this expression is that in Cockney rhyming slang 'brass tacks' are facts.

bread

the best thing since sliced bread

If you say that someone thinks that something is **the best thing since sliced bread**, you mean that they think it is very good, new, and exciting. This expression is often used in a humorous or ironic way. *When your programme first started I thought it was the best thing since sliced bread. But over the last three months I think you have adopted an arrogant attitude.*

bread and butter: 1

If something is your **bread and butter**, it is the most important or only source of your income. *I think I'm more controlled at work. I have to be; it's my bread and butter.*

bread and butter: 2

The **bread-and-butter** aspects of a situation or activity are its most basic or important aspects. *It's the bread and butter of police work, checking if anybody had seen anything suspicious.*

bread and circuses

Bread and circuses is used to describe a situation in which a government tries to divert attention away from real problems or issues, by providing people with things which seem to make their lives more enjoyable. *Metternich proceeded to neutralise political dissent through a policy of bread and circuses backed up by a fearsome secret police.*

◆ This is a translation of a phrase in a satire by the Roman poet Juvenal. It refers to the fact that, in ancient Rome, the authorities provided the people with public amusements and food in order to prevent possible rebellion.

cast your bread upon the waters

If you **cast** your **bread upon the waters**, you do something good or take a risk, usually without expecting very much in return. *You should make time to offer assistance to anyone who needs it. It's a case of casting your bread upon the waters – who knows how the favour will be repaid.*

◆ This is from the Bible: 'Cast thy bread upon the waters: for thou shalt find it after many days.' (Ecclesiastes 11:1)

know which side your bread is buttered

If you **know which side** your **bread is buttered**, you understand fully how you are likely to benefit from a situation, and you know what to do or who to please in order to put yourself in the best possible situation. *I'm in no doubt which side my bread is buttered for the present.*

breadline

on the breadline

People who are living **on the breadline** are extremely poor. *Too many men have children and then forget about them – leaving the children and the mothers living on the breadline.*

◆ In times of hardship, particularly in the last century in the United States, poor people used to line up outside bakeries or soup kitchens for free or very cheap bread.

break

give someone an even break
give a sucker an even break

Mainly American If you **are** never **given an even break**, you do not get the same chances or opportunities to do something as other people. *He* *kept talking about how she never got an even break from the family.*

□ If someone says **'never give a sucker an even break'**, they are saying light-heartedly or ironically that you should not allow less fortunate people to have the same chances and opportunities as yourself. *They had no idea of fair play or giving suckers an even break.*

◆ 'Never Give a Sucker an Even Break' is the title of a film starring W. C. Fields (1941).

breast

make a clean breast of something

If you tell someone to **make a clean breast of** something, you are advising them to tell the whole truth about it, so that they can begin to deal properly with a problem or make a fresh start. *'But how can I go home?' 'You'll have to make a clean breast of it, dear.'*

breath

a breath of fresh air

If you describe someone or something as **a breath of fresh air**, you mean that they are pleasantly different from what you are used to. *Basically, I was bored. Brian never wanted to do anything. Life was stagnant. So Mike, my present husband, was a breath of fresh air.*

take your breath away

If something **takes** your **breath away**, it amazes and impresses you because it is so wonderful. *He had never believed he would come to such power. The more he realized it, the more it took his breath away.*

with bated breath

If you wait for something **with bated breath**, you look forward to it, or you wait in an anxious or interested way to see what happens next. *The institution is now waiting with bated breath to see if the results of the next few surveys confirm its current assessment.*

◆ 'Bate' is an old form of 'abate', which in this context means 'control' or 'hold back'.

breeze

shoot the breeze

If you **shoot the breeze**, you talk with other people in an informal and friendly way. *Goldie does what she likes doing best: shooting the breeze* *about life, love, and her bad reputation.*

brick

drop a brick

British If you **drop a brick**, you say something tactless or inappropriate which upsets or offends other people. *After his comments on the live TV programme, Mr Freeman was immediately aware that he had dropped a political brick of the worst kind.*

bricks

make bricks without straw

If you say that someone **is making bricks without straw**, you mean that they are doing a job, or are trying to do it, without the proper resources that are needed for it. *His job was apparently to make education bricks without straw – that is to say, to be inspiring without having much money.*

◆ This expression is from the Bible and refers to Pharaoh's order that the captive Israelites should not be given any straw to make bricks. (Exodus 5:7)

bridge

cross that bridge when you come to it

If you say **'I'll cross that bridge when I come to it'**, you are saying that you intend to deal with a problem when it happens, rather than worrying about the possibility of it happening. *'You can't make me talk to you.' 'No, but the police can.' 'I'll cross that bridge when I come to it.'*

bridges

build bridges

If you **build bridges** between opposing groups of people, you do something to help them to understand each other or co-operate with each other. *We look for ways to build bridges between our two organizations.*

☐ You can refer to this process as **bridge-building**.

brief

hold no brief for something

British If you say that you **hold no brief for** a particular cause, belief, or group of people, you mean that you do not support it. *This newspaper* *holds no special brief for a committee that has done nothing to distinguish itself in the past.*

◆ A brief is all the papers relating to a particular client's case that are collected by the client's solicitor and given to the barrister who will represent them in court.

bright

bright as a button

Mainly British If you say that someone is as **bright as a button**, you mean that they are intelligent or full of energy. *She was as bright as a button and sharp as anything. If it had been her running the company, it might still be OK.*

bright-eyed

bright-eyed and bushy-tailed

If you describe someone as **bright-eyed and bushy-tailed**, you mean that they are lively, keen, and full of energy. *But for now, go and sleep awhile. I need you bright-eyed and bushy-tailed tomorrow... This will be a busy year, so you need to be bright-eyed and bushy-tailed to cope.*

◆ The comparison here is to a squirrel.

broke

go for broke

If you **go for broke**, you decide to take a risk and put all your efforts or resources into one plan or idea in the hope that it will be successful. *We have to go for broke for victory against Belgium in the World Cup next month.*

◆ If a gambler goes for broke, they put all their money on one game or on one hand of cards.

if it ain't broke, don't fix it

If someone says **'if it ain't broke, don't fix it'**, they mean that things should only be changed or interfered with if they are faulty or wrong. *With regard to proposals for some grand reorganization of the intelligence community: If it ain't broke, don't fix it. And I believe it is not broke.*

◆ The first recorded use of this modern proverb is by the American Bert Lance, President Carter's Director of the Office of Management and Budget (1977). He was referring to governmental reorganization.

broom

a new broom
a new broom sweeps clean

You can refer to someone as **a new broom** when they have just started a new job in a senior position and are expected to make a lot of changes. Compare **make a clean sweep**; see **sweep**. *'At least someone might actually make a decision now,' said one frustrated producer. But there is the usual apprehension you get with any new broom.*

☐ This expression comes from the proverb **a new broom sweeps clean**. *A new broom doesn't always sweep clean, it just brushes some of the worst dirt under the carpet for a while.*

brown

brown as a berry

If you say that someone is as **brown as a berry**, you mean that they are very tanned because they have been out in the sun. *Steve Hobbs had just come back from his holiday. Brown as a berry he was, when he came round here the following Monday.*

◆ The reference may be to juniper or cedar berries, as most other berries are red, purple, or white.

brownie

brownie points

If you say that someone should get **brownie points** for doing something, you mean that they can expect to be rewarded or congratulated for it. You may also be suggesting that this is the only reason that they did it. *Mr Stein would almost certainly win extra brownie points for taking an ultra-cautious view and removing uncertainty from the share price.*

◆ Brownies are junior members of the Girl Guides. They are expected to be well-behaved and helpful.

brush

tar someone with the same brush

If some members of a group behave badly and if people wrongly think that all of the group is equally bad, you can say that the whole group **is tarred with the same brush**. *At a rough guess, only 10 per cent of the inhabitants collaborated with the occupiers. But all have been tarred with* *the collaboration brush.*

◆ This expression comes from the use of tar to mark all the sheep in one flock to distinguish them from another flock.

bubble

the bubble has burst
prick the bubble

If you say that **the bubble has burst**, you mean that a situation or idea which was very successful has suddenly stopped being successful. You can also say that someone or something **has pricked the bubble**. *The bubble has burst. Crowds at the team's World League games are down from last year's 40,000 average to 22,000... The stock market has been unstable for a long time, a result of the economic downturn and the pricking of the property bubble.*

◆ The bubble referred to in these expressions is the South Sea Bubble, a financial disaster which took its name from The South Sea Company. In the early 18th century, this company took over the British national debt in return for a monopoly of trade with the South Seas. A lot of people invested in the company, but it crashed in 1720 and many investors became bankrupt.

on the bubble

American If someone is **on the bubble**, they are in a difficult situation, and are very likely to fail. *I'm always on the bubble, so I'm probably one of the best scoreboard readers you'll ever meet. If I make it, it'll be by one or two shots. If I miss, it'll be by one or two shots.*

◆ The reference may be to a bubble which is about to burst, or to the bubble on a spirit level, which will move off centre if the level is not kept exactly horizontal.

buck

◆ In poker, the buck was a marker or object which was passed to the person whose turn it was to deal the next hand. This person could either keep the marker or pass it on, in order to avoid dealing and being responsible for declaring the first stake.

the buck stops here

If you say **'the buck stops here'**, you are emphasizing that a problem is your responsibility, and that you are not expecting anyone else to deal with it. *I don't want anyone to blame the players. If you are going to point* *the finger at anyone, it must be at the man in charge and that's me. The buck stops here.*

♦ This expression is often associated with President Truman, who had it written on a sign on his desk in the Oval Office to remind him of his responsibilities.

pass the buck

If you accuse someone of **passing the buck**, you are accusing them of failing to take responsibility for a problem, and of expecting someone else instead to deal with it. *He is our responsibility. Canada is the only place he has ever known and to deport him is simply passing the buck because of a legal loophole.*

☐ This kind of behaviour is referred to as **buck-passing**.

bucket

kick the bucket

If you say that someone **has kicked the bucket**, you mean that they have died. This expression is used to refer to someone's death in a light-hearted or humorous way. *All the money goes to her when the old man kicks the bucket.*

♦ The origins of this expression are uncertain. One suggestion is that the 'bucket' was a wooden frame which was used when slaughtering pigs. The pigs were hung from the bucket by their back legs. After they had been killed, their legs often continued to twitch and kick against the bucket. Alternatively, it may refer to someone committing suicide by standing on a bucket, tying a rope around their neck, then kicking the bucket away.

bud

nip something in the bud

If you **nip** a situation or problem **in the bud**, you stop it at an early stage, before it can develop or become worse. *It is important to recognize jealousy as soon as possible and to nip it in the bud before it gets out of hand.*

♦ This expression may refer to extremely cold weather damaging a plant and stopping it flowering. Alternatively, it may refer to a gardener pruning a plant in bud to prevent it flowering.

buffers

hit the buffers

British If something such as an idea, plan, or project **hits the buffers**, it experiences difficulties which cause it to fail. *Their plans may not get very far before they hit the buffers.*

◆ Buffers are barriers at the end of a railway track.

bug

bitten by the bug

If you **are bitten by the** gardening **bug**, for example, or **are bitten by the** acting **bug**, you become very enthusiastic about gardening or acting, and you start doing it a lot. *Bitten by the travel bug, he then set off for a working holiday in Australia.*

bull

a bull in a china shop

If you describe someone as **a bull in a china shop**, you mean that they say or do things which offend or upset people, or which cause trouble, in situations where they ought to act carefully and tactfully. *In confrontational situations I am like a bull in a china shop.*

a red rag to a bull
a red flag before a bull

If something always makes a particular person very angry, you can say that it is like **a red rag to a bull** or **a red flag before a bull**. 'Rag' is used more commonly in British English and 'flag' is used more commonly in American English. Compare **a red flag**; see **flag**. *It's a red rag to a bull when my son won't admit that he's wrong... Our presence may have the effect of a red flag held permanently before a bull.*

◆ It is a common belief that the colour red makes bulls angry. In bullfighting, the matador waves a red cape to make the bull attack.

take the bull by the horns

If you **take the bull by the horns**, you act decisively and with determination in order to deal with a difficult situation or problem. *This is the time to take the bull by the horns and tackle the complex issues of finance.*

◆ In bullfighting, the matador sometimes grasps the bull's horns before killing it.

bullet

bite the bullet

If you **bite the bullet**, you accept a difficult or unpleasant situation. *The same stressful event might make one person utterly miserable, while* *another will bite the bullet and make the best of it.*

◆ During battles in the last century, wounded men were sometimes given a bullet to bite on while the doctor operated on them without any anaesthetic or painkillers.

get the bullet

British If someone **gets the bullet**, they lose their job. *The banks are still making money but they only have to have one bad year and everybody gets the bullet.*

bum

a bum steer

Mainly American If you describe information that you are given as **a bum steer**, you mean that it is wrong and misleading. *Did you give me a bum steer about your name and address?*

◆ This expression may refer to a worthless bullock. Alternatively, it may refer to someone being given directions which are not correct.

get the bum's rush

Mainly American If someone **gets the bum's rush**, they are completely ignored or rejected in an unexpected and upsetting way. *Let's face it, if the Tories give Mr Minor the bum's rush after the European elections he'll be looking for a job.*

◆ A bum is a person who has no permanent home or job, and very little money. This expression refers to a bum being thrown out of a place by force.

bundle

drop your bundle

Mainly Australian If you are failing at something and you **drop** your **bundle**, you give up and stop trying to win or succeed. *At 25 – 6 University were losing badly, but to their credit they did not drop their bundle.*

bunny

not a happy bunny

British If you say that someone is **not a happy bunny**, you mean that they are annoyed or unhappy about something. You use this expression to be humorous or ironic. *Heading off for the recess, then, they are none of them happy bunnies. But the real worry when they face their constituents* *may be deeper than mere party concerns.*

burn

burn your bridges
burn your boats

If you **burn** your **bridges**, you do something which forces you to continue with a particular course of action, and makes it impossible for you to return to an earlier situation. In British English, you can also say that you **burn** your **boats**. *I didn't sell it because I didn't know how long I would be here. I didn't want to burn all my bridges.*

◆ During invasions, Roman generals sometimes burned their boats or any bridges they had crossed, so that their soldiers could not retreat but were forced to fight on.

burner

on the back burner
on the front burner

If you put a project or issue **on the back burner**, you decide not to do anything about it until a later date, because you do not consider it to be very urgent or important. If you put a project or issue **on the front burner**, you start to give it a lot of attention, because you think it is very urgent or important. *She put her career on the back burner after marrying co-star Paul Hogan two years ago.*

◆ A burner is one of the rings or plates on the top of a cooker.

bush

the bush telegraph

British If you talk about **the bush telegraph**, you are talking about the way in which information or news can be passed on from person to person in conversation. *Jean-Michel had heard of our impending arrival in Conflans long before we got there. The bush telegraph on the waterways is extremely effective.*

◆ This expression refers to a primitive method of communication where people who are scattered over a wide area beat drums to send messages to one another.

not beat around the bush
not beat about the bush

If you **don't beat around the bush**, you say what you want to say clearly and directly, without avoiding its unpleasant aspects. In British English, you can also say that you **don't beat about the bush**. *Let's not beat about the bush – they rejected it. The Review Group said it was their most important single recommendation and the Government rejected it.*

◆ In game shooting, beaters drive birds or small animals out of the undergrowth by beating it with sticks. They may have to do this cautiously as they do not know exactly where the birds or animals are.

bushel

hide your light under a bushel

If someone tells you not to **hide** your **light under a bushel**, they mean that you should not be modest about your skills and good features, and instead you should be confident and willing to let people know that you have them. *In these challenging times, it is essential we must go out there and tell the world what we have to offer. We are proud of the facilities in Newmarket and this is not the time to hide our light under a bushel.*

□ People often vary this expression. *Never one to hide her talent under a bushel, she is all set to set up a legal practice with her solicitor husband.*

◆ This is from the Bible, where Jesus says: 'Neither do men light a candle and put it under a bushel, but on a candlestick.' (Matthew 5:15)

bushes

beat the bushes

Mainly American If you say that someone **is beating the bushes**, you mean that they are trying very hard to get or achieve something. *He was tired of beating the bushes for work, and he did not want to ask for help or accept charity.*

busman

a busman's holiday

Mainly British If someone spends part of their holiday doing or experiencing something that forms part of their normal job or everyday life, you can say that they are having **a busman's holiday**. *A fire crew's Christmas outing turned into a busman's holiday when their coach caught fire.*

◆ This expression may refer to bus drivers at the beginning of the 20th century when buses were horse-drawn. Drivers sometimes spent their day off riding on their own bus to make sure that the relief drivers were treating the horses properly.

busy

a busy bee
busy as a bee

If you describe someone as **a busy bee** or say that they are **busy as a bee**, you mean that they enjoy doing a lot of things and always keep themselves busy. *'I enjoyed being a busy bee, getting things done,' she says in her confident way.*

butter

butter wouldn't melt in your mouth

If you say that someone looks as though **butter wouldn't melt in** their **mouth**, you mean that although they look completely innocent, they are capable of doing something unpleasant or horrible. *He may look as though butter wouldn't melt in his mouth, but I wouldn't trust him.*

butterflies

butterflies in your stomach
get butterflies

If you say that you have **butterflies in** your **stomach** or have **got butterflies**, you mean that you feel very nervous about something that you have to do. *Any jockey who says he doesn't get butterflies down at the start is telling lies.*

butterfly

break a butterfly on a wheel

British If you talk about **breaking a butterfly on a wheel**, you mean that someone is using far more force than is necessary to do something. *The Huglets have had their ideology combed over, examined, misinterpreted and rewritten. Talk about breaking a butterfly on a wheel.*

◆ This is a quotation from 'Epistle to Dr Arbuthnot' (1735) by Alexander Pope. In the past, the wheel was an instrument of torture. A person was tied to it and then their arms and legs were broken or they were beaten to death.

button

a hot button

American If you say that a subject or problem is **a hot button**, you mean that it is topical and controversial, and people have very strong feelings about it. *If crime is the city's issue most known to outsiders, rent control is the city's hot button for its residents.*

on the button

Mainly American If you talk about a time or amount being **on the button**, you mean that it is exactly that time or amount. *He'd say he'd meet us at 10.00 on the button.*

press the right button

If you say that someone **presses the right button**, you mean that they cleverly or skilfully do the things which are necessary to get what they want in a particular situation. *In what it describes as a well-judged performance, the newspaper says he pressed all the right buttons to please the representatives.*

right on the button
on the button

If someone says that you are **right on the button** or **on the button**, they mean that you have guessed correctly about something. *The important thing is that the Treasury's forecast was right on the button.*

C

caboodle

the whole caboodle
the whole kit and caboodle

The whole caboodle or **the whole kit and caboodle** means the whole of something. 'The whole caboodle' is used only in British English. *I would probably find that I could borrow the whole lot. I could borrow the whole caboodle.*

◆ 'Caboodle' may come from the Dutch word 'boedal', meaning 'property'.

cage

rattle someone's cage

If you **rattle** someone's **cage**, you do or say something that upsets or annoys them. *If there's one thing I have learnt as an editor, it's that you can't create a truly superb magazine without rattling a few cages.*

Cain

raise Cain

If someone **raises Cain**, they get very angry about something, and show their anger by behaving or speaking violently. *The opposition parties intend to use the budget debates to raise Cain over the relationship between politicians and gangsters revealed by the scandal.*

◆ The reference here is to the Bible story in which Cain murdered his brother Abel in a fit of rage (Genesis 4:1–9).

cake

have your cake and eat it

If you say that someone wants to **have** their **cake and eat it**, you are criticizing them for trying to get all the benefits of two different situations or things, when they are only entitled to benefit from one of them. *What he wants is a switch to a market economy in a way which does not reduce people's standard of living. To many, of course, this sounds like wanting to have his cake and eat it.*

◆ Although 'have your cake and eat it' is now the most common form of the expression, the original was 'eat your cake and have it'. Some people consider the recent version illogical, since it is certainly possible to have a cake and then eat it but not the other way round.

take the cake

If you say that someone or something **takes the cake**, you are surprised or angry about something they have said or done. *With his one good arm the driver tore off his oxygen mask and reached through the wreckage to answer his mobile phone. Officers say they get to see some pretty odd things at times, but that one just about takes the cake.*

◆ Cakes have been awarded as prizes in competitions since classical times but this expression is thought to have its origin among African-Americans in the southern United States in the time of slavery. The competitors walked or danced round a cake in pairs, and the cake was awarded to the couple who moved the most gracefully.

cakes

cakes and ale

British **Cakes and ale** is used to refer to a time or activity when people enjoy themselves greatly and have no troubles. *Devotees of study holidays are quick to claim that being pale and acquiring poetic sensitivity does not necessarily mean stinting on the cakes and ale.*

◆ This expression is used in Shakespeare's 'Twelfth Night'. Sir Toby Belch says to Malvolio, 'Dost thou think, because thou art virtuous, there shall be no more cakes and ale?' (Act 2, Scene 3). 'Cakes and Ale' is also the title of a novel by Somerset Maugham, which was published in 1930.

calf

kill the fatted calf

If someone **kills the fatted calf**, they put on a big celebration to welcome back a person who has been away for a period of time. *He went off to make movies, and rumour has it that, when he returned, his record company didn't exactly kill the fatted calf.*

◆ This expression comes from the story of the prodigal son which is told by Jesus in the Bible (Luke 5: 3– 32). In this story, a young man returns home after wasting all the money his father has given him. However, his father is so pleased to see him that he celebrates his return by killing a calf and preparing a feast.

camp

a camp follower

You refer to someone as **a camp follower** when they follow or associate themselves with a particular person or group, either because they admire or support them, or because they hope to gain advantages from them. This expression is often used to show contempt. It is sometimes used to refer to women who are willing to have sex with the person or people that they want to be associated with. *Even in my day as a player, we had our camp followers.*

◆ Originally, camp followers were civilians who travelled with an army and who made their living selling goods or services to the soldiers.

can

carry the can

British If you **carry the can** for something that has gone wrong, you take the blame for it even though you are not the only person responsible. *It annoys me that I was the only one who carried the can for that defeat.*

◆ This was originally a military expression referring to the man chosen to fetch a container of beer for a group of soldiers.

in the can

If a film or piece of filming is **in the can**, it has been successfully completed. *We had to lie motionless for rehearsal after rehearsal, take after take, until the scene was in the can.*

◆ Cinema film is stored in circular metal containers called cans.

candle

burn the candle at both ends

If you say that someone **is burning the candle at both ends**, you mean that they are going to have problems because they are trying to do too much; for example, they may be regularly going to bed very late even though they have to get up early in the morning. *Frank delighted in burning the candle at both ends. No matter how much of a night-life he was living, he maintained our ritual of an early breakfast.*

can't hold a candle to someone

If you are comparing two people or things and you say that the first **can't hold a candle to** the second, you mean that the second is much better than the first. *Surveys reveal that most people glean their knowledge of science from television. Newspapers, books and radio cannot hold a candle to television.*

◆ This expression implies that the first person is not worthy even to hold a light to help the other person to see.

not worth the candle
the game is not worth the candle

Mainly British If you say that something is **not worth the candle** or **the game is not worth the candle**, you mean that it is not worth the trouble or effort which is needed in order to achieve or obtain it. *If it means falling into my present state afterwards, writing isn't worth the candle. If I can't do it without being in danger of drinking again, it's just not worthwhile... It is some kind of a success story to be able to boast you married the richest woman in the world. But he must sometimes wonder whether the game was worth the candle.*

◆ This expression originally referred to a game of cards where the amount of money at stake was less than the cost of the candle used up during the game.

candy

like a kid in a candy store
like a child in a sweet shop

If you say that someone is **like a kid in a candy store**, you mean that they do whatever they want without restricting or moderating their behaviour in any way. In British English, you can say 'sweet shop' instead of 'candy store'. *Brett Brubaker, a money manager at Abraham and Sons in Chicago, went on a buying binge and 'felt like a kid in a candy store', he recalls... In Westminster the party of law and order seems to have become the party of deception and distortion. They showed all the monetary restraint of a child in a sweet shop.*

like taking candy from a baby

If you say that doing something is **like taking candy from a baby**, you mean that it is very easy. *In the end it was like taking candy from a baby. For the second week in succession the Premier League leaders were offered three points on a plate and took maximum advantage to go four points clear at the top.*

cannon

a loose cannon
a loose cannon on the deck

If you describe someone as **a loose cannon** or **a loose cannon on the deck**, you mean that their behaviour is unpredictable and therefore could have unfortunate or dangerous consequences. *There is a widespread worry that the military command has turned into a loose cannon beyond the control of the government.*

♦ This expression refers to the cannons which used to be carried on the decks of warships. If one of the cannons was not properly fastened down, it could spin round and make a hole in the ship.

canoe

paddle your own canoe

If you **paddle** your **own canoe**, you control what you want to do without help or interference from anyone. *You now have the self-knowledge and energy to paddle your own canoe to a job that's perfect for you.*

♦ This was originally an American expression but it is now more common in British English.

cap

cap in hand

Mainly British If you go **cap in hand** to someone, you ask them very humbly and respectfully for money or help. The usual American expression is **hat in hand**. *On holiday, if you rely on cash and lose the lot you could end up going cap in hand to the nearest British consulate.*

if the cap fits

British You can say **'if the cap fits'** when you are telling someone that unpleasant or critical remarks which have been made about them are probably true or fair. The American expression is **if the shoe fits**. *Promotional and activity have become their unwieldy middle names, but does the corporate cap fit?*

put your thinking cap on

If you **put** your **thinking cap on**, you try hard to solve a problem by thinking about it. *We've got five pairs of boots to give away, so get your thinking caps on and answer the question.*

◆ This expression may refer to the cap which judges used to wear when passing sentence or judgment.

set your cap at someone

British, old-fashioned If a woman **sets** her **cap at** a man, she tries to make him notice her, usually because she wants to marry him. *Now she wanted a big man and she set her cap at the biggest star of them all.*

◆ The idea behind this expression is that in the past women would wear their best cap in order to attract the attention of a man they wished to marry.

carbon

a carbon copy

If one person or thing is **a carbon copy** of another, the two people or things seem to be identical, or very similar. *She's always been quiet. She's a carbon copy of her mother – her mother always hated making a fuss.*

◆ A carbon copy of a document is a copy of it which is made using carbon paper.

card

a calling card

If you describe what someone possesses or has achieved as **a calling card**, you mean that it gives them a lot of opportunities which they would not otherwise have had. *Some cabinet ministers, comparing their likely pension with their lifestyle, are tempted to look for jobs in the City while their present status remains a calling card.*

◆ In American English, a calling card is a small card which has your name and other personal information printed on it, and which you give to people when you visit or meet them.

a wild card

You describe someone or something as **a wild card** when they cause uncertainty, because nobody knows how they will behave or what effects they will have. *The Cossacks are the wild card in Kazakhstan. Armed and anarchic, they claim a million supporters and demand official recognition as a paramilitary force.*

◆ In games such as poker, a wild card is a card that can have any value a player chooses.

cards

lay your cards on the table

If you **lay** your **cards on the table** or **put** your **cards on the table**, you tell someone the truth about your feelings and plans. *I will lay my cards on the table. I am an atheist... We were shy of talking about the future because we hadn't laid our cards on the table... Put your cards on the table and be very clear about your complaints. This should clear the air.*

◆ The reference here is to players in a card game laying their cards face up for the other players to see.

on the cards
in the cards

If you say that something is **on the cards**, you mean that it is very likely to happen. In American English you can also say something is **in the cards**. *If he demands too much, the unions will vote him down. So a compromise is on the cards... He believes an invasion was never in the cards.*

◆ This is a reference to Tarot cards, or to other cards used to predict the future.

play your cards right

Mainly British If you **play** your **cards right**, you use your skills to do everything necessary to succeed or gain an advantage. *Soon, if she played her cards right, she would be head of the London office.*

◆ The reference here is to a player in a card game who can win the game if they use their cards well enough.

carpet

on the carpet
call someone on the carpet

In British English, if someone is **on the carpet**, they are in trouble for doing something wrong. In American English, you say they **are called on the carpet**. *The 22-year-old bad boy of English cricket was on the carpet again this week for storming out of the ground when told to wear one of the club's sponsored shirts.*

◆ This expression may refer to a piece of carpet in front of a desk where someone stands while being reprimanded. Alternatively, it could refer to an employer calling a servant into a drawing room, or other room with a carpet, in order to reprimand them.

roll out the red carpet

If you **roll out the red carpet** for someone, especially someone famous or important, you give them a special welcome and treat them as an honoured guest. *The museum staff rolled out the red carpet; although it was a Sunday, the deputy director came in especially to show us round.*

☐ You can also say that someone receives **red carpet** treatment or a **red carpet** welcome. *Yeltsin arrived in Rome this morning to a red carpet welcome by Italian officials.*

◆ It is customary to lay out a strip of red carpet for royalty or other important guests to walk on when they arrive for an official visit.

sweep something under the carpet

Mainly British If you **sweep** something **under the carpet**, you try to hide it and forget about it because you find it embarrassing or shameful. Other verbs such as 'brush' and 'push' are sometimes used instead of 'sweep'. *People often assume if you sweep something under the carpet the problem will go away, but that is not the case.*

carrot

carrot and stick

If someone uses a **carrot and stick** method to make you do something, they try to make you do it, first by offering you rewards and then by threatening you. Compare **carry a big stick**; see **stick**. *But Congress also wants to use a carrot and stick approach to force both sides to negotiate an end to the war.*

□ 'Carrot' and 'stick' are also used in many other structures with a similar meaning. *Protests continued, however, so the authorities substituted the carrot for the stick... When the Security Council waves a stick at an offending country, the secretary-general can also offer a carrot as encouragement.*

◆ The idea behind this expression is that an animal such as a donkey can be encouraged to move forward either by dangling a carrot in front of it or by hitting it with a stick. The carrot represents the tempting offer and the stick represents the threat.

dangle a carrot in front of someone
offer someone a carrot

If someone **dangles a carrot in front of** you or **offers** you **a carrot**, they try to persuade you to do something by offering you a reward if you do it. *An additional carrot being dangled in front of the Spanish is to move the headquarters of the company running the project from Munich to Madrid... Tax cuts may be offered as a carrot to voters ahead of the next election.*

◆ The image here is of someone encouraging a donkey to move forward by holding a carrot in front of it.

cart

put the cart before the horse

If you say that someone is **putting the cart before the horse**, you are criticizing them for doing things in the wrong order. *Creating large numbers of schools before improving school management is putting the cart before the horse.*

cash

a cash cow

If you refer to a source of money as **a cash cow**, you mean that it continues to produce a large amount of money and profit over a long period, without needing a lot of funding. *The park has been a cash cow for the city. Property and sales taxes there account for approximately 15 per cent of the city's general fund.*

castles
castles in the air
castles in Spain

If you say that someone is building **castles in the air**, you mean that they have unrealistic plans or hopes for the future. In British English, you can also say that they are building **castles in Spain**. *'Along the way I have to become very very rich.' He shook his head in wonder at her. 'You're building castles in the air, Anne.'... However, I also have a rich imaginary life, my equivalent of castles in Spain.*

cat
cat and mouse
a game of cat and mouse

In a contest or dispute, if one person plays **cat and mouse** with another, they know that they can win easily and quickly but they choose to do it slowly so that their opponent suffers more. You can also say that they play **a game of cat and mouse**. *He would play cat-and-mouse with other riders, sometimes waiting until the fourth lap to come from behind and win.*
□ **Cat and mouse** is also used before 'game' or another word. *They were arrested after a cat-and-mouse chase through the fields.*
◆ The reference here is to a cat playing with a mouse before killing it.

a cat on hot bricks
a cat on a hot tin roof

If someone is very nervous or restless, you can say they are like **a cat on hot bricks** or **a cat on a hot tin roof**. *Why are you shifting from one foot to the other like a cat on hot bricks?... The company has unbalanced inventories and executives who are as nervous as a cat on a hot tin roof.*
□ 'Cat On A Hot Tin Roof' is the title of a play by the American writer Tennessee Williams (1955).

the cat's whiskers

British, old-fashioned If you describe someone or something as **the cat's whiskers**, you are saying in a light-hearted way that they are the best person or thing of their kind. *As far as knowing the market and supplying it are concerned, she's the cat's whiskers.*
□ If someone thinks that they are **the cat's whiskers**, they are very pleased with themselves or very proud of themselves. *She had this great dress on with huge skirts, and she thought she was the cat's whiskers as she came out along the gallery.*
◆ This expression was originally American. It became popular in Britain during the 1920s, perhaps because 'cat's whisker' was also the name of a fine wire in a crystal wireless receiver.

a fat cat

You can refer to a businessman or politician as **a fat cat** when you disapprove of the way they use their wealth, power, and privileges, for example because it seems unfair or wrong to you. *The Government should launch an inquiry into the fat cats of commerce making huge profits out of the public.*

fight like cat and dog

If you say that two people **fight like cat and dog**, you mean that they frequently have violent arguments with each other. *They had fought like cat and dog ever since he could remember, and he wondered how they'd got together in the first place.*

grin like a Cheshire cat

If you say that someone **is grinning like a Cheshire cat**, you mean that they are smiling broadly, usually in a foolish way. *Standing on the door step and grinning like a Cheshire Cat was Bertie Owen... A beaming Steve stood in the background, nodding his head up and down and wearing a Cheshire Cat smile on his face.*

◆ The Cheshire cat is a character from 'Alice in Wonderland' (1865) by the English writer Lewis Carroll. This cat gradually disappears until only its huge grin remains. The idea for the character may have come from Cheshire cheese, which was moulded in the shape of a grinning cat. Alternatively, it may have come from signboards of inns in Cheshire, many of which had a picture of a grinning lion on them.

let the cat out of the bag

If someone **lets the cat out of the bag**, they reveal something secret or private, often without meaning to. *'The Mosses didn't tell the cops my name, did they?' 'Of course not,' she said. 'They wouldn't want to let the cat out of the bag.'*

◆ This expression may have its origin in an old trick where one person pretended to sell a piglet in a bag to another, although the bag really contained a cat. If the cat was let out of the bag, then the trick would be exposed. 'A pig in a poke' is based on the same practice: see **pig**.

like the cat that got the cream
like the cat that ate the canary

If you say that someone looks **like the cat that got the cream** or **like the cat that ate the canary**, you mean that they look satisfied and pleased with themselves, for example because they have been successful or done something they are proud of. 'Like the cat that got the cream' is used mainly in British English. *'Thanks a million,' he repeats, grinning like the cat that nearly got the cream... Jule stands at one end, and on his face, more clearly than on those of his colleagues, is the look of the cat that* *ate the canary.*

no room to swing a cat

Mainly British If you say that there is **no room to swing a cat** in a place, you are emphasizing that it is very small and there is very little space. *It was billed as a large, luxury mobile home, but there was barely room to swing a cat... We went into the ward, and my first thought was, how is she going to sleep. You couldn't swing a cat.*

◆ The 'cat' in this expression is probably a 'cat-o'-nine-tails', a whip with nine lashes which was used in the past for punishing offenders in the army and navy. However, the expression could be connected with the practice in the past of swinging cats by their tails as targets for archers.

put the cat among the pigeons

British If a remark or action **puts** or **sets the cat among the pigeons**, it causes trouble or upset. *Once again she set the cat among the pigeons, claiming that Michael was lying.*

see which way the cat jumps

Mainly British If someone waits to **see which way the cat jumps**, they delay making a decision or taking action on something until they are more confident about how the situation will develop. *I'm going to sit tight and see which way the cat jumps.*

◆ This expression could be connected with the old game of 'tip-cat', in which players waited to see which way a short piece of wood called the 'cat' moved before hitting or 'tipping' it.

there's more than one way to skin a cat

People say **'there's more than one way to skin a cat'** when they want to point out that there are several ways to achieve something, not just the conventional way. *Ministers who previously insisted there was no alternative to Britain's ERM policy were last night saying: 'There is more than one way to skin a cat.'*

when the cat's away, the mice will play

If you say **'when the cat's away, the mice will play'**, you mean that people do what they want or misbehave when the person who has authority over them is away. People sometimes just say **'when the cat's away'**. *While the cat's away – when a supervisor was out, some employees began straggling in late.*

catbird
in the catbird seat

American, old-fashioned If someone is sitting **in the catbird seat**, they are in an important or powerful position. *'The sonofabitch couldn't get along without me.' 'Yeah, he'd go broke tomorrow if you left him, right?*

And you, you'd be sitting in the catbird seat, right?'
◆ This expression became widely known in the 1940s and 1950s, when it was used by the baseball commentator Red Barber. Catbirds are North American songbirds. The expression may be explained by the fact that catbirds often sit very high up in trees.

Catch
a Catch 22

A **Catch 22** is an extremely frustrating situation in which one thing cannot happen unless another thing has happened, but the other thing cannot happen unless the first thing has happened. *There's a Catch 22 in social work. You need experience to get work and you need work to get experience… It's a Catch 22 situation here. Nobody wants to support you until you're successful, particularly if you're a woman. But without the support how can you ever be successful?*
◆ This expression comes from the novel 'Catch 22' (1961), by the American author Joseph Heller, which is about bomber pilots in the Second World War. Their 'Catch 22' situation was that any sane person would ask if they could stop flying. However, the authorities would only allow people to stop flying if they were insane.

cats
it's raining cats and dogs

You can say **'it's raining cats and dogs'** to emphasize that it is raining very heavily. *'You mean she wasn't wearing a coat, even though it was raining cats and dogs?'*

◆ There are several possible explanations for this expression, but none of them can be proved. It may refer to the days when drainage in towns was so poor that cats and dogs sometimes drowned in heavy rainfall. Alternatively, 'cats and dogs' could be a corruption or misunderstanding of the Greek word 'catadupe', meaning 'waterfall', so the expression would originally have been 'it's raining like a waterfall'. The origin may also be in Norse mythology, where cats and dogs were sometimes associated with the spirit of the storm.

caution

throw caution to the wind

If you **throw caution to the wind** or **throw caution to the winds**, you do something without worrying about the risks and danger involved. *This was no time to think, he decided. He threw caution to the winds and rang the bell of the ground-floor flat.*

centre (*American* **center**)
centre stage
    If someone or something takes **centre stage**, they become the most significant or noticeable person or item in a situation. *In his fiction, drugs don't take center stage very often, but they are a persistent theme... She has held centre stage for a decade now and has just enjoyed her biggest US hit in years.*

cents
your two cents' worth
    If you have or you put in your **two cents' worth**, you give your opinion about something, even if nobody has asked you for it. *Your father kept telling me to hush up and don't be a damn fool, but you know me, I had to put in my two cents' worth.*

chaff
separate the wheat from the chaff
separate the grain from the chaff
    If you **separate the wheat from the chaff** or **separate the grain from the chaff**, you decide which things or people in a group are good or necessary, and which are not. *The reality is often blurred by an overdose of propaganda. It is becoming more and more difficult to separate the wheat from the chaff.*

☐ You can refer to the good or necessary things or people in a group as 'wheat' or 'grain', and to the others as 'chaff'. *Your health or day-to-day work may undergo a significant change, but it simply means that the chaff is being swept away to reveal the seeds of a better future.*

♦ The 'chaff' is the outer husks of wheat or other cereal which has been separated from the grain by winnowing or threshing. In the Bible (Matthew 3:12; Luke 3:17), John the Baptist uses the image of someone separating the wheat from the chaff to describe how Jesus will separate those who go to heaven from those who go to hell.

chain
pull someone's chain
yank someone's chain
    Mainly American If you **pull** someone's **chain** or **yank** their **chain**, you

tease them about something, for example by telling them something which is not true. *I glared at her, and she smiled. When would I learn to smarten up and ignore her when she yanked my chain?*

◆ The image here is of someone teasing a dog by pulling the chain that it is tied up with.

chalice

a poisoned chalice

British If you refer to a job or an opportunity as **a poisoned chalice**, you mean that it seems to be very attractive but will in fact lead to failure or create a very unpleasant situation. *The contract may yet prove to be a poisoned chalice.*

chalk

by a long chalk

British You can use **by a long chalk** to add emphasis to a statement you are making, especially a negative statement or one that contains a superlative. *Where do you think you're going, Kershaw? You haven't finished by a long chalk.*

◆ This expression may refer to the practice of making chalk marks on the floor to show the score of a player or team. 'A long chalk' would mean 'a lot of points' or 'a great deal'.

chalk and cheese

British If you say two people or two things are like **chalk and cheese**, you are emphasizing that they are completely different from each other. *Our relationship works because we are very aware of our differences, we accept that we are chalk and cheese.*

changes

ring the changes

British If you **ring the changes**, you make changes in the way something is organized or done in order to alter or improve it. *The different varieties within each brand enable you to ring the changes to ensure that your dog never gets bored with his food.*

◆ In bell-ringing, to 'ring the changes' means to ring a number of church bells, each of which gives a different note, one after the other in every possible combination.

chapter

chapter and verse

If you say that someone gives you **chapter and verse** on a subject, you mean that they give you all the details of it, without missing anything out. *When we expressed doubts they handed us the proof, chapter and verse.*

◆ This expression refers to the practice of giving precise chapter and verse numbers when quoting passages from the Bible.

chase

cut to the chase

American If someone **cuts to the chase**, they start talking about or dealing with what is really important, instead of less important things. *The Council ought to cut to the chase and make a political decision based on what Council members feel is the best use for the house.*

◆ In films, when one scene ends and another begins the action is said to 'cut' from one scene to the next. If a film 'cuts to the chase', it moves on to a car chase scene. This expression compares the important matters to be discussed or dealt with to the exciting action in a film, such as car chases.

cheek

cheek by jowl

If you say that people or things are **cheek by jowl**, you mean that they are very close together, especially in a way that seems undesirable or inconvenient. *You'd think living so close would make people friendlier, but it didn't. After about seven years, all this living cheek-by-jowl began to irritate people.*

◆ 'Jowl' is an old-fashioned word for 'cheek'.

turn the other cheek

If you **turn the other cheek** when someone harms or insults you, you decide not to take any action against them in return. *Ian must learn to turn the other cheek, no matter what the provocation.*

◆ This expression comes from Jesus's words to His followers in the Bible: 'Resist not evil: but whosoever shall smite thee on thy right cheek, turn to him the other also.' (Matthew 5:39)

cheese

a big cheese

Old-fashioned If you describe someone as **a big cheese**, you mean that they have an important and powerful position in an organization. *Henri Maire is undoubtedly the big cheese of the Jura wine producers, dominating the industry not only locally but also nationally and internationally... He was a big-cheese divorce lawyer.*

◆ The word 'cheese' in this expression may be a corruption or misunderstanding of the Urdu word 'chiz' or 'cheez', meaning 'thing'. This started being used in English in about 1840 because of the British presence in India. Later the word came to refer to a person or boss.

chest

get something off your chest

If you **get** something **off** your **chest**, you talk about a problem that has been worrying you for a long time, and you feel better because of this. *My doctor gave me the opportunity to talk and get things off my chest.*

play your cards close to your chest
keep your cards close to your chest

If you **play** your **cards close to** your **chest** or **keep** your **cards close to** your **chest**, you do not tell anyone about your plans or thoughts. *Williams is playing his cards close to his chest, especially in terms of his driver line-up for next season.*

□ 'Cards' is often replaced with other nouns. *Taylor kept his thoughts close to his chest, saying only: 'I'm not prepared to comment.'... She looked up, meeting her friend's eye. 'Have you inside information?' 'Afraid not. Dave's playing this one close to his chest.'*

◆ This is a reference to card-players holding their cards close to their chest so that nobody else can see them.

chestnut

an old chestnut

British If you refer to a statement, story, or idea as **an old chestnut**, you mean that it has been repeated so often that it is no longer interesting. *But above all, the feminist struggle is too important to become an old chestnut over which people groan.*

chestnuts

pull someone's chestnuts out of the fire

Old-fashioned If you **pull** someone's **chestnuts out of the fire**, you save them from a very difficult situation which they have got themselves into, or to solve their problems for them. *Presidents frequently try to use the CIA to pull their chestnuts out of the fire.*

◆ This expression is based on the fable of the cat and the monkey. The cat wanted to get some roast chestnuts out of the fire but did not want to burn its paws, so it persuaded the monkey to do the job instead.

chicken

chicken and egg: 1

If you describe something as a **chicken and egg** situation, you mean that you cannot decide which of two related things happened first and caused the other. *It's a chicken-and-egg argument about which comes first: Do people create a neighborhood lifestyle? Or does a neighborhood environment influence how residents live?*

chicken and egg: 2

If you say that something is a **chicken and egg** situation, you mean that it is impossible to deal with a problem because the solution is also the cause of the problem. *The Zoo may close for lack of public support. It is a chicken-and-egg situation in which the high cost of entry keeps people away.*

◆ This expression comes from the unanswerable question, 'Which came first, the chicken or the egg?'

chicken feed: 1

If you refer to an amount, usually of money, as **chicken feed**, you mean that it is very small. *The £70,000-a-year backing received from sponsors is chicken feed compared to the £20m budgets available to some of his rivals.*

chicken feed: 2

If you say that someone or something is **chicken feed**, you mean that they are insignificant, especially in comparison to another person or thing. *There's Masters, too. He's the biggest threat. We're just chickenfeed.*

like a headless chicken
like a chicken with its head cut off

If you say that someone is running around **like a headless chicken** or **like a chicken with its head cut off**, you are criticizing them for behaving in an uncontrolled or disorganized way, and not thinking calmly or logically. *Instead of running round like a headless chicken you're using your efforts in a more productive way, more efficiently… They were all running around like chickens with their heads cut off – they didn't know where to go, where to sit, who to talk to.*

◆ Chickens have been known to run around for a short time after they have had their heads cut off.

chickens

not count your chickens
don't count your chickens before they're hatched

If you say that you **are not counting** your **chickens**, you mean that you are not going to make plans for the future because you do not know for certain how a particular situation will develop. *If we get through, Real Madrid and the Italian side Genoa will be massive hurdles to overcome. Most of the top sides are better now than they were in the early eighties so I'm not counting my chickens.*

☐ This expression comes from the proverb **don't count your chickens before they're hatched**.

chiefs

too many chiefs and not enough Indians
too many chiefs

People say **'too many chiefs and not enough Indians'** when they want to criticize an organization for having too many people in charge and not enough people to actually do the work. Many people find this expression offensive, since the use of the word 'Indian' to refer to Native Americans is is regarded as racist. *Americans should also come to recognize that many of their organizations have too many chiefs and not enough Indians.*

☐ People sometimes just say **'too many chiefs'**. *If he chose to counter-attack against the criticism, he might point to the bank's structure. It includes 21 executive directors. No surprise, then, that some insiders say there are too many chiefs.*

child

child's play

If you say that something is **child's play**, you are emphasizing that it is very easy to deal with. *The problem in Western Europe was described by* *one EU energy expert as child's play compared to that in Eastern Europe.*

chin

keep your chin up

If you **keep** your **chin up**, you stay calm or cheerful in a difficult or unpleasant situation. *Richards was keeping his chin up yesterday despite the continued setbacks.*

lead with your chin

If you say that someone **is leading with** their **chin**, you mean that they are behaving very aggressively, for example by creating a conflict. *We don't plan to attack the administration for not spending more on education. There's nothing to be gained from leading with our chins.*

◆ This expression comes from boxing, and refers to a boxer fighting with their chin sticking out, making it easy for their opponent to hit it.

take it on the chin

If someone **takes it on the chin**, they bravely accept criticism or a difficult situation without making a fuss about it. *When the police arrived, he took it on the chin, apologising for the trouble he'd caused them... Andrew is intelligent, wants to learn, and is therefore very coachable. He is also prepared to take criticism on the chin.*

◆ This refers to someone being punched on the jaw but not falling down.

chink

a chink in someone's armour

If someone or something has **a chink in** their **armour**, they have a weakness that can be taken advantage of, although they appear outwardly to be very strong and successful. *There was always the chance that, with their superior knowledge, they might find the chinks in his armour.*

◆ 'Armour' is spelled 'armor' in American English.

chip

a chip off the old block

If you describe someone as **a chip off the old block**, you mean that they are very similar to one of their parents in appearance, character, or behaviour. *I've known Damon since he was a boy and he's a chip off the old block. He has the same dry sense of humour, and the same dedication and total commitment.*

♦ The 'chip' in this expression is a small piece that has been cut off a block of wood.

a chip on your shoulder

If you say that someone has **a chip on** their **shoulder**, you mean that they feel angry and resentful because they think that they have been treated unfairly, especially because of their race, sex, or background. *My father wasn't always easy to get along with; he had a chip on his shoulder and thought people didn't like him because of his colour... Its leaders have lately seemed to revert to the sort of chip-on-shoulder nationalism that naturally makes neighbouring countries nervous.*

♦ There is a story that in America in the past, men sometimes balanced a small piece of wood on one shoulder in the hope that someone would knock it off and give them an excuse to start a fight.

chips

♦ In the following expressions 'chips' are the coloured tokens or counters which are used to represent money in casinos.

call in your chips

British If you **call in** your **chips**, you decide to use your influence or social connections to gain an advantage over other people. *And the other thing is that China can lobby very hard to call in all its chips from, for example, the African bloc.*

♦ In gambling, if you call in your chips, you ask people to pay you all the money that they owe you.

cash in your chips

If someone **cashes in** their **chips**, they sell something such as their investments, in order to raise money. *ICI was small in over-the-counter drugs in the States. It decided to cash in its chips at a surprisingly good price.*

♦ In a casino, if you cash in your chips, you exchange them for money at the end of a gambling session.

have had your chips

British If you say that someone or something **has had** their **chips**, you mean that they have completely failed in something they were trying to do. *After the 4–1 defeat by Wimbledon which all but scuppered their title ambitions, most of the 10,000 crowd were convinced they'd already had their chips.*

◆ This may refer to gamblers who have lost all their chips and so have to stop playing.

when the chips are down

If you refer to the way people behave **when the chips are down**, you are referring to their behaviour in a difficult or dangerous situation. *'How could you do that, knowing you might be rushing to your death?' And he smiled and he said, 'When the chips are down, you do what you have to do.'*

◆ In casinos, the players lay their chips down on the table to make their bets.

chop

chop and change

British If you say that someone **is chopping and changing**, you mean that they keep changing their plans, often when you think this is unnecessary. *After chopping and changing for the first year, Paul and Jamie have settled down to a stable system of management.*

◆ This expression was originally used to refer to people buying and selling goods. To 'chop' meant to trade or barter, and 'change' came from 'exchange'.

cigar

close but no cigar
nice try but no cigar

You use expressions such as '**close but no cigar**' or '**nice try but no cigar**' to point out to someone that they have failed in what they were trying to achieve or make you believe. *'I detest guards and burglar alarms. They're so vulgar. That's why I carry that dreadful gun in my purse, though I hardly know how to use it.' 'Nice try, Laura baby, but no cigar,' said Frank.*

◆ In the past, cigars were sometimes given as prizes at fairs. This expression may have been used if someone did not quite manage to win a prize.

circle

come full circle
the wheel has come full circle

If you say that something **has come full circle**, you mean that it is now exactly the same as it used to be, although there has been a long period of changes. *Her life had now come full circle and she was back where she started, in misery, alone.*

☐ People also say **the wheel has come full circle** or **the wheel has turned full circle**.

♦ This may refer to the medieval idea of the wheel of fortune which is constantly turning, so that people who have good luck at one time in their lives will have bad luck at another time.

square the circle

If you try to **square the circle**, you try to solve a problem that seems to be impossible to solve. *Chile is trying to square the circle of knowing what poor people ought to have, but not yet being able to afford it.*

a vicious circle

If you describe a difficult situation as **a vicious circle**, you mean that one problem has caused other problems which, in turn, have made the original problem even worse. *Kimelman believes the American economy has been caught in a vicious circle during the past two years. 'The economy couldn't create large numbers of jobs because consumers weren't spending. Consumers weren't spending because the economy wasn't creating jobs.'*

♦ This refers to the error in logic of trying to prove the truth of one statement by a second statement, which in turn relies on the first for proof. The expression is a translation of the Latin 'circulus vitiosus', meaning 'a flawed circular argument'.

circles

go around in circles

If someone **is going around in circles**, they are not achieving very much because they keep coming back to the same point or problem over and over again. *This was one of those debates which simply went round in circles with motions and countermotions being amended, withdrawn and re-submitted.*

run around in circles

If someone **is running around in circles**, they are having very little success in achieving something although they are trying hard, because they are disorganized. *She may waste a lot of energy running around in circles, whereas more careful planning could save a lot of effort and achieve a great deal.*

circus

a three-ring circus

If you describe a situation as **a three-ring circus**, you mean that there is a lot of noisy or very chaotic activity going on. This expression is used more commonly in American English than British. *They might fight among themselves, but grief was a private thing, not something to be turned into a three-ring circus by over-eager reporters.*

clappers

like the clappers

British If you say that someone does something **like the clappers**, you are emphasizing that they do it very quickly. *What is it that makes people run like the clappers for a train?*

◆ The clapper of a bell is the part inside it which strikes it to make it ring.

clean

come clean

If someone **comes clean** about something, they tell the truth about it. *He says it is now essential for the Government to come clean, tell the world exactly how the recent tragedy happened and announce an investigation.*

squeaky clean

If you say that someone is **squeaky clean**, you mean that they live a very moral life and do not appear to have any vices. *Our image has been a little over-exaggerated, saying that we're wholesome and squeaky clean. We're not all that, we're just very positive-minded people... He has a squeaky-clean reputation and would be a tough target for the attacks about family values.*

◆ Clean surfaces sometimes squeak when you wipe or rub them.

cleaners

take someone to the cleaners

If someone **is taking** you **to the cleaners**, they are behaving in an unfair or dishonest way which causes you to lose a lot of money. *Just for a change, the insurers discovered that they had been taken to the cleaners.*

◆ This developed from the expression 'to clean someone out', which has been used since the 19th century. People say that they have been 'cleaned out' when they have lost all their money and valuables, for example through being robbed or cheated.

clear

clear as a bell

If you say that something is as **clear as a bell**, you mean that it is very clear indeed. *Suddenly there is an unmistakable sound. It's as clear as a bell.*

clear as crystal

If you say that something is as **clear as crystal**, you mean that it is very clear indeed. *It was a brilliant blue day, as clear as crystal, with a sun that was just comfortably hot.*

☐ People also use the much more frequent adjective **crystal clear** to mean the same thing. *Let me make certain things crystal clear. This government has no intention of letting its authority be undermined.*

clear as day

If you say that something is as **clear as day**, you mean that it is very easy to see, or very obvious and easy to understand. *Suddenly she stepped out from behind a tree less than ten yards from me. I saw her face as clear as day.*

clear as mud

If you say that something is as **clear as mud**, you are saying in a light-hearted or sarcastic way that it is confusing and difficult to understand. *'It's all written down there! Self-explanatory! Clearly.' 'Clear as mud. Even I can't understand it, and I'm pretty smart.'*

steer clear
steer someone clear of something

If you **steer clear** of something or someone, you deliberately avoid them. If you **steer** someone **clear of** something, you help them to avoid it. *The Princess appealed to young people to steer clear of the dangers of drugs... Friends look out for your welfare. They listen to your problems. They steer you clear of damaging situations.*

clever

box clever

British If you say that someone **is boxing clever**, you mean that they are being very careful and cunning in the way they behave in a difficult situation, so that they can get an advantage over other people. *They have* *boxed clever shaping the market to themselves, and themselves to the market.*

cloak

cloak-and-dagger

You use **cloak-and-dagger** to describe activities, especially dangerous ones, which are done in secret. *They met in classic cloak-and-dagger style beside the lake in St James's Park, both tossing snacks to the listless waterfowl... Why all the cloak and dagger stuff?*

◆ This expression is taken from the name of a type of 17th century Spanish drama, in which characters typically wore cloaks and fought with daggers or swords.

clogs

pop your clogs

British If you say that someone **has popped** their **clogs**, you mean that they have died. This expression is used to refer to someone's death in a light-hearted or humorous way. *Comedians are getting younger and pop stars older and the kids want their heroes young. They want to know that the person they're paying to see isn't going to pop their clogs during the performance.*

◆ This expression may refer to an old sense of 'pop', meaning to pawn something. Clogs used to be the normal footwear of people such as mill workers, especially in the north of England.

close

too close to call

If a contest is **too close to call**, it is impossible to say who will win, because the opponents seem equally good or equally popular. *The presidential race is too close to call.*

closet

come out of the closet: 1

If someone **comes out of the closet**, they talk openly for the first time about beliefs, feelings, or habits which they have kept hidden until now. This expression is usually used to talk about homosexuals revealing their homosexuality for the first time. *This new law doesn't help people to come out of the closet... I suppose it's time I came out of the closet and admit I am a Labour supporter.*

☐ You can also talk about someone being forced back **into the closet**, and people often just talk about homosexuals **coming out**. *The HIV Aids crisis threatened to push us all back into the closet.*

◆ 'Out of the closet' was a slogan used by the Gay Liberation Front in the United States in the late 1960s.

come out of the closet: 2

When a subject becomes widely known or openly discussed for the first time, you can say it **comes out of the closet**. *'Prostate cancer came out of the closet,' he adds, 'and men started to join self-help groups to talk openly about prostate problems and the issue of screening.'*

cloth

cloth ears

British If you accuse someone of having **cloth ears**, you mean that they are not paying attention to something which is important, or that they do not understand it properly. You can also describe someone as **cloth-eared**. *The audience had been sitting there for two hours with cloth ears and they weren't attentive.*

cut from the same cloth

Mainly British If two or more people **are cut from the same cloth**, they are very similar in their character, attitudes, or behaviour. If they **are cut from a different cloth**, they are very different. *The charge I most frequently encounter today is that London critics are all cut from the same cloth: that they are predominantly white, male, middle-aged, middle-class and university-educated.*

cut your cloth
cut your coat according to your cloth

Mainly British If you **cut** your **cloth** according to your situation, you take account of the available resources when you are making plans and decisions. You can also say you **cut** your **coat according to** your **cloth**. *Ford would be forced to cut its cloth according to the demands of the market... He had already made it very plain that it was up to organisations which were supported by the taxpayer to cut their coats according to the cloth available.*

whole cloth

American If you say that a story or statement is made out of **whole cloth**, you mean that it is completely untrue. *According to legend, the flag Old Glory was the result of a collaboration between a well-known*

*Philadelphia seamstress and George Washington. But there are those who
say that story was made of whole cloth.*

clothes

steal someone's clothes

British If one politician or political party **steals** another's **clothes**, they
take their ideas or policies and pretend they are their own. *Here lies
Labour's chance. They could steal the Tories' neglected clothes, by making
Labour the party of lower taxes.*

cloud

on cloud nine

If you are **on cloud nine**, you are very happy because something very
good has happened to you. *I never expected to win, so I'm on cloud nine.*

◆ This may have come from the expression 'in seventh heaven'; see
heaven. The form 'on cloud seven' is still occasionally used in American
English. It is not clear why the number changed to nine.

under a cloud

If someone is **under a cloud**, people disapprove or are critical of them,
because of something they have done or are believed to have done. *He was
under a cloud after his men failed to find who had placed the bomb in the
office.*

clover

in clover

If you are **in clover**, you are happy or secure because you have a lot of
money or are enjoying a luxurious lifestyle. *Developers and bankers were
in clover until Congress abruptly changed the rules again, with the 1986
Tax Reform Act.*

◆ Clover is a plant which often grows in fields of grass. Cows are said to
enjoy grazing in fields which contain a lot of clover.

coach

drive a coach and horses through something

Mainly British If someone **drives a coach and horses through** an
agreement or an established way of doing something, their actions
severely weaken or destroy it. *The judgment appeared to drive a coach and
horses through the Hague agreement.*

coalface

at the coalface

Mainly British When people talk about what is happening **at the coalface** of a particular profession, they are referring to the thoughts, feelings, and actions of the people who are actually doing the job. *The only people who extol the newcomer are politicians and air marshals who are far removed from the feelings 'at the coalface'.*

◆ In a coal mine, the coalface is the part where the coal is being cut out of the rock.

coals

coals to Newcastle

If you say that supplying something to someone is like taking **coals to Newcastle**, you mean that it is pointless because they already have plenty of it. *Taking a gun to the United States would be like taking coals to Newcastle... That Moscow with its dilapidated economic machine would try to sell high technology to Japan, one of the world's high-tech leaders, sounds like a coals-to-Newcastle notion.*

☐ 'Coals' and 'Newcastle' can be replaced with other nouns. *Taking our music to your country would be like selling sand to the Arabs... It's like selling ice to the Eskimos.*

◆ The city of Newcastle was the main centre of England's coal-mining industry for over 150 years.

haul someone over the coals
rake someone over the coals

If you **are hauled over the coals** or **are raked over the coals** by someone, especially someone in authority, they speak to you very severely about something stupid or wrong that you have done. 'Haul someone over the coals' is used only in British English. Compare **rake over the coals**. *I heard later that Uncle Jim had been hauled over the coals for not letting anyone know where we were.*

◆ This expression may refer to a practice in medieval times of deciding whether or not someone was guilty of heresy, or saying things which disagreed with the teachings of the Church. The person accused of heresy was dragged over burning coals. If they burned to death they were considered guilty, but if they survived, they were considered innocent.

rake over the coals
rake over the ashes

Mainly British If you say that someone **is raking over the coals** or is **raking over the ashes**, you mean that they are talking about something that happened in the past which you think should now be forgotten or ignored. Compare **rake** someone **over the coals**. *She is firmly in the camp that says, yes, we made mistakes in the past, but let us not waste time raking over the coals when there is hard work to be done.*

coast

the coast is clear

If you say that **the coast is clear**, you mean that you are able to do something which someone does not want you to do, because they are not there to see you or catch you doing it. *Midge stepped aside, nodding that the coast was clear, and Lettie ran through the lobby and up the main staircase.*

◆ This expression may refer to smugglers and messages that there were no coastguards around and it was safe to land or set sail.

coat

trail your coat

British If you **trail** your **coat**, you risk starting an argument or disagreement. *Never lose your temper, and if you do, apologise for it afterwards. I realise I am trailing my coat; someone will no doubt remember an incident when I myself fell far short of these ideals.*

◆ It is said that it was an old Irish custom for a man to drag his coat along the ground as a sign that he was prepared to fight anyone who dared to tread on it.

coat-tails

on the coat-tails of someone

If someone does something **on the coat-tails of** another person or a trend, they are able to do it because of the success or popularity of that person or trend, and not because of their own efforts. *She was looking for* *fame and glory on the coat-tails of her husband... He said Australia was set to ride the coat tails of economic recovery in the US.*

cock

a cock and bull story
a cock and bull tale

If you describe an explanation or excuse as **a cock and bull story** or **a cock and bull tale**, you mean that you do not believe it. *I wasn't the one who fed her some cock-and-bull story about taking care of you.*

◆ This expression may come from old fables in which animals such as cocks and bulls could talk. Alternatively, it may come from the names of inns, such as 'The Cock' and 'The Bull', where people gathered and told each other stories and jokes.

cockles

warm the cockles of your heart

Old-fashioned If something **warms the cockles of** your **heart**, it makes you feel happy and contented. *In the bold black and white setting, the sunny yellow color of the house warmed the cockles of my heart.*

◆ Cockles are a type of shellfish. They are associated with the heart because they have a similar shape. The zoological name for cockles is 'Cardium', which comes from the Greek word for 'heart'.

coffee

wake up and smell the coffee

Mainly American If you tell someone to **wake up and smell the coffee**, you are telling them to be more realistic and more aware of what is happening around them. *It's time Lewis woke up and smelt the coffee and contacted me.*

coin

the other side of the coin

You can refer to an opposite or contradictory aspect of a situation as **the other side of the coin**. Adjectives such as 'reverse' and 'opposite' are sometimes used instead of 'other'. Compare **two sides of the same coin**. *My husband was often away on business when I was married, so being lonely is nothing new. And the other side of the coin is the amazing freedom you have knowing you don't have to please anybody except yourself... Hate* *is the opposite side of the coin to love, and often co-exists with love in a relationship.*

pay someone back in their own coin

If someone has treated you badly or unfairly and you **pay** them **back in** their **own coin** or **in the same coin**, you treat them in exactly the same way they have treated you. *The European Community has even released lists of American unfair trade practices, paying us back in our own coin.*

◆ 'Coin' is an old-fashioned word for currency.

two sides of the same coin
opposite sides of the same coin

If you say that two things are **two sides of the same coin** or **opposite sides of the same coin**, you mean that they are closely related to each other and cannot be separated, even though they seem to be completely different. Compare **the other side of the coin**. *He says he draws no line between tragedy and comedy. 'I've always felt that they are inseparable, that they are two sides of the same coin.'*

cold

leave someone cold

If something **leaves** you **cold**, it does not excite or interest you at all. *Given the world situation, chit-chat about shopping and hairdos leaves you cold.*

out in the cold
come in from the cold

If a person or organization is left **out in the cold**, they are ignored by other people and are not asked to take part in activities with them. *The Association of South-East Asian Nations has expressed concern that developing countries might be left out in the cold in current world trade talks.*

□ If someone or something **comes in from the cold**, they become popular, accepted, or active again after a period of unpopularity or lack of involvement. *The terrorists have been looking to come in from the cold for five years... Grenada's former Health Minister, who was fired from office two months ago, has been brought in from the cold by the Prime Minister.*

◆ 'The Spy who Came in from the Cold' is the title of a novel by the English writer John Le Carré, published in 1963.

when one person sneezes, another catches cold

Mainly British If you say that **when** one country or person **sneezes,** another **catches cold**, you mean that the things that happen to one country or person have a great effect or influence on other countries or people. *When America sneezes the rest of the world catches a cold. Applying this adage to financial markets, some onlookers fear that this week's necessary increase in American interest rates may hinder equally necessary interest-rate cuts in Europe and Japan.*

collar

hot under the collar

If you get **hot under the collar**, you get annoyed about something. *Judges are hot under the collar about proposals to alter their pension arrangements.*

colour (*American* color)

the colour of someone's money

If you say you want to see **the colour of** someone's **money**, you are expressing your doubts about their ability or willingness to pay for something. *He made a mental note never to enter into conversation with a customer until he'd at least seen the colour of his money.*

colours (*American* colors)

◆ A ship's colours are its national flag.

nail your colours to the mast: 1

British If you **nail** your **colours to the mast**, you state your opinions or beliefs about something clearly and publicly. *Let me nail my colours to the mast straightaway. I both like and admire him immensely.*

nail your colours to the mast: 2

British If you **nail** your **colours to the mast** of a particular person, idea, or theory, you say clearly and publicly that you support them. *If the man is so committed to evangelism, why doesn't he come out and firmly nail his colours to the mast of the group?*

◆ Battleships used to lower their colours to show that they were surrendering. Sometimes the colours were nailed to the mast as a sign of determination to fight to the end.

sail under false colours

If you say that someone **is sailing under false colours**, you mean that they are deliberately deceiving people. *This report sails under false* *colours. It purports to be a fair and rigorous examination of press regulation. But clearly the author had reached his basic conclusions long before he even began gathering any fresh evidence.*

◆ When pirate ships spotted a treasure ship, they often took down their own flag and raised the flag of a friendly nation, in order to get close enough to the ship to attack it.

show your true colours
see someone in their true colours

If someone **shows** their **true colours** or if you **see** them **in** their **true colours**, you become aware that they are not as nice, decent, or honest as you thought they were, because they show some unpleasant aspects of their character. Verbs such as 'declare' and 'reveal' are sometimes used instead of 'show'. *Seeking support, you'll turn to friends but beware, someone you trusted may now show their true colours... These men began to reveal the true colours of their personalities: some shouted, others grew insolent to the point of menacing us, others seemed quite mad.*

◆ Once a pirate ship had got close to a treasure ship by 'sailing under false colours', it then revealed its true identity by raising its own flag.

with flying colours

If you achieve something, such as passing an examination, **with flying colours**, you achieve it easily and are very successful. *I had a medical in April and passed with flying colours.*

◆ The image here is of a victorious battleship sailing back into port with its national flag flying.

comb

with a fine-tooth comb
with a fine-toothed comb

If you go through something **with a fine-tooth comb** or **with a fine-toothed comb**, you go through it very carefully and with great attention to detail. *I have taken the responsibility of going through Ed's personal papers and letters with a fine-tooth comb... Ms Hankin said neighborhoods where resisters were suspected of living were gone over with a fine-toothed comb.*

◆ A fine-tooth comb is a comb with very thin teeth set very close together. It is used to remove nits and lice from people's hair.

come

come out fighting
come out swinging

In a conflict, if someone **comes out fighting** or **comes out swinging**, they show by their behaviour that they are prepared to do everything they can in order to win. *Saudi Arabia and other crude oil producers have come out fighting, claiming the West is using environmental issues as a way of cutting back on oil and developing alternative energy sources.*

◆ If boxers come out fighting, they leave their corner as soon as the bell rings and attack their opponent immediately.

common

common as muck

British If you say that someone is as **common as muck**, you mean that they are lower-class and not sophisticated. This expression is usually considered offensive, but is sometimes used ironically. *Leary guessed correctly that his guests were as common as muck and planned the menu accordingly.*

cookie

caught with your hand in the cookie jar

Mainly American If you say that someone **has been caught with** their **hand in the cookie jar**, you mean that they have been caught stealing or doing something wrong. The usual British expression is **have** your **hand in the till**. *She left me. I got caught with my hand in the cookie jar one time too many, I guess.*

a smart cookie

If you describe someone as **a smart cookie**, you mean that they are clever and have lots of good ideas. *She is too much of a smart cookie to join the fashion circuit which still entices most of her fellow supermodels.*

that's the way the cookie crumbles

People say **'that's the way the cookie crumbles'** when they want to say that you should accept the way things happen or turn out, even if they turn out badly.

a tough cookie

If you describe someone as **a tough cookie**, you admire their qualities of courage, endurance, and independence. *One member of her local hunt said she was 'brave – a tough cookie'... He has a reputation as one tough cookie.*

cooks

too many cooks
too many cooks spoil the broth
too many cooks in the kitchen

If you say that there are **too many cooks**, you mean that a plan or project goes wrong because there are too many people trying to do it at the same time. *So far nothing had worked. One problem was that there were simply too many cooks.*

□ This expression comes from the proverb **too many cooks spoil the broth**.

□ In American English, you can also say there are **too many cooks in the kitchen**. *Declaring that 'there are simply too many cooks in the kitchen', Senator Robert Dole has proposed remedying the problems by creating a single committee to handle this year's legislation.*

cool

cool as a cucumber

If you say that someone is as **cool as a cucumber**, you mean that they are very relaxed, calm, and unemotional. *Never once did she gasp for air or mop her brow. She was as cool as a cucumber.*

coop

fly the coop

If someone **flies the coop**, they leave the situation they are in, for example because they do not like it or because they want to have more freedom to live or work as they please. Compare **fly the nest**; see **nest**. *His wife is so fed up with his coldness she is about to fly the coop.*

◆ A coop is a small cage in which chickens or small animals are kept. 'Coop' is also American slang for a prison.

cop

not much cop

British If you say that someone or something is **not much cop**, you mean that they are not very good. *I'm not making excuses for him, because* *he's not much cop as far as I'm concerned.*

♦ In early twentieth century slang, 'cop' meant 'value' or 'use'.

copybook

blot your copybook

British If you **blot** your **copybook**, you damage your reputation by doing something wrong. *It was just that their relationship had been so perfect. Until he'd blotted his copybook over Susan.*

♦ In the past, schoolchildren had 'copybooks'. These were books of examples of handwriting, with spaces for the children to copy it.

cord

cut the umbilical cord
cut the cord

If you say that someone **cuts the umbilical cord** or **cuts the cord**, you mean that they start acting independently rather than continuing to rely on the person or thing that they have always relied on. *I love you. I'll never forget all you've done for me, but it's time to cut the umbilical cord.*

♦ An unborn baby's umbilical cord is the tube connecting it to its mother, through which it receives oxygen and nutrients.

corn

earn your corn

British If someone **earns** their **corn**, they are successful and therefore justify the money that has been spent, for example on training them or hiring them. *The back four got us through the match. They earned their corn against Middlesbrough and that's why we came off with a win.*

corner

fight your corner

British If you **fight** your **corner**, you state your opinion openly and defend it vigorously. Other verbs such as 'argue', 'defend', and 'stand' are sometimes used instead of 'fight'. *The future of Britain lies in the EU and we must fight our corner from within using honest and intelligent arguments.*

♦ In a boxing match, each boxer is given a corner of the ring. They return to their corner at the end of each round.

in your corner

   If you say that someone is **in** your **corner**, you mean that they are supporting and helping you. *Harry and I were encouraged. We felt we had made a pretty good pitch. From words spoken after our meeting, we felt we already had Bob Uhlein in our corner.*

◆ In a boxing match, each boxer is given a corner of the ring. Trainers and helpers come into a boxer's corner between rounds and give help and encouragement.

paint someone into a corner
box someone into a corner

   If someone **paints** or **boxes** you **into a corner**, they force you into a difficult situation where you have to act in a certain way. If you **paint** or **box** yourself **into a corner**, you put yourself in a difficult situation by your own actions. *You'll fight to the death when you're boxed into a corner unless you're provided with a reasonable way out... The Government has painted itself into a corner on the issue of equalising the State pension age.*

◆ 'Paint someone into a corner' refers to someone who is painting a floor and ends up in a corner of the room with wet paint all round them. 'Box someone into a corner' refers to a boxer being forced into a corner of the ring and having no means of escape.

turn the corner

   If someone or something **turns the corner**, they begin to recover from a serious illness or a difficult situation. *Has California's economy finally turned the corner? In April the official figure for the state's unemployment rate dropped for the second month running.*

corners

cut corners

   If you **cut corners**, you save time, money, or effort by not following the correct procedure or rules for doing something. *Don't try to cut any corners as you'll only be making work for yourself later on.*

☐ You can refer to this activity as **corner cutting**. *It was the Chief Inspector for Police who said that the present working culture was 'shot through with corner cutting and expediency'.*

couch

a couch potato

   If you describe someone as **a couch potato**, you are criticizing them for spending most of their time sitting around watching television, in a very lazy way. *Even a couch potato will be inspired to go walking in this perfect resort in the Bahamas.*

count

◆ The following expressions refer to a 'count' in boxing. If a boxer is knocked to the ground and does not get up before the referee has counted to ten, they lose the contest.

down for the count

Mainly American If someone is **down for the count**, they have failed in something they are doing. *Japan will have to do a lot more if it is to pull the sick economy round but the market is not down for the count just yet.*

out for the count

If someone is **out for the count**, they are temporarily unconscious. You can also use this expression to say that someone is very deeply asleep. *At 10.30am he was still out for the count after another night disturbed by bawling and wailing.*

counter

under the counter

Mainly British If you do something **under the counter**, you do it secretly because it is dishonest or illegal. The usual American expression is **under the table**. *The shirts disappeared from the displays but could still be purchased under the counter or in discreet back rooms as recently as last Friday.*

☐ An **under-the-counter** payment or deal is one that is secret and dishonest or illegal. *It was becoming common practice for athletes to receive under-the-counter payments from organizers to attend meetings.*

◆ During the Second World War, shopkeepers sometimes kept articles that were in great demand under the shop counter. They only sold them to special customers, often charging very high prices for them.

courage

Dutch courage

Mainly British When someone drinks alcohol so that they feel less frightened or nervous about a task they have to do, you can describe the drinks or their effect as **Dutch courage**. *Sometimes before leaving I would drink a glass of vodka on the stairs for Dutch courage and then go out.*

◆ In the past, the Dutch had a reputation for drinking a lot of alcohol.

court

hold court

If you **hold court**, you are surrounded by people who pay you a lot of attention because they consider you interesting or important. This expression is often used to suggest that the person holding court is rather self-important and does not deserve this attention and admiration. *She used to hold court in the college canteen with a host of admirers who hung on her every utterance.*

◆ 'Court' in this expression refers to the court of a king or queen.

laughed out of court

If you or your ideas **are laughed out of court**, people dismiss your ideas and do not take you seriously. *Only a decade ago the idea of an Equal Opportunities Commission championing and strengthening the rights of women would have been laughed out of court as preposterous and ludicrous.*

◆ A plaintiff who is 'out of court' has lost the right to be heard in a court of law.

Coventry

send someone to Coventry

British If you **are sent to Coventry**, other people ignore you and refuse to talk to you because they disapprove of something you have done. *When she complained to bosses of sexual harassment she was sent to Coventry by staff.*

◆ Various origins have been suggested for this expression. During the English Civil War, Royalist prisoners from Birmingham were sent to prison in Coventry, a city which strongly supported the Parliamentarian side. Another suggestion is that the people of Coventry disliked soldiers so much that they refused to have anything to do with any woman who was seen talking to a soldier. As a result, soldiers did not like being sent to Coventry, where it was difficult to have social contact with anyone.

cow

have a cow

American If you **have a cow**, you become very upset or angry. *I won't be bullied into having a cow, understand. I'm going to put my foot down on this one.*

a sacred cow

If you describe a belief, opinion, or tradition as **a sacred cow**, you disapprove of the fact that people are not willing to criticize or question it or to do anything to change it. *Many critics think reservation policies have become a sacred cow and should be abolished.*

◆ In the Hindu religion, cows are regarded as sacred.

cows

until the cows come home

If you say that you could do something **until the cows come home**, you mean that you could do it for a very long time. *You can initiate policies until the cows come home, but unless they're monitored at a senior level, you won't get results.*

cracks

fall through the cracks
slip through the cracks

Mainly American If people **fall** or **slip through the cracks**, the system which is supposed to help or deal with them does not do it properly. The British expression is **slip through the net**. *Patients who are misdiagnosed are falling through the cracks of the new law... This family slipped through the cracks in the system, they are not eligible for aid.*

paper over the cracks

Mainly British If someone **papers over the cracks**, they try to conceal the fact that something has gone badly wrong rather than deal with it effectively and honestly. 'Gloss over' and 'cover' are sometimes used instead of 'paper over'. *David Powers says accepting the minister's resignation will only serve to paper over the cracks of a much more serious rift.*

cradle

cradle-snatching

British If someone has a sexual relationship with a person who is much younger than them, you can say they are **cradle-snatching**. The American expression is **robbing the cradle**. *He was young enough to cause a first reaction of 'My God but she's cradle-snatching now'... His uncle said: 'His dad and I just can't believe it. The woman is even older than his mother. It's cradle snatching.'*

□ You can describe someone who does this as **a cradle-snatcher**. *The ageing actress is a cradle snatcher, says her toyboy's family.*

rob the cradle

American If someone has a sexual relationship with a person who is much younger than them, you can say they **are robbing the cradle**. The British expression is **cradle-snatching**. *'I'll always be younger,' he said, 'and there'll always be those who might accuse you of robbing the cradle.'*

□ You can describe someone who does this as **a cradle robber**. *Women who make off with men 15 to 30 years younger are viewed as neurotic cradle robbers.*

crash

crash and burn

Mainly American To **crash and burn** means to fail badly, for example because of a careless mistake or an unfortunate action. *When unacknowledged stress builds up, it can cause over-achievers to crash and burn, and they can end up suffering from emotional disorders and stress-related illnesses.*

◆ This may be a reference to a plane crashing into the ground and bursting into flames.

crazy

crazy as a bedbug

Mainly American If you say someone is as **crazy as a bedbug**, you are emphasizing that their behaviour is illogical. *By now she'd concluded that Skolnick was crazy as a bedbug.*

◆ Bedbugs are small wingless insects that live in beds and bedding. They feed by biting people and sucking their blood.

creature

creature comforts

Creature comforts are modern sleeping, eating, and washing facilities that most people enjoy but which are not regarded as particularly extravagant or luxurious. *Obviously the camping lifestyle suits him? 'I like my creature comforts. But here I don't seem to need them,' he replies.*

◆ An old meaning of 'creatures' is material comforts, or things that make you feel comfortable.

creek

up the creek
up the creek without a paddle
up shit creek

If you say that someone or something is **up the creek**, you mean that they are in a very difficult situation. *We're up the creek because we don't know where to go from here.*

☐ You can also say someone or something is **up the creek without a paddle**. *It is now becoming increasingly obvious there won't be any boom. That leaves Australia up the creek without a paddle.*

☐ People sometimes say **up shit creek** to emphasize that the situation is extremely difficult. Many people find this expression offensive. *The economy's up shit creek, the recession has become a slump, everyone's unemployed.*

crest

on the crest of a wave
ride the crest of the wave

If you are **on the crest of a wave**, you are having great success in something you are doing. *Founded in 1972, the Front has often been dismissed as a cranky fringe group. But now its members are confident they're on the crest of a wave.*

☐ This expression is very variable. For example, you can say that someone is **riding the crest of the wave**. *Both men have chosen to make foreign tours at a time when they are riding the crest of the wave politically.*

cricket

it's just not cricket

British, old-fashioned People say **'it's just not cricket'** when they are complaining that someone's behaviour is unfair or unreasonable. *Their treatment of staff is definitely not cricket.*

♦ Cricket is traditionally associated with the values of fairness and respect for other players.

critical

go critical

If a project or organization **goes critical**, it reaches a stage of development where it can operate smoothly and successfully. *Bristol airport is about to 'go critical'. That will come when more than a million passengers a year pass through the terminal.*

◆ This expression is more commonly used in talking about nuclear power. When a nuclear power station goes critical, it reaches a state in which a nuclear fission chain reaction can sustain itself.

crocodile

shed crocodile tears

If you accuse someone of **shedding crocodile tears**, you are accusing them of being insincere because they are pretending to sympathize with someone who they do not really care about. Verbs such as 'weep' and 'cry' are sometimes used instead of 'shed'. *Labour MPs who weep crocodile tears over the plight of those who earn £10,000 a year insist that they cannot get by on ten times that amount.*

☐ You can refer to a display of sympathy or grief that is insincere as **crocodile tears**. *If ever I've seen crocodile tears, those are them. It was a con job. Who does she think she's kidding?*

◆ There was an ancient belief that crocodiles sighed and groaned to attract their prey, and wept while they were eating it.

cropper

come a cropper

Mainly British If you say that someone **has come a cropper**, you mean that they have suffered a sudden and embarrassing failure. *Banks dabbling in industry can easily come a cropper.*

◆ 'Cropper' may come from the expression 'to fall neck and crop', meaning to fall heavily. A bird's 'crop' is a pouch in its throat where it keeps food before digesting it.

cross

a cross to bear

If you have **a cross to bear**, you have to accept a responsibility or tolerate an unpleasant or inconvenient situation because you can do nothing about it. *Healy believes broken fingers are crosses every keeper must bear and he is determined not to let the side down.*

◆ The reference here is to Jesus being made to carry the cross on which

He was to die to the place of execution.

crossed

get your wires crossed
get your lines crossed

If you **get** your **wires crossed** or **get** your **lines crossed**, you are mistaken about what someone else means or thinks. 'Get your lines crossed' is used only in British English. *Despite her tone of voice, she still looked vaguely confused. He began to wonder if he'd gotten his wires crossed... He appeared to get his lines crossed. 'What part of America are you from?' he asked. 'Sweden,' came the reply.*

☐ You can refer to this type of misunderstanding as **crossed wires** or, in British English, **crossed lines**. *In a month where crossed wires abound for many people, it is essential to keep things in proportion.*

◆ People say they have a crossed line when their call is connected wrongly and they can hear someone else's conversation.

crossfire

caught in the crossfire

If you say that someone or something **is caught in the crossfire**, you mean that they suffer the unpleasant effects of a disagreement between other people even though they are not involved in it themselves. *Teachers say they are caught in the crossfire between the education establishment and the Government.*

◆ This expression is more commonly used literally to talk about a situation where someone is in the way of two sets of people who are firing guns, and so is likely to be shot by mistake.

crow

as the crow flies

If you say that one place is a particular distance from another **as the crow flies**, you mean that the two places are that distance apart if you measure them in a straight line, although the actual distance when travelled by road would be much greater. *My name is Betty Perkes, and I live at Mesa, Washington, about 10 miles as the crow flies from Hanford.*

☐ People occasionally replace 'crow' with another word which is relevant to the subject they are writing about. *They must travel 44 kilometres to visit relatives on the other side of the canal, one kilometre as the gull flies, unless they can catch the ferry.*

◆ It used to be believed that crows always travelled to their destination by the most direct route possible. 'Make a beeline' is based on a similar idea.

eat crow

Mainly American If someone **eats crow**, they admit they have been wrong and apologize, especially in situations where this is humiliating or embarrassing for them. *But by the end of the year, Safire showed he was willing to eat crow. His first judgments of Watergate, he wrote, had been 'really wrong'.*

◆ This expression is said to relate to an incident during the Anglo-American War of 1812 – 14. An American soldier who had accidentally entered an area occupied by the British was tricked into handing over his gun. He was then forced by a British officer to take a bite out of a crow which he had shot down. When his gun was returned to him, he forced the British officer to eat the rest of the bird.

cry

in full cry

Mainly British You use the expression **in full cry** to emphasize that someone is doing something very actively or that something is happening very intensely. *Her comic timing is impeccable, her gift for mimicry brilliant. There is no better entertainment than La Plante in full cry.*

◆ This expression refers to the noise made by a pack of hounds when they see the animal they are hunting.

cudgels

take up the cudgels

If you **take up the cudgels** for someone or **take up the cudgel** for them, you speak up or fight in support of them. *The trade unions took up the cudgels for the 367 staff who were made redundant.*

◆ A cudgel was a short, thick stick that was used as a weapon in the past.

cuff

off-the-cuff

An **off-the-cuff** remark, opinion, or comment is one that has not been prepared or carefully thought out. *Gascoigne offered an apology last night,* *saying: 'I'm sorry. I didn't mean any offence. It was a flippant, off-the-cuff remark.'... Eisenman was speaking off the cuff, and it's possible that my tape recorder did not catch every last word.*

◆ One explanation for this expression is that after-dinner speakers used to write notes on the cuffs of their shirts, to remind them of what to say. Another explanation is that in the early days of cinema, directors sometimes wrote notes on their cuffs during the filming of a scene, to remind them of what they wanted to say to the actors.

cup

not your cup of tea

If you say that something is **not** your **cup of tea**, you mean that you do not feel very enthusiastic about it or interested in it. *It's no secret that I've never been the greatest traveller. Sitting for hours on motorways is not my cup of tea.*

☐ You can say that something **is** your **cup of tea** when you do feel enthusiastic about it or interested in it. *I don't have much time for modern literature. Chaucer's my cup of tea.*

cupboard

cupboard love

British You use **cupboard love** to refer to the insincere affection shown by children or animals towards someone who they think will give them something they want. *The cat twined himself around her ankles, assuring her of complete agreement. 'Cupboard love,' she accused, freeing her ankles. 'You'd agree with anyone who could open the fridge or cooker.'*

◆ The idea here is that cupboards often contain food or something else that a child might want to have.

curate

a curate's egg

British If you describe something as **a curate's egg**, you think that parts of it are good and parts of it are bad. *Wasserman's collection of duets with famous friends is something of a curate's egg.*

◆ A curate is a clergyman in the Church of England who helps the vicar or rector of a parish. A well-known Victorian cartoon published in the British magazine 'Punch' shows a curate having breakfast with a senior clergyman. The curate has been given a bad egg but he is anxious not to offend anyone, so he says that it is 'good in parts'.

curiosity

curiosity killed the cat

You say **'curiosity killed the cat'** to warn someone that they will suffer harm or damage themselves if they try to find out about other people's private affairs. *'Where are we going?' Calder asked. 'Curiosity killed the cat, dear. You'll find out soon enough.'*

curtain

bring the curtain down on something
the curtain comes down

If someone or something **brings down the curtain on** an event, process, or state of affairs, they cause or mark its end. You can also say **the curtain comes down** on something. *Today's simple but moving ceremonies bring down the curtain on that long and historic period in Philippine history marked by the presence of American troops in our territory.*

◆ In theatres, it is traditional for a curtain to come down in front of the stage at the end of each act and at the end of the play.

curtains

it's curtains
mean curtains
spell curtains

If you say that **it's curtains** for someone, you mean that their career, their period of success, or their life is coming to an end. If you say that **it's curtains** for something, you mean that it will be destroyed or is likely to fail. You can also say that something **means curtains** or **spells curtains** for someone or something. *If the vote is yes, it's curtains for us. A way of life will disappear... I would like what happened to Bryan to give hope to people in a similar position. A diagnosis like that doesn't always mean curtains.*

◆ The curtains referred to here are the curtains at the front of the stage in a theatre.

curve

throw someone a curve
throw someone a curve ball
curve balls

Mainly American If someone **throws** you **a curve** or if they **throw** you **a**

curve ball, they surprise you by doing something unexpected and perhaps putting you at a disadvantage. *Just when they thought they might have the boss figured out, Knight would throw them a curve. No-one could ever put him all together.*

☐ You can refer to unexpected problems as **curve balls**. *Once you learn the person's habits and idiosyncrasies, there will be few curve balls.*

◆ In baseball, a 'curve ball' is a ball that curves through the air rather than travelling in a straight line.

cut

a cut above the rest
a cut above

If you say that someone or something is **a cut above the rest**, you think they are much better than other people or things they are being compared to. You can also describe someone or something as **a cut above**. *Crime fiction now basks in literary respectability, and Joan Smith's detective stories are a cut above the rest... I hate to be predictable, but like the last 18 R.E.M. singles, it's a cut above.*

cut and dried

If you say that a situation or discussion is **cut and dried**, you mean that it is clear and definite, and does not raise any questions or problems. *Now, this situation is not as cut and dried as it may seem... There are no cut-and-dried answers as to why a mother or father kills their baby.*

◆ One explanation for this expression is that it refers to wood which has been cut and dried and is ready to use. Alternatively, it may refer to herbs that have been harvested and dried, to be used for cooking and medicine.

cut and run

If you say that someone has decided to **cut and run** from a difficult situation, you are criticizing them for trying to escape from it quickly, rather than dealing with the situation in a responsible way. *When foreigners own property and corporations in the U.S., they are less likely to cut and run in bad times, and more likely to invest extra capital.*

◆ In the past, ships' anchors were attached to ropes. If a warship was attacked, rather than causing delay by pulling up the anchor, the sailors would sometimes cut the rope.

the cut and thrust

British If you talk about **the cut and thrust** of a particular activity or society, you are talking abut the aspects of it that make it exciting and challenging. *Why then does he want to go back into the harrowing cut and thrust of the airline business at an age when most men are happily retired?*

☐ A **cut-and-thrust** society or contest is one that is very exciting, although it is also competitive and stressful. *She has spent the past two years carving out a career as a production assistant in the cut-and-thrust world of advertising.*

◆ This expression comes from sword fighting.

cylinders

fire on all cylinders

If someone **is firing on all cylinders**, they are doing a task with great enthusiasm and energy. 'Fire' is occasionally replaced with other verbs such as 'operate'. *When Wales are firing on all cylinders, they can beat any country in the world at football, as Germany and Brazil could tell you.*

☐ If someone is not doing a task as well as they should be, you can say they **are not firing on all cylinders** or **are only firing on two cylinders**. *We were only firing on two cylinders instead of four. But people have been told, and you won't see a bad performance like that again.*

◆ This expression refers to the cylinders in an engine. There are usually four of them.

D

dab

a dab hand

British If you are **a dab hand** at something, you are very good at doing it. *She was an avid reader and a dab hand at solving difficult crossword puzzles.*

◆ In the late 17th century, 'dab' meant clever or skilful.

daft

daft as a brush

British If you say that someone is as **daft as a brush**, you are

emphasizing that they are very silly or stupid. *She was as daft as a brush.*
Couldn't say anything with any sense in it.

daggers

at daggers drawn

British If two people or groups are **at daggers drawn**, they are having a
serious disagreement and are very angry with each other. *It is rumoured*
that the publishing and record divisions of the company were at daggers
drawn over the simultaneous release of the book and the album.

look daggers at someone
shoot daggers at someone

If someone **looks daggers** at you or **shoots daggers** at you, they stare
at you in a very angry way. *Christabel stopped caressing her hair and*
looked daggers at Ron.

daisies

push up the daisies

If you say that someone **is pushing up the daisies**, you mean that they
are dead. This expression is used to refer to someone's death in a
light-hearted or humorous way. *'I hope I die before I get old,' sang Pete*
Townshend in 'My Generation'. Instead of pushing up daisies, Townshend is
still among the living, grey whiskers and all.

damper

put a damper on something
put a dampener on something

If someone or something **puts a damper on** a situation, they stop it
being as successful or as enjoyable as it might be. In British English you
can also say that they **put a dampener on** it. *Fear of terrorism and war*
has put a damper on bookings at Mike Dorman's Vacation Hotline in
Chicago.

◆ This expression may refer to either of two meanings of 'damper'. In a
piano, a damper is a device which presses the strings and stops them
vibrating, so stopping the sound. In a chimney or flue, a damper is a
movable metal plate which controls the amount of air getting to the fire,
and so controls how fiercely the fire burns.

dance

lead you a merry dance
lead you a merry chase

British If you say that someone **leads** you **a merry dance** while you are trying to achieve something, you mean that they make a lot of difficulties for you, so that you do not achieve it quickly or easily. You can also say that someone **leads** you **a merry chase**. *They had led the Irish Government a merry dance for the last seven months... He led Vincent Korda a merry chase across Italy before agreeing to take the part.*

dander

get someone's dander up

Old-fashioned If someone **gets** your **dander up**, they make you feel very annoyed and angry. *She was almost speechless with rage and despair. My God, Max thought, once she gets her dander up she catches fire!*

◆ The origin of the word 'dander' is unknown.

dark

keep something dark

If you **keep** something **dark**, you keep it a secret. *She took pleasure in keeping dark the identity of the man who was coming.*

a leap in the dark

British If you take **a leap in the dark**, you do something without knowing what the consequences will be, usually because you feel you have no other choice but to take this course of action. *In the last five months, voters in both Brazil and Nicaragua have rejected old campaigners, preferring to take a leap in the dark by electing outsiders with little or no political experience to the highest office.*

a shot in the dark
a stab in the dark

If you refer to a guess as **a shot in the dark** or **a stab in the dark**, you mean that it is a complete guess, although there is a small chance that it will be right. *The Japanese go about their business much as other nations do – with a pretty standard mixture of good judgment, luck, mistakes and shots in the dark... It is impossible to undertake a wild stab in the dark and take a guess at their roots.*

whistle in the dark

If you say that someone **is whistling in the dark**, you mean that they are trying not to show that they are afraid, or that they are trying to convince themselves that a situation is not as bad as it seems. *Then I waited, trying not to feel as if I were whistling in the dark, but I experienced no easing of my fear and anxiety.*

dash

cut a dash

Mainly British If someone **cuts a dash**, they impress other people with their stylish appearance. *Then Mr Marsh's lawyer, a ruddy-cheeked Irishman who looks as though he would cut a dash on the hunting field, started his cross-examination.*

date

past your sell-by date

British If you say that someone or something **is past** their **sell-by date**, you are saying that they are no longer useful, successful, or relevant. *The feeling is that the broad-shouldered 'power dressing' of the Eighties has passed its sell-by date.*

◆ Most food has a date stamped on its packaging: this is its sell-by date. After this date it is no longer fresh enough to sell.

dawn

a false dawn

Mainly British If you refer to an event as **a false dawn**, you mean that although it seems to mark an improvement in a bad situation, there is in fact no improvement. *The new age of enterprise which the Government hoped would revitalise Britain in the Eighties turned out to be a false dawn.*

day

call it a day: 1
call it a night

If you decide to **call it a day**, you decide to stop doing something, usually because you are tired or are bored with it. *It was late afternoon and I searched for hours but I had to call it a day when darkness fell.*

☐ In the evening, people sometimes say that they are going to **call it a night**. *Tomorrow is going to be busy, so let's call it a night.*

call it a day: 2

If someone **calls it a day**, they retire. *He's finally decided to call it a day and retire as manager.*

carry the day

If a person or their opinion **carries the day** in a contest or debate, they win it. *For the time being, those in favour of the liberalisation measures seem to have carried the day.*

◆ This expression was originally used to say which army had won a battle.

the day of reckoning

If you talk about the **day of reckoning**, you are referring to the time when people are forced to deal with an unpleasant situation which they have avoided until now. *The day of reckoning has arrived. You can't keep writing checks on a bank account that doesn't have any money in it.*

◆ According to the Bible, when the world ends, there will be a day of reckoning or day of judgment, when God will judge everyone's actions and send them either to heaven or hell.

make my day

People sometimes say **'make my day'** when they want to challenge another person to compete or argue with them, in order to have the opportunity to prove that they are stronger and better than the other person. *They threaten dire reprisals to any journalist who dares to write 'propaganda' for the fur trade. All I can say is, go ahead boys, make my day. The only reason I don't have a fur coat yet is that I can't quite afford the one I want.*

◆ In the film 'Sudden Impact' (1983), Clint Eastwood, playing a detective called Harry, uses this expression to challenge a criminal who is threatening to shoot him.

save for a rainy day

If you **are saving for a rainy day**, you are saving some of your money in case there are emergencies or problems in the future. *Job loss fears are forcing millions of consumers to save for a rainy day rather than borrow.*

seize the day

If you tell someone to **seize the day**, you are advising them to do what they want straight away, and not to worry about the future. *I can't wait ten years. Life has taught me to seize the day, if not the hour.*

◆ This is a translation of the Latin phrase 'carpe diem', which is also sometimes used.

daylights

beat the living daylights out of someone: 1

If someone **beats the living daylights out of** you or **beats the daylights out of** you, they attack you physically, hitting you many times. *Steve beat the daylights out of him with a hefty length of bike chain.*

beat the living daylights out of someone: 2

If you **beat the living daylights out of** someone or **beat the daylights out of** them, you defeat them totally in a competition or contest. *Sure, they enjoy the money, the endorsements, the fame. But their true pleasure comes from walking on to a golf course and beating the living daylights out of everyone else.*

◆ The word 'daylights' in this expression may be related to an old threat to 'make daylight shine through' someone by stabbing them or shooting them. Alternatively, it may be related to an old meaning of 'daylights' referring to someone's eyes or internal organs. If they were badly beaten, their 'daylights' would stop working.

scare the living daylights out of someone

If someone or something **scares the living daylights out of** you or **scares the daylights out of** you, they frighten you very much. *You scared the living daylights out of me last night. All that screaming.*

days

dog days: 1

Dog days are the hottest days of the year that occur in July and August in the northern hemisphere. *In the country, midsummer marks the final fling of activity before the lazy, dog days of July and August.*

◆ The ancient Romans named these days 'dies caniculares' or 'dog days' because the Dog Star, Sirius, could be seen in the morning sky at this time of year. They believed that the combination of Sirius and the sun produced very hot weather.

dog days: 2

Mainly British If you talk about the **dog days** of someone's career or period in a position of responsibility, you are referring to a period when they are not having much success or are not making any progress. *These are dog days for Middlesex. Their cricket seems to be meandering purposelessly at the moment.*

have seen better days

If you say that something **has seen better days**, you mean that it is old and in poor condition. *There was an old brass double bed with a mattress that had seen better days.*

someone's days are numbered

If you say that someone's **days are numbered**, you mean that they are not likely to survive or be successful for much longer. *As rebels advanced on the capital it became clear that the President's days in power were numbered.*

dead

cut someone dead

British If someone you know **cuts** you **dead**, they deliberately ignore you or refuse to speak to you, for example because they are angry with you. *You can only slag off people behind their backs for so long. I cut her dead when I realised what she was doing.*

dead as a dodo

British If you say that something is as **dead as a dodo**, you mean that it is no longer active or popular. *The foreign exchange market was as dead as a dodo.*

◆ The dodo was a large flightless bird that lived on the islands of Mauritius and Réunion. It became extinct in the late 17th century as a result of hunting and the destruction of its nests by pigs belonging to settlers on the islands.

dead as a doornail

If you say that someone is as **dead as a doornail**, you are emphasizing that they are dead. If you say that something is as **dead as a doornail**, you mean that it is no longer active or popular. *When Senator Goldwater went down to that thrashing defeat in 1964, people said the Republican Party was deader than a doornail.*

◆ It is not certain what 'doornail' actually refers to. In medieval times, it may have been the plate or knob on a door which was hit by the knocker. It was thought that anything that was struck so often must have been dead. Alternatively, doornails may have been the thick nails which were set into outer doors. It is not clear why these nails should be described as 'dead'.

dead in the water

British If you say that something or someone is **dead in the water**, you mean that they have failed and there seems to be little hope that they will be successful in the future. *People are not going into auto showrooms; they're not buying houses; they're not going into stores. This economy is dead in the water.*

◆ The image here is of a sailing boat which cannot move because there is no wind.

knock 'em dead
knock someone dead

If you say that something will **knock 'em dead**, you mean that it will impress people a great deal. You can also say that something **knocks** you **dead**. *Glamorous make-up is best reserved for evenings, or days when you want to go all out to knock 'em dead... Their debut album is going to knock you dead.*

◆ The word "em" is a form of 'them' which is used in informal or non-standard English.

wouldn't be seen dead
wouldn't be caught dead

If you say that you **wouldn't be seen dead** or **wouldn't be caught dead** in particular clothes, places, or situations, you are emphasizing that you strongly dislike or disapprove of them. *I wouldn't be seen dead in a black straw hat... No true aristocrat would have been caught dead with a tan, which was the mark of a peasant forced to toil for a living in the open fields.*

deaf

deaf as a post

Old-fashioned If you say that someone is as **deaf as a post**, you are emphasizing that they are very deaf. *He must be as deaf as a post, half-blind and verging on the paralytic.*

deal

a done deal

Mainly American If something such as a plan or project is **a done deal**, it has been completed or arranged and it cannot be changed. *The pact is far from being a done deal. It must be ratified by the legislative bodies of all three countries.*

get a raw deal

You can say that someone **gets a raw deal** when you feel that they have been treated unfairly or badly. *We must ask why bank customers get such a raw deal. And then find ways to make sure they get treated fairly in future.*

◆ This may refer to someone being dealt a bad hand in a game of cards.

death

at death's door

If someone is **at death's door**, they are seriously ill and are likely to die. *He has won five golf competitions in three months, a year after being at death's door.*

□ You can say that someone comes back **from death's door** when they have recovered from a very serious illness. *The patient has been brought back from death's door by the radical treatment, say his doctors.*

dice with death

If someone **is dicing with death**, they are taking risks that endanger their life. *I dice with death almost every night crossing the road outside Maidstone Barracks station.*

like death warmed up
like death warmed over

If you say that someone looks **like death warmed up** or **like death warmed over**, you mean that they look very ill, pale, and tired. 'Like death warmed up' is used in British English and 'like death warmed over' is used in American English. *He dragged in just after the funeral, sneezing and sniffing and looking like death warmed over.*

sign someone's death warrant
sign your own death warrant

If one person **signs** another's **death warrant**, the first causes the second's ruin or death. If someone **signs** their **own death warrant**, they behave in a way which brings about their own ruin or death. *The summit in Moscow this week virtually signed the organisation's death warrant... The president persuaded Congress to sign its own death warrant by agreeing to a referendum.*

□ A **death warrant** is used in many other structures with a similar meaning. *The plan is seen by all sides as a death warrant for the Bosnian state.*

◆ A death warrant is an official document which orders that someone is to be executed as a punishment for a crime.

deck

all hands on deck

Mainly British If a situation requires **all hands on deck**, it requires everyone to work hard to achieve an aim or carry out a task. *The agency was given less than three weeks to put together the launch of radical plans to shake up Scottish football. It was all hands on deck, but it was a good test of our ability, and proved we could handle such a large project.*

♦ Members of a ship's crew are sometimes called hands.

hit the deck

If someone or something **hits the deck**, they suddenly fall to the ground. *Instead of pulling up, the plane seemed to go faster and faster before it hit the deck.*

♦ 'Deck' normally means the floor of a ship or, in American English, a raised platform outside a house. Here it means the floor or ground.

not play with a full deck
play with a loaded deck
play with a stacked deck

If someone **is not playing with a full deck**, they are not being completely honest in a contest or negotiation, and therefore have an unfair advantage over other people. Compare **stack the deck**; see **stack**. *This guy is either very good or he's not playing with a full deck.*

□ You can also say that they **are playing with a loaded deck** or **a stacked deck**. *Canadian trade officials say Washington is playing the free trade game with a stacked deck.*

♦ A stacked or loaded deck of cards is one that has been altered before a game in order to give one player an advantage.

decks

clear the decks

If someone **clears the decks**, they make sure that everything that they have been doing is completely finished, so that they are ready to start a more important task. *Clear the decks before you think of taking on any more responsibilities.*

♦ In the past, all unnecessary objects were cleared off the decks of a warship before a battle, so that the crew could move around more easily.

depth

out of your depth

If you are **out of** your **depth**, you feel anxious and inadequate because you have to deal with a situation or subject which you know very little about. *You may feel out of your depth on an honours degree course, in which case a change to a diploma course may be a good idea.*

◆ This expression refers to someone who is in deep water but cannot swim very well, or cannot swim at all.

depths

plumb the depths: 1

If you say that someone's behaviour **plumbs the depths**, you mean that it is extremely bad. *'This crime plumbs the very depths of the abyss into which it is possible for the human spirit to sink,' the judge said.*

plumb the depths: 2

If you **plumb the depths** of something, you find out everything you can about it, including things that are normally secret or hidden. *He doesn't plumb the depths of a text in the way of his contemporaries Deborah Warner and Declan Donnellan.*

plumb the depths: 3

If someone **plumbs the depths** of an unpleasant or difficult situation, they experience it to an extreme degree. *They frequently plumb the depths of loneliness, humiliation and despair.*

◆ In the past, when a ship was in shallow water one of the sailors would find out how deep the water was by dropping a piece of lead on a string, called a 'plumb', over the side of the ship. 'Swing the lead' is also based on this practice.

deserts

just deserts

If you say that someone has got their **just deserts**, you mean that they deserve the unpleasant things that have happened to them, because they did something bad. *Some people felt sympathy for the humbled superstar. Others felt she was getting the just deserts of an actress with a reputation for being difficult.*

◆ 'Deserts' is an old-fashioned word meaning a reward or punishment which is deserved.

devices

left to your own devices

If someone **is left to** their **own devices**, they are left to do what they want, or to look after themselves without any help. *After tea we were left to our own devices, so we decided to take a walk in the neighbouring village.*

♦ An old meaning of 'device' was desire or will.

devil

better the devil you know

Mainly British If you say **'better the devil you know'**, you mean that you would rather deal with someone you already know, even if you do not like them, than deal with someone that you know nothing about, because they may be even worse. *People concluded that he had improved his electoral chances as a result of the speech. And one told me this reflected the old adage, 'Better the devil you know.' His challenger remains an unknown quantity.*

□ This expression comes from the proverb **better the devil you know than the devil you don't**.

between the devil and the deep blue sea

Mainly British If you are **between the devil and the deep blue sea**, you are in a difficult situation where the two possible courses of action or choices that you can take are equally bad. *Now exactly what do we really want? You see we are between the devil and the deep blue sea on this issue and people just do not know exactly what to do.*

♦ The origin of this expression is in shipping, not religion. It is unclear exactly what the 'devil' was, but it is thought to have been some kind of seam or plank that was awkward and dangerous to reach, so a sailor who had to make it waterproof was in a very unsafe position, and risked falling into the water.

the devil take the hindmost
every man for himself and the devil take the hindmost

Old-fashioned If someone says **'the devil take the hindmost'**, they mean that you should protect your own interests or safety without considering anyone else's interests. *Just get your laughs any way you can and the devil take the hindmost.*

♦ This expression comes from the saying 'every man for himself and the devil take the hindmost'. 'Hindmost' is an old word meaning furthest back or last.

speak of the devil
talk of the devil

People say **'speak of the devil'** or **'talk of the devil'** if someone they have just been talking about arrives unexpectedly. *'Speak of the devil,' she greeted him, smiling... 'Well, talk of the devil.' Duncan had wandered up from the beach in red wellies and a duffel coat.*

◆ This expression comes from the saying 'talk of the devil and he will appear'.

diamond

a rough diamond: 1
a diamond in the rough

If you refer to someone, especially a man, as **a rough diamond**, you like and admire them because of the good qualities they have, even though they are not very sophisticated or well-mannered. This form of the expression is used mainly in British English; in American English, the usual form is **a diamond in the rough**. *Marden was the rough diamond of the three, feared for his sardonic ruthlessness but respected for his First World War Military Cross... I liked Neil Murphy, who is somewhat of a diamond in the rough.*

a rough diamond: 2
a diamond in the rough

If you refer to someone or something as **a rough diamond**, you mean that they have a lot of talent or potential which needs hard work before it can be revealed. This form of the expression is used mainly in British English; in American English, the usual form is **a diamond in the rough**. *British first novels are more likely to be rough diamonds, with flashes of inspiration in an imperfect whole... Coach Jim Washburn said: 'This kid is a diamond in the rough.'*

◆ A rough diamond is a diamond that has not yet been cut and polished.

dice

load the dice against someone

If you are in a situation where everything seems to work to your disadvantage so that you are unlikely ever to have success, you can say that **the dice are loaded against** you. *The dice are loaded against black* *people and sometimes the institutions of Britain, seemingly dedicated to ensuring equality, like the law, are the very citadels of racism.*

◆ Players who wanted to cheat at dice games sometimes 'loaded' or weighted the dice so that they tended to fall in a particular way.

no dice: 1

If you are trying to achieve something and you say there's **no dice**, you mean that you are having no luck or success with it. *I spent part of that time calling everyone I knew to see if I could find another job for him. No dice.*

no dice: 2

If someone asks you for something and you reply **'no dice'**, you are refusing to do what they ask. *Nope, sorry, we're not interested, no dice.*

◆ This expression comes from the game of craps, and means that the player's last throw is disqualified and not counted.

die

the die is cast

If you say that **the die is cast**, you mean that you have made an important decision about the future and that it is impossible to change it, even if things go wrong. *Therese is regarded by them as having been singled out by God. The die is cast for her: she goes off to a convent and stays there for 20 years.*

◆ 'Die' is an old singular form of the word 'dice'. Once you have thrown the dice, you cannot do anything to change the way they fall. The first use of the expression is attributed to Julius Caesar, who is believed to have said it before crossing over the river Rubicon into Italy from Gaul, thus invading his own country and starting a civil war. 'Cross the Rubicon' is based on the same incident.

dime

◆ A dime is an American coin worth ten cents.

a dime a dozen

Mainly American If you say that things or people are **a dime a dozen**, you mean that there are a lot of them, and so they are not especially valuable or interesting. The usual British expression is **two a penny**. *Writers are a dime a dozen, a new one will be easy enough to find.*

turn on a dime
on a dime

Mainly American You can say that someone **turns on a dime** when they suddenly do something completely different from what they were doing before. *The new reality in the workplace is based on employers' needs to be flexible and to change and sometimes to turn around on a dime in order to stay competitive.*

☐ If something happens **on a dime**, it happens suddenly or dramatically, in complete contrast to the way it was happening before. *Outdoors I heard the rain stop on a dime.*

dinner
done like a dinner
Mainly Australian If you are **done like a dinner** in a contest or competitive situation, your opponents defeat you completely, often in an unfair way. *Aviation consultant Peter Harbison said US carriers had virtual carte blanche to fly in and out of Tokyo as they pleased. 'The Japanese get done like a dinner,' Mr Harbison said.*

dinners
do something more than someone has had hot dinners
British If you say that you **have done** something **more than** someone **has had hot dinners**, you are emphasizing that you have done it a great number of times. *Robin and Lizzie Hamer of First Ascent activity holidays have climbed more mountains than you and I have had hot dinners.*

dirt
dig up dirt
If you say that one person **is digging up dirt** on another, you mean that the first is trying to find out something that may cause harm to the second. *They hired a detective firm to dig up dirt on their rival.*

☐ You can describe this activity as **dirt-digging**. *In the movie, a dirt-digging reporter is framed by a corrupt district attorney and sentenced for manslaughter.*

dish the dirt
If you say that one person **dishes the dirt** on another, you disapprove of the way that the first person spreads stories about the second, especially when they say things that may embarrass or upset that person, or damage their reputation. *Many politicians who maintain that their private lives are their own, are not above dishing the dirt on a fellow politician, if it suits their own political or personal purposes... Some publishers believe that by*

speaking out as he did, he has pushed up the potential value of any
dirt-dishing memoirs he cares to write.

do someone dirt
do the dirt on someone

American If someone **has done** you **dirt** or **has done the dirt on** you,
they have betrayed you or treated you very badly. The British expression
is **do the dirty on** someone. *They tell me you have done me dirt. Tell me it*
ain't true... There is an unofficial biography out of Nancy Reagan which is
doing the dirt on her all over the place.

dirty

do the dirty on someone

British If someone **has done the dirty** on you, they have betrayed you
or treated you very badly. The American expression is **do** someone **dirt**.
There are plenty of people only too ready to make use of a situation like this
to do the dirty on somebody they don't like.

wash your dirty linen in public
air your dirty laundry in public
do your dirty washing in public

If you say that someone **is washing** their **dirty linen in public** or **is**
washing their **dirty laundry in public**, you are criticizing them for
talking about unpleasant or personal matters in front of other people,
when you consider that such things should be kept private. These forms of
the expression are used mainly in British English; in American English,
the usual forms are **air** your **dirty linen in public** or **air** your **dirty**
laundry in public. *We shouldn't wash our dirty laundry in public and if I*
was in his position, I'd say nothing at all.

□ In British English, you can also say that someone is **doing** their **dirty**
washing in public. *We don't want any more to come out in public. We*
want to stop doing our dirty washing in public.

□ There are many other variations of this expression. *In Spain, it seems,*
airing dirty linen is considered more serious than any offence itself... It is
certainly a huge disadvantage of being famous that everyone wants to see
your dirty linen.

distance

go the distance
go the full distance

If you **go the distance** or **go the full distance**, you complete what you are doing and reach your goal. *She has really worked her way up from someone who was kind of an ingenue of someone who is a true movie star. Geena Davis will go the distance in the nineties.*

◆ A boxer who succeeds in fighting until the end of the match is said to 'go the distance'.

ditch

last ditch

You can describe an action as a **last ditch** attempt or effort to do something when everything else has failed and this action is the only way left of avoiding disaster, although it too seems likely to fail. *The President has been making a last ditch attempt to prevent the rebels taking over the city.*

◆ In this expression, 'ditch' means a trench which has been dug in order to defend a military position. The expression refers to soldiers who are prepared to die in a final effort to defend the position rather than surrender.

divide

divide and rule
divide and conquer

If someone in power follows a policy of **divide and rule** or **divide and conquer**, they stay in power by making sure that the people under their control quarrel among themselves and so cannot unite to achieve their aims and overthrow their leader. *Trade unions are concerned that management may be tempted into a policy of divide and rule by cultural divisions... The same principle of divide and conquer that the Roman Empire used so effectively was applied once again by Yugoslavia's occupiers in 1941.*

◆ This expression has its origin in the Latin phrase 'divide et impera'. It describes one of the tactics which the Romans used to rule their empire.

Dixie

whistle Dixie

Mainly American If you say that you **are not whistling Dixie** or **are not just whistling Dixie**, you mean that you are being honest or realistic in what you are saying and you should not be ignored. *'Is that a threat?' 'I'm not just whistling Dixie.'*

◆ Dixie was the name given to the region of the southern and eastern United States which formed the Confederate side in the Civil War. The area gave its name to several songs which were popular as Confederate war songs.

dog

a dog and pony show

Mainly American If you refer to an event as **a dog and pony show**, you mean that it is very showy because it has been organized in order to impress someone. *I'm bombarding him and the others with charts, graphs, facts, and figures. The boss responds by dozing off during most of our dog and pony show.*

◆ This expression refers to circus acts involving dogs and horses.

dog-eat-dog

You use **dog-eat-dog** to describe a situation in which everyone wants to succeed and is willing to harm other people or to use dishonest methods in order to do this. *The TV business today is a dog-eat-dog business.*

dog-in-the-manger

If you say that someone has a **dog-in-the-manger** attitude, you are criticizing them for selfishly wanting to prevent other people from using or enjoying something that they cannot use or enjoy themselves. *I think there'll be a certain group of intransigent Republicans who'll take a dog-in-the-manger kind of attitude and try to frustrate anything the president wants to achieve.*

◆ One of Aesop's fables tells of a dog which prevented an ox from eating the hay in its manger, even though the dog could not eat the hay itself.

a dog's breakfast
a dog's dinner

British If you refer to a situation, event, or piece of work as **a dog's breakfast** or **a dog's dinner**, you mean that it is chaotic, badly organized, or very untidy. *The act created what many admitted was an over-complex but inadequate system. One senior regulator described it as a dog's breakfast.*

every dog has its day

If you say **'every dog has its day'**, you mean that everyone will be successful or lucky at some time in their life. This expression is sometimes used to encourage someone at a time when they are not having any success or luck. *'I don't have any money to fight him. These people are* *all the time in court, anyway,' Cecchini says. 'But every dog has its day and I have lots of patience.'*

◆ This proverb has been known in English since at least the 16th century. Shakespeare quotes it in 'Hamlet': 'Let Hercules himself do what he may, The cat will mew and dog will have his day.' (Act 5, Scene 1).

it's a dog's life

People say **'it's a dog's life'** when they are complaining that their job or situation is unpleasant or boring. *It's a dog's life being a football manager.*

you can't teach an old dog new tricks

If you say **'you can't teach an old dog new tricks'**, you mean that it is often difficult to get people to try new ways of doing things, especially if these people have been doing something in a particular way for a long time. *It is a convenient myth that a person cannot change their personality. Or as the saying goes: 'You can't teach an old dog new tricks.'*

□ This expression is often varied. For example, if you say **'you can teach an old dog new tricks'**, you mean that it is possible to get people to try new ways of doing something. *Our work shows that you can teach an old dog new tricks.*

doghouse

in the doghouse

If you are **in the doghouse**, people are very annoyed with you because of something you have done. *Insurance companies are already in the doghouse over poor advice on pensions which has left hundreds of thousands of people worse off.*

◆ In American English, a 'doghouse' is a kennel.

dogs

call off the dogs

If you tell someone to **call off the dogs**, you are telling them to stop challenging, attacking, or damaging you or another person. *Lenders will be ordered to call off the dogs, especially for families struggling to pay their mortgage through unemployment.*

go to the dogs

If you say that a country, organization, or business **is going to the dogs**, you mean that it is becoming less powerful, efficient, or successful than it has been in the past. *In the 1960s the country was fast going to the dogs.*

let sleeping dogs lie
a sleeping dog

If someone tells you to **let sleeping dogs lie**, they are warning you not to disturb or interfere with a situation, because you are likely to cause trouble and problems. *Why does she come over here stirring everything up? Why can't she let sleeping dogs lie?*

☐ You can refer to a situation that it would be better not to disturb as **a sleeping dog**. *Since the election, it has suited ministers to treat local government finance as the sleeping dog of British politics.*

throw someone to the dogs

If someone **throws** you **to the dogs**, they allow you to be criticized severely or treated roughly, for example in order to protect themselves from criticism or harm, or because they no longer need you. *He told the judges he felt abandoned by his former commanders and that he had been, as he put it, thrown to the dogs.*

doldrums

in the doldrums: 1
out of the doldrums

If an economy or business is **in the doldrums**, nothing new is happening and it is not doing very well. If an economy or business comes **out of the doldrums**, it improves and becomes stronger after a period of inactivity. *After months in the doldrums, the lira strengthened... We were hoping that the housing market was, in fact, going to come out of the doldrums that it's been in for the last few years.*

in the doldrums: 2
out of the doldrums

If someone is **in the doldrums**, they are very depressed and inactive. If someone comes **out of the doldrums**, they stop being depressed and feel happier. *After what feels like a long time out in the doldrums of depression, I am now, at the age of 27, just learning how to overcome my weaknesses and build on my strengths... With her humour and upbeat spirit, Jane got me right out of the doldrums I'd been in for three years.*

◆ The Doldrums is an area of sea near the equator where there is often little or no wind, which meant that sailing ships could be stuck there for long periods. It is not clear whether sailors named the area after the expression, or whether the name for the area gave rise to the expression, although the first possibility is more likely.

dollar

bet your bottom dollar

If you say that you **bet** your **bottom dollar** that something will happen or is true, you are emphasizing that you are absolutely certain that it will happen or that it is true. *I'd bet my bottom dollar he's around somewhere.*

the 64,000 dollar question

If you describe a question as **the 64,000 dollar question**, you mean that it is very important but very difficult to answer. You can also use other large amounts instead of '64,000' to mean the same thing. *They asked the million-dollar question: 'So what makes a good marriage?'*

◆ In the United States in the 1940s, there was a radio quiz show called 'Take It or Leave It'. Contestants had to answer questions for prizes ranging from two dollars for an easy question to $64 for the hardest. A similar television quiz show in the 1950s increased the prize to $64,000 dollars.

dollars

dollars to doughnuts

Mainly American If you say that it is **dollars to doughnuts** that something will happen, you are emphasizing that you are certain it will happen. *It's dollars to doughnuts that the bank of the future will charge more for its services.*

domino

a domino effect

If one event causes another similar event, which in turn causes a further event, and so on, you can refer to this as **a domino effect**. *We have seen how bad the housing problem can become. Unused houses deteriorate rapidly, affecting the value of nearby homes; in a domino effect, the entire neighborhood can easily fall victim.*

◆ This expression was first used in the 1950s by an American political commentator to describe what some people thought would happen if one country in a region became Communist: they believed that the other countries in that area would also 'fall' to the Communists. The image is of a row of upright dominoes; if one falls, it knocks the next one over and so on, until all of them have fallen over.

done

done and dusted

Mainly British and Australian If you say that something is **done and dusted**, you mean that it is finished or decided and there is nothing more to be said or done about it. *'The deal is done and dusted,' Dorahy told The Sunday Mail.*

donkey

donkey's years

British If you say that something lasts or has been happening for **donkey's years**, you are emphasizing that it lasts or has been happening for a very long time. *I've been a vegetarian for donkey's years.*

◆ This expression was originally 'as long as donkey's ears', which are very long. The change to 'donkey's years' may have come about partly because of the expression is used to talk about time, and partly because the original form is difficult to say clearly.

do the donkey work

British If someone **does the donkey work**, they do all the most physically tiring or boring parts of a job or piece of work. *We've been very fortunate getting a succession of secretaries who've managed to do the donkey work.*

door

beat a path to someone's door

If people **are beating a path to** your **door**, they are eager to talk to you or do business with you. *Business leaders should be beating a path to Mr Eggar's door demanding that tough environmental laws be passed.*

◆ This expression has been attributed to the American writer Ralph Waldo Emerson (1803–82), who used similar words in a lecture: 'If a man write a better book, preach a better sermon, or make a better mousetrap than his neighbour, 'tho he build his house in the woods, the world will make a beaten path to his door.'

by the back door

Mainly British If someone gets or does something **by the back door**, they do it secretly and unofficially. *He said the government would not allow anyone to sneak in by the back door and seize power by force... David Hinchliffe, for Labour, accused the Government of introducing a back door* *method of closing council homes.*

close the stable door after the horse has bolted
close the barn door after the horse has gone

In British English, if you say that an action is like **closing the stable door after the horse has bolted**, you mean that it is too late to take this action now, because the problem which it would have prevented has already occurred. In American English, you say that an action is like **closing the barn door after the horse has gone.** *At best, say critics, this strategy is like shutting the door after the horse has bolted... This all has the feeling of closing the barn door after the horse has gone.*

lay something at someone's door

If you **lay** something **at** someone's **door**, you blame them for something unpleasant that has happened. *The robberies were now laid at Brady's door.*

not darken somewhere's door
never darken someone's door

Old-fashioned If someone never goes to a place, you can say that they **do not darken** its **door**. If someone tells you **never to darken** their **door** again, they are ordering you never to visit them again because you have done something to make them very angry or upset. You can use 'doorstep' instead of 'door'. *He had not darkened the door of a church for a long time... The law firm told them to destroy all dossiers and never darken their doorstep again.*

◆ The image here is of someone's dark shadow falling across the door.

push at an open door

British If you say that someone **is pushing at an open door**, you mean that they are finding it very easy to achieve their aims. *'Most departments were helpful,'* she says, *'although enthusiasm was a bit muted in a few cases. In the main we now seem to be pushing at an open door.'*

the revolving door: 1

If you talk about **the revolving door** of an organization or institution, you are referring to the fact that the people working in it do not stay there for very long, and so, for example, it is difficult for anything effective to be achieved. *For the next 25 years, Caramoo had a revolving door of executives.*

the revolving door: 2

In politics, **the revolving door** is used to refer to a situation in which someone moves from an influential position in government to a position in a private company, especially where this may give them an unfair advantage. Sometimes this expression is used to refer to a situation where someone moves from the private sector to government, and then back again. *Bill Clinton ran a campaign that included a strong pledge to stop the revolving door between public service and the private sector.*

the revolving door: 3

You can use **the revolving door** to refer to a situation where solutions to problems only last for a short time, and then the same problems occur again. *East Palo Alto juveniles, like others nationwide, are caught in the revolving door of the justice system, ending up back on the streets after serving time, faced with their old life.*

doors

behind closed doors

If people have talks or discussions **behind closed doors**, they have them in private because they want them to be kept secret. *While there are many examples of decisions being publicly discussed, there are many other examples of the old approach, with decisions taken in secret behind closed doors... His name was reportedly mentioned in relation to arms during a behind-closed-doors court case.*

dot

on the dot

If you do something **on the dot**, you do it punctually or at exactly the time you are supposed to. *At nine o'clock on the dot, they have breakfast.*

◆ The minutes on a clock face are often marked by dots.

since the year dot

British If you say that something has been the way it is **since the year dot**, you mean it has been like that for a very long time. *Most of these folks have been here since the year dot.*

double

at the double
on the double

If you do something **at the double** or **on the double**, you do it very quickly or immediately. 'At the double' is used only in British English. *He said there was a report of a prowler at this address. I knew it was your place so I came over on the double.*

◆ 'At the double' is a military expression meaning at twice the normal marching pace.

down

down and dirty: 1

American If you describe a person or their behaviour as **down and dirty**, you mean that they behave in an unfair or dishonest way in order to gain an advantage. *Did this campaign get down and dirty?... This isn't a guy who teaches comparative literature at Amherst. This is a down and dirty cop.*

down and dirty: 2

Mainly American Journalists sometimes refer to a performer or their performance as **down and dirty** when they like them because they are bold, direct, and perhaps vulgar. *Get down and dirty with Sandra Bernhard who comes to Britain with her one-woman show, Giving Till It Hurts.*

down and out: 1

If you describe someone as **down and out**, you mean that they have nowhere to live, usually have no job, and have no real hope of improving their situation. *I know what it is to be down and out. One time back in the thirties, I was working in New York and I didn't have enough to rent a room.*

☐ You can refer to a person in this situation as **a down-and-out**.

down and out: 2

In a competition or contest, if someone is **down and out**, they have been beaten, or they are losing and have no hope of winning. *Leicester had looked down and out when they trailed 12 – 3 with only 12 minutes left.*

☐ You can say that someone is **down but not out** when they are losing but still have some hope of winning. *The Democrats are down, but not out.*

◆ If boxers are down and out, they have been knocked down and have failed to get up before the referee counted to ten, and have therefore lost the contest.

down-at-heel
down-at-the-heels

A **down-at-heel** or **down-at-the-heels** person or place looks uncared for and untidy. 'Down-at-heel' is used mainly in British English and 'down-at-the-heels' is used mainly in American English. *The flight to Kathmandu is always full of scruffy, down-at-heel people like Hyde.*

♦ The image here is of a person wearing shoes with worn-down heels because they do not have the money to repair or replace them.

have a down on someone
have a downer on someone

British If you **have a down on** someone or something or you **have a downer on** them, you do not like them or you disapprove of them. *Snobs would have a down on a man with a south London accent.*

drag

drag someone through the mud

If you say that someone **is dragged through the mud**, you mean that they are accused of behaving in an immoral or unacceptable way. This expression has several variations. For example, you can also say that someone's reputation or name **is dragged through the mud**. Nouns such as 'mire', 'dirt', or 'filth' can be used instead of 'mud'. *One doesn't like to see an admired institution dragged through the mud like this.*

drag your feet
drag your heels

If you say that someone **is dragging** their **feet** or **dragging** their **heels** on something, you are criticizing them for deliberately delaying making a decision about something that is important to you. *But there's been more substantial criticism of the United States for dragging its feet on measures to protect the environment... A spokesman strongly denied that the Government was dragging its heels on the issue.*

drawer

the top drawer: 1

Mainly British If you describe someone or something as from or out of **the top drawer**, you mean that they are among the best of their kind. *Castleford produced a performance right out of the top drawer to thrash Wigan 33–2... The dramatisation is wonderfully inventive and superbly played by a top-drawer cast including Maria Aitken and Tim Piggott-Smith.*

the top drawer: 2

Mainly British If you describe someone as from or out of **the top drawer**, you mean that they are from a privileged social background. *Some attenders this year seemed – how should one say it – not exactly out of the top drawer.*

dream

a dream ticket

Mainly British If two people are considered **a dream ticket**, they are expected to work well together and have a great deal of success. This expression is usually used to refer to people who are well known, for example politicians or actors. *It should have been Hollywood's dream ticket: husband and wife Tom Cruise and Nicole Kidman starring together in a romantic blockbuster movie.*

◆ In the United States, a ticket is a list of candidates that a political party has nominated for election. A 'dream ticket' is a pair of candidates that seem to be perfectly matched and who will attract a lot of support. 'Dream ticket' was first used to refer to the nomination of Nixon and Rockefeller for president and vice-president respectively.

dressed

dressed to kill

If you describe someone, especially a woman, as **dressed to kill**, you mean that they are wearing very smart or glamorous clothes which are intended to attract attention and impress people. *We're all familiar with the images – the gorgeous, pouting model, dressed to kill, with cigarette dangling from kissable lips.*

drop

at the drop of a hat

If you do something **at the drop of a hat**, you do it willingly and without hesitation. This expression is often used to suggest that someone does not think carefully enough about their actions. *There is a myth that we are a uniquely uncaring generation, shoving our old folk into institutions at the drop of a hat.*

◆ In the early 19th century, boxing matches were often started by someone dropping a hat.

a drop in the ocean
a drop in the bucket

If you say that something, especially an amount of money, is **a drop in the ocean** or **a drop in the bucket**, you mean that it is very small in comparison with the amount which is needed or expected, so that its effect is insignificant. 'A drop in the bucket' is used mainly in American

English. *The size of the grants have been attacked by welfare groups as merely a drop in the ocean.*

♦ This expression may come from a line in the Bible: 'Behold, the nations are as a drop of a bucket, and are counted as the small dust of the balance.' (Isaiah 40:15)

drum

bang the drum
beat the drum

If you **bang the drum** or **beat the drum** for something or someone, you support them strongly and publicly. *The trade secretary disagreed but promised to 'bang the drum for industry'... Some in the media have been beating the environmental drums for a while.*

drunk

drunk as a skunk

If you say that someone is as **drunk as a skunk**, you are emphasizing that they are very drunk. Nouns such as 'lord' or 'coot' are sometimes used instead of 'skunk'. *I heard he was drunk as a coot last night and got into a big fight at Toby's.*

dry

dry as a bone

If you say that something is as **dry as a bone**, you are emphasizing that it is very dry. *By the end of June the pond is as dry as a bone.*

□ People also use the much more frequent adjective **bone-dry** to mean the same thing. *His throat was bone dry.*

dry as dust: 1

If you say that something is **dry as dust**, you are emphasizing that it is very dry. *The hard-packed dirt of the floor was smooth and solid as cement, and the stone walls were dry as dust and hadn't been disturbed in a century.*

dry as dust: 2

If you describe something as **dry as dust**, you mean that it is very dull and uninteresting. *When you see the law in action, you realise how exciting it can be and what a buzz it gives people. It's so different from the dry-as-dust stuff we study at college.*

duck

a dead duck

If you refer to someone or something as **a dead duck**, you mean that they are a failure. *Chelsea Harbour is known to be something of a dead duck. People have failed to move there in the quantities expected, shops have closed, flats and penthouses are still empty.*

a lame duck

If you refer to someone or something as **a lame duck**, you mean that they are weak or in a vulnerable position. *If he loses it's hard to see how he can ever regain his authority. He's already seen widely as a lame duck Prime Minister... Rover intends to complete the transformation from the lame duck of the motor industry into a quality car maker with a series of 'high image' models.*

◆ The image here is of a duck that has been shot and wounded, and so cannot move properly and is likely to die.

a sitting duck

If you refer to someone as **a sitting duck**, you mean that they are an obvious target, and that it is very easy to attack them or criticize them. *If the Chinese authorities were on to me, I was a sitting duck at the airport.*

◆ A duck is an easy target for hunters when it is sitting on the water or on the ground.

take to something like a duck to water

If you **take to** something **like a duck to water**, you discover that you are naturally good at it and find it very easy to do. *Gilbey decided that farming wasn't for him, and moved up to London, where he became a salesman for BMW. He took to it like a duck to water, quickly becoming Car Salesman of the Year.*

ducks

get your ducks in a row

Mainly American If you say that someone **has got** their **ducks in a row**, you mean they have got everything properly organized and under control. *There is going to always be some disarray when you have a Republican White House and a Democratic Congress, but they do seem to have some trouble getting their ducks in a row.*

◆ The 'ducks' in this expression are duckpins. The game of duckpins is a variation of bowling, with ten smaller pins and a smaller ball with no finger holes. The literal meaning of 'to get your ducks in a row' is to get your duckpins set up for the next game.

play ducks and drakes with someone

British If you accuse someone of **playing ducks and drakes with** people, you are accusing them of treating those people badly, by being dishonest with them or not taking them seriously. *He accepted the ceasefire conditions, but since then has been playing ducks and drakes with the United Nations.*

◆ 'Ducks and drakes' is the game of skimming flat stones across the surface of some water to see how many times you can make the stones bounce. In this expression, the person's attitude to others is perhaps being compared to someone idly and thoughtlessly skimming stones.

dudgeon

in high dudgeon

If you say that someone is **in high dudgeon**, you are criticizing them for being unreasonably angry or annoyed about something. *She had left in high dudgeon after learning that the only perk was free coffee.*

◆ The origin of the word 'dudgeon' is unknown.

dull

dull as ditchwater
dull as dishwater

If you say that someone or something is as **dull as ditchwater** or as **dull as dishwater**, you are emphasizing that they are very boring. *Sherry has an image of being as dull as ditchwater but the reality is that it's a subtle and stylish drink.*

◆ The expression 'dull as ditchwater' is over 200 years old, whereas 'dull as dishwater' is a more recent variant. The reference is to the dull dirty colour of the water in ditches or in washing-up bowls.

dummy

spit the dummy
spit out the dummy

Mainly Australian If you accuse someone of **spitting the dummy** or **spitting out the dummy**, you are accusing them of behaving in a bad-tempered and childish way. *He spat the dummy when his wife decided* *to go back to work.*

◆ The image here is of a bad-tempered baby spitting out its dummy.

dumps

down in the dumps: 1
in the dumps

If you are **down in the dumps** or **in the dumps**, you feel depressed. *Tommy has been a bit down in the dumps and he needs a change.*

in the dumps: 2
down in the dumps

If a business or economy is **in the dumps** or **down in the dumps**, it is doing badly. *California's economy is unlikely to stay in the dumps for more than two years, which gives the Governor plenty of time to take credit for the recovery.*

dust

bite the dust: 1

If you say that something **bites the dust**, you mean that it fails or ceases to exist. *There are over 4,000 such restaurants in and around London. Some make big money. Most break even, and quite a few have bitten the dust.*

bite the dust: 2

If you say that someone **has bitten the dust**, you mean that they have died. This expression is used to refer to someone's death in a light-hearted or humorous way. *A Wild West showman nearly bit the dust when he blew himself up making blank bullets in his garden shed.*

◆ In stories about the Wild West, cowboys and Indians were said to 'bite the dust' when they were shot and fell off their horses.

the dust settles
the dust clears

If you say that **the dust has settled** in a situation, you mean that it has become calmer and steadier after a series of confusing or chaotic events. You can also say that **the dust has cleared**. *Now that the dust has settled, it is clear that nothing much has changed.*

eat someone's dust

In a competitive situation, if you **are eating** someone's **dust**, they are doing much better than you. *Aladdin has proved to be the most successful* *animated film of all time, leaving blockbusters like Home Alone 2 eating its dust.*

◆ If you are riding behind another horse in a race, you have the dust kicked up by the other horse in your face.

gather dust

If something such as a project or problem **gathers dust**, it is not dealt with for a very long time. *A report written in 1951, which has been gathering dust on a shelf at the Institution of Civil Engineers in London, advocates a number of the building projects.*

not see someone for dust

Mainly British If you say that you **can't see** someone **for dust**, you mean that they have left somewhere very quickly and run away. *Come the dawn, I couldn't see him for dust.*

◆ The image here is of someone galloping away on a horse, so that all you see is the cloud of dust kicked up by the horse's feet.

shake the dust of somewhere from your feet

British If you **shake the dust of** a place or situation **from** your **feet**, you leave it with the intention that you will never return to it. *He insisted that the bank shake the dust of third-world debt from its feet.*

◆ This expression occurs in the Bible: 'And whosoever shall not receive you, nor hear your words, when ye depart out of that house or city, shake off the dust of your feet.' (Matthew 10:14)

dusty

a dusty answer
a dusty reply

British If you ask or suggest something and you get **a dusty answer** or **a dusty reply**, you get a sharp and unpleasant response, for example a rejection of what you have asked for. *Plans to allow children into pubs received a dusty answer at the bar.*

Dutch

◆ The use of 'Dutch' in expressions which are negative or critical dates back to the seventeenth century, when the Dutch were commercial and military rivals of the British.

go Dutch
a Dutch treat

Old-fashioned If two or more people **go Dutch**, they share the cost of the bill for something such as a meal or an evening out. *Many women are happy to go Dutch with a new boyfriend on the first date.*

□ You can also say that you have **a Dutch treat**. *He wanted to pay the bill, but I objected and we settled on Dutch treat.*

in Dutch

Mainly American, old-fashioned If you are **in Dutch**, you are in trouble. *Doug wants to get Manatelli in Dutch with his boss.*

E

eagle

an eagle eye: 1

If you say that someone is keeping **an eagle eye** on a person or thing, you mean that they are watching that person or thing very carefully. *Managers of Europe's top clubs are keeping an eagle eye on the World Championships hoping to snap up new talent.*

an eagle eye: 2

You can say that someone has **an eagle eye** when they are very good at finding or noticing things. *No antiques shop, market or junk shop escapes her eagle eye.*

◆ Eagles are able to see small animals or objects from a great height.

ear

bend someone's ear

If you say that someone **is bending** your **ear**, you mean that they keep talking to you about something, often in an annoying way. *You can't go on bending everyone's ear with this problem.*

go in one ear and out the other

If you say that something **goes in one ear and out the other**, you mean that someone pays no attention to it, or forgets about it immediately. *The words went in one ear and out the other. They hardly registered.*

grin from ear to ear
smile from ear to ear

If you say that someone **is grinning from ear to ear** or **is smiling from ear to ear**, you are emphasizing that they look very happy. *Brimming* *with confidence and grinning from ear to ear, China's leaders celebrated last night the end of the Asian Games... He rewarded me with an ear-to-ear smile.*

half an ear

If you listen to someone or something with **half an ear**, you do not give your full attention to them. *She is listening to the news of the siege with half an ear.*

have an ear for something

If you **have an ear for** something, such as music or language, you have the ability to learn quickly how it works or is structured, by listening to the various sounds and being able to reproduce them. Compare **have a tin ear for** something; see **tin**. *He had an ear for languages, which he enjoyed, and by this time he spoke five fluently.*

have someone's ear

If you **have the ear of** someone in a position of power, they pay great attention to what you think and say, and often follow your opinion on important issues. *He has been one of Italy's most influential figures, a man who is said to have had the ear of any Italian prime minister.*

keep your ear to the ground

If you **keep** your **ear to the ground**, you make sure that you find out about the things that people are doing or saying. *I have a company which deals in arms. In that business, we have our ear very close to the ground.*

◆ In films, Native Americans are often shown tracking people or animals by listening carefully to the ground for the sound of their footsteps.

lend an ear to someone

If you **lend an ear to** someone or their problems, you listen to them carefully and sympathetically. *They are always willing to lend an ear and offer what advice they can.*

out on your ear

If you are **out on** your **ear**, you have been suddenly told to leave or are dismissed from a course, job, or group. *I'd failed the first year exam in the History of Art. I had to pass the re-sit or I'd be out on my ear.*

play it by ear

If you **play** it **by ear**, you deal with things as they happen, rather than following a plan or previous arrangement. *'Where will we stay in Gloucestershire?' 'Oh, I guess a bed-and-breakfast place. We'll have to play it by ear.'*

◆ If someone plays a piece of music **by ear**, they play it without looking at printed music.

turn a deaf ear to something

If you **turn a deaf ear to** something such as a request or argument, you refuse to consider it and do not pay any attention to it. *The Mayor of Paris, owner of two dogs, has long turned a deaf ear to Parisians who want tougher laws to protect the cleanliness of their pavements.*

ears

be all ears

If you **are all ears**, you are ready and eager to listen to what someone is saying. *'That's a large question, if not necessarily good. May I answer it frankly?' 'I'm all ears.'*

fall on deaf ears

If something you say to someone **falls on deaf ears**, they take no notice of what you have said. *The mayor spoke privately to Gibson yesterday and asked him to resign, but said that his plea fell on deaf ears.*

have something coming out of your ears

If you say that you **have** something **coming out of** your **ears**, you are emphasizing that you have a great amount of it, often so much that you do not want any more. *I absolutely despise football. I've had football coming out of my ears.*

have steam coming out of your ears

If you **have steam coming out of** your **ears**, you are very angry or irritated about something. *Not that Labour's front-benchers quite see it that way; indeed, steam comes out of their ears at the suggestion.*

pin back your ears: 1

British, old-fashioned If you **pin back** your **ears**, you listen carefully to what someone is saying. *Right, pin back your ears and listen.*

pin someone's ears back: 2

American If you **pin** someone's **ears back**, you tell them off for having done something wrong. *Charles Drake of the Child Support Collection Association doesn't shy away from contacting a grandparent. 'Oh, absolutely. If the absent parent fails to cooperate, that's one of the first places I'm going to go to. I've had some grandparents pin their 40-year-old son's ears back.'*

pin back your ears: 3

Mainly British In sport, if someone **pins back** their **ears**, they run very quickly in an attempt to score and help their team win. *The Newport back division dropped the ball 30 metres out and Hughes pinned back his ears and raced to the line.*

prick up your ears

If someone **pricks up** their **ears**, they start listening eagerly, because they suddenly hear an interesting sound or piece of information. *She stopped talking to prick up her ears – and Kenworthy had heard the same sound.*

◆ When animals such as dogs hear a sudden or unfamiliar noise, they literally prick up their ears; that is, their ears become more erect so that they can hear the sound better.

someone's ears are burning

If you have a conversation about someone who is not present and then you meet them, you can ask them if their **ears were burning** in order to let them know that you were talking about them. *He decided to give Chris a call as promised. 'Dave! Talk about coincidence! Were your ears burning?' 'No, why?' 'I was just wondering if I could justify getting in touch with you.'*

up to your ears

If you say that you are **up to** your **ears** in work or in an unpleasant situation, you mean that you are very busy with it or are deeply involved in it. *He told her openly he had only married her for her money. It seems he is in debt up to the ears.*

wet behind the ears

If you say that someone is **wet behind the ears**, you mean that they are new to a situation and are therefore inexperienced or naive. *Hawking was a research student, still wet behind the ears by scientific standards.*

◆ There are two possible origins for this expression. It may refer to a young animal being washed by its mother. Alternatively, it may refer to children forgetting to dry behind their ears after washing.

earth

down to earth

If you say that someone is **down to earth**, you approve of them because they are very realistic and practical. *Everyone liked her down-to-earth approach to life.*

go to earth

British If you **go to earth**, you hide from someone or something. *The girl who had supplied the gun and plastic explosive device stayed put for a couple of weeks before she, too, went to earth.*

◆ A fox's hole is called an earth. In hunting, this expression is used to refer to a fox hiding in its earth.

promise the earth

If someone **promises the earth**, they promise to give people things that they cannot in fact possibly give them. *'Politicians have lost credibility,' he complained, 'they promise the earth and don't deliver.'*

run someone to earth

British If you **run** someone or something **to earth**, you find them after a long search. *I must admit I thought I had run my man to earth, for although a great many people live there now, there could not be many that would match my description.*

◆ A fox's hole is called an earth. In hunting, this expression is used to refer to a fox being chased back to its earth.

easy

easy as pie
easy as ABC

If you say that something is **easy as pie** or **easy as ABC**, you are emphasizing that it is very easy to do. *Dave could not make head or tail of this, but Michael understood at once. 'What is the solution?' 'Why, that's easy as pie,' he said as the rest of us scratched our heads... With our guide, planning your US fly-drive holiday will be as easy as ABC.*

ebb

at a low ebb

If someone or something is **at a low ebb**, they are very depressed or unsuccessful. *When I have been at a low ebb I have found the friendship and Christian love of my fellow churchgoers to be a great strength.*

◆ The ebb tide is one of the regular periods, usually two per day, when the sea gradually falls to a lower level, as the tide moves away from the land.

eclipse

in eclipse

If something is **in eclipse**, it is much less successful and important than it used to be. *Even when her career was temporarily in eclipse she 'had enough money to swing it'.*

◆ An eclipse of the sun is an occasion when the moon is between the earth and the sun, so that for a short time you cannot see part or all of the sun. An eclipse of the moon is an occasion when the earth is between the sun and the moon, so that for a short time you cannot see part or all of the moon because it is covered by the shadow of the earth.

edge

the cutting edge: 1

To be at or on **the cutting edge** of a particular field of activity means to be involved in its most important, exciting, or advanced developments. *It is unrealistic for any designer to expect to be at the cutting edge of the fashion industry for anything longer than 15 years... These were the men and women doing the cutting-edge research.*

a cutting edge: 2

If someone or something gives you **a cutting edge**, they provide you with the ability to be more successful than your opponents. *We need a cutting edge and hopefully they can provide it.*

lose your edge

If someone or something **loses** their **edge**, they no longer have all the advantages and special skills or talents that they used to have. *Its staff disagrees with criticisms that their magazine is out of date or has lost its edge.*

◆ If a sword or knife has lost its edge, it is blunt.

on the edge of your seat
on the edge of your chair

If something keeps you **on the edge of** your **seat**, it keeps you very interested and eager to know what happens next. In American English, you can also say that something keeps you **on the edge of** your **chair**. You use these expressions especially when talking about things such as plays, films, or books. *Saturday night's final had the spectators on the edge of their seats.*

take the edge off something

If something **takes the edge off** a situation, especially an unpleasant one, it weakens its effect, intensity, or unpleasantness. *My head never seemed to clear completely, and the painkillers only took the edge off the pain.*

◆ If something takes the edge off a blade, it makes it blunt.

edges

fray at the edges

If you say that something or someone **is fraying at the edges**, you mean that they are becoming weaker or less certain or stable, and that they are gradually being damaged or destroyed. *The government's army has begun to fray at the edges.*

rough edges: 1

If you say that a person has **rough edges**, you mean that there are small faults in their behaviour towards other people. You use this expression when you generally approve of the person you are talking about. *He had the reputation of sometimes taking himself a little seriously. Those rough edges have long since worn off.*

☐ You can also talk about a **rough-edged** person. *He is exactly the sort of rough-edged entrepreneur who doesn't fit into a bureaucracy such as Stanford's.*

rough edges: 2

If you say that a performance or piece of entertainment has **rough edges**, you mean that it is not technically perfect, although you generally approve of it. *The show, despite some rough edges, was an instant success.*

☐ You can also talk about a **rough-edged** performer, performance, or piece of entertainment. *She was untutored, rough-edged, but the audiences adored her.*

egg

egg on your face

If you get **egg on** your **face**, you feel embarrassed or humiliated by something you have done or said. *Steve didn't expect to win. He just didn't want to get egg on his face.*

◆ People in crowds sometimes throw eggs at someone such as a politician or performer, to show their anger or dislike for them.

lay an egg

American If something **lays an egg**, it fails because people are not interested in it or do not want it. *Independent studies showed the ad laid an egg.*

eggs

put all your eggs in one basket

If you say that someone **is putting all** their **eggs in one basket**, you are pointing out that they are putting all their efforts or resources into one course of action and this means that they will have no alternatives left if it fails. *Don't put your eggs in one basket; study hard at school and always keep an alternative job in mind.*

eggshells

walk on eggshells
walk on eggs

If you **are walking on eggshells** or **are walking on eggs**, you are very careful about what you say or do because you do not want to upset or offend someone, even though you think they are being over-sensitive. *Healthy or sick, good days or bad, I felt I was always walking on eggshells around him.*

elbow

elbow grease

You can use **elbow grease** to refer to the energy and strength you need for doing physical work such as cleaning or polishing something. *Plenty of elbow grease soon moves all the dirt.*

elbow room: 1

If someone gives you **elbow room**, they give you the freedom to do what you need or want to do in a particular situation. *His overall message to governors, though, was that he intends to give them more elbow room to encourage innovation at the state level.*

elbow room: 2

If you have enough **elbow room**, you have enough space to move freely or feel comfortable, without feeling crowded or cramped. *There was not much elbow room in the cockpit.*

not know your arse from your elbow
not know your ass from your elbow

If you say that someone **doesn't know** their **arse from** their **elbow** or **doesn't know** their **ass from** their **elbow**, you are saying in a very rude way that they have no common sense or that they are ignorant and stupid. The form with 'arse' is used in British English and the form with 'ass' is used mainly in American English. *He's just a boy. A big, enthusiastic kid without an ounce of subtlety in him, who doesn't know his arse from his elbow.*

elbows

rub elbows with someone

Mainly American If you **rub elbows with** someone important or famous, you associate with them for a while. The usual British expression is **rub shoulders with** someone. *He rubbed elbows with dozens of political super-celebrities, including Richard Nixon, Imelda Marcos, and Gerald Ford.*

element

in your element
out of your element

If you say that someone is **in** their **element**, you mean that they are doing something that they enjoy or do well. *My stepmother was in her element, organizing everything.*

□ You can say that someone is **out of** their **element** when they are doing something that they do not enjoy or do not do well. *As I hadn't done much cooking recently I felt a bit out of my element in the kitchen.*

◆ Ancient and medieval philosophers believed that all substances were composed from the four elements: earth, air, fire, and water. To be 'in your element' is to be in your natural surroundings, like a bird in air or a fish in water.

elephant

a white elephant

If you describe something such as a new building, plan, or project as **a white elephant**, you mean that it is a waste of money and completely useless. *Will the complex, constructed at some expense but never used, be regarded as a monumental folly, a great white elephant?*

◆ There is a story that the Kings of Siam used to give white elephants, which are very rare, to courtiers who they did not like. The animals cost so much to keep that their owners spent all their money on them and were ruined.

end

at a loose end
at loose ends

If you are **at a loose end** or **at loose ends**, you have some spare time and you feel rather bored because you do not have anything particular to do. 'At a loose end' is used in British English and 'at loose ends' is used in American English. Compare **loose ends**; see **ends**. *After my return home I was at a loose end. I read the typescript over and over until I knew it by heart... Brenda had agreed to see her at four-thirty, which left Mrs. Dambar at loose ends for two and a half hours.*

◆ This expression may refer to the ropes on a sailing ship. The ends of the ropes had to be tightly bound to stop them fraying, and sailors were often given this job to do when there was nothing more urgent to be done. Alternatively, the expression may refer to a working horse being untied at the end of the day and released into a field.

a dead end: 1

If a plan, project, or course of action leads to **a dead end**, there is no future in it and it will never develop any further. *The investigations into the sensational murder of former Prime Minister Rajiv Gandhi seem to have reached a dead end.*

dead-end: 2

You can use **dead-end** to describe a job or situation when you dislike it or are scornful of it because you think it is boring and will never lead to anything more interesting or successful. *He was a dull, nondescript man in a dull, dead-end job.*

◆ A dead end is a street which is closed at one end.

the end of the road: 1
the end of the line

If someone or something is at **the end of the road** or **the end of the line,** they are at a point where they can no longer continue or survive in a situation. *Failure to beat Poland at Wembley in the next match almost certainly will spell the end of the line for the England manager.*

the end of the road: 2
the end of the line

If you refer to **the end of the road** or **the end of the line,** you are referring to what will eventually happen as a result of someone's actions. *There are many of us who tell kids who don't want to go to school that if drugs don't kill them, there's only jail at the end of the road.*

go off the deep end: 1

Mainly American If you say that someone **has gone off the deep end,** you mean that they have gone mad, or that their behaviour has become strange or extreme. *His Aunt Ellen raised him after his mother went off the* *deep end.*

go off the deep end: 2

British If someone **goes off the deep end**, they become very angry. *I thought that the real trouble would begin when my father got home. In fact, he didn't go off the deep end at all. He just said it wasn't fair to make my mother worry like that.*

◆ The deep end is the end of a swimming pool where the water is deepest.

in at the deep end

If you jump **in at the deep end** or are thrown **in at the deep end**, you start by doing the most difficult part of a job or task, before you have tried to do the easier parts or without any preparation. *I believe you gain confidence by being thrown in at the deep end. Then there's no way out. You have to get on with it and produce the goods.*

◆ See the explanation at 'go off the deep end'.

keep your end up
hold your end up

If you **keep** your **end up** or **hold** your **end up** in a particular situation, you do what you have said you will do or what you are expected to do. *But David, despite being uncharacteristically nervous, holds his end up brilliantly, making his points and still managing to play it for laughs... The pure fact of the matter is that we signed a contract and we've worked hard to keep up our end, and they must keep up their end.*

the sharp end

Mainly British If someone is at **the sharp end** of an activity or type of work, they are the people who are actually involved in it and so know about the reality of the situation. *These men are at the sharp end of law enforcement and when a man is waving a gun, they have to act decisively to protect the public and colleagues.*

◆ In sailors' slang, the bow or front end of a ship is known as the sharp end.

ends

loose ends

If there are **loose ends** in something, small details or parts of it have not yet been sorted out satisfactorily. Compare **at loose ends**; see **end**. *The overall impact of the story is weakened by too many loose ends being left inadequately resolved.*

♦ This expression may refer to the ropes on a sailing ship. The ends of the ropes had to be tightly bound to stop them fraying, and sailors were often given this job to do when there was nothing more urgent to be done.

make ends meet

If you find it difficult to **make ends meet**, you find it difficult to pay for the things you need in life, because you have very little money. *Many people are struggling to make ends meet because wages are failing to keep pace with rising prices under the government's economic reform programme.*

♦ Originally, this expression was 'make both ends of the year meet', which meant to spend only as much money as you received as income.

play both ends against the middle

If someone **plays both ends against the middle**, they pretend to support or favour two opposing people or ideas in order to gain an advantage, or to try to get all the benefits that they can from a situation. You usually use this expression to show that you disapprove of this behaviour. *She plays both ends against the middle by deciding to marry the boy and still sleep with the man.*

Englishman

an Englishman's home is his castle

British When people say **'an Englishman's home is his castle'**, they are referring to the belief that people have the right to do what they want in their own home, and that other people or the state have no right to interfere in people's private lives. *An Englishman's home is his castle, and only recently courts have upheld the right of Englishmen to act in self-defence.*

☐ Journalists often vary this expression, for example by saying that an Englishman's home is a particular thing. *Far from being his castle, an Englishman's home is rapidly becoming a financial millstone.*

envelope

push the envelope

Mainly American If you **push the envelope**, you increase the technical capabilities of something or the extent to which it is developed. *Each time they flew faster or higher they regarded that as pushing the envelope.*

evil

put off the evil day

British If you say that someone **is putting off the evil day**, you mean that they have to do something unpleasant but they are trying to avoid doing it for as long as possible. *Some people find it helps to cut down on the number of cigarettes they smoke before they actually give up. But the danger of doing this is that you can simply go on putting off the evil day and eventually find yourself smoking as much as ever.*

evils

the lesser of two evils
the lesser evil

If you have to choose between two bad things, you can refer to the one which is less bad as **the lesser of two evils** or **the lesser evil**. *Should she choose the isolation of life on the streets or the constant abuse of her father? In the end it seemed the street was the lesser of two evils.*

exception

the exception that proves the rule

If you are making a general statement and you say that something is **the exception that proves the rule**, you mean that although it seems to contradict your statement, in most other cases your statement will be true. People sometimes use this expression to avoid having to justify their statement in detail. *I have this theory that, apart from one or two exceptions that prove the rule, very attractive men do not fall in love.*

eye

cast your eyes on something
cast your eye on something

If someone **casts** their **eyes on** something or someone, they want to have or possess them. You can also say that they **cast** their **eye on** them. *To our amazement, another developer has cast greedy eyes on the field next door.*

catch someone's eye

If something or someone **catches** your **eye**, you notice them because they are very striking, vivid, or remarkable. *When I walked into the coffee shop, a flower arrangement caught my eye.*

□ You can also say that something is **eye-catching** when it is very striking, vivid, or remarkable. *There's an eye-catching headline on the front page of the Sunday Times.*

an eye for an eye
an eye for an eye, a tooth for a tooth

People use **an eye for an eye** or **an eye for an eye, a tooth for a tooth** to refer to a system of justice where the punishment for a crime is either the same as the crime or equivalent to it. *They should bring back the death penalty. A lot of people are getting away with things like this, thinking 'So what, they cannot kill me.' I believe in an eye for an eye... I just believe in justice, James. An eye for an eye, and a tooth for a tooth.*

◆ Variations of this expression occur several times in the Old Testament of the Bible: 'Life shall go for life, eye for eye, tooth for tooth, hand for hand, foot for foot.' (Deuteronomy 19:21)

the eye of the storm

If you are in **the eye of the storm**, you are deeply involved in a difficult or controversial situation which affects or interests a lot of people. *He was often in the eye of the storm of congressional debates related to U.S. troop withdrawals from Vietnam.*

◆ This expression refers to the centre or middle part of a storm. However, in wind storms, such as cyclones and tornados, the eye is in reality a relatively calm area of low pressure in the centre.

get your eye in

British If you **get** your **eye in** when you are doing a particular thing, you become more skilful or experienced in it, because you have been practising it or doing it for a long time. *She had this marvellous knack for wheeling and dealing. I helped her get her eye in, but the instinct was there.*

give someone a black eye

If you **give** someone **a black eye**, you punish them severely for something they have done, but without causing them permanent harm. *Whenever the Liberal Democratic Party gets too cocky or corrupt, voters tend to give it a black eye.*

◆ A black eye is a dark-coloured bruise around a person's eye.

a gleam in your eye

If you say that a plan or project is only **a gleam in** someone's **eye** at present, you mean that it is being planned or considered, but has not yet been properly started. You can replace 'gleam' with 'glint' or 'twinkle'. *The European central bank is still no more than a glint in its creators' eyes.*

the naked eye

If something is big enough or bright enough to be seen with **the naked**

eye, you can see it without the help of equipment such as a telescope or microscope. *There could be some internal problem with the tires that isn't visible to the naked eye.*

not bat an eye: 1

Mainly American If you say that someone does something and nobody **bats an eye**, you mean that nobody seems to be shocked or offended by it, and that this is surprising. The usual British expression is **not bat an eyelid**. *You didn't bat your eye when I told you that your mother was dead.*

not bat an eye: 2

Mainly American If you say that someone does something **without batting an eye**, you are expressing your surprise that they are not nervous or worried about it. The usual British expression is **not bat an eyelid**. *Would you believe he ordered them to fill half a tin mug with that stuff and guzzled it without batting an eye, as if it was water?*

one in the eye for someone

British If you say that something you do is **one in the eye for** someone, you mean that it will annoy them. *I want to show Arsenal they were wrong to let me go. Every goal I score now is one in the eye for them.*

see eye to eye with someone

If you do not **see eye to eye with** someone, you do not agree with them about something. If you **see eye to eye** with someone, you agree with them completely. *The Prime Minister did not see eye to eye with him on this issue... We saw eye to eye on the essentials, and I'd even venture to say that we're now in perfect harmony.*

spit in someone's eye

If you say that someone **spits in** your **eye**, you mean that they deliberately upset or annoy you. *Small businessmen, all typical Tory voters, have seen their companies destroyed by the recession. The minister for Trade and Industry spat in their eye yesterday when he said: 'I won't rescue bankrupt companies. I won't support the weak at the expense of the strong.'*

take your eye off the ball
keep your eye on the ball

If you say that someone **takes** their **eye off the ball**, you mean that they stop paying attention for a moment to something they are doing, and as a result they suffer some harm or things go wrong for them. *His greatest disappointment must have been the coal dispute, which revealed that he had misjudged the mood of the public. He told friends later that the decision had* *been right, but he took his eye off the ball over the presentation.*

□ If you say that someone **keeps** their **eye on the ball**, you mean that they continue to pay close attention to what they are doing. *She won widespread praise for her innovation, her tough negotiating skills and her ability to keep things moving, keep her eye on the ball.*

there's more to something than meets the eye
there's less to something than meets the eye

If you say that **there is more to** something or someone **than meets the eye**, you mean that they are more complicated or more involved than they appear to be at first. *'She was convinced there was more to your friendship than met the eye.' 'Well there isn't.'*

□ You can say that **there is less to** something or someone **than meets the eye** to mean that they are less complicated or less involved than they appear to be at first. *Though there's currently a construction boom in luxury apartments, there's much less to this than meets the eye. Since the war ended, little has been done to rebuild the country as a whole, and the economy is in ruins.*

turn a blind eye to something

If you **turn a blind eye to** something, you deliberately ignore it because you do not want to take any action over it, even though you know you should. *The authorities were turning a blind eye to human rights abuses.*

◆ This expression was first used to describe the action of Admiral Nelson at the Battle of the Nile in 1798. When told that he was being ordered to withdraw, he put a telescope to his blind eye and said that he could not see the signal. He went on to win the battle.

would give your eye teeth for something

If you say that you **would give** your **eye teeth** for something, you are emphasizing that you really want it and that you would do almost anything to get it. *He's the most exciting man I've ever worked with, and I'd give my eye teeth to do something with him again.*

◆ A person's eye teeth are their canine teeth, the pointed teeth near the front of their mouth.

eyeball

eyeball to eyeball

If you say that two people are **eyeball to eyeball**, you mean that they are disagreeing with each other, and may argue or fight as a result. *It was*

*an immensely tough negotiation that led to eyeball-to-eyeball confrontations
with union leaders.*

eyeballs

up to the eyeballs: 1
If you say that someone is drugged **up to the eyeballs**, you mean that
they have taken a lot of drugs which have strongly affected them. *We won't
be able to speak to him today because he will be drugged up to the eyeballs. I
don't even know the phone number of the hospital he's in.*

up to the eyeballs: 2
If you say that someone is **up to the eyeballs** in an unpleasant or
difficult situation, you mean that they are very deeply involved in it.
*The one-time media tycoon is down on his luck, out of a job, and up to his
eyeballs in debt.*

eyebrows

raise eyebrows
If something that you do **raises eyebrows**, it surprises, shocks, or
offends people. *President Clinton raised a few eyebrows when he chose
Laura Tyson as the first woman to chair the Council of Economic Advisers.*

eyelid

not bat an eyelid: 1
not bat an eyelash
Mainly British If you say that someone does something and nobody **bats
an eyelid,** you mean that nobody seems to be shocked or offended by it,
and that this is surprising. You can also say that nobody **bats an eyelash.**
The usual American expression is **not bat an eye.** *I thought Sarah and
David would be acutely embarrassed. But they didn't bat an eyelid.*

not bat an eyelid: 2
not bat an eyelash
Mainly British If you say that someone does something **without batting
an eyelid,** you are expressing your surprise that they are not nervous or
worried about it. You can also say that they **do not bat an eyelash.** The
usual American expression is **not bat an eye.** *Mr Yeltsin said the
conspirators would have killed thousands of people without batting an eyelid.*

eyes

feast your eyes on something

If you **feast** your **eyes on** something, you look at it with a great deal of enjoyment and anticipation. *If family food means more to you than simply satisfying hungry mouths, then feast your eyes on our delicious dishes.*

have eyes in the back of your head

If you say that someone **has eyes in the back of** their **head**, you mean that they are very observant and seem to be aware of everything that is happening around them. *Our daughter is at the stage where you need eyes in the back of your head.*

keep your eyes peeled
keep your eyes skinned

If someone tells you to **keep** your **eyes peeled**, they are telling you to watch very carefully for something. They can also tell you to **keep** your **eyes skinned**. *Keep your eyes peeled so you're not followed... She's on the loose. I doubt if she'll come back here, but keep your eyes skinned.*

make eyes at someone

Fairly old-fashioned If someone **is making eyes at** you, they are trying to get you to notice them because they are sexually attracted to you. *He's making eyes at one of the nurses.*

only have eyes for someone: 1

If you **only have eyes for** one person, they are the only person that you are interested in sexually. *The 26 year-old model is adored by thousands but has eyes for only one man – her husband.*

only have eyes for something: 2

You can say that someone **only has eyes for** a particular thing when they are determined to have it. *The president came seeking investment in Mexico, but found Western Europe had eyes only for the new democracies to its east.*

open someone's eyes: 1

If something **opens** your **eyes**, it causes you to become aware of things for the first time. *The need for female labour created during two world wars opened the eyes of many women to better paid lives in factories and offices.*

open your eyes: 2
keep your eyes open

If someone tells you to **open** your **eyes** or **keep** your **eyes open**, they are telling you to become aware of things that you can do in a particular situation. *Wake up, open your eyes and minds and get angry, because political debate is back on the agenda... Keep your eyes open for any likely study courses starting in February.*

up to your eyes

If you say that you are **up to** your **eyes** in work or in an unpleasant situation, you mean that you are very busy with it or are deeply involved in it. *If you are up to your eyes in debt and already set to lose your home, get advice on bankruptcy.*

with your eyes closed
with your eyes shut

If you say that you can do something **with** your **eyes closed** or **with** your **eyes shut**, you are emphasizing that you can do it very easily. *He reassembled the gun quickly and expertly. It was something he could do with his eyes closed.*

with your eyes glued to something

Someone **with** their **eyes glued to** something is watching it with all their attention. *Goldstone's eyes were glued to the clock.*

F

face

at face value: 1

If you take what someone says **at face value**, you accept it and believe it without thinking about it very much, even though it may be incorrect or untrue. *Clients should know better than to take the advice of a wholesaler at face value.*

at face value: 2

If you take someone **at face value**, you accept the impression that they give of themselves, even though this may be completely false. *For a time I took him at face value. At that time, I had no reason to suspect him.*

♦ The face value of a coin or banknote is the amount that is printed on it, although it may in fact be worth more or less than that amount, for example because it is very old.

fly in the face of something

If you say that something **flies in the face of** accepted ideas, rules, or practices, you mean that it conflicts with them or contradicts them. *The plan to sell rhino horn flies in the face of the international ban.*

◆ The reference here is to a dog attacking someone.

in-your-face

If you describe someone or something as **in-your-face**, you mean that they are unconventional and provocative, and may upset or offend some people. *Christina James plays Perry's widow, a vivacious, in-your-face woman who is sometimes too honest for her own good.*

keep a straight face

If you **keep a straight face**, you manage to look serious, even though you really want to laugh or smile. *'I don't see that there's anything funny about it,' he said, offended. 'Of course there isn't,' she said, trying to keep a straight face.*

□ You can also say that someone or something is **straight-faced**. *It's the way he tells a joke. He is completely straight-faced and I just fall about laughing.*

laugh on the other side of your face

British If someone says **'you'll be laughing on the other side of your face'**, they are warning you that although you are happy or successful at the moment, things are likely to go wrong for you in the future. The American expression is **laugh out of the other side of** your **mouth**. *You'll be laughing on the other side of your face when they get Paul Stewart back from Liverpool.*

a long face

If you say that someone has **a long face**, you mean that they look very serious or unhappy. *There were some long faces in Paris that day. Astoundingly, an American had won the Tour de France.*

make a face
pull a face

If you **make a face** or **pull a face**, you show a feeling such as dislike, disgust, or defiance by twisting your face into an ugly expression, or by sticking out your tongue. 'Pull a face' is used only in British English. *She made a face at the musty smell, and hurried to open the windows... He was taught from an early age to address people as 'Mister' and not to poke his tongue out or pull faces.*

☐ If someone **makes** or **pulls a** particular kind of **face**, they show that feeling in their expression. *'Here I am,' Chee said. 'What can I do?' Janet made a wry face.*

save face
lose face

If you **save face**, you do something so that people continue to respect you and your reputation is not damaged. *Most children have an almost obsessive need to save face in front of their peers.*

☐ You can talk about a **face-saving** action. *The change of heart on aid seems to show that officials are looking for a face-saving way to back down.*

☐ Journalists sometimes refer to an action or excuse which enables someone to save face as **a face-saver**. *Nobody can object to a prisoner exchange between combatants. The hope is that this exchange will also give the kidnappers the face-saver they need to release the hostages.*

☐ If you **lose face**, people think less well of you because you are made to look foolish or because you do something which damages your reputation. *Political observers said the army chief had lost a lot of face because of the government's victory.*

◆ These expressions were first used by English-speaking people living in China. 'Lose face' is a translation of a Chinese expression.

set your face against something

Mainly British If you say that someone **has set** their **face against** something, you mean that they oppose it in a determined way. You often use this expression when you think the person is being stubborn or unreasonable. *Both the government and the major rebel groups appear to have set their faces against a negotiated settlement to the conflict.*

◆ This expression is used several times in the Bible. When God 'set His face against' someone who had sinned, He showed that He was angry with them.

until you are blue in the face

If you say that someone can do something **until** they **are blue in the face**, you mean that however long they do it or however hard they try, they will still fail. *The president can issue decrees until he is blue in the face, but they are ignored.*

fair

all's fair in love and war

In a competition or contest, people say **'all's fair in love and war'** when they want to justify dishonest or unfair behaviour, by suggesting that under difficult circumstances any kind of behaviour is acceptable. *He appears to live by the boorish credo that all is fair in love and war. And being cruel to mistresses and wives isn't wrong.*

☐ Sometimes people use other nouns instead of 'war' depending on the situation they are in. *It seems women are at last realising what men have known for years: All is fair in love and divorce.*

fair and square

If you say that someone won a competition or did something **fair and square**, you mean that they did it honestly and without cheating or lying. *I was beaten fair and square.*

fall

be heading for a fall
be riding for a fall

If you say that someone **is heading for a fall** or **is riding for a fall**, you mean that they are doing something which is likely to have unpleasant consequences for them. *The Tory Party is heading for a great fall.*

♦ This expression was probably first used in fox-hunting to refer to someone who was riding dangerously.

familiarity

familiarity breeds contempt
familiarity breeds content

If you say that **familiarity breeds contempt**, you mean that if you know someone or something very well, you can easily become bored with them and stop treating them with respect or stop paying attention to them. Other nouns are sometimes used instead of 'contempt'. *Familiarity breeds inattention. Typically, family members are so convinced they know what another family member is going to say that they don't bother to listen.*

☐ Sometimes this expression is varied, for example as **familiarity breeds content**, to say that when you know someone or something very well, you grow to like them more or have more respect for them, rather than less. *Through carefully maintaining a less grand image, the Queen has become as familiar to her people as a member of their own family – a familiarity that has bred content.*

farm

farm

buy the farm

If someone **buys the farm**, they die. *The plane spun down and never came out of it; it nosedived into the ground and exploded. He bought the farm.*

◆ A possible explanation for this expression is that, in wartime, American Air Force pilots sometimes said that they wanted to stop flying, buy a farm or ranch, and lead a peaceful life. 'Buy the farm' then came to be used when a pilot was killed in a crash.

fast

play fast and loose

If you accuse someone of **playing fast and loose** with something important, you are accusing them of treating it without proper care or respect. *The banks claim high interest rates are necessary because the government is playing fast and loose with public spending.*

pull a fast one

If someone **pulls a fast one**, they succeed in tricking you in order to get an advantage. *Management recently tried to pull a fast one. Behind the backs of workers, the directors arranged to buy up the majority of shares to be issued. This meant that the number of shares issued to the workers would be far fewer.*

fat

chew the fat

If you **chew the fat** with someone, you chat with them in an informal and friendly way about things that interest you. *We'd been lounging around, chewing the fat for a couple of hours.*

◆ This may refer to sailors in the past talking to each other while they chewed the fat in the dried pork which they were given to eat.

the fat is in the fire

If you say that **the fat is in the fire**, you mean that someone has said or done something which is going to upset other people and cause a lot of trouble. *Immediately the fat was in the fire, for in making an accusation directly and in the open, the minister for education and science had broken all the rules.*

☐ You can say that someone **pulls the fat out of the fire** when they prevent or stop trouble by taking action at a very late stage. *Don't rely on pulling the fat out of the fire by launching a late, last-ditch negative campaign against Clinton.*

◆ When food is being cooked over a fire, if fat or oil falls into the fire, the flames suddenly burn very fiercely.

the fat of the land

If you say that someone is living off **the fat of the land**, you mean that they have a rich and comfortable lifestyle without having to work hard for it. You often use this expression to criticize someone who is rich because they are exploiting people. *He was pretty fed up with these bloated royalists who were living off the fat of the land and off American aid while the rest of the country was starving, literally.*

◆ This is from the story of Joseph in the Bible. During the famine in Israel, Pharaoh invited Joseph's father and brothers to come to Egypt, where there was plenty of food: 'Come unto me: and I will give you the good of the land of Egypt, and ye shall eat the fat of the land.' (Genesis 45:18)

fate

seal someone's fate

If something **seals the fate** of a person or thing, it makes it certain that they will fail or that something unpleasant will happen to them. *The parliament's decision today could seal the Republic's fate.*

feast

enough is as good as a feast

British, old-fashioned If you say **'enough is as good as a feast'**, you mean that there is no point in having more of something than you need or want. *I too am very fond of music; nobody loves a tune better than I do. But I always say enough is as good as a feast; do you not agree?*

◆ This was first used by the Greek writer Euripides in the 5th century BC to explain that it is wrong to be greedy.

feast or famine

If someone says 'it's **feast or famine**', they mean that sometimes they have too much of something such as money, while at other times they do not have enough. *While her life is rich in memories, funds are a problem.*

'It's feast or famine with me,' she says.

☐ People often vary this expression. *After a long famine, a mini-feast: investors are once again providing banks with the capital they need.*

the spectre at the feast
the ghost at the feast
the skeleton at the feast

British If you describe a person or event as **the spectre at the feast**, **the ghost at the feast**, or **the skeleton at the feast**, you mean that they spoil other people's enjoyment, for example because they remind them of an unhappy event or situation. *The party that broke out that night, the sense of liberation and the euphoria that gripped the town was amazing. The only skeletons at the feast were the Russian military.*

◆ According to the Greek writer Plutarch, the Ancient Egyptians used to place a skeleton at the table during a feast, to remind them that they would die one day.

feather

a feather in your cap

If you describe someone's achievement as **a feather in** their **cap**, you mean that they have done very well and you admire them. *Hauptmann's arrest and conviction had been hailed as a triumph for justice and a feather in the cap of the New Jersey police.*

◆ Traditionally, Native American warriors added feathers to their headdresses as a sign of bravery in battle. Medieval knights in England also wore feathers in their helmets as a sign of their bravery.

feathers

ruffle someone's feathers

If someone **ruffles** your **feathers**, they say or do something which upsets or annoys you. *The country has, for example, ruffled a few feathers by breaking with the Western consensus on trade with China.*

smooth ruffled feathers

If someone **smooths ruffled feathers**, they calm things down when an argument or disagreement gets intense and they attempt to solve the problem. *His function was to smooth ruffled feathers. He would go around trying to convince people that they were making a lot of fuss about nothing.*

feet

feet on the ground

If someone keeps their **feet on the ground**, they continue to act in a sensible and practical way even when new or exciting things are happening or even when they become successful or powerful. Compare **get** your **feet on the ground**. *Kevin was always level-headed with both feet on the ground.*

find your feet

If you say that someone in a new situation **is finding** their **feet**, you mean that they are becoming more confident and learning what to do. *It takes a while for people to find their feet at this level and gain the necessary confidence.*

get cold feet

If you **get cold feet** about something, you are not sure whether you want to do it, or you become too nervous and worried to do it. *I feel your boyfriend got cold feet about being in a committed relationship.*

get your feet on the ground

Mainly American If you **get** your **feet on the ground**, you become established in a new situation, or become re-established in an old one. Compare **feet on the ground**. *They have modest two-room apartments, and until they get their feet on the ground, they take most meals at the institute's cafeteria.*

get your feet under the table

British If someone **gets** their **feet under the table**, they establish themselves firmly in a new job or situation. *I think I shall be able to do something about that next year. But let me get my feet under the table.*

get your feet wet

Mainly American If you **get** your **feet wet**, you get involved in something or experience something for the first time. *Charlton thinks it's time for me to get my feet wet. He says I'll be able to help the department a lot more if I learn how police actually solve crimes.*

have feet of clay
clay feet

You say that someone who is greatly admired or respected **has feet of clay** to point out that they have serious faults or weaknesses which people generally do not know about. *For all his right-on posturing about how* *much he cares for his fans, Bruce is just another corporate rock star with feet of clay.*

☐ You can also say that someone has **clay feet**. This form is used mainly in American English. *So do you think he was familiar with the clay feet of the justices and therefore didn't have great heroes among them?*

♦ According to the Bible, King Nebuchadnezzar asked Daniel to explain his dream of a giant idol, which was made of gold, silver, brass, and iron, but had feet made partly from clay. Daniel told the king that the clay feet were a sign of weakness and vulnerability. (Daniel 2:33)

itchy feet

If you say that you have got **itchy feet**, you mean that you have become bored with the place or situation that you are in, and you want to move somewhere new or start doing something new. *I hated living in London, and I started getting itchy feet. Last year, I decided I really wanted to come out to the States.*

land on your feet
fall on your feet

If you say that someone **lands on** their **feet** or **falls on** their **feet**, you mean that they find themselves in a good situation, which you think is the result of luck and not their own efforts. 'Fall on your feet' is used only in British English. *Everything I want, she's got: good marriage, good home, nice children. While I struggle through life, she lands on her feet... He has fallen on his feet with a new career set to earn him a fortune.*

♦ This may refer to the belief that when a cat falls, it always lands on its feet without hurting itself.

stand on your own two feet
stand on your own feet

If you **stand on** your **own two feet** or **stand on** your **own feet**, you show that you are independent and do not need anyone to help you or support you. *Having spent the past decade learning to stand on their own feet, Japan's drug makers now hope to take on the world.*

two left feet

If you say that someone has **two left feet**, you are saying light-heartedly that they dance or move in a clumsy or awkward way. *The first session was good fun, but with two left feet I found myself floundering on some of the steps in the aerobics section.*

vote with your feet

If people **vote with** their **feet**, they indicate what they want through their actions, for example showing their dislike of a place or situation by leaving it. *It seems thousands of people are already voting with their feet, and leaving the country for the hope of a better life.*

fence

sit on the fence
come off the fence

You say that someone **is sitting on the fence** to express your disapproval of them for refusing to state a definite opinion about something or to say who they support in a conflict. *The commission has chosen, extraordinarily, to sit on the fence, murmuring that schools must decide for themselves.*

☐ You can refer to this kind of behaviour as **fence-sitting**, and to someone who behaves like this as **a fence-sitter**. *At his first press conference there was much fence-sitting... I have a sense, just from what I've read and from talking to people, that there are a lot of fence sitters out there.*

☐ If you say that someone **comes off the fence**, you mean that they at last state their opinion about something or show who they support. Verbs such as 'climb' and 'get' can be used instead of 'come'. *It is time for us to get off the fence, to speak up, and to vote.*

fences

mend fences

If you have a difficult relationship with someone and you do something to try to improve it, you can say that you are trying to **mend fences** with them. *Yesterday he was publicly criticised for not doing enough to mend fences with his big political rival.*

☐ You can refer to this process as **fence-mending**. *King Hussein made numerous diplomatic missions. He's even now out of the country on a fence-mending mission to the European Community.*

fiddle

play second fiddle

If you have to **play second fiddle** to someone, you have to accept that you are less important than they are and do not have the same status,

even though you may resent this. *The 44-year-old senator will play second
fiddle to a man who, although of the same political generation, has been
his clear junior in the Democrat hierarchy.*

◆ A fiddle is a violin. The metaphor here refers to the first and second
violins in an orchestra.

field

have a field day

If you say that someone **is having a field day**, you mean that they are
taking advantage of a situation, especially one which other people find
upsetting or difficult. *Debt collectors are having a field day in the recession.*

out in left field
out of left field

If you say that someone or something is **out in left field** or comes **out of
left field**, you mean that they are unusual and unconventional. *Most of the
business tips are common sense, but others are right out of left field.*

□ **Left-field** can be used in many other structures. *Over the last few years,
the most left-field films in world cinema have come from Japan.*

◆ In baseball, left field is the part of the outfield where the sun and the
wind can cause problems with the ball. In addition, the spectators often
shout at the fielder in left field, and so players consider it to be a difficult
position to play.

out of left field

Mainly American A question, statement, or event which comes **out of
left field** is completely unexpected. *'You and Brian got married, didn't
you?' The question came out of left field, but Mary Ann wasn't really
surprised.*

◆ In baseball, left field is part of the outfield. A ball is said to come out of
left field when the pitcher throws it in such a way that it seems to come
out of nowhere.

play the field

If someone **plays the field**, they have many different romantic or sexual
relationships rather than staying with one person. *He gave up playing the
field and married a year ago.*

◆ If gamblers play the field, they bet on all the horses in a race except the
one that is considered most likely to win.

fig

a fig leaf

Something which is intended to hide an embarrassing or awkward situation can be referred to as **a fig leaf**. *My interpretation is that the pledge to rejoin the ERM was a fig leaf, designed to indicate that the government's economic strategy was not dead but merely sleeping.*

◆ According to the Bible, when Adam and Eve ate the apple in the Garden of Eden, they realized that they were naked and felt ashamed, so they covered their genitals with fig leaves. (Genesis 3:7)

fight

a knock-down drag-out fight

American If you describe a debate, argument, or fight as **a knock-down drag-out fight**, you mean that it is very serious, emotional, and angry or even violent. *Nobody had much of a stomach this year for another knock-down, drag-out fight over the state budget.*

◆ This expression refers to a type of boxing match in which a fighter who had been knocked down was dragged out of the ring and replaced by another contestant.

finger

give someone the finger

If someone **gives** you **the finger**, they do something which shows their contempt, anger, or defiance of you. Many people find this expression offensive. *Barker's personal worth has been put at around £30 million, but it could be greater by a factor of as much as five if he didn't give the finger to most of the commercial opportunities that come his way.*

◆ 'To give someone the finger' literally means to make a rude and offensive gesture with one hand, with the middle finger pointing up and the other fingers bent over in a fist.

have a finger in every pie
have a finger in the pie

If you say that someone **has a finger in every pie**, you mean that they are involved in many different activities, often in a way that you disapprove of. *He has a finger in every pie and is never short of ideas for making the next buck.*

□ If you say that someone **has a finger in the pie**, you mean that they **are** involved in the activity you are talking about. *They describe 45 governmental and non-governmental organisations with fingers in the environmental pie.*

◆ The most likely explanation for this expression is that it refers to someone who is involved in making a pie.

not lift a finger
not raise a finger

If you accuse someone of **not lifting a finger** or **not raising a finger** to do something or to help someone, you are criticizing them for not doing it or not helping them. *I'm the one who has to clean it all up. She wouldn't lift a finger if I didn't beg her.*

point the finger at someone

If you **point the finger at** someone, you blame them for a mistake they have made or accuse them of doing something wrong. *I think you have to point the finger at successive governments, which have really underfunded British Rail for years and years and years now.*

□ You can also say, for example, that you **point the finger of blame** or **the finger of suspicion** at someone. *It would be easy to point the finger of blame at individuals, and dismiss the problem by calling them irresponsible and naive.*

□ When people blame or accuse each other in this way, you can refer to this as **finger-pointing**. *Whether or not the investigation succeeds, it is bound to lead to finger-pointing and backbiting.*

pull your finger out
get your finger out

British If you tell someone to **pull** their **finger out** or **get** their **finger out**, you are telling them rudely to start working harder or to start dealing with something. *I have told them to get their fingers out and start winning games. We haven't had a victory for eight matches and it's not good enough.*

put the finger on someone

If you **put the finger on** a particular person, you tell someone in authority that the person has done something wrong or illegal. *It's not like we put the finger on someone real, Janie. Nobody is suffering because of what we told that detective.*

put your finger on something

If you **put** your **finger on** something, for example the cause of a problem or the answer to a question, you realize what it is and identify it. If you cannot see the cause of a problem or the answer to a question, you can say that you **can't put** your **finger on** it. *He had thought that Houston would have arrived at that solution first; but, no, it was Dr. Stockton who had put his finger on the truth... Had they known each other as children? At school? She couldn't put her finger on it.*

twist someone around your little finger
wrap someone around your little finger

If you say that you can **twist** someone **around** your **little finger** or **wrap** them **around** your **little finger**, you mean that you can make them do anything you want them to. *A child who is spoilt is able to wrap her parents around her little finger.*

fingers
get your fingers burned
burn your fingers

If you **get** your **fingers burned** or **burn** your **fingers** when you try do something, it goes wrong, and there are very unpleasant consequences for you, so that you feel nervous about trying again. *The government, after getting its fingers burned so badly, will surely not want to make the same mistake again.*

have green fingers

British If you say that someone **has green fingers**, you mean that they are very good at gardening. The American expression is **have a green thumb**. *Propagating is a skill as well as an art, so even if you were not born with green fingers you can easily learn a few simple techniques to help you achieve success.*

☐ You can describe someone who is good at gardening as **green-fingered**. *Even if you're not green-fingered you can put on a stunning show of flowers right through summer and beyond.*

itchy fingers

Mainly British If you have **itchy fingers**, you are very keen to get involved in a particular activity. *I went into town to watch people playing chess. After a few days of this I started getting itchy fingers. I didn't dare ask my family for money, but I made a chess set for myself out of cardboard and took it to school to play with.*

keep your fingers crossed
cross your fingers
fingers crossed

British If you say that you **are keeping** your **fingers crossed** or **are crossing** your **fingers**, you mean that you are hoping for luck or success in something. *I will be keeping my fingers crossed that everything goes well... We all cross our fingers and hope it never happens. But if long-term illness struck tomorrow, could you keep paying the bills?*

□ People say **'fingers crossed'** when they are wishing someone good luck. *You can take your chance and turn up on the night. Fingers crossed you might be able to get in.*

◆ In the past, people believed that crossing their middle finger over their index finger was a way of protecting themselves from the devil or bad luck.

work your fingers to the bone

If you talk about someone having to **work** their **fingers to the bone**, you mean that they have to work extremely hard. *What sort of life is this if, like a miner, you work your fingers to the bone?*

fingertips

at your fingertips: 1

If you have something **at** your **fingertips**, it is readily available for you to use or reach. *All basic controls are at your fingertips for straightforward, no fuss operation.*

at your fingertips: 2

If you have facts or information **at** your **fingertips**, you know them thoroughly and can refer to them quickly. *He wanted to know all about his latest projects, so that the correct answers were at his fingertips when he was questioned by the right people.*

fire

breathe fire

If you say that someone **is breathing fire** about something, you are emphasizing that they are very angry about it. *Senators, who for months have breathed fire about the need for tougher American trade policies, have meekly endorsed the president's request.*

catch fire

If something such as an event or performance **catches fire**, it becomes exciting, entertaining, and enjoyable. *The play only really catches fire once Aschenbach falls in love.*

come under fire
be under fire

If someone or something **has come under fire** or **is under fire**, they are being strongly criticized. *The president's plan first came under fire from critics who said he didn't include enough spending cuts... Britain's prisons are under fire from an international human rights group.*

◆ This expression is more commonly used literally to talk about a situation where someone is actually being fired at.

draw someone's fire

If you **draw** someone's **fire**, you do or say something which makes them strongly criticize you. *Their first substantial work was the flats at Ham Common in 1957. This immediately drew the fire of the architectural establishment.*

fight fire with fire

If you **fight fire with fire**, you use the same methods of fighting and the same amount of force as your opponent. Other verbs such as 'meet' or 'match' are sometimes used instead of 'fight'. *Down here it is essential to adapt to conditions and meet fire with fire. We have the ability to play any style when required.*

fire in your belly

If you say that someone does something with **fire in** their **belly**, you mean that they do it in a very enthusiastic, energetic, and passionate way. *Ian has played with fire in his belly throughout his career. He would not be the same without the aggressive streak.*

hang fire

If someone **hangs fire**, they wait and do not do anything for a while. If something **hangs fire**, nothing is done about it for a while. *Banks and building societies are hanging fire on interest rates to see how the French vote in their referendum.*

◆ This expression dates from the time when firearms used gunpowder rather than bullets. If a gun hung fire, it did not fire properly because the gunpowder had not caught light. 'Flash in the pan' has a similar origin.

hold your fire
hold fire

If you **hold** your **fire** or **hold fire**, you delay doing something, for example attacking or criticizing someone, because you are waiting to see what will happen. *We are holding fire on our assessment of the situation until a detailed analysis can be made.*

◆ This expression is more commonly used literally to talk about a situation where soldiers stop shooting, or wait before they start shooting.

light a fire under someone

Mainly American If you **light a fire under** someone, you force them to take action or to start behaving in the way you want. *They need to crank up their technical research and light a fire under their marketing force because their stream of new products is too slow.*

◆ There is a story that some American farmers in the early part of the 20th century used to light fires under particularly stubborn mules that were refusing to move, in order to make them do so.

play with fire

If you accuse someone of **playing with fire**, you are warning that they are behaving in a very risky way and are likely to have problems. *It is the Government that is playing with fire. If it carries on in this way, it will cause civil war within the Conservative Party.*

fish

a big fish

If you refer to someone as **a big fish**, you mean that they are important or powerful. *The four who were arrested here last September were described as really big fish by the U.S. Drug Enforcement Agency.*

a big fish in a small pond

If you refer to someone as **a big fish in a small pond**, you mean that they are one of the most important and influential people in a small organization or social group. You often use this expression to suggest that they would be less important or interesting if they were part of a larger organization or group. *In Rhodesia I was a big fish in a small pond. But here there'd be many lean years before I built up a reputation.*

□ You can refer to someone as **a small fish in a big pond** if they are not very important or influential because they are part of a much larger organization or social group. *I was used to being a big fish in a small pond. Now I'm the smallest fish in a very big pond. But that has its own advantages because it stretches you as a designer to try to achieve more.*

a cold fish

If you refer to someone as **a cold fish**, you mean that they seem unemotional, and this makes them appear unfriendly or unsympathetic. *He didn't really show much emotion – he is a bit of a cold fish.*

drink like a fish

If you say that someone **drinks like a fish**, you mean that they regularly drink a lot of alcohol. *When I was younger I could drink like a fish and eat like a pig.*

◆ People used to believe that fish drank constantly because they breathe through open mouths.

a fish out of water

If you feel like **a fish out of water**, you feel awkward or ill at ease because you are in an unfamiliar situation or surroundings. *I think he thought of himself as a country gentleman and was like a fish out of water in Birmingham.*

have other fish to fry
have bigger fish to fry

If you say that someone is not interested in something because they **have other fish to fry** or **have bigger fish to fry**, you mean that they are not interested because they have more important, interesting, or profitable things to do. *I didn't pursue it in detail because I'm afraid I had other fish to fry at the time.*

like shooting fish in a barrel

If you say that a battle or contest is **like shooting fish in a barrel**, you mean that one side is so much stronger than the other that the weaker side has no chance at all of winning. *I heard one case where some of the enemy soldiers had come out and they were saying it was like shooting fish in a barrel.*

neither fish nor fowl

If you say that something or someone is **neither fish nor fowl**, you mean that they are difficult to identify, classify, or understand, because they seem partly one thing and partly another. *By the mid-1980s, Canada had a constitution that was neither fish nor fowl in terms of political philosophy.*

there are plenty more fish in the sea
there are other fish in the sea

If your romance or love affair has ended and someone says to you **'there are plenty more fish in the sea'** or **'there are other fish in the sea'**, they are trying to comfort you by pointing out that there are still many other people who you might have a successful relationship with in the future. *If your daughter is upset because her boyfriend left her, declaring cheerfully 'There are other fish in the sea' won't help.*

fishing

a fishing expedition

Mainly American If you are on **a fishing expedition**, you are trying to find out the truth or the facts about something, often in a secretive way. *You know why you're here. You're on a fishing expedition. You're hunting for material.*

fit

fit as a fiddle

If you say that someone is **fit as a fiddle**, you mean that they are very fit and healthy. *I'm as fit as a fiddle, I'm never ill, I have an iron constitution.*

◆ This expression may originally have applied to a violin player, or fiddler, rather than to a violin, or fiddle. The fiddler had to be fit in order to play all evening at a festival or party. Alternatively, 'fit' could mean 'suitable' rather than 'healthy', so the original meaning may have been 'as suitable for its purpose as a fiddle is for making music'.

fit as a flea

British If you say that someone is **fit as a flea**, you mean that they are very fit and healthy. *He will want to make up for time lost. He is young enough at 33 and fit as a flea. He's a brilliant goalkeeper, no different from when I signed him as a teenager for Aberdeen, just more experienced.*

fit to be tied

Mainly American If you are **fit to be tied**, you are very angry. *Douglas was fit to be tied. He almost killed Harry. He made Harry pay back every last penny.*

fits

in fits and starts

If something happens or is done **in fits and starts**, it does not happen continuously, but regularly stops and then starts again. *The employment picture had been improving in fits and starts during the past several months, and most economists had been predicting more improvement for June. But that didn't happen.*

flag

fly the flag

If you **fly the flag** for your country or a group to which you belong, you represent it at a sporting event or at some other special occasion, or you do something to show your support for it. *It doesn't matter whether you are flying the flag for your country, or the Horse Trials Group, or your sponsor, the image you present is all-important.*

keep the flag flying

If you **keep the flag flying**, you do something to show your support for a group to which you belong, or to show your support for something that you agree with. *I would ask members to keep the flag flying by entering some of their plants in both shows.*

a red flag

Mainly American You can refer to something that gives a warning of a bad or dangerous situation or event as **a red flag**. Compare **a red flag before a bull**; see **bull**. *Cholesterol was the red flag that alerted millions of Americans to the fact that diet really does matter.*

wrap yourself in the flag
drape yourself in the flag

Mainly American If you say that someone, especially a politician, **is wrapping** themselves **in the flag** or **is draping** themselves **in the flag** of their country, you are criticizing them for trying to do something for their own advantage while pretending to do it for the good of their country. *Politicians always try to wrap themselves in the flag on Independence Day, but I think most people can see through that.*

flagpole

run something up the flagpole

If you **run** a new idea **up the flagpole**, you suggest it to people in order to find out what they think of it. *The President should consider running the capital-gains cut back up the flagpole.*

☐ You can also say that you are going to **run** an idea **up the flagpole and see who salutes it**.

flags

put the flags out

British If you **put the flags out** or **put out the flags**, you celebrate something special that has happened. *Birthdays and christenings, or just a spell of good weather, are all the excuse you need to put out the flags.*

flame

an old flame

An old flame is someone who you had a romantic relationship with in the past. *Last week Alec was seen dining with his old flame Janine Turner in New York.*

◆ An old meaning of 'flame' was the person that someone was in love with.

flames

fan the flames

If something that someone says or does **fans the flames**, it makes a bad situation worse. *The mayor's creation of a commission to investigate police corruption further fanned the flames of resentment that finally exploded into race hatred.*

go up in flames
go down in flames

If something **goes up in flames** or **goes down in flames**, it fails or comes to an end, or is destroyed completely. *On May 1st, the proposal went down in flames.*

◆ The expression 'go up in flames' is more commonly used literally to talk about something being destroyed by fire.

shoot down in flames

If an idea or plan **is shot down in flames**, it is criticized strongly or rejected completely. *Just six months ago his idea would have been shot down in flames for its sheer lunacy.*

□ If you **are shot down in flames**, you are severely criticized or made to look foolish for something that you have done or suggested. *I know damn well they'll probably shoot me down in flames and come out with a load of excuses.*

flash

flash in the pan

If you say that an achievement or success is **a flash in the pan**, you mean that it is unlikely to be repeated or to last. If you say that someone who has had a success is **a flash in the pan**, you mean that their success is unlikely to be repeated. *In the days following Beckon's victory, the British establishment has gone out of its way to try and dismiss the result as a flash* *in the pan... Hers is no flash-in-the-pan talent, but a major and mature new voice.*

◆ This expression has its origins in the way that an old-fashioned flintlock gun worked. Pulling the trigger produced a spark which set light to a small amount of gunpowder held in the 'pan'. This in turn lit the rest of the gunpowder. However, if it failed to do so there was just a 'flash in the pan' and the gun did not fire properly. 'Hang fire' has a similar origin.

flat

fall flat on your face

If you say that someone **falls flat on** their **face** when they try to do something, you mean that they fail or make an embarrassing mistake. *I may fall flat on my face or it may be a glorious end to my career.*

flat as a pancake

If you say that something is as **flat as a pancake**, you are emphasizing that it is very flat. *There was barely a breeze and the water was as flat as a pancake.*

flat-footed

catch someone flat-footed

If someone **is caught** or **left flat-footed**, they are put at a disadvantage when something happens which they do not expect, with the result that they do not know what to do next and often look clumsy or foolish. *'The people around were caught flat-footed,' said Mr. Enko. 'Nobody expected floods of such magnitude.'*

flavour (*American* flavor)

flavour of the month

Mainly British If you say that someone or something is **flavour of the month**, you mean that they are currently very popular. This expression is often used to suggest in a critical way that people change their opinions very frequently, so that the people or things that are popular now are unlikely to stay popular for very long. *At the moment the flavour of the month is the fixed-rate loan.*

□ Instead of 'month', you can mention other periods of time such as 'year', 'week', or 'moment'. *Suddenly, he was flavour of the moment on both sides of the Atlantic.*

◆ American ice cream parlours used to select a particular flavour of the month in order to encourage people to try different flavours of ice cream.

flea

a flea in your ear

British If someone sends you away with **a flea in** your **ear**, they angrily reject your suggestions or attempts to do something. *I was prepared to be met with hostility as another nosy outsider, even to be sent off with a flea in my ear. But Moira was happy to chat.*

flesh

flesh and blood: 1

If you say that someone is your own **flesh and blood**, you are emphasizing that they are a member of your family, and so you must help them when they are in trouble. *You can't just let your own flesh and blood go to prison if there's any way you can help.*

flesh and blood: 2

If you say that someone is **flesh and blood**, you are emphasizing that they have human feelings or weaknesses, and that they are not perfect. *We priests are mere flesh and blood. In fact we're often even weaker than others.*

flesh and blood: 3

If you describe someone as a **flesh and blood** person, you are emphasizing that they are real and actually exist, rather than being part of someone's imagination. *His absence ever since her second birthday made her think of him as a picture rather than a flesh-and-blood father.*

put flesh on something
put flesh on the bones of something

If you **put flesh on** something or **put flesh on the bones of** something, you add more detailed information or more substance to it. *The central bankers' blueprint is nevertheless the first clear picture of what a central banking system would look like and puts flesh on the European vision of monetary integration... What would a Middle East at peace actually look like? Somebody needs to start putting flesh on those bones.*

flick

give someone the flick
give someone the flick pass

Mainly Australian If you **give** someone or something **the flick** or **give** them **the flick pass**, you reject them or get rid of them. *Nikki has given Brandon the flick... Adrian Brunker plans to give work the flick pass by the time he hits 30. He reckons that will give him more time to play golf.*

♦ In Australian football, a flick pass is a pass made by hitting the ball with an open hand. Flick passes are against the rules, which state that the ball should be passed by hitting it with the fist.

flies

drop like flies: 1

If you say that people **are dropping like flies**, you mean that large numbers of them are dying within a short period of time, usually for the same reason. *Relief officials say two-thirds of the seven million population are at risk. 'What we are seeing is the complete elimination of a nation. They are dropping like flies.'*

drop like flies: 2

If you say that large numbers of similar things **are dropping like flies**, you mean that they are all failing, within a short period of time. *While other retailers are dropping like flies, supermarkets are making fat profits.*

there are no flies on someone

If you say **there are no flies on** someone, you mean that they are quick to understand a situation and are not easily deceived. *You have to establish that you are an officer with good and tried soldiers: there are no flies on them.*

flip

flip your lid
flip your wig

If someone **flips** their **lid** or **flips** their **wig**, they become extremely angry or upset about something, and lose control of themselves. *'Boy, you are brave,' she said, stroking the bleeding cut. 'A lot of grownups flip their lids when you clean a cut like this.'... Maybe it was the break-up of the old group that finally made him flip his wig.*

floodgates

open the floodgates
the floodgates open

If an event, action, or decision **opens the floodgates** to something, it makes it possible or likely that a particular thing will be done by many

people, perhaps in a way that seems undesirable. You can also say that
the floodgates open. *Giving in to the strikers' demands, government
ministers said, would open the floodgates to demands by workers in other
large state-owned industries like textiles and mining.*

floor

through the floor

If prices or values have fallen **through the floor**, they have suddenly
decreased to a very low level. *Property prices have dropped through the
floor.*

wipe the floor with someone

If you **wipe the floor with** someone, you prove that you are much
better than they are at doing something, or you defeat them totally in a
competition, fight, or discussion. *When you play against people whose
technique is superior and who can match your courage and commitment,
they're going to wipe the floor with you.*

flow

go with the flow

If you **go with the flow**, you let things happen to you or let other people
tell you what to do, rather than trying to control what happens yourself.
*This year I'm going to take a deep breath, leave my troubles and tension in
the departure lounge and go with the flow.*

fly

the fly in the ointment

If you refer to someone or something as **the fly in the ointment**, you
mean that they are the person or thing that prevents a situation from
being as successful or happy as it otherwise would be. *The only flies in the
ointment were the older boys, who objected to the character of their school
changing. They did not care much for Mr Cope's new rules.*

◆ This expression probably comes from the Bible: 'Dead flies cause the
ointment of the apothecary to send forth a stinking savour: so doth a little
folly him that is in reputation for wisdom and honour.' (Ecclesiastes 10:1)

a fly on the wall

If you say that you would like to be **a fly on the wall** when a particular
thing happens, you mean that you would like to hear what is said or to
see what happens, although this is actually impossible because it will take

place in private and you cannot be there. *I'd love to be a fly on the wall at their team meetings.*

☐ You can use **fly-on-the-wall** to describe something such as a documentary film, where the makers of the film record everything that happens in an unobtrusive way, so that the film seems as accurate and natural as possible. *I'd love to work as the personal photographer of a rock star for a year, documenting their life on the road from a fly-on-the-wall perspective.*

like a blue-arsed fly

British If you do something **like a blue-arsed fly**, you do it very quickly and without having much control. Some people find this expression offensive. *I ran around like a blue-arsed fly, packed two suitcases and a trunk, and left everything else.*

on the fly

If you do something **on the fly**, you do it quickly and automatically, without thinking about it or planning it in advance. *The negotiation has been passed out of the hands of the diplomats into the hands of the politicians, people who can make decisions on the fly and don't have to phone home to their boss.*

food

food for thought

If something gives you **food for thought**, it makes you think very hard about an issue. *This event also provided the international selection committee with encouragement and some food for thought when it meets to discuss the team.*

fool

a fool and his money are soon parted

People say **'a fool and his money are soon parted'** to point out that it is easy to persuade someone who is not sensible to spend their money on worthless things. *They can be charming – no one is better at parting a fool from his money – but as the picture opens, they're a little desperate.*

fool's gold

If you say that a plan for making money is **fool's gold**, you mean that it would be foolish to carry it out because you are sure that it will fail. *The Chancellor dismissed as 'pure fool's gold' the idea that devaluing the pound could assist the British economy.*

◆ Fool's gold is another name for iron pyrite, which is a mineral that can easily be mistaken for gold because it is a similar colour.

live in a fool's paradise

If you say that someone **is living in a fool's paradise**, you are criticizing them for believing wrongly and stupidly that their situation is good, when really it is not. *Parents live in a fool's paradise when it comes to drugs. More than 90 per cent refuse to accept that their child would take drugs, but a third think their children's friends do.*

fools

fools rush in where angels fear to tread
fools rush in

People say **'fools rush in where angels fear to tread'** or **'fools rush in'** to comment on or criticize a person who did something hastily without thinking clearly about the likely consequences. *'Sometimes I stop and think, Good God, how did I get into this,' she says with a laugh. 'Fools rush in where angels fear to tread.'*

◆ This proverb comes from Alexander Pope's 'An Essay on Criticism' (1711).

foot

the boot is on the other foot
the shoe is on the other foot

If you say that **the boot is on the other foot**, you mean that a situation has been reversed completely, so that the people who were previously in a better position are now in a worse one, while the people who were previously in a worse position are now in a better one. This form of the expression is used in British English; in American English, the form is **the shoe is on the other foot**. *Comments like that from a manager are better made in private. If the boot was on the other foot and a player went public like that after a game, his club would quickly be looking to slap a fine on him.*

◆ Until the end of the 18th century, shoes could be worn on either foot, as cobblers did not make 'right' and 'left' shoes. If a person found that one of their shoes hurt their foot, they could try wearing it on their other foot to see if it felt better that way.

caught on the wrong foot

If you **are caught on the wrong foot**, something happens quickly and unexpectedly, and surprises you because you are not ready for it. Compare **get off on the wrong foot**. *The recent change of public mood has caught the government clumsily on the wrong foot.*

□ The verb **wrong-foot** is also used, and is much more common. *Again and again European and UN diplomacy has been wrong-footed by events in the Balkans.*

a foot in both camps
a foot in each camp

If someone has **a foot in both camps**, they support or belong to two different groups, without making a firm commitment to either of them. You can also say that someone has **a foot in each camp**. *Sagdeev is trying to promote a compromise because he has one foot in each camp.*

a foot in the door: 1

If someone is trying to get involved in something, for example to start doing business in a new area, and you say that they have got **a foot in the door**, you mean that they have made a small but successful start and are likely to do well in the future. *China is opening its state owned airlines to foreign investors and if British Airways gets a foot in the door, the profits will be enormous.*

foot-in-the-door: 2

If you describe a way of doing something as **foot-in-the-door**, you mean that it is done in an aggressive or forceful way, in order to persuade someone to agree to do something which they probably do not want to do. *Double glazing salesmen have become a bit of a national joke, what with their foot-in-the-door methods.*

◆ If someone manages to put their foot in a doorway, they can prevent another person from closing the door and keeping them out.

get off on the wrong foot
start off on the right foot

If you start doing something and you **get off on the wrong foot**, you start badly or in an unfortunate way. Compare **caught on the wrong foot**. *The last few times I've been at home on leave everything seems to have gone wrong. We seem to get off on the wrong foot from the start. We row a lot.*

□ If you **start off on the right foot**, you immediately have success when you begin to do something. *Share your feelings, both positive and negative. If you decide to go ahead, you will be starting off on the right foot.*

◆ The 'wrong foot' refers to the left foot. There is an ancient superstition that the left side of the body is connected with bad luck and evil. The Romans sometimes placed guards at the entrances to public buildings to ensure that people entered them with their right foot first. 'Get out of bed on the wrong side' is based on a similar belief.

not put a foot wrong

British If you **don't put a foot wrong**, you do not make any mistakes. *He glided smoothly through his news conference, never putting a foot wrong.*

one foot in the grave

If you say that someone has **one foot in the grave**, you mean that they are very ill or very old and are likely to die soon. You use this expression when you are talking about illness and death in a light-hearted way. *The guard and warder are taken in, they're convinced De Fiore's got one foot in the grave.*

put your best foot forward

If you are doing something and you **put** your **best foot forward**, you work hard and energetically to make sure it is a success. *Sir David said that having been faced with a warning of one last chance, the commission should have put its best foot forward and produced something independent.*

put your foot down: 1

If you **put** your **foot down**, you use your authority in order to stop something from happening. *He had planned to go skiing on his own, but his wife had decided to put her foot down.*

put your foot down: 2

If you **put** your **foot down** when you are driving, you start to drive as fast as you can. *Once out of the park and finding a clear stretch of the Bayswater Road, he put his foot down.*

put your foot in it
put your foot in your mouth

If you **put** your **foot in it** or **put** your **foot in** your **mouth**, you say something which embarrasses or offends the person you are with, and embarrasses you as a result. *I put my foot in it straight away, referring to folk music. Tom sat forward and glared. 'It's not folk music, man. It's heritage music.'... To the majority of voters, he is hopelessly unpresidential, a lightweight, forever putting his foot in his mouth.*

☐ Journalists sometimes refer humorously to someone's **foot-in-mouth** tendencies. *I loved Prince Philip's latest attack of foot-in-mouth disease when he asked a Cayman Islander: 'Aren't most of you descended from pirates?'*

shoot yourself in the foot

If you **shoot** yourself **in the foot**, you do or say something stupid which causes problems for yourself or harms your chances of success. *Unless he shoots himself in the foot, in all probability he will become President.*

footloose

footloose and fancy-free

If someone is **footloose and fancy-free**, they are not married or in a long-term relationship, and they have very few responsibilities or commitments. *A divorced man is footloose and fancy-free. He can go to parties and pubs on his own, and come and go as he pleases.*

footsteps

follow in someone's footsteps

If you **follow in** someone's **footsteps**, you do the same thing that they did. *Rudolph Garvin was a college student, the son of a physician, who wanted to follow in his father's footsteps.*

forelock

tug your forelock
touch your forelock

If you think that someone is showing an excessive amount of respect to another person and making themselves seem very humble and inferior, you can say that they **are tugging** their **forelock** or **touching** their **forelock** in order to express your criticism of their behaviour. *These are the same old fogeys who tug the forelock to the British establishment.*

□ You can refer to this kind of behaviour as **forelock-tugging** or **forelock-touching**. *The idea of forelock-tugging is totally alien to us, as is the idea that some people can be bred to rule.*

◆ A forelock is a lock of hair that falls over a person's forehead. In the past, it was customary for lower class people to remove their hats in front of upper class people. If they were not wearing a hat, they touched their forelock instead.

forewarned

forewarned is forearmed

British People say **'forewarned is forearmed'** to mean that if you know about something which is going to happen in the future, you can be ready to deal with it. *The authors' idea is that to be forewarned is to be forearmed: if we know how persuasion works, perhaps we can resist some of it.*

fort

hold the fort
hold down the fort

If you **hold the fort** for someone, you look after things for them while they are somewhere else or while they are busy doing something else. In American English, you can also say that you **hold down the fort**. *Since she entered Parliament five years ago, he has held the fort at their Norfolk home during the week.*

frame

in the frame: 1
the name in the frame

British If you are **in the frame** for promotion or success, you are very likely to get a promotion or to be successful. *Steve has done well. He's close to being back in the frame and I will have a good look at him in training this week.*

□ You can talk about someone being **the name in the frame** when they are very likely to get a promotion or be successful. *Speculation about potential replacements is already rife, with Sir David Scholey of Warburgs and Sir Nigel Wicks at the Treasury and Lord Lawson among the names in the frame.*

in the frame: 2

British If someone is **in the frame** for something, people think that they are responsible for a crime or an unpleasant situation, even though this might be untrue. *The fact is, there's only ever been one guy in the frame for this killing, and that's the husband... After all, wasn't it the Chancellor who originally put Germany in the frame for the pound's failure?*

◆ The 'frame' referred to here is probably one of the frames, or images, in a reel of film.

freefall

go into freefall
in freefall

If the value or level of something **goes into freefall**, it starts to fall very quickly. *Fears are now widespread that shares could go into freefall before Christmas.*

☐ **A freefall** is a situation in which the value or level of something is falling very rapidly. You can also say that the value or level of something **freefalls**. *Others underlined the potential for monetary chaos unleashed by the free fall of sterling... His career seemed about to freefall into oblivion and retirement after a series of drug-related scandals.*

◆ In parachuting, freefall is the part of the jump before the parachute opens.

frenzy

a feeding frenzy

When people refer to **a feeding frenzy**, they are referring to a situation in which a lot of people become very excited about something, often in a destructive or negative way. This expression is often used to refer to journalists writing about a famous person or an exciting or scandalous event. *Parents and other concerned citizens are meeting to discuss the scandal. Lakewood mayor Mark Title says the media feeding frenzy is taking bites out of what he calls an outstanding community.*

◆ This expression was first used to describe the behaviour of groups of sharks when there is blood in the water but not enough food for them all. In this situation the sharks will attack anything that they see, even each other.

fresh

fresh as a daisy
fresh as paint

If you say that someone or something is as **fresh as a daisy**, you are emphasizing that they are very fresh, bright, or alert. In British English, you can also say that they are as **fresh as paint**. *She can sleep through anything and emerge fresh as a daisy at the end of it... Young Hustler looked as fresh as paint despite this being his fourteenth race of the season.*

frighteners

put the frighteners on someone

If someone **puts the frighteners on** you, they threaten you and try to scare you into doing what they want. *He and his chums tried to put the frighteners on Kelley before she had written a single word.*

♦ 'Frighteners' used to be a name for members of criminal gangs who were sent to frighten people into doing something.

fritz

on the fritz

American A piece of machinery that is **on the fritz** is not working properly. *My mother's toaster went on the fritz.*

frog

a frog in your throat

If someone has **a frog in** their **throat**, they find it difficult to speak clearly because they have a cough or a sore throat. Compare **a lump in** your **throat**; see **lump**. *I've got a bit of a cough, excuse me, a frog in my throat.*

♦ In medieval times, there was a belief that if you drank water containing frogspawn, the frogs would grow inside your body. People believed that sore throats and coughing could be caused by the frogs trying to escape from your stomach through your throat.

fruit

bear fruit

If an action **bears fruit**, it produces good results. *People see material conditions getting worse. They don't see the economic reforms championed by the President as bearing fruit.*

forbidden fruit

If you describe something as **forbidden fruit**, you mean that you want it very much but are not allowed to have it, or you are not supposed to have it. *In the days of Maoism, auctions were barred. Now Peking's first auction house, which is highly successful, gives a taste of the forbidden fruit.*

♦ This expression refers to the story in the Bible in which Eve tempts Adam to eat the fruit of the tree of knowledge, which God has forbidden them to touch. (Genesis 3)

frying pan

out of the frying pan into the fire

If you say that someone has gone or jumped **out of the frying pan into the fire**, you mean that they have moved from a bad situation to an even worse one. *If you do decide to take such a drastic step, first take every possible precaution that you do not go from the frying pan into the fire.*

fuel

add fuel to the fire
add fuel to the flames

If something that someone says or does **adds fuel to the fire** or **adds fuel to the flames**, it makes a bad situation worse. *The government is warning that a return to the traditional system of wage indexation will only add fuel to the inflationary fires.*

funeral

it's your funeral

If you are insisting on doing something in a particular way and someone says **'it's your funeral'**, they are pointing out that they think you are wrong but that you will be affected by the bad consequences resulting from it, and they will not. *Have it your own way. You'll be sorry. It's your funeral.*

fur

the fur is flying

If you say that **the fur is flying** over something, you mean that people are arguing very fiercely and angrily about it. *A blazing row between Euro factions at last week's meeting of the 1922 Committee set the fur flying again on the Tory backbenches.*

◆ The image here is of animals tearing out each other's fur during a fight.

furniture

part of the furniture

If you say that someone or something is **part of the furniture**, you mean that they have been present somewhere for such a long time that everyone accepts their presence without questioning it or noticing them. *Once cameras in courts have become part of the furniture, witnesses are so absorbed in answering questions that they forget the cameras are there.*

furrow

plough a lonely furrow
plough a lone furrow

British If someone **ploughs a lonely furrow** or **ploughs a lone furrow**, they do something by themselves and in their own way, without any help or support from other people. *It seems that Shattock was something of an original thinker, ploughing a lonely furrow.*

fuse

blow a fuse

If you **blow a fuse**, you suddenly lose your temper and cannot control your anger. *For all my experience, I blew a fuse in the quarter-final and could have been sent off.*

♦ A fuse is a safety device found in electrical equipment. If the equipment becomes too hot, the fuse blows, or burns. This breaks the electrical circuit, so that the equipment will stop working.

light the fuse

If you say that someone **lights the fuse**, you mean that they do something which starts off a new and exciting development, or which makes a situation become dangerous. *Ghana's independence in 1957 lit the fuse which led to the rapid freeing of colonial Africa.*

♦ The fuse referred to here is the type that is used to set off a firework or explosive device.

on a short fuse
have a short fuse

If you say that someone is **on a short fuse** or **has a short fuse**, you mean that they lose their temper very easily and are quick to react angrily when something goes wrong. *Perhaps he's irritable and has a short fuse, letting you know when he's not pleased.*

♦ See the explanation at 'light the fuse'.

G

gaff

blow the gaff

British If you **blow the gaff**, you tell people something which was supposed to be kept secret. *Scottish Nuclear Ltd has now blown the gaff by saying that it may decide to do without reprocessing altogether.*

♦ 'Blow' here means 'reveal'. In the 19th century, 'gaff' was a slang word used to refer to dishonest behaviour which was intended to deceive people.

gallery

play to the gallery

If you say that someone such as a politician **is playing to the gallery**, you are criticizing them for trying to impress the public and make themselves popular, instead of dealing seriously with important matters. *Her obstinate refusal to play to the gallery had eventually won her the reverent respect of all but a tiny minority among her people.*

◆ The gallery in a theatre is a raised area like a large balcony, that usually contains the cheapest seats. In the past, the poorest and least educated people sat there. Actors and other performers found it easier to get applause from them than from the other members of the audience.

game

beat someone at their own game

If you **beat** someone **at** their **own game**, you do something more successfully than they do, although they have a reputation for doing it better than anyone else. *The East is said to be beating the West at its own game. Its business conglomerates, which lay in ruins only a few decades ago, now outperform those of Europe and America.*

the game is up

If you say that **the game is up** for someone, you mean that they can no longer continue to do something wrong or illegal, because people have found out what they are doing. *He narrowed his eyes as the blue lights of the police car filled the cab. Sensing the game was up, he pulled over.*

a game plan

Someone's **game plan** is the things that they intend to do in order to achieve a particular aim. *So few people stick to their game plan. I stuck to mine. I had always wanted to be a millionaire from a very early age.*

◆ In American football, a game plan is a strategy which the players and coach develop before a match.

give the game away

If someone or something **gives the game away**, they reveal something which someone had been trying to keep secret. *She looks every inch a Beverly Hills native as she leans against a palm tree. Only the English accent gives the game away.*

new to the game

If you say that someone is **new to the game**, you mean that they have no previous experience of the activity that they are taking part in. *Don't forget that she's new to this game and will take a while to complete the task, so you need to be very patient.*

the numbers game

If you say that someone is playing **the numbers game**, you mean that they are using amounts, figures, or statistics to support their argument, often in a way that confuses or misleads people. *The document derides the numbers game which automatically argues that an exhibition receiving 5,000 visitors each day is better than one receiving 3,000.*

♦ In the United States, the numbers game or numbers racket is an illegal lottery. It involves people placing small bets on a series of numbers that appear in particular sections of that day's newspaper, for example the stock market figures.

the only game in town

If you say that someone or something is **the only game in town**, you mean that they are the best or most important of their kind, or the only one worth considering. *This plan is the only game in town that may lead to a durable and viable peace, for the alternatives are too awful to think about.*

♦ This expression may refer to someone being prepared to take part in a game of poker, even if it was dishonest, because it was the only one going on at the time.

play someone at their own game

If you **play** someone **at** their **own game**, you behave towards them in the same unfair or unpleasant way that they have been behaving towards you. *It used to bug me when men used to come in the office and I never used to get introduced. So I've started playing them at their own game. When I had clients to come and see me, I'd never introduce the men either.*

play the game

If you have to **play the game**, you have to do things in the accepted way or in the way that you are told to by your superiors, in order to keep your job or to achieve success. *In order to survive and to prosper in the political system, they have to play the game.*

☐ If you accuse someone of **not playing the game**, you are accusing them of behaving in an unfair and unacceptable way.

♦ This a quotation from the Olympic Creed written by Pierre de

Coubertin, founder of the modern Olympics, in 1896. The expression was then used by Sir Henry Newbolt in his poem 'Vitaï Lampada' (1898); 'But the voice of the schoolboy rallies the ranks: "Play up! Play up! and play the game!"'

a waiting game

If you play **a waiting game**, you delay making any decisions or taking any action, because you think that it is better to wait and see how things develop. *The government seems more inclined to lay aside the contingency plans for air attack and play the waiting game.*

garbage

garbage in, garbage out

Garbage in, garbage out is a way of saying that if you produce something using poor-quality materials, the thing you produce will also be of poor quality. *Hi-fi has hi-jacked the computer industry maxim 'Garbage in equals garbage out', to reinforce the concept that a terrific pair of speakers will show up a shoddy CD player for the piece of junk it is.*

◆ This expression comes from computing. If the wrong information is put into the computer, the output will be useless.

garden

common-or-garden
garden-variety

You can use **common-or-garden** to say that something is of a very ordinary kind and has no special features. This form of the expression is used in British English; in American English, the form is **garden-variety**. *She didn't look remotely like a woman going down with a common or garden head cold... The experiment itself is garden-variety science that normally would attract scant public attention.*

◆ These expressions were originally used to describe the most ordinary variety of a species of plant.

lead someone up the garden path
lead someone down the garden path

If someone **leads** you **up the garden path**, they deceive you by making you believe something which is not true. This form of the expression is used mainly in British English; in American English, the usual form is **lead** someone **down the garden path**. *He may have led me up the garden path. He said everything was over with Penny but now he seems to be seeing* *her again.*

gas

run out of gas

Mainly American If you **run out of gas**, you suddenly feel very tired or lose interest in what you are doing, and so you stop completely or fail. *He ran out of gas, artistically speaking, and retired for roughly a decade.*

♦ The image here is of a car stopping because it has run out of 'gas', or petrol.

gauntlet

♦ Gauntlets are long thick gloves which protect your hands, wrists, and forearms.

run the gauntlet: 1

If you have to **run the gauntlet**, you have to go through a place where people are trying to harm or humiliate you, for example by attacking you or shouting insults at you. *She was forced to run a gauntlet of some 300 jeering demonstrators, waving placards denouncing her as a 'witch'.*

run the gauntlet: 2

If you have to **run the gauntlet** of some kind of unpleasant behaviour, you have to suffer it because of something you are trying to achieve. *He has decided to run the gauntlet of Tory jibes that Labour stands for nothing.*

♦ 'Gatlopp' is a Swedish word meaning 'lane run'. The 'gatlopp' was a Swedish military punishment that came into common use in England during the Thirty Years' War (1618–48). The victim had to run between two rows of soldiers who would whip or beat them. In England, the unfamiliar Swedish word 'gatlopp' was replaced by the more familiar English word 'gauntlet'.

throw down the gauntlet
take up the gauntlet

If you **throw down the gauntlet**, you do or say something that challenges someone to take action or to compete against you. If you **take up the gauntlet**, you accept a challenge. *The truckers threw down their gauntlet to the government after an all-night meeting of their strike committee. They say they will now keep up their action indefinitely until their demands are met.*

♦ In medieval times, a knight would throw one of his gauntlets to the ground as a challenge to another knight to fight. If the second knight picked it up, he accepted the challenge.

genie

the genie is out of the bottle
let the genie out of the bottle
put the genie back in the bottle

If something has been done or created which has made a great and permanent change in people's lives, especially a change which people regret, you can say that **the genie is out of the bottle** or that someone **has let the genie out of the bottle**. *If the President came to believe that parliament was too disruptive, he might dissolve it and call new elections. But having let the democratic genie out of the bottle, he has to be careful.*

□ People often vary this expression, for example by saying that you cannot **put the genie back in the bottle**. *For a generation, the world's nuclear powers have talked about restraining the nuclear 'genie' in its bottle.*

◆ In Arabian mythology, a genie is a mischievous spirit with magical powers. This expression may refer to the story of Aladdin, who rubs a lamp and releases a genie from it. There is a pantomime based on this story.

gentle

gentle as a lamb

If you say that someone is as **gentle as a lamb**, you mean that they are kind and mild. *Brian was as gentle as a lamb and wouldn't hurt anyone.*

ghost

give up the ghost: 1

If you **give up the ghost**, you stop trying to do something, because you no longer believe that you can succeed. *In Manhattan there was no Memorial Day parade this year. The organizers said they've given up the ghost after so few people turned out to see last year's parade.*

give up the ghost: 2

If you say that a machine **has given up the ghost**, you are saying in a humorous way that it has stopped working. *A short way off the return ferry, Danny's car gave up the ghost again.*

◆ This expression originally meant 'to die'. The 'ghost' is the soul, which many people believe is released from a person's body when they die.

lay the ghost of something

If you **lay the ghost of** something bad in your past, you do something which stops you being upset or affected by it. *Jockey Adrian Maguire laid the ghost of a ghastly week with a comprehensive win in the Irish Champion Hurdle yesterday.*

gift

the gift of the gab
the gift of gab

If you say that someone has **the gift of the gab**, you mean that they are able to speak confidently, clearly, and in a persuasive way. In American English, you can also say that someone has **the gift of gab**. *He was entertaining company and certainly had the gift of the gab.*

◆ This expression may be related to the Irish and Gaelic word 'gab', which means mouth.

gift horse

look a gift horse in the mouth

If someone tells you not to **look a gift horse in the mouth**, they mean that you should accept something that is being offered to you, or take advantage of an opportunity, and not try to find faults or difficulties. *When you're an entrepreneur, you don't look a gift horse in the mouth.*

◆ This expression refers to the fact that you can judge the age of a horse by looking at its teeth.

gills

green around the gills

If you say that someone looks **green around the gills**, you mean that they look as if they are going to be sick. *Kenny stumbled out from the washroom. 'I'm all right now.' He still looked quite green around the gills.*

gilt

take the gilt off the gingerbread

British To **take the gilt off the gingerbread** means to spoil something or make it seem less good. *The film has some good jokes, but Martin plays cute and Hawn plays kooky. They've been doing it for years and the gilt is wearing off the gingerbread.*

◆ In the past, gingerbread was sometimes decorated with gilt, which is a very thin layer of gold.

glass

the glass ceiling

When people talk about **the glass ceiling**, they are referring to the invisible barrier formed by such things as attitudes and traditions, which can prevent women, or people from ethnic or religious minorities, from being promoted to the most important jobs. *A woman judge has at last succeeded in breaking through the glass ceiling into the Court of Appeal, the second highest court in the land.*

people who live in glass houses shouldn't throw stones

If you are told **'people who live in glass houses shouldn't throw stones'**, you are being reminded that you have faults and so you should not criticize other people for their faults. *When will they learn? People in glass houses really shouldn't throw stones.*

gloves

the gloves are off

If you are talking about a situation in which people have decided to fight or compete aggressively with each other, you can say **the gloves are off**. *In the software price war, the gloves are coming off.*

◆ The reference here is to boxers fighting with bare fists, which is more dangerous than fighting with gloves on.

gnat

strain at a gnat
strain at a gnat and swallow a camel

If you say that someone **is straining at a gnat**, you mean that they are concerning themselves with something minor or trivial, and perhaps neglecting something important. You can also say that they **are straining at a gnat and swallowing a camel**. *One must beware of straining at a gnat and swallowing a camel in the name of correct spelling. To spell badly is a social rather than a moral or intellectual fault.*

◆ This expression comes from the Bible. Jesus used it when criticizing the scribes and the Pharisees for being too concerned with unimportant areas of the Jewish law. (Matthew 23:24)

go

what goes around comes around

If you say **'what goes around comes around'**, you mean that if someone does something bad or wrong, they will eventually suffer for it in the future. *He still wasn't completely beyond feeling things like guilt and shame. Besides, he thought, what goes around comes around. You ignore the other guy when he asks for help, you might just be setting yourself up for a little of the same later on.*

goal

an own goal

British If someone takes a course of action which fails to achieve the effect that they want and instead harms their own interests, you can say that they score **an own goal**. *He said that the Government must get its act together and stop scoring economic own goals.*

◆ In sports such as football and hockey, if someone scores an own goal, they accidentally score a goal for the team they are playing against by knocking the ball into their own net.

goalposts

move the goalposts

If you accuse someone of **moving the goalposts**, you mean that they have changed the rules, policies, or aims in a situation or activity, in order to gain an advantage for themselves and to make things more difficult for the other people involved. *They seem to move the goalposts every time I meet the conditions which are required.*

goat

act the goat

British If someone **acts the goat**, they behave in a silly way. *I left them there, crossing among the traffic. They stood side by side. I acted the goat a bit, turning and waving umpteen times till she was laughing.*

◆ Goats are often associated with unpredictable behaviour.

get someone's goat

If you say that someone or something **gets** your **goat**, you mean that they annoy you intensely. *It was a bad result and a bad performance, but what really got the media's goat was the manager's refusal to take all the blame.*

◆ This expression may be connected with the early 20th century practice in America of putting goats in the same stable as racehorses, since the goats seemed to have a calming effect. If someone stole the goat, the horse would be upset and its performance would be affected.

gold

all that glitters is not gold
all that glisters is not gold

People say **'all that glitters is not gold'** to warn you that someone or something may not be as good or as valuable as they first appear. In British English, people also say **'all that glisters is not gold'**. 'Glister' is an old word which means the same as 'glitter'. *All that glitters is not gold and it's a good idea to delay finalising any important agreements, otherwise you may jeopardise a valuable relationship.*

a pot of gold
a crock of gold

You can refer to a lot of money or something valuable that someone hopes to get in the future as **a pot of gold** or **a crock of gold**. Compare **the pot of gold at the end of the rainbow**; see **rainbow**. *There are already 11,000 laser disc titles available in Japan and 6,000 in America. That could mean a pot of gold for music companies.*

◆ A crock is an earthenware pot or jar.

strike gold

If you **strike gold**, you find, do, or produce something that brings you a lot of money or success. *The company has struck gold with its new holiday development.*

good

good as gold

If you say that someone, especially a child, is as **good as gold**, you are emphasizing that they are behaving very well. *They were both in the playroom as good as gold.*

goods

deliver the goods

If someone or something **delivers the goods**, they achieve what is expected or required of them. *If he fails to deliver the goods, they could well be looking for a new prime minister by next summer.*

have the goods on someone

Mainly American If you **have the goods on** someone, you know things about them which could harm them if these things were made public. *The Republicans keep saying that they've got the goods on Bill Clinton.*

◆ 'The goods' here refers to stolen property, which can be used as evidence against the person who is in possession of it.

goose

cook your goose
your goose is cooked

If you say that someone **has cooked** their **goose**, you mean that they have done something wrong and spoiled their chances of success. You can also say that someone else **has cooked** your **goose**. *By trying to nick my girlfriend he cooked his goose. After that I just had to sack him.*

☐ If you are in trouble or will certainly fail at something, you can say that your **goose is cooked**. *I fully expected we would be attacked by ground forces. We all felt that our goose was cooked. There was absolutely no way to retreat.*

◆ There is a story that King Eric XIV of Sweden once arrived at a town to find that the people had hung a goose from a tree. This was intended as an insult, perhaps because geese were associated with stupidity. The King announced that he would 'cook their goose', and his soldiers invaded the town and set fire to its main buildings. An alternative theory is that the expression refers to Aesop's fable of the goose which laid golden eggs: see the explanation at 'kill the goose that lays the golden egg'.

kill the goose that lays the golden egg
kill the golden goose

If something **kills the goose that lays the golden egg** or **kills the golden goose**, it results in an important source of income being destroyed or seriously reduced. *Most professionals in the travel and tourism industry know that unregulated tourism can kill the goose that laid their golden egg.*

☐ You can refer to an important source of income as **a golden goose**, especially when it is in danger of being destroyed or seriously reduced. *It was alleged in court that Hewitt treated Whittaker as a 'golden goose'.*

◆ This expression comes from Aesop's fable about a peasant who owned a goose which laid golden eggs. The peasant was so eager to become rich that he cut the bird open, hoping that he would be able to get all the eggs at once.

a wild goose chase

If you complain that you have been sent on **a wild goose chase**, you are complaining that you have wasted a lot of time searching for something that you have little chance of finding, because you have been given misleading information. *Every time I've gone to Rome to try to find out if the story could be true, it has turned out to be a wild-goose chase.*

◆ In medieval times, a wild goose chase was an unusual kind of horse race. It started with an ordinary horse race. The winner then rode in any direction they chose and the other riders had to follow. The race may have been called 'a wild goose chase' because the movements of wild geese are often irregular and unpredictable, which makes them difficult to hunt.

wouldn't say boo to a goose

If you say that someone **wouldn't say boo to a goose**, you mean that they are very timid, gentle, and shy. *'If you remember, at college I wouldn't say boo to a goose.' 'That's right, you were very quiet.'*

gooseberry

play gooseberry

British If you say that someone **is playing gooseberry**, you mean that they are joining or accompanying two people who are having a romantic relationship and who want to be alone together. *He knows you've got a boyfriend and far be it from him to play gooseberry.*

◆ The origin of this expression is not known, although it may refer to the third person picking gooseberries to pass the time while the other two are busy being romantic.

gospel

take something as gospel
the gospel truth

If you **take** something **as gospel**, you accept it as being completely true. *You will read much advice in books and magazines but you should not take it all as gospel.*

☐ If you say that something is **the gospel truth**, you are emphasizing that it is completely true. *When people have asked me how old I am, and I say I don't know, they think I'm coy. But it's the gospel truth.*

◆ In the Christian religion, the gospel is the message and teachings of

Jesus Christ. The four books of the Bible which describe His life and teachings are called the Gospels.

grace

fall from grace

If you talk about someone's **fall from grace** or say that they **have fallen from grace**, you are referring to the fact that they have made a mistake or done something wrong or immoral, and as a result have lost their power or influence and spoiled their good reputation. *Rock Hudson's story represents one of the most spectacular falls from grace in film history.*

☐ Journalists sometimes talk about **the fall from grace** of a company, organization, or institution when people no longer approve of it or trust it. *The increasing number of complaints and the banks' fall from grace in the eyes of the public have also taken effect.*

a saving grace

A **saving grace** is a good quality or feature in someone or something that prevents them from being completely bad or worthless. *She definitely outshone the so-called 'stars' and is one of the film's few saving graces.*

grade

make the grade

If you **make the grade**, you succeed at something, usually by reaching a particular standard. *Top public schools failed to make the grade in a new league table of academic results.*

◆ In American English, a 'grade' is a slope. This expression was originally used in connection with United States railways to refer to a train which succeeded in climbing a steep section of track.

grain

go against the grain

If you say that an idea or action **goes against the grain**, you mean that it is very difficult for you to accept or do, because it conflicts with your ideas, beliefs, or principles. *Heaping such lavish praise on an 18-year-old goes against the grain.*

◆ The grain of a piece of wood is the direction of its fibres. It is easier to cut or plane wood along the direction of the grain, rather than across it.

grandmother

teach your grandmother to suck eggs

British If you tell someone that they **are teaching** their **grandmother to suck eggs**, you are criticizing them for giving advice about something to someone who actually knows more about it than they do. *'It's a sarcophagus. Dig it good and wide,' he said. 'Go teach your grandmother to suck eggs,' said Leshka, and waved him away with a show of irritation.*

grapes

sour grapes

If you describe someone's attitude as **sour grapes**, you mean that they are jealous of another person's success and show this by criticizing the other person or by accusing them of using unfair methods. *The government retorts that Mr Fedorov's criticisms are mere sour grapes.*

◆ In one of Aesop's fables, a fox tries several times to reach a bunch of delicious-looking grapes. In the end he gives up, telling himself that they are probably sour and inedible anyway.

grapevine

hear something through the grapevine
hear something on the grapevine

If you say that you **heard** something **through the grapevine**, you mean that you heard about it informally from your friends, colleagues, or acquaintances. In British English, you can also say that you **heard** something **on the grapevine**. *I hear through the grapevine that you are getting ready to sue us. If that's true, I want to hear it from you.*

☐ **The grapevine** is the way news or gossip spreads among a group of people who know each other. *Spread the word that you are very keen for your guests to choose gifts from your wedding list: tell a few close friends and your family and you will be surprised how effective the grapevine can be.*

◆ One of the early telegraph systems in America was given the nickname 'the grape-vine telegraph' because the wires often became tangled, so that they reminded people of grapevines. During the American Civil War, the telegraph system was used to communicate propaganda and false information, as well as real news about the progress of battles, so that anything heard on the 'grapevine' was likely to be unreliable.

grass

the grass is always greener on the other side of the fence
the other man's grass is always greener

If someone says '**the grass is always greener on the other side of the fence**' or '**the other man's grass is always greener**', they are pointing out that other people may appear to be in a better or more attractive situation than you, but in reality their situation may not be as good as it seems. *The old saying goes that, to many people, the grass is always greener on the other side of the fence, and the majority of Britain's young people are no exception... He had learned the other man's grass was indeed greener.*

put someone out to grass

If someone **is put out to grass**, they are made to retire from their job, or they are moved to an unimportant job, usually because people think that they are too old to be useful. *The Prime Minister refused to be put out to grass. Asked if he would quit, he replied 'The answer is no.'*

◆ When horses have reached the end of their working lives, they are sometimes released into fields to graze.

grave

dig your own grave

If you **dig** your **own grave**, you put yourself in a difficult situation by doing something wrong or making foolish mistakes. *United States prosecutors and other law enforcement officials were more than happy to let Pollard dig his own grave.*

turn in your grave
turn over in your grave

If you say that someone who is dead would **turn in** their **grave**, you mean that they would be very angry or upset about something which is happening now, if they knew about it. This form of the expression is used in British English; in American English, the form is **turn over in** your **grave**. *Churchill and Bevan would turn in their graves if they could hear the pathetic attempts at public speaking made by members of all parties in the past three weeks.*

gravy

a gravy train

If you talk about **a gravy train**, you are referring to a secure and easy way of earning money over a long period, especially by having a job that is easy and well-paid. *Software companies realise that the gravy train can't go on for much longer. Cut-throat competition in the recession is sending computer prices tumbling.*

◆ In the United States, 'gravy' was slang for money or profit. Railway workers invented this expression in the early 1920s to describe a regular journey which provided good pay for little work.

Greek

be Greek to someone
If you say that something **is Greek to** you, you mean that you do not understand it at all. *Soccer is, frankly, all Greek to me.*

◆ The idea behind this expression is that Greek is very difficult to learn and understand, especially because it uses a different alphabet from other European languages.

green

green as grass
British If you say that someone is as **green as grass**, you mean that they are inexperienced or naive. *My brother's a joiner and he said 'You don't want to be a bricklayer.' I was still green as grass so I said 'Oh well, I'll be a painter then.'*

green with envy
If you say that someone is **green with envy**, you mean that they are extremely envious of something that another person has or does. *This is the most unexpected discovery I have made in 20 years of digging. Archaeologists in other parts of the world will be green with envy.*

grips

get to grips with something
If you **get to grips with** a problem, you start dealing with it seriously, for example by getting a proper understanding of it. *The stop-go nature of economic policy is a worrying sign of the country's inability to get to grips with the real problems.*

grist

grist for the mill
grist to the mill
If you say that something is **grist for the mill**, you mean that it can be

put to good use in a particular situation, or that it can be used to support someone's point of view. In British English, you can also say that something is **grist to the mill**. *Mr Kinkel and his senior aides had warned that changes to the nationality laws would be grist to the mill of right wing extremists.*

◆ 'Grist' was grain that was brought to a windmill or watermill to be ground. Millers needed regular supplies of grain to keep their businesses in operation.

groove

in the groove
in a groove

If you say that a sportsperson or a sports team is **in the groove** or **in a groove**, you mean that they are having a continuous series of successes. *Nick is in the groove, as he showed with seven goals last weekend.*

◆ This may refer to the way the needle fits neatly into the groove on a record.

ground

break new ground

If someone **breaks new ground**, they do something completely different, or they do something in a completely different way. You use this expression to show approval of what is being done. *She hopes to break new legal ground by convincing the court that verbal harassment constitutes a wrongful act under Japanese civil law.*

☐ You can talk about **ground-breaking** work. *The impact of Professor Jonker's declaration at this ground-breaking conference has already been substantial.*

cut the ground from under someone
cut the ground from under someone's feet

If you **cut the ground from under** someone or **cut the ground from under** their **feet**, you seriously weaken their argument or position, often by doing something unexpected. *On February 9th, he departed from Labour tradition and cut the ground from under the opposition by promising a cut in corporate-tax rates.*

fall on stony ground

British If something such as a warning or piece of advice **falls on stony ground**, it is ignored. *Dire warnings about the effects on public services fell* *on stony ground.*

◆ This expression comes from Jesus's story in the Bible (Mark 4:5 – 6) about a man sowing seed which falls on different kinds of ground. The seed that falls on stony ground dies because the roots cannot grow properly. In the story, the seed represents Christ's teachings and the stony ground represents the people who soon forget or ignore what He has said.

get in on the ground floor

If you **get in on the ground floor**, you get involved from the very beginning with something, especially something that is likely to be profitable for you. *These smaller companies are getting in on the ground floor of what will be a gigantic industry.*

get something off the ground

If you **get** something **off the ground**, you put it into operation, often after a lot of hard work getting it organized. *Councillor Riley spoke of the dedication and enthusiasm of staff and volunteers in getting the schemes off the ground.*

go to ground

British If you **go to ground**, you hide from someone or something. *He left the hotel and went to ground in the station waiting-room. It was a safe place.*

◆ In hunting, this expression is used to refer to a fox escaping into its hole.

hit the ground running

If you **hit the ground running**, you start a new activity with a lot of energy and enthusiasm, and do not waste any time. *She is in excellent shape and in good spirits. She will hit the ground running when she gets back.*

◆ This image here may be of soldiers landing by parachute or helicopter in a battle area and moving off quickly as soon as they reach the ground.

the moral high ground
the high ground

If you say that a person or organization has taken **the moral high ground** or **the high ground**, you mean that they consider that their policies and actions are morally superior to the policies and actions of their rivals. *The US has taken the moral high ground in telling others what their problems are, while not devoting enough time to its own domestic problems.*

♦ In a battle, the army which is on higher ground has the advantage.

run someone into the ground: 1

If you **run** someone **into the ground**, you make them work so hard and continuously at something that they become exhausted. *Liverpool's young players in particular ran themselves into the ground.*

run something into the ground: 2

If you **run** something **into the ground**, you use it continuously without repairing or replacing it, so that eventually it is destroyed or useless. *Britain's public housing has been virtually run into the ground and the Government shows absolutely no desire to revive it.*

run someone to ground

British If you **run** someone or something **to ground**, you find them after a long search. *Truman eventually ran him to ground, asleep and rather the worse for wear in a hotel.*

♦ In hunting, this expression is used to refer to a fox being chased back to its hole.

stamping ground
stomping ground

If you describe a place as someone's **stamping ground**, you mean that they work there or go there regularly. You can also talk about someone's **stomping ground**. *I'm not fond of the City of London because I'm a West End man, myself. Park Lane, Knightsbridge, Piccadilly and Bond Street are my favourite stamping grounds.*

♦ This expression may refer to the way that stallions stamp while mating. Alternatively, it may come from the dances of male prairie chickens when they gather in spring in order to mate.

suit someone down to the ground

British If something **suits** you **down to the ground**, it completely meets your needs or requirements. *Helen has finally found a method of exercise that suits her outgoing character down to the ground.*

thin on the ground
thick on the ground

British If people or things are **thin on the ground**, there are very few of them. If they are **thick on the ground**, there are a lot of them. *Ideas are thin on the ground in the British film industry... Jobs are not exactly thick on the ground.*

guard

the old guard

You can refer to a group of people as **the old guard** when they have worked in an organization or system for a very long time. You often use this expression to show disapproval of such people when they are unwilling to accept new ideas or practices. *The company's old guard is stepping aside, making way for a new, more youthful team.*

◆ The original 'Old Guard' consisted of the most experienced regiments of Napoleon Bonaparte's Imperial Guard. These soldiers were considered to be the best in the French army.

gum tree

up a gum tree

British, old-fashioned If someone is **up a gum tree**, they are in a very difficult situation. *If you look at any problem like this in terms of right and wrong you'll find yourself nowhere but up a gum tree.*

◆ This expression may be based on the fact that opossums often hide in gum trees when they are being hunted.

gun

jump the gun

If someone **jumps the gun**, they do something before the right, proper, or expected time. You usually use this expression when you disapprove of this behaviour. *Spain has already jumped the gun on diplomatic contacts by announcing earlier this month that its foreign minister would soon visit China.*

◆ If a runner jumps the gun, they begin running before the pistol is fired to start the race.

a smoking gun

Mainly American If you talk about **a smoking gun**, you are referring to a piece of evidence which proves that a particular person is responsible for a crime. *First of all, there's no smoking gun. In the course of our investigation we did not find a single piece of evidence.*

under the gun

Mainly American If you are **under the gun**, you are under great pressure and your future success is being threatened. *Society, in many* *ways, is under the gun. We have a multitude of problems – medical, health problems, drug problems, crime problems, educational, literacy.*

guns

the big guns

If you talk about **the big guns**, you are referring to the most important and powerful people in an organization. *She has been much sought after by the film industry's big guns... Back in the early '70s Arsenal and Leeds were the two big guns in the First Division.*

◆ Cannons used to be referred to as 'big guns' or 'great guns', while rifles or muskets were called 'small guns'.

go great guns

If you say that someone or something **is going great guns**, you mean that they are being very successful at something. *It must have eaten into his confidence when, while his troubles piled up, he heard that Nick Faldo was going great guns.*

◆ See the explanation at 'big guns'.

spike someone's guns

British If you **spike** someone's **guns**, you prevent them from carrying out their plans, or you do something to make their actions ineffective. *Jubilant Tories poured out of the Commons hailing the Chancellor as a genius for spiking Labour's guns with his giveaways for the lower paid.*

◆ In the past, when soldiers captured a large enemy gun which they could not move, they hammered a nail or spike into the hole where the gunpowder was put. This meant that the gunpowder could not be lit and so the gun would not work.

stick to your guns

If you **stick to** your **guns**, you refuse to change your decision or opinion about something, even though other people are trying to tell you that you are wrong. *He should have stuck to his guns, refused to meet her.*

◆ The image here is of soldiers remaining in position, even though they are being attacked by the enemy.

with all guns blazing

If you do something **with all guns blazing**, you do it with a lot of enthusiasm and energy. *Manchester United stormed into the European Cup with all guns blazing.*

guts

spill your guts

If someone **spills** their **guts**, they tell you everything about something secret or private. *People call in and just spill their guts about whatever's bothering them on the job or in a relationship.*

H

hackles

raise someone's hackles
someone's hackles rise

If something **raises** your **hackles**, it makes you angry or annoyed. When something makes you angry or annoyed, you can say that your **hackles rise**. *The taxes will presumably be designed not to raise voters' hackles too much.*

◆ 'Hackles' are feathers on the necks of cockerels and some other birds. They rise up when the bird becomes aggressive.

hair

curl your hair
make your hair curl

If something **curls** your **hair** or **makes** your **hair curl**, it makes you very shocked or worried. *I could tell you stories that would make your hair curl.*

a hair of the dog
a hair of the dog that bit you

Some people believe that you can cure a hangover by having another alcoholic drink. This extra drink is called **a hair of the dog**. You can also talk about **a hair of the dog that bit** you. *I need a drink, chum. A large hair of the dog.*

◆ There was an old belief that if a person was bitten by a mad dog, they could be cured by putting some hairs from the dog's tail on the wound.

a hair shirt

If you say that someone is wearing **a hair shirt**, you mean that they are deliberately making their own life unnecessarily unpleasant or uncomfortable, especially by not allowing themselves any luxuries. *No one is asking you to wear a hair shirt and give up all your luxuries... He has lived a life of almost hair-shirt austerity.*

♦ In the past, hair shirts were very rough, uncomfortable shirts made from horsehair. People sometimes wore them for religious reasons, to show that they were truly sorry for their sins.

in your hair
out of your hair

If you say that someone gets **in** your **hair**, you mean that they annoy you and are a nuisance to you. If you get someone who is a nuisance **out of** your **hair**, you succeed in arranging things so that you are no longer involved with them. *They were very busy and had little time to get into one another's hair... Just do me a favor, will you? Keep her out of my hair from now on.*

keep your hair on

Mainly British If someone tells you to **keep** your **hair on**, they are telling you in a forceful way to calm down and not be angry or impatient. The usual American expression is **keep** your **shirt on**. *His annoyance evaporated in a grin. 'You're right. She's got a tough job. I'll try to keep my hair on in future.'*

let your hair down

If you **let** your **hair down**, you relax and enjoy yourself, and do not worry about being dignified or behaving correctly. *It is only with friends that most people feel they can let their hair down and be themselves.*

make your hair stand on end

If something **makes** your **hair stand on end**, it makes you very frightened or shocked. *The first ten minutes of the film made my hair stand on end.*

not turn a hair

If you say that someone **did not turn a hair** in an unpleasant or difficult situation, you mean that they were very calm, and did not show any sign of being afraid or anxious. *His men were so accustomed to his rages that they never turned a hair.*

tear your hair out

If you say that someone **is tearing** their **hair out**, you mean that they are very angry, upset, or anxious about something. *The nation is tearing its hair out over what to do with these child criminals.*

hairs

by the short hairs

If someone has you **by the short hairs**, they have you completely in their power. *The hard fact is that they have got us by the short hairs. We can't do anything without material support from them.*

◆ 'Short hairs' in this expression may refer to a person's pubic hair, to hair on the back of their neck, or to the hair in a beard.

put hairs on your chest
put hair on the chest

If you say that an alcoholic drink will **put hairs on** someone's **chest** or will **put hair on the chest**, you mean that it is very strong. You can also use this expression to suggest that food is very filling or nourishing. *Some of the concoctions would put hairs on your chest and indeed those brave enough to sample some left with distinct smiles on their faces.*

split hairs

If you accuse someone of **splitting hairs**, you are accusing them of making distinctions in a situation where the differences between things are actually very small and unimportant. *Don't split hairs. You know what I'm getting at.*

☐ You can also accuse someone of **hair-splitting**. *On BBC Radio she accused her critics of hair-splitting.*

halcyon

halcyon days

If you talk about the **halcyon days** of something, you are talking about a time in the past when it was especially successful. *When we ask him whether the wool industry will ever see those halcyon days again, he turns back to his beer and shakes his head.*

☐ You also use **halcyon days** to talk about a time in the past when your life was especially peaceful and happy. *I experienced again the sense of peace and lightness that I associated with the halcyon days at La Chorrera.*

◆ The seven days before and after the shortest day of the year are sometimes called halcyon days. 'Halcyon' comes from the Greek word for kingfisher. According to Greek legend, Halcyone and her husband were turned into kingfishers by the gods. It was believed that these birds built their nests on the sea during the seven days before the shortest day of the year and then sat on their eggs for the next seven days, and that the gods always ensured calm weather during this period.

half

go off half-cocked
go off at half cock

If someone **goes off half-cocked**, they are unsuccessful in what they are trying to do, because they have not taken enough care or prepared properly. You can also say that actions or people **go off at half cock**. *Remember, don't go off half-cocked when we get there. Stick to the plan... In-store guest appearances are usually embarrassing, half-cocked events.*

♦ If a gun goes off at half-cock, it does not fire properly and so the shot is wasted. This is because the firing mechanism has not been raised high enough to connect with the trigger.

hammer

go at it hammer and tongs: 1

British If you **go at it hammer and tongs**, you do something very energetically, vigorously, and enthusiastically. *'He loved gardening,' sniffed Mrs Gascoigne. 'He went at it hammer and tongs as soon as he got back from work.'*

go at it hammer and tongs: 2
go at someone hammer and tongs

Mainly British If you say that two people **are going at it hammer and tongs**, you mean that they are having a noisy argument. You can also say that one person **is going at** the other **hammer and tongs**. *'They were going at it hammer and tongs.' 'What about?' 'I'm not very sure, but they were arguing.'... Goodness knows how long she had been going hammer and tongs at the child like this.*

♦ The image here is of a blacksmith holding a piece of heated iron with a pair of tongs, and striking the iron repeatedly with a hammer.

under the hammer

British If something goes **under the hammer**, it is offered for sale at auction. The American expression is **on the block**. *A portrait by Dutch master Rembrandt went under the hammer for £4.18 million at Sotheby's yesterday.*

♦ In an auction, the auctioneer shows that a sale has been made by banging a hammer on a table.

hand

bite the hand that feeds you

If you talk about someone **biting the hand that feeds** them, you mean that they are ungrateful and behave badly towards the person who has helped them or supported them. *She may be cynical about the film industry, but ultimately she has no intention of biting the hand that feeds her.*

the dead hand

Mainly British If you talk about **the dead hand** of someone or something, you are criticizing them for having a very negative influence on a situation, for example by preventing change or progress. *The North Korean economy had started to shrink under the dead hand of central planning.*

force someone's hand

If someone **forces** your **hand**, they force you to do something that you are not ready to do or do not want to do. *Today's move may be a tactical manoeuvre designed to force the hand of the Prime Minister.*

◆ In card games, to force an opponent's hand means to force them to play a card earlier than they want to.

a free hand

If you have or are given **a free hand** to do something, you have the freedom to make your own decisions on how it should be done. *She was given a totally free hand by her clients to do exactly as she pleased.*

get out of hand

If a situation or person **gets out of hand**, they cannot be controlled any longer. Compare **out of hand**. *At the time of the strike in the Gdansk shipyards in the summer of 1980, the Kremlin felt things were rapidly getting out of hand.*

give with one hand and take away with the other

If you accuse someone of **giving with one hand and taking away with the other**, you mean that they seem to be helping you in one way, but are also doing something which has the opposite effect, for example harming you or preventing you from achieving what you want. *Although my parents were very supportive, in a way they gave with one hand and took back with the other, because I never really learned what it was to be independent.*

hand in glove

If one person or organization is working **hand in glove** with another person or organization, they are working very closely together. You usually use this expression to suggest that the people you are talking about are doing something dishonest or immoral. *Many of the city's politicians are hand in glove with smugglers.*

◆ The original form of the expression was 'hand and glove'. It was used to say that there was a strong connection or similarity between two things.

hand in hand: 1

If two things go **hand in hand**, they are closely connected and cannot be considered separately from each other. You can also say that one thing goes **hand in hand** with another thing. *The principle of the playgroup movement is that play and learning go hand in hand: your child masters new skills and absorbs knowledge while having fun.*

hand in hand: 2

If two people or organizations work **hand in hand**, they work closely together, often with a single aim. You can also say that one person or organization works **hand in hand** with another. *Steelmakers are working hand-in-hand with auto makers to slash the cost of producing automotive parts.*

hand over fist

If someone is making money **hand over fist**, they are making a lot of money very quickly. If they are losing money **hand over fist**, they are losing it very quickly. *The companies had no skills and almost all were losing money hand over fist.*

hand-to-mouth

You can say that someone is acting in a **hand-to-mouth** way when they do not plan ahead, but decide what to do from day to day. You usually use this expression critically or disapprovingly. Compare **live from hand to mouth**. *Unless a government sets its course from the start, it is doomed to spend the rest of its term in hand-to-mouth improvising.*

have someone eating out of your hand
have someone eating out of the palm of your hand

If you **have** someone **eating out of** your **hand** or **have** them **eating out of the palm of** your **hand**, they will do whatever you want because they admire you so much. These expressions are often used to refer to situations where someone is suspicious or uncooperative at first, but then starts to like you and agree to anything you say. *He is a silver-tongued* *lawyer famed for having juries eat out of the palm of his hand.*

◆ The image here is of an animal which is tame and will take food from a person's hand.

in the palm of your hand: 1

If you have a group of people, especially an audience, **in the palm of your hand**, they are giving you their full attention and are responding enthusiastically to everything you say or do. *A cursory look at the audience shows that she's got them in the palm of her hand.*

in the palm of your hand: 2

If you have someone **in the palm of** your **hand**, you have complete control over them and they will do whatever you want. You can also say that you have them **in the hollow of** your **hand**. *The Englishman was staring back at Raisa. The girl clearly thought she already had him in the palm of her hand.*

keep your hand in

If you do something to **keep** your **hand in**, you do it in order to use the skills which you have developed in the past, so that you do not lose them. *I had to wait two years before I was offered another part, and just to keep my hand in, I went on tour with a play that wasn't very good.*

live from hand to mouth
live hand to mouth

Someone who **lives from hand to mouth** or **lives hand to mouth** does not have enough money to live comfortably, and has no money left after they have paid for basic necessities. You can also say that someone like this **is hand to mouth**. Compare **hand-to-mouth**. *I have a wife and two children and we live from hand to mouth on what I earn.*

☐ You can also talk about a **hand-to-mouth** existence or a **hand-to-mouth** economy. *Unloved and uncared-for, they live a meaningless hand to mouth existence.*

an old hand

If someone is **an old hand** at something, they are very skilled at it because they have been doing it for a long time. *Being faced with decorating a flat like this from scratch would have put a lot of people off, but Bryce relished the challenge. He is, after all, an old hand at this kind of project.*

out of hand

If you reject an idea or suggestion **out of hand**, you reject it without hesitating and without discussing it or considering it first. Compare **get out of hand**. *He has rejected out of hand any suggestion that there can be any compromise over the proposals.*

overplay your hand

If someone **overplays** their **hand**, they act more confidently than they should, because they believe they are in a stronger position than they really are. *US officials tried to persuade Nazarbayev he had overplayed his hand, that he would lose any prospects for economic and technical assistance by holding onto the weapons.*

◆ 'Hand' in this expression refers to the cards dealt to you in a card game.

the right hand doesn't know what the left hand is doing

If you say that an organization's **right hand doesn't know what** its **left hand is doing**, you mean that the people in one part of the organization do not know what the people in another part are doing and this is leading to confusion or difficulties. You use this expression when you want to criticize people or organizations for not communicating or co-operating properly. *The great service industries of Britain are still in the situation where their right hand doesn't know what the left is doing. Usually they dig up roads, fill them in and then another service does the same a few days later.*

◆ This expression comes from Jesus's teaching in the Bible, in which He says that when people give money to charity, they should do it without boasting or telling anyone about it. 'But when thou doest alms, let not thy left hand know what thy right hand doeth.' (Matthew 6:3)

show your hand

In a competitive situation, if you **show** your **hand**, you let other people see what your position is and what you intend to do. You can replace 'show' with 'reveal'. *On domestic politics he seemed unwilling to show his hand too clearly.*

◆ If you show your hand in a card game, you reveal your cards to another player.

a steady hand on the tiller

If you describe someone as having **a steady hand on the tiller**, you are showing admiration for the way that they are keeping control of a situation. *'If ever there was an urgent need for a steady hand on the tiller, it is now,' said one European diplomat.*

◆ In a boat, the tiller is the handle with which you steer.

throw in your hand

If you **throw in** your **hand**, you give up trying to do something. *Defeat on this embarrassing issue might just tip Mr Major into throwing in his hand.*

◆ In card games such as poker, if you throw in your hand, you put your cards on the table to show that you accept that you have lost.

the upper hand

If one side has **the upper hand** in a competitive situation, it has more power than the other side and can control things. If one side gains **the upper hand**, it gets more power and becomes able to control things. *Diplomats believe it is still far from clear which side is gaining the upper hand in the economic debate.*

wait on someone hand and foot

If someone **is waited on hand and foot**, another person looks after them, taking care of them in every way and making them very comfortable. This expression is usually used to suggest that it is unreasonable for someone to be looked after in this way. *Many men expect to be waited on hand and foot because they've been spoiled rotten by their mothers.*

handle

fly off the handle

If you **fly off the handle**, you suddenly become very angry about something and behave in an uncontrolled and irrational way. *Unless some decision was reached they might fly off the handle and do something foolish.*

◆ The reference here is to an axe head which has become loose, and so when someone swings the axe, the axe head flies off.

hands

dirty your hands

If you say that someone does not **dirty** their **hands**, you mean that they avoid doing physical work or the parts of a job that they consider unpleasant or distasteful. This expression is often used in criticizing someone for not getting involved in things. Compare **get** your **hands dirty**. *Very few academics of his distinction are willing to dirty their hands with political activity to the extent that he does.*

get your hands dirty

If you **get** your **hands dirty** in your job, you get involved with all aspects of it, including routine, practical, or more junior work, or dealing with people directly. This expression is usually used showing approval. Compare **dirty** your **hands**. *The guys at the top make all the money, while the people actually getting their hands dirty get exploited.*

play into someone's hands

If you **play into** someone's **hands**, you make a foolish mistake or act in the way that they want you to act, so that they gain an advantage over you or defeat you. *The main opposition parties played into his hands by boycotting the election.*

rub your hands

Mainly British If you say that someone **is rubbing** their **hands**, you mean that they are very pleased about something, often something bad which has happened to an enemy or opponent. *Leaders of the Windward Islands opposition parties are rubbing their hands in glee at the news that British banana magnates have suffered a cut in profits.*

a safe pair of hands
safe hands

Mainly British If you refer to someone, especially a politician, as **a safe pair of hands**, you mean that they are good at their job and unlikely to make any serious mistakes. *Douglas Hurd is widely regarded within the party as being what's known as a safe pair of hands.*

☐ You can also refer to someone who is thought of in this way as **safe hands**. *In front of Munich's city hall, Max Streibl and Theo Waigel urge people to vote again for safe hands.*

sit on your hands

If you say that someone **is sitting on** their **hands**, you are criticizing them for not doing something which they ought to be doing. *I think the US troops there are beginning to feel quite embarrassed about sitting on their hands while refugees stream through the lines with tales of horror.*

☐ In American English, you can also use this expression to show your approval of someone for restraining themselves and waiting for the best time to take action. *Force yourself to read the draft in its entirety. Sit on your hands. Give the draft a chance before you begin reworking it.*

sully your hands

If you talk about someone **sullying** their **hands** by doing something, you mean that they would find it unpleasant or distasteful to do it. This expression is often used to criticize people's attitudes towards an activity. *He had no intention of sullying his hands by playing politics: he wished to be, as he so frequently declared, 'above politics'.*

wash your hands of something

If you **wash** your **hands** of a problem or of a person who causes problems, you refuse to be involved with them or to take responsibility for them any longer. *The Macclesfield MP said: 'We cannot wash our hands of responsibility for the state of the economy.'*

◆ According to the Bible, Pontius Pilate washed his hands in a bowl to show that he would not take responsibility for the death sentence which the public demanded he should pass on Jesus. (Matthew 27:24)

win hands down: 1
beat someone hands down

If you say that someone **wins** a contest **hands down**, you are emphasizing that they win it easily. You can also say that they **beat** someone else **hands down**. *They predict that if a general election was held now, the Conservative Party would win hands down.*

win hands down: 2
beat something hands down

When you are comparing things to see which is best, you can say that the thing which is clearly best **wins hands down** or **beats** the others **hands down**. *I had always enjoyed driving through the New Forest, but two-wheeled travel beats the car hands down... We are hands-down, flat-out the leaders of the world in this.*

◆ This expression was originally used in horse racing to describe jockeys who won their races very easily and could cross the winning line with their hands lowered and the reins loose.

wring your hands

If you say that someone **is wringing** their **hands**, you mean that they are expressing sadness or regret about a bad situation, but are not taking any action to deal with it. You usually use this expression to show your disapproval of them for behaving like this. *Mr Ashdown had accused the Government of wringing its hands and doing nothing as the country's jobless figures spiralled.*

☐ When someone behaves like this, you can refer to **hand-wringing** or **wringing of hands**. *Condolences and hand-wringing are not enough.*

your hands are tied

If your **hands are tied**, something such as a law is preventing you from acting in the way that you want to. *He would like to help but he is powerless because his hands are tied by regulations approved by the council of ministers.*

handsome

handsome is as handsome does
pretty is as pretty does

Old-fashioned When people say **handsome is as handsome does** or **pretty is as pretty does**, they mean that you should judge someone by their actions and not by their appearance. *Handsome is as handsome does, my mother and grandmother always said in order to counter self-admiration.*

hang

get the hang of something

If you **get the hang** of an activity, you learn how to do it competently. *'After a few months,' he says, 'you think you are getting the hang of the language and expressing yourself quite well.'*

hang someone out to dry

If you say that someone **has been hung out to dry**, you mean that they are in a very difficult situation and have been abandoned by the people who previously supported them. *Once again, the CIA – apparently unable to resist political manipulation by the administration – is in danger of being hung out to dry.*

hang up your boots

If a sports player, especially a footballer, **hangs up** their **boots**, they stop playing and retire. *I'm slower now and the time has come to hang up my boots.*

□ People often replace 'boots' with another word which relates to a person's job, to mean that they stop doing that job. *Nurse Christine Soutar hung up her uniform to look after her four young sons.*

□ 'Hang up your boots' is used in British English. The other forms are used in both British and American English.

happy

happy as a clam

American If you are **happy as a clam**, you are very happy. *Join the* *other kids. Do that, and before you know it you'll be happy as a clam.*

happy as a lark

If you are **happy as a lark**, you are very happy. *Look at me – eighty-two years old and happy as a lark!*

happy as a pig in muck

British If you are **happy as a pig in muck**, you are very happy. *From day one I adored it. I was as happy as a pig in muck.*

□ This expression has several variations. For example, some people talk about being **happy as a pig in shit**. Many people find this offensive. *I'd much rather be as I am, I couldn't imagine being any different. Happy as a pig in shit.*

happy as a sandboy

British If you are **happy as a sandboy**, you are very happy. *He's all smiles and happy as a sandboy.*

◆ Sandboys were boys or men who sold bags of sand from carts. It is possible that they were described as 'happy' because they had a reputation for spending their money on alcohol.

happy as Larry

British If you are as **happy as Larry**, you are very happy. *I gave her a police badge to wear on her sleeve and she's as happy as Larry.*

◆ 'Larry' may refer to the successful Australian boxer Larry Foley (1847–1917). Alternatively, 'Larry' may come from 'larrikin', a 19th century word for a hooligan or ruffian, used mainly in Australia.

hard

hard as nails

If you say that someone is as **hard as nails**, you mean that they are very unsympathetic towards other people, or do not seem to care about them. *He's a shrewd businessman and hard as nails.*

hardball

play hardball

Mainly American If someone **plays hardball**, they will do anything that is necessary to achieve or obtain what they want, even if this involves being harsh or unfair. Compare **play ball**; see **ball**. *The White House decided to retaliate by taking jobs away from his state, showing they were tough guys who could play hard ball.*

◆ Hardball is the same as baseball.

hare

run with the hare and hunt with the hounds

British If you say that someone **runs with the hare and hunts with the hounds**, you mean that they try to support both sides in an argument or conflict, in order to make their own life easier. *They want to keep the peace and have everybody happy. For this reason they learn very quickly to run with the hares and hunt with the hounds; to side with whoever is nearest in a relentless quest to avoid rows.*

start a hare

British If someone **starts a hare**, they introduce a new idea or topic which other people become interested in. *Some work needs to be done before the connection between aluminium and heart disease is proved to everyone's satisfaction. But Mr Birchall has started a hare that many researchers will be watching.*

◆ To 'start' a hare means to disturb it and cause it to leave its hiding place, so that the hounds start chasing it.

harness

in harness: 1

British You say someone is **in harness** when they are actually doing a job which they have been appointed to do. *They hope to have the Australian Test forward Troy Coker back in harness before the end of the season.*

in harness: 2

Mainly British If two or more people work **in harness**, they work together or produce something together. *Experts in production statistics and computing may work in harness on a single project.*

hat

eat your hat

Old-fashioned You say that you will **eat** your **hat** if a particular thing happens in order to emphasize that you do not believe that it will happen. *He has promised to eat his hat if he is wrong.*

hat in hand

Mainly American If you go **hat in hand** to someone, you ask them very humbly and respectfully for money or help. The usual British expression is **cap in hand**. *He won't go hat-in-hand to the White House to ask that sanctions be lifted against his country.*

♦ In the past, it was customary for lower-class people to remove their hats in front of upper-class people. The expression may also refer to the fact that people sometimes hold out their hats when they are begging, for other people to put money in.

keep something under your hat

If someone tells you something and then asks you to **keep** it **under** your **hat**, they are asking you not to mention it to anyone else. *Look, if I tell you something will you promise to keep it under your hat. Promise now, not a word to anyone?*

knock something into a cocked hat

If you say one thing **knocks** another **into a cocked hat**, you are emphasizing that the first thing is much better or more successful than the second. *I am writing a novel which is going to knock Proust into a cocked hat.*

♦ One explanation for this expression is that it refers to the cocked hats of the 18th century, which were made by folding the edge of a round hat into three corners or points. According to this explanation, the expression originally meant to change something completely. Alternatively, the expression may refer to an American game of skittles where only three pins were set up, in the triangular shape of a cocked hat.

old hat

If you describe something as **old hat**, you are being scornful of it, because you think it is unoriginal or out of date. *The younger generation tell me that religion is old hat and science has proved this, but has it?*

♦ This expression may have developed because in the times when it was customary for women to wear hats, the fashions in hats used to change very quickly.

pass the hat
pass the hat around

If people **pass the hat** or **pass the hat around**, they collect money for someone or something. *The United States is also passing the hat among rich countries to help to pay for our military effort.*

♦ The image here is of people using a hat to collect money in.

pull a rabbit out of the hat
pull something out of the hat

If someone **pulls a rabbit out of the hat**, they unexpectedly do something which solves a problem or helps them to achieve something. *I cannot pull a rabbit out of a hat every time I go into the boxing ring. All I can do is do my best.*

☐ You can also say that someone **pulls** something good or successful **out of the hat**. *The Chancellor failed to pull any economic miracles out of the hat last night when he unveiled his latest strategy for recovery.*

◆ This expression refers to a traditional magician's trick, in which the magician appears to produce a rabbit from an empty hat.

take your hat off to someone
hats off to someone

If you say you **take** your **hat off to** someone, you are expressing admiration for something that they have done. *I take my hat off to them. They've done very well.*

☐ You can also say **hats off to** someone. *Hats off to them for supporting the homeless.*

◆ People sometimes remove their hats as a sign of respect when they meet someone.

talk through your hat

If you say that someone **is talking through** their **hat**, you are saying rudely or scornfully that what they are saying is ridiculous or totally incorrect. *He is talking through his hat when he attributes the overcrowding and over-use of parts of the Lake District to its designation as a national park.*

throw your hat into the ring
throw your cap into the ring

If you **throw** your **hat into the ring** or **throw** your **cap into the ring**, you become one of the people taking part in a competition or contest. Other verbs are sometimes used instead of 'throw'. *She would have been the first woman to serve as Germany's top diplomat, but she lost the nomination after Kinkel threw his hat into the ring at the last moment.*

◆ In the past, prize fighters at showgrounds used to challenge people to fight them. Someone who was willing to accept the challenge would throw their hat into the ring.

hatch

down the hatch

If you say some food or drink goes **down the hatch**, you mean someone eats or drinks it, usually quickly or greedily. *My daughter raised the shell to her lips, closed her eyes and down the hatch went the oyster.*

☐ People sometimes say **'down the hatch!'** just before drinking an alcoholic drink. *She said 'Down the hatch!' and drank the whole lot in one gulp.*

◆ In the 18th century, this expression was used as a toast in the navy. A hatch is an opening in the deck of a ship, through which people and goods can pass.

hatches

batten down the hatches

If you **batten down the hatches**, you prepare for a difficult situation by doing everything you can to protect yourself. *While most companies are battening down the hatches, fearing recession, Blenheim is leading an assault on the US market.*

◆ Battens are strips of wood used for fastening things down. Hatches are openings in the deck of a ship, or the wooden flaps which cover the openings.

hatchet

◆ A hatchet is a small axe.

bury the hatchet

When people who have quarrelled **bury the hatchet**, they agree to forget their quarrel and become friends again. *One employee said Viscount Althorp had been to see his father before his death and this showed the two had finally buried the hatchet after their falling-out.*

◆ In the past, when Native American tribes made peace after fighting each other, it was traditional for each tribe to bury a tomahawk or small axe, as a sign of peace.

a hatchet job

To do **a hatchet job** on someone or something means to say or write a lot of bad things about them in order to harm their reputation. *Tories fear the Shadow Home Secretary can do the same hatchet job on Mr Major as he* *has on Home Secretary Michael Howard.*

◆ See explanation at 'a hatchet man'.

a hatchet man

You describe a man as **a hatchet man** when his job is to destroy things or do unpleasant tasks, often on behalf of someone else. This expression is usually used showing disapproval. *He had to play the hatchet man and it was not pleasant for the many he laid off.*

◆ This expression may relate to violent gang warfare in the United States during the early part of the 20th century. Gangs often hired an assassin or 'hatchet man' to hack an important member of a rival gang to death with a hatchet. This work was known as a 'hatchet job'.

haul

a long haul
in something for the long haul

If you say a task or course of action will be **a long haul**, you mean that it will be very difficult to deal with and will need a great deal of effort and time. *Revitalising the economy will be a long haul... The American Defence Secretary, Mr Dick Cheney, said the United States was prepared for a long haul.*

☐ In American English, if you say that you are **in** something **for the long haul**, you mean that you intend to continue doing it until it is finished, even if it is difficult or unpleasant. *Impatience is not our problem. We're in it for the long haul. Five years is the minimum.*

over the long haul

Mainly American If you talk about the effect that something will have **over the long haul**, you are talking about its effect over a long period of time in the future. *The fact is that over the long haul, most investors would be pleasantly surprised at just how much can be earned by putting their money into good, sound, safe investments.*

hawk

watch someone like a hawk

If you **watch** someone **like a hawk**, you pay close attention to everything they do, usually to make sure that they do not do anything wrong. *If we hadn't watched him like a hawk, he would have gone back to London.*

◆ Hawks have very good eyesight, and are able to see small animals or objects from a great height.

hay

make hay while the sun shines
make hay

If you **make hay while the sun shines**, you take advantage of a good situation which is not likely to last. *Making hay while the sun shines, the Egyptian government has taken radical measures to liberalise the economy.*

☐ You can say that someone **makes hay** out of any situation that they take advantage of, especially if you disapprove of their behaviour. *The New Zealand media made hay with the issue.*

head

bite someone's head off
snap someone's head off

If someone **bites** your **head off**, they speak to you in an unpleasant, angry way, because they are annoyed about something. You can also say that they **snap** your **head off**. *And don't bite my head off just because you're bad tempered.*

bury your head in the sand

If you say that someone **is burying** their **head in the sand**, you mean that they are deliberately refusing to accept the truth about something unpleasant. *Don't be an ostrich and bury your head in the sand, hoping your problems will disappear... I oppose it because it's a stupid, head-in-the-sand approach to the global problem of nuclear waste disposal.*

◆ People used to think that ostriches buried their heads in the sand when they were in danger.

cannot make head or tail of something

If you **cannot make head or tail of** something, you cannot understand it at all. *I couldn't make head or tail of it myself, but it sounded like part of some sort of hymn or prayer.*

come to a head

If a problem or disagreement **comes to a head**, it reaches a state where you have to take action to deal with it. *These problems came to a head in September when five of the station's journalists were sacked.*

◆ This expression may refer to farmers waiting for cabbage leaves to grow together and form a head. Alternatively, the reference may be to a boil on a person's body forming a head just before it bursts.

fall head over heels
be head over heels

If you **fall head over heels** in love with someone, you fall suddenly and deeply in love with them. If you **are head over heels** in love, you are very deeply in love. *It was obvious that Alan had fallen head over heels in love with Veronica.*

◆ Until the late 18th century this expression was 'heels over head', which refers to someone doing a somersault.

get in over your head

If you say that someone **gets in over** their **head**, you mean that they become deeply involved in a situation which is too difficult for them to deal with. *He realized that he was in over his head, and that only his family could help him.*

◆ This expression refers to someone who is in deep water but cannot swim very well, or cannot swim at all.

give someone their head

If you **give** someone their **head**, you allow them to do what they want to do, without trying to advise them or stop them. *By giving nationalism its head, the communists unleashed forces they could not control.*

◆ If a horse is given its head, the rider allows it to gallop as fast as it likes.

go over someone's head: 1

If you **go over the head of** someone who is in authority or who has responsibility for something, you appeal to a higher authority than them in an attempt to get what you want. *He was reprimanded for trying to go over the heads of senior officers.*

go over someone's head: 2
talk over someone's head

If something that someone says or writes **goes over** your **head**, you do not understand it because it is too difficult for you. You can also say that someone **talks over** your **head**. *I bought a handful of photographic magazines last month and when I got home to read them, I found they were completely over my head.*

go to your head: 1

If you say that someone lets success **go to** their **head**, you mean that they start to think that they are better or cleverer than other people, and they begin to behave in an arrogant or silly way. *Ford is definitely not a* *man to let a little success go to his head. He knows he still has a lot to learn.*

go to your head: 2

If alcohol **goes to** your **head**, it makes you slightly drunk and perhaps affects your judgement so that you do silly things. *He was not accustomed to strong liquor and it went to his head.*

hang over your head

If you say that something difficult or unpleasant **is hanging over** your **head**, you mean that it worries you because it may cause something bad to happen to you in the future. *If the post fell vacant, it is unlikely that the Home Office would want to appoint him if an inquiry was hanging over his head.*

◆ This expression may relate to the story of the Sword of Damocles: see **sword**.

have your head in the clouds

If you say that someone **has** their **head in the clouds**, you mean that they are out of touch with reality and perhaps have impractical ideas about achieving success. *When we were leaving school, Rosemary used to say she was going to be a very rich lady one day. We all thought it was typical of her, she seemed to live with her head in the clouds.*

have your head screwed on

If you say that someone **has** their **head screwed on**, you mean that they are sensible and realistic. *Good girl! I always knew you had your head screwed on properly.*

a head of steam: 1

If someone builds up **a head of steam**, they gradually become more and more angry, anxious, or emotional about something until they can no longer hide their feelings. *Bob was the most angry, as if in waiting for the other items to be cleared he had built up a greater head of steam.*

a head of steam: 2

If someone gets **a head of steam** for something such as a plan or cause, they gain a lot of support for it. *While most senior Conservative MPs still believe an election next year is more likely, there's an increasing head of steam behind November.*

◆ A steam engine can only work when the steam has reached a particular pressure level.

hold a gun to someone's head

If someone **holds a gun to** your **head**, they force you to do something by threatening to take extreme action against you if you do not do it. *Not a man to have a gun put to his head, Mr Riordan was soon tearing up the offer and cancelling future meetings with the union.*

keep your head above water

If you are trying to **keep** your **head above water**, you are struggling to survive, for example by keeping out of debt. *Thousands of other small businesses like mine are, at best, struggling to keep their heads above water or, at worst, have gone bust.*

keep your head down: 1

In a difficult or dangerous situation, if you **keep** your **head down**, you try to avoid trouble or involvement by behaving in a quiet way, so that people will not notice you. *I just decided to keep my head down and do my job and eventually I was accepted by the male pilots and everything was going well.*

keep your head down: 2

If you **keep** your **head down**, you continue to concentrate and work hard at something. *When he gets a chance of winning he keeps his head down and really goes for it.*

knock something on the head: 1

British If you **knock** a story or idea **on the head**, you show that it is not true or correct. *I think this is another fallacy that needs to be knocked on the head, the idea that women never went out to work till the First World War.*

knock something on the head: 2

British If you **knock** an activity **on the head**, you decide to stop it, or not to go ahead with it. *I remember us in the early days saying: 'We'll never be like The Rolling Stones. When we stop enjoying ourselves, we'll knock it on the head.'*

off the top of your head: 1

If you say that you are commenting on something **off the top of** your **head**, you mean that what you are about to say is an immediate reaction and is not a carefully considered opinion, and so it might not be correct. *I can't remember off the top of my head which plan they used, but it certainly wasn't the Ordnance Survey plan.*

off the top of your head: 2

If you know something **off the top of** your **head**, you know it well and can remember it easily. *OK, off the top of your head, do you know the capital of South Korea?*

on your head

You can use expressions such as **on** your **own head** and **on** your **head be it** to warn someone that they are responsible for something that they intend to do or something that happens as a consequence The expressions are used more commonly in British English than American.. *If you choose to ignore my generous offer, then on your own heads be it.*

put your head above the parapet
keep your head below the parapet

British If someone **puts** their **head above the parapet**, they do or say something in public that has previously been kept private, and risk being criticized or attacked. *In private, however, some now acknowledge this is a policy option which cannot be ignored – although they are not prepared to put their heads above the parapet to say so.*

☐ If someone **keeps** their **head below the parapet**, they do not risk saying or doing something in public that has previously been kept private, even though they may feel that they ought to. *We are not very good at publicity stunts, at drawing attention to ourselves. We like to keep our heads below the parapet.*

◆ Parapets are banks of earth or walls which soldiers build for protection against enemy attacks.

put your head in a noose
stick your head in a noose

If you **put** your **head in a noose** or **stick** your **head in a noose**, you deliberately do something which will put you in danger or in a difficult situation. *If I have to be caught, OK, but I am damned if I will put my head in a noose and walk into that hotel!*

rear its head
raise its head
rear its ugly head

If you say that something undesirable **rears** its **head** or **raises** its **head**, you mean that it starts to appear or be active. You often use this expression when the thing you are talking about appears again after being hidden or absent for a period of time. *The familiar pattern of violence is raising its head once again in Punjab.*

☐ People often say that something undesirable **rears** or **raises** its **ugly head**. *Inflation may yet raise its ugly head again, affecting both Germany and its eastern neighbours.*

scratch your head

If you **are scratching** your **head** about a problem or question, you are puzzled and unsure about what to do or what the solution is. *A lot of people are scratching their heads and saying, 'What are we doing? Are we getting our money's worth?'*

□ You can also talk about **head-scratching**. *That caused a lot of head scratching and another hour and a half delay, but finally things seemed to work all right.*

turn something on its head
stand something on its head

If you **turn** something such as an argument or theory **on** its **head** or **stand** it **on** its **head**, you use the same facts to produce a different or opposite conclusion. *Instead of pleading for women's rights, the Equal Opportunities Commission should turn the argument on its head and point out the cost of denying women the right to earn.*

headlights

like a rabbit caught in the headlights
like a deer caught in the headlights

If you say that someone is **like a rabbit caught in the headlights** or **like a deer caught in the headlights**, you mean that they are so frightened or nervous that they do not know what to do. *He just sat there, like a rabbit caught in the headlights.*

□ This expression is very variable. For example, you can just say that someone is caught or frozen **in the headlights**. *It often seems, from the outside, that the optimum strategy for a writer caught in the headlights of unexpected celebrity is simply to keep bashing on, to keep writing and publishing.*

◆ Animals such as rabbits or deer sometimes remain still because they do not know which way to run when the light from a vehicle's headlights shines on them at night.

heads

heads roll

If **heads roll** when something goes wrong, the people responsible or in positions of power are punished, usually by losing their job or position. *The widely-held view is that heads should roll over the losses.*

◆ In the past, people in important positions were sometimes beheaded if they were considered responsible for a mistake or problem.

knock people's heads together
bang people's heads together

Mainly British When people disagree and someone in authority **knocks** their **heads together** or **bangs** their **heads together**, they force them to reach an agreement. *John believes that you usually get what you want by talking to people rather than banging heads together.*

turn heads

If someone or something **turns heads**, they are so beautiful, unusual, or impressive that people are attracted to them and cannot help looking at them or paying attention to them. *At the age of 20, the dark-haired actress was already turning heads in the right places.*

☐ Journalists sometimes describe someone or something as **head-turning**, or refer to them as **a head-turner**. *Gardams' designers have created a range of head-turning evening wear in their latest collection... The car is solid, fun to drive, quick off the blocks and a real head-turner.*

headway

make headway

If you **make headway**, you make progress in the thing that you are trying to achieve. *A spokesman said the two sides have agreed on a timetable for the rest of the talks and have also made headway on some security issues.*

heap

the bottom of the heap
the top of the heap

Someone who is at **the bottom of the heap** is low down in society or in an organization. Someone who is at **the top of the heap** is high up in society or in an organization. The expressions **the bottom of the pile** and **the top of the pile** mean the same. *At the bottom of the heap live at least 1 million people – the rural poor... Why do we want to find progress in evolution? He wonders whether it is a device 'to justify our position on the top of the biological heap'.*

heart

a bleeding heart

If you refer to someone as **a bleeding heart**, you are criticizing them for being too sympathetic towards people who claim to be poor or suffering, either because you think the people do not deserve sympathy, or because you think that the person you are criticizing is not sincere. Compare your **heart bleeds for** someone. *I know how the lawmakers and the judges and the bleeding hearts screw things up for the police. Hell, I've been a cop as long as you have... This was precisely the sort of bleeding-heart sentimentality that Charles Lindbergh deplored.*

cross my heart

You can say **'cross my heart'** when you want to assure someone that you are telling the truth. People sometimes also say **'cross my heart and hope to die'**. *And I won't tell any of the other girls anything you tell me about it. I promise, cross my heart.*

◆ This expression refers to the Christian practice of moving your hand across your chest in the shape of a cross.

eat your heart out

When you want to draw attention to something you have done, you can say **'eat your heart out'** and mention the name of a person who is famous for doing the same kind of thing. *I think I have the makings of a novel here. Marcel Proust, eat your heart out.*

a heart of gold

If you say that someone has **a heart of gold**, you mean they are kind and generous, and enjoy helping other people. *He is a tough guy, but with a heart of gold.*

wear your heart on your sleeve

If you **wear** your **heart on** your **sleeve**, you allow your feelings to be obvious to everyone around you. *She simply doesn't wear her heart on her sleeve so it's sometimes difficult to know what she's feeling.*

your heart bleeds for someone

If you say that your **heart bleeds for** someone, you mean that you feel a lot of sympathy for them because they are suffering. Compare **a bleeding heart**. *You looked so sad when you walked up the aisle at the funeral. My heart bled for you when I watched it.*

□ This expression is often used ironically to show that you think someone does not deserve any sympathy, because you do not believe that they are genuinely suffering. *I must say my heart bleeds for the poor BT share issue investors who made a mere 15 per cent on their investment in one day.*

your heart is in the right place

If you say that someone's **heart is in the right place**, you mean that they are kind, considerate, and generous, although they may lack other qualities which you consider to be important. *Whether Johnson's professional judgement was good or not, I decided that his heart was in the right place.*

your heart is in your mouth

If you say that your **heart is in** your **mouth**, you mean that you feel extremely anxious or nervous, because you think something unpleasant or unfortunate may be about to happen. *My heart was in my mouth when I walked into her office.*

heartstrings

tug at the heartstrings

If you say that someone or something **tugs at the heartstrings**, you mean that they cause you to feel a great deal of pity or sadness for them. *Miss Cookson knows exactly how to tug at readers' heartstrings.*

◆ In medieval times, it was believed that 'heartstrings' were tendons which supported the heart.

heat

if you can't stand the heat, get out of the kitchen

If someone is involved in a difficult or unpleasant activity and they start complaining, you can say to them **'if you can't stand the heat, get out of the kitchen'**. This is a way of telling them that they should either learn to tolerate the difficulty or unpleasantness, or give up their involvement in that activity. *If you are a manager of a top football club and you don't like the heat you should get out of the kitchen.*

◆ This expression became very widely known when the American President Harry S. Truman used it in 1952 to announce that he would not stand again for president.

heather

set the heather on fire

Mainly Scottish If you say that something **sets the heather on fire**, you mean that it is very exciting and successful. *Their results have not set the heather on fire.*

heaven

in seventh heaven

If you say that you are **in seventh heaven**, you are emphasizing that you are extremely happy. *After I was given my first camera I was in seventh heaven.*

◆ According to Islam, there are seven heavens. The seventh is the most glorious and is governed by Abraham. In the Jewish religion, the seventh heaven is the dwelling place of God and his angels.

move heaven and earth

If you **move heaven and earth** in order to do something, you do everything you possibly can to make sure that you do it. *He had been moving heaven and earth for six weeks in order to prevent the film being made; and he had failed.*

heel

bring someone to heel
call someone to heel

If you **bring** someone **to heel** or **call** them **to heel**, you force or order them to obey you. *In practice it's still not clear how the president will use his power to bring the republics to heel.*

◆ The image here is of a person making their dog walk obediently at their side.

heels

dig in your heels

If you **dig in** your **heels** or **dig** your **heels in**, you refuse to do something such as change your opinions or plans, especially when someone is trying very hard to make you do so. *I begged her to come home but she dug her heels in.*

hard on the heels of something: 1
hot on the heels of something

If you say that one event follows **hard on the heels of** another or **hot on the heels of** another, you are emphasizing that one happens very quickly or immediately after another. *The news comes hard on the heels of the appointment of new chief executive Cedric Scroggs.*

hard on your heels: 2
hot on your heels

In a competitive situation, if someone is **hard on** your **heels** or **hot on** your **heels**, they are doing nearly as well as you, and it is likely that they will soon be doing better than you. *The next generation of British athletes is pressing hard on the heels of today's champions.*

hard on your heels: 3
hot on your heels

If someone is **hard on** your **heels**, they are close behind you, for example because they are chasing you. You can also say that someone is **hot on** your **heels**. *But the law was hard on their heels. Within two weeks gang leader Michael McAvoy and Brian Robinson were behind bars.*

kick up your heels

If someone **is kicking up** their **heels**, they are enjoying themselves a lot, for example at a party. *Combine music, culture and good food in Jersey this month. Kick up your heels at the annual Jersey Jazz Festival.*

kick your heels
cool your heels

If you **are kicking** your **heels** or **are cooling** your **heels**, you are waiting somewhere and feel bored or impatient because you have nothing to do, or because someone is deliberately keeping you waiting. The form with 'kick' is used more commonly in British English and the form with 'cool' is used more commonly in American English. *The Tunisian authorities wouldn't grant us permission to fly all the way down to Sfax, so I had to kick my heels at Tunis Airport.*

set you back on your heels
rock you back on your heels

If something **sets** you **back on** your **heels** or **rocks** you **back on** your **heels**, it surprises or shocks you, and often puts you at a disadvantage. *Ireland started brightly, only to be rocked back on their heels by the first error just 10 minutes into the match.*

show a clean pair of heels: 1

Mainly British In a sporting contest, if one competitor **shows** the others **a clean pair of heels**, he or she wins clearly and decisively. *Another working-class hero with whom I identified was Alf Tupper, who trained on fish and chips, ran in a borrowed vest and showed the world's best runners a clean pair of heels.*

show a clean pair of heels: 2

Mainly British When journalists are talking about a competitive situation in which one person or organization is clearly better than the rest, they sometimes say that person or organization **shows** the others **a clean pair of heels**. *Only one point stands: Japan has shown all the other rich countries a clean pair of heels.*

take to your heels

If you **take to** your **heels**, you run away. *He took to his heels and rushed out of the room.*

hell

all hell breaks loose

If you say that **all hell breaks loose**, you mean that there is a lot of fuss, arguing, or fighting. *In 'Jungle Fever', a happily-married black architect begins an affair with his Italian-American secretary, but all hell breaks loose when his wife finds out.*

come hell or high water

If you say that you will do something **come hell or high water**, you are emphasizing that you are determined to do it, in spite of the difficulties involved. *The chairman of the Senate Judiciary Committee, Senator Joseph Biden, says the all-male panel will have two female members this year, come hell or high water.*

hell for leather

If you say that someone is going **hell for leather**, you are emphasizing that they are moving or doing something very quickly, and often recklessly. *Once I decide to write a play, I have to go for it hell for leather.*

◆ This expression may originally have related to horse riding. 'Leather' would refer to a saddle.

hell freezes over

If you say that something will not happen until **hell freezes over**, you mean that you are certain that it will never happen. *'Tell them you'll get married when hell freezes over,' she says.*

hell hath no fury like a woman scorned

People say **'hell hath no fury like a woman scorned'** to suggest that women often react to something which hurts or upsets them by behaving very angrily and viciously. This expression is often used to refer to cases where a woman has an unfaithful partner and takes revenge. *Faithless* *husbands who doubt that hell hath no fury like a woman scorned should read Tolleck Winner's novel 'Love With Vengeance' and beware.*

☐ This expression is often exploited, especially by journalists, to make it appropriate to the subject which they are writing about. *Ian Woosnam, having decided to absent himself from next week's International Open competition, has discovered that hell hath no fury like a sponsor spurned.*

◆ This comes from William Congreve's 'The Mourning Bride' (1697): 'Heav'n has no rage, like love to hatred turn'd, Nor Hell a fury, like a woman scorn'd.'

play hell
play merry hell

If you say that someone **plays hell** or **plays merry hell**, you mean that they cause trouble by behaving badly or that they protest strongly or angrily about something. *She played merry hell and stormed out in a rage.*

play hell with something
play merry hell with something

If you say that one thing **plays hell with** another, you mean that the first thing has a bad effect on the second one or causes great confusion. In British English, you can also say that one thing **plays merry hell with** another. *Slugs play merry hell with emerging shoots; earwigs and woodlice gobble the leaves.*

the road to hell is paved with good intentions

You say **'the road to hell is paved with good intentions'** when you are pointing out to someone that it is not enough for them to make plans or promises, but they must also carry them out. Nouns such as 'path' are sometimes used instead of 'road'. *The path to hell is paved with good intentions, and there are many, many pots of vitamin tablets which have been started but never finished.*

there'll be hell to pay
there'll be merry hell to pay

You can say that **there'll be hell to pay** to warn someone that there will be serious trouble if a particular thing happens or if it does not happen. You can also say that **there'll be merry hell to pay**. *If I try to get through the kitchen with these, there'll be hell to pay. You know what she's like.*

to hell and back

If you say that someone has been **to hell and back**, you mean that they have had a terrible experience, although it is now over. *We have been to hell and back but the love of this little boy has kept us going.*

hen
rare as hen's teeth

If you say that something is as **rare as hen's teeth**, you are emphasizing that it is extremely rare. *Record companies are becoming as rare as hen's teeth, and by the end of the decade there probably won't be anybody left except the five international distributors.*

◆ Hens do not have teeth.

herd
ride herd on someone

American If someone **rides herd on** other people or their actions, they supervise them or watch them closely. *His departure would undermine state efforts to ride herd on the oil companies.*

◆ Originally, 'riding herd' involved patrolling on horseback around a herd of animals, in order to make sure none of them wandered away.

herring
a red herring

If you describe a piece of information, a suggestion, or an action as **a red herring**, you mean that it is irrelevant and, often deliberately, is taking people's attention away from the main subject, problem, or situation that they should be considering. *This is a total political red herring and an attempt to divert from the main issues in the campaign.*

◆ A red herring is a herring that has been soaked in salt water for several days, and then dried by smoke. Red herrings were sometimes used when training dogs to follow a scent. They were also sometimes used to distract dogs from the scent they were following during a hunt.

hide
haven't seen hide nor hair of someone

If you **haven't seen hide nor hair of** someone or something, you have not seen them, although you expected to. You can also say that you **haven't seen hair nor hide of** someone or something. *After nearly two weeks in Australia I had seen neither hair nor hide of a kangaroo.*

hiding
on a hiding to nothing

British If you say that someone is **on a hiding to nothing**, you mean that they have absolutely no chance of being successful at what they are trying to do. *A car manufacturer capable of making only 50,000 cars a year is on a hiding to nothing.*

high

high as a kite

If someone is as **high as a kite**, they feel very excited, or they are strongly affected by alcohol or drugs. *When I had finished the course I felt as high as a kite... I felt so strange on the steroid injections. I was as high as a kite some of the time.*

leave someone high and dry

If someone **leaves** you **high and dry**, they leave you in a difficult situation which you are unable to do anything about. *By introducing an element of competition, schools with better reputations will be flooded with applications while poorer schools will be left high and dry.*

♦ The image here is of a boat which is left on a beach after the tide has gone out.

ride high

If you say that someone or something **is riding high**, you mean that they are very popular or successful at the present time. *The elections have come at a time when Labour is riding high in the opinion polls.*

♦ The image here is of a horse rider who sits very straight in their saddle and seems very proud and confident.

search high and low for something

If you **search high and low for** something, you search for it very carefully and thoroughly, looking in every possible place that it could be. *I've hunted high and low for the photos, but I've moved since then and I can't find them.*

hill

over the hill

If you say that someone is **over the hill**, you mean that they are no longer young, and are too old to do a particular thing. *It's true some people regard you as probably over the hill at fifty.*

hilt

to the hilt

You use **to the hilt** to emphasize that someone does something to the greatest possible extent. *He'll be a good candidate. We'll back him up to the hilt.*

◆ The hilt of a sword or knife is its handle. The image here is of a knife or sword being pushed in all the way to the handle.

hip

joined at the hip

If you say that two people are **joined at the hip**, you mean that they are very close to each other emotionally and that they spend a great deal of time together. People often use this expression when they disapprove of this degree of closeness. *Though we often work together, we're not joined at the hip, so we see things differently.*

□ If you say that two problems or factors are **joined at the hip**, you mean that they are very closely linked and cannot be considered or resolved separately. *Trends in world trade and trends in the environment are supposed to be joined together at the hip.*

◆ The reference here is to Siamese twins, who are born with their bodies joined together.

shoot from the hip

If you say that someone **shoots from the hip**, you mean that they give their opinion or react to situations very quickly, without stopping to think them through properly. *She specifically declared that she did not shoot from the hip. She liked to think hard and long before taking decisions.*

◆ The image here is of a cowboy removing his gun from its holster and firing immediately, without raising it to take aim.

hit

hit and miss
hit or miss

If you describe something as **hit and miss** or **hit or miss**, you mean that it is done carelessly or without proper planning, so that it is equally likely to fail or succeed. *His studies did much to make wine making a science, not a hit and miss affair based on country and folk remedies and superstition.*

hit it off

If two people **hit it off** when they first meet, they find that they like each other or get on well together and have many things in common. *After their* *extended two hour talk yesterday, the two leaders actually seem to have hit it off.*

a hit list

If someone has **a hit list** of people or things, they are intending to take action concerning those people or things, for example by getting rid of them or refusing to deal with them. *The report said that none of the 31 pits on the hit-list should close until the consequences for employment had been fully assessed.*

◆ In some terrorist or criminal organizations, 'a hit list' is a list containing the names of important people who they intend to kill.

hit the sack
hit the hay

If someone **hits the sack** or **hits the hay**, they go to bed. *It was raining and we were tired, so we only half-unpacked the car and then hit the sack.*

◆ In the past, people sometimes used sacks and hay as bedding.

Hobson

Hobson's choice

Mainly British You can refer to a decision as **Hobson's choice** when it forces you to choose between two things which are both unsatisfactory, and so you cannot possibly be happy. *Now employers face a Hobson's choice. If they decide not to settle the initial discrimination claim and lose, they pay; if they settle, they're still open to years of litigation brought by white employees.*

◆ This expression may refer to a man called Thomas Hobson, who earned money by hiring out horses at the end of the 16th century. He had a particular system for using each horse in turn, so a customer was given no choice, even if there were many horses available.

hog

◆ A hog is a pig.

go hog wild

American If you **go hog wild**, you behave in an uncontrolled and excited way. *That doesn't mean you should go hog-wild and double the recipe's sugar content. Just keep the word 'moderation' in mind.*

◆ Hogs can sometimes become uncontrolled and aggressive.

go the whole hog
go whole hog

If someone **goes the whole hog**, they do something to the fullest extent possible. This expression is often used ironically to suggest that someone is being too extreme in their behaviour or actions. *Dixons sells a range of hi-fi speakers costing from £10.99 to £72.99. Or you can go the whole hog and buy a dedicated sound output system for £299.00.*

□ In American English, you can also say that someone **goes whole hog**. *The thing to do in life is to find out what gives you pleasure and go for it whole hog.*

◆ This expression may have its origin in butchers asking their customers which part of the pig they wished to buy, or whether they would 'go the whole hog' and buy the whole pig. Alternatively, 'hog' was a slang term for a ten cent piece in America, and also for an Irish shilling, so the expression may originally have meant 'spend the full amount'.

live high on the hog

Mainly American If someone **is living high on the hog**, they have a good life, with plenty of money. *He and Austen were living high on the hog in a flat with three servants.*

holds

no-holds-barred

You use **no-holds-barred** when describing a way of behaving when people act very forcefully or enthusiastically, without paying attention to any restraints, limits, or restrictions that may exist. *We are in a state of war. It is a war with no holds barred and we must prepare to resist.*

◆ This expression refers to a wrestling match in which many of the usual rules do not apply, and so competitors can hold their opponent in any way they like.

hole

burn a hole in your pocket

If money **is burning a hole in** your **pocket**, you are very eager to spend it as soon as possible, especially on something you do not really need but would like to have. *Money always tends to burn a hole in my pocket.*

a hole card

Mainly American **A hole card** is something that you keep secret or hidden until you are ready to use it to gain an advantage over other people. *The fact that I knew where she was and had in my possession a boxful of evidence were my only two remaining hole cards.*

◆ In five card 'stud' poker, the 'hole' card is the only card which is dealt to you face down so that the other players cannot see it.

hole-in-the-corner
hole-and-corner

British If you describe something as **hole-in-the-corner** or **hole-and-corner**, you disapprove of the fact that it is secretive and possibly dishonest. *I think we were treated in a rather hole-and-corner fashion.*

in the hole

American If a person or organization is **in the hole**, they owe money to someone else. *The Federal Housing Administration has just been discovered to be $4 billion in the hole.*

◆ The 'hole' referred to here may have been a slot which was cut in the surface of a poker table in a gambling house. The money which the house charged was placed in the slot, and fell into a locked drawer. Gamblers who owed money to the house were said to be 'in the hole'.

need something like a hole in the head

If you say that you **need** something or someone **like a hole in the head**, you are emphasizing that you do not want them at all, and that they would only add to the problems that you already have. *We need an interest rate rise like we need a hole in the head.*

hollow

beat someone hollow

British If you **beat** someone **hollow**, you defeat them completely. *Waterman was the first independent operator to take on the big boys at the pop game and beat them hollow.*

holy

the holy of holies

If you describe something as **the holy of holies**, you mean that people think it is the most special or important thing of its kind. This expression is sometimes used ironically, to suggest that you do not agree with them. *Last year, his work was performed for the first time at the Aldeburgh Festival, the holy of holies in the contemporary British music scene.*

◆ In a Jewish synagogue, the holy of holies is the inner room which only the chief rabbi may enter.

home

bring home the bacon: 1

The person in a family who **brings home the bacon** is the person who goes out to work and earns enough money for the family to live on. *The question 'Who brings up the baby and who brings home the bacon?' will, increasingly in coming years, be the most important of all political questions.*

bring home the bacon: 2

In sport, if someone **brings home the bacon**, they win or do very well. This expression is used mainly in journalism. *The fact is, Mansell continues to bring home the bacon.*

◆ In the past, large pieces of bacon or even whole pigs were sometimes given as prizes in competitions.

bring something home to someone

If you **bring** something such as a problem, danger, or situation **home to** someone, you make them fully aware of how serious or important it is. Verbs such as 'drive', 'press', and 'hammer' are often used instead of 'bring'. *This tragic death brings it home to people in the drinks trade just how dangerous alcohol can be.*

close to home

If you say that a remark is **close to home**, you mean that it makes people feel uncomfortable or upset because it is about a sensitive or very personal subject. *The spectacle touched too close to home for a man whose grandparents had died in the Holocaust.*

hit a home run

American If someone **hits a home run**, they do something that is very successful. *Bartlett Giamatti, Professor of English at Yale, hits a home run here with his memoir of encounters with W. H. Auden over many years.*

◆ In baseball, when a batter hits a home run, they hit the ball a very long way, so that they are able to run round all the bases and score a run before the other team gets the ball back.

hit home
strike home

If a situation or what someone says **hits home** or **strikes home**, people realize that it is real or true, even though it may be painful for them to accept it. *In many cases the reality of war doesn't hit home with reservists until they're actually called upon to fight.*

home and dry
home and hosed

Mainly British If you say that someone is **home and dry** in a contest or other activity, you mean that they have achieved victory or success, or that you are certain that they will achieve it. *There are still three weeks to polling day and the Labour candidate is not yet home and dry.*

☐ You can also say that someone is **home and hosed**. This form of the expression is used mainly in Australian English. *Queensland almost snatched a draw in the final 90 seconds when Meninga made a 60m sideline run. I thought he was home and hosed.*

◆ These expressions may refer to a long-distance runner who wins comfortably and has already washed by the time the others reach the finishing line.

the home stretch
the home straight

If you are in **the home stretch** or **the home straight** of a long or difficult activity, you are on the last part or stage of it. *As the campaign hits the home stretch, opinion polls show that the Labor Party and a conservative alliance, called the Liberal National Coalition, are running head and head.*

nothing to write home about
something to write home about

If you say that something is **nothing to write home about** or **not much to write home about**, you mean that it is not very interesting, exciting, or special. *Yes, there is cheese, bread and meat in Brighton market and the surrounding shops, but it's nothing to write home about.*

☐ If you say that a thing is **something to write home about**, you mean that it is interesting, exciting, or special. *And you're giving that poor man a new start in life. That's something to be proud of and, incidentally, something to write home about.*

honest

honest as the day is long

If you say that someone is as **honest as the day is long**, you are emphasizing that they are very honest. *This boy's hard-working, ambitious, smart, and honest as the day is long. They don't come any better* *than Russell here.*

hoof

on the hoof: 1

British If you say that someone does something **on the hoof**, you mean that they do it in response to things that happen, rather than as part of a carefully considered plan. *There is nothing more dangerous than policy-making on the hoof.*

on the hoof: 2

If someone does something **on the hoof**, they do it while they are doing something else, or without stopping to sit down. *Presumably, like everybody else, you learnt the job on the hoof.*

♦ To do something 'on the hoof' literally means to do it while on horseback without stopping to get off.

hook

by hook or by crook

If someone says they will do something **by hook or by crook**, they mean that they are determined to do it even if it is very difficult for them, or they have to use dishonest means. *If a man took Antonia's fancy, she would go out of her way to get him by hook or by crook.*

♦ The hook in this expression is a billhook, which is cutting tool with a hooked blade. A shepherd's crook is a long stick with a curve at the top. This expression may refer to a medieval law which allowed ordinary people to collect firewood from forests belonging to the King or a lord, so long as they took only dead wood which they could reach with crooks and billhooks.

hook, line, and sinker: 1

If you say that someone has swallowed something **hook, line, and sinker**, you are criticizing them for being fooled into believing something completely and being deceived by it. *Our president is one heck of a salesman, and people are just swallowing this thing hook, line, and sinker, without knowing what it's all about.*

hook, line, and sinker: 2

You use **hook, line, and sinker** to emphasize that someone does something very intensely, deeply, or fully. *I fell for her hook, line and sinker.*

♦ When fish are caught, they sometimes swallow part of the fishing line and the 'sinker' or weight, as well as the hook.

on your own hook

American If you do something **on** your **own hook**, you do it alone, without any help. *St. Mary's Hospital does not meet incoming flights with its own vehicle. Patients come on their own hook.*

◆ The reference here is to someone catching a fish using their own equipment and without help from others.

ring off the hook

American If your telephone **is ringing off the hook**, so many people are trying to call you that it is ringing all the time. *Since war broke out in the Middle East, the phones at donation centers have been ringing off the hook.*

◆ If you take a telephone off the hook, you take the receiver off the part that it normally rests on, so that the telephone will not ring.

sling your hook

British If someone tells you to **sling** your **hook**, they are telling you to go away. *I've always said that there's no point in keeping unsettled players at a football club. Spurs are entering a new era and if Ruddock doesn't want to be part of it then he should sling his hook.*

◆ The 'hook' in this expression may be a ship's anchor, which had to be taken up and tied up with ropes or chains, which were called a sling, before the ship could move on.

hooks

get your hooks into someone

If you say that someone or something **has got** their **hooks into** you, you mean that they are controlling or influencing you very strongly, often in a way that is not good for you. *But 8mm video faces problems and tough competition. For instance, the rival VHS format has really got its hooks into the American consumer.*

hoops

jump through hoops
go through the hoops

If someone makes you **jump through hoops** or **jump through the hoops** to obtain something that you want, they make you prove your ability and willingness by forcing you to do a lot of difficult things first. You can also say that they make you **go through the hoops**. *Eventually,* *if they jump through enough hoops, illegal workers can get work visas.*

◆ Circus animals are sometimes trained to jump through hoops which are hung or held above the ground and sometimes set on fire.

hoot

not give a hoot
not give two hoots
If you say that you **don't give a hoot** or **don't give two hoots** about something, you mean that you do not care about it at all. *I'm really disgusted with our politicians in Washington. They don't give two hoots about their constituents.*

hop

catch someone on the hop
British If someone **is caught on the hop**, they are unprepared for something that happens and so are unable to respond quickly or appropriately. *In both cases the West was caught on the hop when a brutal dictator decided that it was safe to use force to resolve a long-standing territorial dispute.*

a hop, skip, and a jump
a hop and a skip
If one thing is only **a hop, skip, and a jump** away from another, they are very close together or very closely linked. You can also say that one thing is only **a hop and a skip** away from another. *Wells, Maine, is just a hop and skip from George Bush's place in Kennebunkport.*

horn

blow your own horn
toot your own horn
American If you accuse someone of **blowing** their **own horn** or **tooting** their **own horn**, you are criticizing them for boasting about themselves. The British expression is **blow** your **own trumpet**. *Maybe I am a superstar right now, but I don't go around blowing my own horn; this is a game which kicks you right back in the face.*

◆ 'Horn' is an American word for trumpet. In the past, the arrival of important people in a place was announced by the playing of trumpets.

hornet

stir up a hornet's nest
If you say that someone **has stirred up a hornet's nest**, you mean that

they have done something which has caused a lot of controversy or has produced a situation which is extremely difficult to deal with. *I seem to have stirred up a hornet's nest. Three weeks ago I wrote a column about the teaching of Shakespeare in schools. Letters have poured in ever since.*

□ Sometimes people just talk about **a hornet's nest**. *Wasserman had no idea what a hornet's nest he was stepping into.*

◆ A hornet is a large wasp with a powerful sting.

horns

the horns of a dilemma

If you are on **the horns of a dilemma**, you have to choose between two or more alternatives, which seem to be equally good or equally bad. *I was often caught on the horns of a dilemma. Do I work late in the air-conditioned cool darkness of the office, or retreat to the bar for cold beer?*

◆ In logic, a dilemma is a situation where an argument leads to two choices which are both undesirable. In the Middle Ages, a dilemma was traditionally represented as an animal with two horns such as a bull.

lock horns

If you **lock horns** with someone, you argue or fight with them. *I remember a harrowing few days in the October of 1962 when Mr Khrushchev and President Kennedy locked horns over Russian missiles based in Cuba.*

◆ The reference here is to two male animals, such as deer, fighting over a female and getting their horns caught together or 'locked'.

pull in your horns
draw in your horns

If you **pull in** your **horns** or **draw in** your **horns**, you start behaving more cautiously than you did before, especially by spending less money. *Customers are drawing in their horns at a time of high interest rates, and delaying payment to suppliers.*

◆ When snails sense danger, they pull in their 'horns', which are the stalks that their eyes are on.

horse

back the wrong horse

If someone **backs the wrong horse**, they support the wrong person, for example the loser in a contest or election. *He had a wide following among ambitious younger employees, who now fear they have ruined their prospects* *by backing the wrong horse.*

a dark horse

If you describe someone as **a dark horse**, you mean that very little is known about them, although they may have recently had success or may be about to have success. *To many people, Robert Ayling is an unknown quantity, a dark horse who worked away behind the scenes at BA, only to be thrust into the limelight last February... William Randolph Hearst had briefly been a dark horse candidate for President in 1908.*

◆ This expression may refer to a horse which people do not know very much about, so that it is difficult to predict how well it will do in a race.

eat like a horse

If you say that someone **eats like a horse**, you mean that they eat a lot because they have a large appetite. *When Kelly is on medication, he eats like a horse and when he is off, he has almost no appetite at all.*

flog a dead horse
beat a dead horse

If you say that someone **is flogging a dead horse**, you mean that they are wasting their time trying to achieve something that cannot be done. This form of the expression is used in British English; in American English the form is **beat a dead horse**. *You're flogging a dead horse. You have some talented boys but they're playing like run-down machines.*

from the horse's mouth

If you get a piece of information **from the horse's mouth**, you get it directly from the person who knows best or knows most about it, and so you are sure it is true. *Most of the book is completely true; it comes from the horse's mouth.*

◆ This expression may refer to the fact that you can tell a horse's age by looking at its teeth. Alternatively, it may simply refer to a racing tip which is so reliable that it is as if the horse itself has told you how well it is going to perform.

get on your high horse
come down off your high horse

If you say that someone **is getting on** their **high horse**, you are showing disapproval of them for behaving as if they are superior to other people, and for refusing to accept any criticism of themselves. *When Kuwait was occupied, President Bush and Prime Minister John Major lost no time in getting on their high horses.*

☐ If someone **comes down off** their **high horse** or **gets down off** their

high horse, they stop acting in a superior way. *It is time for the intellectuals to get off their high horses and to really take the struggle into the ghettoes.*

◆ In the past, very large horses were a sign of high rank because they were owned and ridden only by knights.

a one-horse race

Mainly British If you say that a contest is **a one-horse race**, you mean that it is obvious even before it starts that one person or team is much better than the others and will win. *Marseilles are threatening to turn the French championship into a one-horse race.*

a one-horse town

If you describe a town as **a one-horse town**, you mean that it is very small, dull, and uninteresting. *I mean, would you want to live in a small one horse town for your whole life?*

a stalking horse: 1

If you describe something as **a stalking horse**, you mean that it is being used to obtain a temporary advantage so that someone can get what they really want at a later date. This expression is usually used to show disapproval. *The development will act as a stalking horse for further exploitation of the surrounding countryside.*

a stalking horse: 2

In politics, **a stalking horse** is someone who stands against the leader of a party to test the strength of any opposition to the leader. They then withdraw in favour of a stronger challenger, if it looks likely that the leader can be defeated. *These days, she is often touted as a stalking horse in a leadership contest if John Major is forced to quit... The notion of a stalking horse challenge at the autumn party conference seemed highly unlikely.*

◆ Stalking horses were horses that were used by hunters. They were trained to allow their rider to hide behind them, and so get closer to the birds they were hunting.

a Trojan horse

If you describe a policy or activity as **a Trojan horse**, you mean that it seems harmless, but is likely to damage or destroy something important. *Socialist politicians have used the Trojan horse of 'urgent need' to conceal their hidden ambitions for general income redistribution.*

◆ This refers to an ancient Greek story. The city of Troy was under siege from the Greeks. The Greeks built a large hollow wooden horse and left it secretly as a gift for the Trojans, who took it into the city. However, Greek soldiers were hiding inside the horse, and they were able to cause the destruction of the city.

you can lead a horse to water but you can't make him drink

If someone says **'you can lead a horse to water, but you can't make him drink'**, they mean that you can give someone the opportunity to do something, but you cannot force them to do it if they do not want to. This expression is often varied. *You were brought to Pontywen for training. However, as the old proverb says, you can bring a horse to the water but you can't make him drink... You can lead a boy to books, but can you make him read?*

horses

hold your horses

If you say to someone **'hold your horses'**, you are telling them to wait, slow down, or stop for a moment, often when you think that they are going to do something hasty. *Hold your horses a minute, will you, and just take another look at this badge.*

horses for courses

British If you say that something is a matter of **horses for courses**, you mean that different people are suitable for different things or kinds of situation, and this ought to be taken into account when making choices in particular cases. *Companies started practising horses for courses, hiring law firms for their specialities rather than sticking with long-term relationships.*

◆ Some horses are especially suited to particular kinds of races or conditions.

ride two horses at the same time

British If you say that someone **is riding two horses at the same time**, you are criticizing them for trying to follow two conflicting sets of ideas at the same time. *He is not doing his popular appeal much good by continuing to ride two horses at the same time.*

wild horses

You can use **wild horses** in expressions such as 'wild horses would not drag me to something' or 'wild horses would not make me do something' to emphasize that you will not do something even if other people try to force you to. *I would not confess. Wild horses wouldn't drag this secret out of me.*

hostage

a hostage to fortune

Mainly British If you are **a hostage to fortune**, you cannot control how a situation develops, and so you have to accept any bad things that happen. *Charles, then nearly 33, had already made himself a hostage to fortune by declaring that 30 was a suitable age to settle down.*

☐ If you say that you do not want to give any **hostages to fortune**, you mean that you do not want to say or do something which could cause problems for you in the future, because you will have no control over how the situation develops. *Despite persistent questioning, he gave no hostages to fortune in the form of a timetable.*

◆ This expression comes from an essay by Francis Bacon, 'Of Marriage and Single Life' (1625): 'He that hath wife and children hath given hostages to fortune.'

hot

blow hot and cold: 1
blow hot

If you say that someone **blows hot and cold** on something, you mean that their attitude to it keeps changing, so that sometimes they seem enthusiastic or interested, and sometimes they do not. This expression is often used to show disapproval. *The media, meanwhile, has blown hot and cold on the affair.*

☐ In British English, you can also say that someone **is blowing hot** to mean that they are enthusiastic about something or interested in it at the moment, but that you are sure their attitude will soon change. *He was capricious, indeed some would say treacherous, on the issue of mine closures, blowing hot one day in defence of the miners, and backing down a few days later.*

blow hot and cold: 2

If you say that someone **blows hot and cold**, you mean that sometimes their work or performance is good, and sometimes it is not. *They seem to have blown hot and cold in their early matches.*

hot as Hades

If you say that it is as **hot as Hades**, you are emphasizing that it is extremely hot. *The shafts were dug straight down, hundreds of feet into rock and blackness. It was always bone-cold at the top, and hot as Hades as you descended.*

◆ In Greek mythology, Hades is the place where the spirits of the dead live. However, this expression seems to use Hades as a euphemism for hell, as Hades is usually represented as a dark and gloomy place, rather than a fiery hot place.

too hot to handle

If you say that someone or something is **too hot to handle**, you mean that they are so dangerous, difficult, or extreme that people do not want to be involved with them. *Wherever he has been based, his host country has eventually found him too hot to handle.*

hot cakes

sell like hot cakes
sell like hotcakes

If you say that things **sell like hot cakes**, you mean that they are very popular and people buy large quantities of them in a short time. 'Hotcakes' is the usual form in American English, and it is also occasionally used in British English. *Their whisky was selling like hot cakes.*

◆ In American English, 'hotcakes' are pancakes, while in British English 'hot cakes' are cakes which have just been baked.

hots

have the hots for someone

If someone **has the hots for** you, they are very strongly attracted to you sexually. *But it's obvious Catherine has the hots for Curran too and soon the two are locked in each other's arms.*

hour

the eleventh hour

If something happens at **the eleventh hour**, it happens very late or at the last possible moment. *The concert, scheduled for last Saturday, was cancelled at the eleventh hour, after the star Peter Gabriel pulled out on Thursday.*

□ An **eleventh hour** decision or action is one that occurs at the last possible moment. *The company has sold off 31 social clubs to Mansfield Brewery in an eleventh hour deal.*

◆ This expression comes from the Bible, where Jesus uses it in the story of the labourers in the vineyard (Matthew 20:1–16). In Jesus's time the hours were counted from dawn until dusk, with the twelfth hour bringing darkness, and so the eleventh hour was the last hour before dark.

house

bring the house down

If a person or their performance **brings the house down**, the audience claps and cheers loudly for a long time because they liked the performance so much. *We had just one rehearsal and I was petrified but, as Lenny predicted, the sketch brought the house down.*

eat someone out of house and home

If you say that someone **is eating** you **out of house and home**, you are complaining that they eat so much food that it costs you a lot of money to feed them. *They eat everybody out of house and home but nobody minds because they provide such first-rate entertainment.*

get on like a house on fire

If two people **get on like a house on fire**, they quickly become close friends, for example because they have similar interests. *I went over and struck up a conversation, and we got on like a house on fire.*

a halfway house

British **A halfway house** is a compromise between two things, or a combination of two things. *A halfway house between the theatre and cinema is possible.*

a house of cards

If you say that a system, organization, or plan is like **a house of cards**, you mean that it is likely to fail or collapse. *This government could fall apart like a house of cards during the first policy discussion.*

not give someone house room

British You can say that you would **not give** someone or something **house room** when you strongly dislike or disapprove of them and you want to have nothing to do with them. *Conservatives should not give house room to those arguing we can trade a little more inflation for a little more growth.*

put your house in order

If you **put** your **house in order**, you make sure that all your affairs are arranged properly and there is nothing wrong with them. *The government is also trying to put its own house in order and trim its deficit by cracking down on tax evasion.*

houses

round the houses

British If you say that someone is going **round the houses**, you mean that they keep talking about unimportant things, rather than concentrating on what they are supposed to be discussing. *What certainly came into my notes at the last meeting is that although in many cases we talk round the houses, we get to the important issues as well.*

hue

a hue and cry

If there is **a hue and cry** about something, there is a loud protest about it or opposition to it. *There probably will be a hue and cry about my suggestion of more power to the police, but until the criminals realise someone will take them in hand, they will do exactly what they want.*

◆ Until the 19th century, 'hue and cry' was the legal name for the cries of someone who had been robbed and who was calling for others to help. It was an offence for anyone to refuse to join the chase, once they heard the cry. 'Hue' comes from the Old French 'huer', meaning 'to shout'.

hump

get the hump

British If you **get the hump**, you get annoyed or irritated by something. *Dad used to coach me in the back garden when I was about 10 or 11 – but he tried to drum too much into me and I used to get the hump with him.*

over the hump

If you are **over the hump** in an unpleasant or difficult situation, you are past the worst part of it. *I think we're basically over the hump in this instance. We've got an economy now that's likely to grow.*

I

i

dot the i's and cross the t's

If someone **dots the i's and crosses the t's**, they add the final minor details to a piece of work, plan, or arrangement. *Unless all the i's are dotted and the t's are crossed, a contract is not likely to be enforced.*

◆ In old-fashioned styles of handwriting, you write a word with one movement of your pen, and then go back and add the dot to any i's and the cross-strokes to any t's.

ice

break the ice

If you **break the ice** at a party or meeting, or in a new situation, you say or do something to make people feel relaxed and comfortable. *Break the ice with tea or coffee and get to know your client a little better.*

□ **An ice-breaker** is something that you say or do to break the ice. *This presentation was a good ice-breaker. A few laughs go a long way toward making a potential client comfortable.*

□ An **ice-breaking** comment or action is one that breaks the ice. *Graham's breakfast-time phone call to David was an ice-breaking exercise.*

cut no ice

If you say that something **cuts no ice** with you, you mean that you are not impressed or influenced by it. *Flying is dreadful. Statistics cut no ice with anyone scared of going up in the air in a plane.*

◆ This expression refers to ice-skating. In order for the skater to move easily, the blades must be sharp so that they cut into the ice.

put something on ice
on ice

If something such as a plan or project **is put on ice**, it is postponed. If a plan or project stays **on ice** or is **on ice**, no action is taken to put it into operation. *A further cut in base rates to 6% is now likely to stay on ice till next year.*

◆ This expression refers to the use of ice to preserve food and prevent it from decaying.

skate on thin ice

If you say that someone **is skating on thin ice**, you mean that they have got themselves into a difficult situation which may have serious or unpleasant consequences for them. *All through my career I had skated on thin ice on many assignments and somehow had, so far, got away with it.*

icing

the icing on the cake
the frosting on the cake

If you describe something as **the icing on the cake**, you mean that it is an extra good thing that happens and makes a situation or activity even better. In American English, you can also talk about **the frosting on the cake**. *To ride for one's country is the ultimate accolade. To be in a winning team is the icing on the cake.*

☐ You can also use these expressions to refer to something which is only a minor part of the main thing you are talking about. *Finance Minister Vaclav Klaus has dismissed environmental issues as the frosting on the cake.*

inch

give someone an inch and they'll take a mile

If you say **'give** someone **an inch and** they'll **take a mile'**, you mean that if you do a small favour for someone, they will become greedy and ask you to do bigger and bigger favours for them and make you regret doing the first favour. *Gorbachev meant to give the GDR socialism with a human face, not to get rid of the GDR altogether. But when the leaders gave an inch the people took a mile.*

☐ Sometimes people just say **'give them an inch'**, or use another word instead of 'mile'. *The problem with him was that if you gave him an inch he'd take six.*

ink

bleed red ink

If a company **is bleeding red ink**, it has severe financial problems. *Even large companies are bleeding red ink. But they are quickly closing plants and axing thousands of jobs to boost performance.*

◆ This expression comes from the practice in the past of using red ink to fill in entries on the debit side of a book of accounts.

innings

have a good innings: 1

    Mainly British, old-fashioned You can say that someone **has had a good innings** or **has had a long innings** when they have just stopped doing something, for example a job, that they have been doing successfully for a long time. *I had a good innings as a player and I hope it will continue in this new venture.*

have a good innings: 2

    Mainly British, old-fashioned When someone has just died or is about to die, if you say that they **have had a good innings**, you mean that they have lived for a long time and have had a fulfilling and rewarding life. *His mental attitude towards his Aids was stoical: he himself had had a good innings, he said, but he was smitten with pity for younger victims in desolate circumstances.*

    ♦ An innings is a period in a game of cricket during which a particular team or player is batting.

insult

add insult to injury

    If you **add insult to injury**, you make a bad situation worse by doing something that upsets or harms someone, after you have already done something bad to them. *The Council of State opposed the president's unconstitutional referenda and added insult to injury by leaking its hostile and secret comments to the press.*

iron

an iron fist
an iron hand
an iron fist in a velvet glove

    If you say that someone controls a situation with **an iron fist** or **an iron hand**, you mean that they do it with great force, often without regard to other people's welfare. *The Generals have ruled the nation with an iron fist for more than half of its independent existence.*

    □ You can talk about **an iron fist in a velvet glove** or **an iron hand in a velvet glove** when someone actually uses a lot of force although they give the appearance of being caring or gentle. *Milton has a way of handling people. He rules with the iron hand in the velvet glove... While the team is inherently sympathetic, the iron fist in the velvet glove approach is* *occasionally employed.*

strike while the iron is hot

If you say that someone should **strike while the iron is hot**, you mean that they should act immediately, while they have the best chance of succeeding at something. *This is the week to get plans off the ground. It's time to strike while the iron is hot.*

♦ A blacksmith can only bend or work iron when it is hot.

irons

have a lot of irons in the fire

If someone **has a lot of irons in the fire**, they are involved in several different activities or have several different plans at the same time, so that there is likely to be something which succeeds even if others fail. *Be realistic about your goals. Too many irons in the fire can sap your energy and prevent you from seeing which path to take in your career.*

♦ This expression may refer to flat irons, which were used in the past to iron clothes and had to be heated over a fire. Alternatively, it may refer to a blacksmith heating several pieces of iron in the fire at once.

ivory

an ivory tower

If you accuse someone of living in **an ivory tower**, you mean that their lifestyle or their work prevents them from experiencing the problems experienced by other ordinary people, and so they remain generally unaware of these problems. *They're all out of touch – they live up in a little ivory tower, and they don't see what's going on down here.*

♦ This is a translation of a French expression 'tour d'ivoire', which was used by the critic Saint-Beuve to describe the way in which the writer Alfred de Vigny isolated himself from the rest of society.

J

jack

a jack of all trades
a jack of all trades and a master of none

If you say that someone is **a jack of all trades**, or **a jack of all trades but master of none**, you mean that they can do a large number of different things but that they are perhaps not very good at doing any of them. *I believe in specialisation. Too many photographers are jacks of all trades and masters of none.*

jackpot

hit the jackpot: 1

If someone **hits the jackpot** with something, it is very successful and they earn a lot of money from it. *The National Theatre hit the jackpot with its first musical, Guys And Dolls.*

hit the jackpot: 2

You can say that someone **hits the jackpot** when they succeed in getting or finding something which they have been trying to get or find. *I went through all the people called Lasalles in the Sydney phone book until I hit the jackpot.*

◆ This expression was originally used in poker. A 'jackpot' was a sum of money which increased until someone could start the betting with a pair of jacks or higher.

jam

jam tomorrow
jam today

Mainly British If someone says **'jam tomorrow'**, they mean that people are being promised that they will have something in the future, although they cannot have it now. This expression is often used to suggest that people are in fact unlikely to receive what they have been promised. *There is also an element of 'jam tomorrow' about some of the chancellor's measures.*

☐ **Jam today** is used to refer to the idea that people can have or get something immediately, rather than having to wait. *Economists generally assume that most people value jam today more highly than the same quantity of jam tomorrow.*

◆ In 'Through the Looking Glass' (1872) by Lewis Carroll, the Red Queen says: 'The rule is jam tomorrow and jam yesterday, but never jam today'. As Alice points out, this means that nobody will ever get any jam.

Jell-O

like trying to nail Jell-O to the wall

American If you say that something is **like trying to nail Jell-O to the wall**, you are emphasizing that it is extremely difficult or impossible. **Jell-O** is a trademark. *He also complained that pinning down PCC's cost* *formula 'was like trying to nail Jell-O to the wall'.*

◆ This expression was first used by the American President Theodore Roosevelt in a letter to William Roscoe Thayer in 1915. He was describing the difficulty of negotiating with Colombia over the Panama Canal.

jewel

the jewel in someone's crown

If you describe something as **the jewel in** someone's **crown**, you consider it to be the best thing they have, or the achievement that they can be most proud of. *His achievement is astonishing and this book is the jewel in his crown.*

Johnny

Johnny-come-lately

You use **Johnny-come-lately** to refer to someone who becomes involved in an activity or organization after it has already started, when you think that they are less reliable or experienced than the people who have been involved since the beginning. *We advise members who want to rent cars to ensure that they are dealing with a reliable and long-established company – not the Johnny-come-lately firm that's just set up round the corner.*

◆ This name used to be given to new or inexperienced sailors in the American navy.

joker

the joker in the pack

Mainly British If you describe something or someone as **the joker in the pack**, you mean that they are different from the other things or people in a situation and do not seem to fit in, or may cause problems. *Franco Moschino is described as the joker in the pack of Italian fashion.*

◆ The joker in a pack of playing cards is the card which does not belong to any of the four suits.

Joneses

keep up with the Joneses

If you say that someone is trying to **keep up with the Joneses**, you mean that they are trying to have or do the same things as other people that they know, even if they do not really have enough money to do this, or are not really interested in these things. *Her mother, Louise, was very keen on keeping up with the Joneses, and through much of her teens Linda accepted what she now calls 'these false values'.*

◆ This expression comes from the title of a comic strip by Arthur Momand, which was first published in the New York 'Globe' in 1913.

jump

for the high jump

British If you say that someone is **for the high jump**, you mean that it is certain that they will be punished for something they have done wrong. *God help anyone who was sneaking a cup of tea when they shouldn't have been. They'll be for the high jump.*

◆ This expression may refer to criminals in the past being sentenced to death by hanging.

get a jump on someone

Mainly American If you **get a jump on** someone or something, or **get the jump on** them, you do something before they do and so gain an advantage over them. *This year, many stores did try to get a jump on the shopping season by holding promotional sales even before Thanksgiving.*

◆ This expression refers to a competitor in a running race leaving the starting blocks ahead of the other competitors.

jury

the jury is still out

If you say that **the jury is still out** on a particular subject, you mean that people have not yet formed an opinion about it or reached a decision. *Specialists haven't been able to make up their minds whether hair dye is safe or not. 'The jury is still out,' says Dr Venitt firmly. 'There are niggling doubts.'*

K

kangaroos

kangaroos in your top paddock

Mainly Australian If you say that someone has **kangaroos in** their **top paddock**, you mean that they have peculiar ideas or are crazy. 'Roos' can be used instead of 'kangaroos'. *A woman's a dangerous and unpredictable creature. A guy who pretends to understand the sheilas has got roos in his top paddock.*

keel

on an even keel

If someone or something is **on an even keel**, they are calm or are progressing steadily, especially during or after a period of troubles or difficulties. *She sees it as her role to keep the family on an even keel through its time of hardship.*

◆ The image here is of a ship moving along smoothly and steadily, because it is balanced and not leaning to either side.

keen

keen as mustard

Mainly British, old-fashioned You say that someone is **keen as mustard** to emphasize that they are very eager or alert. *I have an adult pupil who scored very low in assessments but is keen as mustard. He's made staggering progress and loves every minute of it.*

keeper

not your brother's keeper
not someone's keeper

You can say that you are **not** your **brother's keeper** to indicate that you do not accept responsibility for other people in any way. *Part of me wants to help him, but part of me realizes I can't be my brother's keeper.*

☐ If you are asked where someone is and you answer that you are **not** their **keeper**, you are saying in quite a rude way that you do not know where they are and you cannot be expected to know. *'I don't know where he is,' Hughes replied, 'I'm not his keeper.'*

◆ This expression comes from a story in the Bible. Cain has killed his brother, Abel, but tries to deny it. 'And the Lord said unto Cain, Where is Abel thy brother? And he said, I know not: Am I my brother's keeper?' (Genesis 4:9)

kettle

◆ 'Kettle' may come from 'kiddle'. Kiddles were baskets or nets which were laid in streams and rivers to catch fish. Alternatively, 'kettle' may refer to a fish kettle, which is a long narrow saucepan that is used for cooking fish.

a different kettle of fish
another kettle of fish

You can say that something is **a different kettle of fish** or **another kettle of fish** to emphasize that it is completely unlike another thing that you are mentioning. *Artistic integrity? Who needs it? Money? Now that's a completely different kettle of fish.*

a pretty kettle of fish
a fine kettle of fish

Old-fashioned If someone describes a situation as **a pretty kettle of fish** or **a fine kettle of fish**, they are being ironic and criticizing it because it is confused and unsatisfactory. *Well, this is a pretty kettle of fish, as Queen Mary said.*

kibosh

put the kibosh on something

If someone **puts the kibosh on** something, they prevent it from happening, continuing, or being successful. *The export boom has also put the kibosh, once and for all, on the old belief that the American economy is relatively self-sufficient.*

◆ The origin of this expression is uncertain, but some people think that 'kibosh' may come from Yiddish.

kick

kick ass
kick butt

If a person in authority **kicks ass**, they behave in an unpleasant and aggressive way towards people, giving them strict orders to carry out, and punishing them if they refuse. You can also say that they **kick butt**. Many people find these expressions offensive. *A whole society is based upon the premise that the man or woman with the power and the money can kick ass whenever or wherever he or she likes.*

kick-off

for a kick-off

You use **for a kick-off** to indicate that you are mentioning just one of a number of things, points, or reasons which you could list or mention if you wanted to. *Is it not in fact the opinion of the public that most dentists earn far too much for a kick-off?*

◆ The kick-off is the beginning of a football match.

kid

treat someone with kid gloves
handle someone with kid gloves

If you **treat** someone **with kid gloves** or **handle** them **with kid gloves**, you treat them very carefully, for example because they are very important or because they are easily upset. People sometimes use this expression when they want to suggest that they do not think this kind of treatment is right or necessary. *To a large degree Mr Sarbutts was treated as a VIP. He was very much our guest at the police station, which I was not too happy about, and everybody was treating him with kid gloves... I'm not suggesting that you all begin handling Bessie with kid gloves.*

◆ Kid is very soft leather.

Kilkenny

fight like Kilkenny cats

British, old-fashioned If you say that people **fight like Kilkenny cats**, you mean that they fight or disagree very violently and destructively. *For six years Mr Wilder and Mr Robb have been fighting like Kilkenny cats.*

◆ This expression comes from the story of two cats in the Irish town of Kilkenny, which are said to have fought each other until only their tails were left.

killing

make a killing

If someone **makes a killing**, they make a large profit very quickly and easily. *The boss of Britain's top pizza concern made a killing on the market yesterday by selling off a parcel of his shares.*

kingdom

blow someone to kingdom come

To **blow** someone or something **to kingdom come** means to destroy them, especially in a very violent way. *There was tremendous damage in these industrial towns down to the South – homes flattened, trailers blown to kingdom come.*

♦ This comes from the line 'Thy kingdom come' in the Lord's Prayer in the Bible. (Matthew 6:10)

kiss

kiss-and-tell

If someone who has had a love affair with a famous person tells the story of their affair in public, for example in a newspaper or book, you can refer to what they say as a **kiss-and-tell** story. *On many occasions we discussed selling details of kiss-and-tell stories.*

☐ If someone tells their story in this way, you can say that they **kiss and tell**. You can also refer to their behaviour as **kissing and telling**. *In no circumstances will I kiss and tell... The girl he picked was a publicity-seeking actress who kissed and told her friends, who told the papers every sordid detail.*

the kiss of death

If you say that a particular event is **the kiss of death** for something, you mean that it is certain to cause that thing to fail or be ruined. *The conventional view of timber extraction is that it is the kiss of death for a rainforest.*

♦ This expression refers to the Bible story of how Judas betrayed Jesus by kissing him. This identified Jesus to the Romans, and led to his arrest and crucifixion.

kite

fly a kite

Mainly British If you say that someone **is flying a kite**, you mean that they are suggesting ideas or possibilities in order to see how people react to them before deciding whether or not to put them into practice. This expression is often used to suggest that the ideas that are being put forward are stupid or unrealistic. *The committee has paid a good deal of attention to what might be politically possible. It is consciously flying a kite.*

☐ You can also talk about **kite-flying**. *Recent kite-flying exercises outlined in your paper concerning health service cuts should not deflect, as they are intended to, the attention of the electorate from the underlying problems facing the Government.*

kittens

have kittens

Mainly British If someone **has kittens**, they are extremely worried or upset by something. *The boss will have kittens if I don't get that dress back inside the hour.*

knee

knee-high to a grasshopper

If you say that you have done something since you were **knee-high to a grasshopper**, you mean that you have done it since you were a very young child. *I've lived here since I was knee-high to a grasshopper.*

□ People sometimes change 'grasshopper' to a word or expression that is relevant to the subject they are talking about. *She had met Irving Berlin, Rodgers and Hammerstein and the Gershwins when only knee-high to a piano stool.*

knell

sound the death knell

If you say that something **sounds the death knell** for an activity or organization, you mean that it is likely to cause the activity or organization to end or fail. *The announcement that the mine would close in March with the loss of more than 980 jobs sounded the death knell for the village.*

♦ A death knell is the ringing of a church bell at a funeral or to announce someone's death.

knickers

get your knickers in a twist

British If you say that someone **gets** their **knickers in a twist**, you are emphasizing that they become extremely upset or worried about something. *The Co-op has its knickers in a twist about Sunday trading.*

□ People sometimes change **knickers** to another word or expression which refers to underpants, or to another word or expression which has some relevance to the person or thing they are talking about. *The government got its Y-fronts in a fine old twist over the Maastricht treaty.*

knife

like a hot knife through butter
like a knife through butter

If you manage to overcome a difficulty quickly and without any problems, you can say that you cut through it **like a hot knife through**

butter or **like a knife through butter**. 'Like a knife through butter' is
used only in British English. *They will be cutting through the competition
like a hot knife through butter... Think about the women who have gone
through life like a knife through butter, slicing through every kind of setback
and discouragement.*

on a knife-edge
walk a knife-edge

Mainly British If someone or something is **on a knife-edge** or **is
walking a knife-edge**, they are in a situation in which nobody knows
what is going to happen next. *With recovery poised on a knife edge the
country needs a leader with vision and stature... She walks an emotional
knife-edge.*

put the knife in

If someone **puts the knife in**, they deliberately do or say things which
will upset another person or cause problems for them. *It is also an attempt
to make those who have put the knife in look bad before the world.*

twist the knife

If someone **twists the knife**, they deliberately do or say things which
make a situation even worse for someone who is already upset or
experiencing problems. *Her daughter manages to twist the knife still
further by claiming Nancy never loved her.*

knight

a knight in shining armour

If a man is kind and brave, and rescues you from a difficult situation,
you can describe him as **a knight in shining armour**. *I just felt dizzy and
then I collapsed. The next thing I woke up in intensive care. I am very, very
grateful to Tom and I always will be – he really was my knight in shining
armour.*

◆ 'Armour' is spelled 'armor' in American English.

knitting

stick to your knitting

If someone, especially a company or organization, **sticks to** their
knitting, they continue to do something that they are experienced at and
do not try to do something different about which they know very little. *It
failed because we did not understand the plumbing business, and it taught
us a lesson about sticking to our knitting!*

knives

the knives are out

Mainly British If you say that **the knives are out** for you, you mean that other people are feeling very angry or resentful towards you, and are trying to cause problems for you. *The knives are out for me at the moment.*

knot

a Gordian knot
cut the Gordian knot

If you describe a situation or problem as **a Gordian knot**, you mean that it is very complicated and difficult to resolve. If someone succeeds in resolving it, you can say that they **cut the Gordian knot**. *The federal deficit has become the Gordian knot of Washington.*

◆ According to an ancient legend, Gordius, the king of Phrygia, tied a knot that nobody could untie. It was said that if anyone untied it, they would become the next ruler of Asia. When Alexander the Great heard this, he solved the problem by cutting through the knot with a sword.

tie the knot

If two people **tie the knot**, they get married. *The couple tied the knot last year after a 13-year romance.*

◆ Tying knots in items of clothing or ribbons worn by the bride and groom is a traditional feature of many wedding ceremonies, symbolizing their unity.

knots

tie someone in knots: 1

In a discussion or argument, if someone **ties** you **in knots**, they confuse you by using clever arguments, so that you cannot argue or think clearly any longer. *He could tie her in knots in an argument and never once missed an opportunity to prove his intellectual superiority.*

tie yourself in knots: 2

If you **tie** yourself **in knots**, you make yourself confused or anxious, and so you are not able to think clearly about things. *The week after Jordan's appointment the New York Times editorial page tied itself in knots trying to find the correct tone with which to treat him.*

know

know something inside out
know something inside and out

If you **know** something or someone **inside out** or **know** them **inside and out**, you know them extremely well. *I used to think I knew my daughter inside out, and I still find it hard to understand what she has done to me... He knows the house inside and out, you know, having stayed there so often when Dolph's aunt and uncle were alive.*

knuckle

near the knuckle

British If you say that something someone says or writes is **near the knuckle**, you mean that it is close to the limits of what people find acceptable, for example because it is sexually explicit or offensive to particular groups. *There are important people who fear the public will be outraged. This kind of material is very near the knuckle.*

knuckles

rap someone on the knuckles

If someone in authority **raps** you **on the knuckles**, they criticize you or blame you for doing something they consider to be wrong. *I was rapped on the knuckles for interfering in things that were not my concern.*

◆ In the past, teachers sometimes punished pupils who behaved badly by hitting them on the knuckles with a ruler or stick.

L

labour (*American* labor)

a labour of love

A **labour of love** is a job or task that you do for pleasure or out of duty without expecting a large reward or payment for it. Often other people may think that the job or task is not worth doing or is unpleasant. *They concentrated on restoring outbuildings such as the Victorian greenhouse, an expensive labour of love.*

lady

it isn't over until the fat lady sings

If you say to someone, for example someone who is losing a contest, **'it isn't over until the fat lady sings'**, you are encouraging them not to give up hope because nothing is certain and there is still time for the situation to change. *The catastrophes are coming, but they're not upon us yet. The game, as they say, isn't over until the fat lady sings, and she hasn't started singing yet.*

lam

on the lam

Mainly American If someone is **on the lam**, they are trying to escape or hide from someone, for example the police or an enemy. *A Rhode Island banker accused of stealing millions has turned himself in after months on the lam.*

◆ 'Lam' is an American slang word meaning to run away.

lambs

like lambs to the slaughter
like sheep to the slaughter

If you say that people go somewhere **like lambs to the slaughter** or **like sheep to the slaughter**, you mean that they behave quietly and obediently without resisting because they have not realized that it will be dangerous or unpleasant, or because they realize that they are powerless. *The record companies have an easy life. We grovel and follow their every word like lambs to the slaughter.*

land

the lay of the land
the lie of the land

If you get **the lay of the land** or get **the lie of the land**, you learn or find out the details of a situation or problem. *I'm not sure what's going to happen. That's why I'm coming in early. I want to get the lay of the land.*

land-office

do a land-office business

Old-fashioned, American If you say that a business **is doing a land-office business**, you mean that they are very successful. *The Paradiso, one of the capital's newest and most luxurious clubs, was doing a land-office business.*

◆ In the United States before the Civil War, the government opened up land offices which sold rights to pieces of land in the West. So many people wanted to buy land to settle on that there were often long queues outside the offices before they opened in the morning.

lane

the fast lane
the slow lane

If you say that someone lives their life in **the fast lane**, you mean that they live in a way which seems full of activity and excitement but which often involves a lot of pressure as well. *Tired of life in the fast lane, Jack, a fifty-ish American businessman, decides to give it all up to fulfil a dream of becoming a painter... He had to quit, and not only did he have to quit, but he had to get away from this fast-lane, high-society lifestyle.*

□ You can say that someone lives their life in **the slow lane** when their life is quiet and boring without any exciting incidents. *For your own sake, pull over and enjoy traveling in the slow lane of life for a while.*

lap

fall into your lap
drop into your lap

If something good happens to you without any effort on your part, you can say that it **falls into** your **lap** or **drops into** your **lap**. *Reid couldn't believe that such good fortune could fall into his lap... It would not be safe to assume that victory will drop into our lap at the next election.*

in the lap of luxury

If you say that someone lives **in the lap of luxury**, you mean that they live in conditions of great comfort and wealth. *We don't live in the lap of luxury, but we're comfortable.*

in the lap of the gods

If you say that something is **in the lap of the gods**, you mean that it will be decided or affected by luck or chance, rather than anything you can do. *Once they had repaired my lung they had to stop the operation. The liver is self-healing anyway, so at that stage, my life was in the lap of the gods.*

land in your lap
be thrown into your lap

If you are forced to deal with a problem which is not really your responsibility, you can say that it **has landed in** your **lap** or **has been thrown into** your **lap**. *These problems have landed in the lap of Donald Jackson, an unassuming manager with little international experience.*

large

large as life
big as life

When you want to say that you have found someone in a place, especially a place where they are not supposed to be, you can say that you found them there **large as life**. In American English, you can also say that you found them there **big as life**. You often use these expressions to suggest that the person should have been embarrassed at being found there. *I called on him one Friday night on some pretext or other and there they all were, large as life.*

larger

larger than life
bigger than life

If you describe someone as **larger than life**, you mean that they seem more interesting or exciting than other people, for example because they are very talented, or because they behave in an unusual or interesting way. In American English, you can also describe them as **bigger than life**. *John Huston was a larger-than-life character, whose temperament was as dramatic as any of the fictional figures in his own films.*

lark

up with the lark

Old-fashioned, mainly British If someone is **up with the lark**, they are up very early in the morning. *Most bakers are up with the lark, but Neville Wilkins is in action hours before the rest.*

last

stick to your last
let the cobbler stick to his last

Fairly old-fashioned If you advise someone to **stick to** their **last**, you mean that they should continue doing what they know about and not try to do new things, at which they are likely to fail. This expression comes from the proverb **let the cobbler stick to his last**. *Looking back, I should have stuck to my last and gone on to get a research job in one of the studios... I was afraid they'd think, 'Why can't the cobbler stick to his last?'*

◆ A last is a foot-shaped object which a cobbler uses as a model or mould to make shoes the right shape and size.

lather

in a lather

If someone gets **in a lather** or works themselves **into a lather**, they become very agitated about something. *The truth of the matter is that you have spent the past six months worrying and working yourself up into a lather over situations which are really none of your business.*

◆ When horses get very hot, the sweat on their coats sometimes forms a foamy substance called 'lather'.

laugh

have the last laugh

If you **have the last laugh**, you make your critics or opponents look foolish or wrong, by becoming successful when they said that you would fail. *Singer Des O'Connor is expecting to have the last laugh on his critics by soaring to the top of the Christmas hit parade.*

laundry

a laundry list

Mainly American If you have a large number or long list of things, you can say that you have **a laundry list** of them. *The president then went through a laundry list of proposals, some old, some new, which make up his agenda for American renewal.*

laurels

◆ In ancient Greece, the laurel or bay tree was associated with the god Apollo. The winning competitors in the Pythian games, which were held in honour of Apollo, were given crowns or wreaths of laurel.

look to your laurels

If you tell someone to **look to** their **laurels**, you are telling them to work hard or think seriously about what they are doing, in order to make sure that they continue to be successful and do not start to fail. *The City of London maintains a dominant role, but it must now look to its laurels.*

not rest on your laurels

If you say that someone **is not resting on** their **laurels**, you mean that they do not rely on their previous successes and that they carry on working hard to make sure that they have continued success. *The trouble with all successful restaurants, however, is the tendency to rest on their laurels and stagnate.*

law

the law of the jungle

You use **the law of the jungle** to describe a situation where the normal rules or codes of civilized life do not exist, and so, for example, strength, power, and aggressiveness have more effect than moral codes and legal rights. *The streets are subject to the law of the jungle and policing has been entrusted to private law enforcement agencies.*

a law unto yourself

If you say that a person or organization is **a law unto** themselves, you mean that they behave in an independent way, ignoring laws, rules, or conventional ways of doing things. *When he goes about his work, he does it well but in an unconventional way. He is truly a law unto himself.*

lay down the law

If you say that a person in authority **lays down the law**, you mean that they tell people very forcefully and firmly what to do. *The Prime Minister laid down the law and said he would accept no weakening of the bill.*

lead

go down like a lead balloon
a lead balloon

If you say that something **went down like a lead balloon**, you mean that it was completely unsuccessful and people did not like it at all. This form of the expression is used in British English; the usual American expression is **go over like a lead balloon**. *A senior source said the memo had gone down like a lead balloon.*

☐ You can refer to something that is unsuccessful or unpopular as **a lead balloon**. *Truman knew that this cause was a lead balloon at the UN.*

◆ Lead is a very heavy metal.

put lead in your pencil
have lead in your pencil

Old-fashioned, British If someone says that something **will put lead in** a man's **pencil**, they are suggesting humorously that it will improve his sexual ability. If they say that he **has lead in** his **pencil**, they are praising his sexual ability. *Back then, he'd been blessed with amazing stamina and a lot of lead in his pencil.*

◆ The lead in a pencil is the part in the centre which makes a mark on paper.

swing the lead

British If you accuse someone of **swinging the lead**, you are accusing them of pretending to be ill and not doing something they should be doing, such as going to work. *There is no question of taking money away from those who are genuinely sick. It is a question of getting the right benefits to the right people, and we want to stop anyone swinging the lead.*

◆ In the past, when a ship was in shallow water, one of the sailors would drop a piece of lead on a string, called a plumbline, over the side of the ship to find out how deep the water was. Sometimes sailors would just swing the plumbline, because they were too lazy to do the work properly. 'Plumb the depths' is also based on this practice.

leaf

◆ The 'leaf' in these expressions is a page of a book.

take a leaf out of someone's book

If you **take a leaf out of** someone's **book**, you copy them and behave or do something in the same way as them, usually because they were successful when they acted in that way. *If he wants a better rapport with the British public, it's high time he took a leaf out of Frank Bruno's book and started doing the media things – chat and game shows, even pantomimes.*

turn over a new leaf

If someone **has turned over a new leaf**, they have started to behave in a better or more acceptable way than previously. Compare **turn the page**; see **page**. *While Emilio has turned over a new leaf, his 31-year-old brother Charlie can still be spotted in the bars along Sunset Strip.*

lease

a new lease of life
a new lease on life

If someone or something is given **a new lease of life** or **a new lease on life**, something makes them successful once again or improves their condition. 'A new lease of life' is used in British English and 'a new lease on life' is used in American English. *The old oak table which is used for family breakfasts was another bargain, picked up for just £4 and subsequently given a new lease of life by Kim's mother… After a career as a comedian, he found a new lease of life as an actor.*

leash

◆ A 'leash' is a long thin piece of leather or chain, which you attach to a dog's collar so that you can keep the dog under control.

on a short leash
on a tight leash
a longer leash

If someone is kept **on a short leash** or **on a tight leash**, another person controls them carefully and only allows them a small amount of freedom to do what they want. *The rightwing leadership strove to impress the country with its calm reasonableness and kept its troops on a tight leash.*

□ If someone is given **a longer leash**, another person allows them more freedom to do what they want. *At the beginning of the 1992 campaign, Dan*

Quayle was given a longer leash than ever before.

strain at the leash

If you say that someone **is straining at the leash**, you are emphasizing that they are very eager to do things. *Most Labour delegates at Blackpool this week are straining at the leash, raring to go.*

least

least said, soonest mended

Old-fashioned, British If someone says **'least said, soonest mended'**, they mean that it is a good idea to say very little, because you might upset someone or make a situation worse if you say too much. *'Say nothing. It's the only thing they can't hold against you.' 'Least said, soonest mended is what I always say,' nodded another. 'Especially in court.'*

left

left, right, and centre
left and right

You use **left, right, and centre** or **left and right** to emphasize that something is happening or being done a great deal. 'Left, right, and centre' is used in British English and 'left and right' is used in American English. *They're all expecting the state to pay out money left right and centre... The Postal Service has been losing customers left and right to the alternative mail facilities.*

leg

break a leg

People say **'break a leg'** to a performer who is about to go on stage as a way of wishing them good luck. *Jason sent Phillip a fax from the airport before Monday's show, with the greeting: 'Break a leg and enjoy yourself.'*

◆ There are many superstitions associated with the theatre. For example, many performers consider that it is unlucky to say 'good luck' directly to anyone. Instead, they pretend to wish them bad luck.

give someone a leg up

If you **are given a leg up** or **get a leg up**, someone helps you to achieve something and become successful, especially by giving you an advantage that other people do not have. *Two highly-favoured ministers, Peter Lloyd and Brian Mawhinney, get a leg up the political ladder with their appointment as Privy Counsellors.*

◆ To give a rider a leg up means to help them get on to the horse.

not have a leg to stand on

If you say that someone **does not have a leg to stand on**, you are emphasizing that they are in a very weak position, for example because they are unable to prove a claim or statement they have made. *It's my word against his. I haven't got a leg to stand on. I had no witnesses.*

pull someone's leg

If you **pull** someone's **leg**, you tease them about something, for example by telling them something which is not true. *Is he serious or just pulling our legs?*

☐ You can refer to a joke like this as **a leg-pull**. *I never know what to say about this kind of painting anyway, still less how to explain its virtues to those who consider it a leg-pull.*

◆ There are two possible explanations for this expression, although there is no proof for either. One suggestion is that in the past, when someone was being hanged, their friends or family sometimes pulled their legs hard so that they died more quickly and suffered less. Alternatively, the expression may refer to thieves tripping people up before they robbed them.

talk the hind leg off a donkey

British If you say that someone can **talk the hind leg off a donkey**, you are emphasizing that they are very talkative. *He could talk the hind leg off a donkey. It took real perseverance to get through to him on the telephone.*

legs

have legs

Mainly American If you say that an idea, plan, or story **has legs**, you consider that it is likely to work or be true. *Mr Blucher was confident that his concept had legs, so he persisted and pressed Mr Cooper for a meeting.*

on your last legs

If you say that something or someone is **on** their **last legs**, you mean that they are no longer as useful, successful, or strong as they were and are about to fail altogether. *By the mid-1980s, the copper industry in the US was on its last legs.*

leopard

a leopard does not change its spots

Mainly British If you say that **a leopard does not change its spots**, you mean that it is not possible for someone bad or unpleasant to change and become good or pleasant. *It only goes to show how this racist leopard has in no way changed his spots.*

♦ A form of this proverb is used in the Bible, by the prophet Jeremiah, to say that wicked people never change: 'Can the Ethiopian change his skin, or the leopard his spots? Then may ye also do good, that are accustomed to do evil.' (Jeremiah 13:23)

letter

a dead letter

If you say that a law or agreement is **a dead letter**, you mean that people do not pay any attention to it, although it still exists. *In this conflict, international humanitarian law is a dead letter. Unacceptable practices are going on.*

♦ A dead letter is a letter that the post office is unable either to deliver or to return to the sender, because it does not have the right addresses.

the letter of the law

If you say that someone keeps to **the letter of the law**, you mean that they act according to what is actually written in the law, rather than according to the moral principles on which it is based. You usually use this expression to show disapproval. *Michael Brower says such transactions violate the spirit, if not the letter, of the law.*

to the letter

If you follow instructions, rules, or advice **to the letter**, you carry them out exactly in every detail. *Even if that international agreement is followed to the letter, the ozone layer won't recover fully until the year 2060.*

level

on the level

Someone who is **on the level** is honest and truthful. Something that is

on the level is true or legal. *Wait a minute, is this guy on the level or not?... I can offer you something better than this, Trish. And all on the level.*

licence (*American* license)

a licence to print money
Mainly British If you describe a commercial activity as **a licence to print money**, you disapprove of the fact that it allows people to get a lot of money with little effort or responsibility. *Under this Government the privatised utilities have become a licence to print money at the expense of the consumer.*

lid

keep the lid on something
put the lid on something
To **keep the lid on** or **put the lid on** a particular situation or problem means to keep its true nature hidden, or to control it and stop it becoming worse. *But I understand that Murray was desperately trying to keep the lid on a potential scandal.*

put the tin lid on something
Old-fashioned, British You say that something **puts the tin lid** on a bad situation when it is a final unpleasant event in a series. *Next day, to put the tin lid on things, a hospital appointment letter for Jane was forwarded from the clinic.*

take the lid off
To **take the lid off** a difficult or dangerous situation or problem means to reveal its true nature which has previously been hidden. You can replace 'take' with 'blow' or 'lift'. *'The Knowledge' is a new documentary series blowing the lid off music business scandals.*

☐ You can also say that a place or situation is seen **with the lid off** when its true nature or problems are revealed. *Morag Karius is a British cook who spent 18 years working in the kitchens of the rich and famous. What she saw was Hollywood with the lid off – a side the movie-goer never sees.*

lie

a white lie
If you tell **a white lie**, you say something which is untrue, often in order

to protect someone or to avoid hurting someone's feelings. *The issue here for me was whether doctors are justified in telling these little white lies in order to benefit the patient.*

life

get a life

You tell someone to **get a life** to express scorn, criticism, or ridicule of them, for example because they never do anything interesting, or because they are being unrealistic and stupid, or because you want them to go away. *This is silly, you've pursued this much too long. Get a life, Joan.*

the life and soul of the party
the life of the party

If you refer to someone as **the life and soul of the party**, you mean that they are very lively and entertaining on social occasions, and are good at mixing with people. This form of the expression is used in British English; in American English, the form is **the life of the party**. *She was having a very enjoyable time and was clearly the life and soul of the party.*

life is a bowl of cherries

If someone says **'life is a bowl of cherries'**, they are saying that they think life is full of pleasure and enjoyment. This expression is often used negatively to comment on an unpleasant or difficult situation. *'He had an impish sense of fun and so much zest,' says one admirer. 'To him, life was a bowl of cherries.'*

live the life of Riley

If you say that someone **is living the life of Riley**, you mean that they are having a very enjoyable time because they have no worries about money or work. This expression is sometimes used to show disapproval or envy. *He was living the life of Riley, enjoying holidays in Italy, weekend breaks in mid-Wales and trips to the theatre, while we had barely enough to eat.*

♦ 'Riley' may refer to a character from various 19th century songs.

light

give the green light

If a plan or action **is given the green light**, someone in authority says that it can be carried out. *Despite local planning opposition he has finally* *been given the green light to develop a terrace of 11 derelict houses he owns in South Kensington.*

in the cold light of day

If you think about a problem, feeling, or event **in the cold light of day**, you think about it some time later and in a calmer or more practical way than was possible at the time it happened. Nouns such as 'dawn' and 'morning' are sometimes used instead of 'day'. *He has to sit down in the cold light of day and analyse what needs to be done to prevent the club from being relegated.*

a leading light

Mainly British If you say that someone is **a leading light** of an organization or campaign, you mean that they are considered to be one of the most important, active, and successful people in it. *He is a leading light in the just launched campaign to rid football of racism.*

♦ A leading light was a light which was placed at the entrance to a harbour or shallow channel of water, as a guide for ships.

light as a feather

You can say that someone or something is as **light as a feather** to emphasize that they weigh very little. *'Put me down,' I said. 'I'm too heavy.' 'Light as a feather,' he retorted, ignoring my request.*

the light at the end of the tunnel

If you refer to **the light at the end of the tunnel**, you are referring to something which gives you hope about the future and for the end of a difficult or unpleasant situation. *People feel hopeless. They don't see any light at the end of the tunnel.*

out like a light

If someone is **out like a light**, they are very deeply asleep. If someone goes **out like a light**, they fall asleep very quickly. *Dad gently closed the door again. 'She's out like a light,' I heard him whisper to my anxious mother.*

see the light

If someone **sees the light**, they come to understand or agree with something, especially after a long period when they have not understood or agreed with it. This expression is sometimes used about people who suddenly start believing in God. *'People these days realise that they don't have to put up with discrimination,' says Jill Chesworth. But male bosses* *have been slow to see the light.*

lightning

lightning does not strike twice

You say that **lightning does not strike twice** when you want to say that someone who has been exceptionally lucky or unlucky is unlikely to have the same good or bad luck again. You can also say that **lightning strikes twice** or that **lightning strikes again** when someone actually does have the same good or bad luck again. *Observers reckon he will be very lucky to repeat the performance. Lightning rarely strikes in the same place twice, particularly in big business... Then, several years later, lightning struck again. Her other son Stephen died suddenly at the age of 13.*

lights

the lights are on but nobody is at home

If you say of someone that **the lights are on but nobody is at home**, you think that although they seem to be normal or satisfactory, they are in fact very stupid or useless. *According to Mark Harrington, many projects are insufficiently co-ordinated or thought through: 'You get the feeling that the lights are on but no one's at home.'*

lily

gild the lily

If you say that someone **is gilding the lily**, you mean that they are trying to improve something which is already very good, and so what they are doing is unnecessary. *Here in Europe I'm gilding the lily. There they really need advice.*

◆ This expression may be based on lines in Shakespeare's 'King John' (1595): 'To gild refined gold, to paint the lily... Is wasteful and ridiculous excess.' (Act 4, Scene 2)

limb

out on a limb

If you go **out on a limb**, you do something risky or extreme, which puts you in a position of weakness. If you are left **out on a limb**, you are left in a position of weakness without any help or support. *No company wants to be the first to put its rates up. The companies who have tried have found themselves out on a limb.*

◆ In this expression, a 'limb' is a branch of a tree. The image here is of someone who climbs out along a limb, away from the main trunk.

line

the bottom line

In a discussion or argument, if you describe one particular point as **the bottom line**, you mean that it is the most important and fundamental part of what you are discussing. *The bottom line is that the great majority of our kids are physically unfit... This is a cracking good story, and that is the bottom-line criterion for any novel.*

◆ This expression refers to the last line in a set of accounts, which states how much money has been made.

cross the line

If you say that someone **has crossed the line**, you mean that they have started behaving in an unacceptable way, for example by getting involved in something extreme or anti-social. *The show's pretty outrageous, but I don't think it crosses the line.*

◆ The 'line' in this expression may refer to boxing matches in the past, when a line was drawn on the ground which neither boxer could cross. 'Draw the line' may be based on a similar idea.

draw a line under something

If you say that something **draws a line under** a bad situation which has now ended, you mean that it enables the situation to be considered as over, so that people can start again or continue with things more productively. *He said the document draws a line under the painful chapters of our past and clears the way for a new beginning.*

draw the line

If you talk about knowing where to **draw the line**, you are talking about knowing at what point an activity or situation stops being reasonable and starts to be unacceptable. *It is difficult for charities to know where to draw the line between acceptable and unacceptable sources of finance.*

☐ If you say that you would **draw the line** at a particular activity, you mean that you would not do it, because you disapprove of it or because it is so extreme. *I'll do virtually anything – although I think I'd draw the line at running naked across the set!*

◆ There are several theories about the origin of this expression. It may come from early versions of tennis, in which the court had no fixed size: players agreed their own limits and drew lines accordingly. Alternatively, it may be connected with the 16th century practice of using a plough to cut a line across a field to indicate a boundary between two plots of land. A third possibility is that it refers to boxing matches in the past, when a line was drawn in the ring which neither boxer could cross. 'Cross the line' may be based on a similar idea.

get a line on someone

Mainly American If you **get a line on** someone or something, you get some information about them. *We've been trying to get a line on you, and the more we try, the less we find.*

in the firing line
in the line of fire
out of the firing line

If you are **in the firing line** or **in the line of fire**, you are in a position where you are likely to be criticized or attacked. If you are taken **out of the firing line** or **out of the line of fire**, you are removed from a position where you are likely to be criticized or attacked. *Governor-designate Eddie George is in the firing line of the committee's criticisms… All very well to say that, when you're not in the line of fire like me… He was a caring man, concerned for his client. He wanted her to first leave home, to get her out of the firing line before applying for any court orders.*

◆ These expressions are often used literally to talk about the fact that someone is in the way of people who are firing guns, and therefore likely to be shot.

in the front line
on the front line

If someone is **in the front line** or **on the front line**, they have a very important part to play in achieving or defending something. *Local authorities of course are in the front-line of providing help, but they're starved of resources due to the government's policy.*

◆ The image here is of soldiers in the front line during a battle.

not your line of country

British If you say that something is **not** your **line of country**, you mean that it is not a subject that you know a great deal about, or one in which you are very interested. *I am rather ignorant on this matter – it is not quite my line of country.*

on line

Mainly American If a plan or a project comes **on line**, it begins to operate fully. The usual British expression is **on stream**. *Boeing officials say the charter plane was the first 767 to be lost since the popular model came on line in 1982.*

out of line

Mainly American If you tell someone that they are **out of line**, you mean that they are completely wrong to say or do a particular thing. Compare **step out of line**. *Addressing a fellow officer like that is out of line, and I won't stand for it, hear me?*

◆ The line referred to here is a line of soldiers, who are expected to act as a unit.

put something on the line: 1

If you **put** something such as your reputation or your job **on the line**, you do something which causes you to risk losing it. *He had put his career on the line and I wasn't prepared to allow what he had done to be diminished in significance... Using a small, one-man business can also be a good idea. You are likely to get more care and attention because his reputation is on the line.*

□ You can say that you **put** yourself **on the line** when you risk something such as your reputation or your job. *Ferguson has to take the responsibility for everything, and in that sense, he did put himself on the line.*

put something on the line: 2
lay it on the line

If someone **puts** or **lays** their heart or their emotions **on the line**, they speak truthfully and directly about their feelings. You can also say that someone **puts** or **lays** himself or herself **on the line**. *You have to put your emotions on the line with love, but he cannot do this... There's incredible vulnerability in it. He's really laying himself on the line.*

□ If someone **lays** or **puts it on the line**, they say what needs to be said truthfully and directly. *Then he laid it on the line and said without* *treatment I had only three months to live.*

◆ Originally, 'lay it on the line' may have been connected with gambling. It meant to lay a bet on the sideline in the game of craps, or on the counter of a betting window at a racecourse.

put your neck on the line
put your ass on the line

If you **put** your **neck on the line**, you do something although it is risky and you may lose your reputation or money as a result. *Gere put his neck on the line to make Sommersby.*

□ In American English, you can say that someone **puts** their **ass on the line**. Many people find this form of the expression offensive. *I appreciate your putting your ass on the line.*

shoot a line

British You say that someone **is shooting a line** when you think that what they are saying is exaggerated, untrue, or difficult to believe. *He'd been looking for new blood for his office in Vienna. That was the line he shot, though knowing him as I did I'm sure he had a more personal, ulterior motive.*

step out of line

If someone **steps out of line**, they do something that they should not do or they behave in an unacceptable way. Compare **out of line**. *Values and traditions were accepted and agreed by everyone. If you stepped out of line, you knew what to expect.*

◆ See the explanation at 'out of line'.

toe the line

If you refuse to **toe the line**, you refuse to behave in the way that people in authority expect you to behave. If you **toe the line**, you behave in the way they expect. *The new legislation could force them out of business if they don't toe the line... He was sacked for not toeing the Party line.*

◆ At the start of a race, runners stand in a row with their toe just behind the starting line.

lines

on the right lines
along the right lines

British If someone is **on the right lines** or is proceeding **along the**

right lines, they are behaving in a way which is likely to result in success. *Sometimes all you really require is just a friendly voice to tell you that you are on the right lines.*

□ You can also use this expression to suggest that someone is almost, but not completely, managing to achieve the required result. *The treatment offered so far has been along the right lines, but not successful in curing the condition completely.*

read between the lines

If you **read between the lines**, you understand what someone really means, or what is really happening in a situation, even though it is not stated openly. You can also talk about the message **between the lines**. *He was reluctant to go into details, but reading between the lines it appears that the Bank of England has vetoed any idea of a merger between British banks... He didn't give a reason, but I sensed something between the lines.*

link

a weak link
a weak link in the chain

If you describe someone or something as **a weak link** or **a weak link in the chain**, you mean that they are an unreliable part of a system, and because of them the whole system may fail. *It was automatically assumed that Edward would be the weak link in the partnership.*

□ People sometimes say that a system **is only as strong as** its **weakest link**. *A rail system is only as strong as its weakest link, as any commuter trapped behind a broken-down train can testify.*

lion

the lion's share

If you get **the lion's share** of something, you get the largest part of it, leaving very little for others. *Defence has taken the lion's share of this year's budget.*

◆ This refers to Aesop's fable 'The Lion and his Fellow Hunters', in which a lion goes hunting with several other animals and takes everything that they catch for himself, instead of sharing it with them.

put your head into the lion's mouth

If you **put** your **head into the lion's mouth**, you deliberately place yourself in a dangerous or difficult situation. *Put your head in the lion's mouth and just say 'I don't know what the hell is going on.'*

◆ This expression refers to the traditional circus act where a lion-tamer puts his or her head in a lion's mouth.

walk into the lion's den
Daniel in the lion's den

If you **walk into the lion's den**, you deliberately place yourself in a dangerous or difficult situation. Other verbs can be used instead of 'walk'. *With the confidence of a man who believes that he has done no wrong, the Minister last night walked into the lion's den of his press accusers, looked them in the eye, and fought back.*

☐ People also say that they feel like **Daniel in the lion's den** when they are in a dangerous or difficult situation and feel very alone and nervous. *When I first went in the hostility from some sections of the newsroom was palpable. I felt rather like Daniel in the lion's den.*

◆ This expression comes from the story in the Bible of Daniel, who was thrown into a den of lions because he refused to stop praying to God. However, he was protected by God and the lions did not hurt him. (Daniel 6)

lions

throw someone to the lions

If someone **throws** you **to the lions**, they allow you to be criticized severely or treated roughly, and they do not try to protect you. *Tanya isn't sure exactly why she's been thrown to the lions. She traces it back to quotes she made about the business that were reproduced out of context.*

◆ In Roman times and at other periods in the past, people were sometimes put to death by being thrown into a den of lions.

lip

pay lip service to something

If you say that someone **pays lip service** to an idea, you are being critical of them because they appear to be in favour of it, but are not doing anything to support it. *Nearly all Western manufacturers now pay lip-service to Japanese management techniques.*

☐ You can also just talk about **lip service**. *All the talk about nation-building is pure lip-service, because people who are selfish will never join with others to build the nation and preserve the good welfare of others.*

a stiff upper lip

If someone is keeping **a stiff upper lip**, they hide their emotions and do not let other people see what they are feeling. *I shared my feelings with no one because I had always believed in keeping a stiff upper lip, crying in private, and putting on my best face for family and friends.*

lips

lick your lips
lick your chops

If someone is looking forward eagerly to a future event, you can say that they **are licking** their **lips** or **licking** their **chops**. *His home supporters licked their lips in anticipation of a first Scottish-born winner since Tommy Armour in 1931... After hearing the president's plan for economic recovery, they were licking their chops.*

read someone's lips

If someone tells you to **read** their **lips**, they are telling you to believe and trust what they are saying. *Mr Bush won the White House in 1988 thanks, in large part, to his now infamous pledge 'read my lips: no new taxes'.*

litmus

a litmus test

If you say that something is **a litmus test** of the quality or success of a particular thing, you mean that it is an effective and conclusive way of proving it or measuring it. *The success of wind power represents a litmus test for renewable energy.*

◆ Litmus paper is used to test the acidity of substances. It turns red in acid conditions and blue in alkaline conditions.

lives

have nine lives

If you say that someone **has nine lives**, you mean that they keep managing to get out of difficult or dangerous situations without being hurt or harmed. This expression is sometimes used to suggest surprise that they have survived so long. *I think this is probably going to be the end, although he has shown he is a political cat with far more than nine lives.*

◆ This expression comes from the saying 'a cat has nine lives', which refers to the fact that cats seem to survive a lot of very dangerous situations or events.

loaf

half a loaf is better than none

If you say that **half a loaf is better than none**, you mean that it is better to take what you can get, even if it is very little, than to risk having nothing at all. *Leeds are now a point behind Manchester United, who have a game in hand. Their manager said: 'Half a loaf is better than none. We'll just have to get on with it.'*

lock

lock, stock, and barrel

You use **lock, stock, and barrel** to emphasize that you do something completely or include every part of something. *He has moved down from the north-east, lock, stock and barrel.*

◆ The three main parts which make up a complete gun are the lock, the stock, and the barrel.

lockstep

in lockstep
in lock step

Mainly American If two people or things move **in lockstep**, they are very closely linked and dependent on one another, so that if one changes, the other changes too. *Many criminologists argue that support for the death penalty moves in lockstep with the crime rate.*

◆ Lockstep is a way of marching in which the marchers follow as close behind each other as possible.

log

easy as falling off a log
simple as falling off a log

If you say that something is as **easy as falling off a log**, you are emphasizing that it is very easy to do. You can also say it is as **simple as falling off a log** or **like falling off a log**. *The band had only been together for a year when they got signed to Epic. 'Getting signed was like falling off a log,' they said.*

loggerheads

at loggerheads

If one person or group is **at loggerheads** with another, they strongly disagree about something. *Social workers and doctors are at loggerheads over how well the new system will work.*

◆ In medieval times, loggerheads were implements with long handles and a round bowl on one end. In battles, the bowl was filled with hot tar, and then thrown at the enemy.

loins

gird your loins

If you say that someone **is girding** their **loins**, you mean that they are preparing themselves to deal with a difficult or stressful situation, especially by preparing themselves mentally or psychologically. *Conservation organisations are girding their loins to take on the European Community.*

◆ This expression is used several times in the Bible. The Hebrews wore long loose robes which they tied up with a girdle or belt when they were working or travelling.

loop

throw someone for a loop
knock someone for a loop

Mainly American If someone or something **throws** you **for a loop** or

knocks you **for a loop**, they shock you or surprise you very much. *The banker was surprised to find Johnson in his usual high spirits. If Kravis's offer had thrown him for a loop, Johnson wasn't letting it show.*

loose

cut loose

If someone **cuts loose**, they become free from the influence or authority of other people. *Italy has not cut loose from the ERM as determinedly as Britain.*

loss

a dead loss

If you describe someone or something as **a dead loss**, you think that they are completely useless. *I have always been a dead loss at competitive sports and games.*

losses

cut your losses

If you **cut** your **losses**, you decide to stop spending time, energy, or money on an activity or situation on which you have already spent a lot without having any success. *Only you can decide if you should push on to the end of your degree or cut your losses and get out.*

lot

all over the lot

American If something is **all over the lot**, it is spread across a large area or over a wide range of things. *IBM's investments have been all over the lot – in fiber-optic technology, data-retrieval systems, computer networks and so on.*

◆ In American English, a lot is an area of land.

throw in your lot with someone
cast your lot with someone

If you **throw in** your **lot with** someone, or **cast** your **lot with** them, you decide to join them and to share whatever good or bad things happen to them. *That does not mean that France is ready to throw in its lot with other*

Community states on defence matters.

◆ In the past, 'lots' were objects such as pieces of straw or paper which people used when making a decision or choice. Each lot represented, for example, a different piece of property or course of action. All the lots were put together and then chosen at random to decide who would receive the different pieces of property or what action would be taken.

love

for love nor money

If you say that you cannot get something **for love nor money**, you are emphasizing that it is very difficult to get. *You won't get a room here, not for love nor money.*

no love lost
little love lost

If you say that there is **no love lost** between two people or groups, or **little love lost** between them, you mean that they do not like each other at all. *There was no love lost between the country's two most powerful politicians.*

◆ Originally this expression had the opposite meaning to its present one. It used to mean that the two people liked each other a lot.

luck

the luck of the draw

If something that happens depends on **the luck of the draw**, it depends on chance rather than on the efforts or merits of the people involved. *On better acquaintance, you may decide that there's no basis for a real friendship. That's just the luck of the draw.*

◆ This expression refers to the act of drawing a card at random from a pack of playing cards.

lucky

strike lucky

British If someone **strikes lucky** or **strikes it lucky**, they suddenly have some good luck, for example by winning some money. *I arrived at 12.30 to give myself time to find a parking meter, but struck lucky* *immediately.*

◆ This expression has its origins in mining in the 19th century. It refers to someone finding the minerals or oil that they were looking for. 'Strike oil' is based on the same idea.

lump

like it or lump it
have to lump it
If you say that someone has to **like it or lump it** or that they will **have to lump it**, you mean that they will have to accept a situation even though they do not like it, because they cannot do anything to change it. *If you're a shareholder in the club then you have some sort of say in the way things are run. But as a paying customer you like it or lump it... When we pointed out they'd effectively taken part of our garden, they said they hadn't even noticed. We just had to lump it.*

a lump in your throat
bring a lump to your throat
If you say that you have **a lump in** your **throat**, you mean that you have a tight feeling in your throat because of a strong emotion such as sorrow, nostalgia, or gratitude. You can also say that something **brings a lump to** your **throat**. Compare **a frog in** your **throat**; see **frog**. *It brings a lump to my throat. We are so proud of her.*

lunch

out to lunch
If you say that someone is **out to lunch**, you mean that they do not seem aware of what is happening around them, or they do not seem intelligent or capable. *He has failed to fulfil his role as the mayor who could take charge. He is seen as a man who is out to lunch.*

there's no such thing as a free lunch
People say **'there's no such thing as a free lunch'** or **'there is no free lunch'** to mean you cannot expect to get things for nothing, since most things that are worth having need to be paid for or worked for. *The government has spent 14 years telling the nation that there is no such thing as a free lunch and lecturing us on the virtues of sound economics.*

◆ This expression dates back to at least 1840 in the United States. It recently became popular again when the American economist Milton Friedman used it in the 1970s.

lurch

leave someone in the lurch

If you say that someone **has left** you **in the lurch**, you are complaining that they have put you in a difficult situation by suddenly going away or abandoning you, without giving you very much notice of their plans. *Chicago-based Midway Airlines has shut down, leaving thousands of ticket holders in the lurch.*

lying

not take something lying down

If something bad is happening and you say that you **will not take** it **lying down**, you mean that you will complain about it or resist it. *It is clear that he means to push everyone out, and I for one am not going to take it lying down.*

M

mad

mad as a hatter

Mainly British If you say that someone is as **mad as a hatter**, you think that they are very strange, foolish, or crazy. *Her sister's as mad as a hatter and if you ask me she's not much better herself.*

◆ In the 19th century, 'hatters' or hat-makers used nitrate of mercury to treat fabrics such as felt. This substance is poisonous, and if the hat-makers breathed it in, they often suffered brain damage. As a result, hatters were traditionally thought of as mad. In Lewis Carroll's children's story 'Alice in Wonderland' (1865), one of the characters is a hatter who behaves very strangely. Carroll may have based the character on a well-known Oxford furniture dealer, Theophilus Carter, who was known as the 'Mad Hatter'.

mad as a hornet

Mainly American If you say that someone is as **mad as a hornet**, you mean that they are extremely angry. *Bob grinned. 'I'll bet he's as mad as a hornet.' 'He did not sound at all pleased,' Jerry admitted.*

◆ A hornet is a large wasp.

map

on the map

If someone or something puts a person, place, or thing **on the map**, they cause them to become well-known or important. *The film which really put Ellen Barkin on the map was The Big Easy.*

marbles

lose your marbles
have all your marbles

If you say that someone **has lost** their **marbles**, you mean that they are mad or senile. *At 83 I have not lost my marbles and my memory is, thank God, as clear as it ever was.*

☐ You can say that someone **has all** their **marbles** when it is obvious that they are completely sane and rational. *The producer Mirian Adhtar has found four particularly fearless old ladies; they have all their marbles, crystal clear recollections and, at ninety-odd, no false modesty.*

pick up your marbles and go home

American If you say that someone **picks up** their **marbles and goes home**, you mean that they leave a situation in which they are involved because they are dissatisfied with the way things are going. You can use this expression to suggest that you think they are wrong to do this. *Many Asians regard a U.S. presence as a desirable counterweight to Japanese influence. No one wants the U.S. to pick up its marbles and go home.*

◆ The reference here is to a player in a game of marbles who is annoyed about losing and therefore stops playing and takes the marbles away so that nobody else can play either.

march

march to a different drummer
march to the beat of a different drummer
march to a different tune

If you say that someone **marches to a different drummer** or **marches to the beat of a different drummer**, you mean that they act in accordance with beliefs or expectations which are different from those of their colleagues or associates. *Can't Congress see that this only compounds the problem? Or does Congress march to a different drummer?... The state-supported school marches to the beat of a different drummer, and I will permit it to continue to do so.*

☐ This expression is sometimes varied, for example by replacing 'drummer' with 'drum'. *As a player Lindner has always marched to the beat of a different drum.*

☐ In British English, you can also say that someone **marches to a different tune**. *Clough has always marched to a different tune, but this time his perversity may finally be his undoing.*

steal a march

If you **steal a march** on someone, you do something before they do and so gain an advantage over them. *The bold move is designed to entice shoppers away from Tesco, which stole a march by opening more stores on the Sundays in the run-up to Christmas.*

◆ If an army steals a march on the enemy, it moves secretly and takes the enemy by surprise.

mark

a black mark

If people form a low opinion of you as a result of something that you have done or that they think you have done, you can say that you get **a black mark**. *I knew I had no history of bad debts and couldn't think why there should be a black mark against my name.*

◆ This expression may refer to a practice in schools in the past. If children misbehaved, the teacher put black marks against their names on a list.

get off the mark

Mainly British In a sporting contest, when someone **gets off the mark**, they score or win for the first time. If you **get off the mark** in another activity, you start to do it quickly. *The goal was Atkinson's second of the season, having got off the mark against Ipswich Town on Saturday... Don't waste time with small talk; you might have only five minutes to present your case. Get off the mark right away.*

♦ The 'mark' in this expression is the line which runners stand behind at the start of a race.

hit the mark
miss the mark

If you say that something such as a film, a book, or a performance **hits the mark**, you mean that it is very good and succeeds in pleasing people. *The band have really hit the mark. 'Call It What You Want' is destined to be one of the successes of the year.*

□ If you say that something such as a film, a book, or a performance **misses the mark**, you mean that it is unsuccessful, unsatisfactory, or inadequate. *But along the way, hospitals got wrapped up in image advertising that missed the mark with consumers, the study says.*

♦ The 'mark' in this expression is the target used in archery or shooting.

off the mark: 1
on the mark

If something that you say or write is **off the mark**, it is incorrect or inaccurate. If something someone says or writes is **on the mark**, it is correct or accurate. *They're sometimes called 'Poor Man's Oyster', but I think that name is way off the mark. Mussels are every bit as good as the more expensive oyster... A thousand thanks for your interview with Michael Medved. He's right on the mark about movies being out of step with American culture.*

off the mark: 2

Mainly British If you describe someone's words or behaviour as **off the mark**, you are criticizing them for being unfair. *There are good and bad decisions in every Test Match you play in, even in England. Mistakes are being made, but to question the umpires' integrity is off the mark.*

♦ See the explanation at 'hit the mark'.

overshoot the mark

If you **overshoot the mark**, you do something to a greater extent than is necessary or desirable. *I quite unwittingly overshot the mark, and I still feel embarrassed about it.*

♦ See the explanation at 'hit the mark'.

overstep the mark

If someone **oversteps the mark**, they behave in a way that is considered unacceptable, for example by doing something which they are not allowed to do. *Sometimes newspapers overstep the mark but overall they do more good than harm.*

◆ The 'mark' in this expression may be the line behind which runners stand before the race. Alternatively, it may refer to boxing matches in the past, when a line was drawn in the ground which neither boxer could cross.

quick off the mark
first off the mark
slow off the mark

Mainly British If someone is **quick off the mark**, they are quick to understand or respond to something, or to take advantage of an opportunity. If they are **first off the mark**, they act more quickly than anyone else. *These price cuts are great news for the holidaymaker who is quick off the mark... The new fine art season moved into top gear yesterday with Christie's and Sotheby's announcing big collections for the autumn sales in London and New York. Christie's were first off the mark with a collection of seven paintings by Paul Cézanne.*

☐ If someone is **slow off the mark**, they are slow to act or to react to a situation or event. *International relief efforts on behalf of the refugees were slow off the mark, partly because of a belief that the refugees would soon be repatriated.*

◆ See the explanation at 'get off the mark'.

up to the mark

If you say that something is **up to the mark**, you mean that it is of a satisfactory standard or quality. *They get rid of those whose work is not up to the mark.*

◆ The 'mark' in this expression is a hallmark, which is an official symbol put on gold and silver items that reach a particular standard.

wide of the mark

If something that you say or write is **wide of the mark**, it is incorrect or inaccurate. *The SIB said last night: 'Any suggestions that we are putting any pressure on Sir Gordon to step down are very wide of the mark.'*

◆ See the explanation at 'hit the mark'.

market

a cattle market
a meat market
    If you refer to a situation as **a cattle market** or **a meat market**, you
mean that people are being treated in an undignified way which shows no
respect for them as individuals. For example, you might refer to a beauty
contest as **a cattle market** or **a meat market** if you disapprove of the fact
that the contestants are being considered only in terms of their physical
attractiveness. 'A cattle market' is used mainly in British English. *The
parade of beautiful girls from every nation in the world was rightly called a
cattle market... 'Is it a meat market?' 'Yes, of course, but no more than any
other nightclub.'*

marrow

to the marrow
    -You can use **to the marrow** to emphasize the intensity of someone's
beliefs or feelings. *I wasn't expecting to be thrilled to the marrow with it.*

◆ 'Marrow' is the fatty substance inside the bones of a person or animal.

masters

not serve two masters
    If you say that a person **cannot serve two masters**, you mean that it is
impossible to be loyal to two opposing principles, beliefs, or organizations.
*But there is something more fundamentally wrong: the inherent conflict of
interest in Sir Nicholas's job. He is expected to serve two masters: politics
and the law.*

◆ This expression is used in the Bible. In the Sermon on the Mount, Jesus
says: 'No man can serve two masters: for either he will hate the one, and
love the other; or else he will hold to the one, and despise the other.'
(Matthew 6:24, Luke 16:13)

mat

go to the mat
    Mainly American If someone **goes to the mat**, they fight very fiercely

about something. *To civil rights leaders, this talk is rank heresy. So they will go to the mat to destroy him.*

◆ This expression refers to a wrestler who fights fiercely and is willing to risk a fall.

match

the whole shooting match

You can use **the whole shooting match** to refer to the whole of something. *The head of this division would run the whole shooting match. He would have to get products, write presentations, devise campaigns, hire, fire, and a hundred other things.*

◆ This may be a reference to someone winning all the prizes in a shooting contest.

McCoy

the real McCoy

If you describe something as **the real McCoy**, you mean that it is genuine or the original, rather than a fake or copy, and is therefore often considered to be the best. *Unlike some other products which are promoted as the real McCoy, Cobra is a genuine Indian product.*

◆ There are several suggestions about who the original 'McCoy' was, including an American boxer, a liquor smuggler, and a Kansas cattle dealer. However, it is more likely that the expression was originally British, and that 'McCoy' was originally 'Mackay'. There was a 19th century whisky manufacturer called Mackay who advertised his product as 'the real Mackay' to distinguish it from other brands with similar names. Alternatively, the expression may come from a dispute between two branches of the MacKay clan over which was older. Eventually the MacKays of Reay, or the 'Reay MacKays', won the dispute.

meal

make a meal of something

Mainly British If you say that someone **is making a meal of** something, you are criticizing them for spending more time or energy on it than is necessary. *Alexander has made such a meal out of a mildly mistaken* *newspaper report.*

a meal ticket

If you describe something as **a meal ticket**, you mean that it is a way of getting money on a regular basis and securing a good lifestyle. *Four out of ten men fear their partner may be after a life-long meal ticket.*

a square meal

If you have **a square meal**, you have a large, filling, nutritious meal. *The troops are very tired. They haven't had a square meal for four or five days.*

♦ On sailing ships in the past, sailors ate off square wooden plates.

means

by fair means or foul

If someone tries to achieve something **by fair means or foul**, they are prepared to use any possible method to achieve it, and they do not care if their behaviour is dishonest or unfair. *He accused the company of being hell bent on achieving its cuts by whatever means, fair means or foul, irrespective of the financial and emotional impact.*

meat

dead meat

If someone says a person is **dead meat**, they mean that person is in serious trouble which may result in them suffering unpleasant consequences, or even being injured or killed. *They can follow you when you go to the bathroom at two or three in the morning and beat you up and if the man on duty isn't quick to intervene, you're dead meat.*

meat and drink to someone

Mainly British If something is **meat and drink to** you, it is something you find easy to cope with and enjoy doing. *What normal people considered pressure was meat and drink to Robert Maxwell.*

one man's meat is another man's poison

If you say that **one man's meat is another man's poison**, you are pointing out that different people like different things. *Art is everywhere. Because it is a question of personal taste, the cliché of one man's meat being another's poison is in this case especially fitting.*

□ People sometimes vary this expression to include nouns which are relevant to the subject they are talking about. *You've got to remember that one person's junk mail is another person's source of interesting information.*

◆ The Roman author Lucretius said in 'De Rerum Natura': 'What is food to one person may be bitter poison to others.'

medicine

give someone a taste of their own medicine
give someone a dose of their own medicine
If someone has behaved badly and you **give** them **a taste of** their **own medicine** or **a dose of** their **own medicine**, you treat them badly in return. *The cowardly thugs who mug old people should be given a taste of their own medicine with the return of corporal punishment.*

melting pot

in the melting pot
Mainly British If something is **in the melting pot**, it is constantly changing, so that you do not know what will finally happen to it. *Their fate is still in the melting-pot, and much suffering may lie ahead.*

◆ A 'melting pot' is a container in which metal is melted down before being made into new objects.

men

sort out the men from the boys
separate the men from the boys
If a difficult or challenging situation **sorts out the men from the boys** or **separates the men from the boys**, it tests people and shows who is strong and capable and who is not. *This is the game that will sort out the men from the boys. It is absolutely vital to win the replay and get to the final.*

messenger

shoot the messenger
If someone accuses you of **shooting the messenger**, they are criticizing you for unfairly blaming a person who has given you unpleasant news or information, when you should instead be angry with the people who are

really responsible for the situation. *Nobody enjoys paying tax, but at least be sure of your facts before you criticize the Inland Revenue, and remember the government makes the rules which the Revenue then has to enforce. If you don't like the message, don't shoot the messenger.*

mickey

take the mickey
take the mick
British If you **take the mickey** or **take the mick** out of someone or something, you tease them or make jokes about them in a way that causes them to seem ridiculous. *He started taking the mickey out of this poor man just because he is bald.*

☐ When someone behaves like this, you can refer to their behaviour as **mickey-taking**. You can refer to an instance of it as **a mickey-take**. *Until puberty I was really quite plump and had to put up with all the mickey-taking that went with it.*

◆ This expression may be based on rhyming slang. 'To take the Mickey Bliss' means 'to take the piss', an offensive expression which means to tease or make fun of someone.

middle

middle-of-the-road: 1
If you describe a person or their political ideas as **middle-of-the-road**, you mean that they are neither very left-wing nor very right-wing. *He has represented himself as being a moderate, middle-of-the-road kind of person who understands and takes into consideration both sides of the issues.*

middle-of-the-road: 2
If you describe someone or something as **middle-of-the-road**, you mean that they are very ordinary, rather than unusual, exciting, or extreme. *These are, for the most part, ordinary middle-of-the-road people who want the usual things out of life.*

midnight

burn the midnight oil
If you **burn the midnight oil**, you stay up very late at night in order to

finish a piece of work. *Chris is asleep after burning the midnight oil trying to put together his article on the Bosnian situation.*

◆ The image here is of someone working late into the night by the light of an oil lamp.

midstream

change horses in midstream

If someone who is involved in an activity **changes horses in midstream**, they stop using one method or thing and start using another one, or they stop supporting one person and start supporting someone else. You can also just say that someone **changes horses**. These expressions are often used to advise someone against doing one of these things. *I think we were very wise not to change horses in mid-stream.*

☐ Sometimes people replace 'horses' with another noun. *They haven't hesitated to change the rules in midstream in order to try to thwart the President.*

mile

go the extra mile

If you say that someone is willing to **go the extra mile**, you mean that they are willing to make a special effort to do or achieve something. *The President is determined to go the extra mile for peace.*

☐ People sometimes replace 'mile' with 'yard'. *He has enormous compassion for people and a willingness to go the extra yard to help them.*

milk

it's no use crying over spilled milk

If you tell someone **'it's no use crying over spilled milk'**, you are telling them that it is pointless to worry or be upset about something that has happened and cannot be changed. *I'm a man, I can take it. I ain't going to cry over spilt milk, I was beaten fair and square.*

milk and honey
the land of milk and honey

You can describe a time or a situation in which you are very contented and have plenty of money as a time of **milk and honey**. *The days of milk* *and honey are back – at least for US equity salesmen in the City.*

□ This expression is a shortened form of **the land of milk and honey**, which describes a place where people will be happy and have plenty of food and wealth.

◆ This expression is used in the Bible to describe the Promised Land of the Israelites. (Exodus 3:8)

milk and water

British If you describe something or someone as **milk and water**, you mean that they are weak and ineffectual. *The only time we have ever won an election, is when as in 1945 it was fought on principle; every other time we've put forward this milk and water liberalism, and we've lost.*

mill

go through the mill
put through the mill

If you **go through the mill** or **are put through the mill**, you experience a very difficult period or situation. *'Oh I've been through the mill,' said Shirley. 'Single parent, no money, and a boyfriend who beat me up.'... Richard confesses he'll put a junior through the mill for the first few months, and work them hard to see if they can keep their temper.*

◆ The reference here is to grain passing through a mill and being made into flour.

run-of-the-mill

You use **run-of-the-mill** to describe something or someone that you think is ordinary and unexciting. *They must organise their staff photographers to ensure that daily run-of-the-mill events are covered.*

◆ This expression may be using the image of a watermill making the same movements continuously and regularly so long as the flow of water stays the same. Another suggestion is that it comes from the use of 'run-of-the-mill' in the United States as a term for timber which has been sawn at a sawmill but has not yet been graded.

millstone

a millstone around your neck

If you say that something is like **a millstone around** your **neck**, you mean that it is a very unpleasant problem or responsibility that you cannot escape from. *Argentina's notoriously inefficient telephone company, Entel, has been a millstone round the government's neck.*

☐ **Millstone** is often used on its own with this meaning. *There is the continuing millstone of the country's enormous foreign debt.*

◆ A millstone is one of a pair of very heavy round flat stones which are used to grind grain.

mincemeat

make mincemeat of someone
If you **make mincemeat of** someone, you defeat them completely in a fight, argument, or competition. *Naturally, Lord Goodman will make mincemeat of this absurd claim.*

◆ In British English, mincemeat is meat that has been cut into very small pieces by being forced through the small holes in a machine called a mincer.

mind

bear something in mind
keep something in mind
If you tell someone to **bear** something **in mind** or **keep** something **in mind**, you are reminding or warning them about something important which they should remember. *There are a few general rules to bear in mind when selecting plants.*

blow your mind
If you say that something **blows** your **mind**, you mean that you find it so exciting, amazing, or interesting that it is hard to believe it. *Oxford really blew his mind. He loved the feeling of the place, he loved the people.*

☐ You can also say that you find something **mind-blowing**. *In the museum, the artist's impression of how Delphi must once have looked is mind-blowing in its majesty.*

cross your mind
If something **crosses** your **mind**, you suddenly think of it. *The thought instantly crossed my mind that she might be lying about her age.*

give someone a piece of your mind

If someone has annoyed or upset you and you **give** them **a piece of** your **mind**, you angrily tell them what you think of them. *You can't let people get away with that sort of thing. You should have given her a piece of your mind.*

have a one-track mind

If you say that someone **has a one-track mind**, you mean that they seem to only ever think or talk about one subject. This expression is often used light-heartedly to refer to people who think or talk about sex a lot. *In my view Saunders is the complete modern striker, busy, quick, and with a one-track mind for scoring goals.*

in your mind's eye

If you see something **in** your **mind's eye**, you have a clear picture of it in your imagination or memory. *Susie had a clear picture in her mind's eye of how she wanted the house to look.*

in your right mind

If you say that nobody **in** their **right mind** would do a particular thing, you mean that it is an irrational thing to do, and you do not expect anyone would ever do it. *Those places are so barren, dangerous and inhospitable that no one in their right mind would go there unless they had a contract to fulfil.*

minds

in two minds
of two minds

If you are **in two minds** about something, you are very hesitant and cannot reach a decision about it. In American English, you can also say that you are **of two minds**. *Roche was in two minds whether to make the trip to Oslo... Her family was of two minds about what was happening, proud that Miss Kim was being honored by the state and distressed that she had to leave home.*

miss

miss the boat
miss the bus

If someone **misses the boat**, they fail to act in time to take advantage of an opportunity, with the result that they lose the chance to do something or to benefit from something. You can also say that someone **misses the bus**. *My mother and my grandmother were both married at 24 and at that age, I suddenly thought I'd missed the boat – but I have a wider world than they ever had.*

mockers

put the mockers on something
If someone **puts the mockers on** something, they prevent it from happening or from being successful. *When it was first suggested that the group might tour with them back in 1990, the Happy Mondays themselves put the mockers on it.*

◆ The origin of this expression is uncertain, but some people think that 'mockers' may come from Yiddish.

money

money for old rope
money for jam
British If you say that someone is getting **money for old rope** or **money for jam**, you mean that they are getting money very easily and with very little or no effort on their part. *I had always believed that the fashion model's job was money for old rope... Who on earth can afford five pounds per hour? This is robbery, money for jam.*

money talks
If you say that **money talks**, you mean that people with a lot of money have power and influence and they can get whatever they want. *As far as he is concerned, money talks and he can do what he likes.*

put your money where your mouth is
If you **put** your **money where** your **mouth is**, you give practical support to causes or activities that you believe are right, especially by giving money. *If the minister is so keen on the school he should put his money where his mouth is and give us more resources.*

□ Journalists sometimes replace 'money' or 'mouth' with other nouns in order to refer to a particular situation or to the type of support someone might give. *We'll be watching to see how many Members of the Rules Committee end up putting their votes where their rhetoric is.*

right on the money

Mainly American If you say that someone is **right on the money**, you mean that they are completely right. *They say his analysis of what was wrong with General Motors was right on the money.*

◆ This expression was originally used to describe a bet which turned out to be exactly right.

the smart money: 1

You say that **the smart money** is on a particular event when that event seems very likely to happen, or is expected to happen by the people who know a lot about it. *The smart money is on him losing his seat to the Labour challenger.*

the smart money: 2

People who have a lot of experience and knowledge of investing money are sometimes referred to as **the smart money**. *Vietnam's cost advantage explains why Asia's smart money expects the nation to grow so rapidly from its low base.*

throw good money after bad

If you say that someone **is throwing good money after bad**, you are criticizing them for spending a lot of money in an attempt to get back money which they have already lost, for example in a bad investment, even though this is unlikely to be successful. *Germany is pledging trust and goodwill but no more cash. As one senior official put it, we don't want to throw good money after bad.*

monkey

have a monkey on your back
get the monkey off your back

Mainly American If you **have a monkey on** your **back**, you have a serious problem that is making your life difficult or unpleasant. If you **get the monkey off** your **back**, you put an end to the problem. *That job has been foisted upon us actually. We've got a monkey on our backs of having to reveal the character of our candidates, because the parties are no longer screening them... 'This is a big monkey off my back,' said McEnroe. 'It's been so long since I had such a big win.'*

◆ 'To have a monkey on your back' originally meant to be angry. Later it came to be used to say that someone was addicted to drugs; it is still used in this way today.

make a monkey out of someone

If someone **makes a monkey out of** you, they make you seem ridiculous or stupid. *If it makes any difference, I'm not here to make monkeys out of the police, I'm a cop myself.*

monkey business

If you refer to someone's activities as **monkey business**, you are suggesting that they are dishonest or unacceptable. *Senator Jose Maria Sala runs the party machine in Catalonia, where the monkey business is alleged to have gone on.*

not give a monkey's

British If you say that you **don't give a monkey's** about something, you mean that you do not care about it at all. Some people find this expression offensive. *They constantly said they would not injure the maid or the child because they had children of their own, but they said they didn't give a monkey's about what they did to me.*

monkeys

a cartload of monkeys

British, old-fashioned If you say that someone is as cunning or as clever as **a cartload of monkeys**, you are emphasizing that they are extremely cunning or clever. You can use 'barrel load' or 'barrel' instead of 'cartload'. *They are engaging creatures, cunning as a cartload of monkeys.*

month

a month of Sundays: 1

You say that a period of time seems to last for **a month of Sundays** to emphasize that it seems to be very long. *Torrential rain and jet-black skies can make each day seem like a month of Sundays.*

a month of Sundays: 2

If you say that something will not happen in **a month of Sundays**, you are emphasizing that it is very unlikely to happen. *'I think I know what you're about,' he growled, 'but it'll never work – not in a month of Sundays.'*

monty

the full monty

British If you say that something is **the full monty**, you are emphasizing that it is as complete or extreme as possible. *The band opened with two new songs. They're promising the full monty at their two Brixton Academy shows.*

◆ 'Monty' is sometimes spelled 'monte'. The origin of the word 'monty' is unknown.

moon

ask for the moon
cry for the moon

If you say that someone **is asking for the moon** or **is crying for the moon**, you mean that they are asking for something that they cannot possibly have. *We're not asking for the moon, but we are asking for some stability so that we can continue the progress that has been made.*

bay at the moon
howl at the moon

If you say that someone **is baying at the moon**, you mean that they are wasting their time and energy trying to do something which is impossible or to get something which they cannot have. You can also say that they **are howling at the moon**. *Asking for improved childcare provision has so far proved as fruitful as baying at the moon.*

once in a blue moon

Something that happens **once in a blue moon** is very rare and hardly ever happens. *I only get over to Cambridge once in a blue moon and I'm never in London.*

◆ The moon occasionally looks blue because there is dust in the earth's atmosphere caused by something such as a volcanic eruption or a forest fire.

over the moon

Mainly British If you are **over the moon** about something, you are very happy about it. *I'm over the moon about the way this album turned out.*

moth

like a moth to a flame

If you say that a person is attracted to another person or thing **like a moth to a flame**, you mean that the attraction is so powerful that they cannot resist. This expression is very variable. For example, you can talk about 'moths around a flame', or replace 'flame' with 'candle'. *The bright lights of west London drew Kharin like a moth to a flame.*

motions

go through the motions

If you say that someone **is going through the motions**, you mean that they are doing something that they have to do or are expected to do, but without any real effort or enthusiasm. *Many of the students who did attend classes with any regularity were just going through the motions.*

mould (*American* mold)

◆ The 'mould' in these expressions is a container that is used to make something into a particular shape. Soft or liquid substances are put into the mould, and when they harden they form objects with the shape or pattern of the mould.

break the mould

If someone or something **breaks the mould**, they completely change the way something has traditionally been done, and do it in a new way. 'Shatter' and 'crack' are sometimes used instead of 'break'. *Mayall would shortly become associated with the new vanguard of alternative, left-wing comics who were to break the British comedy mould in the late Seventies.*

☐ You can use **mould-breaking** to describe someone or something that completely changes the way something has traditionally been done. *Southwold, a sleepy fishing town on the extreme eastern edge of England, might seem an odd place from which to launch a mould-breaking wine business.*

☐ You can refer to someone who has done something in a completely new way as **a mould-breaker**. *She is frequently praised as a mould-breaker: in the words of Steve Rider, 'Julie Welch demonstrated that a woman's opinion on the game is as valid as a man's.'*

they broke the mould when they made someone

If you say that **they broke the mould when they made** someone or something, you are emphasizing that the person or thing is special or unique, and that there is nobody else or nothing else quite like them. *He is a most remarkable man. They broke the mould when they made him.*

☐ You can also just say that **they broke the mould**. *But they don't make them like that any more – I think they broke the mold.*

mountain

if Mohammed will not go to the mountain, the mountain must go to Mohammed

People use expressions such as **'the mountain must come to Mohammed'** or **'Mohammed comes to the mountain'** to say that if someone you want to see does not come to you, then you must go to them. *Another member of the RAF staff added that all the freed hostage's needs would be met on the base. The mountain would come to Mohammed, he said.*

☐ People do not normally use the full expression, but refer to it partially or indirectly. *Rudge admits that the market is very quiet, and has decided, on the Mahomet and the Mountain principle, to go out and get the clients.*

◆ These expressions are based on a story about the prophet Mohammed, who was asked to show his power by making Mount Safa come to him.

make a mountain out of a molehill

If you say that someone **is making a mountain out of a molehill**, you are criticizing them because you think that they are making a small, unimportant problem seem big and important. *The Kremlin's initial reaction to western reports was an attempt to say the West was trying to make a mountain out of a molehill.*

a mountain to climb

Mainly British If you say that someone has **a mountain to climb**, you mean that it will be difficult for them to achieve what they want to achieve. *His government has an economic mountain to climb.*

mountains

move mountains

People sometimes say that something such as faith or love can **move**

mountains in order to emphasize that it can be a very powerful force. *We should all repeat five times a day, 'It is possible to change!' With this belief, you can move mountains.*

◆ This is from the proverb 'Faith will move mountains', which is based on the words of Jesus to his followers in the Bible: 'If ye have faith as a grain of mustard seed, ye shall say unto this mountain, Remove hence to yonder place; and it shall remove'. (Matthew 17:20)

mouth

all mouth and trousers
all mouth and no trousers
British If you say that someone is **all mouth and trousers**, you disapprove of the fact that they talk a lot about doing something but never actually do it. People also say **all mouth and no trousers**, or use other nouns instead of 'trousers'. *He wants to write a play about two Scottish brothers, the one a none-too-successful West of Scotland man with vague criminal connections; the other a fast-talking, London media type, all mouth and trousers... Sandra is all mouth and no talent.*

□ Sometimes people just say that someone is **all mouth**. *They are all mouth in the name of the cause, and are always seen to be saying the right thing.*

down in the mouth
British If you feel **down in the mouth**, you feel unhappy or depressed. *As for George, I hear he's rather down in the mouth.*

foam at the mouth: 1
froth at the mouth
If you say that someone **is foaming at the mouth** or **is frothing at the mouth**, you mean that they are very angry. *Stewart was foaming at the mouth about an incident at Gooch's private hospital the previous afternoon... It is now taken for granted that 'political correctness' is undesirable. Its mere mention is enough to cause journalists to froth at the mouth.*

foam at the mouth: 2
froth at the mouth
If you say that someone **is foaming at the mouth** or **is frothing at the mouth**, you mean that they are very excited about something. *At that time*

the newspaper had foamed at the mouth in favour of agreement with Fascist countries.

laugh out of the other side of your mouth

American If someone says **'you'll be laughing out of the other side of your mouth'**, they are warning you that although you are happy or successful at the moment, things are likely to go wrong for you in the future. The British expression is **laugh on the other side of** your **face**.

make your mouth water

If you say that something **makes** your **mouth water**, you are emphasizing that it is very attractive or appealing. *London Zoo now has fewer visitors than its counterpart in Chester. Its site in Regent's Park would make any developer's mouth water.*

☐ People also use the much more frequent adjective **mouth-watering** to mean the same thing. *The perks that go with the governorship are mouth-watering.*

shoot your mouth off: 1

If you say that someone **is shooting** their **mouth off**, you are criticizing them for talking loudly and boastfully about themselves or their opinions. *He'd been shooting his mouth off saying he could sing, when of course, he couldn't.*

shoot your mouth off: 2

If you say that someone **has been shooting** their **mouth off** about something, you are criticizing them for talking publicly about something which is secret. *What if he decides to try for a little more money, or to shoot his mouth off around town?*

speak out of both sides of your mouth
talk out of both sides of your mouth

American If you accuse someone of **speaking** or **talking out of both sides of** their **mouth**, you are criticizing them because in different situations they give completely different advice or opinions, even though they are talking about the same thing. *This whole thing shows one of Larry's problems, which is speaking out of both sides of his mouth. At Harvard he panders constantly to the students with his radical rhetoric. But then, in the outer world, he is Laurence Tribe, national figure, who has to pull back from these positions.*

movers

the movers and shakers

If you refer to people as **the movers and shakers** of a particular event, organization, or movement, you admire them because they are the people who take an active part in it and make things happen, or who bring in new developments. *She and her husband, the millionaire author Ken Follett, have become movers and shakers behind the scenes of the Labour Party.*

mud

mud sticks

Mainly British If you say that **mud sticks**, you mean that when something bad is said about someone, people will continue to believe it, although it may have been proved to be completely untrue. *Whether he's innocent or not, some of the mud has stuck.*

sling mud
throw mud

If you say that one person **is slinging mud** or **is throwing mud** at another, you disapprove of the first person because you think that they are trying to spoil the second person's reputation by saying bad things about them or by telling lies. *The elections have been straight personality contests, with the candidates slinging as much mud at their opponents as they can muster.*

☐ You can refer to this kind of behaviour as **mud-slinging**. *A fragile truce seemed to be holding last night as Labour and Tory chiefs ordered an end to political mud-slinging.*

a stick-in-the-mud

If you refer to someone as **a stick-in-the-mud**, you disapprove of them because they do not like doing new things or having fun. *I felt sorry for him because he obviously wanted to enjoy himself but was married to a real stick-in-the-mud.*

murder

scream blue murder
scream bloody murder

If you say that someone **is screaming blue murder** or **is screaming**

bloody murder, you mean that they are making a lot of noise or fuss about something. 'Scream blue murder' is used only in British English. *People are screaming blue murder about the amount of traffic going through their town.*

muscles

flex your muscles

If people or organizations **flex** their **muscles**, they behave in a way intended to show that they have power and are considering using it. *The National Party is certainly flexing its muscles in the early days of this new Government.*

music

face the music

If you **face the music**, you accept responsibility for something that you have done wrong and you prepare yourself to be criticized or punished for it. *We were foreigners in a forbidden area, the authorities had found out and we were about to face the music.*

◆ The 'music' in this expression may refer to the orchestra at an opera or musical. The orchestra sits in front of the stage, so when a performer faces the audience, they also face the orchestra, or 'music'. Alternatively, the expression may come from an army practice in which a soldier who had been dismissed for dishonourable behaviour was sent away with drums beating.

music to your ears

If you say that something is **music to** your **ears**, you mean that it makes you feel very happy when you hear it, for example because you have been hoping or waiting to hear it for a long time. *'There'll be another big bonus in it for you.' 'Music to my ears.'*

mustard

not cut the mustard

If you say that someone **doesn't cut the mustard**, you mean that their work or performance is not as good as it should be. *You have to be on form every week and people soon start noticing if you're not cutting the mustard.*

☐ You say that someone can **cut the mustard** to emphasize that their work or performance is as good as or better than you expected it to be. *The first backstage reports are that Sarah is okay. She has great presence and can really cut the mustard.*

◆ In the United States, 'mustard' used to be slang for 'the best' or 'the genuine article'.

muster

pass muster

If someone or something **passes muster**, they are considered to be satisfactory for a particular purpose or job. *Only Azerbaijan has yet to fulfil all the membership requirements, but it is expected to pass muster soon.*

◆ In the army and navy, a 'muster' is an inspection of the soldiers' or sailors' uniforms and equipment.

mutton

mutton dressed as lamb

British If someone describes a middle-aged or old woman as **mutton dressed as lamb**, they disapprove of her because she dresses in a style which they consider suitable only for younger women. *You would never be able to describe her as mutton dressed up as lamb because she obviously still feels young and fresh in herself so she carries off the look extremely well.*

□ This expression is occasionally applied to things rather than people, in order to suggest that something old is being falsely made to look new. *Union leader, Jim Thomas described the move as 'mutton dressed up as lamb'. He said the jobs were not new but part of a relocation deal with Germany, in which the UK lost more jobs than were gained.*

N

nail
another nail in the coffin
the final nail in the coffin

If you say that an event is **another nail in the coffin** of something or someone, you mean that it is the latest in a series of events which are seriously harming that thing or person. *The vote is another nail in the coffin of the one-party system.*

☐ If you say that an event is **the final nail in the coffin** of something, you mean that it finally destroys that thing. If you say that an event is **the final nail in the coffin** for a person, you mean that it finally puts an end to that person's hopes or plans. *Historians may well record the past three days in Moscow as driving the final nail into the coffin of more than seventy years of Soviet communism.*

hit the nail on the head

If someone makes a comment and you say that they **have hit the nail on the head**, you mean that they have described a situation or problem exactly. *I agree with Dr Carey, everything he says. I think he's hit the nail right on the head.*

on the nail: 1

British If you pay cash **on the nail** for something, you pay for it immediately and in cash. The American expression is **on the barrelhead**. *You have to pay cash on the nail sometimes, and this was one of them.*

☐ If you pay money **on the nail**, you pay it at exactly the time you are supposed to. *The Marwood family has subsequently said that the money was never repaid but Violet, who was handling Ford's affairs, said it was, and on the nail.*

on the nail: 2
hit it on the nail

If you talk about a particular time or amount **on the nail**, you mean that time or amount exactly. If you say that someone **has hit it on the nail**, you mean that they have described a situation exactly. *'When did Captain Schmidt come to see you?' 'Six o'clock, just about on the nail.'... 'It sounds as if he almost depended on you as much as you depended on him.' 'You just hit it on the nail.'*

◆ This expression may refer to cylindrical counters called 'nails' that were sometimes used by traders in the Middle Ages. When a price had been agreed, the money was placed on the nail, so that everyone could see that the correct amount was being paid.

name

the name of the game

If you say that something is **the name of the game**, you mean that it is the most important aspect of the activity that you are talking about. *In the current economic climate, survival is the name of the game.*

a name to conjure with

Mainly British If you say that someone or something is **a name to conjure with**, you mean that they are very important, influential, or memorable. *Bugattis, Bentleys, Ferraris – motoring names to conjure with, and all part of a breath-taking display of classic cars.*

◆ In this expression, the importance and influence associated with a person or thing are regarded as a kind of magical power which you can call on by using their name.

take someone's name in vain

If someone says that another person **takes** God's **name in vain**, they mean that the person uses it disrespectfully, especially by swearing. *He persevered, and always gently corrected us when we took the Lord's name in vain.*

☐ You can say that someone **is taking** another person's or a thing's **name in vain** when you think that they are using them for their own purposes in an inappropriate or disrespectful way. *The minister for science cited Green's work as an example of good British research. Green feels that his name was being taken in vain. 'There is a tremendous amount of bitterness at what has been done by the government,' he says. 'If there has been good research, it has been in spite of what the government has done.'*

◆ This is from the second of the Ten Commandments in the Bible: 'Thou shalt not take the name of the Lord thy God in vain.' (Exodus 20:7)

your name is mud

If you say that someone's **name is mud**, you mean that they have said or done something which has made them very unpopular with a particular group of people. *His name has been mud at the Telegraph since he left to work for a rival newspaper.*

◆ This expression may refer to Dr Samuel Mudd. John Wilkes Booth, the assassin of Abraham Lincoln, broke his leg while trying to escape and was treated by Dr Mudd. Although Mudd did not know what his patient had done and acted in good faith, he was put in prison and he and his family were hated for many years.

nature

the nature of the beast

If you say that something is **the nature of the beast**, you mean that it is an essential part of the character of the person or thing that you are talking about. *Baker likes to say that negotiations always get tougher towards the end. That's the very nature of the beast.*

☐ If you say that someone knows or understands **the nature of the beast**, you mean that they know or understand a particular person or thing very well. *Why did he join the army in the first place, when he must have been aware of the nature of the beast?*

navel

navel-gazing
contemplate your navel

If you accuse someone of **navel-gazing** or **navel-contemplation**, you are criticizing them for thinking only about themselves and their own problems or activities, rather than concerning themselves with the problems or activities of other people. *I'm very good at motivating people to do things, so I'm a doer rather than a thinker. I've never really done much navel-gazing!*

☐ You can also say that someone **contemplates** their **navel** or **gazes at** their **navel**. *The Institute has always been famous for contemplating its own navel.*

neck

breathe down someone's neck: 1

In a race, contest, or other competitive situation, if someone **is breathing down** your **neck**, they are close behind you and may soon catch up with you or beat you. *No doubt Jones and Armstrong maintain a consistently high standard because both have talented rivals breathing down their necks.*

breathe down someone's neck: 2

If you say that someone **is breathing down** your **neck**, you mean that they are closely watching and checking everything that you do. *Most farmers have bank managers breathing down their necks, so everything has to have an economic reason.*

dead from the neck up

British If you say that someone is **dead from the neck up**, you are saying very rudely that they are stupid. If you say that something is **dead from the neck up**, you mean that it is not intellectually challenging or original in any way. *The debate on Labour's future has been dead from the neck upwards. It has utterly failed to excite the party, let alone the country.*

get it in the neck

British If someone **gets it in the neck**, they are punished or strongly criticized for something wrong that they have done. *This film is an attack on the media, especially the television news media. It's quite nice to see them get it in the neck for once.*

neck and neck

In a race or contest, if two competitors are **neck and neck**, they are exactly level with each other, so that it is impossible to say who will win. *The latest opinion polls show both parties running neck and neck... Philippe Jeantot of France and the South African John Martin are involved in a neck and neck race to finish second across the line.*

♦ Two horses are said to be neck and neck when they are exactly level and it is impossible to say which one is winning the race.

risk your neck

If you do something dangerous which could result in your being killed or injured, you can say that you **risk** your **neck** doing it. *I won't have him risking his neck on that motorcycle.*

stick your neck out

If you **stick** your **neck out**, you say or do something which other people are afraid to say or do, even though this may cause trouble or difficulty for you. *First of all, I'll stick my neck out here and I will say that Aston Villa won't go into the Second Division next season... At the risk of sticking my neck out, I doubt whether the compensation fund will be needed.*

♦ This expression may come from boxing, where fighters need to keep their necks and chins drawn in or protected in order to avoid being hit by their opponent.

up to your neck

If you say that someone is **up to** their **neck** in something bad such as debt or corruption, you mean that they are very deeply involved in it. *The Prime Minister was up to his neck in scandal.*

your neck of the woods

You can refer to the place where you live as your **neck of the woods**. *I discovered, however, that stone troughs were pretty scarce in my neck of the woods and expensive as well.*

□ You can refer to the place where you are at the moment as **this neck of the woods**. *What's there to do in this neck of the woods?*

♦ This expression originated in the United States. 'Neck' comes from 'naiack' which means 'point' or 'corner' in an Algonquian Native American language.

needle

like looking for a needle in a haystack

If you say that trying to find something is **like looking for a needle in a haystack**, you mean that it is extremely difficult or even impossible to find it. *Police have told Mrs Barrow that searching for the dog will be like looking for a needle in a haystack.*

nelly

not on your nelly

British, rather old-fashioned You can say **'not on your nelly'** to emphasize that there is no chance at all of something happening. *They finally become adults, thanks to all your hard work, and do they turn up for mum's birthday? Not on your nellie.*

◆ 'Nelly' is sometimes spelled 'nellie'. This expression may come from cockney rhyming slang. 'Not on your Nellie Duff' stands for 'not on your puff', 'puff' being slang for 'life'.

nerve

touch a nerve
strike a raw nerve

If something that you say **touches a nerve** or **touches a raw nerve**, it upsets someone, because you have mentioned a subject that they feel strongly about or are very sensitive about. You can also say that it **strikes a nerve** or **a raw nerve**. *Buchanan's speech touched a raw nerve here at the Capitol... She seemed to strike a nerve when she asked Dr. Lowe about his past life.*

☐ You can also talk about a remark **finding** or **exposing a raw nerve**. *In making their call for a neutral inspection team, the government have exercised their talent for finding a raw nerve, as doubts have been raised about the neutrality of some of the weapons inspectors.*

nerves

a bundle of nerves
a bag of nerves

If you say that someone is **a bundle of nerves**, you mean that they are extremely nervous, worried, or tense. In British English, you can also say that they are **a bag of nerves**. *What's the matter? You're a bundle of nerves.*

get on someone's nerves

If you say that someone or something **gets on** your **nerves**, you mean that they annoy or irritate you. *It was so hot, and there we were, just cooped up together, getting on each other's nerves.*

live on your nerves

British If you say that someone **is living on** their **nerves**, you mean that they are always worried and anxious, because they are in a difficult situation. *Once this is all over and done with I've told her she's to go into*

*the clinic for a complete rest to get her strength back, because she's living on
her nerves.*

a war of nerves
a battle of nerves

If two opposing people or groups are carrying on **a war of nerves** or **a
battle of nerves**, they are trying to weaken each other psychologically,
for example by frightening each other, in order to get what they want
without taking any direct action. *There may be a truce in the long war of
nerves between the White House and Congress over how this country
conducts secret intelligence operations abroad.*

nest

feather your nest

If you accuse someone of **feathering** their **nest**, you are accusing them
of taking advantage of their position in order to get a lot of money, so that
they can lead a comfortable life. *The politicians seem anxious to feather
their nests at the expense of the people.*

◆ Some birds line their nests with soft feathers which they pluck from
their own breasts or gather from the ground.

fly the nest
leave the nest

When children **fly the nest** or **leave the nest**, they leave their parents'
home to live on their own. Compare **fly the coop**; see **coop**. *When their
children had flown the nest, he and his wife moved to a thatched cottage in
Dorset.*

foul your own nest

If you say that someone **has fouled** their **own nest**, you mean that they
have done something which damages their own interests or chances of
success. *Man has invented a hundred brilliant ways of fouling his own nest
– the grime, the pollution, the heat, the poisons in the air, the metals in the
water.*

a nest egg

A **nest egg** is a sum of money that you are saving for a particular
purpose. *He collected about $450m as a retirement nest-egg when he sold
most of his controlling stake to Canadian Pacific.*

net

cast a wide net
cast the net wider

If you **cast a wide net**, you involve a large number of things or people in what you are doing. If you **cast the net wider**, you increase the number of things or people that are involved. *The U.S. has cast a wide diplomatic net, asking a variety of other nations to deliver the same message to Iran and to Syria... We will cast the net wider to look at many other factors too.*

slip through the net: 1
fall through the net

British If people **slip through the net** or **fall through the net**, the system which is supposed to help or deal with them does not do it properly. The American expression is **fall through the cracks**. *Vulnerable adults may be slipping through the social work net.*

slip through the net: 2

Mainly British If someone who is behaving illegally **slips through the net**, they avoid being caught by the system or trap that is meant to catch them. *Government officials fear some of the thugs identified by British police may have slipped through the net.*

☐ If illegal goods **slip through the net**, the system which is meant to discover them does not find them. *A shipment of 44 kilos of cocaine slipped through the customs net at Gatwick.*

nettle

grasp the nettle

Mainly British If someone **grasps the nettle**, they deal with a problem or unpleasant task quickly and in a determined way. *It's better to grasp the nettle, speak to your superior and make it clear you regret your mistake and are determined it will never happen again.*

♦ If you grasp a nettle firmly, it is less likely to sting you than if you just touch it lightly.

nice

nice as pie

If you say that someone is as **nice as pie**, you mean that they are very kind, friendly, and charming. You usually say this when their behaviour is not what you expect, or when it contrasts with their behaviour at other times. Compare **sweet as pie**; see **sweet**. *He is nice as pie when you meet him, then you hear he is going around bad-mouthing you.*

niche

carve a niche

If you **carve a niche** for yourself or **carve out a niche**, you create a secure position for yourself, especially at work. *The firm is carving out what could be a lucrative niche in the market for microprocessors.*

nick

in the nick of time

If you say that something happens **in the nick of time**, you mean that it happens at the last possible moment, when it is almost too late. *She woke up in the nick of time and raised the alarm.*

nickel

nickel and dime: 1

Mainly American If you describe someone or something as **nickel and dime**, you mean that they are not very important or only function on a small scale. *The boss is dead and now every nickel and dime drug dealer and money launderer can come in here and ply his trade.*

nickel and dime: 2

American If you accuse a person of **nickel and diming** someone or something, you are criticizing that person for weakening or exhausting them, for example by continually taking small amounts of money away from them, or by continually making small changes or requests. *Oakland, like other cities, has been reeling from financial crisis and consequently has been nickel-and-diming essential services for years.*

◆ A nickel is a five cent coin and a dime is a ten cent coin.

a wooden nickel

American If you refer to something as **a wooden nickel**, you mean that it is completely false or worthless. *He looked at the card as though it were a wooden nickel. 'That doesn't prove a thing,' he said.*

night

a night owl

If you describe someone as **a night owl**, you mean that they regularly stay up late at night, or prefer to work late at night. *The street noise and late-night parties make this hotel a haven for night owls.*

ninepins

fall like ninepins

British If you say that things **are falling like ninepins**, you mean that they are rapidly being damaged or destroyed, one after another. *Conservative council seats fell like ninepins.*

◆ Ninepins are skittles.

nines

dress to the nines

If you say that someone **is dressed to the nines**, you mean that they are wearing very smart or glamorous clothes. This expression is often used to suggest that someone is dressed in an exaggerated or inappropriate way. *They dress to the nines when they go out on the town.*

☐ In British English, you can also say that someone **is done up to the nines**. *You're more likely to find the genuine rogue done up to the nines in an Armani suit.*

nineteen

talk nineteen to the dozen

British If you say that someone is talking **nineteen to the dozen**, you mean that they are talking very quickly, without pausing. *Ms Wallace visited them on February 28th and found them 'vivacious and chatty and talking nineteen to the dozen'.*

nip

nip and tuck

In a competition or contest, if it is **nip and tuck**, it is impossible to say who will win because both sides are performing equally well. *It was nip and tuck throughout as the players struck the ball with equal venom.*

◆ One explanation for this expression is that it comes from sword-fighting, where a 'nip' is a light touch and a 'tuck' a heavier blow. Another is that it comes from horse racing, where it means the same as 'neck and neck'.

nits

pick nits

If you say that someone **is picking nits**, you mean that they are pointing out small problems or faults with something, often ones which seem relatively unimportant. *He then spent the second half of his intervention picking nits, particularly about the environmental impact for 'the beautiful' Bluebell Hill.*

◆ The verb 'nitpick' has a similar meaning, and there is also a much more frequent word 'nitpicking'. These words are generally used more disapprovingly than 'pick nits', to express criticism of someone who is deliberately trying to find faults.

nod

a nod and a wink

British If someone gives you **a nod and a wink**, they communicate something to you by saying it indirectly or by giving you some kind of signal. This expression is usually used to show disapproval, often because something illegal or dishonest is taking place. *A nod and a wink from the chairman is all it takes to move share prices up or down... There has been so-called 'nod and wink' diplomacy on the sidelines.*

□ If you say **'a nod's as good as a wink'**, you mean that it is not necessary to explain something further, because you understand what someone has already signalled to you or told you indirectly.

◆ This comes from the saying 'a nod's as good as a wink to a blind horse', which suggests that both the nod and the wink are equally useless, as the horse would not be able to see either.

on the nod

British If a proposal goes through **on the nod**, it is accepted without being questioned or argued about. *The party cannot be seen to let the treaty through on the nod.*

◆ One explanation for this expression is that it comes from auctions, where bidders nod as a sign that they want to buy something.

noises

make noises

If you say that someone **is making noises** about something, you mean that they are talking about it in a vague, indirect, or indefinite way. *John Major has been making noises about making government more open.*

make the right noises

If you say that someone **is making the right noises** about a problem or issue, you mean that their remarks suggest that they will deal with the situation in the way that you want them to. *The President was making all the right noises about multi-party democracy and human rights.*

nooks

the nooks and crannies

If you talk about **the nooks and crannies** of a place or object, you are talking about the smaller or less accessible parts which are not normally noticed. *In the weeks before Christmas, we would scour the house, searching all the nooks and crannies trying to find our presents.*

◆ 'Nook' is an old word for a corner, and a 'cranny' is a crack or crevice.

nose

cut off your nose to spite your face

If you say that someone **is cutting off** their **nose to spite** their **face**, you mean they are doing something in order to hurt another person, without realizing or caring that they will hurt themselves just as much or even more. *It is clear that while the manager would not be prepared to cut off his nose to spite his face by leaving out the centre-half, he is concerned that the player should realise the error of his ways.*

follow your nose: 1

If you **follow** your **nose**, you make decisions and behave in a particular way because you feel instinctively that this is what you should do, rather than because you are following any guidelines or rules. *I'd started a bit of journalism, so I had a source of income. And I've just followed my nose doing that ever since.*

follow your nose: 2

If someone tells you to **follow** your **nose** when you are looking for a place, they are telling you to go straight ahead, or to follow the most obvious route. *More or less follow your nose till you come to Marks and Spencer's. Bear right there. And it's there.*

get up someone's nose

Mainly British If you say that something or someone **gets up** your **nose**, you mean that they irritate you a great deal. *This producer looks as if he's going to get up everybody's nose. He has only been here for a few hours and already he has been babbling about 'discipline' to Annie.*

give someone a bloody nose: 1
bloody someone's nose

In a contest or competition, if one side **is given a bloody nose**, it is defeated in a way that does not cause permanent damage but makes it look foolish or inferior. *Most are so fed up with this current attack on the elderly they are threatening to give the Government more than a bloody nose in the forthcoming by-election.*

□ You can also say that one side in a contest **bloodies the nose of** the other side. *A full-scale ambush is almost certainly beyond the Welsh team. But they'll be looking for a few opportunities to bloody English noses, all the same.*

give someone a bloody nose: 2

In a war or conflict, if one side **is given a bloody nose**, it is damaged sufficiently to cause it to withdraw, at least for a time. *Giving the national army a bloody nose is one thing. Taking on its full might is another.*

□ You can also say that one side in a conflict **bloodies the nose of** the other side. *He never forgave the rebels for bloodying the nose of the army he sent against them in 1979.*

keep your nose clean

If you **keep** your **nose clean**, you behave well and avoid trouble. *The best advice I can give is tell you to keep your nose clean.*

keep your nose out of something

If someone tells you to **keep** your **nose out of** something, they are telling you rather rudely not to interfere in it, because it does not concern you. Compare **poke** your **nose into** something. *Nancy realized that this was his way of telling her to keep her nose out of his business.*

keep your nose to the grindstone

If you **keep** your **nose to the grindstone**, you concentrate on working hard at your job, and do not concern yourself with other things. *There is more to life than keeping one's nose to the grindstone and saving for a rainy day.* A grindstone is a revolving stone disc which is used to sharpen metal tools. The reference here is to a person bending over the grindstone while they are working, so that their nose is close to it. The person sharpening the tools bent over the grindstone when they were working hard, so their nose would be close to the grindstone.

lead someone by the nose

If someone **leads** you **by the nose** or **leads** you **around by the nose**, they control you completely so that you do whatever they want. This expression is often used to suggest that the person being led is foolish or wrong to let this happen. *The Government has let itself be led by the nose by the timber trade into suppressing the report for the narrow commercial advantage of those involved.*

◆ Bulls and other animals sometimes have rings through their noses so that a rope can be tied to the ring in order to lead them along.

look down your nose at something

If you say that someone **looks down** their **nose at** a thing or person, you mean that they regard that thing or person as inferior and treat them with scorn or disrespect. You use this expression to show disapproval of this attitude. *If anyone leaves my shop feeling that we'd looked down our noses at them for not buying expensive cheese, I would be very ashamed.*

a nose for something

If you say that someone has **a nose for** something, you mean that they have a natural talent for finding it. *How does he rate a good record over an indifferent one? 'You just feel it, somehow, if it's good,' he says. 'You develop a nose for it.'*

not see beyond your nose
not see beyond the end of your nose

If you say that someone **can't see beyond** their **nose**, or **can't see**

beyond the end of their **nose**, you are criticizing them for thinking only about themselves and their immediate needs, rather than about other people or wider and longer-term issues. *We want our people to be able to see beyond their own noses and to keep things in perspective... It is high time that British industry started thinking beyond the end of its nose. The trouble is that what companies perceive to be in their own interest is not necessarily what the country needs.*

on the nose: 1

If you talk about a time or amount being **on the nose**, you mean that it is exactly that time or amount. *This is Radio One FM. Precisely on the nose seven sixteen.*

◆ The origin of this expression is in broadcasting. When a show was running on time, the producer signalled this fact to the performers by putting a finger on his or her nose.

on the nose: 2

If you describe someone or something as **on the nose**, you mean that they are considered to be unpleasant or offensive. This expression is used mainly in Australian English. *North West Airlines might be on the nose here and in Japan but it's definitely flavour of the month in the United States.*

pay through the nose for something

If you **pay through the nose** for something, you pay more for it than you consider fair or reasonable. *Some restaurateurs have cottoned on to the fact that we do not like paying through the nose for our wines when eating out.*

poke your nose into something
stick your nose into something

If you say that someone is **poking** their **nose into** something or **sticking** their **nose into** it, you mean that they are interfering in something that does not concern them. Compare **keep** your **nose out of** something. *We don't like foreigners who poke their noses into our affairs.*

put someone's nose out of joint

If something **puts** someone's **nose out of joint**, it offends or upsets them, because they think that they have not been treated with the respect that they deserve. You often use this expression to suggest that the person who is offended thinks that they are more important than they really are. *Gillian's sons, 17 and 15, were resentful of the female invasion. Barry, the youngest, had his nose put out of joint by Lucy's aloof sophistication, although she was his junior.*

rub someone's nose in it
rub someone's nose in the dirt

If you **rub** someone's **nose in it** or **rub** their **nose in the dirt**, you embarrass or upset them by reminding them of something that they do not want to think about, such as a failure or a mistake that they have made. *You obviously delight in the defeat of a fellow performer! And proceed to rub his nose in it, don't you?... If he agrees to withdraw his forces, should there be some other arrangement which would be a let-out rather than rubbing his nose in the dirt?*

□ You can also say that someone's nose **is rubbed in** a particular failing or mistake. *America should have basked in triumph after the fall of communism, but instead found its nose rubbed in inadequacies at home.*

thumb your nose at someone

If you **thumb** your **nose at** someone or something powerful or influential, you behave in a way that shows disrespect or contempt for them. *There is a hard-core of young persistent offenders, and too many of them are simply laughing at authority and thumbing their noses at the court.*

□ You can describe this behaviour as **nose-thumbing**. *These women's lives, as portrayed by Hollywood, were a nose-thumbing at stuffy Victorian England.*

◆ To thumb your nose at someone literally means to make a rude gesture by placing the end of your thumb on the end of your nose, spreading out your fingers, and wiggling them. 'Cock a snook at someone' means the same.

turn up your nose at something

If you say that someone **turns up** their **nose at** something, you mean that they reject it because they think that it is not good enough for them. You use this expression to show disapproval of the person's behaviour, because you think that they are being foolish or too proud. *You should never turn your nose up at inexpensive plants.*

nuclear

go nuclear

British If someone **goes nuclear**, they get extremely angry and start behaving in a forceful or irrational way as a result. *Labour's tabloids were ready to go nuclear against the Tories if personal smears were deployed against Neil Kinnock and his team during the general election campaign.*

nudge

a nudge and a wink
nudge-nudge, wink-wink

You use expressions such as **a nudge and a wink** or **nudge-nudge, wink-wink** to indicate that someone is talking about something in a sly, suggestive way, because the subject is embarrassing or because they may get into trouble if they say it openly. *The article then listed a series of nudge-nudge, wink-wink rumors that have appeared in broadsheet and tabloid newspapers over the last two years, insinuating the Prime Minister was having an affair.*

◆ This expression became popular as a result of the 1970s British TV comedy series 'Monty Python's Flying Circus'. One of the characters in a sketch made suggestive remarks and followed them by saying 'nudge-nudge, wink-wink, say no more'. People sometimes nudge each other or wink at each other as a way of hinting at something.

number

a back number

If you refer to someone as **a back number**, you are saying in a rather unkind way that they are no longer useful or successful. *The film gives us a real sense of the way the Japanese still honour those who might in other societies be considered back numbers.*

◆ A back number of a magazine or newspaper is an edition of it that was published some time ago and is not the most recent.

do a number on someone

If someone **does a number on** you, they harm you in some way, for example by cheating you or by totally defeating you in a game or match. *I really did a number on him. I'm going to try and make it up to him, if he'll let me... The Irish team are looking to do a number on England in Dublin tomorrow.*

have someone's number

If you **have** someone's **number**, you understand what kind of person they are, and so you know how to treat them or deal with them. *If they have your number from the start, and it is a small hotel, you are bound to get extra attention.*

look after number one

If you say that someone **looks after number one**, you mean that they selfishly put their own needs and interests before everyone else's. *This sums up the attitude of many greedy big earners – look after Number One* *and to hell with everyone else.*

someone's number is up

If you say that someone's **number is up**, you mean that something unpleasant is going to happen to them, and that there is nothing that they can do about it. This expression is sometimes used to say that someone is certain to fail at something, or that they are about to lose their job. It can also be used to say that someone is going to die. *When Michael Stich found himself two match points down to Marc Rosset of Switzerland last night, he thought his number was up.*

nut

do your nut

British If someone **does** their **nut**, they become very angry about something. *I wanted to ask Lorraine out and I knew that Wendy would do her nut if she found out.*

◆ Nut is a slang word for head.

a sledgehammer to crack a nut

British If you say that someone is using **a sledgehammer to crack a nut**, you mean that the methods they are using to solve a problem are far stronger than is necessary. People sometimes replace 'sledgehammer' with 'hammer'. *Bankers say that the proposed law is a sledgehammer to crack a nut.*

◆ A sledgehammer is a large heavy hammer which is used for smashing rocks and concrete.

a tough nut to crack
a tough nut

If you say that a problem is **a tough nut to crack**, you mean that it is difficult to resolve. If you say that someone is **a tough nut to crack**, you mean that they are difficult to deal with or to defeat in an argument or competition. You can also describe a person or problem like this as **a tough nut**. *Despite not having won a title of note, Harrington has taken 17.5 points from a possible 20 in international singles, making him a tough nut to crack... But the tough nut is the economy and health care, those two issues that do cost money and that require some complex strategy and a lot of risk taking.*

nuts

the nuts and bolts of something

The nuts and bolts of something are the detailed facts about it and its practical aspects, as opposed to abstract ideas about it. *Tonight Margaret*

Atwood will discuss the nuts and bolts of the writer's craft... I've always taken a nuts and bolts approach.

nutshell

in a nutshell

You say **'in a nutshell'** when you are summarizing something in a concise or brief way. *She wants me to leave the company. I want to stay. That's it in a nutshell.*

nutty

nutty as a fruitcake

British If you say that someone is as **nutty as a fruitcake**, you think that they are very strange, foolish, or crazy. *He sounds a trifle defensive, but there's no need for it. Despite his maddening fidgeting, the man is a charmer – intense, funny, and nutty as a fruitcake.*

O

oaks

great oaks from little acorns grow

People say **'great oaks from little acorns grow'** when they want to point out that something large and successful began in a small and insignificant way. Other adjectives can be used instead of 'great' and 'little'. *Henry Ford did not start his operations by hiring 330,000 employees and opening hundreds of factories in his first year. Remember, mighty oaks from tiny acorns grow.*

◆ Acorns are the nuts that grow on oak trees.

oar

put your oar in

Mainly British If someone **puts** their **oar in** during a discussion or argument, they give their opinion, even if other people have not asked them for it. Verbs such as 'stick' and 'get' can be used instead of 'put'. *He is modest enough to let them say their piece without feeling the need to put his oar in; he is obviously a good listener.*

◆ This comes from an old expression 'to have an oar in every man's boat', meaning to interfere in other people's business.

oars

rest on your oars
lean on your oars

British If you say that someone **is resting on** their **oars** or **is leaning on** their **oars**, you are criticizing them for not working hard, so that they are in danger of suffering harm or defeat. *In the absence of any other source of pressure, many boards take their time over making necessary changes, leaning on their oars while another study is done and another year goes by.*

oats

sow your wild oats

If you say that someone, especially a young man, **is sowing** their **wild oats**, you mean that they have many sexual relationships, without expecting or wanting any of them to become serious or permanent. *I got all that sowing wild oats out of my system before I got married.*

◆ In this expression, the behaviour of young people is compared to someone sowing wild oats, which cannot be eaten, on good ground instead of edible oats.

odds

at odds with someone: 1

If one person is **at odds with** another, or if two people are **at odds**, they disagree about something. *The region has reportedly been at odds with the central government both militarily and politically... The authorities, the security forces and the politicians remain at odds over how to deal with the campaign by militants for a separate independent homeland.*

at odds with something: 2

If you say that one thing is **at odds with** another, you mean that it does not match or correspond to that other thing. *He was a good piano player, but slightly ashamed of it, as it seemed at odds with his macho image.*

pay over the odds

British If you **pay over the odds** for something, you pay more for it than it is really worth. *Over the years, London's beer drinkers have got used to having to pay a little bit over the odds for their pint. It has been the price of living in a prosperous area where costs are higher.*

◆ This expression refers to someone paying more than the agreed or usual price when they are betting on a horse in a race.

odour (*American* odor)

in bad odour
in good odour

Fairly old-fashioned If you are **in bad odour** with someone, they disapprove of you because they think you have done something bad or wrong. You can say that you are **in good odour** with someone when they think you have done something good or right. *The republic's policy of repression has put them in bad odour with Western human rights groups... He became director of central intelligence in 1987. The agency has managed to keep out of trouble since then and he is keen to leave while it is still in good odour.*

off-chance

on the off-chance

If you do something **on the off-chance** that something good or pleasant will happen, you do it because there is a small chance that the good or pleasant thing will happen. *I just thought I'd call on the off chance.*

oil

no oil painting

British If you say that someone is **no oil painting**, you mean that they are unattractive or ugly. *I started seeing a guy who was no oil painting but wonderfully bright and interesting.*

oil and water

If you say that you cannot mix **oil and water**, you mean that if two people or things are very different they cannot work together or exist together successfully. *'One might just as well try mixing oil and water,' Marianne replied, 'as people from the arts with those who have cash registers where their hearts should be.'*

☐ You say that two people or things are **like oil and water**, or that they **are oil and water**, to emphasize that they are very different. *We got along well despite being oil and water.*

pour oil on troubled waters

If you **pour oil on troubled waters**, you do or say something to make an angry or tense situation calmer or more peaceful. *He is an extremely experienced politician, who some diplomats believe may be able to pour oil on the troubled waters.*

◆ It has been known for a long time that pouring oil on rough water could calm it. The Greek author Plutarch mentioned it in about 95 AD: 'Why does pouring oil on the sea make it still and calm?'

strike oil

If you say that someone **has struck oil**, you mean that they have suddenly become successful in finding or doing something. *'It won't tell us where he was at the time of the murder.' 'Work on it. The police aren't likely to strike oil in the King Edward. Not the sort of pub where people take time to stand and stare.'*

◆ This expression is more commonly used literally to say that someone discovers oil in the ground as a result of drilling. 'Strike lucky' is based on the same idea.

old

old as the hills

If you say that something is as **old as the hills**, you mean that it is very old, and perhaps old-fashioned or very traditional. *Their equipment may be modern, but the techniques remain as old as the hills.*

olive

an olive branch

If you hold out **an olive branch** to someone, you say or do something to indicate that you want to end a disagreement with them or stop them feeling resentful, bitter, or angry with you. *He held out an olive branch to the 500,000-strong Hungarian minority, some of whom feel their future in an independent Slovakia may be less than secure.*

◆ The story of the Flood in the Bible tells how Noah sent out first a raven, then a dove, to see if there was any sign of land. If they found some land, it would mean that God had forgiven man: 'And the dove came in to him in the evening; and, lo, in her mouth was an olive leaf pluckt off; so Noah knew that the waters were abated from off the earth.' (Genesis 8:11)

omelette

you can't make an omelette without breaking eggs

If you say that you **can't make an omelette without breaking eggs**, you mean that it is impossible to achieve something without there being bad or unpleasant side-effects. *You can't make an omelette without breaking eggs. If you want universal health care there's just no way of* *getting it without us putting more money into it.*

♦ 'Omelette' is also spelled 'omelet' in American English.

omnibus

the man on the Clapham omnibus

British When people talk about **the man on the Clapham omnibus**, they mean ordinary, average people. Other place names are sometimes used instead of 'Clapham'. *The wealthy and powerful never liked the man on the Clapham omnibus knowing what they were about.*

♦ Clapham is an area of London and 'omnibus' is an old-fashioned word for bus. This expression was first used by a British judge, Lord Bowen, in 1903 when he was hearing a case of negligence in court: 'We must ask ourselves what the man on the Clapham omnibus would think.'

one

be one up on someone

If you **are one up on** someone, you have an advantage over them, because you have done something which they have not done or because you know something that they do not know. *You don't want the competitive kind who will see this as the opportunity to be one up on you.*

got it in one

British If someone guesses something and you say **'got it in one'** or **'you've got it in one'**, you mean that they have guessed correctly. *'Is that a Birmingham accent?' I asked, explaining that all my family were originally from that part of the world. 'You got it in one. I grew up in Birmingham.'*

☐ You can also use these expressions after asking a question, to indicate that the answer is obvious. *Guess who objected strongly to the scheme? You've got it in one!*

put one over on someone

If you **put one over on** an opponent or rival, you gain a victory or advantage over them. *Clark insisted: 'It's nice to put one over on your old boss but I don't hold any grudges.'*

onions

know your onions

British, old-fashioned If you say that someone **knows** their **onions**, you mean that they know a great deal about a particular subject. *It shows she really knows her onions in the historical field too.*

open

open and shut

If you say that something, especially a legal case, is **open and shut**, you mean that it is easily decided or solved because the facts are very clear. *The prosecution behaved as if they had an open-and-shut case.*

order

the order of the day

If you say that something is **the order of the day**, you mean that it is what is happening in a particular situation, or what someone considers should be happening then. *Informality is the order of the day among all the Princess Royal's household.*

a tall order

If you describe a task as **a tall order**, you mean that it is going to be very difficult. *Financing your studies may seem like a tall order, but there is plenty of help available.*

◆ An old meaning of 'tall' is large or excessive.

orders

marching orders: 1

British If you are given your **marching orders**, you are made to leave something such as a job or a relationship. If a player in a team sport is given their **marching orders**, they are ordered to leave the pitch because they have behaved in an unacceptable way. The American expression is **walking papers**. *What does it take for a woman to say 'that's enough' and give her man his marching orders?*

marching orders: 2

American Your **marching orders** are the instructions that you are given in order to carry out a plan or achieve an aim. *As one mid-level White House official put it, 'We're still waiting for our marching orders.'*

◆ When soldiers are given marching orders, they are ordered to march to a particular place.

organ

the organ grinder's monkey

British If you refer to someone as **the organ grinder's monkey**, you mean that they are closely associated with a powerful person and act on their behalf, but have no real power themselves. This expression is often used to show contempt or dislike for both of the people you are talking about, but especially for the 'monkey'. *'Do you feel that you've been squeezed out?' 'Well, I feel more like the organ-grinder's monkey, actually.'*

☐ The wording of this expression is not very fixed, and people often refer to it partially or indirectly. *Why bother with monkeys when you can deal with the organ-grinder?*

♦ Organ grinders are street entertainers who play barrel organs. Sometimes they have a monkey that performs to the music.

overdrive

go into overdrive

If someone or something **goes into overdrive**, they begin to work very hard or to perform intensely or very well. *The campaign that began in the cold of New Hampshire is in overdrive now with the candidates crisscrossing the nation in a final push for votes.*

♦ Overdrive is an extra gear on some vehicles, which enables them to go faster than they can with ordinary gears.

own

hold your own

If you **hold** your **own**, you are able to defend your position against someone who is attacking you or threatening you. *Some areas of heavy industry, such as shipbuilding, were able to hold their own in international markets.*

P

p

mind your p's and q's

If you **mind** your **p's and q's**, you try to speak and behave politely or to act in an acceptable way, so that you do not offend people. *She always put on her best act and minded her p's and q's in front of the queen, but their relationship wasn't that close.*

◆ This expression may originally have been a warning to children not to confuse p's and q's when learning the alphabet. Alternatively, 'p's and q's' may stand for 'pleases and thankyous', or expressions of politeness.

pace

can't stand the pace

If someone **can't stand the pace**, they do not work or function effectively when they are under pressure, and so cannot compete or do things as well as other people. *Most journalists know of a colleague who abandoned journalism for advertising. We curl our lips at such a fellow. He is a sell-out, a loser, somebody who couldn't stand the pace in the real game.*

set the pace

If someone **sets the pace**, they do something which is regarded as a good example, and other people then do the same thing. *The consensus is that Versace has got it right this season and has set the pace for mainstream fashion.*

□ You can refer to someone who does this as a **pacesetter** and to this activity as **pacesetting**. *Politically and geographically isolated and with no history of overt opposition to communist rule, it seemed an unlikely candidate as the pacesetter for political change in Asia... Though consumer-electronics companies may have failed to come up with a new pace-setting product quite as novel as the video cassette recorder, never have they been more inventive.*

paces

put someone through their paces

If you **put** someone or something **through** their **paces**, you get them to show you how well they can do something. Other verbs can be used instead of 'put'. *The eleven boxers on the British team are in the hands of the British coach, Ian Irwin, who is putting them through their paces.*

◆ To put a horse through its paces means to test it to see how well it has been trained.

pack

ahead of the pack

If a person or organization is **ahead of the pack**, they are being more successful than their competitors or rivals. *This decentralized management system has kept the company far ahead of the pack in terms of* *product development.*

page

on the same page

American If two or more people are **on the same page**, they are in agreement about what they are trying to achieve. *We're all on about the same page in our careers, we all have the same professional needs.*

turn the page

If someone **turns the page**, they make a fresh start after a period of difficulties and troubles. Compare **turn over a new leaf**; see **leaf**. *Shareholders at Fiat's annual meeting will be looking for signs that the troubled company really does mean to turn the page.*

paid

put paid to something

Mainly British If an unexpected event **puts paid to** someone's hopes, chances, or plans, it completely ends or destroys them. *Great Britain gave a limp performance here last night that put paid to their chances of reaching the Olympic finals.*

pain

a pain in the neck

If you think that someone or something is very annoying, you can say that they are **a pain in the neck**. *He was a pain in the neck. I was glad when he left my department.*

pains

growing pains

If an organization or a relationship suffers from **growing pains**, it experiences temporary difficulties and problems as it develops and grows stronger. *Their three-year-old marriage has been going through some growing pains.*

◆ Growing pains are pains that children sometimes get in their muscles and joints. Many people wrongly think that they are caused by the children growing too fast.

pale

beyond the pale

If you say that someone's behaviour goes **beyond the pale**, you mean that it is completely unacceptable. *There will be no more compromises with people whose views are beyond the pale.*

◆ 'Pale' comes from the Latin 'palum', meaning 'stake', and in English it came to refer to a territorial boundary marked by a line of stakes. The area inside was regarded as civilized, but the area beyond the pale was seen as barbaric.

palm

grease someone's palm

If you accuse someone of **greasing** an official's **palm**, you are accusing them of giving money to the official in order to gain an unfair advantage over other people or in order to get something that they want. You can replace the verb 'grease' with the verb 'oil'. *Italy's continuing corruption probe took a fresh turn with the confession by Carlo De Benedetti, Olivetti's chairman, that he, too, was forced to grease a few palms along the way.*

◆ The idea behind this expression is that grease and oil help machines work smoothly. In the same way, bribing people will make it easier to get what you want.

Pandora

a Pandora's box

If someone opens **a Pandora's box**, they do something that unintentionally causes a lot of problems, which they did not know existed before. *This latest controversy has opened up a Pandora's box of intrigue amongst the coalition government's different factions.*

◆ According to Roman mythology, Prometheus offended the gods and in revenge Jupiter ordered the creation of Pandora, the first woman. Jupiter gave Pandora a box which she was to offer to the man she married. Pandora married Prometheus's brother Epimethius. He opened the box and all the problems and wickedness that now trouble the world flew out and could never be put back.

pants

catch someone with their pants down
catch someone with their trousers down

If someone **is caught with** their **pants down** or **is caught with** their **trousers down**, something happens that they are not prepared for and that reveals an embarrassing or shocking fact about them. 'Catch someone with their trousers down' is used only in British English. *In July 1991, the Department of Transport was caught with its pants down and took seven months to produce the consultative document needed to change legislation.*

paper

can't fight your way out of a paper bag

If you say that someone **can't fight** their **way out of a paper bag**, you are saying in a contemptuous way that they are very bad at fighting. *We've already shown you that they are no use to you as allies. They couldn't fight their way out of a paper bag.*

☐ You can replace 'fight' with other verbs that state what someone is incapable of doing. *Certainly, too, the democratic parties that support Mr Yeltsin could not organise their way out of a paper bag.*

not worth the paper it's written on

If you say that a promise, agreement, or guarantee **is not worth the paper it's written on**, you mean that although it appears to be official or definite, it is in fact worthless. 'Printed' can be used instead of 'written'. *The certificate is not worth the paper it is printed on.*

on paper

If you say that something looks or sounds good **on paper**, you mean that it seems to be a good idea, plan, or argument when you read or hear about it, but may not be good in reality. *These reforms are more impressive on paper than in reality.*

a paper tiger

If you say that a person, country, or organization is **a paper tiger**, you mean that although they seem to be powerful, they do not really have any power. *Russia's Asian forces are a paper tiger these days. Starved of fuel and spare parts, low on morale, they are barely in shape even for manoeuvres, let alone war.*

◆ This is an old Chinese expression which Chairman Mao applied to the United States in the 1950s.

a paper trail

Mainly American Written evidence of someone's activities can be referred to as **a paper trail**. *The criminal proceedings were raised after investigations found a paper trail of checks that were written on dummy bank accounts.*

papers

walking papers

American If you are given your **walking papers**, you are made to leave something such as a job or a relationship. The British expression is **marching orders**. *Sol Siegel having been ousted several months earlier, it was Vogel's turn to get his walking papers from the board of directors.*

par

par for the course

If you say that something that happens is **par for the course**, you mean that you are not pleased with it but it is what you expected to happen. *He said long hours are par for the course. 'I'm up every morning at six, or even earlier.'*

♦ In golf, 'par' is the number of strokes a good golfer is expected to take for a particular hole or for the whole course.

parade

rain on someone's parade

If someone **rains on** your **parade**, they do something which spoils a plan of yours, usually a plan that is very important to you. *Damon Hill is ready to rain on Nigel Mansell's comeback parade in Sunday's French Grand Prix.*

parker

a nosey parker

British If you say that someone is **a nosey parker**, you are criticizing them for being interested in things that are nothing to do with them. *The village's resident nosey parker, Olive, likes to spy on her neighbours with binoculars.*

♦ 'Nosey' is sometimes spelled 'nosy'. 'Parker' may refer to Matthew Parker, who became Archbishop of Canterbury in 1559, and had a reputation for interfering in people's business.

parrot

parrot fashion

British If a child learns something **parrot fashion**, they learn it by repeating it many times, but they do not really understand what it means.

Under the old system pupils often had to stand to attention and repeat lessons parrot fashion.

♦ Some parrots are able to imitate human speech, and repeat words and phrases, although they do not really understand what they are saying.

part

look the part: 1

If someone **looks the part**, they dress or behave in the way that is characteristic of a particular kind of person. *You look the part of an English gentleman, so he is half ready to believe you as soon as you meet.*

look the part: 2

Mainly British If you want to say that someone or something seems impressive, you can say that they **look the part**. *The Alpha 5 CD player certainly looks the part with a stylish slimline design, moulded front panel and finely-textured paint finish.*

part and parcel

If one thing is **part and parcel** of another, it is involved or included in it and cannot be separated from it. *There comes a time during every player's season when his form dips and the goals don't go in. It's part and parcel of being a professional.*

take something in good part

British If someone **takes** something such as criticism **in good part**, they are not offended or upset by it. *I tried to eliminate from the critical comments the casual, the superficial and the trivial, but I nevertheless agonized over having to pass on to Pasternak even the sort of objections with which I could not myself agree. But he took it all, however unusual, in good part.*

party

bring something to the party

If you talk about what someone **brings to the party**, you are talking about the contribution they make to a particular activity or situation. *Johnson asked, 'What do they bring to the party?' 'They bring a lot to the party,' Cohen replied, 'principally $3 billion in capital.'*

pass

sell the pass

British, old-fashioned If you say that someone **has sold the pass**, you are accusing them of betraying their friends or allies by giving an enemy or opponent what they wanted. *English Heritage has been notably inactive in defending ancient battlefields in the past, and was widely blamed for selling the pass at a public enquiry in 1985 which enabled a new motorway to be built over the site of the battle of Naseby.*

◆ This expression relates to a story in Irish history. The soldiers of Crotha, Lord of Atha, were blocking a pass between the mountains, against the enemy army of Trathal, the King of Cael. One of Crotha's soldiers was bribed to let Trathal's army through, and so he 'sold the pass'. Because of this, Trathal's army invaded successfully, and Trathal became king of all Ireland.

past

wouldn't put it past someone

If you say that you **wouldn't put it past** someone to do something bad, you mean that you would not be surprised if they did it. *I wouldn't put it past him to double-cross Schrader, especially after the rumour I heard the other day.*

pasture

put someone out to pasture

If someone **is put out to pasture**, they are made to retire from their job, or they are moved to an unimportant job, usually because people think that they are too old to be useful. *I'm retiring next month. They're putting me out to pasture... At 28, I'm hardly ready to be put out to pasture and it's not so long ago I was England's No 1 strike bowler for 18 months.*

◆ When horses have reached the end of their working lives, they are sometimes released into fields to graze.

pastures

greener pastures

If someone seeks **greener pastures**, they try to leave a situation which they do not like, in order to find a new and better one. *There are drawbacks for nurses seeking greener pastures overseas, and many are put off by the lengthy process involved in going to work in the US.*

pastures new
fresh pastures

British If someone moves on to **pastures new**, they leave their current situation and enter a new one. *Michael decided he wanted to move on to pastures new for financial reasons.*

☐ You can also talk about moving on to **new pastures** or **fresh pastures**. *No matter how much we long for new pastures, when we reach them they can seem like a bad idea.*

◆ This is a quotation from 'Lycidas' (1638) by the English poet Milton: 'At last he rose, and twitch'd his Mantle blew: Tomorrow to fresh Woods, and Pastures new.' This is sometimes wrongly quoted as 'fresh fields and pastures new'.

pat
a pat on the back
pat someone on the back
If you give someone **a pat on the back**, you congratulate them or show your appreciation for something they have done. If you give yourself **a pat on the back**, you feel pleased about something you have done. *Any mail order shop that gives such rapid response to a customer's complaint deserves a pat on the back.*

☐ You can also say that one person **pats** another **on the back**, or that someone **pats** themselves **on the back**. *I decided if giving up smoking was going to be so hard, I'd need more pleasurable things in my life, so each day I kept patting myself on the back and treating myself.*

stand pat
Mainly American If someone **stands pat**, they do not change something or they refuse to change their mind about something. *Building society managers are willing to stand pat on mortgage rates for the moment.*

◆ In the game of poker, if a player stands pat, they are satisfied with the hand dealt to them and do not exchange any of their cards.

patch
not a patch on someone
British If you say that one person or thing **is not a patch on** another, you mean that the first is not nearly as good as the second. *Of course, the facilities aren't a patch on those of richer schools, but the boys think they're terrific.*

path
path-breaking
break a new path
Mainly American You describe someone's achievement as **path-breaking**

when they have done something completely different and new which will affect the way in which things are done or considered in the future. *Russia's Parliament today approved a path-breaking measure that gives individual farmers a right to buy and sell their own land.*

☐ You can refer to someone who achieves something path-breaking as **a path-breaker**. You can also say that they **break a new path**.

pay dirt

hit pay dirt
strike pay dirt

Mainly American If you **hit pay dirt** or **strike pay dirt**, you find or achieve something important and valuable. *The first two people with whom she spoke hung up on her. The third was not rude, but he refused to help her. With the fourth, she struck pay dirt.*

♦ This expression probably refers to earth which contains enough gold dust to make it financially worthwhile to look for gold in it.

peanuts

if you pay peanuts, you get monkeys

British If you say **'if you pay peanuts, you get monkeys'**, you mean that if an employer pays very low wages, they cannot expect to find good staff. *The present pay policy will inevitably have an adverse effect on quality. As Sir Roger put it, 'The truth of the matter is that if they pay peanuts, they will get monkeys.'*

♦ People sometimes refer to small or trivial amounts of money as 'peanuts'.

pearls

cast pearls before swine

If you say that someone **is casting pearls before swine**, you mean that they are wasting their time by offering something that is helpful or valuable to someone who does not appreciate or understand it. *I have wonderful costumes. I scour second-hand shops for interesting pieces like feathers and top hats, but it's like casting pearls before swine, they don't care what you wear.*

☐ You can vary this expression in several ways, for example by saying that something **is pearls before swine**. *The Musical Times, she tells me, is written by professionals for those with a genuine understanding of the finer*

*points. I certainly hope so, or else my piece on some new Rossini editions, due
to appear in the September issue of MT, will be pearls before swine.*

♦ This expression comes from the Bible, from the Sermon on the Mount,
when Jesus is giving His followers advice on how they should live: 'Give
not that which is holy unto dogs, neither cast ye your pearls before swine,
lest they trample them under their feet, and turn again and rend you.'
(Matthew 7:6)

pearls of wisdom

If you describe something that someone has said or written as **pearls of
wisdom**, you mean that it sounds very wise or helpful. You can also talk
about **a pearl of wisdom**. People usually use this expression ironically, to
suggest that in fact they think the person is saying something very
obvious or boring. *'Never be afraid of failure; just be afraid of not trying.'
Another pearl of wisdom.*

peas

like two peas in a pod

If you say that two people are **like two peas in a pod**, you mean that
they are very alike in appearance or character. *She is convinced the men
are brothers. She said: 'It was uncanny. They were like two peas in a pod.'*

pebble

not the only pebble on the beach

Mainly British If you say that someone is **not the only pebble on the
beach**, you mean that they are not the only person who is important or
should be considered in a particular situation, although they may think
they are. *You should encourage him to understand that he is very definitely
not the only pebble on the beach.*

pecker

keep your pecker up

British If someone tells you to **keep** your **pecker up**, they are
encouraging you to remain cheerful in a difficult situation. *'I'll give you a
ring later because I must go now.' 'Fine. Well, keep your pecker up.' 'I'll try.'*

♦ 'Pecker' was a slang term for the nose, comparing it to a bird's beak. If
someone is unhappy, they tend to look downwards so that their nose
points towards the ground. 'Pecker' is also a slang word for 'penis'.

pecking

the pecking order

The pecking order in a group is the order of importance of the people or things within that group. *As a player in category 12, he is way down the pecking order.*

♦ When groups of hens are kept together, a 'pecking order' tends to form. This means that a stronger bird can peck a weaker bird without being pecked in return.

pedestal

♦ A pedestal is a base on which something such as a statue stands.

knock someone off their pedestal

If someone or something **knocks** you **off** your **pedestal**, they show that you are not as good or talented as people generally think, or make people realize that you are not perfect. *The tabloids have been trying for several years now to knock Jackson from his pedestal.*

☐ If you say that someone should come **down from** their **pedestal**, you mean that they should stop behaving as though they think they are perfect. *My advice to Paula is to climb down off her pedestal and get in touch with reality.*

put someone on a pedestal

If someone **puts** you **on a pedestal**, they think you are extremely good or talented, or they seem not to realize that you are not perfect. *I put my own parents on a pedestal. I felt they could do no wrong.*

peg

a square peg in a round hole

If you say that someone is **a square peg in a round hole**, you mean that they are in a situation or are doing a task that does not suit them at all. *Taylor is clearly the wrong man for the job – a square peg in a round hole.*

☐ People often vary this expression. *The system too often leads to round pegs being appointed to square holes.*

take someone down a peg or two

If you say that someone needs **taking down a peg or two**, you mean that they are behaving in an arrogant and unpleasant way and they should be made to realize that they are not as important or talented as they think. *I do think he needed taking down a peg or two.*

♦ This expression may refer to the tuning of musical instruments such as guitars or violins, where pegs are used to keep the strings tight. Alternatively, it may refer to the game of cribbage, where pegs are used to keep the score.

pegged

have someone pegged

If you say that you **have** someone **pegged**, you mean that you understand completely the way they are or who they are. *I want you to know that the drinkers in the cocktail lounge have you pegged for a detective.*

pennies

pinch pennies

If someone **pinches pennies**, they try to spend as little money as possible. *Markets are shrinking and customers are pinching pennies.*

♦ The verb 'pennypinch' has a similar meaning, and there is also a much more frequent word 'pennypinching'. These words are generally used more disapprovingly than 'pinch pennies'.

penn'orth

your two penn'orth

British If you have or put in your **two penn'orth**, you give your opinion about something, even if nobody has asked you for it. The American expression is your **two cents' worth**. *I'm just putting my two penn'orth in, that's all. The same as you are.*

♦ 'Two penn'orth' means 'two pennies' worth'.

penny

in for a penny, in for a pound

You say **'in for a penny, in for a pound'** to indicate that you are firmly committed to a particular course of action, even though it will probably cost a lot of money or use a lot of resources if you continue. *In for a penny, in for a pound. I took the wine to the counter.*

the penny drops

Mainly British When someone finally understands or realizes something, you can say that **the penny has dropped**. *It seems the penny has finally dropped – house prices won't budge until first-time buyers are tempted into the market.*

◆ This expression probably refers to slot machines, which only operate when you put in a coin.

penny-wise and pound-foolish

British, old-fashioned If you say that someone is **penny-wise and pound-foolish**, you are criticizing them for being careful in small matters but careless in more important ones. *If we had the right number of auditors to go out and check on this, we would have saved billions of dollars. In other words, we have been penny-wise and really pound-foolish here.*

turn up like a bad penny

Mainly British, old-fashioned If you say that someone or something **turns up like a bad penny**, you mean that they appear again in a place where they are not welcome or wanted. You often use this expression to indicate that they keep doing this. *Her husband was able to trace her, to turn up again on her doorstep like the proverbial bad penny.*

two a penny
ten a penny

British If you say that things or people are **two a penny** or **ten a penny**, you mean that there are a great deal of them, and so they are not especially valuable or interesting. The American expression is **a dime a dozen**. *Books on golf are two a penny. There are ones on personalities; others on how to play the game; more on courses; and so on.*

perch

fall off the perch

British, old-fashioned If you say that someone **falls off the perch** or **falls off** their **perch**, you are saying in a humorous or light-hearted way that they die. *He fell off the perch years ago.*

knock you off your perch
fall off your perch

British If someone or something **knocks** you **off** your **perch**, they cause you to fail, or they damage your status or position. When this happens, you can say that you **fall off** your **perch**. *For the leading regional firms this is an excellent time to knock London firms off their perch and seize the advantages of lower fees and local contacts.*

petard

hoist by your own petard

If someone **is hoist by** their **own petard**, their plan to benefit themselves or to harm someone else results instead in benefit to the other person or harm to themselves. In American English you usually use 'on' instead of 'by'. *When Japan and America were negotiating a bilateral commercial treaty, the Americans insisted on a provision that ensured American multinationals could put their own people into top positions in their Japanese subsidiaries. Now that Japanese multinationals are leading the way, America finds itself hoist by its own petard.*

◆ 'Petards' were metal balls filled with gunpowder which were used to blow up walls or gates. The gunpowder was lit by a slow-burning fuse, but there was always a danger that the device would explode too soon and 'hoist' the person lighting it, that is, blow them up in the air.

Peter

rob Peter to pay Paul

If someone **is robbing Peter to pay Paul**, they are using money meant for paying off one debt to pay off a different debt and so they are still in debt. *His mortgages ran into arrears and he borrowed from loan companies. He started robbing Peter to pay Paul.*

phrase

to coin a phrase

You say **'to coin a phrase'** when you are making a pun or using a cliché or colloquial expression, in order to show that you realize people might think that it is a silly or boring thing to say, but you think it is relevant in spite of this. *Being gay is what I am, not the easiest of roads to follow, but it wasn't a choice. To coin a phrase, 'I am what I am.'*

picnic

be no picnic

If you say that an experience, task, or activity **is no picnic**, you mean that it is difficult or unpleasant. *'Poor little mites,' she said of the evacuees. 'It's no picnic for them being taken away from their homes.'*

picture

get the picture

If someone **gets the picture**, they understand what another person is trying to explain or describe to them. This expression is often used in contexts where you are saying that someone does not understand something immediately. *Anna was giggling. She was beginning to get the picture.*

in the picture: 1
out of the picture

If you say that someone is **in the picture**, you mean that they are involved in the situation you are talking about. If you say that they are **out of the picture**, you mean that they are no longer involved in the situation. *Some people don't believe it will ever be safe to go home as long as the terrorists are still in the picture... Once Derek was out of the picture, however, Malcolm's visits to the Swires became more frequent.*

in the picture: 2
out of the picture

If you are **in the picture** for promotion or success, you are very likely to get a promotion or be successful. If you are **out of the picture**, you are not one of the people who are being considered for a promotion or place on a team. *He told me that Annabella was back in the picture. She was the best one they could find... But I've been told I'm fifth-choice striker, so I'm totally out of the picture.*

put someone in the picture
keep someone in the picture

British If you **put** someone **in the picture**, you tell them about a situation which they need to know about. If you **keep** them **in the picture**, you keep them aware of any changes or developments in the situation. *Has Inspector Fayard put you in the picture?*

pie

eat humble pie

If someone **eats humble pie**, they admit that they have been wrong and apologize, especially in situations where this is humiliating or embarrassing for them. *The critics were too quick to give their verdict on us. We hope they'll be eating humble pie before the end of the season.*

□ **Humble pie** is sometimes used in other structures with a similar meaning. *Nigel Mansell's critics may be helping themselves to a slice of humble pie this morning after his hard-won third place in yesterday's race.*

◆ 'Umbles' is an old word for the guts and offal of deer. When nobles had venison or deer to eat, the 'umbles' were made into a pie for their servants. As 'umbles' pie was eaten by 'humble' people, the two words gradually became confused. 'Humble pie' came to be used to refer to something humiliating or unpleasant.

pie in the sky

If you describe an idea, plan, or promise as **pie in the sky**, you mean that it is very unlikely to happen. *Ideally what I would like to see would be free childcare, but I think that's a bit pie in the sky at the moment... Is it all just a pie-in-the-sky idea? It is certainly a major job, and not cheap.*

◆ This expression comes from the song 'The Preacher and the Slave' (1911) by Joe Hill, an American songwriter and workers' organizer: 'You'll get pie in the sky when you die. (That's a lie.)'

piece

all of a piece

If something is **all of a piece**, each part or aspect of it is consistent with all the others. You can also say that one thing is **all of a piece** with another. *Thus the biosphere is all of a piece, an immense, integrated, living system.*

a piece of cake

If you say that something is **a piece of cake**, you mean that it is very easy to do. *Fathoming the complexities of maternity benefits makes the actual process of childbirth look like a piece of cake.*

a piece of piss

British If you say that something is **a piece of piss**, you mean that it is very easy to do. Many people find this expression offensive. *The one thing people think is how difficult touring is, but really, it's a piece of piss.*

say your piece

If you **say** your **piece**, you give your opinion about a particular matter, although you are aware that other people may not agree with you, or be interested in what you have to say. *Each preacher stood for two minutes on a box, said his piece, and stepped down.*

pieces

go to pieces: 1

If you **go to pieces**, you are so upset or distressed by something that you cannot control your emotions or cope with the things that you have to do. *She's a strong woman, but she nearly went to pieces when Arnie died.*

go to pieces: 2

If you say that something such as your work or a relationship **has gone to pieces**, you mean that it is no longer as good as it once was and you cannot stop it getting worse. *My work is all going to pieces.*

pick up the pieces

If you **pick up the pieces** after something bad has happened, you do what you can to get the situation back to normal again. *Louie had sent his business manager into my life to help pick up the pieces of my shattered career and finances.*

shot to pieces

If you say that something such as your confidence or a plan is **shot to pieces**, you mean that it is completely ruined. *The economy is shot to pieces, thousands are losing their jobs every day, and the chances of economic recovery have receded for yet another year.*

pig

like a greased pig

Mainly American If someone moves **like a greased pig**, they move very fast and nobody can catch them or stop them.

◆ This may come from a fairground competition which was popular in the past, in which a piglet that had been covered in grease was let loose and the person who caught it won a prize.

make a pig's ear of something

British If you say that someone **makes a pig's ear of** something that they are doing, you are saying in a forceful way that they are doing it very badly. *I made a pig's ear of it last time and I'm going to make sure that won't happen again.*

◆ This expression may refer to the fact that most parts of a pig can be eaten, but the ears are the least useful part.

a pig in a poke

Fairly old-fashioned If you buy or accept **a pig in a poke**, you buy or accept something without examining it or thinking about it carefully first, with the result that you do not know what you are getting, or you get something that you do not want. *The state was going to get a building that they could redevelop. But what's really happening here is that the state may* *be stuck with a pig in a poke.*

♦ In the past, traders selling piglets at markets often had one pig on show and the rest in bags, or 'pokes', ready to sell. Dishonest traders used to put cats in the bags instead of pigs to cheat their customers. 'Let the cat out of the bag' is based on the same practice: see **cat**.

squeal like a stuck pig

If you say that someone **is squealing like a stuck pig**, you mean that they are screaming very loudly, as though they are in a lot of pain. *Alan tried to calm him while Miller continued to scream like a stuck pig.*

pigeon

be someone's pigeon

British, old-fashioned If something **is** your **pigeon**, you have to deal with it. *I'm sorry to load this on you, Harry, but I'm selfishly glad it's your pigeon rather than mine.*

♦ Originally this expression was 'that's not my pidgin'. The word 'pidgin' represents a 17th century Chinese pronunciation of the word 'business'. The expression literally meant the same as 'that's not my business'.

piggy

the piggy in the middle

British You can say that someone is **the piggy in the middle** when they are involved against their will in a conflict between two other people or groups, which leads to a very unpleasant situation for them. *When the men in boiler suits arrive on Doug's cruiser it's not to service his engine. He finds himself piggy in the middle of a cannabis smuggling outfit and the Customs.*

♦ 'Piggy in the middle' is a children's game in which two children throw a ball to each other over the head of a third child, who tries to catch the ball.

pigs

pigs might fly

If you say **'pigs might fly'** after someone has said that something might happen, you mean that you think it is very unlikely. *'There's a chance he isn't involved in this, of course.' 'And pigs might fly.'*

□ People often vary this expression, for example by saying they saw **a pig flying by**. *'Maybe one day we'll be seen as entertaining.' 'Oh look, I just saw a pig fly by my window.'*

pike

come down the pike

American If something **is coming down the pike**, it is starting to happen or to become available. *There's been threats out of the White House to veto any legislation that comes down the pike, like family leave or a civil rights bill.*

◆ The reference here is to someone travelling along a turnpike or toll road.

pill

sugar the pill
sweeten the pill
sugar-coat the pill

If you **sugar the pill** or **sweeten the pill**, you try to make bad news or an unpleasant situation more acceptable for someone by giving them or telling them something good or pleasant at the same time. These forms of the expression are used in British English; in American English, the usual form is **sugar-coat the pill**. *Ministers may reprieve Harefield hospital, the world's leading heart transplant centre, to sugar the pill of a further round of hospital cuts and closures in London and the South-east.*

swallow a bitter pill
a bitter pill to swallow

If someone has to **swallow a bitter pill**, they have to accept a difficult or unpleasant fact or situation. *Gordon Hodgson, Cowie's chief executive, said the failure to win was 'a little bit of a bitter pill to swallow'... I'm not going to tell you this is not a bitter pill for the armed forces, because clearly it is.*

pillar

from pillar to post

If someone is moved **from pillar to post**, they are moved repeatedly from one place or position to another, usually in a hurried or disorganized way so that they suffer as a result. This expression is used in British English and in old-fashioned American English. *I didn't want the children pushed from pillar to post.*

◆ This expression comes from an early form of tennis that was played indoors. Players often played shots back and forth across the court, from the posts supporting the net to the pillars at the back of the court.

pillar to post

British In sport, especially horse racing, a **pillar to post** victory is one in which the winner was in the lead from the start of the race. *Sally Prosser held off the best of the Far East to top the Asian circuit, thanks largely to a pillar to post victory in the JAL Malaysian Open.*

◆ This may refer to the posts that mark the start and finish of a racecourse.

pilot

on automatic pilot
on autopilot

If you are **on automatic pilot** or **on autopilot**, you are acting without thinking about what you are doing, usually because you have done it many times before or because you are very tired. *When the kids came home I just switched on to autopilot, making the tea, listening to them fight.*

◆ In aircraft, automatic pilot is a device which automatically keeps the plane on course without the need for the pilot to do anything.

pinch

at a pinch
in a pinch

If you say that it is possible to do something **at a pinch** or **in a pinch**, you mean that it can just be done if it is absolutely necessary. 'At a pinch' is used in British English and 'in a pinch' is used in American English. *Six people, and more at a pinch, could be seated comfortably at the table.*

feel the pinch

If a person or company **is feeling the pinch**, they do not have as much money as they used to have, and so they cannot buy the things they would like to buy. *Japanese car makers are feeling the pinch of an economic slowdown at home.*

pink

in the pink

Old-fashioned If you say that someone is **in the pink** or **in the pink of condition**, you mean that they are very fit and healthy. You can also say that they are **in the pink of health**. *He insists that Mr Harris, a non-smoker, appeared in the pink of health.*

tickled pink

If you are **tickled pink** about something, you are extremely pleased about it. *'As a developer, I'm tickled pink by the dropping prices,' he said.*

◆ This expression may refer to someone's face becoming pink or redder when they are being tickled.

pins

for two pins

Mainly British, old-fashioned People say **'for two pins'** to indicate that they would definitely do something if they were able to, but other factors or considerations make it impossible to do it. *Now his eyelids were smarting and heavy and he could feel that his face was flushed in the hot little room. For two pins he'd have fallen asleep there and then.*

on pins and needles

Mainly American If you are **on pins and needles**, you are very anxious or nervous because you are waiting to see if something happens the way you want it to. *We were approaching Cape Horn, where we had almost lost our lives two years ago, and so until we would get around Cape Horn, I was definitely on pins and needles.*

pipe

put that in your pipe and smoke it

People sometimes say **'put that in your pipe and smoke it'** to tell you that although you may dislike or disagree with something they have just said, you must accept that it is a fact or true. *As for rules, the only person who makes rules in this house is me. So you can tell Miss Underwood from me: she can put that in her pipe and smoke it.*

pipeline

in the pipeline

If something is **in the pipeline**, it is being planned or is in progress. *New security measures are in the pipeline, including closed-circuit TV cameras in most stores plus secret tags on goods.*

piper

he who pays the piper calls the tune

When people say **'he who pays the piper calls the tune'**, they are referring to the idea that the person who pays for something has the right to decide how that thing operates or is organized. **Call the tune** is also used on its own as an expression: see **tune**. *He who pays the piper should call the tune. It's important our customers have a real say on the balance between demands for improved services and increasing charges.*

☐ People often vary this expression. *If Europe and Japan are to pay the piper, they will expect at least some say in his choice of tune.*

◆ This may come from the custom, dating back to the 17th century, of hiring travelling musicians to play at festivals and weddings. The people who paid for the music were able to choose the tunes they wanted to hear.

piss

take the piss

British If someone **is taking the piss** out of another person or thing, they are teasing them or making jokes about them in a way that causes them to seem ridiculous. Some people find this expression offensive. *Men will not worry about how powerful their Hoover is, but they'll hit each other if one thinks the other is taking the piss out of his car.*

☐ You can refer to an instance of this behaviour as **a piss-take**. *In a long-overdue piss-take of the cop movie, Emilio Estevez and Samuel L Jackson crash through 83 minutes of slam-bam entertainment.*

pitch

make a pitch: 1

If someone **makes a pitch** for something, they tell people how good that thing is and try to persuade them to support it or buy it. *The president also used his remarks to make a pitch for further space exploration.*

make a pitch: 2

If someone **makes a pitch** for something, they try to obtain that thing. *So far Federal Reserve Chairman Alan Greenspan hasn't made a pitch for the job.*

queer someone's pitch

Mainly British If someone **queers** your **pitch**, they make it very difficult for you to achieve what you are trying to do. *We did everything we could for you here, and you repay the school by doing your best to queer the pitch for us.*

◆ In the past, a pitch was the place where a showman set up his tent or stall. If anyone, especially the police, spoiled or interrupted his show, they were said to queer the pitch. There is an old verb 'queer' which means 'cheat' or 'spoil'.

place

a place in the sun

If you say that someone has found their **place in the sun**, you mean that they are in a job or situation where they will be happy and well-off, and have everything that they want. *I've done what everybody's done. I've fought my way in. I think I've earned my place in the sun.*

put someone in their place

If you **put** someone **in** their **place**, you show them that they are less important or clever than they think they are. *In a few words she had not only put him in his place, but delivered a precise and damning assessment of his movie.*

places

go places

If you say that someone **is going places**, you mean that they are showing a lot of talent or ability and are likely to become very successful. *If we can play like that every week, then this club is going places.*

plague

avoid something like the plague

If you say that you **avoid** someone or something **like the plague**, you are emphasizing that you deliberately avoid them because you dislike them so much. *I normally avoid cheap Chianti like the plague.*

plain

plain as a pikestaff

British, old-fashioned If you say that something is as **plain as a pikestaff**, you are emphasizing that it is very obvious or easy to understand. *The Inspector sat back, relaxed. 'You're on to a loser here, Lennox. Plain as a pikestaff, the whole thing.'*

◆ This expression was originally 'plain as a packstaff'. A packstaff was a long stick that pedlars used to carry their bundles. The word 'pikestaff' was substituted at a later time: a pikestaff was a long walking stick. Both packstaffs and pikestaffs were very plain and simple.

plain as day

If you say that something is as **plain as day**, you mean that it is very easy to see, or that it is very obvious and easy to understand. *The good sense behind moves to develop mutually supportive economic policies is plain as day.*

plain as the nose on your face

If you say that something is as **plain as the nose on** your **face**, you are emphasizing that it is very obvious or easy to understand. *It's plain as the nose on your face that this company is wildly undervalued.*

plank

walk the plank

If something goes wrong and someone in a position of authority **walks the plank**, they accept responsibility for what has happened and leave their position. *If they think that the President is going to lose, they might decide, 'OK, why should I walk the plank for him?'*

♦ Many people believe that pirates used to kill their prisoners by forcing them to walk off the end of a plank or gangplank, sticking out from the side of the ship, into the sea.

plate

hand someone something on a plate

Mainly British If you say that someone **was handed** something desirable **on a plate**, you are showing disapproval of the fact that they were given it without having to work for it or make an effort to get it. *He had had everything, the whole world handed to him on a plate.*

have enough on your plate
have a lot on your plate
have your plate full

If you **have enough on** your **plate** or **have a lot on** your **plate**, you have a lot of work to do or a lot of things to deal with. *I'm sorry to bother you with it, Mark, but John's got enough on his plate.*

☐ You can also say that someone **has** their **plate full** or **has a full plate**. *I'm making no promises. My staff have their plate full at the present time.*

step up to the plate

American If someone **steps up to the plate**, they do or say something which shows that they are willing to accept responsibility for something or to take a particular course of action. *People are very concerned about who is going to step up to the plate and buy municipal bonds in the absence of institutional buyers.*

♦ In baseball, the plate is the home base where the batter stands.

platter

on a silver platter
on a platter

If you are given something **on a silver platter** or **on a platter**, you are given it without having to work or make an effort to get it. *The Opposition has been handed this issue on a platter*.

playing field

a level playing field
level the playing field

You use **a level playing field** to refer to a situation that is fair. You usually use this expression when talking about the fact that a situation is not fair, or when saying that you think it should be fair. *At the moment we are not competing on a level playing field*.

□ If you say that you want to **level the playing field**, you mean that you want to make a situation fair, by ensuring that nobody has an advantage over other people. *Industry analysts say the agreement should help level the playing field*.

plot

the plot thickens

If you say 'the plot thickens' when you are describing a complicated situation or series of events, you mean that it starts to become even more complicated or mysterious. *At this point the plot thickened further. A link emerged between the attempt to kill the Pope and the kidnapping of the American*.

plug

pull the plug on something

If someone with power **pulls the plug on** a project or activity, they stop supporting it, so that the project or activity fails and has to stop. You usually use this expression to talk about financial support being withdrawn. *Theoretically, the banks have the power to pull the plug on the project if they do not like the companies' sums*.

plum

a plum in your mouth

British If you say that someone speaks with **a plum in** their **mouth**, you are showing your disapproval of them for having an upper-class accent or for being upper-class. *I heard Mr Downer speaking on the radio on the previous day. I was not conscious of the 'plum in the mouth', but I was aware of his clear diction.*

plunge

take the plunge

If you decide to **take the plunge**, you decide to do something that you have been thinking of doing for some time, even though it is difficult, risky, or unpleasant. *Helen decided to take the plunge and turned professional in 1991.*

poacher

poacher turned gamekeeper

British If you say that someone is **poacher turned gamekeeper**, you mean that they have changed their job or opinion and now have one which seems the opposite of the one they had before. *Gary Mason, boxing's poacher turned gamekeeper, will make his managerial debut tomorrow.*

☐ You can also say that someone is **gamekeeper turned poacher**, especially when you think they have gone from a respectable position to a less respectable one. *Gamekeeper turned poacher: after two years with the Financial Times, energy reporter Jane Sayers resigned yesterday to join a public relations firm.*

pocket

dip into your pocket
dig deep into your pocket
dig deep

If someone **dips into** their **pocket** or **digs into** their **pocket** in order to pay for something, they pay for it with their own money. *Potential lenders will need to be persuaded that the government is tackling its economic problems before they dig into their pockets again.*

☐ If you say that someone **digs deep into** their **pocket** in order to pay for something or that they **dig deep**, you mean that they use a lot of their own money to pay for it. *Adrian dug deep into his own pocket and published the book himself... At Christmas, most will dig deep and spend more than last year.*

in someone's pocket

If you are **in** someone's **pocket**, they control you or have power over you and so you do everything that they tell you. *The Labour party suffered badly in the election from Conservative claims that it was in the pockets of the unions.*

out of pocket: 1

If you are left **out of pocket**, you have less money than you should have or than you intended, for example because something was more expensive than you expected or because of a mistake. *The promoter claims he was left £36,000 out of pocket.*

out of pocket: 2

Out-of-pocket expenses are expenses which someone pays out of their own money, and which are normally paid back later. *I charge twenty dollars an hour plus out-of-pocket expenses.*

☐ In American English, if you **pay out of pocket**, you pay for something yourself and claim the money back later. *As long as people have to pay out of pocket to see a physician, there will be a deterrent to seeking necessary care.*

pockets

line your pockets

If you accuse someone of **lining** their **pockets**, you are accusing them of making a lot of money in a dishonest or unfair way. If you say that they **are lining** another person's **pockets**, you mean that they are making a lot of money for the other person in a dishonest or unfair way. *He has been lining his pockets for 27 years while his country has festered in poverty.*

live in each other's pockets

Mainly British If you say that two or more people **live in each other's pockets**, you mean that they spend a great deal of time together. You usually use this expression to suggest that this is a bad thing, because they do not have enough time on their own or with other people as a result. *Just because you're married doesn't mean you have to live in each other's pockets.*

point

boiling point

If a situation reaches **boiling point**, it becomes very tense or dangerous because the people involved are so angry that they are likely to go out of control. *Tempers were already close to boiling point as the dispute remained deadlocked for the ninth day.*

not to put too fine a point on it

British You say **'not to put too fine a point on it'** in order to indicate that what you are about to say may sound unpleasant, unkind, or critical. *Sun City has had, not to put too fine a point on it, a slightly tacky reputation.*

a sticking point

A **sticking point** is a problem which stops you from achieving something, especially in a series of negotiations or a discussion. *Sources say a Republican call for a cut in the capital gains tax is the main sticking point in budget negotiations.*

points

score points: 1

If someone **scores points** off you, they gain an advantage over you, especially in a discussion or argument. This expression is often used to suggest that they are not really interested in the issues being discussed, but are just trying to show that they are better than you. *They're not remotely concerned about the disabled. They're concerned about trying to score points off Willie Brown, the Democratic speaker of the State Assembly.*

□ You can refer to this type of behaviour as **point-scoring**. *We can see our leaders looking shifty in close-up every night on television. There is no frankness, only point-scoring.*

score points: 2

If you **score points** with someone, you do something that impresses them or makes them think favourably of you. *Again, Laine paused, clearly confident in his arguments. He was scoring points with the judge and the spectators.*

pole

the greasy pole

British If you say that someone is moving up **the greasy pole**, you mean that they are reaching a more successful position as a result of working very hard and dealing with all the difficulties they meet. This expression is often used disapprovingly, to suggest that their ambitions are wrong or their methods are dishonest. *He was just another, albeit particularly hardworking, local politician climbing assiduously up the greasy pole.*

◆ In the past, climbing up or along a greasy pole in order to get a prize at the end of it was a popular fairground competition.

pole position

Mainly British If you are in **pole position**, you are in a very strong position in a competition or competitive situation, and are likely to win or be successful. *They've been favourites all season and are in pole position now.*

◆ This expression comes from motor racing, where the driver who starts the race in front of all the other drivers is said to start in pole position.

wouldn't touch something with a barge pole
wouldn't touch something with a ten-foot pole

If you say that you **wouldn't touch** something or someone **with a barge pole**, you mean that you do not want to have anything to do with them, because you do not trust them or like them. This form of the expression is used in British English; in American English, the form is **wouldn't touch** something or someone **with a ten-foot pole**. *The history of the place kept the price down. No one would touch it with a barge pole.*

◆ A barge pole is a very long pole that is used to move a barge forward.

poles

poles apart

If you say that two people, ideas, or systems are **poles apart**, you are emphasizing that they are very different. *In social and political terms, they were poles apart.*

◆ The reference here is to the north and south poles, which are at opposite ends of the earth.

poor

poor as a church mouse

Old-fashioned If you say that you are as **poor as a church mouse**, you are emphasizing that you have very little money. *I was as poor as a church mouse, but I bought that wreck of a car.*

◆ Mice living in a church are unlikely to find much to eat as there is no kitchen or food cupboard.

port

a port in a storm

You can refer to a person, place, or organization where you can get help in a difficult situation as **a port in a storm**. *She was sweet to take me in the way she did, hardly any notice at all, just told me to come right to her. A port in a storm is a welcome thing.*

☐ You say **any port in a storm** when you are in a position where you have to accept help from anyone who will give it to you, even if it is from someone who you do not like or approve of.

possum

play possum

If someone **plays possum**, they try to make people ignore them by pretending to be dead or asleep. *'Playing possum, huh?' said Joe. 'Right,' said Frank. 'I figured it might be interesting to hear what they had to say to each other when they thought I was unconscious.'*

◆ The possum or opossum is a North American and Australian animal. If it is threatened by another animal it sometimes lies still, as if it is dead, so that the animal will lose interest.

post

◆ The following expressions refer to the finishing post in a horse race.

first past the post

If you say that someone is **first past the post** in a race or competitive situation, you mean that they finish first or achieve something first. *Britain's bid to stage the Olympics in the year 2000 failed to be the first past the post. Manchester lost the race to host the biggest sporting festival in the world.*

◆ This expression is often used in talking about electoral systems. A first-past-the-post electoral system is one in which the candidate who gets the most votes wins.

pip someone at the post

British If you **pip** someone **at the post** or **pip** them **to the post**, you narrowly beat them in a competition or race to achieve something. *They were concerned that their rivals might pip them to the post.*

posted

keep someone posted

If someone asks you to **keep** them **posted**, they are asking you to continue giving them the latest information about a situation that concerns them. *She made me promise to keep her posted on developments.*

pot

go to pot

If you say that something **is going to pot**, you mean that its condition is becoming very bad, because it has not been properly looked after. *The neighbourhood really is going to pot.*

♦ This expression may refer to meat which is chopped into pieces and cooked in a pot. Alternatively, the 'pot' may have been a melting pot, where metal objects were melted down.

keep the pot boiling

If you do something in order to **keep the pot boiling**, you do it in order to make sure that a process does not stop. *I threw in a question, just to keep the pot boiling while my brain caught up.*

the pot calling the kettle black

When someone with a particular fault accuses someone else of having the same fault, you can say this is a case of **the pot calling the kettle black**. *Ferguson publicly questioned the Leeds players nerves before the weekend, which is a bit like the pot calling the kettle black.*

☐ People often vary this expression. *It is all very well for Washington State to assume moral superiority. There is a bit of pot-and-kettle about its outrage.*

♦ In the past, both pots and kettles were hung over fires, and would be burned black.

a watched pot never boils

Old-fashioned If you say **'a watched pot never boils'**, you mean that if you wait and watch anxiously to see something happen, it will seem to take a very long time, or it will not happen at all. *This strategy is doomed from the start because it is far too public: a watched pot never boils.*

potato

drop something like a hot potato
drop something like a hot brick

If you **drop** something or someone **like a hot potato** or **drop** them **like a hot brick**, you get rid of them as quickly as possible because they are difficult to deal with, or because you do not want them any more. *If a place gains a reputation for being unwelcoming, the trade drops it like a hot potato... He panicked and dropped his lover like a hot brick. But the* *scandal was already brewing.*

a hot potato

If you say that a subject or problem is **a hot potato**, you mean that it is very topical and controversial and most people would rather not have to deal with it. *When she is confronted with a political hot potato such as abortion or tightening the gun laws, she is not beyond voicing her opinion.*

potatoes

small potatoes

If you say that something is **small potatoes**, you mean that it is not important or significant. *While a total tour attendance of around 20,000 is small potatoes by British standards, it is very big in this country.*

pot luck

◆ 'Pot luck' is usually written as 'potluck' in American English. A potluck is a meal at which different guests bring different parts of the meal.

be pot luck

If you ask someone to have a meal at your house and you tell them it will be **pot luck**, you mean that you have not planned it or prepared any special food. *'We'll just be casual and eat in the kitchen. It's just pot luck,' Moira said. 'Hope you don't mind.'*

take pot luck

If you **take pot luck**, you make a choice from what is available, although you do not have any knowledge to help you, and so it is a matter of luck whether you get something good. *We'd take potluck at whatever restaurants might still be open... Travel firms stuck with hundreds of unsold package holidays are offering great breaks on a pot-luck basis.*

pottage

a mess of pottage

Old-fashioned If you accuse someone of selling or exchanging something of lasting value for **a mess of pottage**, you mean that they have foolishly sold or exchanged it for something which has no lasting value at all. *She was not going to lower herself for the sake of a fifty-dollar mess of pottage.*

◆ A mess of pottage is a dish of vegetables. This expression comes from a story in the Bible, which tells how Esau was hungry and sold his privileges as first-born son to his brother Jacob in return for this meal. (Genesis 25:29 – 33)

pound

your pound of flesh

If you say that someone demands or gets their **pound of flesh**, you mean that they insist on getting something they are entitled to, even though they might not need it and it will cause problems for the people they are getting it from. *Banks are quick enough to demand their pound of flesh from the small businessman and other regular customers when overdrafts run a little over the limit.*

◆ This expression comes from Shakespeare's play 'The Merchant of Venice' (Act 4, Scene 1). Shylock is owed money by Antonio, and attempts to carry out an agreement which allows him to cut off a pound of Antonio's flesh.

powder

keep your powder dry

If someone **keeps** their **powder dry**, they are ready to take immediate action in case a situation suddenly gets worse. *The only course upon which the government could agree was to move cautiously, keep its powder dry, and await the outcome of events abroad.*

◆ The powder referred to here is gunpowder. The expression comes from a story about the English leader Oliver Cromwell. He is said to have ended a speech to his soldiers, who were about to cross a river and go into battle, by saying: 'Put your trust in God, my boys, and keep your powder dry.'

powder keg

sit on a powder keg

If you say that someone **is sitting on a powder keg**, you mean that they are in a very dangerous situation, in which something could suddenly go seriously wrong at any time. *The Prime Minister was all too aware that he was sitting on a powder keg which could explode at any moment.*

☐ People often use **powder keg** to refer to a dangerous situation or to a place where disaster could suddenly happen. *The region has long been regarded as the powder keg of Europe.*

◆ A powder keg was a small barrel which was used to store gunpowder.

power

all power to your elbow

British People say **'all power to** your **elbow'**, to wish someone luck and to encourage them to be successful. *Bobby Gould is a good man and he's now paving the way for a very good third division campaign. So all power to his elbow.*

the power behind the throne

If you refer to someone as **the power behind the throne**, you mean that although another person appears to have all the power and control in an organization, it is in fact the first person who has all the power and control. *She was the real power behind the throne, a strong and single-minded woman manipulating a weaker husband for her own ends.*

practise (*American* practice)

practise what you preach

If someone **practises what** they **preach**, they behave in the way in which they encourage other people to behave. *Grown-ups don't know all the answers, don't practise what they preach, and must be held responsible for the poor state of society.*

□ People sometimes vary this expression, for example by saying that someone **preaches what** they **practise**. *The Bishop said the government had let the people down badly: it had preached love but practised hate.*

praise

damn with faint praise

If you **damn** someone **with faint praise**, you say something about them which sounds nice but which shows that you do not really have a high opinion of them. *Why you English seem oblivious to his talents and damn him with faint praise is totally beyond us.*

□ You can also just talk about **faint praise**. *Mr Robinson acknowledged Mr Golub this week as 'the most obvious internal candidate'. That sounds like ominously faint praise.*

◆ This expression was first used by the English writer Alexander Pope in his 'Epistle to Dr Arbuthnot' (1735): 'Damn with faint praise, assent with civil lear, And, without sneering, teach the rest to sneer.'

praises

sing the praises of someone

If you **sing the praises of** someone or something, you praise them in an enthusiastic way. *All parties are singing the praises of the multi-party system and the virtues of a market economy.*

prawn

come the raw prawn

Mainly Australian If you accuse someone of **coming the raw prawn**, you are accusing them of trying to cheat or trick you. *It pains me to say this but I'm afraid the Italians were caught trying to come the raw prawn, as it were.*

prayer

not have a prayer

If you say that someone **does not have a prayer** of achieving something, you mean that it is impossible for them to achieve it. *He did not seem to have a prayer of regaining the world title.*

pregnant

you can't be half pregnant

If you say **'you can't be half pregnant'**, you are pointing out that it is often necessary to commit yourself fully to an idea or project, and you cannot keep changing your mind about it. *We did, however, pick up a valuable lesson: you can't be half-pregnant. An entrepreneur must be able to give his enterprise a full commitment.*

press

a full-court press

American If there is **a full-court press** on something or someone, people are making a lot of effort and putting a lot of pressure on them in order to get a particular result. *The administration steps up the full-court press on the president's economic plan today.*

◆ In basketball, a full-court press is where the defending players stay close to the attacking players over the whole area of the court, rather than just in front of their own basket.

pretty

sit pretty

If someone **is sitting pretty**, they are in a good, safe, or comfortable situation. *When the war started, they thought they were sitting pretty, because they had all that extra surplus grain.*

pricks

kick against the pricks

Mainly British If someone **kicks against the pricks**, they show their opposition to people in authority. *Kicking against the pricks when you're 30 or 40 or more strikes me as a better test of one's convictions.*

◆ This expression occurs in the Bible (Acts 9:5). It refers to cattle kicking out when people try to drive them by jabbing them with sticks.

pride

swallow your pride

If you **swallow** your ⎩ride, you decide to do something even though it is shameful or embarrassing, and you would prefer not to. *However, if political compulsions demand, he can swallow his pride and ally himself with his political enemies.*

print

the small print
the fine print

If you refer to **the small print** or **the fine print** in a contract, agreement, or advertisement, you mean the part which contains important legal information, often in very small print. Most people do not read this information and so may not understand fully what their legal rights are. *Patients who thought they were fully covered are being hit by huge bills because they did not read the small print on their insurance forms.*

prisoners

take no prisoners

If you say that someone **takes no prisoners** when they are carrying out a plan or an action, you mean that they do it in a very forceful and determined way, without caring if they harm or upset other people. *It's a team packed with experienced and mature professionals. They won't be* *taking prisoners... We had a take no prisoners attitude, which was we didn't care who we infuriated.*

production

make a production of something

If you say that someone **is making a production of** something, you are criticizing them for doing it in a complicated or exaggerated way, when it could be done much more simply. *He made a production of brushing his hands clean on his pant legs.*

profile

keep a low profile

If someone **keeps a low profile**, they avoid doing things that will make people notice them. *The Home Secretary was keeping a low profile yesterday when the crime figures were announced in the House of Commons... He turned eventing from a low profile sport into a commercial success.*

proof

the proof of the pudding is in the eating

If you say that **the proof of the pudding is in the eating**, you mean that something new can only be judged to be good or bad after it has been tried or used. *Such therapies should not be dismissed out of hand, particularly when the proof of the pudding can be in the eating.*

□ People often vary this expression, for example by just talking about **the proof of the pudding**. *The proof of the pudding, so to speak, will be if sales of English cheese hold up after the dispute is over.*

pudding

over-egg the pudding

Mainly British If you say that someone **over-eggs the pudding**, you are criticizing them for trying so hard to improve something that they spoil it, for example by making it seem exaggerated or extreme. *The movie obviously over-eggs the glowing childhood pudding with lots of cuddles, warm milk and snow pattering against the window panes.*

pull

pull the other one
pull the other one, it's got bells on it

British If someone tells you something and you say **'pull the other one'** or **'pull the other one, it's got bells on it'**, you mean that you do not believe them. *'The Duchess gave it to me.' 'Think I'd believe that? Pull the other one, there's bells on it.'*

♦ 'One' in this expression refers to someone's leg. See the explanation for 'pull someone's leg' at **leg**.

pump

prime the pump

If someone **primes the pump**, they take action to help something succeed or grow, usually by spending money on it. *The budget in December is likely to prime the pump by tax cuts.*

☐ You can also talk about **pump-priming**, or say that someone **pump-primes** an economy or project. *I think we are going to have to do some more spending and some pump-priming in order to get the economy going.*

♦ To prime a water pump means to pump it until it is full of water and all the air has been forced out, so that it is ready to be used.

punch

pack a punch

If something **packs a punch**, it has a very powerful effect. 'Wallop' is sometimes used instead of 'punch'. *Huge uniformed orchestras with vast brass sections packed a powerful punch and filled the dance halls during the depression years of the Thirties.*

pleased as punch

If you say that someone is as **pleased as punch** about something, you are emphasizing that they are very pleased about it. *Branfoot announced he was as pleased as punch with his team's performance.*

♦ 'Punch' is a character from traditional 'Punch and Judy' puppet shows, who enjoys making trouble for people. The puppet usually has a big grin.

punches

not pull your punches
pull no punches

If someone does **not pull** their **punches** or **pulls no punches**, they speak very frankly about something and do not moderate their comments or criticism in any way. *I didn't pull any punches. We all knew we had a* *problem, a critical one, and that decisions would have to be reached quickly.*

◆ If boxers pull their punches, they do not hit their opponent as hard as they could do.

roll with the punches

If someone **rolls with the punches**, they do not allow difficulties or criticism to discourage them or affect them badly. *He has impressed all sides by his ability to negotiate and willingness to roll with the punches.*

◆ If boxers roll with the punches, they move their head and body backwards, away from their opponent's punch.

pup

sell someone a pup

British If someone **is sold a pup**, they buy or accept something and then feel deceived because it is not as good as they thought it would be. *No-one is being sold a pup. What you see is what you get.*

purse

hold the purse strings
tighten the purse strings
loosen the purse strings

If someone **holds the purse strings**, they control the way that money is spent in a particular family, organization, or country. *Six out of ten women think that financial institutions treat them like simpletons, even though they usually hold the domestic purse strings.*

□ You can also say that someone **tightens the purse strings** when they reduce the amount of money that you can spend, or that they **loosen the purse strings** when they allow you to spend more money.

push

get the push

British If someone **gets the push**, they lose their job. *This time white-collar workers and professionals are getting the push, not just factory workers and low-level clerks.*

when push comes to shove
if push comes to shove

If you talk about what you will do **when push comes to shove** or **if push comes to shove**, you are talking about what you will do when a situation reaches a critical point and you must make a decision on how to progress. *They knew they could sit back, and when push came to shove I'd do all the work.*

pusher

a pen pusher
a pencil pusher
a paper pusher

If you refer to someone who works in an office as **a pen pusher, a pencil pusher,** or **a paper pusher,** you are expressing scorn for the sort of work which typically goes on in offices, in contrast to more active kinds of work. 'Pen pusher' is used mainly in British English; 'pencil pusher' is used only in American English; 'paper pusher' is used in both British and American English. *Many of the men who now sit on company boards are pencil pushers with PhDs and MBAs from top schools, but lack operating experience in business.*

□ You can refer to office work as **pen-pushing, pencil-pushing,** or **paper-pushing.** You can also say that office workers **push papers** or **push pens.** *I want our uniformed services freed from paper pushing, so that we can put police officers on the beat again.*

putty

putty in your hands

If you say that someone is **putty in** your **hands,** you mean that they will do anything you ask or tell them to do. *I was completely in awe of him, I was putty in his hands.*

♦ Putty is a stiff paste which is used to fix glass panes into frames. You roll the putty in your hands until it is soft and smooth and ready to use.

Q

QT

on the QT

Old-fashioned If you do something **on the QT,** you do it secretly. *Many of the companies in which he had a financial interest had been selling to the Russians for years, openly or on the q.t.*

◆ In this expression, 'QT' is short for 'quiet'.

quart

a quart into a pint pot

British If you say someone is trying to get **a quart into a pint pot**, you mean that they are trying to put a large amount of something into a container or space that is too small. *In putting together a 'brief' article on the Tay Bridge Disaster, I was faced with the problem of fitting a quart into a pint pot, there being so much material available.*

◆ A quart is a unit of measure for liquids. It is equal to two pints.

quarterback

a Monday morning quarterback

American If you accuse someone of being **a Monday morning quarterback**, you mean they are criticizing or judging something unfairly, because although they now have full knowledge of the way things happened, the people involved could not possibly have had that knowledge and so could not have behaved any differently. *Some Monday-morning quarterbacks said the initial lower bid, without junk bonds, was a factor in his losing the company.*

☐ You can also accuse someone of **Monday morning quarterbacking**. *The Los Angeles County District Attorney rejects such Monday-morning quarterbacking, insisting that his lawyers did, quote, 'an excellent job'.*

◆ In American football, the quarterback is usually the player who calls out signals which tell the team which moves to make. In the United States, most professional football games are played on Sunday. Someone who tells people what the team should have done to win the game is known as a Monday morning quarterback.

question

beg the question: 1

If you say something **begs the question** or **begs** a particular **question**, you mean that it makes people want to ask that question. *Hopewell's success begs the question, why aren't more companies doing the same?*

beg the question: 2

If you say someone's statement **begs the question**, you mean that they can only make that statement if they assume that a particular problem has already been dealt with. By using this expression, you are suggesting that the problem has not in fact been dealt with, and so their statement may not be valid or reasonable. *Even the New York Times in 1988 stated that 'the warming of the earth's climate is no longer in dispute', somewhat begging the question of whether or not that warming is a greenhouse effect or, indeed, necessarily part of a continuing long-range trend.*

◆ This is a rough translation of the Latin expression 'petitio principii', a technical term used in logic to describe a situation in which the truth of something is assumed before it has been proved.

quick

cut someone to the quick

If something **cuts** you **to the quick**, it makes you very upset. *That tone of hers always cut him to the quick.*

◆ The quick is the very sensitive flesh under the fingernails or toenails.

quits

call it quits

If you say that you are going to **call it quits**, you mean that you have decided to stop doing something or stop being involved in something. *He and Moira had finally called it quits.*

quote

quote, unquote
quote, end quote

Mainly American If you use a word which someone else has used and you say **quote, unquote**, you are drawing attention to the word, and showing that it is not an accurate or precise way to describe the situation you are referring to. You sometimes use this expression to suggest that a word is being used with almost the opposite meaning to its normal meaning. In American English, you can also say **quote, end quote**. *She gathered around her a group of 'bodyguards', quote, unquote, who were essentially a bunch of thugs... The book was given to several school libraries, and in every case a vice principal of the particular school took the book out and then reported it, quote, 'lost', end quote.*

R

rack

on the rack
put someone on the rack

Mainly British If you say that someone is **on the rack**, you mean that they are in a state of anxiety, distress, or difficulty. You can also say that someone **puts** them **on the rack**. *In the flat Vangelis waited, still on the rack, not daring to believe.*

◆ The rack was an instrument of torture which was used in the past. Prisoners were tied to the rack, and their arms and legs were stretched until they confessed or told secrets, or died.

rack and ruin

If you say that something is going to **rack and ruin**, you mean that it is falling into a very bad condition, because nobody is looking after it or dealing properly with it. *The country is going to rack and ruin. No one is discussing the economic crisis.*

◆ The old-fashioned spelling 'wrack' is occasionally used instead of 'rack' in this expression. 'Wrack' means the same as 'wreck'.

rag

lose your rag

British If you **lose** your **rag**, you suddenly lose your temper with someone and get very angry. *The bloke pushed Melvin out of the way and he lost his rag and hit him.*

ragged

run someone ragged

If someone **runs** you **ragged**, they make you do so much that you get extremely tired. *Their defence was run ragged by a rampant Portsmouth in front of a crowd of 11,000.*

rags

rags to riches
riches to rags

If you describe someone's life as a **rags to riches** story, you are saying that even though they were very poor when they were young, they became very rich and successful. You can also say that they went from **rags to riches**. *His life sounds to me like the classic rags to riches story. He married some money, I gather, but he made a lot more… When asked how he went from rags to riches, Plunkett said, 'I saw my opportunities and I took them.'*

□ People sometimes use the expression **riches to rags** to mean that you have been very rich but have lost a lot of money and so have become very poor. *The country went from riches to rags in a generation.*

rails

jump the rails
Mainly British If something such as a plan or project **jumps the rails**, it suddenly goes wrong. *You never know when or where you'll find examples of how life in this modern society has jumped the rails.*

off the rails: 1
Mainly British If someone goes **off the rails**, they start to behave in an unacceptable or peculiar way. *Our family was so happy until our daughter went off the rails.*

off the rails: 2
Mainly British If something goes **off the rails**, it starts to go wrong. *By the Spring, the project seemed to be going off the rails.*

on the rails: 1
Mainly British If something stays **on the rails**, it continues to be as successful as it has been in the past. If something is back **on the rails**, it is beginning to be successful again after a period when it almost failed. *Co-ordinated action is needed more than ever to put the European economy back on the rails.*

on the rails: 2
If someone stays **on the rails**, they live and behave in a way which is acceptable and orderly. If someone is back **on the rails**, their life is going well again after a period when it was going badly. *I was released from prison last year. I have managed to get part of my life back on the rails by finding a flat and a part-time job.*

rain

it never rains but it pours
People say **'it never rains but it pours'** to comment on the fact that when one bad thing happens, other bad things often happen too and make

the situation worse. *He had a legitimate goal disallowed for 'handball' and later had a shot handled by a defender, only to see no penalty given. It never rains but it pours.*

take a rain check

If you offer something to someone or invite them to do something, and they say that they will **take a rain check**, they are refusing your offer or invitation politely, or saying that they would like to accept it, but at a different time. *I'm simply exhausted, Mimi. It's all been such a strain. Could I take a rain-check?*

◆ This expression refers to baseball. If a baseball game was cancelled because of rain, people were entitled to see another game by showing their original ticket or receipt. This ticket was called a rain check.

rainbow

at the end of the rainbow
the pot of gold at the end of the rainbow

If you say that something is **at the end of the rainbow** or is **the pot of gold at the end of the rainbow**, you mean that although you dream of getting it, in reality it will be very difficult to achieve. Compare **a pot of gold**; see **gold**. *There's a great big prize at the end of the rainbow and we both want it... I would rather be honest with people than mislead them that there is going to be some pot of gold at the end of the rainbow.*

◆ There is an old legend that a pot of gold is buried at the point where the end of the rainbow meets the ground.

rainbows

chase rainbows

If you say that someone **is chasing rainbows**, you mean that they are wasting their time by trying to get something which they can never have. *Only time will tell whether or not you're still chasing rainbows.*

ranch

bet the ranch

American If you say that someone **bets the ranch**, you mean that they spend all the money they have in order to achieve something, and risk losing it if they fail. *We thought that if we could do it, it would give us an important lead over our competition in future years. We've taken risks before and so we bet the ranch.*

rank

pull rank

If you say that someone in authority **pulls rank**, you disapprove of the fact that they make unfair use of their power or position to make people do what they want. *He was a chief superintendent and just occasionally he pulled rank.*

ranks

◆ A rank of soldiers is a line of them standing side by side.

break ranks
break rank

If someone **breaks ranks**, they disobey the instructions of a group or organization of which they are a member, and express their own opinion. You can also say that someone **breaks rank**. *Would you break ranks with your party and vote against the president's tax bill?*

◆ When soldiers break ranks, they stop standing in a line and move apart.

close ranks

If the members of a group **close ranks**, they support each other totally and oppose any criticism or attacks from outside on individual members. *They would more likely close ranks and support their president rather than abandon him in an election year.*

◆ When soldiers close ranks, they stand closer together so that it is hard for anyone to break through the line.

ransom

hold someone to ransom

British If you say that one person **is holding** another **to ransom**, you mean that the first person is using their power or influence to force the second to do something they do not want to do. *But who are the powerful men at the Bundesbank who have the power to hold Europe to ransom?*

a king's ransom

Mainly British If you refer to a sum of money as **a king's ransom**, you are emphasizing that it is very large. *Actress Julia Roberts is asking a king's ransom for her next film role.*

rap

take the rap

If someone **takes the rap**, they accept the blame or responsibility for something that has been done badly or has gone wrong, even if it is not their fault. *He had tried, and failed, to get someone to take the rap for a corruption scandal.*

◆ 'Rap' is slang for a criminal charge.

rat

the rat race

If you talk about getting out of **the rat race**, you are talking about giving up a job or way of life in which people compete aggressively with each other in order to be successful. *I had to get out of the rat race for a while and take a look at the real world again.*

smell a rat

If you **smell a rat**, you suspect that something is wrong in a particular situation, for example that someone is trying to deceive you or harm you. *If only I'd used my head, I'd have smelt a rat straight away and never touched the proposition.*

rate

at a rate of knots

British If someone does something **at a rate of knots**, they do it very quickly. *By 1935, Blyton was publishing at a rate of knots – adventures, fairy tales, mysteries.*

◆ The speed of ships is measured in knots. A knot is one nautical mile per hour, equivalent to 1.15 land miles per hour.

ray

a ray of sunshine

If you describe someone or something as **a ray of sunshine**, you mean that they make you feel better because there is something positive and refreshing about them. This expression is sometimes used ironically, for example to describe someone who is depressing and miserable. *Kim is like a ray of sunshine, a wonderful and beautiful girl who has changed my life.*

reap

reap the harvest

If you say that someone **reaps the harvest** of past actions, you mean that they suffer or benefit as a result of those actions. *Russia is reaping the vicious harvest of 74 years of Soviet rule.*

reap the whirlwind
sow the wind and reap the whirlwind

If you say that someone **is reaping the whirlwind**, you mean that they are suffering now because of mistakes that were made in the past. *There has been a permissive revolution and now we all reap the whirlwind.*

☐ You can also say someone **has sown the wind and is now reaping the whirlwind**. *The new Chancellor has tended to flit from job to job, staying long enough to sow the wind but leaving someone else to reap the whirlwind... Events beyond the Prime Minister's control mean that he is likely to reap the economic whirlwind he helped to sow.*

♦ This is a quotation from the Bible. It refers to the punishment of the Israelites for disobeying God: 'For they have sown the wind, and they shall reap the whirlwind.' (Hosea 8:7)

you reap what you sow
as you sow, so shall you reap

You use the expression **you reap what you sow** to say that everything that happens is a result of things which you have done in the past. *It seems to me that if we create areas of such bleakness and social deprivation we should expect to reap what we sow.*

☐ People sometimes say **'as you sow, so shall you reap'**. *In the final analysis our future lies in our own hands. Let us ensure that it is ethically and spiritually orientated, for without doubt as we sow so shall we reap!*

♦ This is based on a quotation from the Bible: 'Whatsoever a man soweth, that shall he also reap.' (Galatians 6:7)

rearguard

fight a rearguard action

If you say that someone **is fighting a rearguard action**, you mean that they are trying hard to stop something happening, but you do not think that they will succeed. *National telephone companies are fighting a rearguard action against competition from beyond their frontiers.*

☐ You can also just talk about **a rearguard action**. *The government move is being seen as a rearguard action to protect the corrupt among its own ranks.*

♦ The rearguard of a retreating army is a unit which separates from the rest and acts as a defence while the rest of the army is getting away.

record

off the record

If you say that your remarks are **off the record**, you mean that you do not want anyone to report what you said. *That's off the record. You boys! I forgot you were here! Don't go repeating what I've said, you hear... Downing Street was furious last night at further revelations of the Prime Minister's 'off-the-record' remarks to journalists.*

red

in the red
out of the red

If a person or organization is **in the red**, they owe money to someone or to another organization. Compare **in the black**; see **black**. *Banks are desperate to get your custom – even if you're in the red... The network faces the prospect of falling back into the red for the first time in five years.*

☐ You can say that you have come **out of the red** when you have paid back your debt. *Life may be more complicated these days, but it means we're climbing out of the red.*

◆ This expression comes from the practice in the past of using red ink to fill in entries on the debit side of a book of accounts.

red as a beetroot
red as a beet

If you say that someone goes as **red as a beetroot** or as **red as a beet**, you mean that their face goes very red, for example because they are very hot or very embarrassed. 'Red as a beetroot' is used in British English and 'red as a beet' is used in American English. *He turned as red as beetroot when I told him.*

a red letter day

You refer to a day as **a red letter day** when something very important or exciting happens then. *Back in 1986 Jim had his first picture published in BBC Wildlife Magazine. 'That was a real red letter day for me!' he confesses.*

◆ In the past, important feast days and saints' days were printed in red in some calendars.

see red

If you **see red**, you suddenly become very angry or annoyed because of something which has been said or done. *I cannot stand humiliation of any kind. I just see red. I could pick up a bottle and just smash it in someone's face because of it.*

◆ This is a reference to the traditional belief that the colour red makes bulls angry. In bullfighting, the matador waves a red cape to make the bull charge.

red-handed

catch someone red-handed

If someone **is caught red-handed**, they are caught while they are doing something illegal or wrong. *Three smugglers caught red-handed with several kilograms of uranium and other radioactive materials were detained last week in the southern Polish city of Rzeszow.*

◆ The reference here is to a guilty person whose hands are covered in blood.

reed

a broken reed

British If you refer to one of the members of a group as **a broken reed**, you mean that they are very weak and so you cannot depend on them in difficult situations. *They recognized that their allies were a broken reed.*

reign

a reign of terror

A reign of terror is a period during which there is a lot of violence and killing, especially by people who are in positions of power. *The president last night dismissed the government, accusing it of maladministration, corruption and nepotism, and of having unleashed a reign of terror against its political opponents.*

◆ The original Reign of Terror was during the French Revolution between April 1793 and July 1794, when many thousands were put to death by the government.

rein

◆ The reference in these expressions is to a rider using the reins to control a horse.

give someone free rein

If someone **is given free rein** to do something, they are given all the freedom they want or need to do it. *Most husbands, Barker discovered, insist that their tastes should dominate in areas like the living room. Their wives are allowed free rein only in private rooms like the bedroom.*

keep a tight rein on someone
hold someone on a tight rein

If you **keep a tight rein on** someone or something, you control them firmly. *The recession has forced people to keep a very tight rein on their finances when on holiday.*

rhyme

without rhyme or reason

If you say that something happens **without rhyme or reason**, you mean that there seems to be no logical or obvious reason for it to happen. *Sometimes I still get so depressed. There's no rhyme or reason for why all these awful things have happened.*

rich

rich as Croesus

British If you say that someone is as **rich as Croesus**, you mean that they are very rich. *He may be nearly as rich as Croesus, but that's still not rich enough for him.*

♦ Croesus was the ruler of Lydia, a kingdom in Asia Minor, in the 6th century BC. He was famous for being very rich.

strike it rich

If you **strike it rich**, you suddenly earn or win a large amount of money. *She says the graduates' perception is that commerce offers more opportunities to strike it rich.*

ride

a free ride

If you say that someone is getting **a free ride** in a particular situation, you disapprove of the fact that they are getting some benefit from it without putting any effort into achieving it themselves. *I never wanted anyone to think I was getting a free ride or special treatment from the boss.*

go along for the ride

If you say that someone **is going along for the ride**, you mean that they have decided to join in an activity but are not doing it seriously or getting deeply involved in it. *Your boyfriend is not likely to be serious about anything this week except having a good time. Go along for the ride.*

take someone for a ride

If you say that someone **has been taken for a ride**, you mean that they have been deceived or cheated. *You've been taken for a ride. Why did you give him five thousand francs?*

◆ This expression comes from American gangsters' slang. When gangsters 'took someone for a ride', they took them away in a car in order to kidnap them or kill them.

right

right as rain

If you say that someone is as **right as rain**, you mean that they are feeling well or healthy again after an illness or injury. *We put a bandage on his knee, gave him a biscuit and a cup of tea and he was right as rain.*

your right-hand man
your right-hand woman

Someone's **right-hand man** is their close assistant and the person they trust to help and support them in everything they do. People occasionally talk about someone's **right-hand woman** or their **right-hand person**. *Paddy Ashdown's speech to the Liberal Democrat conference yesterday was the last drafted for him by Alan Leaman, his right-hand man for the past 10 years.*

◆ There are several possible explanations for this expression. The right side of the body is traditionally associated with skill and strength. In the past, the position on the right of the leader at political or social gatherings was the place of honour. Alternatively, it may refer to the soldier who was responsible for the right side of a troop of horses.

rights

bang to rights: 1
dead to rights

If you have got someone **bang to rights** or **dead to rights**, you have got enough evidence against them to accuse them of a crime and to prove that they are guilty. *You've got your man – got him bang to rights – evidence,* *witnesses, the lot… Now, Captain Millard, how do you intend to proceed in the Rafaelli case? I mean, you have him pretty well dead to rights.*

bang to rights: 2
dead to rights

If someone gets you **bang to rights** or **dead to rights**, they show a good understanding of you and describe you accurately. *I read Matthew Sura's piece on you last month and I thought he got you bang to rights.*

ringer

a dead ringer for someone

If you say that one person is **a dead ringer for** another, you mean that the first person looks or sounds exactly like the second. *An ordinary guy from Baltimore, Dave Kovic is extraordinary in one respect: he's a dead ringer for the US President.*

◆ The word 'ringer' may originally have come from a name for dishonest traders at fairs who sold brass rings, pretending they were gold. In American horse racing, a 'ringer' is a horse that has been dishonestly substituted for another in a race.

rings

run rings round someone

If someone **runs rings round** you, they are much better at a particular activity than you and can beat or outwit you. *Mentally, he can still run rings round men half his age.*

ringside

a ringside seat
a ringside view

If you have **a ringside seat** or **a ringside view**, you have an excellent and clear view of what is happening. *The first US presidential election for which I had a ringside seat was that which brought John F. Kennedy to office over 30 years ago.*

◆ In boxing, the ringside seats are the seats that are closest to the ring and have the best view.

riot

read the riot act

If someone in authority **reads the riot act**, they angrily tell someone off for having done something stupid or wrong. *I'm glad you read the riot act to Billy. He's still a kid, you know. He still needs to be told what to do.*

◆ The Riot Act was a law passed in Britain in 1715. It made it an offence for a group of twelve or more people to refuse to break up and leave if someone in authority read them the relevant section of the Act.

run riot: 1

If someone **runs riot**, they get out of control. *Besides, there can be no parts of Britain which are no-go areas, where gangs run riot terrorising the innocent while the police stay safely away.*

run riot: 2

If something such as imagination or speculation **runs riot**, it expresses itself or spreads in an uncontrolled way. *We have no proof and when there is no proof, rumour runs riot.*

◆ In hunting, if the hounds run riot, they follow the scents of other animals rather than the one they are supposed to be chasing.

rise

◆ The reference in these expressions is to a fish rising to the surface of the water to take the bait, and getting caught.

get a rise out of someone

If you **get a rise out of** someone, you deliberately make them angry by teasing them or making fun of them. *If he told Livvy he had my backing, my guess is he did it to taunt her, to get a rise out of her.*

take the rise out of someone

If you **take the rise out of** someone or something, you make fun of them. *It should be fun taking the rise out of some love songs.*

river

sell someone down the river

If someone **sells** you **down the river**, they betray you or do something which harms you in order to gain an advantage for themselves. *He has been sold down the river by the people who were supposed to protect him.*

◆ This is a reference to slave-owners on the Mississippi river selling unwanted slaves to other slave-owners further down the river, where the conditions were harsher.

road

down the road

If you talk about something happening a particular number of years or months **down the road**, you are talking about its happening after that amount of time. *Twenty-five years down the road from independence, we have to start making some new priorities.*

hit the road

If you **hit the road**, you begin a journey. *The band plan to release a new single and hit the road for a tour in November.*

take the high road
take the low road

American If you say that someone **takes the high road**, you mean that they follow the course of action which is the most moral or most correct and which is least likely to harm or upset other people. *US diplomats say the president is likely to take the high road in his statements about trade.*

☐ You can say that someone **takes the low road** when they follow an immoral or dishonest course of action. *He was charged with taking the low road, which he seemed to do with relish.*

robbery

highway robbery
daylight robbery

If you are charged a lot of money for something that should cost a lot less or even nothing at all, you can refer to it as **highway robbery** to express your outrage at it. In British English, the expression **daylight robbery** is also used. *They are charging three bucks for the comics, which sounds like highway robbery to us... They're not doing a service, they're just taking the tickets away from the fans who have to buy them back again later at triple the price. They're just ripping the fans off; it's daylight robbery.*

rock

between a rock and a hard place

If you are caught **between a rock and a hard place**, you are in a difficult situation where you have to choose between two equally unpleasant courses of action. *Goss is caught between a rock and a hard place. If he bows to pressure and makes concessions on proposed cuts, middle-ground voters could see him as the typical Labor Premier in the grip*

*of union bosses. If he ignores the unions he runs the risk of further
alienating his traditional party supporters.*

hit rock bottom: 1
reach rock bottom
at rock bottom

If something **hits rock bottom** or **reaches rock bottom**, it is at an
extremely low level and cannot go any lower. You can also say that it is **at
rock bottom**. *The UK motor industry slumped to one of its blackest days
yesterday as new car sales hit rock bottom... Morale is at rock-bottom and
constant talk of job losses does nothing to make them feel any safer in their
jobs.*

□ If people buy or sell things at **rock-bottom** prices, they buy or sell them
when prices are extremely low. *He has been buying property at rock-bottom
prices.*

hit rock bottom: 2
reach rock bottom
at rock bottom

If someone **hits rock bottom** or **reaches rock bottom**, they are in a
hopeless or difficult situation, and so feel very depressed. You can also say
that they are **at rock bottom**. *I've hit rock bottom. I want a job so bad it's
cracking me up. I keep a smile on my face but inside I'm like stone... She
was at rock bottom. Her long-term love affair was breaking up and so was
she.*

rocker

off your rocker

If you say that someone is **off** their **rocker**, you mean that they are
crazy or completely illogical. *Mrs. Stevens will think I'm off my rocker
handing out my money like that before the bankruptcy business is even
settled.*

rocket

a rocket scientist
not rocket science

You can use expressions such as 'it doesn't take **a rocket scientist**' to
point out that doing a particular thing does not need much intelligence or
skill, and is actually very easy or obvious. *It doesn't take a rocket scientist
to make a rock record.*

☐ If you say that something **isn't rocket science**, you are emphasizing that it is very easy. *In 1981, it didn't take long for our people at CBS to learn these techniques. As I'd told Sauter, this isn't rocket science.*

rocks

on the rocks

If something such as a relationship or business is **on the rocks**, it is experiencing many difficulties and is likely to end or fail. *Their marriage was on the rocks, but they had determined not to divorce until the children were grown up.*

◆ The image here is of a ship that is stuck on some rocks.

rod

make a rod for your own back

British If you say that someone **has made a rod for** their **own back**, you mean that they have unintentionally done something which will cause them many problems. *The transport secretary, who expects to be flooded with angry drivers dialling from car phones, said 'I know I am making a rod for my own back. But if people see examples where contractors have clearly got long stretches of cones with nothing happening, they should let me know.'*

◆ This expression refers to someone providing the stick with which they themselves will be beaten.

roll

on a roll

If you say that you are **on a roll**, you mean that things are going very well for you, for example in your work or personal life. *We're on a roll and we're winning, which gives the players that extra belief in themselves.*

Rome

fiddle while Rome burns

If you accuse someone of **fiddling while Rome burns**, you mean that they are doing nothing or are spending their time on unimportant things when they have very serious issues or problems to deal with. *He said that the Australian community did not realise the gravity of the situation. We think it does: it is the Federal Government that has been fiddling while Rome burns.*

☐ This expression is very variable. For example, people sometimes replace 'Rome' with a different place name or other word so that this expression is more relevant to the subject they are talking about. *People talk about choice, people talk about educational reform but while the politicians fiddle, Los Angeles and Chicago are burning and these kids' educational opportunities are going down in flames as well... Far from fiddling while depositors got burnt, the Bank of England spent years containing BCCI's losses.*

◆ There is a story that the Emperor Nero set fire to Rome, and then played his lyre and sang as he watched the flames. Afterwards he denied this and blamed the Christians for the destruction.

Rome was not built in a day

People say **'Rome was not built in a day'** to point out that it takes a long time to do a job or task properly, and you should not rush it or expect to do it quickly. *Only two shoppers I interviewed were charitable about the new government. 'Rome wasn't built in a day,' one man said. 'Let's give them more time.'*

when in Rome
when in Rome, do as the Romans do

You say **'when in Rome'** to mean that people should follow the customs of the people they are visiting or living with. This expression comes from the proverb **when in Rome, do as the Romans do**. *When in Rome (or Palo Alto) do as the Romans do. Close up shop for a month or so for vacation. That's why the restaurant has been quiet and empty for the last two weeks.*

roof

go through the roof: 1
hit the roof
go through the ceiling

If the level of something such as the price of a product or the rate of inflation suddenly increases very rapidly, you can say that it **goes through the roof** or **hits the roof**. You can use 'ceiling' instead of 'roof'. *Interest rates were going through the roof... In 1990, wool prices hit the roof.*

go through the roof: 2
hit the roof
hit the ceiling

If someone **goes through the roof** or **hits the roof**, they suddenly become very angry, and usually show their anger by shouting at someone. You can use 'ceiling' instead of 'roof'. *I admitted I had ordered a racing car, and found myself in terrible trouble. He went through the roof!... I don't know what to think. Everyone seems angry with me. My parents have hit the roof.*

raise the roof
lift the roof

If a person or a crowd of people **raises the roof**, they make a very loud noise, for example by cheering, singing, or shouting. In British English, you can also say that someone **lifts the roof**. *Best audience I've ever had in my life – they practically raised the roof.*

rooftops

shout something from the rooftops

If you **shout** something **from the rooftops**, you let a lot of people know about something that you are particularly angry or excited about. *I would love to be able to shout our results from the rooftops.*

room

a smoke-filled room

If someone says that a political or business decision is made in **a smoke-filled room**, they mean that it is made by a small group of people in a private meeting, rather than in a more democratic or open way. *Richards doesn't think that a return to the smoke-filled room, in which a few bosses make the decision, would be possible.*

roost

come home to roost
the chickens come home to roost

If someone has done something bad or unacceptable, and you say that it **has come home to roost**, you mean that they will now have to deal with the unpleasant consequences of their actions. *You ought to have known that your lies would come home to roost in the end.*

☐ You can also say **the chickens are coming home to roost** to mean the same thing. People sometimes say 'pigeons' instead of 'chickens'. *Politicians can fool some people some of the time, but in the end, the chickens will come home to roost.*

◆ This expression is taken from the poem 'The Curse of Kehama' by the

English poet Robert Southey: 'Curses are like young chickens, they always come home to roost.'

rule the roost

If someone **rules the roost**, he or she is the most powerful and important person in a group. *In Germany, scientists will be found at the top of many manufacturing companies; in Britain, accountants rule the roost.*

☐ People sometimes say that something **rules the roost** when it is more popular than the things that it is being compared to. *By now you would expect CD to rule the roost, having relegated the venerable black vinyl record to a dark and dusty corner of the Science Museum.*

◆ This expression seems to refer to the dominant cock in a chicken coop. However, 'rule the roost' may have developed from the earlier expression 'rule the roast', which refers to the head of the household who carves and serves the meat.

root

money is the root of all evil
the love of money is the root of all evil

People say **'money is the root of all evil'** when they want to suggest that greed is the cause of a particular problem or the cause of society's problems in general. *From what I gather, Mr Smith owed Mr Morris some money. I believe the amount involved is a substantial sum and money is the root of all evil, as they say.*

☐ This expression comes from the proverb **the love of money is the root of all evil.**

◆ This proverb comes from a letter in the Bible from St. Paul to his disciple Timothy. (1 Timothy 6:10)

root and branch

If something is changed or reformed **root and branch**, it is changed or reformed completely, so that none of the old or traditional parts remain. *These genuinely radical measures, in contrast to the half-measures of the previous reforms, should change our economic system root and branch... Britain's schools are struggling daily to cope with the massive task of implementing the Government's root-and-branch reform of our education system.*

take root

If an idea, belief, or custom **takes root**, it becomes established or begins to develop. *When communism fell in Poland, it was said that time would be needed for democracy to take root.*

roots

put down roots: 1

If someone **puts down roots**, they make a place their home, for example by taking part in activities there or by making a lot of friends there. *Servicemen and women are seldom in the same place long enough to put down roots and buy their own home.*

put down roots: 2

If something **puts down roots** somewhere, it becomes firmly established there, so that it is likely to last and to be successful in the future. *Despite evident parliamentary disarray, democracy is putting down roots.*

rope

at the end of your rope

Mainly American If you say that you are **at the end of** your **rope**, you mean that you feel desperate because you are in a difficult situation and do not know how to deal with it. You can also use this expression to show your impatience or annoyance with someone. The usual British expression is **at the end of** your **tether**. *Everything is dreadful and I am at the end of my rope.*

◆ The image here is of an animal which cannot move very far because it is tied to something with a length of rope.

give someone enough rope to hang themselves
give someone enough rope

If you **give** someone **enough rope to hang** themselves, you give them the freedom to do something in the way they want to do it, usually in the hope that they will fail or become weak by doing it the wrong way. *We're worried that we're being set up. Being given enough rope to hang ourselves.*

□ If you **give** someone **enough rope** or **give** them **the rope** they **need**, you give them the freedom to do what they want in their own way. *He would give you enough rope and see what you did with it.*

ropes

learn the ropes
know the ropes

If you **learn the ropes**, you learn how to do a particular job or task. If you **know the ropes**, you know how a particular job or task should be done. *He tried hiring more salesmen to push his radio products, but they took too much time to learn the ropes.*

◆ The origin of this expression is on sailing ships, where the sailors had to get to know the complicated system of ropes which made up the rigging.

on the ropes

If you say that someone is **on the ropes**, you mean that they are very close to failing or being defeated. *The Denver-based developer has been on the ropes because of depressed housing markets in Denver, Texas and Arizona.*

◆ The image here is of a boxer who has been pushed back against the ropes around the edge of the ring.

show someone the ropes

If you **show** someone **the ropes**, you show them how to do a particular job or task. *We had a patrol out on the border, breaking in some young soldiers, showing them the ropes.*

◆ See the explanation at 'learn the ropes'.

roses

come up smelling of roses

If someone has been in a difficult situation and you say that they **have come up smelling of roses**, you mean that they are now in a better or stronger situation than they were before. You usually use this expression to show your surprise or resentment that this has happened. *Tom Ellis, who walked out on Monday after a boardroom row, has come up smelling of roses. He has been snapped up by a rival engineering company and the word is that his financial package is even healthier… No matter the problem, he manages to wriggle out of it and come up smelling of roses.*

everything is coming up roses

If you say that **everything is coming up roses** for someone, you mean that they are having a lot of success and everything is going well for them. *For Rachel Ashwell, everything's coming up roses both in her home and her working life.*

not a bed of roses
not all roses

If you say that a situation is **not a bed of roses** or **not all roses**, you mean that it is not all pleasant, and that there are some unpleasant aspects to it as well. *Life as a graduate is not a bed of roses.*

rose-tinted

rose-tinted spectacles
rose-coloured glasses

If you say that someone looks at something through **rose-tinted**

spectacles or **rose-coloured glasses**, you mean that they only notice the good things about it and so their view is unrealistic. *He accused diplomats of looking at the world through rose-tinted spectacles... Real estate broker Tom Foye believes that many buyers tend to look at houses with rose-colored glasses. Consequently, they end up feeling cheated.*

◆ 'Rose-coloured' is spelled 'rose-colored' in American English.

rough

cut up rough

British If you say that someone **cuts up rough**, you mean that they suddenly become extremely angry or violent. *I was detailed to take a revolver and accompany the sailor who brought him his meals in case he cut up rough.*

rough and ready: 1

If you describe something as **rough and ready**, you mean that it is rather simple and basic, or it is not very exact, because it has been thought of or done in a hurry. *We put up for the night at the town's only hostelry, a rough-and-ready bar with rooms attached.*

rough and ready: 2

If you describe someone as **rough and ready**, you mean that they are not very well-mannered or refined. *At first the rough and ready sailors did not know what to make of the young cleric.*

rough and tumble

You can use **rough and tumble** to refer to a situation in which the people involved try hard to get what they want, and do not worry about upsetting or harming others. You use this expression when you think that this is normal or acceptable behaviour. *Whoever expected leaders in the rough and tumble of electoral politics to be nice or fair?*

◆ Originally, a rough and tumble was a boxing match in which there were no rules or restrictions.

take the rough with the smooth

British If you **take the rough with the smooth**, you are willing to accept both the unpleasant and pleasant aspects of something. *You have to take the rough with the smooth. I never promised there would be no risk.*

roughshod

ride roughshod over someone

British If someone **rides roughshod over** other people, they pay no attention to what those people want, or they take decisions without considering their feelings or interests. *Bosses nowadays seem to think they can ride roughshod over unions and I like to see them fighting back.*

◆ In the past, a roughshod horse had nail heads sticking out from its shoes, so it would not slip on icy roads. These shoes could cause terrible injuries if the horse was ridden over a person in a battle or by accident.

roulette
Russian roulette

If you say that someone is playing **Russian roulette**, you are critical of them for doing something which is very dangerous because it involves unpredictable risks. *One ex-employee said security was so lax that the airline was, in effect, playing Russian roulette with passengers' lives.*

◆ If someone plays 'Russian roulette', they put one bullet in a revolver and fire it at their head without knowing whether the bullet will be fired or not.

row
a hard row to hoe
a tough row to hoe

If you say that you have **a hard row to hoe** or **a tough row to hoe**, you mean that you are in a situation which is very difficult to deal with. *She is the first to admit that being a woman in politics has been a hard and sometimes isolated row to hoe... I think, however, that in a criminal prosecution against the police, the prosecutor has a very tough row to hoe.*

rub
not have two pennies to rub together
not have two nickels to rub together

If you say that someone **doesn't have two pennies to rub together**, you are emphasizing that they have very little money. *And from all those interviews her family gave to the Press they sounded as if they hadn't two pennies to rub together.*

☐ You can also use these expressions without a negative when you are suggesting that someone or something has more of a quality than other people or things. *Anyone with two brain cells to rub together could have spotted she wasn't to be trusted.*

the rub of the green

Mainly British If you say that you have **the rub of the green** in an activity or sport, you mean that you have good luck. *Providing we have the* *rub of the green, there is no reason why we can't do really well in the summer.*

◆ This expression probably comes from golf or bowls. The 'rub' is the direction in which the grass is bent when it is cut, which affects the movement of the ball.

Rubicon

cross the Rubicon

If someone **has crossed the Rubicon**, they have made an important decision which cannot be changed and which will have very important consequences. *Mr Major's clear support for military action has come at a time when President Bush himself is said by his spokesmen to have crossed the Rubicon in his mind about the use of force.*

◆ The Rubicon was a small river which separated Roman Italy from Gaul, the province ruled by Julius Caesar. Caesar crossed the Rubicon in 49 BC, invaded Roman Italy, and started a civil war. 'The die is cast' is based on the same incident.

rug

pull the rug from under you
pull the rug from under your feet

If someone **pulls the rug from under** you or **pulls the rug from under** your **feet**, they suddenly stop helping and supporting you. *Every time we have been close to saving the shipyard, the Government has pulled the rug from under our feet.*

sweep something under the rug

Mainly American If you **sweep** something **under the rug**, you try to hide it and forget about it because you find it embarrassing or shameful. The usual British expression is **sweep** something **under the carpet**. *By sweeping the wrongdoing under the rug, executives seek to avoid being accused of mismanagement by directors and shareholders.*

rule

a rule of thumb

A rule of thumb is a general rule about something which you can be confident will be right in most cases. *As a rule of thumb, drink a glass of water or pure fruit juice every hour you are travelling.*

◆ This expression probably dates back to the use of the first joint of the thumb as a unit of measurement.

run

a dummy run

British **A dummy run** is a trial or test procedure which you carry out in order to see if a plan or process will work properly. *Before we started we did a dummy run, checking out all the streets and offices we would use, and planning our escape route.*

give someone a run for their money

If you **give** someone **a run for** their **money**, you put up a very strong challenge in a contest which they are expected to win fairly easily. *We think the Irish will give the Welsh a good run for their money.*

run before you can walk

British If you say that someone is trying to **run before** they **can walk**, you mean that they are trying to do something which is very difficult or advanced before they have made sure that they can successfully achieve something simpler. *They tried to run before they could walk. They made it too complicated.*

runaround

give someone the runaround

If someone **gives** you **the runaround**, they deliberately try to mislead or confuse you and they do not tell you the truth about something which you need or want to know. *Someone close could give you the runaround, especially where it concerns money or other joint matters... In the early days of their questioning, they felt they were getting the runaround.*

runes

read the runes

British If someone **reads the runes**, they interpret a situation in a particular way and decide what is likely to happen. *Of course, reading the runes on US interest rates may all seem irrelevant next month if the President goes to war.*

◆ Runes were a form of writing used particularly in Scandinavia until medieval times. The letters were often thought to have magical properties.

running

in the running
out of the running

If someone is **in the running** for a job or prize, they have a good chance of getting it or winning it. If they are **out of the running**, they no longer have a chance of getting it or winning it. *The US needs a win tonight to still be in the running for the gold.*

◆ If a horse is 'in the running', it has a good chance of winning a race.

rush

a rush of blood
a rush of blood to the head

If you say that you have **a rush of blood** or **a rush of blood to the head**, you mean that you suddenly do something foolish or daring which you would not normally do. *You can't have a sudden rush of blood to the head and speak about something which hasn't been brought up before.*

S

sabre (*American* saber)

sabre-rattling
rattle your sabre

If you describe someone's behaviour as **sabre-rattling**, you mean that they are behaving very aggressively and making threats, often of military action, although it is not certain how serious they are or whether they will actually carry out their threats. *After more than a week of sabre-rattling, the two countries have agreed to talk about their differences.*

□ You can also say that people **are rattling** their **sabres**. *There is a sliver of territory called Nakhichevan that several countries are rattling their sabers over.*

◆ A sabre is a heavy sword with a curved blade that was used in the past by soldiers on horseback.

saddle

in the saddle

You can say that someone is **in the saddle** when they are in charge of their country's affairs, or when they make the important decisions in an organization. *It is his bad luck to be in the saddle when his country has to decide which road it is now going to follow.*

ride high in the saddle

If you say that someone **is riding high in the saddle**, you mean that they are currently very successful and are showing this in their behaviour and attitudes. *Australia are riding a little higher in the saddle after their first Test victory.*

safe

safe as houses

British If you say that something is as **safe as houses**, you mean that it is very safe and reliable. *Both managers can count on one thing – their jobs are safe as houses.*

sailing

plain sailing
clear sailing
smooth sailing

In British English, if you say that an activity or task will not be **plain sailing**, you mean that it will be difficult to do or achieve. In American English, you say that it will not be **clear sailing**, **smooth sailing**, or **easy sailing**. *As Phillippa found, even with the ideal tenant it isn't all plain sailing. 'If you are used to having your home to yourself, it's difficult at first to get used to sharing the kitchen and the bathroom and so on,' she admits... It's not going to be easy sailing. He's bound to come up with some tough opposition.*

□ When an activity or task is easy to do, you can say that it is **plain sailing**. *Once I got used to the diet it was plain sailing.*

◆ 'Plain sailing' is sailing in favourable conditions, without any difficulties. However, the expression may have come from 'plane sailing', a method of working out the position of a ship and planning its route using calculations based on the earth being flat rather than round. This is a simple and easy method which is fairly accurate over short distances, especially near the equator.

sails

trim your sails

If you **trim** your **sails**, you adapt your behaviour to deal with a difficult situation, for example by limiting your demands, needs, or expectations. *Mr Lee, for his part, has already begun trimming his sails in preparation* *for dealing with the new government.*

♦ To trim sails means to adjust them according to the strength and direction of the wind.

salad

your salad days

If you talk about your **salad days**, you are talking about the time when you were young and inexperienced. *The Grand Hotel did not seem to have changed since her salad days.*

♦ This is a quotation from Shakespeare's 'Antony and Cleopatra' (Act 1, Scene 5), when Cleopatra is talking about her youth: 'My salad days, When I was green in judgment'.

saloon

the last chance saloon
drinking in the last chance saloon

British If someone is doing something and you say that it is **the last chance saloon** for them, you mean that it is their final opportunity to succeed in what they are doing. You can also say that they **are drinking in the last chance saloon**. *Boxers Coetzer, 31, and Bruno, 30 and 11 months, understand one thing clearly. As far as the world title goes, Saturday is the last chance saloon for both of them... David Mellor, who was the Cabinet minister in charge of media regulation, told the tabloid editors they were drinking in the last-chance saloon and to clean up their act or face government legislation.*

salt

rub salt into the wound

If you are in an unpleasant situation and you accuse someone of **rubbing salt into the wound**, you are accusing them of making things even worse for you, for example by reminding you of your failures or faults or by increasing your difficulties. *The Rovers players were quick to rub salt into United's wounds, cheering and chanting through the paper-thin walls separating the dressing rooms.*

the salt of the earth

If you describe someone as **the salt of the earth**, you are showing admiration for their honesty and reliability. *These are good people, rough-hewn, but the salt of the earth... Proceeds this time go to Centacare,*

the salt-of-the-earth Catholic family welfare service which provides
counselling and aid for the unhappy.

◆ This comes from the Bible, when Jesus is talking to His disciples: 'Ye
are the salt of the earth: but if the salt have lost his savour, wherewith
shall it be salted?' (Matthew 5:13)

take something with a pinch of salt
take something with a grain of salt

If you say that a piece of information should **be taken with a pinch of
salt**, you mean that it should not be relied on, because it may not be
accurate or true. This expression is used mainly in British English; in
American English, the usual form is **take** something **with a grain of salt**.
*You have to take these findings with a pinch of salt because respondents in
attitude surveys tend to give the answers they feel they should.*

◆ A pinch of salt is a small amount of salt held between your thumb and
your first finger. Some people believe that this expression refers to the
King of Pontus, Mithridates VI, who lived in the first century BC. It is said
that he made himself immune to poison by swallowing small amounts of it
with a grain of salt. However, other people think that it is a medieval
English expression, which suggests that you need to be suspicious of
unlikely stories in the same way that you need salt with food.

worth their salt

If you say, for example, that no teacher **worth** their **salt** or no actor
worth their **salt** would do a particular thing, you mean that no teacher or
actor who was good at their job would consider doing that thing. *No
racing driver worth his salt gets too sentimental about his cars.*

◆ In the past, salt was expensive and rare. Roman soldiers were paid a
'salarium' or salt money, so they could buy salt and stay healthy.

sand

build something on sand

If you say that something **is built on sand**, you mean that it does not
have a strong or proper basis, and so is likely to fail or come to an end. *He
moved into the newspaper business in the Seventies. It was an empire built
on sand. The newspapers folded, and in 1981 he was charged with
fraudulent bankruptcy.*

◆ This expression relates to a story in the Bible, where Jesus compares
the people who follow his teachings to a wise man, who built his house on
rock, and those who did not to a foolish man, who built his house on sand.

When floods came, the house built on rock remained standing but the house built on sand collapsed. (Matthew 7:24–27).

sands

shifting sands

You can talk about the **shifting sands** of a situation when it keeps changing, and this makes it difficult to deal with. *Arrogant and authoritarian he might be, but he had been a rock in the shifting sands of her existence.*

sandwich

the meat in the sandwich
the filling in the sandwich

British If you say that you are **the meat in the sandwich** or **the filling in the sandwich**, you mean that you are in a very awkward position because you have been caught between two people or groups who are in conflict with each other. *Previously, the idea of a closely united Europe was unpopular because Europeans feared being the filling in a superpower sandwich.*

sardines

packed like sardines

If a group of people are together in an enclosed space and you say that they **are packed like sardines**, you mean that there are far more of them than the space was intended to hold, and so they are very close to each other and cannot move about easily. *The people are in an appalling condition. They're packed like sardines on the ship.*

sauce

what's sauce for the goose is sauce for the gander

Fairly old-fashioned People say **'what's sauce for the goose is sauce for the gander'** when they are arguing that what applies to one person should apply to others, because people should be treated fairly and equally. This expression is often shortened or varied. *If we're going to have equality, let's have real equality. There's been more male nudity in films lately and I think it's very refreshing – sauce for the goose and all that.*

say

before you could say Jack Robinson
before you could say knife

If you say that something happened **before you could say Jack**

Robinson or **before you could say knife**, you are emphasizing that it happened very suddenly and quickly. *The pair of them were out of the door and down the steps before you could say Jack Robinson... The money they'd sent their son for gold teeth had gone on booze before you could say knife.*

☐ People often change 'Jack Robinson' or 'knife' to a name or a word or expression that is relevant to the context they are talking about. *She was on the phone to New York before you could say long-distance.*

scales

the scales fall from your eyes

When someone suddenly realizes the truth about something after a long period of not understanding it or of being deceived about it, you can say that **the scales have fallen from** their **eyes**. *It was only at that point that the scales finally fell from his eyes and he realised he had made a dreadful mistake.*

◆ This is a reference to the Bible story of Saul, who became blind after he had a vision of God on the road to Damascus. Saul became a Christian after Ananias, a follower of Jesus, restored his sight. The Bible says: 'And immediately there fell from his eyes as it had been scales: and he received sight forthwith, and arose, and was baptized.' (Acts 9:18)

scene

set the scene: 1

If you **set the scene**, you briefly tell people what they need to know about a subject or topic, so that they can understand what is going to happen or be said next. *To set the scene for this latest example of the improvement in East-West relations, here's Kevin Connolly from Moscow.*

☐ Introducing a subject like this can be described as **scene-setting**. *The purpose of this chapter was scene-setting – to clarify our goals and the approach being taken.*

set the scene: 2

If something **sets the scene** for an event, it creates the conditions in which that event is likely to happen. *Some members feared that Germany might raise its interest rates. That could have set the scene for a confrontation with the US, which is concerned that increases could cut demand for its exports.*

scenes
behind the scenes
If something is done **behind the scenes**, it is done in private or in secret, rather than publicly. *The Prime Minister's remarks put in the public arena a debate which has been going on behind the scenes for months... The debate was postponed for a third time after another day of intensive behind-the-scenes negotiations.*

scent
throw someone off the scent
If you are looking for something or trying to find out the truth about something and someone **throws** you **off the scent**, they deliberately confuse or mislead you by making you believe something that is not true. *We decided that if anyone was following us, it would be wiser if we split up to throw them temporarily off the scent.*

◆ This is a reference to hounds that get distracted from the trail of an animal they are hunting, for example because of another smell.

school
the old school
If you say that someone is of **the old school**, you mean that they have traditional ideas and values and are fairly old-fashioned. *As a builder of the old school, he did not always see eye to eye with designers of new houses... She is very much an old-school nurse and her outlook leads to clashes with other staff.*

the old school tie
British When people talk about **the old school tie**, they are referring to the belief that men who have been to the most famous British private schools use their positions of influence to help other men who went to the same school as themselves. *Ray Illingworth's appointment as chairman of selectors was a triumph of commonsense and a blow for sporting virtue ahead of the old school tie network.*

the school of hard knocks
If you say that someone has graduated from **the school of hard knocks**, you mean that their life in the past has been very difficult or unpleasant. *He graduated from the school of hard knocks as well – most of his family perished in the war.*

science

blind someone with science

If someone **blinds** you **with science**, they tell you about something in a complex or technical way so that you have great difficulty in understanding it. *We want facts and figures but don't want to be blinded by science.*

score

know the score

If you **know the score**, you know what the real facts of a situation are and how they affect you, even though you may not like them. *Now I know the score and know everything that's going on around there.*

settle a score
settle an old score

If someone **settles a score** or **settles an old score**, they take revenge for something that someone has done to them in the past. *The ethnic groups turned on each other to settle old scores, leaving millions dead.*

☐ You can talk about people or groups being involved in **score-settling** or **the settling of scores**. *Some of the changes that have taken place since the war may amount to little more than the settling of scores.*

scratch

from scratch

If you start **from scratch**, you create something completely new, rather than adding to something that already exists. *She moved to a strange place where she had to make new friends and start a new life from scratch.*

◆ In the past, the starting line for races was often a line scratched in the earth.

not up to scratch

British If you say that something or someone is **not up to scratch**, you mean that they are not as good as they ought to be. *Athletes have no one to blame but themselves if their performances are not up to scratch.*

◆ In the past, boxers started a fight with their left feet on a line drawn on the ground, known as the scratch. When a boxer was knocked down, they were allowed thirty seconds' rest before coming 'up to the scratch' once more. A boxer who was not at the line in time lost the fight.

screw

have a screw loose

If you say that someone **has a screw loose**, you mean that their behaviour is very strange or that they are slightly mad. *Do you honestly think if I had a screw loose, I would be allowed to work with the elderly?*

turn the screw on someone
tighten the screw on someone

If someone **turns the screw on** you, they increase the pressure on you to make you do what they want. You can also say that they **tighten the screw** or **tighten the screws on** you. *Perhaps it's a final attempt to turn the screw and squeeze a last concession out of us.*

□ In a process like this, you can refer to each action that puts pressure on someone as **a turn of the screw**, **a twist of the screw**, or **a tightening of the screw**. *Opposition parties and immigrant organisations see the changes as a further tightening of the screw.*

◆ This is a reference to a method of torture called the thumbscrew. The prisoner's thumbs were pressed between two bars of iron which were then tightened by means of a screw.

screws

put the screws on someone

If someone **puts the screws on** you, they use pressure or threats to make you do what they want. *They had to put the screws on Harper. So far, he was the only person who might know something.*

◆ See the explanation at 'turn the screw on someone'.

Scylla

between Scylla and Charybdis

If you are **between Scylla and Charybdis**, you have to choose between two possible courses of action, both of which seem equally bad. *The middle course was felt to be between the Scylla of democratic tyranny and the Charybdis of arbitrary rule.*

◆ In Greek mythology, Scylla and Charybdis were monsters who lived on either side of the Straits of Messina. Scylla lived on a rock on the Italian side, and had twelve heads, with which she swallowed sailors. Charybdis lived on the coast of Sicily and swallowed the sea three times a day, creating a whirlpool.

sea

all at sea
at sea

If you say that someone is **all at sea** or is **at sea**, you mean that they are very confused by a situation and do not understand it. 'All at sea' is used only in British English. *While he may be all at sea on the economy, his changes have brought the West real and lasting political benefits.*

◆ The reference here is to a ship or a boat that has got lost.

a sea change

You can describe a complete change in someone's attitudes or behaviour as **a sea change**. *There has also been a sea-change in attitudes to drinking – a major cause of death on the roads – thanks to greater public awareness and the use of breathalysers.*

seams

burst at the seams

If you say that a place **is bursting at the seams**, you mean that it is very full of people or things. *The tiny Abbey Stadium was bursting at the seams with a capacity crowd of just under 10,000.*

come apart at the seams: 1
fall apart at the seams

If you say that a system or relationship **is coming apart at the seams** or **is falling apart at the seams**, you mean that it is in a very bad state, and is about to collapse and completely fail. *University lecturers have given a warning that Britain's university system is in danger of falling apart at the seams because of cuts in government funding.*

come apart at the seams: 2

If you say that someone **is coming apart at the seams**, you mean that they are behaving in a strange or illogical way, because they are under severe mental strain. *He stood for a moment, breathing deeply; he was coming apart at the seams, something he had never thought would happen to him.*

season

open season

If you say that it is **open season** on someone or something, you mean that a lot of people are currently criticizing or attacking them. *Open season has been declared on the royal family*.

◆ In hunting, the open season is the period of the year when it is legal to hunt particular types of animals or birds.

seat

fly by the seat of your pants

If you say that someone **is flying by the seat of** their **pants**, you mean that they are doing something difficult or dangerous using only their instincts, because they do not have the right kind of experience or information. You often use this expression to show disapproval of this situation. *To a great extent, all of us fly by the seat of our pants and try to learn quickly from experience.*

□ A **seat-of-the-pants** method of doing something depends on instinct rather than on careful planning or knowledge. *I don't know much law, never did. A seat-of-the-pants barrister, that's me.*

◆ If you fly an aircraft by the seat of your pants, you do not use maps or instruments.

in the driving seat
in the driver's seat

In British English, if you say that someone is **in the driving seat**, you mean that they have control of a situation. In American English, the form is **in the driver's seat**. *The radicals were in the driving seat, much to the anxiety of the moderates… Those who had access to money were in the driver's seat.*

in the hot seat

If someone is **in the hot seat**, they are in a position where they have to make important or difficult decisions, or where they have to answer difficult questions. In American English, you can also say that they are **on the hot seat**. *She decided to end the interview by putting me in the hot seat. 'And you? What about your background?' I was stuck for words.*

take a back seat: 1

If you **take a back seat**, you allow other people to have all the power, importance, or responsibility. *You will be aware that there are some situations when it is wise to take a back seat and some where it is appropriate to fifight for your, and others', rights.*

take a back seat: 2

If one thing **takes a back seat** to another, people give the first thing less attention because they think that it is less important or less interesting than the other thing. *His own private life takes a back seat to the problems and difficulties of his patients.*

security

a security blanket

If you refer to something as **a security blanket**, you mean that it provides someone with a feeling of safety and comfort when they are in a situation which worries them or makes them nervous. *He never gave a second thought to leaving behind the security blanket of his family and friends to head north.*

◆ A young child's security blanket is a piece of cloth or clothing which the child holds and chews in order to feel comforted.

seed

go to seed: 1
run to seed

If you say that someone **has gone to seed**, you mean that they have allowed themselves to become unfit, untidy, or lazy as they have grown older. You can also say that they **have run to seed**. *Once he had carried a lot of muscle but now he was running to seed.*

go to seed: 2
run to seed

If a place **has gone to seed** or **has run to seed**, it has become dirty and neglected because people have not bothered to care for it. *When she died, the place lost its focus and went to seed.*

◆ When vegetables such as lettuce go to seed, they produce flowers and seeds, and are no longer fit to eat.

seed corn
eat your seed corn

If you refer to resources or people as **seed corn**, you mean that they will produce benefits in the future rather than immediately. *I regard the teachers as the people who are planting the seed corn for the future and therefore I regard their work as crucially important.*

☐ If you say that people **are eating** their **seed corn**, you mean that they are using up their resources, and they will suffer for this in the future. *A society that's unwilling to invest in its future is a society that's living off capital. It's eating its seed corn and I'm afraid that's what we're doing too much in the United States today.*

♦ A farmer's seed corn is the grain that is used for planting rather than being sold or eaten.

seeds

sow the seeds of something
plant the seeds of something

If something **sows the seeds of** a future problem, it starts the process which causes that problem to develop. You can also say that something **plants the seeds of** a future problem. *The birth of a second child may upset a previously satisfactory relationship between the mother and the first child and sow the seeds of a long-standing behaviour problem.*

□ You can also **sow** or **plant the seeds of** something good. *Ministers had spent five years planting the seeds of reform.*

send

send someone packing

If someone **is sent packing**, they are told very forcefully or in an unsympathetic way to leave a place, or to leave their job or position. *Mr Cawley was sent packing from his home on the estate after 26 years as park manager.*

shade

put someone in the shade

If one person or thing **puts** another **in the shade**, they are so impressive that they make the other person or thing seem unimportant by comparison. *The celebrations put Mardi Gras in the shade.*

shades

shades of

If you have just mentioned a person or thing and you say **shades of** another person or thing, you mean that the first person or thing reminds you of the second one. *The debate had been brought forward by a week, in an effort to avert the protest planned for it by the school students' leaders. Shades of 1968, perhaps?*

♦ 'Shade' is an old word for 'ghost'.

shadow

afraid of your own shadow

If you say that someone is **afraid of** their **own shadow**, you mean that are very timid or nervous. *They're all afraid of their own shadows. Can't say I blame them. After all, this is a police state.*

a shadow of your former self

If you say that someone or something is **a shadow of** their **former self**, you mean that they are much less powerful or capable than they used to be. *The federal Communist party that resumed its Congress on Saturday after a break of four months was a pale shadow of its former self.*

shakes

in two shakes of a lamb's tail
in two shakes

Fairly old-fashioned If you say that you will do something **in two shakes of a lamb's tail**, you mean that you will do it very soon or very quickly. You can also just say **in two shakes**. *If you were an incompetent buffoon, I would have you out of office in two shakes of a lamb's tail... I'll just dash up to the phone and be back in two shakes.*

no great shakes

If you say that someone or something is **no great shakes**, you mean that they are ineffective, useless, or of poor quality. *As a thriller, 'A Death in Paris' is no great shakes.*

♦ This expression probably refers to shaking dice and getting a poor result, although there are other possible explanations.

shape

knock something into shape
whip something into shape
lick something into shape

If you **knock** something **into shape** or **whip** it **into shape**, you use whatever methods are necessary to change or improve it, so that it is in the condition that you want it to be in. In British English, 'lick' can be used instead of 'knock' or 'whip'. *Most experts agree that the country's agriculture can quickly be knocked into shape and be successful... We were licked into shape by the long-serving departmental managers to whom we reported.*

◆ The variation 'lick someone into shape' relates to an ancient belief that bear cubs were born as shapeless lumps. It was thought that their mothers then licked them until they developed their proper form.

shape up or ship out

If you tell someone to **shape up or ship out**, you are telling them that they should start behaving in a more reasonable or responsible way, or else leave the place where they are or give up what they are doing. *You've either got to take all this, you've got to stomach it, join in, or you'll go under. Shape up or ship out.*

shave

a close shave

If you say that someone had **a close shave**, you mean that they very nearly had an accident or disaster, or very nearly suffered a defeat. *Admittedly you had a close shave, but you knew when you accepted this job that there would be risks involved.*

sheep

the black sheep
the black sheep of the family

If you describe someone as **the black sheep** or **the black sheep of the family**, you mean that they are very different from the other people in their family or group and are considered bad or worthless by them. *While to her family she might seem the rebellious black sheep, when Janet compared herself to friends like Nancy or Margaret, she saw herself as bourgeois, neat, and timid... My aunt was very famous in those days, but because she was the black sheep of the family I was never encouraged to talk about her.*

◆ Black sheep are less valuable than white sheep since their wool cannot be dyed. In addition, people used to associate the colour black with evil and wrongdoing.

make sheep's eyes

Old-fashioned If you **make sheep's eyes** at someone, you look at them in an adoring and admiring way. *I kissed her hand, made sheep's eyes and followed her, humming, up the winding stairs.*

might as well be hanged for a sheep as a lamb

If someone says '**I might as well be hanged for a sheep as a lamb**', they mean that they will suffer or be punished whatever they do, so they might as well do something really bad if they can get some enjoyment or profit from it. 'Hung' is sometimes used instead of 'hanged'. *If they are going to hang me for what has already been done why should I sue for peace? I might as well be hanged for a sheep as well as a lamb.*

◆ For a long time in the past in England, the penalty for sheep stealing was death.

separate the sheep from the goats
sort out the sheep from the goats

If you **separate the sheep from the goats** or **sort out the sheep from the goats**, you examine a group of things or people and decide which ones are good and which are bad. *It is getting harder and harder to sort out the sheep from the goats among the 4,000 or so titles for children that pour off the publishers' presses every year.*

◆ The Bible says that on the Day of Judgement, Jesus will divide His sheep from the goats. The sheep represent those who are going to heaven, and the goats represent those who are going to hell. (Matthew 25:32)

sheet

a clean sheet: 1
a clean sheet of paper

If you are allowed to start with **a clean sheet** or with **a clean sheet of paper**, you are allowed to forget previous debts or mistakes, and so are given a new chance to succeed at something. *The Christmas break has erased unhappy memories and allowed the Government to start the new year with a clean sheet.*

a clean sheet: 2

British In a football match, if a team keeps **a clean sheet**, no goals are scored against them.

sheets

three sheets to the wind

Old-fashioned If you say that someone is **three sheets to the wind** or **three sheets in the wind**, you mean that they are drunk. *He's probably three sheets to the wind down at Toby's, wondering where the hell he left his truck.*

◆ On a boat, the ropes that control the position of the sails are called sheets. If the sheets are left hanging loose, the sails flap freely in the wind and cannot be controlled.

shelf

on the shelf

British When a woman is no longer young and has not married, people sometimes say that she is **on the shelf**, meaning that she will not get married because she is too old for men to find her attractive. Many people dislike this expression because of the attitude which it represents. *I certainly don't equate being single with being on the shelf!*

shelf life

If you say that something has a particular **shelf life**, you mean that it will only last for that length of time, rather than continuing indefinitely. *A large proportion of small businesses have a short shelf life.*

◆ The shelf life of a food, drink, or medicine is the length of time it can be kept before it is too old to sell or use.

shell

come out of your shell
go into your shell

If you **come out of** your **shell**, you become less shy and more talkative and friendly. *She used to be very timid and shy but I think she's come out of her shell.*

☐ If you **go into** your **shell**, you become more timid and less friendly. Verbs such as 'withdraw' and 'retreat' can be used instead of 'go'. *Brian withdrew increasingly into his shell, inhibited by a growing but unrecognized sense of inferiority.*

a shell game

Mainly American If you say that someone is playing **a shell game**, you mean that they are deliberately deceiving people, for example by changing things or pretending to change things, in order to gain an advantage. *The union had accused the mine owners of playing a kind of corporate shell game, in which mines could be opened in the future under a variety of names with the intent of hiring non-union miners.*

◆ The shell game is an old confidence trick. An object is hidden under one of three cups, which are then moved out of their original order. The victim bets on where the object is, and typically gets it wrong. The trick may have become known as the shell game because it was originally done with walnut shells rather than cups.

shine

take a shine to someone

British If you **take a shine to** someone or something, you like them a lot from the very first time that you come into contact with them. *Laura took a shine to her and offered her the job without any prompting from me.*

take the shine off something

Mainly British If something **takes the shine off** a pleasant event or achievement, it makes it less enjoyable than it should be. *For Labour, their reverses in parts of London have taken the shine off what they otherwise describe as their best local election performance ever.*

ship

don't spoil the ship for a ha'porth of tar

Old-fashioned; mainly British People say **'don't spoil the ship for a ha'porth of tar'** when someone risks ruining something because they do not want to spend a relatively small amount of money on a necessity. *Don't spoil the ship for a ha'porth of tar. If you give away a miniature replica of a bottle that won a prize for design, you will attract more new customers than the same perfume in a plain bottle.*

◆ 'Ship' in this expression was originally 'sheep'. A 'ha'porth' is a 'halfpenny's worth'; a halfpenny was a British coin of very low value. Shepherds used to put tar on their sheep's wounds and sores to protect them from flies, and it would be foolish to risk the sheep's health in order to save a small amount of money.

jump ship
abandon ship

If you accuse someone of **jumping ship** or of **abandoning ship**, you are accusing them of leaving an organization or cause, either because they think it is about to fail or because they want to join a rival organization. *Cheers rang out a week ago when the Liberal Democrat government lost a vote of confidence. Some ruling party members immediately jumped ship and created new parties.*

◆ If sailors jump ship, they leave their ship without permission and do not return.

run a tight ship

If you say that someone **runs a tight ship**, you mean that they keep firm control of the way their business or organization is run, so that it is well organized and efficient. *Harvard runs a tight ship: it spends less than a quarter of a percent of its portfolio on management, comfortably below many other universities.*

a sinking ship
abandon a sinking ship
like a rat leaving a sinking ship

If you say that an organization or cause is **a sinking ship**, you mean that it is failing and unlikely to recover. *The television company is not a sinking ship. There is ample finance in the system to produce an original schedule which can be refreshed and renewed year-on-year with innovative new programmes.*

☐ If you say that someone **is abandoning a sinking ship**, you mean that they are leaving an organization or cause which is about to fail completely. You can use verbs such as 'leave' or 'desert' instead of 'abandon'. If you disapprove strongly of their behaviour, you can say that they are **like a rat leaving a sinking ship**. *It's looking more and more as though Communists across the country have realised this is the time to abandon their sinking ship... I know people are saying things about rats deserting the sinking ship, but Tinsley was very junior. She hadn't the least idea of what was going on.*

when your ship comes in

When people talk about what they will do **when** their **ship comes in**, they are talking about what they will do if they become rich and successful. *Sims is convinced that one day his ship will come in, if only he waits long enough.*

♦ This is a reference to a merchant's ship returning home with a heavy load of goods.

shirt

keep your shirt on
keep your pants on

Mainly American If someone tells you to **keep** your **shirt on**, they are telling you to calm down and not be angry or impatient. 'Shirt' is sometimes replaced with 'pants'. The usual British expression is **keep** your **hair on**. *The doorbell rang. Helen told the caller to keep his shirt on – snappish because she felt the ringing had been excessive.*

put your shirt on something
lose your shirt

Mainly British If you **put** your **shirt on** something, you bet or risk a large amount of money on it, because you are convinced that it will win or succeed. *I was just thinking you might put your shirt on Golden Boy. It's bound to be a winner, isn't it?*

☐ If you **lose** your **shirt**, you lose all your money on a bad investment or bet. *His father warned him that he knew nothing about shipping and could easily lose his shirt.*

a stuffed shirt

If you refer to a man who has an important position as **a stuffed shirt**, you mean that he behaves in a very formal or pompous way. *He takes well-deserved credit for his pioneering stand against the stuffed-shirts of the organization... I have little patience with the dress rules of stuffed-shirt establishments.*

shit

the shit hits the fan

If someone talks about what will happen when **the shit hits the fan**, they are talking about what will happen when a situation becomes very bad or when some serious trouble begins. Many people find this expression offensive. *There's so much shit going to hit the fan in the next few days, my getting fired won't matter a bit.*

☐ People sometimes use less offensive words instead of 'shit'. *The governor and his staff thought they'd be safely away when it hit the fan around here.*

shoe

drop the other shoe

American If someone **drops the other shoe**, they complete a task by doing the second and final part of it. *Time Warner Inc. dropped the other shoe in its two-step $13.86 billion acquisition of Warner Communications Inc.*

if the shoe fits

American You can say **'if the shoe fits'** when you are telling someone that unpleasant or critical remarks which have been made about them are probably true or fair. The British expression is **if the cap fits**. *'You said something about me being in a bad mood,' Jack said. 'What made you say that? If I wasn't in a bad mood before you said it, it's enough when you say it to put me in one.' 'If the shoe fits,' Mary said.*

shoes

dead men's shoes

British If you talk about **dead men's shoes**, you are talking about a situation in which people cannot make progress in their careers until someone senior to them retires or dies. *At that particular time, jobs were rather difficult to obtain. It was more or less dead men's shoes.*

in someone's shoes
in someone's boots

If you talk about being **in** someone's **shoes**, you are describing how you would feel or act if you were in the same situation as them. *I hope you'll stop and consider how you would feel if you were in my shoes.*

□ If you say that you **wouldn't like to be in** someone's **shoes**, you mean that you would not like to be in the same situation as them. *He hasn't made any friends and has upset a lot of powerful people. I wouldn't like to be in his shoes if he comes back to work.*

□ You can also talk about being **in** someone's **boots**. *'I suppose Monsieur will start early.' Sharpe nodded. 'I would if I was in his boots.'*

step into someone's shoes
fill someone's shoes

If you **step into** someone's **shoes**, you take over their job or position. If you **fill** someone's **shoes**, you do their job or hold their position as well as they did. Compare **step into** someone's **boots**; see **boots**. *In America, if a president resigns or dies in office, the vice-president steps into his shoes... It'll take a good man to fill her shoes.*

shoestring

on a shoestring

If you do something **on a shoestring**, you do it using very little money. *Newly divorced with two children to raise, she was living on a shoestring... A British science fiction film made on a shoestring budget is taking America by storm.*

◆ In American English, shoelaces are called shoestrings. The reference here is to the very small amount of money that is needed to buy shoelaces.

shoo-in

be a shoo-in

Mainly American If you say that someone **is a shoo-in** for something such as an election or contest, you mean that they are certain to win. *The* *president seemed a shoo-in for a second term, even though the election was some 20 months away.*

◆ 'Shoo-in' is sometimes spelled 'shoe-in'.

shop

all over the shop

British If you say that something is **all over the shop**, you mean that it is spread across a large area or over a wide range of things. *Big government majorities gave backbenchers the freedom to make trouble all over the shop without fear of retribution.*

shut up shop
close up shop

If a person or organization has to **shut up shop** or **close up shop**, they are forced to close their business, for example because of difficult economic conditions. 'Shut up shop' is used only in British English and 'close up shop' is used mainly in American English. *Unless business picks up soon, some of the 245 foreign-owned banks in Switzerland may have to shut up shop.*

a talking shop
a talk shop

Mainly British If you describe something such as a conference or an organization as **a talking shop** or **a talk shop**, you are being critical of it because you think that its discussions have no practical results. *Governments which used to dismiss the UN as a mere 'talking shop' now see possibilities for the international body to act more as a world policeman.*

talk shop
shop talk

If people who do the same kind of work **are talking shop**, they are talking to each other about their work. This expression is often used to suggest that this is boring for other people who are present and who do not do the same work. *With the pressures of the day behind them, they would gather in small, informal groups and talk shop.*

☐ Talking about your work like this can be referred to as **shop talk**. *Conversation over dinner began with catching up on family matters, then turned to shop talk.*

shopping

a shopping list

Someone's **shopping list** is a list of demands or requirements that they want to get from a particular person or organization. *Mr Baker presented a shopping list of additional help the United States was requiring from its allies.*

short

by the short and curlies

British If someone has you **by the short and curlies**, they have you completely in their power. *The unions' chief negotiator last night said: 'We had the company by the short and curlies.'*

◆ In this expression, 'short and curlies' may refer to a person's pubic hair, to hair on the back of their neck, or to the hair in a beard.

one sandwich short of a picnic
several cards short of a full deck

Short of is used in expressions such as 'one sandwich short of a picnic' or 'several cards short of a full deck' to indicate in a humorous way that you think someone is very stupid or is behaving very strangely. 'Short' is sometimes replaced with 'shy' in American English. *His daughter confirmed that her father was definitely one sandwich short of a picnic.*

☐ This expression is used very creatively, and people often use it simply for the humorous effect of a new and amusing variation. *He's also a few gallons shy of a full tank, if you catch my drift.*

sell someone short

If you accuse someone of **selling** you **short**, you are accusing them of failing to provide you with all the things which you think they ought to provide. *Students don't necessarily want to cope with too much complexity. But, on the other hand, if the tutor makes things too simple, that's selling them short too.*

◆ The reference here is to someone being cheated by being given less of something than they have paid for.

sell yourself short

If you **sell** yourself **short**, you are modest about your achievements and good qualities, so that other people do not realize just how good you are. *He had not risen to his lofty position by selling himself short or underestimating his own potential.*

☐ You can also say that someone **sells** themselves **short** when they do something which is well below their capabilities. *Almond is an artist more than capable of scaling dizzying heights – here he is simply, woefully,* *selling himself short.*

◆ See the explanation at 'sell someone short'.

shot

by a long shot

You can use **by a long shot** to add emphasis to a statement, especially a negative statement or one that contains a superlative. Compare **a long shot**. *No city has escaped the ravages of recession, but Seattle has fared best by a long shot.*

get shot of something
be shot of something

British If you want to **get shot of** someone or something or to **be shot of** them, you want to get rid of them quickly. *City experts still reckon the company wants to get shot of its brewing division.*

give something your best shot

If you **give** something your **best shot**, you try as hard as you can to achieve it, even though you know how difficult it is. *I gave it my best shot, but I wasn't quite good enough.*

☐ You can describe a course of action as someone's **best shot** when it is the best chance they have of achieving something. *Mazankowski and other analysts say Canada's best shot at economic recovery is continued growth in the United States.*

a long shot

If you describe a way of solving a difficulty or problem as **a long shot**, you mean that there is little chance that it will succeed, but you think it is worth trying. Compare **by a long shot**. *Could he forestall a deal with Johnson? It was a long shot, but Bagley had little to lose.*

☐ You can also say that something is **a long shot** when it is very unlikely to happen. *Observers say a deal between the White House and Congress is a long shot in an election year, when both political parties are trying to get the upper hand.*

◆ The reference here is to someone shooting at a target from a very long distance.

one shot in your locker

If you have only **one shot in** your **locker**, you have only one thing left that you can do in order to achieve success, and if this fails you will have to give up. *It's hard to see what kind of concessions the government could* *make before it's too late to call off the strike. Having already offered talks and announced the wage rise, it can have few shots left in its locker.*

◆ A locker is a small cupboard with a lock. In this case, it might be a cupboard containing ammunition.

a shot across someone's bows
a warning shot across someone's bows
a warning shot

If you fire **a shot across** someone's **bows** or **a warning shot across** their **bows**, you do something which shows that you are prepared to oppose them strongly if they do not stop or change what they are doing. You can also simply say that someone fires **a warning shot**. *The election result wasn't entirely responsible for the market's worries, but political analysts regard it as a warning shot across the government's bows... The United States has fired a warning shot in its ongoing trade dispute with China.*

◆ The bows are the front part of a ship.

a shot in the arm

If something gives you **a shot in the arm**, it gives you help and encouragement at a time when you badly need it. *Joe really helped us out of a hole and it was really exciting. It gave us a real shot in the arm at a time when we needed it most.*

◆ A 'shot' is an injection, in this case an injection of a drug that stimulates you.

shots

call the shots

If you **call the shots**, you are the person who makes all the important decisions in an organization or situation. *The days of the empire are over. Britain must realise that she does not call the shots any more.*

◆ This may refer to someone shooting and saying which part of the target they intend to hit. Alternatively, it may refer to a snooker or pool player saying which ball they intend to hit or which pocket they intend to hit it into.

shoulder

give someone the cold shoulder

If someone deliberately ignores you, you can say that they **give** you **the**

cold shoulder. *He gives him the cold shoulder; he doesn't talk to him very much, if at all.*

☐ You can also say that someone or something **is cold-shouldered** or talk about **cold-shouldering**. *Even her own party considered her shrewish and nagging, and cold-shouldered her in the corridors.*

◆ A shoulder is a cut of meat which includes the upper part of the animal's front leg. This expression refers to a medieval practice where important guests were given roast meat. Less important people were only given cold meat left over from previous meals.

put your shoulder to the wheel

If you **put** your **shoulder to the wheel**, you put a great deal of effort into a difficult task. *Is there anybody here that is not willing to put his or her shoulder to the wheel and do it?*

◆ In the days when people travelled in carriages or carts on roads that often got very muddy, people would help free vehicles that were stuck by leaning against a wheel and pushing.

a shoulder to cry on
cry on someone's shoulder

If you refer to someone as **a shoulder to cry on**, you mean that you can rely on them to give you emotional support when you are upset or anxious. *For a lot of new mums the health visitor becomes a real friend, full of sound advice and the perfect shoulder to cry on when it all gets too much.*

☐ You can also say that one person **cries on** another's **shoulder**. *He had let her cry on his shoulder when she was upset, bringing her flowers and taking her on a late-night walk to help her feel better.*

shoulder to shoulder

If you stand **shoulder to shoulder** with a group of people, you work co-operatively with them to achieve a common aim. *He was working shoulder to shoulder with enthusiastic theatre folk for the first time in twenty-five years, and sharing in the creative spirit.*

straight from the shoulder

If you say something **straight from the shoulder**, you say it directly and with complete honesty. *His opinions about top politicians in Washington and New York come straight from the shoulder.*

◆ In boxing, a blow that is straight from the shoulder is a direct and powerful blow, delivered with a straight arm.

shoulders

rub shoulders with someone

Mainly British If you **rub shoulders with** someone important or famous, you associate with them for a while. The usual American expression is **rub elbows with** someone. *She went to Cambridge before the First World War and rubbed shoulders with the likes of George Bernard Shaw and Sidney and Beatrice Webb.*

□ You can also say that two groups of people **rub shoulders**. *Farmers, painters and retired colonels rub shoulders at an inn which used to entertain smugglers and coachmen.*

show

♦ The show referred to in the following expressions is a theatrical performance.

get the show on the road

If you **get the show on the road**, you put a plan or idea into action. *He checked his watch. 'Shouldn't we get this show on the road, now that Rolfe's here?'*

run the show

If you say that someone **is running the show**, you mean that they are in control of an organization, event, or situation. *This is the first summit in which the Americans are just another player; Germany is now running the show.*

steal the show

If you say that someone or something **steals the show**, you mean that they get more attention or praise than the other people or things in a show or other event. *It's Jack Lemmon who finally steals the show, turning in his finest performance in years.*

□ You can describe someone or something that gets more attention than other people or things as **a show-stealer**. *The latest Steven Spielberg epic, Jurassic Park, had theatre patrons squirming in their seats at a special preview in Hollywood this week. The show-stealer is Tyrannosaurus Rex, a 5 tonne dinosaur.*

stop the show

If you say that someone **stops the show**, you mean that they give an outstanding performance in a show or other event. *Twelve-year-old Reggie*

Jackson stopped the show last night with 'America the Beautiful'.

☐ You can describe an impressive person, performance, or thing as **show-stopping** or say that they are **a show-stopper**. *Her first encore was a real show-stopper, 'Je Suis Comme Je Suis'.*

showers

send someone to the showers
a trip to the showers

American If someone **is sent to the showers**, they are disqualified from a game or excluded from an activity, because of their bad behaviour or poor performance. You can also say that they earn **a trip to the showers**. Compare **an early bath**; see **bath**. *Investors, like savvy team owners, would be wise to weigh a variety of factors before sending a manager to the showers.*

◆ In baseball and other sports, players who are sent off cannot return to the field and so can take a shower before the game is finished.

shrift

short shrift

If someone or something gets **short shrift**, they are treated very rudely or very little attention is paid to them. *Southerners are justifiably angry at the way their interests get short shrift.*

◆ 'Shrift' is an old word meaning confession to a priest. In the past, condemned criminals were allowed only a few minutes to make their confession before they were executed.

shuffle

lost in the shuffle

Mainly American If you say that someone or something gets **lost in the shuffle**, you mean that nobody notices them or pays them any attention. *He worries campaign finance reform will get lost in the shuffle of White House priorities.*

◆ When packs of cards are properly shuffled, it is impossible to know where a particular card is.

sick

sick as a dog

If you say that you are as **sick as a dog**, you are emphasizing that you feel very ill or upset. *The superintendent had looked as sick as a dog when told of Jacobs's guilt.*

sick as a parrot

British If you say that you are as **sick as a parrot**, you mean that you are very annoyed or disappointed about something. *Sportsnight presenter Des Lynam will be as sick as a parrot if his new TV show fails to score with viewers.*

◆ The origin of this expression is uncertain. References to people being 'as melancholy as a sick parrot' have been found as early as the 17th century. In the 1970s in West Africa, there was an outbreak of the disease of psittacosis or parrot fever, which humans can catch from birds. At about this time, footballers and football managers started using this expression a lot to say how they felt when they had lost a match.

sick as a pig

British If you say that you are as **sick as a pig**, you mean that you are very annoyed and upset about something. *I've had Les in my office and he's been disciplined the maximum. He's as sick as a pig.*

side

let the side down

British If you accuse someone of **letting the side down**, you are criticizing them for disappointing people by doing something badly or by doing something which people do not approve of. *The workers are the best in the world – it is the managements who let the side down.*

look on the bright side

If you try to **look on the bright side**, you try to be cheerful about a bad situation by concentrating on the few good things in it or by thinking about how it could have been even worse. *I tried to look on the bright side, to be grateful that I was healthy. I hid my feelings completely and didn't talk to other people at all about what was going on.*

☐ You can talk about **the bright side** of a bad situation. *If there is a bright side for the Prime Minister, however, it is that the elections were a judgment on the whole party, not just him.*

sunny side up

Mainly British If you describe things or people as **sunny side up**, you mean that they are bright and cheerful. *This book should keep you and your family feeling sunny-side-up throughout your vacation.*

◆ In American English, if you ask for a fried egg to be cooked 'sunny side up', you want it to be cooked on one side only and not turned over in the pan.

sieve

a brain like a sieve

If you say that you have **a brain like a sieve**, you mean that you have a bad memory and often forget things. *He lost the key to his Ferrari but admitted that his brain was like a sieve.*

sight

out of sight, out of mind

If you say **'out of sight, out of mind'**, you mean that it is easy to forget about someone or something, or to stop caring about them, when you have not seen them for a long time. *After the drought is over, the systems are going to be out of sight, out of mind, They definitely will not be maintained after that.*

□ People often vary this expression. *In the years he spent imprisoned on Robben Island, Mandela was out of sight, but much in mind.*

a sight for sore eyes

If you say that someone is **a sight for sore eyes**, you mean that you are pleased to see them. If you say that something is **a sight for sore eyes**, you mean that it gives you pleasure to look at it. *Jack. You're a sight for sore eyes. It's been too long. Far too long... The sunset over the Strait of Malacca is a sight for sore eyes.*

sights

◆ The sights on a weapon such as a rifle are the part that helps you to aim it more accurately.

have something in your sights

If you **have** something **in** your **sights**, you are aiming or trying hard to achieve it, and you have a good chance of success. If you have someone **in** your **sights**, you are determined to catch, defeat, or overcome them. *Usually, at this stage of the season, Liverpool are lying first or second in the table and have the Championship firmly in their sights.*

◆ This expression are also used literally to say that someone is looking at a target through the sights of a gun.

set your sights on something

If you **set** your **sights on** something, you decide that you want it and try very hard to get it. *Although she came from a family of bankers, Franklin set her sights on a career in scientific research.*

□ You can say that someone **sets** their **sights high** when they are trying to get something that is hard to achieve. If you say that someone **sets** their **sights low**, you mean that they are unambitious and do not achieve as much as they could. *Women tend to end up in low-status jobs with low pay. Often we only have ourselves to blame. We just do not set our sights high enough.*

signed

signed and sealed
signed, sealed, and delivered

If you say that an agreement is **signed and sealed**, you mean that it is official and cannot be changed. You can also say that it is **signed, sealed, and delivered**. *Although a peace agreement has been signed and sealed, many of these villagers say they're afraid to return to their homes... A government spokesman said the bill must be signed, sealed and delivered by tomorrow.*

◆ In the past, documents were 'sealed' with a blob of wax into which a special mark or design was pressed using a device called a seal. The mark or design in the wax proved that the document was authentic and had not been opened.

silk

you can't make a silk purse out of a sow's ear

If you say that you **can't make a silk purse out of a sow's ear**, you mean that it is impossible to make something really successful or of high quality out of something which is unsuccessful or of poor quality. People often vary this expression. *It takes more than a good swimming pool and an indoor tennis court or two to make a sow's ear of a resort into a silk purse.*

silver

born with a silver spoon in your mouth

If you say that someone **was born with a silver spoon in** their **mouth**, you mean that their family was very rich and they had a privileged upbringing. You usually use this expression to show resentment or disapproval. *People like Samantha and Timothy had been born with a silver spoon in their mouth; they hadn't a worry in the world, and there was* *always someone to pay their bills if their own inheritance was not sufficient.*

◆ This expression goes back to the 17th century. The reference is to babies from wealthy families being fed using silver spoons.

a silver lining
every cloud has a silver lining

If you say that a bad or unpleasant situation has **a silver lining**, you mean that there is a good or pleasant side-effect of it. *The fall in inflation is the silver lining of the prolonged recession.*

☐ When you are using **a silver lining** in this way, you often refer to the bad or unpleasant situation as **the cloud**. *Even Kenneth Clarke, usually a man to find a silver lining in the blackest cloud, admitted that the government was in 'a dreadful hole'.*

☐ These expressions come from the proverb **every cloud has a silver lining**, which is used to say that every bad or unpleasant situation has some benefits or pleasant side-effects.

sing

sing a different tune: 1
sing the same tune
sing the same song

If you say that someone **is singing a different tune**, you mean that they are expressing ideas or opinions which are in complete contrast to the ones which they were expressing a short time ago. If you say that someone **is singing the same tune**, you mean that they are continuing to express the same ideas or opinions that they have expressed before. You can replace 'tune' with 'song' in these expressions. *Then he said: 'As employees of the county clubs, their first and only loyalty should be to English cricket.' Yesterday he was singing a different tune, hoping 'there is no acrimony from players who disagree with the decision'... The president basically sent the signal that he's going to keep singing the same tune he's been singing.*

sing a different tune: 2
sing the same tune
sing the same song

If you say that a group of people **are singing the same tune**, you mean that they are all expressing the same opinions about something. You can also say that one person **is singing the same tune** as the others. If people **are singing a different tune**, they are expressing different opinions

sink

468

about something. You can replace 'tune' with 'song' in these expressions. *It doesn't help when politicians argue in public and so confuse our case. We should all be singing the same tune... The burden of homelessness in Tower Hamlets is great enough without two Government departments singing different songs.*

sing from the same hymn sheet
sing from the same song sheet

British If you say that two or more people **are singing from the same hymn sheet** or **are singing from the same song sheet**, you mean that they agree about something, and are saying the same things in public about it. *The main theme is to bring together the departments so that we're all singing from the same hymn sheet.*

sink

sink or swim

If you say that someone will have to **sink or swim**, you mean that they are being left to do something on their own, and whether they succeed or not will depend entirely on their own efforts or abilities. *By some estimates, 70–80 per cent of the country's enterprises are technically bankrupt. Many will certainly fail once they are transferred to private ownership and forced to sink or swim on their own.*

six

knock someone for six
hit someone for six

Mainly British If something **knocks** you **for six** or **hits** you **for six**, it gives you a surprise or shock which you have difficulty recovering from. *Many people are very positive and see redundancy as a chance to start a new career, but the emotional impact of being made redundant can knock others for six.*

◆ In cricket, six runs are scored when a batsman hits the ball so that it lands outside the playing area without bouncing. When this happens, you can say the bowler has been hit for six.

six of one and half a dozen of the other

If you describe two people, situations, or possible courses of action as **six of one and half a dozen of the other**, you mean that both are equally bad or equally good. *To me it was six of one and half a dozen of the other. They were both at fault.*

sixes

at sixes and sevens
Mainly British If something or someone is **at sixes and sevens**, they are disorganized and confused. *They are at sixes and sevens over their tax and spending plans.*

size

cut someone down to size
If you **cut** someone **down to size** when they are behaving arrogantly, you do or say something which shows that they are less important or impressive than they think they are. *It is time the big bosses were cut down to size. They are the ones to blame for much of the country's economic misery.*

try something on for size
If you **try** something **on for size**, you consider it carefully or try using it in order to decide whether you think it is any good or whether you believe it. *We are able to a limited extent to try models on for size to see which may be compatible with us, but it is important to give time to the experiment.*

skates

get your skates on
Mainly British If someone tells you to **get** your **skates on**, they are telling you to hurry up. *Bargain hunters had better get their skates on – the best properties are selling fast.*

skeleton

a skeleton in the closet
a skeleton in the cupboard
If you say that someone has **a skeleton in the closet**, you mean that they are keeping secret something which would be scandalous or embarrassing for them if other people knew about it. In British English, you can also say that they have **a skeleton in the cupboard**. *But everybody's got vices, haven't they? There's always a skeleton in the closet somewhere.*

skid

skid row
You say that someone is on **skid row** when they have lost everything in

their life, for example because they have become alcoholic or gone bankrupt. *Business is very tough right now, so if it wasn't for all my trinkets and paintings I would be on skid row.*

◆ 'Skid row' is used, especially in American English, to refer a poor part of a city where many drunks and homeless people live. 'Skid Row' has developed from 'skid road', a track made of logs that was used to haul logs to a loading platform or mill. The area of town where loggers lived and worked was often considered very rough and not respectable.

skids

on the skids
If you say that something is **on the skids**, you mean that it is doing badly and is very likely to fail. *My marriage was on the skids.*

put the skids under something
British If you **put the skids under** something or someone, you cause them to do badly or fail. *Two new witnesses in the murder case have put the skids under his alibi.*

skin

by the skin of your teeth
If you do something **by the skin of** your **teeth**, you just manage to do it but very nearly fail. *Premier John Major breathed a sigh of relief last night as he avoided a disastrous rise in interest rates by the skin of his teeth.*

◆ This expression seems to come from the book of Job in the Bible, although its meaning has completely changed. Job loses everything and then says 'I am escaped with the skin of my teeth' (Job 19:20), meaning that the skin of his teeth is all he has left.

get under your skin: 1
If something **gets under** your **skin**, it annoys or worries you. *The continuing criticism, which is getting harsher, is getting under his skin a little bit.*

get under your skin: 2
If someone or something **gets under** your **skin**, they begin to affect you in a significant way, so that you become very interested in them or very fond of them. *After a slow start, his play gets under your skin because of its affection for its characters and sympathy with the frustrations of small town life.*

get under someone's skin: 3

If you try to **get under** someone's **skin**, you try to find out how they feel and think, so that you are able to understand them better. *Geoffrey Beattie's book is presented as 'an attempt to get under the skin of the Protestant people of Ulster'.*

it's no skin off my nose

Mainly British If someone says **'it's no skin off my nose'** when something bad happens, they mean that they are not worried about it, because it only affects or harms other people, or because it is not their responsibility. *Let them publish it. It's no skin off my nose, if it turns out to be wrong. They wrote it, not me.*

jump out of your skin

If you say that something made you **jump out of** your **skin**, you mean that it gave you a sudden unpleasant shock or surprise. *The first time I heard shots I jumped out of my skin, but now I hardly notice the continuous gunfire.*

make your skin crawl

If you say that something **makes** your **skin crawl**, you mean that you find it unpleasant and it makes you frightened, distressed, or uncomfortable. *I hated this man, his very touch made my skin crawl.*

save your skin

If someone tries to **save** their **skin**, they try to save themselves from something dangerous or unpleasant, often without caring what happens to anyone else. *He appeared to be condemning the entire movement. Maybe this was because he was trying to save his skin.*

skin and bone
skin and bones

If you describe someone as **skin and bone** or **skin and bones**, you mean that they are very thin, because they have not had enough to eat for a long time, or because they are suffering from a serious illness. *A man like me can't live on beans – I'll soon be skin and bone.*

a thick skin
thick-skinned

If you say that someone has **a thick skin**, you mean that they are not easily hurt or upset by criticism. You can also describe someone as being **thick-skinned**. Compare **a thin skin**. *A woman who survives in politics needs a thick skin... She worked as a nurse in a psychiatric emergency clinic in South London, a job that made her thick-skinned and able to handle abuse.*

a thin skin
thin-skinned

If you say that someone has **a thin skin**, you mean that they are very easily hurt or upset by criticism. You can also describe someone as being **thin-skinned**. Compare **a thick skin**. *Evidence of such a thin skin and lack of tenacity means that he is certainly not cut out to be a journalist... At each level the judging gets more critical, and if you're thin-skinned, it's better to start slowly and build up your confidence.*

sky

blow something sky-high

If you **blow** someone's hopes or beliefs **sky-high**, you do or say something which completely destroys them. *They knew nothing about me, apart from what I encouraged them to think. She could have blown all that sky-high.*

out of a clear blue sky

If you describe something as happening **out of a clear blue sky**, you mean that it happens completely unexpectedly. People sometimes omit 'clear' or 'blue'. *It certainly cannot be bad news when, out of a clear blue sky and after 34 months of successive increases, unemployment drops by 22,000.*

◆ This expression compares an unexpected event to a bolt of lightning from a blue sky. The expressions 'out of the blue' and 'a bolt from the blue' are based on a similar idea.

the sky's the limit

You can say **'the sky's the limit'** when you are talking about the possibility of someone or something being very successful. *Asked how far Agassi could go, McEnroe said simply: 'The sky's the limit.'*

slack

cut someone some slack

If you **cut** someone **some slack**, you make things slightly easier for them than you normally would, because of their special circumstances or situation. *When you're new at a job, colleagues and bosses cut you a little slack. They forgive minor mistakes because you're new.*

take up the slack

If someone **takes up the slack** in an industry, economy, or organization, they start making full use of all its resources or potential. *The export market has not taken up the slack, so redundancies are coming thick and fast.*

◆ If you take up the slack in a rope, you tighten it.

slap

a slap in the face

You can describe someone's behaviour as **a slap in the face** when they upset you by insulting you or appearing to reject you. *Mr Nakajima was the first Japanese to win a high UN office; if he were not re-elected, it would be a slap in the face.*

a slap on the wrist

You can refer to a very light punishment or reprimand as **a slap on the wrist**. *The fine they gave her is just a slap on the wrist.*

slate

◆ In the past, people used pieces of slate for writing on, for example in schools, shops, and pubs. Shopkeepers and publicans would write customers' debts on their slates, and wipe them clean when the debts were paid.

on the slate

British If you buy something **on the slate**, you buy it on credit and will need to pay for it later. *He'd call at the pub coming back from work and it was all put on the slate until Friday night.*

wipe the slate clean: 1
a clean slate

If you **wipe the slate clean**, you get rid of an existing system so that you can replace it with a new one. You can then say that you are beginning with **a clean slate**. *He wanted to wipe the slate clean of anything that had gone before. He wanted his new Council to make up its own mind about everything… The new chief executive has clearly decided to start with a clean slate as he embarks on one of the toughest jobs in British retailing.*

wipe the slate clean: 2
a clean slate

If you **wipe the slate clean**, you earn enough money to pay off your debts, so that you no longer owe money to anyone. *Over a decade he wiped the firm's slate clean of debt and brought it up to record earnings.*

☐ When you begin something without owing any money, you can say that you are beginning with **a clean slate**. *The proposal is to pay everything you owe, so that you can start with a clean slate.*

wipe the slate clean: 3

If you **wipe the slate clean**, you are punished for something wrong that you have done, or you make amends for it by your good behaviour, so that you can start your life again without feeling guilty about it. *Serving a prison sentence makes them believe they have 'wiped the slate clean', but the anger and hurt felt by those close to them remains long after their release.*

sleeve

have something up your sleeve
have an ace up your sleeve
have a card up your sleeve

If someone **has** something **up** their **sleeve**, they have a secret idea or plan which they can use to gain an advantage over other people. *He's nothing if not a tough campaigner, and he has one final option up his sleeve.*

□ The expressions **have an ace up** your **sleeve** and **have a card up** your **sleeve** mean the same. *Even those who regard him as ruthless and brutal admit, however, that he seems always to have a card up his sleeve.*

◆ If someone wanted to cheat at cards, they could hide a good card up their sleeve to use at an appropriate time.

laugh up your sleeve

If you say that someone **is laughing up** their **sleeve**, you mean that they are secretly amused by something, for example because someone else has done something badly or because they know something that nobody else knows. This expression is usually used to show disapproval. *He wondered just how smugly she was laughing up her sleeve at his ineptitude.*

◆ The image here is of someone trying to hide the fact that they are laughing by putting their hand or arm in front of their mouth.

slings

slings and arrows

If you talk about the **slings and arrows** of something, you are referring to the unpleasant things that it causes to happen to you and that are not your fault. *He received lectures on handling the press from his wife, who had suffered her own share of slings and arrows in the quest for publicity.*

◆ This is a quotation from a speech in Shakespeare's play 'Hamlet', where Hamlet is considering whether or not to kill himself: 'To be, or not to be - that is the question; Whether 'tis nobler in the mind to suffer The slings

and arrows of outrageous fortune, Or to take arms against a sea of
troubles, And by opposing end them?' (Act 3, Scene 1)

slip

a slip of the tongue

If you refer to something you said as **a slip of the tongue**, you mean
that you said it by mistake. *'Did you say Frank Sinatra?' 'Oh, did I? I'm
sorry. That was a slip of the tongue. I don't know what got into me.'*

there is many a slip twixt cup and lip

If people say **'there is many a slip twixt cup and lip'**, they are warning
that a plan may easily go wrong before it is completed, and they cannot be
sure of what will happen. *Most Italians had thought it a foregone
conclusion. But Mario Segni, the rebel Christian Democrat who first
championed the referendum, fears the possibility of a slip twixt cup and lip.*

☐ People sometimes just say **'there's many a slip'**, or vary the second half
of the expression. *He knows, too, after the much postponed title fight against
Tyson, that there's many a slip between signing a contract and pulling on
the gloves.*

◆ 'Twixt' is an old-fashioned word meaning 'between'.

slippery

slippery as an eel

If you say that someone is as **slippery as an eel**, you mean that it is
very difficult to catch them or to get the information that you want from
them. *The boy raided 36 homes. The judge said 'the invasion of homes by a
boy as slippery as an eel' was a horrifying experience.*

slope

a slippery slope

If someone is on **a slippery slope**, they are involved in a course of action
that cannot be stopped and that will lead to failure or serious trouble. *The
company started down the slippery slope of believing that they knew better
than the customer, with the inevitable disastrous results.*

smoke

blow smoke
blow smoke in someone's face
blow smoke in someone's eyes

Mainly American If you accuse someone of **blowing smoke** or of

blowing smoke in your **face** or **eyes**, you are accusing them of deliberately confusing you or misleading you in order to deceive you. *I just can't shake the feeling that he's up to something. Sounds to me like he's blowing smoke... Everyone knew Philip Morris was growing faster than RJR. But now we know they've been growing faster than faster. RJR has been blowing smoke in our faces.*

go up in smoke

If something that is important to you **goes up in smoke**, it fails or ends without anything being achieved. *But with just eight minutes to go, their dreams of glory went up in smoke. Liverpool scored twice within minutes and went three – two ahead.*

smoke and mirrors

Mainly American If you say that something is full of **smoke and mirrors**, you mean that it is full of things which are intended to deceive or confuse people. *The president and his aides claim that their economic plan is free of the gimmicks and smoke and mirrors that have characterized previous presidential budget proposals.*

◆ Magicians sometimes use smoke and mirrors when they are performing tricks, in order to confuse or deceive people.

smoke signals

If someone sends out **smoke signals**, they give an indication of their views or intentions, often in an unclear or vague form which then needs to be interpreted. *Recent economic smoke-signals suggest that the economy began to pick up in May.*

◆ Smoke signals are columns of smoke which were used to send messages over long distances, for example by Native American tribes.

there's no smoke without fire
where there's smoke there's fire

If you say **'there's no smoke without fire'** or **'where there's smoke there's fire'** when you are referring to an unpleasant rumour or unlikely story, you mean that it is likely to be at least partly true, as otherwise nobody would be talking about it. *The story was the main item on the news and people were bound to think there was no smoke without fire.*

snail

at a snail's pace

If you say that something is moving or developing **at a snail's pace** or **at snail's pace**, you mean that it is moving or developing very slowly.

You usually use this expression when you think that it would be better if it went more quickly. *The economy grew at a snail's pace in the first three months of this year.*

snake

a snake in the grass

If you describe someone as **a snake in the grass**, you are expressing strong dislike and disapproval of them because they pretend to be your friend while actually being an enemy and betraying you. *Sofia Petrovna would tell Kolya everything about that snake in the grass, the accountant's wife.*

snake oil
a snake oil salesman

Mainly American You use **snake oil** to refer to something which someone is trying to sell you or make you believe in when you think that it is false and not to be trusted. *He's ready to be president. And he's a good salesman, even if he's selling snake oil.*

□ A **snake-oil salesman** is someone who tries to sell you something or make you believe in something like this. *This is the national headquarters for slick-talking snake-oil salesmen who use the telephone to extract money from the gullible and the greedy and then vanish.*

◆ In the United States, snake oil was a substance typically made from the plant snakeroot. Dishonest salesman tried to persuade people to buy it, claiming that it was a medicine which would cure their illnesses.

snook

cock a snook at someone

Fairly old-fashioned If you **cock a snook at** someone, you show your contempt or lack of respect for them by deliberately insulting or offending them. *They drove around in Rolls-Royces, openly flaunting their wealth and cocking a snook at the forces of law and order.*

◆ To cock a snook at someone literally means to make a rude gesture by placing the end of your thumb on the end of your nose, spreading out your fingers, and wiggling them. 'Thumb your nose at someone' means the same.

snow

a snow job

Mainly American You refer to what someone has said as **a snow job** to express your disapproval of the fact that it is full of lies and exaggerations, and was intended to deceive or flatter you. *They have the experience to know the difference between getting information and getting a snow job. You can lie to a member of Congress once, and that's it.*

snug

snug as a bug in a rug

If you say that someone is as **snug as a bug in a rug**, you are saying light-heartedly that they are in a very comfortable situation. This expression is considered old-fashioned in British English. *Jamieson went to the galley, ordered coffee for himself and his men and sat beside McKinnon. 'Ideal working conditions, you said. Snug as a bug in a rug, one might say.'*

sober

sober as a judge

Old-fashioned, British If you say that someone is as **sober as a judge**, you are emphasizing that they are not drunk. *After all, he was as sober as the proverbial judge. And when Tom was sober, they just couldn't find anything wrong with him.*

sock

put a sock in it

Old-fashioned, British If you tell someone to **put a sock in it**, you are rudely telling them to stop talking. *'Can he not speak for himself?' 'He can,' Dermot said. 'Put a sock in it, all of you.'*

socks

knock your socks off
knock the socks off someone

If you say that something or someone **knocks** your **socks off**, you are saying in a light-hearted way that they are very good and that you are very impressed by them. If they **knock the socks off** other people or things, they are much better than the others. *If you fancy an Amazonian holiday that will knock your socks off then keep listening... As a dancer he knocked the socks off everybody.*

pull your socks up

British If someone tells you to **pull** your **socks up**, they want you to try hard to improve your behaviour or work. *In a way what happened last season gave us a necessary jolt. Maybe we needed to pull our socks up and we are trying to do just that.*

work your socks off

If you **work** your **socks off**, you work as hard and as well as you can. You can use this expression with many other verbs, especially verbs related to performing such as 'dance', 'act', and 'play'. *I can see that the lecturers have really tried their hardest. They've worked their socks off to produce something that's vivid and dynamic and vital... 'We're going to dance our socks off tonight,' said Chris de Burgh at the start of his show last Friday.*

song

for a song

If something is going **for a song**, it is being sold for an unexpectedly low price. *I know of good, solid, stone-built houses which have been sold by councils for a song.*

◆ This expression may be a reference to printed song sheets, which were very cheap. Alternatively, it may refer to small amounts of money that passers-by give to someone who is singing in the street.

make a song and dance about something

Mainly British If you accuse someone of **making a song and dance about** something, you mean that they are reacting in a very anxious, excited, or angry way to something that is not important. *You'll be relieved to know I'm not going to make a song and dance about it.*

on song

British If a sports player is **on song**, they are playing very well. *When I was on song, I knew opponents couldn't stop me. I felt I could take anyone on.*

sorrows

drown your sorrows

If someone **drowns** their **sorrows**, they drink a lot of alcohol in order to forget something sad or upsetting that has happened to them. *His girlfriend dumped him so he went off to the pub to drown his sorrows.*

soul

bare your soul

If you **bare** your **soul** to someone, you tell them all the thoughts and feelings that are most important to you. *We all need someone we can bare our souls to, someone we can confide in.*

sell your soul

If someone **sells** their **soul** for something, they do whatever they need to in order to get what they want, even if it involves abandoning their principles or doing something they consider wrong. *As the Co-operative movement approaches its 150th anniversary, Clive Woodcock examines growing fears that it may have sold its soul to commercial pressures.*

◆ There are many stories about people who sold their souls to the devil in return for wealth, success, or pleasure. The most famous is about Dr Faustus, whose story was first told in a book published in Germany in 1587, and later told by writers such as the English writer Marlowe and the German poet Goethe.

sound

sound as a bell

If you say that something is as **sound as a bell**, you mean that it is in a very good condition or is very reliable. *Timber that is as sound as a bell after 50 years under water or in dry air is quite capable of rotting completely in two years or less at the junction of soil and air.*

◆ 'Sound' in this expression means whole and undamaged. A bell that has a crack in it will not ring clearly.

soup

in the soup

If you are **in the soup**, you are in trouble. *A recession could put oil markets right back in the soup.*

spade

call a spade a spade

If you **call a spade a spade**, you speak frankly and directly about something, especially if it is controversial or embarrassing, rather than being careful about what you say. *I'm not at all secretive, and I'm pretty good at calling a spade a spade.*

☐ If you want to say that someone is being extremely frank and direct about something, or more frank and direct than you think is necessary, you can say that they **call a spade a shovel**. *Nicola is refreshingly down-to-earth and not afraid to call a spade a bloody shovel if she has to.*

spanner

throw a spanner in the works

British If someone or something **throws a spanner in the works**, they cause problems which prevent something from happening in the way that it was planned. The American expression is **throw a wrench** or **a monkey wrench into the works**. *For Britain to throw a spanner in the works could damage the prospects of a treaty being successfully concluded.*

spark

a bright spark

Mainly British If you refer to someone as **a bright spark**, you mean that they are intelligent and lively. *It was totally demoralizing because in the third form we'd been real bright sparks.*

□ You usually use this expression ironically to criticize someone for being foolish, or to refer scornfully to someone. *You'd think the bright sparks who come up with these madcap ideas would have learned their lesson.*

sparks

sparks fly: 1

If **sparks fly** between two people, they discuss something in an angry or excited way. *France's bank may initially have to take an even harder line on interest rates than Germany's. Wait for the sparks to fly.*

sparks fly: 2

You can say that **sparks fly** when you are describing a situation or relationship that is very exciting. *Whenever two such quality artists meet, you know sparks will fly.*

strike sparks off each other

Mainly British If people who are trying to achieve something together **strike sparks** off each other, they react to each other in a very exciting or creative way. *It was to be a fertile association, the two men striking the creative sparks from each other that ensured whatever they did was an assault on traditional ideas of architectural propriety.*

speed

bring someone up to speed: 1

If you **bring** someone **up to speed**, you give them all the latest information about something. *I guess I should bring you up to speed on what's been happening since I came to see you yesterday.*

bring something up to speed: 2

If you **bring** something **up to speed**, it reaches its highest level of efficiency. *Protected industries would have time to come up to speed before being exposed to market forces.*

spick

spick and span

If you say that a place or a person is **spick and span**, you mean that they are very clean, neat, and tidy. *When she arrived here this morning she had found Ann dusting the furniture, making sure her home was spick and span... Barbara lives in a spick and span bungalow.*

♦ 'Spick' is sometimes spelled 'spic'. This expression has developed from an old-fashioned expression 'spick and span-new', meaning 'very new'. 'Spick' probably came from a Dutch word meaning 'new', and 'span-new' meant 'completely new'.

spin

in a spin
in a flat spin

Mainly British If someone is **in a spin**, they are so angry, confused, or excited that they cannot act sensibly or concentrate on what they are doing. You can also say that they are **in a flat spin**. *The flautist's long blonde hair and sexy evening frocks have set the classical music world into a spin... There's no need to go into a flat spin. It was a perfectly reasonable request to make.*

♦ If a plane goes into a spin, it goes out of control and falls very rapidly towards the ground in a spiralling movement. If it goes into a flat spin, it turns round and round as it falls, but remains horizontal.

spit

spit and polish

You can talk about **spit and polish** when you are talking about a place or person being very clean or being made very clean. *The bar, which had been open for two months now, was all spit and polish and good taste.*

spit and sawdust

British If you describe a place such as a pub or a bar as a **spit and**

sawdust place, you mean that it looks dirty, untidy, and not very respectable. *There's the Compasses in the High Street if it's spit and sawdust you're after.*

◆ In the past, the public bars of many pubs had sawdust on the floor to soak up the mess caused by people spitting and spilling their drinks.

the spitting image
the spit and image
the dead spit

If you say that one person is **the spitting image** of another, you mean that the first person looks exactly like the second. *He is the spitting image of his father.*

☐ People occasionally use **the spit and image** or **the dead spit** to mean the same thing. *He had a handsome face, the dead spit of Tikhonov, the film actor.*

◆ The origin of this expression is uncertain, but it may have developed from 'spirit and image'. If one person was the spirit and image of another, they were alike both in character and physical appearance.

splash

make a splash

If someone **makes a splash**, they attract a lot of attention because of something successful that they do or by the way they behave on a particular occasion. *Japan has made a major splash here at the Earth Summit by demonstrating its technological prowess in the area of the environment.*

spoke

put a spoke in someone's wheel

Mainly British If you **put a spoke in** someone's **wheel**, you deliberately make it difficult for them to do what they are planning to do. *If she had known he was seeing Tinsley, she undoubtedly would have tried to put a spoke in his wheel.*

◆ Cartwheels used to be made of solid wood, with holes in them through which a wooden bar or 'spoke' could be pushed in order to make the cart slow down or stop.

spoon

the wooden spoon

British If someone is last in a race or competition or is the worst at a particular activity, you can say that they get **the wooden spoon**. *England must beat the defending champions Scotland today to avoid their first wooden spoon in the event's 49-year history.*

◆ At one time, the student who got the lowest marks in their final mathematics exam at Cambridge University was given a wooden spoon.

spot

have a soft spot for someone

If you say that you **have a soft spot for** someone or something, you mean that you like them or care about them a lot. *It looked to me as if he had a soft spot for Mrs Frazer and didn't like what was happening to her.*

hit the spot

If you say that something **hits the spot**, you mean that it is very good and succeeds in pleasing people. *When she was asked what she thought, she reckoned the advert hit the right spot perfectly.*

on the spot

If you say that someone puts you **on the spot**, you mean that they put you in a difficult situation which you cannot avoid, for example by making you answer difficult questions. *You shouldn't ask a player about how his manager is coping. You put Gary on the spot and that's very unfair.*

spots

knock spots off something

British If you say that one thing or person **knocks spots off** another, you mean that the first is much better than the second. *I'm looking forward to the return of their chat show. It knocks spots off all the others.*

◆ The reference here is probably to someone who is shooting so well that they are able to knock out the spots or marks on a playing card that they are aiming at.

spout

up the spout: 1

British If you say that something is **up the spout**, you mean that it is completely ruined or hopeless. *The economy's up the spout.*

up the spout: 2

British If someone says that a woman is **up the spout**, they mean that she is pregnant, and usually that this is a problem rather than a good thing. Some people find this expression offensive. *There was always somebody up the spout, and there were some very strange marriages between young girls in the village and quite middle-aged farmers.*

◆ Originally, this expression was used to refer to items which had been pawned. The 'spout' was the lift in which an item was taken from the pawnbroker's shop to the storeroom above.

sprat

a sprat to catch a mackerel

British, old-fashioned If you describe something you do as **a sprat to catch a mackerel**, you mean that it involves a small sacrifice or a small amount of effort, but you are expecting that it will bring you great rewards or benefits. *As a sprat to catch the American mackerel, MITI is now offering to share the patents resulting from the joint research with foreign participants.*

spring

no spring chicken

If you say that someone is **no spring chicken**, you mean that they are no longer young. You often use this expression when you think someone's behaviour is inappropriate or surprising for their age. *At 85, he is no spring chicken, but Enrico Cuccia is busier than ever.*

spur

on the spur of the moment

If you do something **on the spur of the moment**, you do it suddenly and without planning it in advance. *He had decided on the spur of the moment to make the journey south to Newcastle... Judges currently cannot reflect in their sentencing the difference between a planned killing and a spur-of-the-moment emotional crime.*

spurs

earn your spurs
win your spurs

Mainly British If you say that someone **has earned** their **spurs** or **has won** their **spurs**, you mean that they have shown they are capable of doing something well, and can be relied on to do it well in the future. *Kampelman had won his spurs as U.S. negotiator at the Madrid talks.*

◆ In medieval times, when a man was made a knight, he was sometimes given a pair of golden spurs.

square

back to square one
back at square one
from square one

If you say that someone is **back to square one**, you are emphasizing that they have failed completely in what they were trying to do, so that now they have to start again. You can also say that someone is **back at square one** or starts **from square one**. *So we are back to square one. Their costly intervention has been for nothing, a carefully-constructed peace process lies in ruins… The new board will apparently be starting from square one.*

◆ This expression may refer to board games where the players move counters along a series of squares, and sometimes have to start again at the beginning.

on the square

Mainly American If you say that someone is **on the square**, you mean that they are being totally honest with you. *Most say they plan to vote for the Clinton-Gore ticket. 'Anything is better than what we got. At least he's on the square.'*

◆ This expression probably comes from the use of a square, a measuring device used to check that a right angle is completely accurate.

squib

a damp squib

Mainly British If you describe something as **a damp squib**, you are criticizing it for being much less impressive or exciting than you expected it to be. *Those pictures we were promised turned out to be a damp squib – I thought they would be much more exciting.*

◆ A squib is a small firework. A damp squib would not go off properly, and so it would be a disappointment.

stack

blow your stack

Mainly American If you **blow** your **stack**, you become very angry with someone and shout at them. *'You told me that your parents were very forgiving. They let you do anything.' 'Yeah, that used to be true. But my father really blew his stack over this.'*

stack the deck
stack the cards

If someone **stacks the deck** or **stacks the cards**, they arrange a situation unfairly against you, or in their own favour. 'Stack the deck' is used only in American English. Compare **not play with a full deck**; see **deck**. *The President is doing everything in his power to stack the cards in his favour and guarantee his regime's return to power.*

◆ The literal meaning of this expression is to cheat when shuffling cards by secretly putting them in an order which is to your advantage.

stage

set the stage for something

To **set the stage for** something means to make preparations so that the thing can happen. *The agreement sets the stage for renewed nuclear arms reduction talks and paves the way for a superpower summit later this year.*

stake

go to the stake

Mainly British, old-fashioned If you say that you would **go to the stake** to defend something, you mean that you are absolutely certain that you are right about it, and you are prepared to suffer the consequences of defending it. *He admitted several staff had keys but said: 'They are all trustworthy. I would go to the stake for all of them.'*

◆ A stake is a wooden post. In the past, people were sometimes tied to a stake and burned alive for refusing to give up beliefs which the church considered heretical and wrong.

stall

set out your stall

British If you **set out** your **stall** to achieve something, you make all the necessary plans or arrangements, and show that you are determined to achieve it. *He has set out his stall to retain his place in Europe's Ryder Cup team.*

stand

stand up and be counted

If you are willing to **stand up and be counted**, you are willing to state publicly your support for or rejection of something, especially when this is difficult or controversial. *This kind of demonstration should not be necessary but we are here because we want to stand up and be counted.*

standard

the standard bearer

If you say that someone is **the standard bearer** of an organization or a group of people who have the same aims or interests, you mean that they act as the leader or representative of the organization or group. *Inevitably, the public perception of her is that of a standard-bearer for women jockeys.*

◆ A standard is a flag with badges or symbols on it, which represent a person or organization. In the past, a standard bearer was the person who led an army into battle carrying a standard.

stars

reach for the stars
reach for the sky
reach for the moon

If you **reach for the stars** or **reach for the sky**, you are very ambitious and try hard to achieve something, even though it may be very difficult. You can also say that you **reach for the moon**. *If you're ready to move on in your career, keep your feet firmly on the ground while reaching for the stars!*

stars in your eyes

If you say that someone has **stars in** their **eyes**, you mean that they are very hopeful and excited about things which they expect to happen to them in the future. You often use this expression to suggest that they are naive and their hopes are unlikely to come true. *With stars in my eyes, I set about becoming a guitarist, singer and songwriter.*

starter

under starter's orders

British If you say that someone is **under starter's orders**, you mean that they are ready to do a task or job, and can begin doing it immediately if necessary. *The Tories have been effectively put under starter's orders as they gather for tomorrow's party conference.*

◆ This expression is more commonly used in talking about horse racing. When the horses in a race are under starter's orders, they are in position at the start of the race, and are waiting for the signal for the race to begin.

state

the state of play

British If someone tells you what **the state of play** is, they tell you about the current situation. *Ben Willmott gives you the state of play on marijuana and the law.*

steam

◆ The following expressions refer to the use of steam to provide power for a machine, especially a steam engine.

full steam ahead

If you go **full steam ahead** with a project, you start to carry it out in a thorough and determined way. *The Government was determined to go full steam ahead with its privatisation programme.*

let off steam
blow off steam

If you **let off steam** or **blow off steam**, you do or say something which helps you to get rid of your strong feelings about something. 'Let off steam' is used mainly in British English and 'blow off steam' is used mainly in American English. *This special session will give politicians a chance to let off steam... He may also experience reactions to stress, blowing off steam by turning violently on his wife and children.*

◆ The reference here is to steam escaping noisily from the safety valve of a steam engine.

pick up steam

If something such as a process **picks up steam**, it starts to become stronger or more active. *Boskin said the economy should pick up steam next year.*

run out of steam

If something such as a process **runs out of steam**, it becomes weaker or less active, and often stops completely. *The promised recovery ran out of steam.*

under your own steam: 1

If you go somewhere **under** your **own steam**, you make your own arrangements for the journey, rather than letting someone else organize it for you. *Most hotels organise tours to inland beauty spots, but car hire is cheap enough to consider taking off into the hills under your own steam.*

under your own steam: 2

If you do something **under** your **own steam**, you do it on your own and without help from anyone else. *He left the group convinced he could do better under his own steam.*

stew

in a stew

Fairly old-fashioned If you say that someone is **in a stew**, you mean that they are very worried about something. *'She was having trouble finding something, wasn't she?' 'Yeah, she was in a bit of a stew.'*

let someone stew in their own juice
let someone stew

If you **let** someone **stew** in their **own juice** or **let** them **stew**, you deliberately leave them to worry about something, for example the consequence of their actions, and do not do anything to comfort or help them. *'I thought you might have pressed him on that, sir.' 'I'd rather let him stew,' said Thorne. 'We'll get more out of him that way in the end.'*

stick

carry a big stick
wield a big stick

If someone **carries a big stick**, they have a lot of power, and so they can get what they want. If they **wield a big stick**, they have this power and use it. Compare **carrot and stick**; see **carrot**. *The company has a history of talking softly. But it wields a big stick. Over the past 107 years it has built itself up into the biggest brand in the world and now controls 44 per cent of the global market.*

□ **Big stick** is used in many other structures with a similar meaning. *They wanted peace, he said, but this big stick policy was forcing them into war.*

◆ This expression comes from a saying which became widely known through a speech made by Theodore Roosevelt in 1903: 'There is a homely old adage which runs, "Speak softly and carry a big stick; you will go far."'

get the short end of the stick

Mainly American If someone **gets the short end of the stick**, they end up in a worse position than other people in a particular situation, although this is not their fault. *As usual it's the consumer who gets the short end of the stick.*

get the wrong end of the stick
get hold of the wrong end of the stick

If someone **gets the wrong end of the stick** or **gets hold of the wrong end of the stick**, they completely misunderstand something, or completely miss someone's point. *People are so easily confused, so readily get hold of the wrong end of the stick.*

in a cleft stick

British If someone is **in a cleft stick**, they are in a difficult situation which they cannot get out of easily. *Debbie now finds herself in a cleft stick. On the one hand, Social Security refuse to pay her more money. On the other hand, she is being pursued and hassled by debt collectors, wanting just that money which she doesn't have.*

♦ This expression may refer to the practice of trapping snakes by holding them down behind the head with a forked stick.

more things than you can shake a stick at

If you say that you have **more** things **than** you **can shake a stick at**, you are emphasizing that you have a very large number of them. *I've replanted more geraniums than you can shake a stick at.*

a stick to beat someone with

British If you say that something is **a stick to beat** someone **with**, you mean that it can be used to cause embarrassment or difficulty for them. *Surprisingly, the opposition, usually eager to find any stick to beat the government with, is refusing to comment on the affair.*

stiff

stiff as a board

If your body is very stiff, you can say that you are as **stiff as a board** or that your body is as **stiff as a board**. *His lower back felt as stiff as a board.*

sting

a sting in the tail

British If you say that something such as a remark or proposal has **a**

sting in the tail, you mean that although most of it seems welcome or pleasing, it contains an unpleasant part at the end. *The resolution had a sting in the tail. It said that the entire military aid package would be suspended if the country failed to make progress on the economic front.*

♦ This is a reference to a scorpion, which is small and looks harmless, but has a poisonous sting in its tail.

take the sting out of something

If something **takes the sting out of** an unpleasant situation, it makes it less unpleasant or painful. *His calmness surprised her and helped to take the sting out of her anger.*

stitch

a stitch in time
a stitch in time saves nine

If someone says **'a stitch in time'**, they mean that it is better to deal with a problem in its early stages, in order to prevent it getting worse. *The adage 'a stitch in time' is never more true than with a steel boat's paintwork: one must be immediately ready to touch up the chips that inevitably occur in order to prevent a bigger job later.*

□ This expression comes from the proverb **a stitch in time saves nine**.

stone

leave no stone unturned

If you **leave no stone unturned** in your efforts to find something or achieve something, you consider or try every possible way of doing it. *In the difficult weeks ahead, we'll leave no stone unturned in our search for a peaceful solution of the crisis.*

not set in stone

If you say that something such as an agreement, policy, or rule is **not set in stone**, you are pointing out that it is not permanent and that it can be changed. *He is merely throwing the idea forward for discussion, it is not cast in stone.*

a rolling stone gathers no moss
a rolling stone
gather moss

People say **'a rolling stone gathers no moss'** when they want to point out that if a person keeps moving from one place to another, they will not get many friends or possessions. *If he was going to say that a rolling stone* *gathers no moss, that never having a family would be one of the penalties I would have to pay if I spent my life on the road, I was going to prove him wrong on that, too.*

☐ You can refer to a person who does not settle down as **a rolling stone**. *But throughout it all, Greta has found the desire and courage to keep in contact with her absentee father, who is a rolling stone to this day.*

☐ If you say that someone **is gathering moss**, you mean that they have stayed in the same place for a long time. *The old families die out or move on, or stay and gather moss.*

a stone's throw

If you describe one place as **a stone's throw** from another, you mean that the first place is very close to the second. *Burke found employment and rented a flat a stone's throw from their former, rather grand house.*

stools

fall between two stools
caught between two stools

Mainly British If someone or something **falls between two stools**, they are in an unsatisfactory situation because they do not belong to either of two groups or categories, or because they are trying to do two different things at once and are failing at both. You can also say that someone **is caught between two stools**. *Labour says that young people on waiting lists for youth training fall between two stools. They can't get unemployment benefit, nor can they get the allowance for the scheme they're waiting to get on.*

stops

pull out all the stops

If you **pull out all the stops**, you do everything you possibly can to make something happen in the way that you want it to. *Don't worry about taking foreign assignments, because if anything goes wrong, we're going to pull out all the stops to get you out.*

◆ On a church organ, the stops are the knobs which you pull or push in order to control the type of sound that comes out of the pipes. The organ plays loudest when all the stops are out.

storage

into cold storage

If you put something **into cold storage**, you delay doing it or dealing with it, for example because other more important things need your attention or because you are not ready to do it. *A few years ago I was asked by a publisher to consider writing a novel with a motor racing background, and the idea has been in cold storage ever since.*

store

give away the store

American If you accuse someone of **giving away the store**, you are criticizing them for giving away an advantage or for giving in to other people very easily. *They literally gave away the store to the unions and it has been very detrimental.*

storm

the calm before the storm
the lull before the storm

If you describe a very quiet period as **the calm before the storm** or **the lull before the storm**, you mean that it is likely to be followed, or was followed, by a period of trouble or intense activity. *Things are relatively calm at the moment, but I think it probably is the calm before the storm.*

a storm in a teacup

British If you say that something is **a storm in a teacup**, you mean that it is not very important but people are making a lot of unnecessary fuss about it. The American expression is **a tempest in a teapot**. *Ella likes you. I'm sure it's all a storm in a teacup. It'll blow over in no time.*

take somewhere by storm

If someone or something **takes** a place **by storm**, they are very successful or popular and make a good impression on people there. *Hailed as the next Sophia Loren, the dark-eyed Italian is set to take the fashion world by storm.*

◆ This expression originally meant to capture something such as a fort or a military position by means of a sudden, violent attack.

weather the storm
ride out the storm

If you **weather the storm** or **ride out the storm**, you survive a difficult situation or period without being seriously harmed or affected very badly by it. *Rover has weathered the storm of the current recession better than most. As car sales have plummeted, it's seen its share of the market actually increase... By the late 1960s, there were three options for dealing with the crisis. The first option was to ride out the storm, and hope that the crisis* *would be dissipated through the beneficial effects of EU membership.*

story

to cut a long story short
to make a long story short

When you are giving an account of something, you can say **'to cut a long story short'** in British English or **'to make a long story short'** in American English to indicate that you are only going to mention the final result or point, without any further details. *To cut a long story short, a freak accident over four years ago left Paul prone to painful dislocations of the kneecaps... This handsome man stepped off another airplane. I thought, Boy! I could go for him, and to make a long story short, we're getting married.*

straight

the straight and narrow

If someone keeps you on **the straight and narrow**, they help you to live an honest, decent life and prevent you from doing immoral or illegal things. *The Education Secretary, a devout Catholic, is determined to introduce a new classroom culture of morality to set youngsters on the straight and narrow.*

◆ 'Straight' was originally 'strait', which meant 'narrow'. Some people still use 'strait'. The expression probably refers to a passage in the Bible: 'Because strait is the gate, and narrow is the way, which leadeth unto life, and few there be that find it.'(Matthew 7:14)

straight as a die: 1

British If you say that someone is **straight as a die**, you mean that they are completely honest. *But I got the impression that deviousness is not one of his characteristics. He is, as the English would say, as straight as a die.*

straight as a die: 2

British If you say that something is **straight as a die**, you are emphasizing that it is very straight. *The streets are lined up, straight as a die, along the left bank of the Guadiana estuary.*

◆ A die is a specially shaped block of metal which is used to cut or form other metal into a particular shape. This expression may refer to dies which were used to produce designs on coins. The metalworkers needed to strike the die with a hard straight blow from a hammer, in order to leave a clear impression on the coin.

straw

draw the short straw

Mainly British If you **draw the short straw**, you are chosen from a number of people to perform a task or duty that nobody wants to do. *Brenner drained his glass with a sense of relief, thankful that it was someone else, probably Hean, who had drawn the short straw.*

◆ This expression comes from the practice of using pieces of straw to draw lots. One person holds several pieces of straw in their hand with the ends poking out. Each person in the group takes a piece of straw and the person with the shortest piece loses.

the last straw
the final straw

If you say that something is **the last straw** or **the final straw**, you mean it is the latest in a series of unpleasant or difficult events, and it makes you feel that you cannot tolerate a situation any longer. *The increased hardship caused by water and power cuts appears to have been the last straw and provoked open rebellion.*

◆ This is a reference to the expression 'the straw that breaks the camel's back'.

a man of straw
a straw man

Mainly British If you say that a man is **a man of straw**, you mean that he does not have the ability or the courage necessary to carry out a particular task or fulfil a particular role. *The problem of the Labour Party is that it is once again firmly in the grip of men of straw without guts and without principles.*

☐ You can also talk about **straw men**. This form of the expression is used in both British and American English *These also represent the reflex responses of straw men with straw policies.*

the straw that breaks the camel's back
the last straw that breaks the camel's back

You can say that something is **the straw that breaks the camel's back** when it is the latest in a series of unpleasant or difficult events, and it makes you feel that you cannot tolerate a situation any longer. See also **the last straw**. *Last week, I broke my wrist skateboarding. I'm a good skateboard rider and love the sport – but that was the straw that broke the camel's back as far as my dad was concerned.*

☐ In British English, you can also say that something is **the last straw that breaks the camel's back**. *He tried to reassure my father, but said all the wrong things: 'I wouldn't worry about it. You've educated your daughter, she can work!' My father went berserk. This was the last straw that broke the camel's back. He ordered him out of the house.*

◆ The reference here is to an animal which is already carrying a great deal on its back and which collapses when one more thing is added.

straws

clutch at straws
grasp at straws
a drowning man will clutch at a straw
    If you say that someone **is clutching at straws** or **is grasping at straws**, you mean that they are relying on ideas, hopes, or methods which are unlikely to be successful, because they are desperate and cannot think of anything else to try. In American English 'grasp at straws' is more common. *This disparaging speech was made by a man clutching at straws to gain much-desired publicity.*

☐ You can also say that an idea, hope, or method is **the straw** which someone **clutches at** or **the straw** which someone **grasps**. *The drop in bank base rates to their lowest levels since June 1988 may have given the property industry a much needed, if fragile, straw to clutch at.*

☐ This expression comes from the proverb **a drowning man will clutch at a straw**.

◆ The image here is of a drowning person who is desperately trying to grab hold of anything to save himself or herself, even a straw.

straws in the wind
    Mainly British If you say that events are **straws in the wind**, you mean that they are signs of the way in which a situation may develop. *Day by day evidence mounts that the economy is starting to climb out of recession. The latest straw in the wind is a pick-up in sales among the nation's retail giants.*

◆ People sometimes drop pieces of straw in order to see which way they move as they fall, so that they can tell which way the wind is blowing.

streak

talk a blue streak
    American If you say that someone **talks a blue streak**, you mean that

they are talking a lot and very fast. *They say I talked a blue streak from the time I opened my mouth.*

◆ This expression refers to a blue streak of lightning flashing quickly across the sky.

stream

on stream

Mainly British If a plan or a project comes **on stream**, it begins to operate fully. The usual American expression is **on line**. *Faults at Romania's first nuclear power plant must be repaired before it goes on stream.*

street

in Queer Street

British, old-fashioned If you say that someone is **in Queer Street**, you mean that they are having difficulties, especially financial difficulties. *Had he spent more time then listening to the educators, he might not now be in Queer Street.*

◆ In the 19th century, 'queer' was used in many slang terms applied to dishonest or criminal people or activities. However, 'Queer Street' may have developed from 'Carey Street', in London, where the law courts dealing with bankrupts were. Another possibility is that 'queer' may come from 'query', as traders might have put a question mark in their records by the names of customers who could not be trusted to pay their bills.

the man in the street

When people talk about **the man in the street**, they mean ordinary, average people. Nouns such as 'woman' and 'person' are sometimes used instead of 'man'. *The man in the street will be able to buy all that he could reasonably need anywhere in Europe.*

right up your street
just up your street

Mainly British If you say that something is **right up** your **street** or **just up** your **street**, you mean that it is the kind of thing you like or know about. *Actor Roy Barraclough has taken on a role that's right up his street*

– as Sherlock Holmes' bumbling sidekick Watson.

streets

streets ahead

British If you say that one person or thing is **streets ahead** of another, you are emphasizing that the first one is much better than the other one. *Even after its relative decline over the last three years, the South East is still streets ahead of the rest.*

stretch

at full stretch

British If someone or something is operating **at full stretch**, they cannot work any harder or more efficiently, because they are already using all their resources. You can also say that someone or something is **fully stretched**. *Police are warning that emergency services are at full stretch and they are advising motorists to travel only if their journey is absolutely necessary... The Commission's resources were fully stretched.*

stride

get into your stride
hit your stride

If you **get into** your **stride** or **hit** your **stride**, you start to do something easily and confidently, after being slow and uncertain at the beginning. 'Get into your stride' is used only in British English. *The Government is getting into its stride and seems, for the moment, to be fulfilling its promises.*

put someone off their stride

British If something **puts** you **off** your **stride**, it stops you from concentrating on what you are doing, so that you do not do it as well as usual. *His many opponents are suggesting that it is all a tactic designed to put his opponent off his stride.*

take something in your stride
take something in stride

British If you are in a difficult situation and you **take** it **in** your **stride**, you deal with it calmly and successfully. The American expression is **take** something **in stride**. *'Tim is absolutely dreading having to give a speech – he would rather have a tooth pulled!' said Christie, who takes such things in her stride... Across the country, many people took yesterday's events in stride, while remaining generally uneasy about the stock market in general.*

strikes

three strikes against someone
two strikes against someone

Mainly American If there are **three strikes against** someone or something, there are three factors which make it impossible for them to be successful. *There was one lady that said to me, 'Listen young man, you got three strikes against you. You're black, you're poor, and you're blind.'*

☐ If there are **two strikes against** someone or something, there are two factors which make it difficult, but not impossible, for them to be successful, or they have only one more chance of succeeding. *The hotel has two strikes against it. One, it's an immense ugly concrete building. Second, it lies just inside the border so that all doorstep activities involve a fussy border crossing.*

◆ In baseball, the batter is out after three strikes. A 'strike' is a legal pitch or ball which the batter fails to hit.

string

another string to your bow
many strings to your bow

British If you have **another string to** your **bow**, you have more than one useful skill, ability, or thing you can use in case you are unsuccessful with your first attempt. If you have **many strings to** your **bow**, you have several skills, abilities, or things to use. *Looking, as it were, for another string to his bow, he turned to art and design, for which he had always shown a particular talent.*

◆ Archers used to carry a spare bowstring in case the first one broke.

have someone on a string

If someone **has** you **on a string**, they can make you do whatever they want, because they control you completely. *He was once again in serious difficulties. The Germans had him on a string.*

strings

pull strings

If someone **pulls strings** to get something they want, they get it by using their friendships with powerful and influential people, often in a way which is considered unfair. *Anyway, I'm not going to play in the tournament if it's part of a deal; it would look as if I was pulling strings.*

☐ You can also talk about **string-pulling**. *Recent news stories have raised questions about whether he engaged in the kind of string-pulling and backroom deal-making that he accuses his opponents of.*

pull the strings

If someone **pulls the strings**, they control everything that another person or an organization does. *Mike worked sixteen hours a day, pulling the strings to make Apple a raging success.*

◆ The image here is of a puppet which is controlled by means of strings.

with no strings attached
without strings
with strings
with strings attached

If you say that an offer of help comes **with no strings attached** or **without strings**, you mean that it has no unpleasant conditions which must be accepted as part of the offer, or that the person making it does not expect anything in return. *I am grateful to them for their co-operation, which was also given with absolutely no strings attached... He wanted aid quickly and without strings.*

☐ You can say that an offer is **with strings** or **with strings attached** if it has unpleasant conditions which must be accepted as part of the offer, or if the person making it expects something in return. *Western money came with strings such as commercial openings.*

strip

tear a strip off someone
tear someone off a strip

British If you **tear a strip off** someone or **tear** them **off a strip**, you speak angrily or seriously to them, because they have done something wrong. *After breakfast he heard Nora tearing a strip off an orderly for not returning the food bins to the kitchen soon enough... We turned up together on the first day and got torn off a strip for being late.*

stroke

put someone off their stroke

British If something **puts** you **off** your **stroke**, it stops you from concentrating on what you are doing, so that you do not do it as well as usual. *'Is that what you wanted to tell me?' 'What? Oh no, sorry, this business of Ivor has quite put me off my stroke.'*

◆ The reference here is to rowing, in which all the members of a team have to pull on their oars at exactly the same moment. Each pull of the oars is called a stroke.

strokes

broad strokes
broad brush strokes

If someone describes something in **broad strokes** or in **broad brush strokes**, they describe it in general terms rather than giving details. *The speech will lay out in broad strokes the two candidates' differing approaches towards how best to stimulate the economy.*

◆ The image here is of an artist painting a picture roughly or quickly.

different strokes for different folks

People say **'different strokes for different folks'** to point out that people are different, and some individuals or groups have different needs and wants from others. This expression is used more commonly in American English than British. *The federal government has, by tradition, been respectful of local standards in local communities, and therefore you had different strokes for different folks.*

strong

strong as an ox
strong as a horse
strong as a bull

If you say that someone is as **strong as an ox**, you are emphasizing that they are extremely strong. You can replace 'ox' with the name of another large animal. For example, you can say that someone is as **strong as a horse** or as **strong as a bull**. *Big Beppe, as everybody calls him, is enormous for his age and as strong as an ox.*

stubborn

stubborn as a mule

If you say that someone is as **stubborn as a mule**, you mean that they are determined to do what they want and are unwilling to change their mind. This expression is usually used to show disapproval. *He is, without question, a man of his word, and he can certainly be stubborn as a mule.*

stuff

strut your stuff

If you **strut** your **stuff**, you do something which you know you are good at in a proud and confident way in order to impress other people. *This weekend, in parades across the nation, Irish Americans are strutting their stuff.*

stuffing

knock the stuffing out of someone

If you say that something **knocks the stuffing out of** someone, you mean that it destroys all their energy and self-confidence, and leaves them feeling weak and nervous. *Bath knocked the stuffing out of us early on and we never got into the game.*

stump

on the stump

If politicians are **on the stump**, they are travelling to different places and speaking to voters as part of their election campaign. *Despite his falling popularity, the president braved it on the stump today on behalf of his fellow Republicans.*

◆ This expression comes from politicians using tree stumps as platforms when giving a speech in the open air.

style

cramp someone's style

If someone or something **cramps** your **style**, they prevent you from behaving freely in the way that you want. *Like more and more women with good jobs, independent spirits and high standards, she believes wedlock would cramp her style.*

suck

suck it and see

British If you are considering doing something new and someone tells you to **suck it and see**, they mean that the only way to find out if it is a good idea and likely to be successful is to actually try it. *These results do not mean, however, that the Japanese will automatically like Western products. The only sure way to prove that, says Prescott, is to suck it and* *see... Before Prozac, anti-depressant drugs were too unpleasant to give to people on a suck-it-and-see basis.*

suit

◆ The following expressions refer to the four suits in a pack of cards: diamonds, hearts, clubs, and spades.

follow suit

If someone **follows suit**, they do the same thing that someone else has just done. *BP also make nursery provisions for the children of staff members. If only other employers would follow suit.*

◆ If you follow suit in a card game, you play a card of the same suit as the previous player.

your long suit

If you say that something is your **long suit**, you mean that you are good at it or know a lot about it, and this gives you an advantage. *Our long suit is our proven ability to operate power plants.*

◆ If a large number of a player's cards belong to a particular suit, you can call that suit their long suit.

suits

the men in suits
the men in grey suits

Mainly British If you talk about **the men in suits** or **the men in grey suits**, you are referring to the men who are in control of an organization or company and who have a lot of power. *A lot of young people feel detached from older, stereotype politicians – the men in grey suits.*

summer

an Indian summer

Mainly British If someone enjoys **an Indian summer** in their life or career, they have a period of great success late in their life or career, perhaps after a period of not being successful. *The Sixties revival in international fashion is proving an Indian summer for Mr Rabanne, better known for his perfumes in the Seventies and Eighties.*

◆ An Indian summer is a period of unusually warm sunny weather during the autumn. This use occurs in both British and American English, although it is of American origin. Indian summers got their name because they typically occurred more in the lands formerly occupied by Native Americans.

supper

sing for your supper

Fairly old-fashioned If someone tells you that you will have to **sing for your supper**, they mean that you will have to do a particular job before you are allowed to do or have something that you want. *'You only gave me the box number for that bureau, Jo,' I said. 'Is there more?' She took a while to answer. 'Very well,' she said finally. 'But you'll have to sing for your supper.'*

sure

sure as eggs is eggs
sure as eggs

British If you say that something will happen as **sure as eggs is eggs** or **sure as eggs**, you are emphasizing that you are very certain it will happen. *The new magazine, out this month, will sell, sure as eggs.*

◆ This expression may be a corruption or mishearing of 'as sure as x is x', referring to the use of x to represent a variable in algebra and logic.

surface

scratch the surface

If you only **scratch the surface** of something, you deal with or experience only a small part of it. *This is the most exciting aspect of my career at present. I realise now I've only scratched the surface of what I can do.*

swallow

one swallow doesn't make a summer

People say **'one swallow doesn't make a summer'** when they want to point out that although something good has happened, the situation may not continue to be good, and you cannot rely on it. *Sales into the new year are also up about 1 percent, which is a sharp contrast to the 9 percent dive in the previous six months. One swallow, however, doesn't make a summer.*

◆ Swallows are a type of bird. The reference here is to the arrival of swallows in Europe at the beginning of summer, after spending the winter further south.

sweat

by the sweat of your brow

If you do something such as earning your living **by the sweat of** your **brow**, you do it by means of hard physical work, without any help from anyone else. *Most people are no longer earning their bread by the sweat of their brow.*

sweep

make a clean sweep: 1

If someone wins something very easily, or wins a series of victories, you can say they **make a clean sweep** of it. *China were back on top again in the Women's Weightlifting. They have made a clean sweep of all nine titles in that event with three more gold medals today.*

☐ **A clean sweep** is used in many other structures with a similar meaning. *The Italians look well placed to repeat their clean sweep of 1990.*

make a clean sweep: 2

If someone who has just taken up a position of authority in an organization **makes a clean sweep**, they make a lot of changes, for example getting rid of a large number of employees, in order to make the organization more efficient or profitable. Compare **a new broom**; see **broom**. *When Don arrived he said he was going to make a clean sweep, but I didn't think he would go quite this far.*

sweet

cop it sweet

Mainly Australian If you **cop it sweet**, you accept harsh treatment or a punishment without reacting violently or complaining. *Bullies tend to lose interest in a victim very quickly if that victim refuses to 'cop it sweet'.*

sweet as pie

Mainly British If you say that someone is as **sweet as pie**, you mean that they are very kind, friendly, and charming. If a situation is as **sweet as pie**, it is very satisfactory. Compare **nice as pie**; see **nice**. *Everything was as sweet as pie, after that.*

swing

get into the swing of something

If you **get into the swing of** something, you get used to it and you start doing it well or start enjoying it. If you **get back into the swing of things**, you get used to something again after a period of not doing it. *It didn't take people long to relax and get into the swing of things, with a little help from some champagne.*

go with a swing

British If a party or other event **goes with a swing**, it happens in a lively and exciting way. *These impressive recipes are guaranteed to make the party go with a swing.*

in full swing

If something is **in full swing**, it is operating fully or has already been happening for some time, rather than being in its early stages. *Dieppe has plenty to attract cross-Channel visitors. While I was there, a national dog show and a jazz festival were in full swing.*

swings

swings and roundabouts
what you lose on the swings you gain on the roundabouts

British If you say that a situation is **swings and roundabouts**, you mean that there are as many advantages as there are disadvantages in it. *It's swings and roundabouts at Fuji, who have made welcome price reductions on its C-cassettes, but increased the cost of its 8mm tapes, without any significant changes to the product.*

☐ This expression comes from the proverb **what you lose on the swings you gain on the roundabouts**.

Swiss cheese

more holes than Swiss cheese

Mainly American If you say that something such as an argument or theory has **more holes than Swiss cheese**, you mean that it has so many faults that it cannot be taken seriously. *'The current laws,' he says, 'have more holes than Swiss cheese.'*

☐ **Swiss cheese** is used in various other ways to describe an argument or theory like this. *Paglia disparages Wolf as an ill-educated hustler peddling a Swiss-cheese thesis.*

◆ 'Swiss cheese' is an American term for cheese such as Gruyère or Emmenthal, which has round holes in it.

sword

a double-edged sword
a two-edged sword

If you say that something is **a double-edged sword** or **a two-edged sword**, you mean that it has both a good and a bad side. *The strong yen is a double-edged sword for Japan. It increases the spending power of consumers and it helps the nation's banks, but it also raises the costs of exports for car and electronics manufacturers.*

the Sword of Damocles

If you say that someone has **the Sword of Damocles** hanging over their head, you mean that they are in a situation in which something very bad could happen to them at any time. *Franco's power to fulfill or crush their hopes hung over the Spanish royal family like a Sword of Damocles.*

◆ This expression comes from a Greek legend. Dionysius, the ruler of Syracuse, was annoyed by Damocles, who kept flattering him and saying how much he admired him. Dionysius invited Damocles to a feast, and asked him to sit in his own seat. When Damocles looked up during the feast, he noticed a sword hanging by a single thread above his head, and so he could no longer enjoy the feast. The sword symbolized the dangers and fears that rulers have, in addition to all the privileges.

swords

beat swords into ploughshares
turn swords into ploughshares

If you talk about **beating swords into ploughshares** or **turning swords into ploughshares**, you are talking about plans or efforts to stop war or conflict and to use the resources and technology of warfare to do other things to improve people's lives. *Public opinion at the grassroots is now reacting with great warmth to the Gorbachev vision of a world that turns swords into ploughshares.*

◆ 'Ploughshares' is spelled 'plowshares' in American English. A ploughshare is one of the blades on a plough. This expression may come from the Bible: 'They shall beat their swords into ploughshares, and their spears into pruninghooks: nation shall not lift up sword against nation, neither shall they learn war any more.' (Isaiah 2:4).

cross swords

If you **cross swords** with someone, you disagree and argue with them or oppose them. *As a member of Indira Gandhi's Congress Party, he repeatedly crossed swords with Mrs Gandhi in the early 1970s.*

system

get something out of your system

If you **get** something **out of** your **system**, you say or do something that you have been wanting to for a long time, and so you begin to feel less worried or angry about it. *If something awful happens to you at least you can write about it. I'm sure you feel better if you get it out of your system.*

systems

all systems go

You can say 'it's **all systems go**' when you want to indicate that people are very busy with a particular project, or that you expect there will be a lot of activity in a particular field. *Work started on the indoor arena at the beginning of the year and it's now all systems go for a full programme of events over the winter.*

♦ This expression became popular as a result of its use during the launch of spacecraft in the United Sates in the 1960s and 1970s. It indicated that the spacecraft was functioning correctly and was ready for takeoff.

T

table

drink someone under the table

If you say that someone can **drink** you **under the table**, you mean that they can drink much more alcohol than you can without getting drunk. *Donna is the only person I know who can drink me under the table.*

on the table

If you put a proposal, plan, or offer **on the table**, you present it formally to other people so it can be discussed and negotiated, in the hope that it will be accepted. *The United States said Europe must put a new offer on the table to save the talks.*

under the table

American If you do something **under the table**, you do it secretly because it is dishonest or illegal. The usual British expression is **under** the counter. *Athletes sometimes cheated, sometimes lied, or took money under the table... Councillor Doctor Leong Che-Hung said the Hong Kong people could not tolerate any more political cover-ups and under the table deals.*

tables

turn the tables

If you **turn the tables** on someone, you do something to change a situation so that you gain an advantage over them or cause them problems, after a time when they have had the advantages or have been causing problems for you. *In his response, Kissinger sought to turn the tables on his critics.*

◆ The image here is of a player in a game such as chess turning the board through 180 degrees, so that the situations of the two players are reversed.

tabs

keep tabs on someone

If someone **keep tabs on** you, they make sure that they always know where you are and what you are doing, often in order to control you. *We do know that somebody was keeping tabs on her. Perhaps we should have done the same.*

◆ Originally, this was an American expression which uses an American sense of 'tab', meaning an account or bill, which can be used to keep a record of what someone spends.

tail

chase your own tail

If you say that someone **is chasing** their **own tail**, you are being critical of them for spending a lot of time and energy doing something, but achieving nothing. *Any striving for military superiority means chasing one's own tail.*

on your tail

If someone is **on** your **tail**, they are following you closely or are chasing you and trying to catch you. *He heard the wail of sirens, loud and close by. They must be on his tail at last.*

the tail wags the dog

If you say that **the tail is wagging the dog**, you are criticizing the fact that a small or unimportant part of something is becoming too important and is controlling the whole thing. *To avoid the impression of the tail wagging the dog, the Chancellor cannot be seen bending to the wishes of a minority party.*

turn tail

If you **turn tail**, you turn and run away from someone or something because you are frightened of them. *Rebels were forced back from position after position until they turned tail and fled.*

with your tail between your legs

If someone goes off **with** their **tail between** their **legs**, they go off feeling very ashamed, embarrassed, and humiliated, because of a defeat or foolish mistake that they have made. *His team retreated last night with tails tucked firmly between their legs.*

◆ Dogs often go off with their tails down when they have been hit or shouted at.

with your tail up

If you say that someone is doing something **with** their **tail up**, you mean that they seem to be very happy or confident about their chances of success. *We'll go to court with our tails up.*

◆ Dogs often raise their tails and wag them when they are happy or excited.

tales

dead men tell no tales

People say **'dead men tell no tales'** when they want to say that someone who is dead cannot reveal anything about the circumstances of their death. *Hanley told police the gun went off accidentally while Mr Khan was playing with it. 'These statements were a cover-up,' Mr Spencer told the jury. 'Mr Hanley did it on purpose, his thoughts being that dead men tell no tales.'*

tall

tall tales
tall stories

Tall tales or **tall stories** are stories or statements which are difficult to believe because they are so exaggerated or unlikely. *I have met older, more senior scientists who tell tall tales of the 'old days', the 'golden days' of research, when money was plentiful and there were lots of research jobs.*

◆ 'Tall' used to be used to describe language that was considered extremely formal or exaggerated.

tangent

go off on a tangent
go off at a tangent

If someone **goes off on a tangent**, they start saying or thinking something that is not directly connected with what they were saying or thinking before. In British English, you can also say that someone **goes off at a tangent**. *He would occasionally go off on a tangent totally unrelated to the textbook or curriculum.*

♦ In geometry, a tangent is a straight line which touches a curve at one point but does not cross it.

tango

it takes two to tango

If you say that **it takes two to tango**, you mean that a situation or argument involves two people and they are both therefore responsible for it. *It would be very sad if we don't settle this. It takes two to tango, however, and I suspect we'll still be here tomorrow discussing it.*

♦ This is the title of a song by Hoffman and Manning, written in 1952.

tap

on tap: 1

If something is **on tap**, it is available and ready for immediate use. *The enterprise agency's close links with the University of Sheffield as well as other business institutions provides local entrepreneurs with a wealth of knowledge and business expertise on tap.*

on tap: 2

American If an event or activity is **on tap**, it is scheduled to happen very soon. *It's Detroit against Chicago and Dallas against Pittsburgh in the two pro football games on tap this afternoon.*

♦ If drink such as beer is available on tap, it is kept in a barrel fitted with a tap, so it can be drawn off as required.

tape

red tape

People refer to official rules and procedures as **red tape** when they seem unnecessary and cause delay. *Two lawyers have written a book in a bid to help people cut through the red tape when dealing with British immigration and nationality laws.*

◆ Lawyers and government officials used to tie documents together with red or pink tape.

taped

have got something taped

British If you think that you **have got** something **taped**, you think that you fully understand it and are in control of it. *The one certainty of parenthood is that whenever you feel you've got it taped, something or someone will come along to throw you off balance!*

target

shoot for the same target

If two people **are shooting for the same target**, they are in agreement about what they are trying to achieve together. *Just so we can be sure we're both shooting at the same target, here's a summary of what will happen on Friday night.*

taste

leave a bad taste in your mouth

If you say that something someone does **leaves a bad taste in** your **mouth**, you mean that it makes you feel angry or disgusted with them because it was a very unpleasant thing to do. *There's no doubt that some of the magazine's jokes about Jews, women and gays leave a bad taste in the mouth.*

tea

not for all the tea in China

If you say that you would **not** do something **for all the tea in China**, you are emphasizing that you definitely do not want to do it. *I wouldn't go through that again for all the tea in China.*

◆ In the past, all tea came from China.

tee

to a tee
to a T

You can use **to a tee** or **to a T** to mean that something is perfectly or exactly right. *The police soon left, apologizing that they had just been responding to a call about robbers, whose description fit us to a tee.*

◆ T stands for 'tittle', a small mark in printing such as the dot over an i. The expression refers to writing being very clear and exactly right.

teeth

armed to the teeth

Someone who is **armed to the teeth** is armed with a lot of weapons or with very effective weapons. *The police are grossly underpaid and underequipped while the criminals are armed to the teeth with the most modern equipment.*

cut your teeth

If you do something new which gives you experience and helps you learn how to do more advanced or complicated things, you can say that you **cut** your **teeth** doing that thing. *He cut his teeth in the sixties as director of Edinburgh's Traverse Theatre.*

◆ When a child cuts a tooth, the tooth begins to appear through the gum.

fed up to the back teeth
sick to the back teeth

British If you are **fed up to the back teeth** with something or **sick to the back teeth** with it, you feel annoyed, irritated, or tired because it has been going on for a long time and you think it should be stopped or changed. *I've always been a very strong Conservative but I am fed up to the back teeth with them at the moment.*

get your teeth into something
sink your teeth into something

If you **get** your **teeth into** something or **sink** your **teeth into** it, you become deeply involved with it and do it with a lot of energy and enthusiasm. *Half the trouble is having nothing interesting to do. We've not had a case to get our teeth into for weeks.*

gnashing of teeth
wailing and gnashing of teeth
weeping and gnashing of teeth

When people become very worried or agitated by something unexpected or unnecessary that has happened, you can say that there is **gnashing of teeth** or **wailing and gnashing of teeth**, especially when you want to suggest that they are overreacting or showing their concern in an excessive way. You can also say that there is **weeping and gnashing of**

teeth. *In times of widespread strife and much gnashing of teeth, a sense of community is needed to stop everyone plummeting into the dark depths of despair… It was the biggest earthquake to hit LA in years. Radio preachers gibbered about the end of the world. There was a whole lot of wailing and gnashing of teeth.*

◆ The phrases 'weeping and gnashing of teeth' and 'wailing and gnashing of teeth' both appear several times in the Bible in descriptions of the people who are sent to hell.

gnash your teeth

If you say that someone **is gnashing** their **teeth**, you mean that they are showing their anger or annoyance about something in a very obvious way. *If Blythe heard that piece, I bet he was gnashing his teeth.*

grind your teeth

If someone **is grinding** their **teeth**, they are very angry or frustrated about something, but feel that they cannot say or do anything about it. *Men respond that if women are in charge they don't do anything for other women either. The predominantly female audience was grinding its teeth.*

grit your teeth

If you **grit** your **teeth**, you decide to carry on even though the situation you are in is very difficult. *He says that there are no simple solutions, that it's going to take time, that there is going to be hardship, but we have to grit our teeth and get on with it.*

have teeth

If you say that an organization or law **has teeth**, you mean that it has the necessary authority or power to make people obey it. *Trade union committees should have teeth, and not be convenient partners for management.*

lie through your teeth

If you say that someone **is lying through** their **teeth** or **is lying in** their **teeth**, you mean that they are telling very obvious lies and do not seem to be embarrassed about this. *'We were on vacation in Barbados a few years ago and we met Freddie Mercury in a bar,' says Phil, lying through his teeth.*

like pulling teeth

Mainly American If you say that doing something is **like pulling teeth**, you mean that it is very difficult. *Identifying excess and duplication of work is easy. Doing something about it is like pulling teeth.*

◆ When a dentist pulls someone's tooth, they pull it out of their gum. In the past, this was done without anaesthetic and so it was difficult and painful.

set your teeth on edge

If something **sets** your **teeth on edge**, you find it extremely irritating or unpleasant. *His casual arrogance never failed to set my teeth on edge.*

show your teeth

If you **show** your **teeth**, you show that you are capable of fighting or defending yourself. *The bureaucracy was still showing its teeth, resisting and trying to sabotage our efforts.*

teething

teething problems
teething troubles

British If a project or new product has **teething problems** or **teething troubles**, there are problems in its early stages or when it first becomes available. *The Council has conceded there have been teething problems with the new voucher system but said these were being corrected.*

tell

tell someone where to get off

If someone **tells** you **where to get off**, they are telling you in a rude and forceful way that they cannot accept what you are saying or doing. *But if somebody tried to do that to you, you'd just go right up to them and tell them where to get off.*

tempest

a tempest in a teapot

American If you say that something is **a tempest in a teapot**, you mean that it is not very important but people are making a lot of unnecessary fuss about it. The British expression is **a storm in a teacup**. *'It's a tempest in a teapot,' he said of the controversy over the painting.*

tenterhooks

on tenterhooks

If you are **on tenterhooks**, you are very nervous or excited, because you are keen to know what is going to happen. *'It was a good match wasn't it? Very exciting.' 'Yes, we were on tenterhooks.'*

◆ In the past, when cloth had been woven, it was stretched on a frame called a tenter and held in place by hooks. The person's emotional state is being compared to the tension in the cloth.

territory

go with the territory

If you are talking about a particular situation or activity and you say that something **goes with the territory**, you mean that it often occurs in that kind of situation or activity, and so you have to be prepared for it. *For Robbins, activism goes with the territory. 'Art and politics have always been connected,' he says.*

test

stand the test of time

If you say that something **has stood the test of time**, you mean that it has proved its value and has not failed or has not gone out of fashion since it first appeared. *Fashions in floor coverings come and go, but wooden floors have stood the test of time.*

tether

at the end of your tether

British If you say that you are **at the end of** your **tether**, you mean that you feel desperate because you are in a difficult situation and you do not know how to deal with it. You can also use this expression to show your impatience or annoyance with someone. The usual American expression is **at the end of** your **rope**. *I'm at the end of my tether trying to find support and a cure for this condition which I have suffered from for 13 years.*

◆ A tether is a length of rope, used for tying animals up. The image is of an animal which cannot move very far because it is tied to something with a tether.

thick

in the thick of it
in the thick of something

If you are **in the thick of it** or **in the thick of** an activity or situation, you are deeply involved in the activity or situation. *Although he was not a member of the Army Operational Staff, he soon put himself in the thick of it... He was in the thick of the action for the full 90 minutes of the game.*

lay it on thick

If you say that someone **is laying it on thick**, you mean that they are exaggerating a statement, experience, or emotion in order to impress people. *Gerhardt explained the position to the Press Officer, laying it on thick about Adrian Winter's importance.*

thick as mince

Mainly Scottish If you say that someone is as **thick as mince**, you mean that they are very stupid. *No point in expecting any real help from Personnel – most of them are as thick as mince.*

thick as thieves

If two or more people are as **thick as thieves**, they are very friendly with each other. You usually use this expression to suggest that the people you are describing are doing something that is not moral or honest. *Old man Grant went to school with Maloney, the other lawyer in town. They're thick as thieves. Maloney does all his business.*

thick as two planks
thick as two short planks

British If you say that someone is as **thick as two planks** or as **thick as two short planks**, you mean that they are very stupid. *His people regarded him as a great and wise monarch. In fact he was as thick as two planks... Paul Crook was immature, inexperienced and as thick as two short planks.*

through thick and thin

If you do something **through thick and thin**, you continue doing it even when circumstances make it very difficult for you. *I will go on loving James through thick and thin no matter what happens.*

◆ This comes from a hunting expression 'through thicket and thin wood'. A thicket is a small group of trees or bushes which are growing closely together.

thin

spread yourself too thin

If you **spread** yourself **too thin**, you try to do a lot of different things at the same time, with the result that you cannot do any of them properly. *If you spread yourself too thin on the social circuit, you will not be able to keep up with everyone.*

thin as a rake
thin as a stick

If you say that someone is as **thin as a rake** or **thin as a stick**, you are emphasizing that they are very thin. *I was so shocked by his appearance,*

his face so gaunt, his eyes sunk in their sockets and his body thin as a rake
as though he were suffering from some wasting disease.

thorn

a thorn in your side
a thorn in your flesh

If you describe someone or something as **a thorn in** your **side**, you
mean that they continually annoy or irritate you. You can also say that
they are **a thorn in** your **flesh**. *She has become a thorn in the side of the*
government since publishing a number of reports pointing out that public
cash was being mishandled.

◆ This refers to a passage in the Bible, in which St Paul talks about an
illness or other problem: 'There was given to me a thorn in the flesh, the
messenger of Satan to buffet me, lest I should be exalted above measure.'
(2 Corinthians 12:7) Some Pharisees, who were strictly orthodox Jews,
used to deliberately hurt themselves by putting thorns in their clothes to
prick them when they walked.

thread

hang by a thread: 1

If you say that something **hangs by a thread**, you mean that it is very
likely to fail, although it has not failed yet. *It's clear that the ceasefire is*
hanging by a thread with as yet no appropriate impartial body to monitor
or supervise it.

hang by a thread: 2

If you say that someone's life **hangs by a thread**, you mean that they
are seriously ill and are very likely to die. *His kidneys had failed and his*
life was hanging by a thread.

◆ This expression may relate to the story of the Sword of Damocles: see
sword.

throat

cut your own throat

If you say that someone **is cutting** their **own throat**, you mean that
they are making a mistake by doing something which is going to result in
disaster for them. *I think the union is cutting its own throat because the fact*
of the matter is, if General Motors can't get its costs in line, then its market
share will continue to fall, and there will be even more jobs lost.

grab someone by the throat: 1
take someone by the throat

   If you **grab** someone or something **by the throat** or **take** them **by the throat**, you make a determined attempt to control, defeat, or deal with them. *Gloucestershire took the game by the throat from the start.*

grab someone by the throat: 2

   If something **grabs** you **by the throat**, it is so powerful, interesting, or exciting that you are forced to pay attention to it. *The film still grabs you by the throat.*

jump down someone's throat

   If you say something to someone and you complain that they then **jump down** your **throat**, you are complaining that they react in a very impatient, angry, and unpleasant way which you consider unjustified and unreasonable. *If I even asked her about her day, she'd jump down my throat, as if I were interrogating her.*

ram something down someone's throat

   If you accuse someone of trying to **ram** something **down** your **throat**, you mean that they are trying to force you to accept, believe, or learn something against your will. Verbs such as 'shove', 'force', and 'cram' are sometimes used instead of 'ram'. *'In America, you get religion shoved down your throat as soon as you're born,' says Paul, disgusted.*

throats

at each other's throats

   If you describe two people or groups as **at each other's throats**, you mean that they are continually arguing or fighting. *He and Stevens didn't get on, they'd been at each other's throats for years.*

throttle

at full throttle
in full throttle

   If someone does something **at full throttle**, they do it with all their energy and effort. You can also say that someone is **in full throttle**. *He started at full throttle, denouncing 'the poll tax which the Tories believe they can use to drive down living conditions and force poverty and suffering on working people'.*

   ☐ You can use **full throttle** in many other ways. *She was a high-powered Western businesswoman who went at things full throttle... Robert Palmer*

turns on his oh-so-suave and silky touch and gives it full throttle on his
latest album, Ridin' High.

◆ If an engine is operating at full throttle, it is operating at its maximum
speed.

thumb

have a green thumb

American If you say that someone **has a green thumb**, you mean that
they are very good at gardening. The British expression is **have green
fingers**. *She had a green thumb and using only instinct and countless
loads of cow manure, casually grew tomatoes, scallions, peonies, roses and
bumper crops of fruit.*

☐ You can describe someone who is good at gardening as
green-thumbed. *The green-thumbed gardeners will share the secrets of
their success at a series of nine gardening workshops.*

stick out like a sore thumb
stand out like a sore thumb

If you say that someone or something **sticks out like a sore thumb** or
stands out like a sore thumb, you mean that they are very noticeable
because they are very different from the other people or things around
them. *'Does the new housing stick out like a sore thumb or blend into its
surroundings?'*

under someone's thumb

If you say that someone is **under** another person's **thumb**, you
disapprove of the fact that the other person keeps them under their control
or has a very strong influence on them. *National television is firmly under
the thumb of the hardline president.*

thumbs

all thumbs
all fingers and thumbs

If you do something in a clumsy way and keep making mistakes while
you are doing it, you can say that you are **all thumbs**. In British English,
you can also say that you are **all fingers and thumbs**. *Can you open this?
I'm all thumbs.*

the thumbs down

If you give a plan, suggestion, or activity **the thumbs down**, you show
that you do not approve of it and are not willing to accept it. *Out of 58,000*

thunder

replies, 79 per cent gave the thumbs down to compulsory testing.

◆ In ancient Rome, a signal in which the thumb was bent down was used at the games to tell a victorious gladiator not to kill his opponent.

the thumbs up

If you give a plan, suggestion, or activity **the thumbs up**, you show that you approve of it and are willing to accept it. *The ski school gets the thumbs up from visitors.*

◆ In ancient Rome, a signal in which the thumb was straight was used at the games to tell a victorious gladiator to kill his opponent.

twiddle your thumbs

If you say that someone **is twiddling** their **thumbs,** you mean that they do not have anything to do or are wasting their time, and are not achieving anything useful. *The Government must address this problem. It cannot expect graduates who have invested time and their parents' money to go to university then to twiddle their thumbs on the dole.*

thunder

steal someone's thunder

If someone **steals** your **thunder**, they stop you from getting attention or praise by doing something better or more exciting than you, or by doing what you had intended to do before you can do it. *Be wary. He's liable to be either a bad boss or an insecure one and afraid that you might steal some of his thunder.*

◆ This expression may come from an incident in the early 18th century. A British playwright, John Dennis, invented a new way of making the sound of thunder for his play 'Appius and Virginia'. However, the play was unsuccessful and soon closed. Soon afterwards, Dennis went to see a production of 'Macbeth' by another company and found that they had stolen his idea for making thunder sounds. He is said to have jumped up and accused them of stealing his thunder.

ticket

a one-way ticket

If you describe something as **a one-way ticket** to a particular situation or state, usually an undesirable or unpleasant one, you mean that it is certain to lead to that situation. *She knew that the succession of secretarial jobs she'd picked up since leaving college were a one-way ticket to nowhere, professionally speaking.*

tide

swim against the tide
swim with the tide

If you say that someone **is swimming against the tide**, you mean that they are doing or saying something which is the opposite of what most other people are doing or saying. *Adenauer generally appeared to be swimming against the tide in international politics.*

☐ If you say that someone **is swimming with the tide**, you mean that they are acting in the same way as most other people. *In promoting in Britain a more co-operative, less confrontational form of capitalism we are swimming with the tide of the future.*

tightrope

walk a tightrope

If you say that someone **is walking a tightrope**, you mean that they are in a difficult or delicate situation and need to be very careful what they do or say, because they need to take account of the interests of opposing groups. *He is walking a tightrope between the young activists and the more traditional elements within the democracy movement.*

☐ You can refer to someone's attempt to satisfy the interests of opposing groups as **a tightrope walk**. *The strategy is something of a tightrope walk.*

tiles

on the tiles

British If someone has a night **on the tiles**, they go out in the evening, for example to a bar or disco, and do not return home until very late or until the following morning. *You look as though you've been out on the tiles, Ken.*

◆ This may be a reference to cats spending the night out on the rooftops.

till

have your hand in the till
have your fingers in the till

Mainly British If you say that someone **has had** their **hand in the till** or **has had** their **fingers in the till**, you mean that they have been caught stealing or doing something wrong. The usual American expression is **caught with** your **hand in the cookie jar**. *Thirteen company directors* *were found with their hands in the till in the first quarter of this year.*

time

big time

Mainly American You can use **big time** to emphasize the importance or extent of something that is happening. *Wall Street does not like surprises and DEC is surprising Wall Street big time.*

the big time
hit the big time

The big time means fame and success. When someone becomes famous and successful, you can say that they **hit the big time**. *After a series of small but critically acclaimed roles in the Eighties, she has now moved into the big time... He opened his own salon in 1923 and hit the big time in 1935, when he designed the wedding dress for the Duchess of Gloucester.*

□ You can use **big-time** to describe someone or something that is very successful, powerful, or important. *I said something like, 'Do you want to be a big-time rock 'n' roll star?'*

live on borrowed time

If you say that someone or something **is living on borrowed time**, you mean that you do not expect them to survive for much longer. *The organization is living on borrowed time. Its state funding runs out in June of this year, and beyond that, the future is in doubt.*

mark time

If you **mark time**, you do not do anything new or decisive, because you are waiting to see how a situation develops. *Today's gathering of European finance ministers in Bath can do little more than mark time pending the French referendum on September 20th.*

◆ When soldiers mark time, they march on the spot without moving forward.

play for time

If you **play for time**, you try to delay doing or saying something definite until you have decided what is the best course of action to take. *The republic's government is playing for time by asking for clarification of the nature of the economic sanctions.*

time on your hands

If you have **time on** your **hands**, you have a lot of free time and you do not know what to do with it. *Jimmy needed discipline and planned* *activities. He had too much time on his hands and that caused him to get into trouble.*

tin

have a tin ear for something

If you say that someone **has a tin ear for** something, you mean that they do not have any natural ability for it and cannot appreciate or understand it fully. Compare **have an ear for** something; see **ear**. *For a playwright specializing in characters who use the vernacular, he has a tin ear for dialogue.*

a tin god
a little tin god

Mainly British If you accuse someone of behaving like **a tin god** or like **a little tin god**, you are accusing them of behaving as if they are much more important and powerful than they actually are. *So what are his qualifications for acting like a little tin god?*

tinker

not give a tinker's damn
not give a tinker's cuss

Old-fashioned If you say that you **don't give a tinker's damn** or **don't give a tinker's cuss** about something, you mean that you do not care about it at all. *For 50 weeks of the year, give or take the odd Davis Cup disaster, the great British public couldn't give a tinker's cuss about tennis.*

□ You can also say that someone or something is **not worth a tinker's damn** when you think they are useless or worthless. *The real truth is you haven't been worth a tinker's damn all week.*

tip

on the tip of your tongue: 1

If you say that a remark or question was **on the tip of** your **tongue**, you mean that you really wanted to say something but decided not to. *'What do you make of it?' he said after a while. It was on the tip of my tongue to tell him he'd have to ask Charlie. But I said nothing.*

on the tip of your tongue: 2

If you say that something such as a word, answer, or name is **on the tip of** your **tongue**, you mean that you are sure you know what it is even though you cannot remember it at the moment. *I know this, no, no, don't* *tell me, oh, it's on the tip of my tongue.*

the tip of the iceberg

If you describe something as **the tip of the iceberg**, you mean that it is part of a very large problem or a very serious situation, although the rest may not be obvious or fully known about. *Mr Gunn said the Fitzgerald inquiry only touched the tip of an iceberg of corruption.*

♦ Only a very small part of an iceberg is visible above the water. About nine-tenths of it is below the surface.

tip the balance
tip the scales

When two possible outcomes of a situation seem equally likely, and then something happens which is sufficient to produce one outcome rather than the other, you can say that this thing **tips the balance** or **tips the scales**. *As the election looms, the two main parties appear so evenly matched that just one issue could tip the balance.*

tod

on your tod

British If you do something **on** your **tod**, you do it by yourself, without help from anyone else. If you are **on** your **tod**, you are alone. *Oliver knows it's odds against me picking up his trail on my tod.*

♦ This expression comes from Cockney rhyming slang 'on your Tod Sloan' meaning 'on your own'. Tod Sloan was a famous American jockey at the beginning of the 20th century.

toe

a toe in the water

If you dip your **toe in the water**, you start slowly and carefully doing something that you have not done before, because you are not sure if you will like it or if it will be successful. This expression is used more commonly in British English than American. *Recently, judges have been encouraged to dip a cautious toe into the waters of public debate.*

toe to toe

Mainly American If you go or stand **toe to toe** with someone, you fight, argue, or compete with them fiercely, openly, and directly. *The company might seem to be strong enough to go toe-to-toe with their rivals. But Borden has no such intentions.*

toes

keep you on your toes

If you say that someone or something **keeps** you **on** your **toes**, you mean that they cause you or force you to be alert and ready for anything that might happen. *She kept us on our toes right from the moment she took command.*

make your toes curl

If something **makes** your **toes curl**, you react to it very strongly, and, for example, find it very embarrassing or very exciting. *He reminds us of every time our toes curled in the past watching TV presenters making idiotic comments or squirm-inducing jokes.*

□ You can also talk about a **toe-curling** experience. *Movies about famous explorers rarely work, as some recent toe-curling efforts show.*

step on someone's toes
tread on someone's toes

If you **step on** someone's **toes** or **tread on** their **toes**, you offend them by criticizing the way they do something or by interfering in something that is their responsibility. *'Small shopkeepers know who sells what,'* Sue explains, *'and so you don't step on one another's toes.'*

turn up your toes

British If you say that someone or something **turns up** their **toes**, you mean that they die. This expression is used to refer to death in a light-hearted or humorous way. *She gives birth to an alarmingly ugly baby boy which must have made Keaton regret not turning up his toes a darn sight earlier.*

toffee

can't do something for toffee

British If you say, for example, that you **can't** dance **for toffee** or you **can't** sing **for toffee**, you are emphasizing that you are very bad at dancing or singing. *We set off, and within a step or two it was clear she couldn't dance for toffee; she was as rigid as a telegraph pole and quite unwilling to be led.*

Tom

every Tom, Dick, and Harry

The expression **every Tom, Dick, and Harry** is used to refer informally or scornfully to ordinary people who do not have any special skills or qualities. *You cannot sell a gun to any Tom Dick or Harry, can you? It's very difficult to obtain a legally held gun.*

◆ All of these names used to be very common, and so they began to be used to refer to ordinary people in general.

ton

come down on someone like a ton of bricks
If you do something wrong and someone with authority **comes down on** you **like a ton of bricks**, they reprimand or punish you very severely. *If I owed them any money, they'd be down on me like a ton of bricks.*

like a ton of bricks
Like a ton of bricks is used to indicate that something happens very suddenly and dramatically. For example, if something hits you **like a ton of bricks**, you suddenly become aware of it. If you fall for someone **like a ton of bricks**, you fall suddenly and very deeply in love with them. *She was twenty when Orpen met her and he fell for her like a ton of bricks.*

tongue

bite your tongue
hold your tongue
If you **bite** your **tongue** or **hold** your **tongue**, you do not say a particular thing, even though you want to or are expected to, because it would be the wrong thing to say in the circumstances, or because you are waiting for a more appropriate time to speak. *I'm perfectly prepared to bite my tongue until I've learned what the system is all about. Then when I've got something to contribute, they will hear from me... Douglas held his tongue, preferring not to speak out on a politically sensitive issue he felt was best left to politicians.*

find your tongue
If you **find** your **tongue**, you begin to talk, when you have previously been too shy, frightened, or embarrassed to say anything. *After a pause in which the gallery's distinguished visitor seemed lost for words, he eventually found his tongue.*

get your tongue round something
British If you say that you cannot **get** your **tongue round** a word or phrase, you mean that you find it difficult to pronounce. *The Americans are as notorious as the British for their inability to get their tongues around foreign words.*

give someone the rough side of your tongue
give someone the rough edge of your tongue

British, old-fashioned If you **give** someone **the rough side of** your
tongue or **the rough edge of** your **tongue**, you speak angrily or harshly
to them about something that they have done wrong. *He's really going to
give the boy the rough side of his tongue.*

speak with forked tongue

If you accuse someone of **speaking with forked tongue**, you are
accusing them of lying or of deliberately misleading people. *He speaks with
forked tongue. I don't trust him and I don't like him.*

tongue in cheek

If you describe a remark or piece of writing as **tongue in cheek**, you
mean that it is meant to be funny and ironic, and is not meant to be taken
seriously. You can also say that someone is talking or writing **with
tongue in cheek**. *I think people are taking all this more seriously than we
intended. It was supposed to be tongue in cheek... We ran that ad just one
time and it was meant to be a light-hearted, tongue-in-cheek approach. We
never intended to offend anyone.*

tongues

tongues are wagging

If you say that **tongues are wagging**, you mean that people are
gossiping as a result of someone's behaviour. *They spent an evening
together at his Knightsbridge flat. He said they played bridge but added: 'No
doubt tongues will be wagging.'*

tooth

fight tooth and nail
fight tooth and claw

If you **fight tooth and nail** or **fight tooth and claw** for something, you
make a determined effort to keep it or get it, when other people are trying
to take it away from you or prevent you from having it. *Our autonomous
republics are fighting tooth and nail to preserve their special status.*

□ If you **fight** something **tooth and nail** or **tooth and claw**, you make a
determined effort to stop it. *As a member of the council I fought the
proposal tooth and claw.*

long in the tooth

If you describe someone as **long in the tooth**, you mean that they are getting old. If you describe something such as a machine or system as **long in the tooth**, you mean that it is old and outdated and should be replaced. This expression is sometimes used light-heartedly about a person or thing that is not really old at all. *'Why don't you enrol in the University and take a proper course?' 'Aren't I a bit long in the tooth to start being an undergraduate?'*

◆ This expression refers to the fact that you can judge the age of a horse by looking at its teeth. As horses get older, their teeth look longer because their gums are receding.

red in tooth and claw
nature red in tooth and claw

If you describe something as **red in tooth and claw**, you mean that it involves competitive and ruthless behaviour. *My wife and I both now work for companies that are red in tooth and claw.*

☐ People sometimes talk about **nature red in tooth and claw** when they are describing the way wild creatures hunt and kill each other for food. *We had left orderly Canberra with its just-so boulevards and civic monuments and were heading into the bush to take on nature red in tooth and claw.*

◆ This is a quotation from the poem 'In Memoriam' (1850) by the English poet Alfred, Lord Tennyson. (Part 56, stanza 4)

a sweet tooth

If you have **a sweet tooth**, you like eating things that are sugary or taste sweet. *The cream tea is especially authentic with its traditional fresh farmhouse clotted cream. For those without a sweet tooth, savoury snacks are also available.*

top

blow your top

If you **blow your top**, you become very angry with someone and shout at them. *I never asked personal questions because she'd always blow her top.*

over the top: 1
OTT

If you describe something as **over the top**, you are being critical of it because you think it is extreme and exaggerated. *Perhaps I was a bit over the top, accusing you at the inquiry of being a traitor.*

☐ In British English, you can also use the abbreviation **OTT**. *Each design* *is very different in style. Some are subtle, some gloriously OTT.*

◆ During the First World War, 'to go over the top' meant to climb out of the trenches and run into no-man's land in order to attack the enemy.

over the top: 2

   American In a competition or contest, if something puts someone **over the top**, it results in them winning. *The Pepsi Challenge had pushed us over the top, allowing us to unseat Coke as the number-one soft drink in supermarkets.*

torch

◆ The torch referred to in these expressions is a long stick with burning material at one end which provides a light. This kind of torch is sometimes used in processions or parades.

carry a torch for someone

   If you **carry a torch for** someone, you are in love with them but they do not love you or they are already involved with another person. *What makes a woman so special that a man will carry a torch for her all his life?*

carry the torch

   If you **carry the torch** for something such as a political party or a particular belief, you support it very strongly and try to persuade other people to support it too. *This group aims to carry the torch for the millions of people who demonstrated and the thousands who died.*

toss

argue the toss

   British If someone **argues the toss**, they waste their time by arguing about something which is not important or which cannot be changed anyway. *Anyway, while London and Paris were still arguing the toss, the whole situation changed.*

◆ This may refer to someone tossing a coin in the air in order to reach a decision.

not give a toss

   If you say that you **don't give a toss** about something, you mean that you do not care about it at all. Some people find this expression offensive. *'We couldn't give a toss what journalists think,' says Dave Chambers, Cornershop's drummer.*

◆ In this expression, 'toss' comes from a slang word meaning to masturbate.

toss-up

be a toss-up

If two or more courses of action seem equally likely to succeed or fail, you can say **it's a toss-up** which one you choose. Similarly, if two or more things are equally likely to happen, you can say **it's a toss-up** which one will happen. *Some said it's a toss-up whether oil prices will go up or down over the days ahead.*

◆ When you toss a coin, there is an equal chance that the coin will land heads or tails.

touch

the common touch

If you say that someone in a position of power has **the common touch**, you mean that they understand how ordinary people think and feel, and that they are able to communicate well with them. *The Bishop is said to have the common touch but his left-of-centre political views are said to weigh against him.*

kick something into touch

Mainly British If you **kick** something **into touch**, you reject it or postpone it. *She kicked the booze into touch, came back from the brink and emerged a whole person again.*

◆ In rugby football, when the ball is kicked into touch it is kicked over one of the boundary lines along each side of the pitch.

a soft touch
an easy touch

If you say that someone is **a soft touch** or **an easy touch**, you mean that it is easy to make them do what you want or agree with you. *He did not get where he is today by being either a soft touch or a poor judge of his core businesses.*

◆ To touch a person for money means to approach them and persuade them to let you have some money as a loan or a gift.

touch and go

If you say it is **touch and go** whether something will happen, you mean that you cannot be certain whether it will happen or not. *I thought I was* *going to win the race, but it was still touch and go.*

touch paper

light the blue touch paper
light the touch paper

   British If you say that someone **lights the blue touch paper** or **lights the touch paper**, you mean that they do something which causes other people to react in an angry or aggressive way. *This kind of remark is guaranteed to light the blue touch paper with some Labour politicians.*

◆ The touch paper on a firework is a small piece of dark blue paper attached to one end. When it is lit, it burns slowly until it sets off the firework.

tough

tough as old boots
tough as nails

   If you say that someone is **tough as old boots** or **tough as nails**, you are emphasizing that they have a strong and independent character. 'Tough as old boots' is only used in British English. *Barbara is tough as old boots and rules her husband with an iron hand... This man was a very easy-going type of person in a large group, but across a negotiating table was just tough as nails.*

towel

throw in the towel
throw in the sponge

   If someone **throws in the towel**, they stop trying to do something, because they know that they cannot succeed. Verbs such as 'chuck' and 'toss' are sometimes used instead of 'throw'. *One day I will be brave enough (or fed up enough) to chuck in the towel and start again.*

☐ You can also say that someone **throws in the sponge**. This expression is used mainly in British English. *You're not the kind of man who throws in the sponge. You're a fighter and it's your fighting spirit which is ultimately going to save you.*

◆ In boxing, a fighter's trainer sometimes throws a towel or sponge into the ring as a signal of defeat in order to stop the fight before there are any more injuries.

tower

a tower of strength
a pillar of strength

If you say that someone was **a tower of strength** during a difficult period in your life, you mean that they gave you a lot of help or support and you are very grateful to them for this. You can also say that they were **a pillar of strength**. *My eldest daughter, Therese, who's six, was a tower of strength for me then. When I was sick she would clean up after me and look after the other kids.*

town

go to town

If you say that someone **goes to town** on something or someone, you mean that they deal with them with a lot of enthusiasm or energy. *You could really go to town and give her a night at the Sheraton at the Mother's Day rate of $120.*

paint the town red

If you **paint the town red**, you go out and enjoy yourself. *Preparing yourself to paint the town red on a Saturday night just doesn't have the same buzz without a suitable soundtrack to help you shower down, zip up and step out.*

♦ This expression is said to have originated in the Wild West. It may have been used to describe groups of Native Americans setting fire to towns. Another possibility is that it referred to cowboys threatening to 'paint the town red' with the blood of anyone who tried to stop their drunken behaviour.

traces

kick over the traces

If someone **kicks over the traces**, they pay no attention to rules and conventions and behave exactly as they want to. *Harry had kicked over the traces when his father died, and quit going to church.*

♦ When a horse pulling a cart or carriage kicks over the traces, it steps over the side straps attached to its harness, so it can no longer be controlled effectively by the driver.

track

the fast track

The fast track to something is the quickest way of achieving it. If you are on **the fast track** to a particular goal or state, you are likely to achieve it very soon or very easily. *Like many of his classmates, Chris Urwin believes a university degree will be his passport to the fast track into a company.*

□ You can also talk about a **fast-track** approach to something or a **fast-track** way of achieving something. *They offer fast-track promotion schemes for promising young executives.*

have the inside track

Mainly American If you say that someone **has the inside track**, you mean that they have an advantage, for example special knowledge about something. *Denver has the inside track among 10 sites being considered for the airline's new $1 billion maintenance facility.*

◆ On a racing track, the inside track is the shortest, and so the competitors want to use it in order to take advantage of this fact.

off the beaten track
off the beaten path

If a place is **off the beaten track**, it is isolated and quiet, because it is far from large cities or their centres, and so few people go there or live there. In American English, you can also say that a place is **off the beaten path**. *The house is sufficiently off the beaten track to deter all but a few tourists.*

on the right track

If you are **on the right track**, you are acting or progressing in a way that is likely to result in success. *We are finding that guests for lunch and dinner are returning in increasing numbers – a sure sign that we are on the right track.*

on the wrong track

If you are **on the wrong track**, you are acting or progressing in a way that is likely to result in failure. *The standard of careers advice given to school-leavers is generally appalling, setting us off on the wrong track from the start.*

a track record

If you talk about the **track record** of a person, company, or product, you are referring to the reputation they have, which is based on all their successes and failures in the past. *The region is known to have a poor track record in research.*

◆ An athlete's track record is a record of the performances he or she has achieved.

tracks

cover your tracks

If someone **covers** their **tracks**, they hide or destroy evidence of their identity or actions, because they want to keep them secret. *The killer may have returned to the scene of the crime to cover his tracks.*

from the wrong side of the tracks

If you say that someone comes **from the wrong side of the tracks**, you mean that they come from a poor, unfashionable, and lower-class area of town. *I know kids back home who come from the wrong side of the tracks. When they go to school, they haven't eaten and their clothes are all torn.*

◆ Railway tracks sometimes mark boundaries between different parts of a town, for example between richer and poorer areas.

make tracks

If you **make tracks**, you leave the place where you are, usually in a hurry. *Webb looked at the bar clock. 'Ten past nine. We might as well be making tracks.'*

stop someone in their tracks: 1
stop in your tracks

If something **stops** you **in** your **tracks** or if you **stop in** your **tracks**, you suddenly stop moving or doing something because you are very surprised, impressed, or frightened. *They stopped in their tracks and stared at him in amazement... We wandered over to the first glass case. When I saw its contents I stopped in my tracks.*

stop something in its tracks: 2
stop something dead in its tracks

If someone or something **stops** a process or activity **in** its **tracks** or **stops** it **dead in** its **tracks**, they make it immediately stop continuing or developing. *Francis felt he would like to stop this conversation in its tracks. He wished neither to confirm nor deny Cosmo's suspicions.*

trail

blaze a trail

If you say that someone **is blazing a trail**, you mean that they are the first person to do or discover something new and important, and this will make it easier for other people to do the same thing. *The party is blazing the trail for the advancement of women in politics.*

□ You can use **trail-blazing** to describe someone who does something new and important or you can refer to them as **a trail-blazer**. You can also describe what they do as **trail-blazing** or refer to it as **a trail-blazer**. *This trail-blazing study went into immense detail on the habits of pub-goers.*

◆ New trails or routes through forests were often marked by 'blazing', which involved making white marks called 'blazes' on tree trunks, usually by chipping off a piece of bark.

trap

fall into the trap

If someone **falls into the trap** of doing something, they make a very common mistake, or one that is very easy to make. *Many of the world's economies were falling into the same trap as Australia in trying to boost their economy through increased government spending.*

tree

bark up the wrong tree

If you say that someone **is barking up the wrong tree**, you mean that they are following the wrong course of action because their beliefs or ideas about something are incorrect. *Scientists in Switzerland realised that most other researchers had been barking up the wrong tree.*

out of your tree

If you say that someone is **out of** their **tree**, you mean that they are crazy or behaving very strangely, perhaps because of alcohol or drugs. *It was obvious they were on something dodgy. They were both out of their tree.*

the top of the tree

British If you say that someone is at **the top of the tree** or is **top of the tree**, you mean that they have reached the highest level in their career or profession. *She has been at the top of the acting tree for 35 years... As a cricketer he is top of the tree.*

trees

not grow on trees

Mainly British If you say that people or things of a particular kind **do not grow on trees**, you are emphasizing that they are very difficult to obtain. *Mitchell could not be replaced in a hurry: agents with his expertise did not grow on trees.*

☐ When people talk about money **growing on trees**, they are talking about situations in which it is possible to obtain or earn large amounts of money. *The merchant bank was purchased in 1987 for £777 million in hard cash at a time when money was growing on trees.*

not see the wood for the trees
not see the forest for the trees

If you say that someone **can't see the wood for the trees**, you mean that they are so involved in the details of something that they forget or do not realize the real purpose or importance of the thing as a whole. This form of the expression is used in British English; in American English, the form is **not see the forest for the trees**. *His fairness and clarity of vision often helped those who could not see the wood for the trees reach the correct decision… Colonel Vardagas accused congressmen of looking at the problem simplistically. 'They failed to see the forest for the trees,' he said.*

trial

a trial balloon

Mainly American **A trial balloon** is an idea or plan which is suggested in order to find out about public opinions on a controversial subject. *It's hard to say what's a trial balloon and what is a policy in a process of being formed.*

♦ Balloons were formerly used to find out about weather conditions.

trick

do the trick

If something **does the trick**, it achieves what you want. *If these self-help remedies don't do the trick, consult a qualified homoeopath.*

every trick in the book

If you say that someone uses **every trick in the book**, you mean that they do everything they can think of in order to succeed in something. *Companies are using every trick in the book to stay one step in front of their competitors.*

not miss a trick

If you say that someone **does not miss a trick**, you mean that they always know what is happening and take advantage of every situation. *When it comes to integrating their transport systems, the French don't miss a trick.*

♦ The reference here is to a player winning every trick in a card game such as whist or bridge.

the oldest trick in the book

If someone has done something deceitful, dishonest, or unfair and you

describe it as **the oldest trick in the book,** you mean that people should
have expected it because it is a very common or obvious thing to do. *Well,
that's the oldest trick in the book – to blame someone else for your problems.*

tricks

up to your tricks
up to your old tricks

If you say that someone is **up to** their **tricks** or **up to** their **old tricks,**
you mean that they are behaving in a deceitful, dishonest, or foolish way
which is typical of them. *They seemed to be up to their old tricks of
promising one thing and doing the opposite.*

trim

in fighting trim

Mainly American If someone or something is **in fighting trim,** they are
in very good condition. *They argue that it isn't doing much to get Air
France into fighting trim for the 1990s, when domestic competition may
increase.*

◆ A boxer who is in fighting trim is fit and ready to fight.

trolley

off your trolley

British If you say that someone is **off** their **trolley,** you are saying in a
light-hearted way that you think they are crazy or very foolish. *If they
think officers are going to give up their cars, they're off their trolley.*

trowel

lay it on with a trowel

British If you say that someone **is laying it on with a trowel,** you mean
that they are exaggerating a statement, experience, or emotion, in order
to impress people. *There must have been some moments of comfort. Mr
Harris skips them and lays on the squalor with a trowel.*

truck

have no truck with something

If you **have no truck with** something or someone, you strongly
disapprove of them and refuse to become involved with them. *As an
American, she had no truck with the painful formality of English life.*

♦ 'Truck' is an old term which referred to trading goods by bartering. 'To have no truck with someone' literally means to have no dealings with them.

trump

a trump card
play your trump card
   Someone's **trump card** is something which gives them a decisive advantage over other people. You can say that someone holds **the trump card** when they have an advantage like this. If someone **plays** their **trump card**, they do something unexpected which gives them a decisive advantage over other people. *After only two days, the distribution of goods was suffering: and that, ultimately is the railwaymen's trump card... If she wished, she could threaten to play her trump card, an autobiography of embarrassing disclosures.*

♦ In card games such as whist and bridge, one of the four suits is chosen as trumps for each hand. Cards of that suit then rank higher than cards of the other three suits.

trumpet

blow your own trumpet
   British If you accuse someone of **blowing** their **own trumpet**, you are criticizing them for boasting about themselves. The American expression is **blow** your **own horn**. *The three candidates traded insults and blew their own trumpets yesterday as each one claimed to be heading for victory.*

□ You might say **'I'm not blowing my own trumpet'** when you are reporting something good about yourself but do not want other people to think you are boastful or vain. *I am not blowing my own trumpet but I can claim I work a lot quicker than a lot of people.*

♦ In the past, the arrival of important people in a place was announced by the playing of trumpets.

trumps

come up trumps: 1
   British If you say that someone **has come up trumps**, you mean that they have achieved an unexpectedly good result. *Sylvester Stallone has come up trumps at the US box office with his new movie Cliffhanger.*

come up trumps: 2
turn up trumps

British If you say that people or events **come up trumps** or **turn up trumps**, you mean that they unexpectedly help you with your problems. *Much of this luck will come from an unexpected direction. The most unlikely people or events will come up trumps... In moments of crisis for me, you always turn up trumps!*

◆ In card games such as whist and bridge, one of the four suits is chosen as trumps for each hand. Cards of that suit then rank higher than cards of the other three suits. The reference here is to a player drawing a trump from the pack.

tub

tub-thumping
thump the tub

British **Tub-thumping** is used to describe people's attitudes or behaviour when they are supporting an idea or course of action in a very vigorous and sometimes aggressive way. This expression is usually used to show disapproval of this kind of behaviour. *Conservatives know they still have a lot of hard work to do and the Environment Secretary rammed home their tax message in a tub-thumping speech.*

□ You can refer to someone who behaves in this way as **a tub-thumper**. *Marsh was far from being a woolly-minded idealist and tub-thumper.*

□ You can also say that someone **is thumping the tub**.

◆ People sometimes used to refer to pulpits as 'tubs', especially when talking humorously about nonconformist preachers. The image is of a preacher banging the pulpit with his fist to emphasize his message.

tune

call the tune

If someone **calls the tune**, they are in control of a situation and make all the important decisions. *The government will thus reduce this country to one in which the claims of business, commerce and technology will call the tune.*

◆ This expression comes from the proverb **he who pays the piper calls the tune**: see **piper**.

change your tune

If someone **changes** their **tune**, they express a different opinion about something from the one they had expressed previously, or they show a completely different attitude to something or someone. *He had maintained for many years that the Earl was dead. But these days he has changed his tune.*

dance to someone's tune

If you **dance to** someone else's **tune**, you do whatever they want or tell you to do, usually without challenging them or hesitating. This expression is often used to criticize someone for allowing themselves to be controlled in this way. *I know the cathedral is desperate for money and has to raise cash somehow. But the danger of commercialism is that the churches end up dancing to the tune of their big business sponsors.*

□ You can also say that someone **is dancing to** a particular **tune** when they are behaving in a particular way, especially if this is different from the way they were behaving before. *With different circumstances in Germany and Britain, we cannot dance to the same tune.*

tunnel

tunnel vision

If you accuse someone of **tunnel vision**, you are accusing them of focusing all their energy and skill on the task which is most important to them and ignoring things that other people might consider important. *The implication of his letter is that only perfect human beings should be allowed to live in dignity in the community and gain self-respect. Such tunnel-vision appals me... The experts sometimes have a bureaucratic, tunnel-vision view of their mission.*

□ This expression can also be used to express admiration for someone who has achieved a lot by concentrating on a single thing. *They always say that you have to have tunnel vision to be a champion. You can't have any outside distractions at all.*

◆ Tunnel vision is a medical condition in which someone can only see things that are immediately in front of them, and cannot see things that are to the side.

turkey

talk turkey

Mainly American If people **talk turkey**, they discuss something in a frank and serious way. *Suddenly government and industry are talking turkey. Last month the Prime Minister promised a partnership to improve* *the climate for business.*

◆ This expression is said to have its origin in an American story about a white man who went hunting with a Native American. They caught several wild turkeys and some other birds. After the trip the white man divided the birds unfairly, keeping the turkeys for himself and giving the Native American the less tasty birds. The Native American protested, saying he wanted to 'talk turkey'.

a turkey shoot

If someone refers to a battle or other conflict as **a turkey shoot**, they mean that one side is so much stronger or better armed than the other that the weaker side has no chance at all. This expression is usually used to suggest that the situation is unfair. *After weeks of bombing, it was a one-sided battle. The fighting stopped earlier than expected partly because of public disquiet at the 'turkey-shoot'.*

◆ A turkey shoot is an occasion when people hunt turkeys, which are very easy to shoot.

turkeys

like turkeys voting for Christmas

Mainly British If you say that someone choosing to do a particular thing would be **like turkeys voting for Christmas**, you are emphasizing that they are very unlikely to do it because it would very obviously be bad for them. *To expect Lloyd's workers to vote against the status quo would be like expecting turkeys to vote for Christmas.*

◆ In Britain and some other countries, people traditionally eat turkey at Christmas.

turn

at every turn

If something happens **at every turn**, it happens very frequently or continuously, and usually prevents you from doing what you want to do. *Although the government has had a coherent economic plan, parliament has set out to block it at every turn.*

turn-up

a turn-up for the books
a turn-up

British If you say that something is **a turn-up for the books**, you mean that it is very surprising and unexpected, and usually very pleasing. You can also just say that something is **a turn-up**. *How about that for a turn-up for the books? I knew nothing about it, I can tell you.*

♦ The reference here is to a horse that unexpectedly wins a race. The 'books' are the bookmakers' records of the bets taken on the race.

turtle

turn turtle

If a boat **turns turtle**, it turns upside down when it is in the water. *The voyage took six months. The tug nearly turned turtle twice, but I managed to keep her upright.*

♦ Turtles are helpless when they are turned onto their backs.

twain

never the twain shall meet

People say **'never the twain shall meet'** when they believe that there are so many differences between two groups of people or two groups of things that they can never exist together in the same place or situation. People also say **'ne'er the twain shall meet'**. *The British education system is notorious for separating the sciences and the humanities. This academic 'ne'er the twain shall meet' policy unfortunately does not always reflect the requirements of the real world.*

□ People often vary this expression. For example, they say that **the twain do meet** or **the twain are not supposed to meet**. *Although they recognised differences and that East is east and West is west, they would have gone on to argue not that the twain shall never meet but that the two should and must meet.*

♦ 'Twain' is an old-fashioned word meaning two. This is a quotation from 'The Ballad of East and West' (1889) by the English poet Rudyard Kipling: 'Oh, East is East, and West is West, and never the twain shall meet.'

twist

round the twist

British If you say that someone is **round the twist**, you mean that their ideas or behaviour are very strange or foolish. *You would have to be really round the twist to get pleasure out of this.*

two

put two and two together

If you **put two and two together**, you correctly guess the truth about something from the information that you have. You can replace 'put' with 'add'. *He never came out and said, 'I am Jewish', but after a period of time, I put two and two together, and I assumed he was.*

☐ If you say that someone **puts two and two together and makes five**, you mean that they reach the wrong conclusion about something. *Mr Lane's solicitor said after the case that police put two and two together and made five.*

U

unglued

come unglued: 1

American If you say that someone **has come unglued**, you mean that they have lost control of their emotions and are behaving in a strange or crazy way. *She had apparently come unglued since losing her job as social columnist for Western Gentry magazine.*

come unglued: 2

American If someone or something **comes unglued**, they fail. The British expression is **come unstuck**. *Their marriage finally came unglued. Much of his behaviour had become unacceptable to her, and she had withdrawn more and more into herself.*

unstuck

come unstuck

British If someone or something **comes unstuck**, they fail. The American expression is **come unglued**. *Australia's Greg Norman came badly unstuck in the third round of the Memorial golf tournament yesterday.*

up

on the up
on the up and up

British If someone or something is **on the up**, they are becoming very successful and doing well. You can also say that they are **on the up and up**. *I was pretty depressed sometimes at Dundee, but I never reached rock bottom. Now things are on the up.*

on the up and up

Mainly American To be **on the up and up** means to be honest or legal. *We'd like to know where the money came from. It may have been on the up-and-up. He was a frugal type, and he hit the lottery for twenty grand a while back.*

swear up and down

American If someone **swears up and down** that something is true, they insist that they are telling you the truth, even though you are not sure whether or not to believe them. The usual British expression is **swear blind**. *He'd sworn up and down he was going to get the cash and bring it right back.*

up and coming

An **up and coming** person is someone who is likely to be successful in the future. *Beaton wants to help build up the pioneering 198 Gallery in Brixton which regularly exhibits up and coming artists.*

up and running

If a system, business, or plan is **up and running**, it has started well and is working or functioning successfully. *We've invested in the people, tools, and technology to get your system up and running quickly and keep it that way.*

uppers

on your uppers
down on your uppers

British If you say that a person or a company is **on their uppers** or **down on their uppers**, you mean that they have very little money. *The company is on its uppers and shareholders can forget about receiving dividends for a couple of years.*

◆ The upper of a shoe is the top part of it, which is attached to the sole and heel. If you are on your uppers, you have worn through the sole and heel.

upstairs

kick someone upstairs

British If someone **is kicked upstairs**, they are given a job or position which appears to have a higher status but actually has less power or influence. *The radicals kicked him upstairs to the then ceremonial job of president.*

V

vacuum

in a vacuum

If something exists or happens **in a vacuum**, it seems to exist or happen separately from the things that you would expect it to be connected with. *Property values do not exist in a vacuum. The market value of a well-maintained property can fall if the biggest employer in town closes or an all-night service station opens next door.*

variety

variety is the spice of life

If you say that **variety is the spice of life**, you are pointing out that doing and seeing a lot of different things makes life more enjoyable and interesting. *It is important to vary the training program so that boredom is avoided. Exercise should be fun and variety is the spice of life.*

◆ This proverb may come from 'The Task' (1785) by the English poet William Cowper: 'Variety's the very spice of life That gives it all its flavour.'

veil

draw a veil over something

If you **draw a veil over** something, you deliberately do not talk about it or give any details, because you want to keep it private or because it is embarrassing. *It would be kinder, perhaps, to draw a veil over the party's career from 1906 to the outbreak of the War.*

vessels

empty vessels make the most sound
empty vessels make the most noise

Old-fashioned People say **'empty vessels make the most sound'** or **'empty vessels make the most noise'** to point out that people who talk a lot about their knowledge, talent, or experience are often not as knowledgeable, talented, or experienced as they claim to be. *There's a lot of truth in that old saying, 'Empty vessels make the most sound'. Those who are actually content with their choices are not usually interested in evangelising to the rest of us.*

vest

play your cards close to the vest

American If you **play** your **cards close to the vest**, you do not tell anyone about your plans or thoughts. *He plays his cards very close to the vest, leaving some attorneys with whom he's worked to describe him as secretive and manipulative.*

☐ 'Cards' is often replaced with other nouns. *The military's playing this whole operation pretty close to the vest – they generally don't like to talk about future operations.*

◆ In American English, a vest is a waistcoat. This is a reference to card-players holding their cards close to their chest so that nobody else can see them.

view

a bird's-eye view

If you have **a bird's-eye view** of a situation, you are able to form a clear impression of what is happening. Compare **a worm's eye view**. *Before I left England, I was a parliamentary lobby correspondent, getting a bird's eye view of the way politicians encourage people to believe in dreams.*

☐ People often change 'bird' to a word that is relevant to what they are talking about. *He has a child's eye view of the war based on his own experiences.*

◆ The expression 'a bird's-eye view' is more commonly used to indicate that someone who is looking down from a great height gets a clear view of everything below them.

a worm's eye view

If you say that someone has **a worm's eye view** of something, you mean that they are able to form an impression of what is happening in a situation, but that they have a low status, or are considered inferior in some way. Compare **a bird's-eye view**. *Let me offer, then, a worm's eye view of what Thatcherism was, and what its legacy may be.*

◆ This expression can also be used to indicate that something can be seen from very low on the ground, or from below the ground.

villain

the villain of the piece

British If you describe someone as **the villain of the piece**, you mean that they are responsible for all the trouble or all the problems in a situation. *The real villains of the piece are the motor manufacturers. In a country where the top speed limit is 70mph, why do they make 140mph cars?*

◆ In this expression, the 'piece' is a play.

vine

wither on the vine
die on the vine

If something **withers on the vine**, it dies or comes to an end because people show no enthusiasm for it or deliberately ignore it. You can also say that something **dies on the vine**. *The chance to make peace certainly exists, and has seldom been riper, but could still wither on the vine.*

violet

no shrinking violet

If you say that someone is **no shrinking violet**, you mean that they are very self-confident. *Amber is no shrinking violet. She is a brash colourful character.*

◆ In the past, violets were considered to be a symbol of modesty, because of their small size and the fact that the flowers remain hidden among the leaves until they open.

volumes

speak volumes

If you say that something **speaks volumes**, you mean that it reveals or implies a lot about a situation. *What you wear speaks volumes.*

◆ In this expression, a 'volume' is a book.

W

wagon

hitch your wagon to someone
hitch your wagon to a star

If someone **hitches** their **wagon** to a particular person or policy, they try to become more successful by forming a relationship with someone who is already successful. You can also say that they **hitch** their **wagon to a star**. *The increasing power of the Pacific rim provides a reason why Russia should not hitch its wagon too closely to America... Giammetti had the good fortune to hitch his wagon to a brilliant star – one that, without him, might just as easily have fallen as risen.*

♦ This is a quotation from the essay 'Civilization' (1870) by the American writer Ralph Waldo Emerson: 'Now that is the wisdom of a man, in every instance of his labor, to hitch his wagon to a star, and see his chore done by the gods themselves.'

on the wagon
fall off the wagon

If someone is **on the wagon**, they have given up drinking alcohol. You can say that someone **has fallen off the wagon** when they have begun to drink alcohol again after a period of not drinking it. *I'm on the wagon for a while. Cleaning out my system... He has finally fallen off the wagon after 12 long, dry years.*

♦ Originally the expression was 'on the water wagon' or 'water cart'. Water carts were horse-drawn carts used for transporting water or for sprinkling the streets. If someone was 'on the wagon', they were drinking water and not alcohol.

wagons

circle the wagons
pull your wagons in a circle

If a group of people who are in difficulty or danger **circle the wagons**, they unite in order to protect themselves and fight whoever is attacking them. You can also say that people **pull** their **wagons in a circle**. *Some African-Americans who initially opposed Thomas because of his politics are circling the wagons to support him because of his race... When the overall budget shrinks, the services, by and large, pull their wagons in a circle around the next generation of hardware programs.*

♦ According to some Wild West stories, when wagon trains were attacked by Native Americans, the settlers drove the wagons into a circle in order to defend themselves better.

wake

♦ The wake of a ship is the trail of white foaming water behind it.

in something's wake

You say that an event leaves an unpleasant situation **in** its **wake** when that situation happens after that event or is caused by it. *A deadly cloud of gas swept along the valleys north of Lake Nyos in western Cameroon, leaving a trail of death and devastation in its wake.*

in the wake of something

If an event, especially an unpleasant one, follows **in the wake of** a previous event, it happens after the earlier event, often as a result of it. *He remained in office until 1985 when he resigned in the wake of a row with the Socialist government.*

wake-up

a wake-up call

Mainly American You can refer to an event as **a wake-up call** when it shocks people into taking action about a difficult or dangerous situation. *The jury said the damages were intended to send a wake-up call to the firm and other big companies that sexual harassment would not be tolerated.*

♦ If you have a wake-up call, you arrange for someone to telephone you at a certain time in the morning so that you are sure to wake up at that time.

wall

bang your head against a brick wall
bang your head against a wall

If you say that you **are banging** your **head against a brick wall** or **banging** your **head against a wall**, you mean that you feel frustrated because someone is stopping you from making progress in what you are trying to do. 'Bang your head against a brick wall' is used mainly in British English. *I was left out of the side and stuck in the reserves with no chance of playing for the first team again. I was banging my head against a brick wall.*

come up against a brick wall

If you say that you **have come up against a brick wall**, you mean that something is stopping you from doing what you want and preventing you from making any progress. *I was tired, I had been working real hard for a long time and I felt that I'd come up against a brick wall.*

drive someone up the wall

If you say that something or someone **is driving** you **up the wall**, you mean that they are annoying and irritating you a lot. *He's so bloody unco-operative he's beginning to drive me up the wall.*

go to the wall: 1

British If a person or company **goes to the wall**, they lose all their money and their business fails. *Over the last year, two football clubs have gone to the wall.*

go to the wall: 2

British If you are willing to **go to the wall** for a person or a principle, you support them so strongly that you are prepared to suffer on their behalf. *Above all, he prizes loyalty. He'll go to the wall for someone or something he believes in.*

◆ One explanation for this expression is that it refers to someone who is trapped with their back to a wall and no way of escape. Another explanation is that it refers to medieval chapels in which healthy people used to stand, but which had seats around the walls for sick people. A third explanation is that it refers to someone standing in front of a wall before being executed by a firing squad.

hit the wall

If you **hit the wall** when you are trying to do something, you reach a point where you cannot go any further or achieve any more. *To ensure their businesses do not hit the wall, operators must ensure their financial management is strong and streamlined.*

nail someone to the wall

If someone **nails** you **to the wall**, they make you suffer, because they are very angry with you. *If he could not pay off his debt, they would nail him to the wall.*

off the wall

If you describe something or someone as **off the wall**, you mean that they are unusual, unconventional, or eccentric. You can use this expression both when you like this kind of person or thing, and when you do not like them. *The new channel is so off-the-wall and unlike anything we see at the moment that you really have to watch it to appreciate how it will be... At other times the band plays a kind of off-the-wall lounge music, a kind of soundtrack to a hip science fiction movie.*

◆ This may be a reference to a shot in a game such as squash or handball, where the ball bounces off the wall at an unexpected angle.

the writing is on the wall
the handwriting is on the wall

If you say that **the writing is on the wall** or **the handwriting is on the**

wall, you mean that you have noticed things which strongly suggest that a situation is going to become difficult or unpleasant. The form with 'writing' is used mainly in British English and the form with 'handwriting' is used mainly in American English. *The writing was on the wall for Capriati when she lost the first set 6– 1 in less than 20 minutes.*

◆ This expression comes from a Bible story in which a mysterious hand appears and writes a message on the wall, announcing that Belshazzar's kingdom will soon come to an end. (Daniel 5)

walls

climb the walls
If you say that you **are climbing the walls**, you are emphasizing that you feel very frustrated, nervous, or anxious. *Sitting at home would only have had him climbing the walls with worry and frustration.*

walls have ears
You can say **'walls have ears'** in order to warn someone that they should be careful about what they are saying because people might be listening. *Take care. This place is like a village. Assume all walls have ears.*

war

a war of words
If two people or groups of people have **a war of words**, they argue or criticize each other because they strongly disagree about a particular issue. *This latest move signals an escalation in the three-year-old war of words between the two countries.*

warpath

on the warpath
If you say that someone is **on the warpath**, you mean that they are very angry and getting ready for a fight or quarrel. *St Vincent and Grenadines' biggest businessmen are on the warpath after claims that foreign nationals are trying to con them out of thousands of dollars.*

◆ Native Americans were said to be 'on the warpath' when they were on an expedition to attack their enemies. The warpath was the path or route that they took.

wars

in the wars
If you say that someone has been **in the wars**, you mean that they have

been hurt or injured. You usually use this expression in a fairly light-hearted way. *Charlotte's four-year-old brother, Ben, has also been in the wars. He is still in plaster after breaking a leg.*

warts

warts and all

If you describe or accept someone or something **warts and all**, you describe or accept them as they are, including all their faults. *'Jagger Unauthorised' is a sensational warts-and-all biography of the Rolling Stones' living legend.*

◆ The 17th century English leader Oliver Cromwell is said to have told an artist who was painting his portrait that he did not wish to be flattered: 'Remark all these roughnesses, pimples, warts, and everything as you see me, otherwise I will never pay a farthing for it.'

wash

come out in the wash: 1

If you say that something will **come out in the wash**, you mean that people will eventually find out the truth about it. *It will make great listening at an industrial tribunal. Everything will come out in the wash, and Flashman will deserve it all.*

come out in the wash: 2

You can say that everything will **come out in the wash** when you want to reassure someone that everything will be all right. *That will be the end of that. This will all come out in the wash – I promise you.*

watch

on someone's watch

American If something happens **on** someone's **watch**, it happens during a period when they are in a position of power, and are therefore considered to be responsible for it. *A leader is judged for what happens on his watch.*

◆ When someone such as a soldier is on watch, they have been ordered to remain alert, usually while others sleep, so that they can warn of danger or an attack.

water

blow something out of the water

If something **is blown out of the water**, it is destroyed completely, suddenly, and violently. *The government is in a state of paralysis. Its main economic and foreign policies have been blown out of the water.*

◆ The image here is of a ship which is completely destroyed by a missile or torpedo.

in deep water

If you are **in deep water**, you are in a difficult or awkward situation. *It's the same in any business that gets into deep water. As soon as it becomes known that some outfit's down on its luck, all the creditors send in their bills.*

in hot water

If you say that someone is **in hot water**, you mean that they have done something wrong and people are angry with them. *His forthright opinions have sometimes gotten him into hot water.*

like water off a duck's back

You can say that criticism is **like water off a duck's back** when it is not having any effect at all on the person being criticized. *Every time you discipline him he will smile sweetly so that you may think your rebukes are streaming away like water off a duck's back.*

◆ The feathers on a duck's back are covered with an oily substance which stops them absorbing water so that it flows straight off them.

not hold water

If you say that a theory or an argument **does not hold water**, you do not believe that it can possibly be true or right. You can say that a theory or an argument **holds water** when you think that it is true or right. *They make it clear that the British Government's argument does not hold water.*

of the first water

Fairly old-fashioned You can use **of the first water** after a noun to indicate that someone is very good at something or is an extreme example of something. *Best of all there's a performance by M-People, proving themselves to be entertainers of the first water.*

◆ The brilliance of a diamond is called its water. Diamonds 'of the first water' are of very high quality.

pour cold water on something

If someone **pours cold water on** an idea or plan, they point out all its problems, rather than sharing other people's enthusiasm for it. *During the session, the Bank of Japan tried to pour cold water on expectations of early interest rate cuts.*

talk under water

Mainly Australian If you say that someone can **talk under water**, you mean that they always talk a lot in any situation, and it is sometimes difficult to stop them talking. *My friends tell me that I can talk under water*.

test the water
test the waters

If you **test the water** or **test the waters**, you try to find out what the reaction to an idea or plan might be before taking action to put it into effect. *I was a bit sceptical. I decided to test the water before committing the complete management team*.

tread water

If you say that someone **is treading water**, you mean that they are in an unsatisfactory situation where they are not progressing, but are just continuing doing the same things. *I could either tread water until I was promoted, which looked to be a few years away, or I could change what I was doing*.

◆ When swimmers tread water, they move their arms and legs in order to keep their head above the water without actually making progress in any direction.

water under the bridge
water over the dam

You say that an event or situation is **water under the bridge** when you want to say that it happened in the past and so it is no longer worth thinking about or worrying about. In American English, you can also say that something is **water over the dam**. *'I am sorry that I did not go to the 1992 Olympics,' says Timmis, 'but that is water under the bridge.'*

□ You say things such as **'a lot of water has gone under the bridge'** when you want to say that a lot of time has passed or a lot of things have happened since the event that you are referring to. *It's almost two years since it happened. A lot of water has gone under the bridge but we're just about on speaking terms with Marcia*.

waterfront

cover the waterfront

Mainly American If you **cover the waterfront**, you cover a very wide range of things, or cover every aspect of something. *We have three partners and five employees looking after this whole category. They cover the entire* *waterfront: oil, real estate, high-tech, and everything else.*

Waterloo

meet your Waterloo

If you say that someone **meets** their **Waterloo**, you mean that they suffer a very severe defeat or failure, especially one which causes them to finally give up what they are trying to do. *At the foot of the fourth pinnacle I met my Waterloo. The face of the fifth pinnacle rose sheer above us, and it was evident even to me that we would not be attempting it.*

◆ In 1815, the French leader Napoleon suffered his final defeat at the Battle of Waterloo in Belgium.

waters

fish in troubled waters

If you say that someone **is fishing in troubled waters**, you mean that they are involved in a very difficult or delicate situation, which could cause them problems. *Mr Khan said firmly that Pakistan is not fishing in the troubled waters of Central Asia. 'It is not part of any of our policies,' he said, adding that the Central Asian region was far from Pakistan's borders.*

muddy the waters

If you accuse someone of **muddying the waters**, you mean that they are deliberately trying to make a situation or an issue more confusing and complicated than it really is. *'It's really difficult to see what they want,' said a Hong Kong source in London. 'They keep on muddying the waters by raising other political issues.'*

still waters run deep

People say **'still waters run deep'** when they are talking about someone who seems to be unemotional or who is hard to get to know, to suggest that they are in fact interesting and complex. *He's extremely shy and withdrawn, though it may be that still waters run very deep.*

wave

catch the wave

If someone **catches the wave**, they seize an opportunity that is presented to them, especially an opportunity to do something new. *With parliamentary elections still officially scheduled for October, politicians are hoping to catch the wave of rising discontent.*

◆ Surfers need to catch a wave just as it breaks in order to ride it successfully.

wavelength

on the same wavelength

If you say that two people are **on the same wavelength**, you mean that they understand each other well because they share the same attitudes, interests, and opinions. *Although I belonged to their children's generation I found myself very much on their wavelength, often exchanging friendly and amused glances with them.*

◆ A radio programme cannot be heard unless the radio is tuned to the correct wavelength.

waves

make waves

If you say that someone **is making waves**, you mean that they are disturbing a situation by changing things or by challenging the way things are done. You sometimes use this expression to suggest that this is making things better or more exciting. *They are part of the new breed of furniture makers who are starting to make waves on the British scene.*

way

pave the way

If one thing **paves the way** for another, the first thing makes it easier for the second to happen. *A peace agreement last year paved the way for this week's elections.*

rub someone up the wrong way
rub someone the wrong way

If you say that someone **rubs** you **up the wrong way**, you mean that you find them or their behaviour very annoying. This form of the expression is used in British English; in American English, the expression is **rub** you **the wrong way**. *Ella Armstrong had an uncommon knack of rubbing everyone up the wrong way... 'I'm surprised at you for acting like that.' 'I know, and I'm sorry. But that woman just rubbed me the wrong way.'*

◆ Cats do not like having their fur rubbed in the opposite direction to the way it naturally grows.

ways

cut both ways
cut two ways

If something **cuts both ways**, it has two different effects, usually one good and one bad. You can also say that something **cuts two ways**. *For Britain, the impact cuts both ways. The immediate effect of cheaper oil is to reduce North Sea oil revenue. But it also produces lower domestic inflation and stronger export markets.*

mend your ways

If someone **mends** their **ways**, they stop behaving badly or illegally and improve their behaviour. *He seemed to accept his sentence meekly, promising to work hard in prison and to mend his ways.*

wayside

fall by the wayside

If someone **has fallen by the wayside**, they have failed in something they were doing and have given up trying to achieve success in it. If an activity **has fallen by the wayside**, people have stopped doing it and forgotten about it. 'Way' is sometimes used instead of 'wayside'. *Thousands of new diets are dreamed up yearly; many fall by the wayside, but a few are sufficiently effective to become popular.*

◆ This expression comes from the story of the sower told by Jesus in the Bible. The seed which falls by the wayside and is eaten by birds represents the people who listen to what Jesus says, but are soon tempted by Satan and disregard what they have heard. (Mark 4:4)

wear

wear the trousers
wear the pants

The person in a couple who **wears the trousers** or **wears the pants** is the one who makes all the important decisions. This expression is usually used about women who seem to dominate their husbands or partners. 'Wear the trousers' is used only in British English. *She may give the impression that she wears the trousers but it's Tim who makes the final decisions.*

weather

keep a weather eye on something

British If you **keep a weather eye on** something or someone, you watch them carefully so that you are ready to take action when difficulties arise or anything goes wrong. *It is necessary always to keep a weather-eye on your symptoms and stay alert to the changes which occur.*

◆ This expression was originally used by sailors, who had to keep a constant watch on the weather and wind direction.

make heavy weather of something

British If you say that someone **is making heavy weather of** an activity or task, you are criticizing them for making it much more difficult or taking more time than it needs to. *To an outsider, though, the surprising thing is not that Spain's conservatives are inching ahead but that they are making such heavy weather of it.*

◆ Ships were said to make heavy weather when they handled badly and were difficult to control in rough seas.

under the weather

If you are feeling **under the weather**, you do not feel very well. *There are many things a child who is under the weather can do to stimulate his mind and imagination.*

web

a tangled web

If you refer to a situation as **a tangled web**, you mean that it is very confused and difficult to understand. *It is sometimes difficult to cut through the tangled web of government information in order to know the benefits you can claim.*

wedge

drive a wedge between people

If someone **drives a wedge between** two people who are close, they cause bad feelings between them in order to weaken their relationship. *I started to feel Toby was driving a wedge between us.*

the thin end of the wedge

British If you refer to something as **the thin end of the wedge**, you mean that it is the beginning of something which seems harmless or unimportant at present but is likely to become important, serious, or harmful in the future. *I think it's the thin end of the wedge when you have armed police permanently on patrol round a city.*

weight

carry the weight of the world on your shoulders

If you say that someone **is carrying the weight of the world on** their **shoulders**, you mean that they have very many troubles or responsibilities. *You look as if you're carrying the weight of the world on those lovely shoulders.*

◆ This expression may be a reference to Atlas, a giant in Greek mythology, who was punished by Zeus by being made to carry the heavens on his shoulders, and who is often portrayed with the world on his back.

a dead weight

If you talk about the **dead weight** of something, you are referring to the fact that it makes change or progress extremely difficult. *It's time for him to see that Labour must be free of the dead weight of union power.*

pull your weight

If someone **pulls** their **weight**, they work as hard as everyone else who is involved in the same task or activity. This expression is often used in negative structures to suggest that someone is not working as hard as everyone else. *You must remember that your performance will be judged by the performance of your team, and you cannot afford to carry members who are not pulling their weight.*

throw your weight around
throw your weight about

If you accuse someone of **throwing** their **weight around**, you are accusing them of behaving aggressively and of using their authority over other people more forcefully than they need to. In British English, you can also say that someone **is throwing** their **weight about**. *Some people regarded him as a bully who was inclined to throw his weight around.*

throw your weight behind something

If you **throw** your **weight behind** a person, plan, or campaign, you do everything you can to support them. *The U.S. government is promising now to throw its weight behind the peace negotiations.*

worth your weight in gold

If you say that someone or something is **worth** their **weight in gold**, you mean that they are very useful, helpful, or valuable. *Francine was* *turning out to be worth her weight in gold. Many things that Bill hadn't the heart for these days, she attended to cheerfully and responsibly.*

west

go west

Old-fashioned When someone **goes west**, they die. When something **goes west**, it stops existing or working. *His hopes of a professional singing career long ago went west.*

◆ The sun 'goes west' when it sinks below the horizon in the west at the end of the day. The comparison between going west and dying has been used in many different languages and cultures for many centuries. For example, people sometimes associate this expression with Native Americans, who used to say that a dying person went west to meet the sinking sun.

whale

have a whale of a time

If you say that someone **is having a whale of a time**, you are emphasizing that they are enjoying themselves a lot. *We were having a marvellous time, a whale of a time. We saw Edinburgh from top to bottom and had great fun.*

wheel

a big wheel

If you describe someone as **a big wheel** in an organization or society, you mean that they have an important and powerful position in it. *They flew Robin to New York, where George's uncle was a big wheel at Memorial Hospital.*

a fifth wheel
a third wheel

American If you describe someone as **a fifth wheel** in a situation, you mean that they are unwanted, unimportant, out of place, or superfluous. You can also describe them as **a third wheel**. *Women really do suffer more as widows. The fifth woman at a couples dinner party is a fifth wheel; the fifth man is a social coup.*

◆ A fifth wheel on a car or a third wheel on a bicycle would be unnecessary.

reinvent the wheel

If you say that someone **is reinventing the wheel**, you are criticizing them for working on an idea or project that they consider new or different, when it is really no better than something that already exists. *We have created foundations for other countries to follow. Each country's organization does not need to reinvent the wheel.*

☐ People sometimes use this expression when someone has got a new idea or project that does improve on the thing that already exists. *It is new territory for the industry. We are reinventing the wheel here, and there is likely to be a massive change.*

wheels

oil the wheels
grease the wheels

If someone or something **oils the wheels** or **greases the wheels** of a process or system, they help things to run smoothly and successfully. The forms with 'oil' are used only in British English. *Credit cards greased the wheels of the consumer boom by allowing us to buy what we want, when we want.*

set the wheels in motion

If you **set the wheels in motion** to carry out an important plan or project, you do what is necessary to start it. *I have set the wheels in motion to sell Endsleigh Court: the sooner I get out of this block, the better.*

spin your wheels

Mainly American If you accuse someone of **spinning** their **wheels**, you are criticizing them for failing to do or achieve anything satisfactory. *He is not getting anywhere. He's just spinning his wheels.*

the wheels are turning

If you say that **the wheels are turning** in a process or situation, you mean that the process or situation is continuing to develop and progress. *The wheels continue to turn on plans to convert the building into a bookstore.*

wheels within wheels

If you say that there are **wheels within wheels** in a situation, you mean that it is very complicated because many different things, which influence one another, are involved in it. *Our culture is more complex than he knows. Wheels within wheels. Hierarchies.*

◆ This expression comes from the Bible: 'And their appearance and their work was as it were a wheel in the middle of a wheel.' (Ezekiel 1:16)

whip

crack the whip

If a person in authority **cracks the whip**, they make people work very hard and treat them firmly, strictly, and perhaps harshly. *Donna stayed at home and cooked and cracked the whip over her three girls and son.*

a fair crack of the whip

British If you get **a fair crack of the whip**, you get the chance to prove how good you are at something. *None of them is expecting any favours, just a fair crack of the whip.*

have the whip hand

If you **have the whip hand** in a situation, you have more power than the other people involved, and so you have an advantage or control over them. *Consumers will be in the unusual position of having the whip hand over the agents.*

whirl

give something a whirl

If you **give** something **a whirl**, you try it in order to see whether you like it or think you can be successful doing it. *Why not give acupuncture a whirl?*

whisker

by a whisker

If you succeed in doing something **by a whisker**, you almost fail. If you fail to do something **by a whisker**, you almost succeed. *The French government only scraped a Yes vote by a whisker... At the end we lost by a whisker and I feel terribly disappointed.*

within a whisker of something

If you come **within a whisker of** doing something, you nearly succeed in doing it. If something is **within a whisker of** a particular amount, it is almost that amount. *He came within a whisker of scoring a spectacular goal... Unemployment, at 6.4 per cent of the labour force, is now within a whisker of the rate at which inflation has often started to climb.*

whistle

blow the whistle on someone

If you **blow the whistle on** someone who is doing something illegal, dishonest, or immoral, you tell the authorities about them because you feel strongly that what they are doing is wrong and they should be stopped. *The week he died, Foreign Minister Ouko was planning to blow the whistle on corrupt top-level officials.*

☐ You can refer to this activity as **whistle-blowing**. A **whistle-blower** is someone who does this. *The department needs to protect whistle-blowers, health professionals who want and care to make a change in the system.*

◆ In games such as football, the referee blows a whistle to stop play when a player has committed a foul.

wet your whistle

Fairly old-fashioned If you **wet** your **whistle**, you have a drink, especially an alcoholic drink. *Dine at the Griechenbeisel where Mozart, Strauss and Beethoven went to wet their whistles – see their signatures on the walls.*

◆ 'Whistle' is an old slang word for mouth or throat.

whistle for something

If you tell someone that they **can whistle for** something, you are telling them rudely that you will not give it to them. *Rejecting all overtures about the possibility of a compromise, she refused to open her books to the auditors, closed the show and told the city it could whistle for its money.*

◆ There was an old superstition among sailors that they could make the wind blow by whistling.

white

white as a sheet
white as a ghost

If someone looks as **white as a sheet** or as **white as a ghost**, they look very pale and frightened. *There was another lady lorry driver who pulled in in front of me, who it affected badly. She was as white as a sheet... In 30 years of marriage I have never seen my husband in such a state. He was as white as a ghost and trembling.*

white as snow

If you say that something is as **white as snow**, you are emphasizing that it is very white in colour. *When it's warm enough to go bare-legged but your skin's as white as snow, a fake tan's the answer.*

whiter than white

If you describe someone as **whiter than white**, you mean that their actions are always honest and moral. You usually use this expression when you are referring to doubts about the person's character or behaviour, or when you are being ironic and trying to suggest that the person is less honest or moral than they appear to be. *You can't pretend that somehow or other the police are whiter than white. We're living in a real world... This brush with the law seems to have been the only taint in an otherwise whiter than white lifestyle.*

whys

the whys and wherefores

If you talk about **the whys and wherefores** of something, you are talking about the reasons for it. *Even successful bosses need to be queried about the whys and wherefores of their actions.*

◆ 'Wherefore' is an old-fashioned word meaning 'for what' or 'why'.

wick

get on someone's wick

British If you say that someone or something **gets on** your **wick**, you mean that they irritate you a great deal. *Let's face it, after three or four songs that voice really does get on your bloody wick.*

◆ 'Wick' comes from 'Hampton Wick', cockney rhyming slang for 'prick'. 'Prick' is a slang term for penis, which many people find offensive.

wicket

on a sticky wicket
bat on a sticky wicket

British If you say that someone is **on a sticky wicket** or **is batting on a sticky wicket**, you mean that they are in a difficult situation, and they will find it hard to deal with their problems. *It seemed to me that we were on rather a sticky wicket. We couldn't admit that we had got the figures without provoking a major explosion and the certain sacking of Mary Waller.*

□ You can refer to a difficult situation as **a sticky wicket**. *Well, that's a really sticky wicket. As you know, the United Nations will be meeting again on that question later today.*

◆ On a cricket pitch, the wicket is the area of grass between the two sets of stumps. When a lot of rain has fallen on the wicket it becomes soft or 'sticky', and in these conditions, it is difficult for the batsmen to predict which way the ball will bounce.

wide

be wide open

If a contest or competition **is wide open**, it is very difficult to say who will win because the competitors are all equally good. *The competition has been thrown wide open by the absence of the world champion.*

blow something wide open: 1

If someone **blows** a way of doing things **wide open**, they change it completely by doing things in a totally different way. *Pamela has blown the old newsreader image wide open.*

blow something wide open: 2

If someone **blows** something **wide open**, they reveal something secret that other people have been trying to hide. *Has it occurred to you that he can blow the operation wide open?*

leave yourself wide open
lay yourself wide open

If you **leave** yourself **wide open** to something such as criticism or ridicule, you make it very easy for other people to criticize or ridicule you, because you behave in a naive or foolish way. You can also say that you **lay** yourself **wide open** to something. *The statement leaves us wide open to attack.*

wilderness

in the wilderness

British If you refer to someone's time **in the wilderness**, you are referring to a part of their career when they are inactive and ignored, and do not have an influential role. *He is delighted to get another chance to represent his country after a period in the wilderness.*

a voice crying in the wilderness
a lone voice in the wilderness

If you describe someone as **a voice crying in the wilderness** or **a lone voice in the wilderness**, you mean that they are pointing out the dangers in a situation or the truth about it, but nobody is paying any attention. *Ishmael Reed has been a frequent critic of television news coverage of African-Americans, but he says he considered himself a voice crying in the wilderness... For years, he was a lone voice in the wilderness, and a lot of it came across as self-serving. But I'll tell you, the man was right.*

◆ This is from the Bible, and refers to John the Baptist who preached the coming of the Messiah but was often ignored. (Matthew 3:3)

wildfire

spread like wildfire

If something, especially news or a rumour, **spreads like wildfire**, it very quickly reaches or affects a lot of people. *When final confirmation of his release came, the news spread like wildfire.*

◆ This expression may refer to the way that fires which start in the countryside spread very quickly and are difficult to control.

willies

give you the willies

If something **gives** you **the willies**, it makes you feel very nervous or frightened. *Oh, living on the mountainside is enough to give anyone the willies – especially when the wolves howl like the wind and the bobcats screech.*

wind

blow in the wind

If something such as an idea or agreement **is blowing in the wind**, it is being thought about and discussed, but no decision has yet been taken about it. *The agreement blowing in the wind at Montreal signaled a change in business conditions.*

get wind of something

If you **get wind of** something such as a plan or information, you get to know about it, often when other people did not want you to. *I want nothing said about this until I give the word. I don't want the public, and especially not the press, to get wind of it at this stage.*

◆ This expression refers to animals being able to smell hunters or other animals when they are some way off, because the smell is carried to them on the wind.

in the wind

If something such as change is **in the wind**, it is likely to happen. *Change is in the wind and this England team will alter as the year unfolds.*

it's an ill wind
it's an ill wind that blows nobody any good

People say **it's an ill wind** when they want to point out that unpleasant events and difficult situations often have unexpected good effects. *It's an ill wind, of course, and what is bad for the oil companies is good for the consumer and inflation.*

☐ This expression comes from the proverb **it's an ill wind that blows nobody any good**.

put the wind up someone
get the wind up

Mainly British If someone or something **puts the wind up** you, they make you scared or worried. *He has already put the wind up his management team by detailing his strategy of globalisation.*

☐ If you become scared or worried, you can say that you **get the wind up**. *She won't crack, but Denny might when he gets the wind up.*

sail close to the wind

Mainly British If you **sail close to the wind**, you take a risk by doing or saying something which may get you into trouble. *Max warned her she was sailing dangerously close to the wind and risked prosecution.*

◆ If someone sails a boat too close to the wind, they try to sail in the direction from which the wind is blowing, and stop or capsize as a result.

a second wind

If you get **a second wind** when you are tired or unsuccessful, you suddenly find the strength or motivation to go on and succeed in what you are doing. *The president said today that this would be a programme for the nineties, and give the party a second wind.*

◆ If runners who are out of breath get their 'second wind', their breathing becomes easier and they are able to continue.

spit in the wind

If you say that someone **is spitting in the wind**, you mean that they are wasting their time by trying to do something which has little or no chance of success. *But the idea that you can talk about a single currency today is to spit in the wind of economic reality.*

take the wind out of someone's sails
take the wind out of someone's sail

If something **takes the wind out of** your **sails** or **takes the wind out of** your **sail**, it makes you feel much less confident in what you are doing or saying. The form with 'sail' is used only in American English. *This concession succeeded in taking much of the wind out of the opposition's sails. Criticism of the measure has been distinctly muted.*

twist in the wind
swing in the wind

If you say that someone **is twisting in the wind** or **is swinging in the wind**, you mean that they have been left in a very difficult and weak position, often by people who hope to gain advantage from this for themselves. These expressions are used more commonly in American English than British. *For seven and a half months, it now seems clear, she was left twisting mutely in the wind to cover up a failed policy... Critics accused the Prime Minister of leaving the minister swinging in the wind, neither giving him unreserved backing, nor being prepared to end the agony by sacking him.*

which way the wind is blowing
how the wind is blowing

If someone sees **which way the wind is blowing**, they understand or realize how a situation is developing and use this in deciding what to do. You can also say that someone sees **how the wind is blowing**. *He wasn't one to make pronouncements before he was sure which way the wind was blowing.*

whistle in the wind

If you say that someone **is whistling in the wind**, you mean that what they are saying is empty or pointless. *The leader of the Liberal Democrats accused the Prime Minister of whistling in the wind to raise Conservative party morale.*

windmills

tilt at windmills

If you say that someone **is tilting at windmills**, you mean that they are wasting their time on problems or issues which in your opinion are not really problems at all. *The supporters of this act are tilting at windmills. They imagine that America is being leached of technology by predatory foreigners. That could not be further from the truth.*

◆ This expression refers to the novel 'Don Quixote' (1605) by the Spanish writer Cervantes, in which Don Quixote sees some windmills, thinks that they are giants, and tries to attack them.

window

go out the window
go out of the window

If something such as a plan or a particular way of thinking or behaving

has gone out the window or **has gone out of the window**, it has disappeared completely. 'Out of the window' is used only in British English. *It seems Britons are ready to sacrifice almost anything to have an annual holiday. Home improvements go out of the window and one in three people will even give up going to the pub to save for a break.*

wing

on a wing and a prayer

If you do something **on a wing and a prayer**, you do it in the hope that you will succeed, even though you do not have the proper resources for it, or are not properly equipped or prepared. *Whatever the cause, large parts of the government seem to be running on a wing and a prayer.*

◆ This is the title of a song by H. Adamson, written in 1943, which referred to the emergency landing of an aircraft: 'Tho' there's one motor gone, we can still carry on, Comin' In On A Wing And A Pray'r.'

take someone under your wing

If you **take** someone **under** your **wing**, you protect them and make sure that they are all right. *I let him tag along because he had not been too well recently. I took him under my wing and looked after him.*

◆ The image here is of a hen gathering her chicks under her wing.

under the wing of someone

If you are **under the wing of** someone, they control you or take responsibility for you. *What the government has not done, then or now, is to remove the office from under the wing of the economics ministry.*

◆ See the explanation at 'take someone under your wing'.

wings

clip someone's wings

If someone **clips** your **wings**, they limit your freedom to do what you want. *The opposition has been trying to clip his wings by making his actions and his appointments subject to parliamentary approval.*

◆ People sometimes clip the wings of captive birds to prevent them from flying away.

in the wings

If you say that someone is waiting **in the wings**, you mean that they are waiting for an opportunity to take action, especially to take over another person's job or position. *He was one of a number of young, up and* *coming American players who were waiting in the wings for the next Major Championship.*

☐ You can also say that something is **in the wings** when it is about to happen or be made public. *More bad news could be in the wings in the form of more rises in licence fees.*

◆ In a theatre, the wings are the hidden areas to the left and right of a stage, where the actors wait before going on to the stage.

spread your wings

If you **spread** your **wings**, you do something new that is more ambitious than anything you have done before. *Given the firm's high profile in Scotland, it is perhaps surprising that it has not spread its wings across the border.*

try your wings

If you **try** your **wings**, you try to do something new to see if you can succeed. *He was very keen to try his wings and be a deputy on his own.*

wink

not sleep a wink
not get a wink of sleep

If you say that you **did not sleep a wink** or that you **did not get a wink of sleep**, you mean that you tried to go to sleep but could not. *This was my first Grand Prix win of the season and I was so excited I couldn't sleep a wink that night... Unfortunately, I didn't get a wink of sleep because the tablets I was given made me sick.*

tip someone the wink

British, old-fashioned If you **tip** someone **the wink**, you quietly or secretly give them information that could be important or helpful to them. *Back in Italy in 1945, he resolved to help them either by tipping them the wink to flee, or by fudging the evidence.*

winks

forty winks

Fairly old-fashioned If you have **forty winks**, you have a short sleep or rest. *There's nothing like 40 winks to ease away the tension and stresses of a hard day.*

wire

down to the wire

Mainly American If you do something **down to the wire**, you continue doing it until the last possible moment. *Contract negotiations between General Motors and the United Auto Workers are going down to the wire in Detroit. The strike deadline is midnight tonight.*

◆ See the explanation at 'under the wire'.

a live wire

If you describe someone as **a live wire**, you mean that they are very lively and energetic. *She is a wonderful girl, a real live wire and full of fun.*

◆ A live wire is an electric wire or cable that has an electric current running through it.

under the wire

Mainly American If you get in **under the wire**, you get in somewhere or do something at the last possible moment. *He has been running ads in publications like the Wall Street Journal, urging clients to get in under the wire.*

◆ The 'wire' here is a an imaginary one which the horses pass under at the end of a race. A horse that gets in 'under the wire' just manages to beat another horse and finish in one of the winning places.

wives

an old wives' tale

An old wives' tale is a commonly held belief that is based on traditional ideas, often ones which have been proved to be incorrect or inaccurate. *My mother used to tell me to feed a cold and starve a fever. Is it just an old wives' tale?*

wobbly

throw a wobbly
throw a wobbler

British If someone **throws a wobbly** or **throws a wobbler**, they lose their temper in a noisy, uncontrolled, and childish way, often about something unimportant. *I can't even lie in the bath without him throwing a wobbly because there are a few shampoo bottles with the lids off.*

wolf

cry wolf

If you say that someone **is crying wolf**, you mean that they are continually asking for help when it is not needed, or warning about danger when it does not really exist. Because of this, people have stopped believing them and so will not help them when it is really necessary. *Wall Street analysts who have been telling clients to avoid Philadelphia Electric shares are starting to feel like the little boy who cried wolf. Nobody believes them.*

◆ In one of Aesop's fables, a little boy who looks after sheep amuses himself by calling for help and making the villagers rush to rescue him when in fact there is no danger. One day a wolf comes and attacks the sheep, but the villagers do not believe him when he calls for help, and the sheep are all killed.

keep the wolf from the door

Something which **keeps the wolf from the door** provides you with enough money to live on. *Government pension provisions will keep the wolf from the door, but for a comfortable old age you need to make maximum use of the financial choices now open to you.*

◆ For many centuries in the past, wolves were symbols of hunger.

a lone wolf

If you refer to someone as **a lone wolf**, you mean that they are independent and like doing things on their own, rather than doing them with other people. *Furness was a maverick, a lone wolf. A woman who didn't follow Standard Operating Procedures.*

a wolf in sheep's clothing
a sheep in wolf's clothing

If you refer to someone or something as **a wolf in sheep's clothing**, you mean that although they appear harmless or ordinary, they are really very dangerous or powerful. *John Major's grey image may disguise a wolf in sheep's clothing.*

☐ People sometimes describe someone as **a sheep in wolf's clothing** to mean that the person seems dangerous or powerful, but is really harmless or ordinary. *His protruding jaw, combined with his teeth, gave him a vicious appearance. However, he was a sheep in wolf's clothing, a gentle, amiable parish priest, loved by his people in Aberconwy.*

◆ In one of Aesop's fables, a wolf wraps itself in a fleece and manages to get into a sheepfold without being noticed. It then attacks the sheep and eats them. This image is also used in the Bible: 'Beware of false prophets, which come to you in sheep's clothing, but inwardly they are ravening wolves.' (Matthew 7:15)

wolves

throw someone to the wolves

If someone **throws** you **to the wolves,** they allow you to be criticized severely or treated roughly, and they do not try to protect you. *Suddenly he was thrown to the wolves with the stigma of being incompetent, no good, even a fool. It was a dreadful end to a distinguished career.*

wonder

a one-day wonder
a nine-day wonder

If you refer to something or someone as **a one-day wonder** or **a nine-day wonder**, you mean that they are interesting, exciting, or successful for only a very short time, and they do not have any lasting value. *If the goal was simply to make people aware of environmental problems it was a great success. The fear of environmentalists, though, is that this may prove to be a one-day wonder.*

♦ 'A nine-day wonder' may be related to the Catholic 'Novena' festivals, which last for nine days.

wood

dead wood

If you refer to someone or something as **dead wood**, you mean that they are no longer useful or effective in a particular organization or situation and you want to get rid of them. *Mr Hill said the Government's policies, designed to streamline the industry and remove some of the dead wood, had 'gone too far'.*

touch wood
knock on wood
knock wood

When you are talking about how well things are going for you, you say **'touch wood', 'knock on wood'**, or **'knock wood'** to mean that you hope the situation will continue to be good and that you will not have any bad luck. 'Touch wood' is used mainly in British English, and 'knock on wood' and 'knock wood' are used mainly in American English. *She's never even been to the doctor's, touch wood. She's a healthy happy child and anyone can see that.*

☐ People sometimes actually touch or knock on a wooden surface as they say this.

◆ This expression may come from the ancient belief that good spirits lived in trees and people used to tap on them to ask the spirits for help or protection. Alternatively, it may be related to the Christian practice of touching a rosary or crucifix.

woods

out of the woods

If someone or something is not yet **out of the woods**, they are still having difficulties with something or are still in a bad condition. *The Prime Minister is by no means out of the woods, and must fight to defend his leadership at a crisis Cabinet meeting to be called early today.*

◆ This may come from the proverb 'Don't halloo till you are out of the wood', which is a warning not to celebrate something before you have actually achieved your aim.

woodwork

come out of the woodwork

You can say that people **are coming out of the woodwork** if they suddenly start publicly doing something or saying something, when previously they did nothing or kept quiet. You often use this expression when you are critical of them for not having done this earlier. *People are starting to come out of the woodwork to talk about fraudulent practices in the industry.*

wool

dyed-in-the-wool

You use **dyed-in-the-wool** to describe a supporter of a particular philosophy or a member of a particular group to suggest that they have very strong beliefs or feelings about that philosophy or group, and are unlikely ever to change. *I am a dyed-in-the-wool Labour man. He'll not get my vote.*

◆ In medieval times, wool was often dyed before it was spun and woven. This meant that colour was more evenly distributed in the wool, and lasted longer.

pull the wool over someone's eyes

If you accuse someone of **pulling the wool over** your **eyes**, you mean that they are trying to deceive you, in order to get an advantage over you.

'I just told them I was ten years younger than I really was,' says Liliana, speaking yesterday for the first time about how she pulled the wool over the medical profession's eyes.

◆ In the past, wigs for men were sometimes called 'wool' because they looked like a sheep's fleece. It was easy to pull wigs over people's eyes, either as a joke or in order to rob them.

word

a dirty word

If you say that something is **a dirty word** to someone, you mean that they disapprove of it and do not want to have anything to do with it. *A lot of younger women in the '80s and '90s somehow thought feminism was a dirty word.*

get a word in edgeways
get a word in edgewise

If you cannot **get a word in edgeways** or **get a word in edgewise** in a conversation, you find it difficult to say anything because someone else is talking so much. 'Get a word in edgeways' is used only in British English and 'get a word in edgewise' is used mainly in American English. *For heaven's sake, Sue, will you let me get a word in edgeways!*

someone's word is law

If someone's **word is law** in an organization or group, everyone has to obey them. This expression is sometimes used to suggest that this kind of behaviour is unreasonable. *His father was the kind of parent who saw no reason to discuss anything with his son; his word was law.*

a word in someone's ear

British If you have **a word in** someone's **ear**, you speak to them quietly and privately about a delicate or difficult matter. *I'll go and see Quennell. It won't be official, mind. Just a word in his ear over a drink.*

words

eat your words

If someone has given an opinion about something and is now proved to be wrong, you can say that they will have to **eat** their **words**. *The company's embattled chairman has had to eat his words about the company being recession-proof. 'When I suggested that I saw no return to the dark days of recession, I was clearly wrong,' he acknowledges.*

famous last words

If you claim that something will definitely happen in a certain way and then say **'famous last words'**, you are suggesting light-heartedly that it is quite possible that you will be proved wrong. *'All under control,' said Bertie. 'Famous last words,' added Idris with a wide grin.*

□ You can also use **famous last words** to point out that you were in fact wrong about something. *When I set out from Birmingham I thought, at least I'm going to get an early finish. Famous last words.*

not mince your words

If you **do not mince** your **words** or **do not mince words** when you are giving an opinion, you state it clearly and directly, even though you know that some people will not like what you are saying. *I tell it like it is. I don't mince words.*

put words into someone's mouth

If you accuse someone of **putting words into** your **mouth**, you mean that they are reporting opinions or statements which they claim are yours, but which you have never actually held or made. *At medical school, students are shown videos of bad doctors being arrogant, reaching for the prescription pad as soon as patients walk in, putting words in patients' mouths.*

take the words out of someone's mouth

If you **take the words out of** someone's **mouth**, you say the thing that they were just about to say. *'Well, it's been amazing,' she said in closing. 'You took the words right out of my mouth, Lisa.'*

work

do someone's dirty work

If you **do** someone's **dirty work**, you do something unpleasant or difficult on their behalf because they do not want to do it themselves. *He's always got other people to do his dirty work for him.*

have your work cut out

If you say that someone **has** their **work cut out** for them, you mean that they have a very big problem to deal with, and they will not find it easy to do. *The Prime Minister has his work cut out for him as most analysts see little chance of resolving the constitutional crisis.*

works

in the works

Mainly American If something is **in the works**, it is being planned or is in progress. *He said there were dozens of economic plans in the works.*

the works
the whole works
When you are describing something, you can mention a number of things and then say **the works** or **the whole works** to refer to many other things of the same kind or to refer to all the other things which would normally be included. *Amazing place he's got there – squash courts, swimming pool, jacuzzi, the works.*

world

dead to the world
If someone is **dead to the world**, they are sleeping very deeply. *Sarah was dead to the world and would probably sleep for twelve hours.*

it's a small world
small world
You say **'it's a small world'** or **'small world'** to express your surprise when you unexpectedly meet someone you know in an unusual place. You can also use these expressions when you are talking to someone and are surprised to discover that you both know the same person. *I had no idea you knew the Proberts. Well, well, it's a small world... I'm only just recovering from the surprise of running into you like this. Small world.*

not long for this world
If you say that someone **is not long for this world**, you mean that they are likely to die soon. *Peter Hastings asked Ian to become his assistant earlier that year, perhaps knowing that he was not long for this world.*

not set the world on fire
If you say that someone **won't set the world on fire**, you are saying in a light-hearted or ironic way that they are not very exciting or they are not having much success. *Andy Caddick has not set the world on fire in his first two Tests but his day will come.*

on top of the world
If you feel **on top of the world**, you feel extremely happy. *When she came back from that holiday she was so happy, on top of the world.*

out of this world
If you say something is **out of this world**, you are emphasizing that you think it is very good or impressive. *The show was really good. The music was great and the costumes were out of this world.*

the world is your oyster

If someone says **'the world is your oyster'**, they mean that you have the opportunity to achieve great success in your life. *You're young, you've got a lot of opportunity. The world is your oyster.*

◆ This expression suggests that success can be taken from the world in the same way that pearls can be taken from oysters. This idea was used by Shakespeare in 'The Merry Wives Of Windsor': 'Why, then the world's mine oyster, Which I with sword will open.' (Act 2, Scene 2)

worm

the worm turns

If someone who has tolerated a lot of bad treatment from other people without complaining unexpectedly changes their behaviour and starts to behave in a more forceful way, you can say that **the worm has turned**. *Then my mother came home and started bossing us around. She said, 'The worm has turned. Things are going to be different around here.'*

worms

a can of worms
a bag of worms

If you describe a situation as **a can of worms**, you mean that it is much more complicated, unpleasant, or difficult than it seems at first. If you say that someone is opening **a can of worms**, you mean that they are doing something which would be better left alone. 'Bag' is occasionally used instead of 'can'. *Now we have uncovered a can of worms in which there has not only been shameful abuse of power, but a failure of moral authority of the worst kind.*

wounds

lick your wounds

If you say that someone **is licking** their **wounds**, you mean that they are feeling sorry for themselves after being thoroughly defeated or humiliated. *England's cricketers are licking their wounds after being soundly defeated in the second Test against Australia at Melbourne.*

◆ Some animals, such as dogs and cats, lick their wounds when they are injured.

open old wounds
reopen old wounds

If you say that something **opens old wounds**, you mean that it reminds people of an unpleasant or embarrassing experience in the past that they would rather forget about. You can also say that something **reopens old wounds**. *But that afternoon my world was overturned. Ted's diagnosis had opened old wounds and I no longer felt secure... Our Political Correspondent, Andrew Whitehead, says the row is reopening old wounds among Conservative MPs.*

wraps

keep something under wraps

If something **is kept under wraps**, it is kept secret and not revealed to anyone. *The official report has been kept under wraps for months by legal objections from BA.*

take the wraps off something
the wraps come off

If someone **takes the wraps off** something such as a proposal or a new product, they tell people about it for the first time. *The Clinton administration has taken the wraps off its proposals to enhance American technology.*

☐ You can also say that **the wraps come off**. *A breath of spring arrives today as the wraps come off the first Renault convertible to be sold in the UK for more than 20 years.*

wrench

throw a wrench into the works
throw a monkey wrench into the works

American If someone or something **throws a wrench into the works** or **throws a monkey wrench into the works**, they cause problems which prevent something from happening in the way that it was planned. The British expression is **throw a spanner in the works**. *When Elton was robbed it threw a monkey wrench into the works.*

☐ Instead of saying 'into the works', people often mention the process in which the problem is caused. *The federal government has thrown a wrench in the multi-billion dollar Japanese buyout of an American company.*

wringer

go through the wringer

If you **go through the wringer**, you go through a very difficult period or situation which upsets you greatly and makes you ill or unhappy. *I felt* *as though I'd been through a wringer. My life seemed a wreck.*

YZ

yards

the whole nine yards

American If someone goes **the whole nine yards**, they do something to the fullest extent possible. *She's been the whole nine yards with the disease, has come through it, and has now taken up sailing.*

◆ This expression refers to the amount of cement, nine cubic yards, which is contained in a cement-mixer truck.

yonder

into the wide blue yonder
into the wild blue yonder

If someone goes **into the wide blue yonder** or **into the wild blue yonder**, they go on a journey to a faraway place which is unfamiliar or mysterious. *Sailing into the wide blue yonder, Colin discovers his very own Treasure Island.*

zero-sum

a zero-sum game

If you refer to a situation as **a zero-sum game**, you mean that if one person gains an advantage from it, someone else involved must suffer an equivalent disadvantage. Other nouns are sometimes used instead of 'game'. *The idea that foreign investment is a zero-sum game – that one country's gain is another's loss – is mistaken.*

◆ A zero-sum game is one in which the winnings and losses of all the players add up to zero.

INDEX

arms
 up in **arms**
arrow
 a straight **arrow**
arrows
 slings and arrows
arse
 not know your arse
 from your **elbow**
ashes
 rake over the ashes: see
 coals
ask
 ask for the **moon**
ass
 kick ass
 not know your ass
 from your **elbow**
 put your ass on the **line**
ate
 like the **cat** that ate the
 canary
attached
 with no **strings** attached
automatic
 on automatic **pilot**
autopilot
 on autopilot: see **pilot**
avoid
 avoid something like
 the **plague**
ax: see **axe**
axe
 an **axe** hanging over
 something
 get the **axe**
 have an **axe** to grind
babes
 babes in the wood
baby
 leave someone holding
 the **baby**
 like taking **candy** from
 a baby
 throw the **baby** out
 with the bath water
back
 a back **number**
 back the wrong **horse**
 behind your **back**
 break the **back** of
 something
 by the back **door**
 fed up to the back **teeth**
 get off someone's **back**

get someone's **back** up
get the **monkey** off
 your back
get your own **back**
have a **monkey** on
 your back
have **eyes** in the back
 of your head
have your **back** to the
 wall
the last **straw** that
 breaks the camel's
 back
like **water** off a duck's
 back
make a **rod** for your
 own back
off the **back** of a lorry
on someone's **back**
on the back **burner**
a **pat** on the back
pat someone on the back
sick to the back **teeth**
stab someone in the
 back
the **straw** that breaks
 the camel's back
take a back **seat**
you scratch my **back**
 and I'll scratch yours
backward
 lean over backward:
 see **backwards**
backwards
 bend over **backwards**
bacon
 bring **home** the bacon
 save someone's **bacon**
bad
 a bad **apple**
 a bad **apple** spoils the
 barrel
 bad **blood**
 in bad **odour**
 in someone's bad **books**
 leave a bad **taste** in
 your mouth
 throw good **money**
 after bad
 turn up like a bad
 penny
bag
 a bag of **nerves**
 a bag of **worms**
 be someone's **bag**

can't fight your way
 out of a **paper** bag
in the **bag**
leave someone holding
 the **bag**
let the **cat** out of the **bag**
a mixed **bag**
someone's **bag** of tricks
bait
 fish or cut **bait**
 rise to the **bait**
 take the **bait**
baker
 a **baker**'s dozen
balance
 in the **balance**
 tip the balance
balancing
 a balancing **act**
ball
 a **ball** and chain
 the **ball** is in your court
 behind the eight **ball**
 a crystal **ball**
 a different **ball** game
 drop the **ball**
 have a **ball**
 keep your **eye** on the
 ball
 a new **ball** game
 on the **ball**
 play **ball**
 set the **ball** rolling
 take the **ball** and run
 with it
 take your **eye** off the
 ball
 throw someone a **curve**
 ball
 the whole **ball** of wax
ballistic
 go **ballistic**
balloon
 the **balloon** goes up
 go down like a **lead**
 balloon
 a **lead** balloon
 a **trial** balloon
ballpark
 a **ballpark** estimate
 a **ballpark** figure
 in the **ballpark**
 in the same **ballpark**
balls
 break someone's **balls**

cold enough to freeze
the balls off a **brass**
monkey
curve balls
keep **balls** in the air

banana
slip on a **banana** peel
slip on a **banana** skin

band
a one-man **band**
a one-woman **band**

bandwagon
jump on the
bandwagon

bang
bang people's **heads**
together
bang the **drum**
bang to **rights**
bang your head against
a brick **wall**
more **bang** for the buck
not with a **bang** but a
whimper

bangs
more bangs for your
bucks: see **bang**

bank
break the **bank**

baptism
a **baptism** of fire

bare
the bare **bones**
bare your **soul**

barge
wouldn't touch
something with a
barge **pole**

bark
bark up the wrong **tree**
your **bark** is worse
than your bite

barn
close the barn **door**
after the horse has
gone

barrel
a bad **apple** spoils the
barrel
have someone over a
barrel
like shooting **fish** in a
barrel
lock, stock, and barrel
on the barrel: see
barrelhead

scrape the **barrel**
scrape the bottom of the
barrel

barrelhead
on the **barrelhead**

barrels
give someone both
barrels

base
get to first **base**
get to second **base**
off **base**
touch **base**

bases
cover all the **bases**
touch all the **bases**

basket
a **basket** case
put all your **eggs** in
one basket

bat
bat on a sticky **wicket**
blind as a bat
go to **bat** for someone
like a **bat** out of hell
not bat an **eye**
not bat an eyelash: see
eyelid
not bat an **eyelid**
off your own **bat**
play a straight **bat**
right off the **bat**

bated
with bated **breath**

bath
an early **bath**
take a **bath**
throw the **baby** out
with the bath water

baton
pass the **baton**
pick up the **baton**

bats
have **bats** in your belfry

batten
batten down the
hatches

batteries
recharge your **batteries**

battle
the **battle** lines are
drawn
a battle of **nerves**
fight a losing **battle**
join **battle**

lose the **battle**, win the
war
a running **battle**
win the **battle**, lose the
war

bay
bay at the **moon**
bay for **blood**
keep something at **bay**

beach
not the only **pebble** on
the beach

bead
draw a **bead** on
take a **bead** on

beam
be way off **beam**

bean
a **bean** counter
not have a **bean**

beans
count the beans: see
bean
full of **beans**
know how many **beans**
make five
not amount to a hill of
beans
not worth a row of
beans
spill the **beans**

bear
bear **fruit**
bear something in **mind**
a **cross** to bear
like a **bear** with a sore
head
loaded for **bear**

bearer
the **standard** bearer

beast
the **nature** of the beast
no good to man or **beast**
no use to man or **beast**

beat
beat a dead **horse**
beat a path to
someone's **door**
beat someone at their
own **game**
beat someone **hands**
down
beat someone **hollow**
beat **swords** into
ploughshares

beat the **bushes**
beat the **drum**
beat the living
   daylights out of
   someone
beat your breast
beat your chest
march to the beat of a
   different drummer
miss a **beat**
not beat about the **bush**
not beat around the
   bush
a **stick** to beat someone
   with

beaten
off the beaten path: see
   track
off the beaten **track**

beaver
an eager **beaver**

beck
at someone's **beck** and
   call

bed
get into **bed** with
   someone
get out of **bed** the
   wrong side
not a bed of **roses**
put something to **bed**
you have made your
   bed and will have to
   lie on it

bedbug
crazy as a bedbug

bee
the **bee**'s knees
busy as a bee
a **busy** bee
have a **bee** in your
   bonnet

beeline
make a **beeline** for
   something

beer
not all **beer** and skittles
small **beer**

bees
the **birds** and the bees

beet
red as a beet

beetroot
red as a beetroot

beg
beg the **question**

beggars
beggars can't be
   choosers

belfry
have **bats** in your belfry

bell
clear as a bell
ring a **bell**
ring someone's **bell**
saved by the **bell**
sound as a bell

bells
alarm **bells** ring
bells and whistles
pull the other one, it's
   got bells on it
warning **bells** ring

belly
fire in your belly

belly-up
go **belly-up**

belt
below the **belt**
belt and braces
tighten your **belt**
under your **belt**

bend
bend over **backwards**
bend someone's **ear**
round the **bend**

berry
brown as a berry

berth
give someone a wide
   berth

best
the best thing since
   sliced **bread**
give something your
   best **shot**
put your best **foot**
   forward
your best **bib** and
   tucker

bet
bet the **ranch**
bet your bottom **dollar**

bets
hedge your **bets**

better
better the **devil** you
   know
half a **loaf** is better
   than none
have seen better **days**

bib
your best **bib** and
   tucker

big
big as life: see **large**
a big **cheese**
a big **fish**
a big **fish** in a small
   pond
the big **guns**
big **time**
the big **time**
a big **wheel**
carry a big **stick**
get too **big** for your
   boots
get too **big** for your
   britches
hit the big **time**
wield a big **stick**

bigger
bigger than life: see
   larger
have bigger **fish** to fry

bike
on your **bike**

bill
bill and coo
a clean **bill** of health
fill the **bill**
fit the **bill**
foot the **bill**
sell someone a **bill** of
   goods

bind
a double **bind**

bird
the **bird** has flown
a **bird** in the hand
a **bird** in the hand is
   worth two in the bush
a **bird** of passage
an early **bird**
the early **bird** catches
   the worm
eat like a **bird**
give someone the **bird**
a little **bird** told me
a rare **bird**

birds
the **birds** and the bees
birds of a feather
birds of a feather flock
   together
for the **birds**

kill two **birds** with one
stone
bird's-eye
a bird's-eye **view**
biscuit
take the **biscuit**
bit
the **biter** gets bit
champ at the **bit**
chomp at the **bit**
get the **bit** between
your teeth
a **hair** of the dog that
bit you
bite
bite off more than you
can chew
bite someone's **head** off
bite the **bullet**
bite the **dust**
bite the **hand** that
feeds you
bite your **tongue**
a second **bite** at the
cherry
your **bark** is worse
than your bite
biter
the **biter** gets bit
bites
two bites of the cherry:
see **bite**
bitten
bitten by the **bug**
once **bitten**
once **bitten**, twice shy
bitter
a bitter **pill** to swallow
swallow a bitter **pill**
black
black and white
a black **box**
a black **mark**
the black **sheep**
the black **sheep** of the
family
give someone a black **eye**
in **black** and white
in the **black**
not as **black** as you are
painted
the **pot** calling the
kettle black
blank
draw a **blank**

blanket
a **security** blanket
a wet **blanket**
blanks
fire **blanks**
blaze
blaze a **trail**
blazing
with all **guns** blazing
bleed
bleed red **ink**
bleed someone dry
bleed someone white
your **heart** bleeds for
someone
bleeding
a bleeding **heart**
blind
a blind **alley**
blind as a bat
the **blind** leading the
blind
blind someone with
science
fly **blind**
swear **blind**
turn a blind **eye** to
something
blink
on the **blink**
block
a **chip** off the old block
on the **block**
put your head on the
block
put your neck on the
block
a stumbling **block**
blocks
off the **blocks**
off the starting **blocks**
out of the **blocks**
blood
after your **blood**
bad **blood**
bay for **blood**
blood and thunder
blood is thicker than
water
blood, sweat, and tears
flesh and blood
fresh **blood**
have **blood** on your
hands
in cold **blood**

in your **blood**
like getting **blood** out
of a stone
like getting **blood** out
of a turnip
make your **blood** boil
make your **blood** freeze
make your **blood** run
cold
new **blood**
out for **blood**
a **rush** of blood
a **rush** of blood to the
head
scent **blood**
sweat **blood**
taste **blood**
young **blood**
bloody
bloody someone's **nose**
give someone a bloody
nose
scream bloody **murder**
blot
a **blot** on your
escutcheon
blot your **copybook**
blow
blow a **fuse**
blow **hot**
blow **hot** and cold
blow in the **wind**
blow off **steam**
blow **smoke**
blow **smoke** in
someone's eyes
blow **smoke** in
someone's face
blow someone to
kingdom come
blow something out of
the **water**
blow something
sky-high
blow something **wide**
open
blow the **gaff**
blow the **whistle** on
someone
blow your **mind**
blow your own **horn**
blow your own **trumpet**
blow your **stack**
blow your **top**
a **body** blow

strike a **blow** against
something
strike a **blow** for
something

blowing
how the **wind** is
blowing
which way the **wind** is
blowing

blows
come to **blows**
it's an ill **wind** that
blows nobody any
good

blue
between the **devil** and
the deep blue sea
a **bolt** from the blue
into the wide blue
yonder
into the wild blue
yonder
light the blue **touch
paper**
once in a blue **moon**
out of a clear blue **sky**
out of the **blue**
scream blue **murder**
talk a blue **streak**
until you are blue in
the **face**

blue-arsed
like a blue-arsed **fly**

blue-eyed
your blue-eyed **boy**

bluff
call someone's **bluff**

board
above **board**
across the **board**
back to the drawing
board
go by the **board**
stiff as a **board**
sweep the **board**
take something on
board

boards
go by the boards: see
board

boat
float someone's **boat**
in the same **boat**
miss the boat
push the **boat** out

rock the **boat**

boats
burn your boats

Bob
Bob's your uncle

body
a **body** blow
hold **body** and soul
together
keep **body** and soul
together
over my dead **body**

boil
bring something to a
boil
come to the **boil**
make your **blood** boil
off the **boil**
on the **boil**
a watched **pot** never
boils

boiling
boiling **point**
keep the **pot** boiling

bold
bold as brass

bolt
a **bolt** from the blue
shoot your **bolt**

bolted
close the stable **door**
after the horse has
bolted

bolts
the **nuts** and bolts of
something

bone
a **bone** of contention
close to the **bone**
cut to the **bone**
dry as a bone
have a **bone** to pick
with someone
near to the **bone**
skin and bone
work your **fingers** to
the bone

bones
the bare **bones**
feel something in your
bones
make no **bones** about
something
put **flesh** on the bones
of something

skin and bones

bonnet
have a **bee** in your
bonnet

boo
wouldn't say boo to a
goose

book
bring someone to **book**
by the **book**
a closed **book**
close the **book** on
something
every **trick** in the book
in your **book**
the oldest **trick** in the
book
an open **book**
take a **leaf** out of
someone's book
throw the **book** at
someone
you can't judge a **book**
by its cover

books
cook the **books**
in someone's bad **books**
in someone's good
books
a **turn-up** for the books

boot
the boot is on the other
foot
get the **boot**
put the **boot** in
put the **boot** into
someone

boots
die with your **boots** on
fill someone's **boots**
fill your **boots**
get too **big** for your
boots
hang up your boots
in someone's boots: see
shoes
lick someone's **boots**
step into someone's
boots
tough as old boots

bootstraps
pull yourself up by
your **bootstraps**

born
born with a **silver**

spoon in your mouth
borrowed
live on borrowed **time**
bottle
the **genie** is out of the bottle
let the **genie** out of the bottle
put the **genie** back in the bottle
bottom
at **rock** bottom
bet your bottom **dollar**
the **bottom** falls out of something
the bottom **line**
the bottom of the **heap**
hit **rock** bottom
reach **rock** bottom
scrape the bottom of the **barrel**
bow
another **string** to your bow
bow and scrape
many strings to your bow: see **string**
bowl
life is a bowl of cherries
bows
a **shot** across someone's bows
a warning **shot** across someone's bows
box
a black **box**
box clever
box someone into a **corner**
out of the **box**
out of your **box**
a **Pandora**'s box
boy
a whipping **boy**
your blue-eyed **boy**
your fair-haired **boy**
boys
separate the **men** from the boys
braces
belt and braces
brain
a brain like a **sieve**
brains
pick someone's **brains**
rack your **brains**

branch
an olive **branch**
root and branch
brass
bold as brass
the **brass** ring
cold enough to freeze the balls off a **brass** monkey
get down to **brass** tacks
bread
the best thing since sliced **bread**
bread and butter
bread and circuses
cast your **bread** upon the waters
know which side your **bread** is buttered
breadline
on the **breadline**
break
all **hell** breaks loose
break a **butterfly** on a wheel
break a **leg**
break a new **path**
break new **ground**
break rank: see **ranks**
break **ranks**
break someone's **balls**
break the **back** of something
break the **bank**
break the **ice**
break the **mould**
give a sucker an even **break**
give someone an even **break**
the last **straw** that breaks the camel's back
the **straw** that breaks the camel's back
breakfast
a **dog**'s breakfast
breaking
you can't make an **omelette** without breaking eggs
breast
beat your breast
make a clean **breast** of something

breath
a **breath** of fresh air
take your **breath** away
with bated **breath**
breathe
breathe down someone's **neck**
breathe **fire**
breeches: see **britches**
breed
familiarity breeds contempt
familiarity breeds content
breeze
shoot the **breeze**
brick
bang your head against a brick **wall**
come up against a brick **wall**
drop a **brick**
drop something like a hot brick: see **potato**
bricks
a **cat** on hot bricks
come down on someone like a **ton** of bricks
like a **ton** of bricks
make **bricks** without straw
bridge
cross that **bridge** when you come to it
water under the bridge
bridges
build **bridges**
burn your bridges
brief
hold no **brief** for something
bright
bright as a button
a bright **spark**
look on the bright **side**
bright-eyed
bright-eyed and bushy-tailed
bring
bring a **lump** to your throat
bring **home** the bacon
bring someone to **book**
bring someone to **heel**
bring someone up to **speed**

bring something **home**
to someone
bring something to a
boil
bring something to the
party
bring the **curtain** down
on something
bring the **house** down

britches
get too **big** for your
britches

broad
broad brush **strokes**
broad **strokes**

broke
go for **broke**
if it ain't **broke**, don't
fix it
they broke the **mould**
when they made
someone

broken
a broken **reed**

broom
a new **broom**
a new **broom** sweeps
clean

broth
too many **cooks** spoil
the broth

brother
not your brother's
keeper

brow
by the **sweat** of your
brow

brown
brown as a berry

brownie
brownie points

brush
broad brush **strokes**
daft as a brush
tar someone with the
same **brush**

bubble
the **bubble** has burst
on the **bubble**
prick the **bubble**

buck
the **buck** stops here
more **bang** for the buck
pass the **buck**

bucket
a **drop** in the bucket

kick the **bucket**

bucks
more bangs for your
bucks: see **bang**

bud
nip something in the
bud

buffers
hit the **buffers**

bug
bitten by the **bug**
snug as a bug in a rug

build
build **bridges**
build something on
sand

built
Rome was not built in
a day

bull
a **bull** in a china shop
a **cock** and bull story
a **cock** and bull tale
a red flag before a **bull**
a red rag to a **bull**
strong as a bull
take the **bull** by the
horns

bullet
bite the **bullet**
get the **bullet**

bum
a **bum** steer
get the **bum**'s rush

bundle
a bundle of **nerves**
drop your **bundle**

bunny
not a happy **bunny**

burn
burn a **hole** in your
pocket
burn the **candle** at
both ends
burn the **midnight** oil
burn your boats
burn your bridges
burn your **fingers**
crash and burn
fiddle while **Rome**
burns

burned
get your **fingers** burned

burner
on the back **burner**

on the front **burner**

burning
someone's **ears** are
burning

burst
the **bubble** has burst
burst at the **seams**

bury
bury the **hatchet**
bury your **head** in the
sand

bus
miss the bus

bush
a **bird** in the hand is
worth two in the bush
the **bush** telegraph
not beat about the **bush**
not beat around the
bush

bushel
hide your light under a
bushel

bushes
beat the **bushes**

bushy-tailed
bright-eyed and
bushy-tailed

business
do a **land-office**
business
monkey business

busman
a **busman**'s holiday

busy
busy as a bee
a **busy** bee

butt
kick butt

butter
bread and butter
butter wouldn't melt
in your mouth
like a hot **knife**
through butter

buttered
know which side your
bread is buttered

butterflies
butterflies in your
stomach
get **butterflies**

butterfly
break a **butterfly** on a
wheel

button
  bright as a button
  a hot **button**
  on the **button**
  press the right **button**
  right on the **button**
buy
  buy the **farm**
caboodle
  the whole **caboodle**
  the whole kit and
    caboodle
cage
  rattle someone's **cage**
Cain
  raise **Cain**
cake
  the frosting on the
    cake: see **icing**
  have your **cake** and
    eat it
  the **icing** on the cake
  a **piece** of cake
  take the **cake**
cakes
  cakes and ale
  sell like **hot cakes**
calf
  kill the fatted **calf**
call
  at someone's **beck** and
    call
  call a **spade** a spade
  call in your **chips**
  call it a **day**
  call it a night: see **day**
  call it **quits**
  call off the **dogs**
  call someone on the
    carpet
  call someone's **bluff**
  call someone to **heel**
  call the **shots**
  call the **tune**
  he who pays the **piper**
    calls the tune
  too **close** to call
  a **wake-up** call
calling
  a calling **card**
  the **pot** calling the
    kettle black
calm
  the calm before the
    storm

camel
  the last **straw** that
    breaks the camel's
    back
  strain at a **gnat** and
    swallow a camel
  the **straw** that breaks
    the camel's back
camp
  a **camp** follower
  a **foot** in each camp
camps
  a **foot** in both camps
can
  a can of **worms**
  carry the **can**
  in the **can**
canary
  like the **cat** that ate the
    canary
candle
  burn the **candle** at
    both ends
  can't hold a **candle** to
    someone
  the game is not worth
    the **candle**
  not worth the **candle**
candy
  like a kid in a **candy**
    store
  like taking **candy** from
    a baby
cannon
  a loose **cannon**
  a loose **cannon** on the
    deck
canoe
  paddle your own **canoe**
cap
  cap in hand
  a **feather** in your cap
  if the **cap** fits
  put your thinking **cap**
    on
  set your **cap** at someone
  throw your cap into the
    ring: see **hat**
carbon
  a **carbon** copy
card
  a calling **card**
  have a card up your
    sleeve
  a **hole** card

  play your **trump** card
  a **trump** card
  a wild **card**
cards
  a **house** of cards
  in the **cards**
  keep your cards close
    to your **chest**
  lay your **cards** on the
    table
  on the **cards**
  play your cards close
    to the **vest**
  play your cards close
    to your **chest**
  play your **cards** right
  several cards **short** of a
    full deck
  stack the cards
carpet
  call someone on the
    carpet
  on the **carpet**
  roll out the red **carpet**
  sweep something under
    the **carpet**
carrot
  carrot and stick
  dangle a **carrot** in
    front of someone
  offer someone a **carrot**
carry
  carry a big **stick**
  carry a **torch** for
    someone
  carry the **can**
  carry the **day**
  carry the **torch**
  carry the **weight** of the
    world on your
    shoulders
cart
  put the **cart** before the
    horse
cartload
  a cartload of **monkeys**
carve
  carve a **niche**
case
  a **basket** case
cash
  a **cash** cow
  cash in your **chips**
cast
  cast a wide **net**

cast **pearls** before swine
cast the **net** wider
cast your **bread** upon the waters
cast your **eye** on something
cast your eyes on something: see **eye**
cast your **lot** with someone
the **die** is cast

castle
an **Englishman**'s home is his castle

castles
castles in Spain
castles in the air

cat
cat and mouse
a **cat** on a hot tin roof
a **cat** on hot bricks
the **cat**'s whiskers
curiosity killed the cat
a fat **cat**
fight like **cat** and dog
a game of **cat** and mouse
grin like a Cheshire **cat**
let the **cat** out of the bag
like the **cat** that ate the canary
like the **cat** that got the cream
no room to swing a **cat**
put the **cat** among the pigeons
see which way the **cat** jumps
there's more than one way to skin a **cat**
when the **cat**'s away, the mice will play

catbird
in the **catbird** seat

catch
a **Catch** 22
catch **fire**
catch someone **flat-footed**
catch someone on the **hop**
catch someone **red-handed**
catch someone's **eye**
catch someone with

their **pants** down
catch someone with their trousers down: see **pants**
catch the **wave**
the early **bird** catches the worm
a **sprat** to catch a mackerel
when one person sneezes, another catches **cold**

cats
fight like **Kilkenny** cats
it's raining **cats** and dogs

cattle
a cattle **market**

caught
caught between two **stools**
caught in the **crossfire**
caught on the wrong **foot**
caught with your hand in the **cookie** jar
like a deer caught in the **headlights**
like a rabbit caught in the **headlights**
wouldn't be caught **dead**

caution
throw **caution** to the wind

ceiling
the **glass** ceiling
go through the ceiling: see **roof**
hit the ceiling: see **roof**

center: see **centre**

centre
centre **stage**
left, right, and centre

cents
your two **cents**' worth

chaff
separate the grain from the **chaff**
separate the wheat from the **chaff**

chain
a **ball** and chain
pull someone's **chain**
a weak **link** in the chain

yank someone's **chain**

chair
on the **edge** of your chair

chalice
a poisoned **chalice**

chalk
by a long **chalk**
chalk and cheese

champ
champ at the **bit**

chance
chance your **arm**
drinking in the last chance **saloon**
the last chance **saloon**

change
change horses in **midstream**
change your **tune**
chop and change
a **leopard** does not change its spots
a **sea** change

changes
ring the **changes**

chapter
chapter and verse

Charybdis
between **Scylla** and Charybdis

chase
chase **rainbows**
chase your own **tail**
cut to the **chase**
lead you a merry chase: see **dance**
a wild **goose** chase

check
take a **rain** check

cheek
cheek by jowl
tongue in cheek
turn the other **cheek**

cheese
a big **cheese**
chalk and cheese
more holes than **Swiss** cheese

cherries
life is a bowl of cherries

cherry
a second **bite** at the cherry
two bites of the cherry: see **bite**

clogs

Cheshire
grin like a Cheshire **cat**

chest
beat your chest
get something off your **chest**
keep your cards close to your **chest**
play your cards close to your **chest**
put hair on the chest: see **hairs**
put **hairs** on your chest

chestnut
an old **chestnut**

chestnuts
pull someone's **chestnuts** out of the fire

chew
bite off more than you can chew
chew the **fat**

chicken
chicken and egg
chicken feed
like a **chicken** with its head cut off
like a headless **chicken**
no **spring** chicken

chickens
the chickens come home to **roost**
don't count your **chickens** before they're hatched
not count your **chickens**

chiefs
too many **chiefs**
too many **chiefs** and not enough Indians

child
child's play
like a child in a sweet shop: see **candy**

chin
keep your **chin** up
lead with your **chin**
take it on the **chin**

china
a **bull** in a china shop
not for all the **tea** in China

chink
a **chink** in someone's armour

chip
a **chip** off the old block
a **chip** on your shoulder

chips
call in your **chips**
cash in your **chips**
have had your **chips**
when the **chips** are down

choice
Hobson's choice

chomp
chomp at the **bit**

choosers
beggars can't be choosers

chop
chop and change

chops
lick your **chops**: see **lips**

Christmas
like **turkeys** voting for Christmas

church
poor as a church mouse

cigar
close but no **cigar**
nice try but no **cigar**

circle
circle the **wagons**
come full **circle**
pull your **wagons** in a circle
square the **circle**
a vicious **circle**
the wheel has come full **circle**

circles
go around in **circles**
run around in **circles**

circus
a three-ring **circus**

circuses
bread and circuses

clam
happy as a **clam**

Clapham
the man on the Clapham **omnibus**

clappers
like the **clappers**

class
a class **act**

claw
fight **tooth** and claw
red in **tooth** and claw

clay
clay **feet**
have **feet** of clay

clean
a clean **bill** of health
a clean **sheet**
a clean **sheet** of paper
a clean **slate**
clean up your **act**
come **clean**
keep your **nose** clean
make a clean **breast** of something
make a clean **sweep**
a new **broom** sweeps clean
show a clean pair of **heels**
squeaky **clean**
wipe the **slate** clean

cleaners
take someone to the **cleaners**

clear
clear as a bell
clear as crystal
clear as day
clear as mud
clear **sailing**
clear the **air**
clear the **decks**
the **coast** is clear
the **dust** clears
out of a clear blue **sky**
steer **clear**
steer someone **clear** of something

cleft
in a cleft **stick**

clever
box **clever**

climb
climb the **walls**
a **mountain** to climb

clip
clip someone's **wings**

cloak-and-dagger
cloak-and-dagger

clogs
pop your **clogs**

close
close but no **cigar**
close **ranks**
a close **shave**
close the barn **door**
  after the horse has
  gone
close the **book** on
  something
close the stable **door**
  after the horse has
  bolted
close to **home**
close to the **bone**
close up **shop**
keep your cards close
  to your **chest**
play your cards close
  to your **vest**
play your cards close
  to your **chest**
sail close to the **wind**
too **close** to call

closed
behind closed **doors**
a closed **book**
with your **eyes** closed

closet
come out of the **closet**
a **skeleton** in the closet

cloth
cloth **ears**
cut from the same **cloth**
cut your **cloth**
cut your **coat** according
  to your **cloth**
whole **cloth**

clothes
steal someone's **clothes**

clothing
a sheep in **wolf's**
  clothing
a **wolf** in sheep's
  clothing

cloud
every cloud has a
  silver lining
on **cloud** nine
under a **cloud**

clouds
have your **head** in the
  clouds

clover
in **clover**

clutch
clutch at **straws**
a drowning man will
  clutch at a straw: see
  straws

coach
drive a **coach** and
  horses through
  something

coalface
at the **coalface**

coals
coals to Newcastle
haul someone over the
  coals
rake over the **coals**
rake someone over the
  coals

coast
the **coast** is clear

coat
cut your **coat** according
  to your **cloth**
trail your **coat**

coat-tails
on the **coat-tails** of
  someone

cobbler
let the cobbler stick to
  his **last**

cock
a **cock** and bull story
a **cock** and bull tale
cock a **snook** at
  someone
go off at **half** cock

cocked
knock something into a
  cocked **hat**

cockles
warm the **cockles** of
  your heart

coffee
wake up and smell the
  coffee

coffin
another **nail** in the
  coffin
the final **nail** in the
  coffin

coin
opposite sides of the
  same **coin**
the other side of the
  coin

pay someone back in
  their own **coin**
to coin a **phrase**
two sides of the same
  coin

cold
blow **hot** and cold
cold enough to freeze
  the balls off a **brass**
  monkey
a cold **fish**
come in from the **cold**
get cold **feet**
give someone the cold
  shoulder
in cold **blood**
in the cold **light** of day
into cold **storage**
leave someone **cold**
make your **blood** run
  cold
out in the **cold**
pour cold **water** on
  something
when one person
  sneezes, another
  catches **cold**

collar
hot under the **collar**

color: see **colour**

colors: see **colours**

colour
the **colour** of someone's
  money

colours
nail your **colours** to
  the mast
sail under false **colours**
see someone in their
  true **colours**
show your true **colours**
with flying **colours**

comb
with a fine-tooth **comb**
with a fine-toothed **comb**

come
come out fighting
what goes around
  comes around: see **go**

comforts
creature comforts

coming
everything is coming
  up **roses**
have something coming
  out of your **ears**

have steam coming out
of your **ears**
up and coming
common
common as muck
the common **touch**
common-or-garden
common-or-**garden**
conjure
a **name** to conjure with
conquer
divide and conquer
contemplate
contemplate your **navel**
contempt
familiarity breeds
contempt
content
familiarity breeds
content
contention
a **bone** of contention
coo
bill and coo
cook
cook the **books**
cook your **goose**
your **goose** is cooked
cookie
caught with your hand
in the **cookie** jar
a smart **cookie**
that's the way the
cookie crumbles
a tough **cookie**
cooks
too many **cooks**
too many **cooks** in the
kitchen
too many **cooks** spoil
the broth
cool
cool as a cucumber
cool your **heels**
coop
fly the **coop**
cop
cop it **sweet**
not much **cop**
copy
a **carbon** copy
copybook
blot your **copybook**
cord
cut the **cord**

cut the umbilical **cord**
corn
earn your **corn**
eat your **seed** corn
seed corn
corner
box someone into a
corner
fight your **corner**
in your **corner**
paint someone into a
corner
turn the **corner**
corners
cut **corners**
cost
cost an **arm** and a leg
couch
a **couch** potato
count
count the beans: see
bean
don't count your
chickens before
they're hatched
down for the **count**
not count your
chickens
out for the **count**
counted
stand up and be
counted
counter
a **bean** counter
under the **counter**
country
not your **line** of country
courage
Dutch **courage**
course
par for the course
courses
horses for courses
court
the **ball** is in your court
hold **court**
laughed out of **court**
Coventry
send someone to
Coventry
cover
cover all the **bases**
cover the **waterfront**
cover your **tracks**
you can't judge a **book**
by its cover

cow
a **cash** cow
have a **cow**
a sacred **cow**
cows
until the **cows** come
home
crack
crack the **whip**
a fair crack of the **whip**
a sledgehammer to
crack a **nut**
a tough **nut** to crack
cracks
fall through the **cracks**
paper over the **cracks**
slip through the **cracks**
cradle
rob the **cradle**
cradle-snatching
cradle-snatching
cramp
cramp someone's **style**
crannies
the **nooks** and crannies
crash
crash and burn
crawl
make your **skin** crawl
crazy
crazy as a bedbug
go **ape** crazy
cream
like the **cat** that got the
cream
creature
creature comforts
creek
up shit **creek**
up the **creek**
up the **creek** without a
paddle
crest
on the **crest** of a wave
ride the **crest** of the
wave
cricket
it's just not **cricket**
critical
go **critical**
crock
a **crock** of gold
crocodile
shed **crocodile** tears

Croesus
rich as Croesus
crook
by **hook** or by crook
cropper
come a **cropper**
cross
cross my **heart**
cross **swords**
cross that **bridge** when
you come to it
cross the **line**
cross the **Rubicon**
a **cross** to bear
cross your **fingers**
cross your **mind**
dot the i's and cross the
t's
crossed
fingers crossed
get your lines **crossed**
get your wires **crossed**
keep your **fingers**
crossed
crossfire
caught in the **crossfire**
crow
as the **crow** flies
eat **crow**
crown
the **jewel** in someone's
crown
crumble
that's the way the
cookie crumbles
cry
cry for the **moon**
cry on someone's
shoulder
cry **wolf**
a **hue** and cry
in full **cry**
a **shoulder** to cry on
crying
it's no use crying over
spilled **milk**
a voice crying in the
wilderness
crystal
clear as crystal
a crystal **ball**
cucumber
cool as a cucumber
cudgels
take up the **cudgels**

cup
not your **cup** of tea
there is many a **slip**
twixt cup and lip
cupboard
cupboard love
a **skeleton** in the
cupboard
curate
a **curate's** egg
curiosity
curiosity killed the cat
curl
curl your **hair**
make your **hair** curl
make your **toes** curl
curlies
by the **short** and curlies
curtain
bring the **curtain** down
on something
the **curtain** comes down
curtains
it's **curtains**
mean **curtains**
spell **curtains**
curve
curve balls
throw someone a **curve**
throw someone a **curve**
ball
cuss
not give a **tinker's** cuss
cut
a **cut** above
a **cut** above the rest
cut a **dash**
cut and dried
cut and run
the **cut** and thrust
cut both **ways**
cut **corners**
cut from the same **cloth**
cut **loose**
cut no **ice**
cut off your **nose** to
spite your face
cut someone **dead**
cut someone down to
size
cut someone some **slack**
cut someone to the
quick
cut the **cord**
cut the Gordian **knot**

cut the **ground** from
under someone
cut the **ground** from
under someone's feet
cut the umbilical **cord**
cut to the **bone**
cut to the **chase**
cut two **ways**
cut up **rough**
cut your **cloth**
cut your coat according
to your **cloth**
cut your **losses**
cut your own **throat**
cut your **teeth**
fish or cut **bait**
have your **work** cut out
like a **chicken** with its
head cut off
not cut the **mustard**
to cut a long **story** short
cutting
a cutting **edge**
the cutting **edge**
cylinders
fire on all **cylinders**
dab
a **dab** hand
daft
daft as a brush
daggers
at **daggers** drawn
look **daggers** at someone
shoot **daggers** at
someone
daisies
push up the **daisies**
daisy
fresh as a daisy
dam
water over the dam
damn
damn with faint **praise**
not give a **tinker's** damn
Damocles
the **Sword** of Damocles
damp
a damp **squib**
dampener
put a dampener on
something: see
damper
damper
put a **damper** on
something

dance
dance to someone's **tune**
lead you a merry **dance**
make a **song** and dance about something

dancing
all-singing, all-dancing

dander
get someone's **dander** up

dangle
dangle a **carrot** in front of someone

Daniel
Daniel in the **lion**'s den

dark
a dark **horse**
keep something **dark**
a leap in the **dark**
a shot in the **dark**
a stab in the **dark**
whistle in the **dark**

darken
never darken someone's **door**
not darken somewhere's **door**

dash
cut a **dash**

date
past your sell-by **date**

dawn
a false **dawn**

day
call it a **day**
carry the **day**
clear as day
the **day** of reckoning
every **dog** has its day
have a **field** day
honest as the day is long
in the cold **light** of day
make my **day**
the **order** of the day
plain as day
put off the **evil** day
a **red** letter day
Rome was not built in a day
save for a rainy **day**
seize the **day**

daylight
daylight **robbery**

daylights
beat the living **daylights** out of someone
scare the living **daylights** out of someone

days
dog **days**
halcyon days
have seen better **days**
someone's **days** are numbered
your **salad** days

dead
beat a dead **horse**
cut someone **dead**
dead as a dodo
dead as a doornail
a dead **duck**
a dead **end**
dead from the **neck** up
the dead **hand**
dead in the water
a dead **letter**
a dead **loss**
dead **meat**
dead men's **shoes**
dead men tell no **tales**
a dead **ringer** for someone
the dead **spit**
dead to **rights**
dead to the **world**
a dead **weight**
dead **wood**
flog a dead **horse**
knock 'em **dead**
knock someone **dead**
over my dead **body**
wouldn't be caught **dead**
wouldn't be seen **dead**

dead-end
dead-**end**

deaf
deaf as a post
fall on deaf **ears**
turn a deaf **ear** to something

deal
a done **deal**
get a raw **deal**

death
at **death**'s door

dice with **death**
the **kiss** of death
like **death** warmed over
like **death** warmed up
sign someone's **death** warrant
sign your own **death** warrant
sound the death **knell**

deck
all hands on **deck**
hit the **deck**
a loose **cannon** on the deck
not play with a full **deck**
play with a loaded **deck**
play with a stacked **deck**
several cards **short** of a full deck
stack the **deck**

decks
clear the **decks**

deep
between the **devil** and the deep blue sea
dig deep: see **pocket**
dig deep into your **pocket**
go off the deep **end**
in at the deep **end**
in deep **water**
still **waters** run deep

deer
like a deer caught in the **headlights**

deliver
deliver the **goods**

delivered
signed, sealed, and delivered

den
Daniel in the **lion**'s den
walk into the **lion**'s den

depth
out of your **depth**

depths
plumb the **depths**

deserts
just **deserts**

devices
left to your own **devices**

devil
better the **devil** you know

between the **devil** and
the deep blue sea
the **devil** take the
hindmost
every man for himself
and the **devil** take
the hindmost
speak of the **devil**
talk of the **devil**

diamond
a **diamond** in the rough
a rough **diamond**

dice
dice with **death**
load the **dice** against
someone
no **dice**

Dick
every **Tom**, Dick, and
Harry

die
the **die** is cast
die on the **vine**
die with your **boots** on
straight as a die

different
a different **ball** game
a different **kettle** of fish
different **strokes** for
different folks
march to a different
drummer
march to a different
tune
march to the beat of a
different drummer
sing a different tune

dig
dig deep: see **pocket**
dig deep into your
pocket
dig in your **heels**
dig up **dirt**
dig your own **grave**

dilemma
the **horns** of a dilemma

dime
a **dime** a dozen
nickel and dime
on a **dime**
turn on a **dime**

dinner
a **dog's** dinner
done like a **dinner**

dinners
do something more
than someone has had
hot **dinners**

dip
dip into your **pocket**

dirt
dig up **dirt**
dish the **dirt**
do someone **dirt**
do the **dirt** on someone
hit **pay** dirt
rub someone's **nose** in
the dirt
strike **pay** dirt

dirty
air your **dirty** laundry
in public
a dirty **word**
dirty your **hands**
do someone's dirty
work
do the **dirty** on someone
down and dirty
do your **dirty** washing
in public
get your **hands** dirty
wash your **dirty** linen
in public

dish
dish the **dirt**

dishwater
dull as dishwater

distance
go the **distance**
go the full **distance**

ditch
last **ditch**

ditchwater
dull as ditchwater

divide
divide and conquer
divide and rule

Dixie
whistle **Dixie**

do
do a **land-office**
business
do a **number** on
someone
do someone **dirt**
do someone's dirty
work
do the **dirt** on someone
do the **dirty** on someone

do the **donkey** work
do the **trick**
do your **nut**

dodo
dead as a dodo

dog
a **dog** and pony show
dog **days**
a **dog's** breakfast
a **dog's** dinner
every **dog** has its day
fight like **cat** and dog
a **hair** of the dog
a **hair** of the dog that
bit you
it's a **dog's** life
sick as a dog
a sleeping dog: see **dogs**
the **tail** wags the dog
you can't teach an old
dog new tricks

dog-eat-dog
dog-eat-dog

doghouse
in the **doghouse**

dog-in-the-manger
dog-in-the-manger

dogs
call off the **dogs**
go to the **dogs**
it's raining **cats** and
dogs
let sleeping **dogs** lie
throw someone to the
dogs

doldrums
in the **doldrums**
out of the **doldrums**

dollar
the 64,000 **dollar**
question
bet your bottom **dollar**

dollars
dollars to doughnuts

domino
a **domino** effect

done
done and dusted
a done **deal**
done like a **dinner**

donkey
donkey's years
do the **donkey** work
talk the hind **leg** off a
donkey

door
at **death**'s door
beat a path to
someone's **door**
by the back **door**
close the barn **door**
after the horse has
gone
close the stable **door**
after the horse has
bolted
a **foot** in the door
keep the **wolf** from the
door
lay something at
someone's **door**
never darken
someone's **door**
not darken
somewhere's **door**
push at an open **door**
the revolving **door**

doornail
dead as a doornail

doors
behind closed **doors**

dose
give someone a dose of
their own **medicine**

dot
dot the i's and cross the
t's
on the **dot**
since the year **dot**

double
at the **double**
a double **bind**
on the **double**

double-edged
a double-edged **sword**

doughnuts
dollars to doughnuts

down
down and dirty
down and out
down for the **count**
down in the **dumps**
down in the **mouth**
down on your **uppers**
down the **hatch**
down the **road**
down to **earth**
down to the **wire**
have a **down** on
someone

down-at-heel
down-at-heel

down-at-the-heels
down-at-the-heels

downer
have a downer on
someone: see **down**

dozen
a **baker**'s dozen
a **dime** a dozen
six of one and half a
dozen of the other
talk **nineteen** to the
dozen

drag
drag someone through
the mud
drag your feet
drag your heels

drag-out
a knock-down drag-out
fight

drakes
play **ducks** and drakes
with someone

drape
drape yourself in the
flag

draw
draw a **bead** on
draw a **blank**
draw a **line** under
something
draw a **veil** over
something
draw in your **horns**
draw someone's **fire**
draw the **line**
draw the short **straw**
the **luck** of the draw

drawer
the top **drawer**

drawing
back to the drawing
board

drawn
at **daggers** drawn
the **battle** lines are
drawn

dream
a **dream** ticket

dress
dress to the **nines**

dressed
dressed to kill

mutton dressed as lamb

dried
cut and dried

drink
drink like a **fish**
drink someone under
the **table**
meat and drink to
someone
you can lead a **horse** to
water but you can't
make him drink

drinking
drinking in the last
chance **saloon**

drive
drive a **coach** and
horses through
something
drive a **wedge** between
people
drive someone up the
wall

driver
in the driver's **seat**

driving
in the driving **seat**

drop
at the **drop** of a hat
drop a **brick**
a **drop** in the bucket
a **drop** in the ocean
drop into your **lap**
drop like **flies**
drop something like a
hot brick: see **potato**
drop something like a
hot **potato**
drop the **ball**
drop the other **shoe**
drop your **bundle**
the **penny** drops

drown
drown your **sorrows**

drowning
a drowning man will
clutch at a straw: see
straws

drum
bang the **drum**
beat the **drum**

drummer
march to a different
drummer
march to the beat of a
different drummer

drunk
  drunk as a skunk
dry
  bleed someone dry
  dry as a bone
  dry as dust
  hang someone out to
    dry
  home and dry
  keep your powder dry
  leave someone high
    and dry
duck
  a dead duck
  a lame duck
  like water off a duck's
    back
  a sitting duck
  take to something like
    a duck to water
ducks
  get your ducks in a row
  play ducks and drakes
    with someone
dudgeon
  in high dudgeon
dull
  dull as dishwater
  dull as ditchwater
dummy
  a dummy run
  spit out the dummy
  spit the dummy
dumps
  down in the dumps
  in the dumps
dust
  bite the dust
  dry as dust
  the dust clears
  the dust settles
  eat someone's dust
  gather dust
  not see someone for
    dust
  shake the dust of
    somewhere from your
    feet
dusted
  done and dusted
dusty
  a dusty answer
  a dusty reply
Dutch
  Dutch courage

a Dutch treat
go Dutch
in Dutch
dyed-in-the-wool
  dyed-in-the-wool
eager
  an eager beaver
eagle
  an eagle eye
ear
  bend someone's ear
  a flea in your ear
  go in one ear and out
    the other
  grin from ear to ear
  half an ear
  have an ear for
    something
  have a tin ear for
    something
  have someone's ear
  keep your ear to the
    ground
  lend an ear to someone
  make a pig's ear of
    something
  out on your ear
  play it by ear
  smile from ear to ear
  turn a deaf ear to
    something
  a word in someone's ear
  you can't make a silk
    purse out of a sow's
    ear
early
  an early bath
  an early bird
  the early bird catches
    the worm
earn
  earn your corn
  earn your spurs
ears
  be all ears
  cloth ears
  fall on deaf ears
  have something coming
    out of your ears
  have steam coming out
    of your ears
  music to your ears
  pin back your ears
  pin someone's ears back
  prick up your ears

someone's ears are
  burning
up to your ears
walls have ears
wet behind the ears
earth
  down to earth
  go to earth
  move heaven and earth
  promise the earth
  run someone to earth
  the salt of the earth
easy
  easy as ABC
  easy as falling off a log
  easy as pie
  an easy touch
eat
  eat crow
  eat humble pie
  eat like a bird
  eat like a horse
  eat someone out of
    house and home
  eat someone's dust
  eat your hat
  eat your heart out
  eat your seed corn
  eat your words
  have your cake and
    eat it
eating
  have someone eating
    out of the palm of
    your hand
  have someone eating
    out of your hand
  the proof of the
    pudding is in the
    eating
ebb
  at a low ebb
eclipse
  in eclipse
edge
  a cutting edge
  the cutting edge
  give someone the rough
    edge of your tongue
  lose your edge
  on the edge of your
    chair
  on the edge of your seat
  set your teeth on edge
  take the edge off
    something

edges
fray at the **edges**
rough **edges**

edgeways
get a **word** in edgeways

edgewise
get a **word** in edgewise

eel
slippery as an eel

effect
a **domino** effect

egg
chicken and egg
a **curate's** egg
egg on your face
kill the **goose** that lays
  the golden egg
lay an **egg**
a **nest** egg

eggs
put all your **eggs** in
  one basket
sure as eggs
sure as eggs is eggs
teach your
  grandmother to
  suck eggs
walk on eggs: see
  eggshells
you can't make an
  omelette without
  breaking eggs

eggshells
walk on **eggshells**

eight
behind the eight **ball**

elbow
all **power** to your elbow
elbow grease
elbow room
not know your arse
  from your **elbow**
not know your ass
  from your **elbow**

elbows
rub **elbows** with
  someone

element
in your **element**
out of your **element**

elephant
a white **elephant**

eleventh
the eleventh **hour**

empty
empty **vessels** make

the most noise
empty **vessels** make
  the most sound

end
at a loose **end**
at the end of the
  rainbow
at the end of your **rope**
at the end of your
  tether
a dead **end**
the **end** of the line
the **end** of the road
get hold of the wrong
  end of the **stick**
get the short end of the
  stick
get the wrong end of
  the **stick**
go off the deep **end**
hold your **end** up
in at the deep **end**
keep your **end** up
the **light** at the end of
  the tunnel
make your **hair** stand
  on end
not see beyond the end
  of your **nose**
the pot of gold at the
  end of the **rainbow**
quote, end quote
the sharp **end**
the thin end of the
  wedge

ends
at loose ends: see **end**
burn the **candle** at
  both ends
loose **ends**
make **ends** meet
play both **ends** against
  the middle

Englishman
an **Englishman's** home
  is his castle

envelope
push the **envelope**

envy
green with envy

escutcheon
a **blot** on your
  escutcheon

estimate
a **ballpark** estimate

even
give a sucker an even
  break
give someone an even
  break
on an even **keel**

everything
everything is coming
  up **roses**

evil
the lesser evil: see **evils**
the love of money is the
  root of all evil
money is the **root** of all
  evil
put off the **evil** day

evils
the lesser of two **evils**

exception
the **exception** that
  proves the rule

expedition
a **fishing** expedition

extra
go the extra **mile**

eye
the **apple** of your eye
cast your **eye** on
  something
catch someone's **eye**
an **eagle** eye
an **eye** for an eye
an **eye** for an eye, a
  tooth for a tooth
the **eye** of the storm
get your **eye** in
give someone a black **eye**
a gleam in your **eye**
in your **mind's** eye
keep a **weather** eye on
  something
keep your **eye** on the
  ball
the naked **eye**
not bat an **eye**
one in the **eye** for
  someone
see **eye** to eye with
  someone
spit in someone's **eye**
take your **eye** off the
  ball
there's less to
  something than meets
  the **eye**

there's more to
something than meets
the **eye**
turn a blind **eye** to
something
a worm's eye **view**
would give your **eye**
teeth for something
eyeball
eyeball to eyeball
eyeballs
up to the **eyeballs**
eyebrows
raise **eyebrows**
eyelash
not bat an eyelash: see
eyelid
eyelid
not bat an **eyelid**
eyes
blow **smoke** in
someone's eyes
cast your eyes on
something: see **eye**
feast your **eyes** on
something
have **eyes** in the back
of your head
keep your **eyes** open
keep your **eyes** peeled
keep your **eyes** skinned
make **eyes** at someone
make **sheep**'s eyes
only have **eyes** for
someone
open someone's **eyes**
open your **eyes**
pull the **wool** over
someone's eyes
the **scales** fall from
your eyes
a **sight** for sore eyes
stars in your eyes
up to your **eyes**
with your **eyes** closed
with your **eyes** glued
to something
with your **eyes** shut
face
at **face** value
blow **smoke** in
someone's face
cut off your **nose** to
spite your face
egg on your face

face the **music**
fall **flat** on your face
fly in the **face** of
something
keep a straight **face**
laugh on the other side
of your **face**
a long **face**
lose **face**
make a **face**
plain as the nose on
your face
pull a **face**
save **face**
set your **face** against
something
a **slap** in the face
until you are blue in
the **face**
faint
damn with faint **praise**
fair
all's **fair** in love and
war
by fair **means** or foul
fair and square
a fair crack of the **whip**
fair-haired
your fair-haired **boy**
fall
be heading for a **fall**
be riding for a **fall**
the **bottom** falls out of
something
fall apart at the **seams**
fall between two **stools**
fall by the **wayside**
fall **flat** on your face
fall from **grace**
fall **head** over heels
fall into the **trap**
fall into your **lap**
fall like **ninepins**
fall off the **perch**
fall off the **wagon**
fall off your **perch**
fall on deaf **ears**
fall on stony **ground**
fall on your **feet**
fall through the **cracks**
fall through the **net**
the **scales** fall from
your eyes
falling
easy as falling off a log

simple as falling off a
log
false
a false **dawn**
sail under false **colours**
familiarity
familiarity breeds
contempt
familiarity breeds
content
family
the black **sheep** of the
family
famine
feast or famine
famous
famous last **words**
fan
fan the **flames**
the **shit** hits the fan
fancy-free
footloose and fancy-free
farm
buy the **farm**
fashion
parrot fashion
fast
the fast **lane**
the fast **track**
play **fast** and loose
pull a **fast** one
fat
chew the **fat**
a fat **cat**
the **fat** is in the fire
the **fat** of the land
it isn't over until the
fat **lady** sings
fate
seal someone's **fate**
fatted
kill the fatted **calf**
fear
fools rush in where
angels fear to tread
feast
enough is as good as a
feast
feast or famine
feast your **eyes** on
something
the **ghost** at the feast
the skeleton at the **feast**
the spectre at the **feast**
feather
birds of a feather

birds of a feather flock
together
a **feather** in your cap
feather your **nest**
light as a feather
feathers
ruffle someone's
feathers
smooth ruffled **feathers**
fed
fed up to the back **teeth**
feed
bite the **hand** that
feeds you
chicken feed
feeding
a feeding **frenzy**
feel
feel something in your
bones
feel the **pinch**
feet
clay **feet**
cut the **ground** from
under someone's feet
drag your feet
fall on your **feet**
feet on the ground
find your **feet**
get cold **feet**
get your **feet** on the
ground
get your **feet** under the
table
get your **feet** wet
have **feet** of clay
itchy **feet**
land on your **feet**
pull the **rug** from under
your feet
shake the **dust** of
somewhere from your
feet
stand on your own **feet**
stand on your own two
feet
two left **feet**
vote with your **feet**
fence
come off the **fence**
the **grass** is always
greener on the other
side of the fence
sit on the **fence**

fences
mend **fences**
fiddle
fiddle while **Rome**
burns
fit as a fiddle
play second **fiddle**
field
have a **field** day
a level **playing field**
level the **playing field**
out in left **field**
out of left **field**
play the **field**
fifth
a fifth **wheel**
fig
a **fig** leaf
fight
can't fight your way
out of a **paper** bag
fight a losing **battle**
fight a **rearguard** action
fight **fire** with fire
fight like **cat** and dog
fight like **Kilkenny** cats
fight **tooth** and claw
fight **tooth** and nail
fight your **corner**
a knock-down drag-out
fight
fighting
come out fighting
in fighting **trim**
figure
a **ballpark** figure
fill
fill someone's **boots**
fill someone's **shoes**
fill the **bill**
fill your **boots**
filling
the filling in the
sandwich
final
the final **nail** in the
coffin
the final **straw**
find
find your **feet**
find your **tongue**
fine
a fine **kettle** of fish
the fine **print**
not to put too fine a
point on it

fine-tooth
with a fine-tooth **comb**
fine-toothed
with a fine-toothed **comb**
finger
get your **finger** out
give someone the **finger**
have a **finger** in every
pie
have a **finger** in the pie
not lift a **finger**
not raise a **finger**
point the **finger** at
someone
pull your **finger** out
put the **finger** on
someone
put your **finger** on
something
twist someone around
your little **finger**
fingers
all fingers and **thumbs**
burn your **fingers**
cross your **fingers**
fingers crossed
get your **fingers** burned
have green **fingers**
have your fingers in
the **till**
itchy **fingers**
keep your **fingers**
crossed
work your **fingers** to
the bone
fingertips
at your **fingertips**
fire
add **fuel** to the fire
a **baptism** of fire
be under **fire**
breathe **fire**
catch **fire**
come under **fire**
draw someone's **fire**
the **fat** is in the fire
fight **fire** with fire
fire **blanks**
fire in your belly
fire on all **cylinders**
get on like a **house** on
fire
hang **fire**
have a lot of **irons** in
the fire

hold **fire**
hold your **fire**
in the **line** of fire
light a **fire** under
someone
not set the **world** on fire
out of the **frying pan**
into the fire
play with **fire**
pull someone's
chestnuts out of the
fire
set the **heather** on fire
there's no **smoke**
without fire
where there's **smoke**
there's fire

firing
in the firing **line**
out of the firing **line**

first
first off the **mark**
first past the **post**
get to first **base**
of the first **water**

fish
another **kettle** of fish
a big **fish**
a big **fish** in a small
pond
a cold **fish**
a different **kettle** of fish
drink like a **fish**
a fine **kettle** of fish
fish in troubled **waters**
fish or cut **bait**
a **fish** out of water
have bigger **fish** to fry
have other **fish** to fry
like shooting **fish** in a
barrel
neither **fish** nor fowl
a pretty **kettle** of fish
there are other **fish** in
the sea
there are plenty more
fish in the sea

fishing
a **fishing** expedition

fist
hand over fist
an **iron** fist
an **iron** fist in a velvet
glove

fit
fit as a fiddle

fit as a flea
fit the **bill**
fit to be tied
if the **cap** fits
if the **shoe** fits

fits
in **fits** and starts

five
know how many **beans**
make five

fix
if it ain't **broke**, don't
fix it

flag
drape yourself in the
flag
fly the **flag**
keep the **flag** flying
a red **flag**
a red flag before a **bull**
wrap yourself in the
flag

flagpole
run something up the
flagpole

flags
put the **flags** out

flame
like a **moth** to a flame
an old **flame**

flames
add **fuel** to the flames
fan the **flames**
go down in **flames**
go up in **flames**
shoot down in **flames**

flash
flash in the pan

flat
fall **flat** on your face
flat as a pancake
in a flat **spin**

flat-footed
catch someone
flat-footed

flavor: see flavour

flavour
flavour of the month

flea
fit as a flea
a **flea** in your ear

flesh
flesh and blood
put **flesh** on something

put **flesh** on the bones
of something
a **thorn** in your flesh
your **pound** of flesh

flex
flex your **muscles**

flick
give someone the **flick**
give someone the **flick**
pass

flies
as the **crow** flies
drop like **flies**
there are no **flies** on
someone

flip
flip your lid
flip your wig

float
float on **air**
float someone's **boat**

flock
birds of a feather flock
together

flog
flog a dead **horse**

floodgates
the **floodgates** open
open the **floodgates**

floor
get in on the **ground**
floor
through the **floor**
wipe the **floor** with
someone

flow
go with the **flow**

flown
the **bird** has flown

fly
fly a **kite**
fly **blind**
fly by the **seat** of your
pants
fly in the **face** of
something
the **fly** in the ointment
fly off the **handle**
a **fly** on the wall
fly the **coop**
fly the **flag**
fly the **nest**
like a blue-arsed **fly**
on the **fly**
pigs might fly

sparks fly

flying
the **fur** is flying
keep the **flag** flying
with flying **colours**

foam
foam at the **mouth**

folks
different **strokes** for
different folks

follow
follow in someone's
footsteps
follow **suit**
follow your **nose**
a hard **act** to follow

follower
a **camp** follower

food
food for thought

fool
a **fool** and his money
are soon parted
fool's gold
live in a **fool**'s paradise

fools
fools rush in
fools rush in where
angels fear to tread

foot
the boot is on the other
foot
caught on the wrong
foot
a **foot** in both camps
a **foot** in each camp
a **foot** in the door
foot the **bill**
get off on the wrong
foot
not put a **foot** wrong
one **foot** in the grave
put your best **foot**
forward
put your **foot** down
put your **foot** in it
put your **foot** in your
mouth
the shoe is on the other
foot
shoot yourself in the
foot
start off on the right
foot
wait on someone **hand**

and foot

foot-in-the-door
foot-in-the-door

footloose
footloose and fancy-free

footsteps
follow in someone's
footsteps

forbidden
forbidden **fruit**

force
force someone's **hand**

forearmed
forewarned is
forearmed

forelock
touch your **forelock**
tug your **forelock**

forest
not see the forest for
the **trees**

forewarned
forewarned is
forearmed

forked
speak with forked
tongue

former
a **shadow** of your
former self

fort
hold down the **fort**
hold the **fort**

fortune
a **hostage** to fortune

forty
forty **winks**

forward
put your best **foot**
forward

foul
by fair **means** or foul
foul your own **nest**

fowl
neither **fish** nor fowl

frame
in the **frame**
the name in the **frame**

fray
fray at the **edges**

free
a free **hand**
a free **ride**
give someone free **rein**
there's no such thing

as a free **lunch**

freefall
go into **freefall**
in **freefall**

freeze
cold enough to freeze
the balls off a **brass**
monkey
hell freezes over
make your **blood** freeze

frenzy
a feeding **frenzy**

fresh
a **breath** of fresh air
fresh as a daisy
fresh as paint
fresh **blood**
fresh **pastures**

frighteners
put the **frighteners** on
someone

fritz
on the **fritz**

frog
a **frog** in your throat

front
in the front **line**
on the front **burner**

frosting
the frosting on the
cake: see **icing**

froth
froth at the **mouth**

fruit
bear **fruit**
forbidden **fruit**

fruitcake
nutty as a fruitcake

fry
have bigger **fish** to fry
have other **fish** to fry

frying
out of the **frying pan**
into the fire

fuel
add **fuel** to the fire
add **fuel** to the flames

full
at full **stretch**
at full **throttle**
come full **circle**
the full **monty**
full of **beans**
full **steam** ahead
go the full **distance**

have your **plate** full
in full **cry**
in full **swing**
in full **throttle**
not play with a full
    deck
several cards **short** of a
    full deck
the wheel has come full
    circle
full-court
    a full-court **press**
funeral
    it's your **funeral**
fur
    the **fur** is flying
furniture
    part of the **furniture**
furrow
    plough a lone **furrow**
    plough a lonely **furrow**
fury
    hell hath no fury like a
        woman scorned
fuse
    blow a **fuse**
    have a short **fuse**
    light the **fuse**
    on a short **fuse**
gab
    the **gift** of gab
    the **gift** of the gab
gaff
    blow the **gaff**
gain
    what you lose on the
        swings you gain on
        the roundabouts
gallery
    play to the **gallery**
game
    beat someone at their
        own **game**
    a different **ball** game
    the game is not worth
        the **candle**
    the **game** is up
    a game of **cat** and mouse
    a **game** plan
    give the **game** away
    the **name** of the game
    a new **ball** game
    new to the **game**
    the numbers **game**
    the only **game** in town

play someone at their
    own **game**
play the **game**
a **shell** game
a waiting **game**
a **zero-sum** game
gamekeeper
    poacher turned
        gamekeeper
gander
    what's **sauce** for the
        goose is sauce for the
        gander
garbage
    garbage in, garbage out
garden
    lead someone down the
        garden path
    lead someone up the
        garden path
garden-variety
    garden-variety
gas
    run out of **gas**
gather
    gather **dust**
    gather moss: see **stone**
gathers
    a rolling **stone** gathers
        no moss
gauntlet
    run the **gauntlet**
    take up the **gauntlet**
    throw down the
        gauntlet
genie
    the **genie** is out of the
        bottle
    let the **genie** out of the
        bottle
    put the **genie** back in
        the bottle
gentle
    gentle as a lamb
ghost
    the ghost at the **feast**
    give up the **ghost**
    lay the **ghost** of
        something
    white as a ghost
gift
    the **gift** of gab
    the **gift** of the gab
    look a **gift horse** in the
        mouth

gild
    gild the **lily**
gills
    green around the **gills**
gilt
    take the **gilt** off the
        gingerbread
gingerbread
    take the **gilt** off the
        gingerbread
gird
    gird your **loins**
glass
    the **glass** ceiling
    people who live in
        glass houses
        shouldn't throw stones
glasses
    rose-coloured glasses:
        see **rose-tinted**
gleam
    a gleam in your **eye**
glister
    all that glisters is not
        gold
glitter
    all that glitters is not
        gold
glove
    hand in glove
    an **iron** fist in a velvet
        glove
gloves
    the **gloves** are off
    handle someone with
        kid gloves
    treat someone with **kid**
        gloves
glued
    with your **eyes** glued
        to something
gnash
    gnash your **teeth**
gnashing
    gnashing of **teeth**
    wailing and gnashing
        of **teeth**
    weeping and gnashing
        of **teeth**
gnat
    strain at a **gnat**
    strain at a **gnat** and
        swallow a camel
go
    the **balloon** goes up

what goes around
  comes around: see **go**
goal
  an own **goal**
goalposts
  move the **goalposts**
goat
  act the **goat**
  get someone's **goat**
goats
  separate the **sheep**
    from the goats
god
  a little **tin** god
  a **tin** god
gods
  in the **lap** of the gods
gold
  all that glisters is not
    gold
  all that glitters is not
    gold
  a crock of **gold**
  fool's gold
  good as gold
  a **heart** of gold
  a pot of **gold**
  the pot of gold at the
    end of the **rainbow**
  strike **gold**
  worth your **weight** in
    gold
golden
  kill the golden **goose**
  kill the **goose** that lays
    the golden egg
good
  enough is as good as a
    feast
  good as gold
  have a good **innings**
  in good **odour**
  in someone's good
    books
  it's an ill **wind** that
    blows nobody any
    good
  no good to man or **beast**
  the road to **hell** is
    paved with good
    intentions
  take something in good
    part
  throw good **money**
    after bad

goods
  deliver the **goods**
  have the **goods** on
    someone
  sell someone a **bill** of
    goods
goose
  cook your **goose**
  kill the golden **goose**
  kill the **goose** that lays
    the golden egg
  what's **sauce** for the
    goose is sauce for the
    gander
  a wild **goose** chase
  wouldn't say boo to a
    goose
  your **goose** is cooked
gooseberry
  play **gooseberry**
Gordian
  cut the Gordian **knot**
  a Gordian **knot**
gospel
  the **gospel** truth
  take something as
    gospel
grab
  grab someone by the
    throat
grace
  fall from **grace**
  a saving **grace**
graces
  airs and graces
  put on **airs** and graces
grade
  make the **grade**
grain
  go against the **grain**
  separate the grain from
    the **chaff**
  take something with a
    grain of **salt**
grandmother
  teach your
    grandmother to
    suck eggs
grapes
  sour **grapes**
grapevine
  hear something
    through the
    grapevine
grasp
  grasp at **straws**

  grasp the **nettle**
grass
  the **grass** is always
    greener on the other
    side of the fence
  green as grass
  the other man's **grass**
    is always greener
  put someone out to
    grass
  a **snake** in the grass
grasshopper
  knee-high to a
    grasshopper
grave
  dig your own **grave**
  one **foot** in the grave
  turn in your **grave**
  turn over in your **grave**
gravy
  a **gravy** train
gray: see **grey**
grease
  elbow grease
  grease someone's **palm**
  grease the **wheels**
greased
  like a greased **pig**
greasy
  the greasy **pole**
great
  go great **guns**
  great **oaks** from little
    acorns grow
  no great **shakes**
Greek
  be **Greek** to someone
green
  give the green **light**
  green around the **gills**
  green as grass
  green with envy
  have a green **thumb**
  have green **fingers**
  the **rub** of the green
greener
  the **grass** is always
    greener on the other
    side of the fence
  greener **pastures**
  the other man's **grass**
    is always greener
grey
  a grey **area**
  the men in grey **suits**

grin
grin from **ear** to ear
grin like a Cheshire **cat**
grind
grind your **teeth**
have an **axe** to grind
grinder
the **organ** grinder's
monkey
grindstone
keep your **nose** to the
grindstone
grips
get to **grips** with
something
grist
grist for the mill
grit
grit your **teeth**
groove
in a **groove**
in the **groove**
ground
break new **ground**
cut the **ground** from
under someone
cut the **ground** from
under someone's feet
fall on stony **ground**
feet on the ground
get in on the **ground**
floor
get something off the
ground
get your **feet** on the
ground
go to **ground**
the high **ground**
hit the **ground** running
keep your **ear** to the
ground
the moral high **ground**
run someone into the
ground
run someone to **ground**
stamping **ground**
stomping **ground**
suit someone down to
the **ground**
thick on the **ground**
thin on the **ground**
grow
great **oaks** from little
acorns grow
not grow on **trees**

growing
growing **pains**
guard
the old **guard**
gum
up a **gum** tree
gun
hold a gun to
someone's **head**
jump the **gun**
a smoking **gun**
under the **gun**
guns
the big **guns**
go great **guns**
spike someone's **guns**
stick to your **guns**
with all **guns** blazing
guts
spill your **guts**
hackles
raise someone's
hackles
someone's **hackles** rise
Hades
hot as Hades
hair
curl your **hair**
a **hair** of the dog
a **hair** of the dog that
bit you
a **hair** shirt
haven't seen **hide** nor
hair of someone
in your **hair**
keep your **hair** on
let your **hair** down
make your **hair** curl
make your **hair** stand
on end
not turn a **hair**
out of your **hair**
put hair on the chest:
see **hairs**
tear your **hair** out
hairs
by the short **hairs**
put **hairs** on your chest
split **hairs**
halcyon
halcyon days
half
go off at **half** cock
half a **loaf** is better
than none

half an **ear**
six of one and half a
dozen of the other
you can't be half
pregnant
half-cocked
go off **half**-cocked
halfway
a halfway **house**
hammer
go at it **hammer** and
tongs
go at someone
hammer and tongs
under the **hammer**
hand
the **ace** in your hand
a **bird** in the hand
a **bird** in the hand is
worth two in the bush
bite the **hand** that
feeds you
cap in hand
caught with your hand
in the **cookie** jar
a **dab** hand
the dead **hand**
force someone's **hand**
a free **hand**
get out of **hand**
give with one **hand** and
take away with the
other
hand in glove
hand in hand
hand over fist
hand someone
something on a **plate**
hat in hand
have someone eating
out of the palm of
your **hand**
have someone eating
out of your **hand**
have the **whip** hand
have your hand in the
till
in the palm of your
hand
an **iron** hand
keep your **hand** in
live from **hand** to
mouth
live **hand** to mouth
an old **hand**

out of **hand**
overplay your **hand**
the right **hand** doesn't
  know what the left
  hand is doing
show your **hand**
a steady **hand** on the
  tiller
throw in your **hand**
the upper **hand**
wait on someone **hand**
  and foot
handle
  fly off the **handle**
  handle someone with
    kid gloves
  too **hot** to handle
hands
  all hands on **deck**
  beat someone **hands**
    down
  beat something **hands**
    down
  dirty your **hands**
  get your **hands** dirty
  have **blood** on your
    hands
  play into someone's
    hands
  putty in your hands
  rub your **hands**
  safe **hands**
  a safe pair of **hands**
  sit on your **hands**
  sully your **hands**
  time on your hands
  wash your **hands** of
    something
  win **hands** down
  wring your **hands**
  your **hands** are tied
handsome
  handsome is as
    handsome does
hand-to-mouth
  hand-to-mouth
handwriting
  the handwriting is on
    the **wall**
hang
  get the **hang** of
    something
  give someone enough
    rope to hang
    themselves

hang by a **thread**
hang **fire**
hang over your **head**
hang someone out to
  dry
hang up your boots
hanged
  might as well be
    hanged for a **sheep** as
    a lamb
hanging
  an **axe** hanging over
    something
ha'porth
  don't spoil the **ship** for
    a ha'porth of tar
happy
  happy as a clam
  happy as a lark
  happy as a pig in muck
  happy as a sandboy
  happy as Larry
  not a happy **bunny**
hard
  between a **rock** and a
    hard place
  a hard **act** to follow
  hard as nails
  hard on the **heels** of
    something
  hard on your **heels**
  a hard **row** to hoe
  the **school** of hard
    knocks
hardball
  play **hardball**
hare
  run with the **hare** and
    hunt with the hounds
  start a **hare**
harness
  in **harness**
Harry
  every **Tom**, Dick, and
    Harry
harvest
  reap the harvest
hat
  at the **drop** of a hat
  eat your **hat**
  hat in hand
  keep something under
    your **hat**
  knock something into a
    cocked **hat**

old **hat**
pass the **hat**
pass the **hat** around
pull a rabbit out of the
  hat
pull something out of
  the **hat**
take your **hat** off to
  someone
talk through your **hat**
throw your **hat** into the
  ring
hatch
  down the **hatch**
hatched
  don't count your
    chickens before
    they're hatched
hatches
  batten down the
    hatches
hatchet
  bury the **hatchet**
  a **hatchet** job
  a **hatchet** man
hath
  hell hath no fury like a
    woman scorned
hats
  hats off to someone: see
    hat
hatter
  mad as a hatter
haul
  haul someone over the
    coals
  in something for the
    long **haul**
  a long **haul**
  over the long **haul**
hawk
  watch someone like a
    hawk
hay
  hit the hay
  make **hay**
  make **hay** while the
    sun shines
haystack
  like looking for a
    needle in a haystack
head
  bang your head against
    a brick **wall**
  bang your head against
    a **wall**

be **head** over heels
bite someone's **head** off
bury your **head** in the
  sand
cannot make **head** or
  tail of something
come to a **head**
fall **head** over heels
get in over your **head**
give someone their **head**
go over someone's **head**
go to your **head**
hang over your **head**
have **eyes** in the back
  of your head
have your **head** in the
  clouds
have your **head**
  screwed on
a **head** of steam
hit the **nail** on the head
hold a gun to
  someone's **head**
keep your **head** above
  water
keep your **head** below
  the parapet
keep your **head** down
knock something on
  the **head**
like a **bear** with a sore
  head
like a **chicken** with its
  head cut off
need something like a
  hole in the head
off the top of your **head**
on your **head**
put your **head** above
  the parapet
put your **head** in a
  noose
put your head into the
  lion's mouth
put your head on the
  block
raise its **head**
rear its **head**
rear its ugly **head**
a **rush** of blood to the
  head
scratch your **head**
snap someone's **head** off
stand something on its
  head

stick your **head** in a
  noose
talk over someone's
  head
turn something on its
  head
heading
  be heading for a **fall**
headless
  like a headless **chicken**
headlights
  like a deer caught in
    the **headlights**
  like a rabbit caught in
    the **headlights**
heads
  bang people's **heads**
    together
  heads roll
  knock people's **heads**
    together
  turn **heads**
headway
  make **headway**
health
  a clean **bill** of health
heap
  the bottom of the **heap**
  the top of the **heap**
hear
  hear something
    through the
    grapevine
heart
  a bleeding **heart**
  cross my **heart**
  eat your **heart** out
  a **heart** of gold
  warm the **cockles** of
    your heart
  wear your **heart** on
    your sleeve
  your **heart** bleeds for
    someone
  your **heart** is in the
    right place
  your **heart** is in your
    mouth
heartstrings
  tug at the **heartstrings**
heat
  if you can't stand the
    heat, get out of the
    kitchen
heather
  set the **heather** on fire

heaven
  in seventh **heaven**
  move **heaven** and earth
heavy
  make heavy **weather**
    of something
hedge
  hedge your **bets**
heel
  bring someone to **heel**
  call someone to **heel**
heels
  be **head** over heels
  cool your **heels**
  dig in your **heels**
  drag your heels
  fall **head** over heels
  hard on the **heels** of
    something
  hard on your **heels**
  hot on the **heels** of
    something
  hot on your **heels**
  kick up your **heels**
  kick your **heels**
  rock you back on your
    heels
  set you back on your
    heels
  show a clean pair of
    heels
  take to your **heels**
hell
  all **hell** breaks loose
  come **hell** or high water
  hell for leather
  hell freezes over
  hell hath no fury like a
    woman scorned
  like a **bat** out of hell
  play **hell**
  play **hell** with
    something
  play merry **hell**
  play merry **hell** with
    something
  the road to **hell** is
    paved with good
    intentions
  there'll be **hell** to pay
  to **hell** and back
hen
  rare as **hen**'s teeth
herd
  ride **herd** on someone

here
the **buck** stops here
herring
a red **herring**
hide
haven't seen **hide** nor
hair of someone
hide your light under a
bushel
hiding
on a **hiding** to nothing
high
come down off your
high **horse**
come **hell** or high water
for the high **jump**
get on your high **horse**
high as a kite
the high **ground**
in high **dudgeon**
leave someone **high**
and dry
live high on the **hog**
the moral high **ground**
ride **high**
ride high in the **saddle**
search **high** and low for
something
take the high **road**
highway
highway **robbery**
hill
not amount to a hill of
beans
over the **hill**
hills
old as the hills
hilt
to the **hilt**
hind
talk the hind **leg** off a
donkey
hindmost
the **devil** take the
hindmost
every man for himself
and the **devil** take
the hindmost
hip
joined at the **hip**
shoot from the **hip**
hit
hit a **home** run
hit and miss
hit **home**

hit it off
hit it on the **nail**
a **hit** list
hit or miss
hit **pay** dirt
hit **rock** bottom
hit someone for **six**
hit the big **time**
hit the **buffers**
hit the ceiling: see **roof**
hit the **deck**
hit the **ground** running
hit the hay
hit the **jackpot**
hit the **mark**
hit the **nail** on the head
hit the **road**
hit the **roof**
hit the sack
hit the **spot**
hit the **wall**
hit your **stride**
the **shit** hits the fan
hitch
hitch your **wagon** to a
star
hitch your **wagon** to
someone
Hobson
Hobson's choice
hoe
a hard **row** to hoe
a tough **row** to hoe
hog
go **hog** wild
go the whole **hog**
go whole **hog**
live high on the **hog**
hoist
hoist by your own
petard
hold
can't hold a **candle** to
someone
get hold of the wrong
end of the **stick**
hold a gun to
someone's **head**
hold all the **aces**
hold **body** and soul
together
hold **court**
hold down the **fort**
hold **fire**
hold no **brief** for

something
hold someone on a tight
rein
hold someone to
ransom
hold the **fort**
hold the **purse** strings
hold your **end** up
hold your **fire**
hold your **horses**
hold your **own**
hold your **tongue**
not hold **water**
holding
leave someone holding
the **baby**
leave someone holding
the **bag**
hole
burn a **hole** in your
pocket
have an **ace** in the hole
a **hole** card
in the **hole**
need something like a
hole in the head
a square **peg** in a
round hole
hole-and-corner
hole-and-corner
hole-in-the-corner
hole-in-the-corner
holes
more holes than **Swiss**
cheese
holiday
a **busman**'s holiday
holies
the **holy** of holies
hollow
beat someone **hollow**
holy
the **holy** of holies
home
bring **home** the bacon
bring something **home**
to someone
the chickens come
home to **roost**
close to **home**
come home to **roost**
eat someone out of
house and home
an **Englishman**'s home
is his castle

hit a **home** run
hit **home**
home and dry
home and hosed
the **home** straight
the **home** stretch
the **lights** are on but nobody is at home
nothing to write **home** about
pick up your **marbles** and go home
something to write **home** about
strike **home**
until the **cows** come home

honest
honest as the day is long

honey
the land of **milk** and honey
milk and honey

hoof
on the **hoof**

hook
by **hook** or by crook
hook, line, and sinker
on your own **hook**
ring off the **hook**
sling your **hook**

hooks
get your **hooks** into someone

hoops
go through the **hoops**
jump through **hoops**

hoot
not give a **hoot**

hoots
not give two hoots: see **hoot**

hop
catch someone on the hop
a **hop** and a skip
a **hop**, skip, and a jump

horn
blow your own **horn**
toot your own **horn**

hornet
mad as a hornet
stir up a **hornet's** nest

horns
draw in your **horns**

the **horns** of a dilemma
lock **horns**
pull in your **horns**
take the **bull** by the horns

horse
back the wrong **horse**
beat a dead **horse**
close the barn **door** after the horse has gone
close the stable **door** after the horse has bolted
come down off your high **horse**
a dark **horse**
eat like a **horse**
flog a dead **horse**
from the **horse's** mouth
get on your high **horse**
look a **gift horse** in the mouth
put the **cart** before the horse
a stalking **horse**
strong as a horse
a Trojan **horse**
you can lead a **horse** to water but you can't make him drink

horses
change horses in **midstream**
drive a **coach** and horses through something
hold your **horses**
horses for courses
ride two **horses** at the same time
wild **horses**

hosed
home and hosed

hostage
a **hostage** to fortune

hot
blow **hot**
blow **hot** and cold
a **cat** on a hot tin roof
a **cat** on hot bricks
do something more than someone has had hot **dinners**
drop something like a

hot brick: see **potato**
drop something like a hot **potato**
hot **air**
hot as Hades
a hot **button**
hot on the **heels** of something
hot on your **heels**
a hot **potato**
hot under the **collar**
in hot **water**
in the hot seat
like a hot **knife** through butter
sell like **hot cakes**
strike while the **iron** is hot
too **hot** to handle

hotcakes
sell like hotcakes: see **hot cakes**

hots
have the **hots** for someone

hounds
run with the **hare** and hunt with the hounds

hour
the eleventh **hour**

house
bring the **house** down
eat someone out of **house** and home
get on like a **house** on fire
a halfway **house**
a **house** of cards
not give someone **house** room
put your **house** in order

houses
people who live in **glass** houses shouldn't throw stones
round the **houses**
safe as houses

howl
howl at the **moon**

hue
a **hue** and cry

humble
eat humble **pie**

hump
get the **hump**

over the **hump**
hunt
  run with the **hare** and
  hunt with the hounds
hymn
  sing from the same
  hymn sheet
i
  dot the **i**'s and cross the
  t's
ice
  break the **ice**
  cut no **ice**
  on **ice**
  put something on **ice**
  skate on thin **ice**
iceberg
  the **tip** of the iceberg
icing
  the **icing** on the cake
ill
  it's an ill **wind**
  it's an ill **wind** that
  blows nobody any
  good
image
  the **spit** and image
  the spitting image: see
  spit
inch
  give someone an **inch**
  and they'll take a mile
Indian
  an Indian **summer**
Indians
  too many **chiefs** and
  not enough Indians
injury
  add **insult** to injury
ink
  bleed red **ink**
innings
  have a good **innings**
inside
  have the inside **track**
  know something
  inside and out
  know something
  inside out
insult
  add **insult** to injury
intentions
  the road to **hell** is
  paved with good
  intentions

in-your-face
  in-your-**face**
iron
  an **iron** fist
  an **iron** fist in a velvet
  glove
  an **iron** hand
  strike while the **iron** is
  hot
irons
  have a lot of **irons** in
  the fire
itchy
  itchy **feet**
  itchy **fingers**
ivory
  an **ivory** tower
jack
  before you could **say**
  Jack Robinson
  a **jack** of all trades
  a **jack** of all trades and
  a master of none
jackpot
  hit the **jackpot**
jam
  jam today
  jam tomorrow
  money for jam
jar
  caught with your hand
  in the **cookie** jar
Jell-O
  like trying to nail
  Jell-O to the wall
jewel
  the **jewel** in someone's
  crown
job
  a **hatchet** job
  a **snow** job
Johnny-come-lately
  Johnny-come-lately
join
  join **battle**
joined
  joined at the **hip**
joint
  put someone's **nose** out
  of joint
joker
  the **joker** in the pack
Joneses
  keep up with the
  Joneses

jowl
  cheek by jowl
judge
  sober as a judge
  you can't judge a **book**
  by its cover
juice
  let someone **stew** in
  their own juice
jump
  for the high **jump**
  get a **jump** on someone
  a **hop**, skip, and a jump
  jump down someone's
  throat
  jump on the
  bandwagon
  jump out of your **skin**
  jump **ship**
  jump the **gun**
  jump the **rails**
  jump through **hoops**
  see which way the **cat**
  jumps
jungle
  the **law** of the jungle
jury
  the **jury** is still out
just
  it's just not **cricket**
  just **deserts**
  just up your **street**
kangaroos
  kangaroos in your top
  paddock
keel
  on an even **keel**
keen
  keen as mustard
keeper
  not someone's **keeper**
  not your brother's
  keeper
keg
  sit on a **powder keg**
kettle
  another **kettle** of fish
  a different **kettle** of fish
  a fine **kettle** of fish
  the **pot** calling the
  kettle black
  a pretty **kettle** of fish
kibosh
  put the **kibosh** on
  something

kick
kick against the **pricks**
kick ass
kick butt
kick over the **traces**
kick someone **upstairs**
kick something into **touch**
kick the **bucket**
kick up your **heels**
kick your **heels**
kick-off
for a **kick-off**
kid
handle someone with **kid** gloves
like a kid in a **candy** store
treat someone with **kid** gloves
Kilkenny
fight like **Kilkenny** cats
kill
dressed to kill
kill the fatted **calf**
kill the golden **goose**
kill the **goose** that lays the golden egg
kill two **birds** with one stone
killed
curiosity killed the cat
killing
make a **killing**
king
a king's **ransom**
kingdom
blow someone to **kingdom** come
kiss
the **kiss** of death
kiss-and-tell
kiss-and-tell
kit
the whole kit and **caboodle**
kitchen
if you can't stand the **heat**, get out of the kitchen
too many **cooks** in the kitchen
kite
fly a **kite**
high as a kite

kittens
have **kittens**
knee-high
knee-high to a grasshopper
knees
the **bee's** knees
knell
sound the death **knell**
knickers
get your **knickers** in a twist
knife
before you could **say** knife
like a hot **knife** through butter
like a **knife** through butter
put the **knife** in
twist the **knife**
knife-edge
on a **knife**-edge
walk a **knife**-edge
knight
a **knight** in shining armour
knitting
stick to your **knitting**
knives
the **knives** are out
knock
knock 'em **dead**
knock on **wood**
knock people's **heads** together
knock someone **dead**
knock someone for a **loop**
knock someone for **six**
knock someone off their **pedestal**
knock something into a cocked **hat**
knock something into **shape**
knock something on the **head**
knock **spots** off something
knock the **socks** off someone
knock the **stuffing** out of someone
knock **wood**

knock you off your **perch**
knock your **socks** off
knock-down
a knock-down drag-out **fight**
knocks
the **school** of hard knocks
knot
cut the Gordian **knot**
a Gordian **knot**
tie the **knot**
knots
at a **rate** of knots
tie someone in **knots**
tie yourself in **knots**
know
better the **devil** you know
know how many **beans** make five
know something inside and out
know something inside out
know the **ropes**
know the **score**
know which side your **bread** is buttered
know your **onions**
not know someone from **Adam**
not know your arse from your **elbow**
not know your ass from your **elbow**
the right **hand** doesn't know what the left hand is doing
knuckle
near the **knuckle**
knuckles
rap someone on the **knuckles**
labor: see labour
labour
a **labour** of love
lady
it isn't over until the fat **lady** sings
lam
on the **lam**
lamb
gentle as a lamb

in two **shakes** of a lamb's tail
might as well be hanged for a **sheep** as a lamb
mutton dressed as lamb

lambs
like **lambs** to the slaughter

lame
a lame **duck**

land
the **fat** of the land
land in your **lap**
the land of **milk** and honey
land on your **feet**
the lay of the **land**
the lie of the **land**

land-office
do a **land-office** business

lane
the fast **lane**
the slow **lane**

lap
be thrown into your **lap**
drop into your **lap**
fall into your **lap**
in the **lap** of luxury
in the **lap** of the gods
land in your **lap**

large
large as life

larger
larger than life

lark
happy as a lark
up with the **lark**

Larry
happy as Larry

last
drinking in the last chance **saloon**
famous last **words**
have the last **laugh**
the last chance **saloon**
last **ditch**
the last **straw**
the last **straw** that breaks the camel's back
let the cobbler stick to his **last**
on your last **legs**

stick to your **last**

lather
in a **lather**

laugh
have the last **laugh**
laugh on the other side of your **face**
laugh out of the other side of your **mouth**
laugh up your **sleeve**

laughed
laughed out of **court**

laundry
air your **dirty** laundry in public
a **laundry** list

laurels
look to your **laurels**
not rest on your **laurels**

law
the **law** of the jungle
a **law** unto yourself
lay down the **law**
the **letter** of the law
someone's **word** is law

lay
kill the **goose** that lays the golden egg
lay an **egg**
lay down the **law**
lay it on the **line**
lay it on **thick**
lay it on with a **trowel**
the lay of the **land**
lay something at someone's **door**
lay the **ghost** of something
lay your **cards** on the table
lay yourself **wide** open

lead
go down like a **lead** balloon
have **lead** in your pencil
a **lead** balloon
lead someone by the **nose**
lead someone down the **garden** path
lead someone up the **garden** path
lead with your **chin**
lead you a merry chase: see **dance**

lead you a merry **dance**
put **lead** in your pencil
swing the **lead**
you can lead a **horse** to water but you can't make him drink

leading
the **blind** leading the blind
a leading **light**

leaf
a **fig** leaf
take a **leaf** out of someone's book
turn over a new **leaf**

lean
lean on your **oars**
lean over backward: see **backwards**

leap
a leap in the **dark**

learn
learn the **ropes**

lease
a new **lease** of life
a new **lease** on life

leash
a longer **leash**
on a short **leash**
on a tight **leash**
strain at the **leash**

least
least said, soonest mended

leather
hell for leather

leave
leave a bad **taste** in your mouth
leave no **stone** unturned
leave someone **cold**
leave someone **high** and dry
leave someone holding the **baby**
leave someone holding the **bag**
leave someone in the **lurch**
leave the **nest**
leave yourself **wide** open

leaving
like a rat leaving a sinking **ship**

left
left and right
left, right, and centre
left to your own **devices**
out in left **field**
out of left **field**
the right **hand** doesn't
know what the left
hand is doing
two left **feet**

leg
break a **leg**
cost an **arm** and a leg
give someone a **leg** up
not have a **leg** to stand
on
pull someone's **leg**
talk the hind **leg** off a
donkey

legs
have **legs**
on your last **legs**
with your **tail** between
your legs

lend
lend an **ear** to someone

length
at **arm**'s length

leopard
a **leopard** does not
change its spots

less
there's less to
something than meets
the **eye**

lesser
the lesser evil: see **evils**
the lesser of two **evils**

letter
a dead **letter**
the **letter** of the law
a **red** letter day
to the **letter**

level
a level **playing field**
level the **playing field**
on the **level**

licence
a **licence** to print
money

license: see **licence**

lick
lick someone's **boots**
lick someone's shoes:
see **boots**

lick something into
shape
lick your chops: see **lips**
lick your **lips**
lick your **wounds**

lid
flip your lid
keep the **lid** on
something
put the **lid** on something
put the tin **lid** on
something
take the **lid** off

lie
let sleeping **dogs** lie
the lie of the **land**
lie through your **teeth**
a white **lie**
you have made your
bed and will have to
lie on it

life
big as life: see **large**
bigger than life: see
larger
get a **life**
it's a **dog**'s life
large as life
larger than life
the **life** and soul of the
party
life is a bowl of cherries
the **life** of the party
live the **life** of Riley
a new **lease** of life
a new **lease** on life
shelf life
variety is the spice of
life

lift
lift the **roof**
not lift a **finger**

light
give the green **light**
hide your light under a
bushel
in the cold **light** of day
a leading **light**
light a **fire** under
someone
light as a feather
the **light** at the end of
the tunnel
light the blue **touch
paper**

light the **fuse**
light the **touch paper**
out like a **light**
see the **light**

lightning
lightning does not
strike twice

lights
the **lights** are on but
nobody is at home

lily
gild the **lily**

limb
out on a **limb**

limit
the **sky**'s the limit

line
the bottom **line**
cross the **line**
draw a **line** under
something
draw the **line**
the **end** of the line
get a **line** on someone
hook, line, and sinker
in the firing **line**
in the front **line**
in the **line** of fire
lay it on the **line**
line your **pockets**
not your **line** of country
on **line**
on the front **line**
out of **line**
out of the firing **line**
put something on the
line
put your ass on the **line**
put your neck on the
line
shoot a **line**
step out of **line**
toe the **line**

linen
wash your **dirty** linen
in public

lines
along the right **lines**
the **battle** lines are
drawn
get your lines **crossed**
on the right **lines**
read between the **lines**

lining
every cloud has a
silver lining

a **silver** lining
link
a weak **link**
a weak **link** in the chain
lion
Daniel in the **lion**'s den
the **lion**'s share
put your head into the
lion's mouth
walk into the **lion**'s den
lions
throw someone to the
lions
lip
pay **lip** service to
something
a stiff upper **lip**
there is many a **slip**
twixt cup and lip
lips
lick your **lips**
read someone's **lips**
list
a **hit** list
a **laundry** list
a **shopping** list
litmus
a **litmus** test
little
great **oaks** from little
acorns grow
a little **bird** told me
little **love** lost
a little **tin** god
twist someone around
your little **finger**
wrap someone around
your little **finger**
live
live from **hand** to
mouth
live **hand** to mouth
live high on the **hog**
live in a **fool**'s paradise
live in each other's
pockets
live on borrowed **time**
live on your **nerves**
live the **life** of Riley
a live **wire**
people who live in
glass houses
shouldn't throw stones
lives
have nine **lives**

living
beat the living
daylights out of
someone
scare the living
daylights out of
someone
load
load the **dice** against
someone
loaded
loaded for **bear**
play with a loaded **deck**
loaf
half a **loaf** is better
than none
lock
in lock step: see
lockstep
lock **horns**
lock, stock, and barrel
locker
one **shot** in your locker
lockstep
in **lockstep**
log
easy as falling off a **log**
simple as falling off a
log
loggerheads
at **loggerheads**
loins
gird your **loins**
lone
a lone voice in the
wilderness
a lone **wolf**
plough a lone **furrow**
lonely
plough a lonely **furrow**
long
by a long **chalk**
by a long **shot**
honest as the day is
long
in something for the
long **haul**
a long **face**
a long **haul**
long in the **tooth**
a long **shot**
not long for this **world**
over the long **haul**
to cut a long **story** short
to make a long **story**
short

your long **suit**
longer
a longer **leash**
look
look after **number** one
look a **gift horse** in the
mouth
look **daggers** at
someone
look down your **nose**
at something
look on the bright **side**
look the **part**
look to your **laurels**
looking
like looking for a
needle in a haystack
loop
knock someone for a
loop
throw someone for a
loop
loose
all **hell** breaks loose
at a loose **end**
at loose ends: see **end**
cut **loose**
have a **screw** loose
a loose **cannon**
a loose **cannon** on the
deck
loose **ends**
play **fast** and loose
loosen
loosen the **purse** strings
lorry
off the **back** of a lorry
lose
lose **face**
lose the **battle**, win the
war
lose your **edge**
lose your **marbles**
lose your **rag**
lose your **shirt**
what you lose on the
swings you gain on
the roundabouts
win the **battle**, lose the
war
losing
fight a losing **battle**
loss
a dead **loss**

losses
  cut your **losses**
lost
  little **love** lost
  lost in the **shuffle**
  no **love** lost
lot
  all over the **lot**
  cast your **lot** with
    someone
  have a lot of **irons** in
    the fire
  have a lot on your **plate**
  throw in your **lot** with
    someone
louder
  actions speak louder
    than words
love
  all's **fair** in love and
    war
  cupboard love
  for **love** nor money
  a **labour** of love
  little **love** lost
  the love of money is the
    root of all evil
  no **love** lost
low
  at a low **ebb**
  keep a low **profile**
  search **high** and low for
    something
  take the low **road**
luck
  be **pot** luck
  the **luck** of the draw
  take **pot** luck
lucky
  strike **lucky**
lull
  the lull before the **storm**
lump
  bring a **lump** to your
    throat
  have to **lump** it
  like it or **lump** it
  a **lump** in your throat
lunch
  out to **lunch**
  there's no such thing
    as a free **lunch**
lurch
  leave someone in the
    lurch

luxury
  in the **lap** of luxury
lying
  not take something
    lying down
mackerel
  a **sprat** to catch a
    mackerel
mad
  mad as a hatter
  mad as a hornet
man
  a drowning man will
    clutch at a straw: see
    straws
  every man for himself
    and the **devil** take
    the hindmost
  a **hatchet** man
  the man in the **street**
  a man of **straw**
  the man on the
    Clapham **omnibus**
  no good to man or **beast**
  no use to man or **beast**
  one man's **meat** is
    another man's poison
  the other man's **grass**
    is always greener
  a **straw** man
  your **right**-hand man
map
  on the **map**
marbles
  have all your **marbles**
  lose your **marbles**
  pick up your **marbles**
    and go home
march
  march to a different
    drummer
  march to a different
    tune
  march to the beat of a
    different drummer
  steal a **march**
marching
  marching **orders**
mark
  a black **mark**
  first off the **mark**
  get off the **mark**
  hit the **mark**
  mark **time**
  miss the **mark**

  off the **mark**
  on the **mark**
  overshoot the **mark**
  overstep the **mark**
  quick off the **mark**
  slow off the **mark**
  up to the **mark**
  wide of the **mark**
market
  a cattle **market**
  a meat **market**
marrow
  to the **marrow**
mast
  nail your **colours** to
    the mast
master
  a **jack** of all trades and
    a master of none
masters
  not serve two **masters**
mat
  go to the **mat**
match
  the whole shooting
    match
McCoy
  the real **McCoy**
meal
  make a **meal** of
    something
  a **meal** ticket
  a square **meal**
mean
  mean **curtains**
means
  by fair **means** or foul
meat
  dead **meat**
  meat and drink to
    someone
  the meat in the
    sandwich
  a meat **market**
  one man's **meat** is
    another man's poison
medicine
  give someone a dose of
    their own **medicine**
  give someone a taste of
    their own **medicine**
meet
  make **ends** meet
  meet your **Waterloo**
  never the **twain** shall
    meet

there's less to
something than meets
the **eye**
there's more to
something than meets
the **eye**
melt
butter wouldn't melt
in your mouth
melting
in the **melting pot**
men
dead men's **shoes**
dead men tell no **tales**
the men in grey **suits**
the men in **suits**
separate the **men** from
the boys
sort out the **men** from
the boys
mend
mend **fences**
mend your **ways**
mended
least said, soonest
mended
merry
lead you a merry chase:
see **dance**
lead you a merry **dance**
play merry **hell**
play merry **hell** with
something
there'll be merry **hell**
to pay
mess
a mess of **pottage**
messenger
shoot the **messenger**
mice
when the **cat**'s away,
the mice will play
mick
take the mick: see
mickey
mickey
take the **mickey**
middle
the **piggy** in the middle
play both **ends** against
the middle
middle-of-the-road
middle-of-the-road
midnight
burn the **midnight** oil

midstream
change horses in
midstream
mile
give someone an **inch**
and they'll take a mile
go the extra **mile**
milk
it's no use crying over
spilled **milk**
the land of **milk** and
honey
milk and honey
milk and water
mill
go through the **mill**
grist for the mill
grist to the mill
put through the **mill**
millstone
a **millstone** around
your neck
mince
not mince your **words**
thick as mince
mincemeat
make **mincemeat** of
someone
mind
bear something in **mind**
blow your **mind**
cross your **mind**
give someone a piece of
your **mind**
have a one-track **mind**
in your **mind**'s eye
in your right **mind**
keep something in
mind
mind your **p**'s and **q**'s
out of **sight**, out of
mind
minds
in two **minds**
of two **minds**
mirrors
smoke and mirrors
miss
hit and miss
hit or miss
miss a **beat**
miss the boat
miss the bus
miss the **mark**
not miss a **trick**

mixed
a mixed **bag**
mockers
put the **mockers** on
something
Mohammed
if Mohammed will not
go to the **mountain**,
the mountain must
go to Mohammed
mold: see **mould**
molehill
make a **mountain** out
of a molehill
moment
on the **spur** of the
moment
Monday
a Monday morning
quarterback
money
the **colour** of someone's
money
a **fool** and his money
are soon parted
for **love** nor money
give someone a **run** for
their money
a **licence** to print
money
the love of money is the
root of all evil
money for jam
money for old rope
money is the **root** of all
evil
money talks
put your **money** where
your mouth is
right on the **money**
the smart **money**
throw good **money**
after bad
monkey
cold enough to freeze
the balls off a **brass**
monkey
get the **monkey** off
your back
have a **monkey** on
your back
make a **monkey** out of
someone
monkey business
not give a **monkey**'s

the **organ** grinder's
   monkey
throw a monkey
   wrench into the
   works
monkeys
   a cartload of **monkeys**
   if you pay **peanuts**,
   you get monkeys
monte: see **monty**
month
   flavour of the month
   a **month** of Sundays
monty
   the full **monty**
moon
   ask for the **moon**
   bay at the **moon**
   cry for the **moon**
   howl at the **moon**
   once in a blue **moon**
   over the **moon**
   reach for the moon: see
      stars
moral
   the moral high **ground**
morning
   a Monday morning
      quarterback
moss
   gather moss: see **stone**
   a rolling **stone** gathers
      no moss
moth
   like a **moth** to a flame
motion
   set the **wheels** in
      motion
motions
   go through the **motions**
mould
   break the **mould**
   they broke the **mould**
      when they made
      someone
mountain
   if Mohammed will not
      go to the **mountain**,
      the mountain must
      go to Mohammed
   make a **mountain** out
      of a molehill
   a **mountain** to climb
mountains
   move **mountains**

mouse
   cat and mouse
   a game of **cat** and mouse
   poor as a church mouse
mouth
   all **mouth** and no
      trousers
   all **mouth** and trousers
   born with a **silver**
      spoon in your mouth
   butter wouldn't melt
      in your mouth
   down in the **mouth**
   foam at the **mouth**
   from the **horse**'s mouth
   froth at the **mouth**
   laugh out of the other
      side of your **mouth**
   leave a bad **taste** in
      your mouth
   live from **hand** to mouth
   live **hand** to mouth
   look a **gift horse** in the
      mouth
   make your **mouth**
      water
   a **plum** in your mouth
   put **words** into
      someone's mouth
   put your **foot** in your
      mouth
   put your head into the
      lion's mouth
   put your **money** where
      your mouth is
   shoot your **mouth** off
   speak out of both sides
      of your **mouth**
   take the **words** out of
      someone's mouth
   talk out of both sides of
      your **mouth**
   your **heart** is in your
      mouth
move
   move **heaven** and earth
   move **mountains**
   move the **goalposts**
movers
   the **movers** and shakers
muck
   common as muck
   happy as a pig in muck
mud
   clear as mud

   drag someone through
      the mud
   mud sticks
   sling **mud**
   throw **mud**
   your **name** is mud
muddy
   muddy the **waters**
mule
   stubborn as a mule
murder
   scream bloody **murder**
   scream blue **murder**
muscles
   flex your **muscles**
music
   face the **music**
   music to your ears
mustard
   keen as mustard
   not cut the **mustard**
muster
   pass **muster**
mutton
   mutton dressed as lamb
nail
   another **nail** in the
      coffin
   fight **tooth** and nail
   the final **nail** in the
      coffin
   hit it on the **nail**
   hit the **nail** on the head
   like trying to nail
      Jell-O to the wall
   nail someone to the **wall**
   nail your **colours** to
      the mast
   on the **nail**
nails
   hard as nails
   tough as nails
naked
   the naked **eye**
name
   the name in the **frame**
   the **name** of the game
   a **name** to conjure with
   take someone's **name**
      in vain
   your **name** is mud
narrow
   the **straight** and narrow
nature
   the **nature** of the beast

navel
contemplate your **navel**
navel-gazing
navel-gazing
near
near the **knuckle**
near to the **bone**
neck
breathe down
someone's **neck**
dead from the **neck** up
get it in the **neck**
a **millstone** around
your neck
neck and neck
a **pain** in the neck
put your neck on the
block
put your neck on the
line
risk your **neck**
stick your **neck** out
up to your **neck**
your **neck** of the woods
need
need something like a
hole in the head
needle
like looking for a
needle in a haystack
needles
on **pins** and needles
nellie: see **nelly**
nelly
not on your **nelly**
nerve
strike a raw **nerve**
touch a **nerve**
nerves
a bag of **nerves**
a battle of **nerves**
a bundle of **nerves**
get on someone's
nerves
live on your **nerves**
a war of **nerves**
nest
feather your **nest**
fly the **nest**
foul your own **nest**
leave the **nest**
a **nest** egg
stir up a **hornet**'s nest
net
cast a wide **net**

cast the **net** wider
slip through the **net**
nettle
grasp the **nettle**
new
break a new **path**
break new **ground**
a new **ball** game
new **blood**
a new **broom**
a new **broom** sweeps
clean
a new **lease** of life
a new **lease** on life
new to the **game**
pastures new
turn over a new **leaf**
you can't teach an old
dog new tricks
Newcastle
coals to Newcastle
nice
nice as pie
nice try but no **cigar**
niche
carve a **niche**
nick
in the **nick** of time
nickel
nickel and dime
a wooden **nickel**
nickels
not have two nickels to
rub together
night
call it a night: see **day**
a **night** owl
nine
have nine **lives**
on **cloud** nine
a **stitch** in time saves
nine
the whole nine **yards**
nine-day
a nine-day **wonder**
ninepins
fall like **ninepins**
nines
dress to the nines
nineteen
talk **nineteen** to the
dozen
nip
nip and tuck
nip something in the
bud

nits
pick **nits**
nod
a **nod** and a wink
on the **nod**
no-holds-barred
no-**holds**-barred
noise
empty **vessels** make
the most noise
noises
make **noises**
make the right **noises**
nooks
the **nooks** and crannies
noose
put your **head** in a
noose
nose
bloody someone's **nose**
cut off your **nose** to
spite your face
follow your **nose**
get up someone's **nose**
give someone a bloody
nose
it's no **skin** off my nose
keep your **nose** clean
keep your **nose** out of
something
keep your **nose** to the
grindstone
lead someone by the
nose
look down your **nose**
at something
a **nose** for something
not see beyond the end
of your **nose**
not see beyond your
nose
on the **nose**
pay through the **nose**
for something
plain as the nose on
your face
poke your **nose** into
something
put someone's **nose** out
of joint
rub someone's **nose** in it
rub someone's **nose** in
the dirt
stick your **nose** into
something

thumb your **nose** at someone

turn up your **nose** at something

nosey
a nosey **parker**

nosy: see **nosey**

nothing
much **ado** about nothing

nothing to write **home** about

on a **hiding** to nothing

nuclear
go **nuclear**

nudge
a **nudge** and a wink

nudge-nudge
nudge-nudge, wink-wink

number
a back **number**

do a **number** on someone

have someone's **number**

look after **number** one

someone's **number** is up

numbered
someone's **days** are numbered

numbers
the numbers **game**

nut
do your **nut**

a sledgehammer to crack a **nut**

a tough **nut**

a tough **nut** to crack

nuts
the **nuts** and bolts of something

nutshell
in a **nutshell**

nutty
nutty as a fruitcake

oaks
great **oaks** from little acorns grow

oar
put your **oar** in

oars
lean on your **oars**

rest on your **oars**

oats
sow your wild **oats**

ocean
a **drop** in the ocean

odds
at **odds** with someone

at **odds** with something

pay over the **odds**

odor: see **odour**

odour
in bad **odour**

in good **odour**

off-chance
on the **off-chance**

offer
offer someone a **carrot**

off-the-cuff
off-the-**cuff**

oil
burn the **midnight** oil

no **oil** painting

oil and water

oil the **wheels**

pour **oil** on troubled waters

snake oil

a **snake** oil salesman

strike **oil**

ointment
the **fly** in the ointment

old
a **chip** off the old block

money for old rope

old as the hills

an old **chestnut**

an old **flame**

the old **guard**

an old **hand**

old **hat**

the old **school**

the old **school** tie

an old **wives'** tale

open old **wounds**

reopen old **wounds**

settle an old **score**

tough as old boots

up to your old **tricks**

you can't teach an old **dog** new tricks

oldest
the oldest **trick** in the book

olive
an **olive** branch

omelet: see **omelette**

omelette
you can't make an

omelette without breaking eggs

omnibus
the man on the Clapham **omnibus**

once
once **bitten**

once **bitten**, twice shy

once in a blue **moon**

one
back to **square** one

be **one** up on someone

from **square** one

give with one **hand** and take away with the other

go in one **ear** and out the other

got it in **one**

kill two **birds** with one stone

look after **number** one

one **foot** in the grave

one in the **eye** for someone

one man's **meat** is another man's poison

one sandwich **short** of a picnic

one **shot** in your locker

one **swallow** doesn't make a summer

pull a **fast** one

pull the other one

pull the other one, it's got bells on it

put all your **eggs** in one basket

put **one** over on someone

six of one and half a dozen of the other

there's more than one way to skin a **cat**

when one person sneezes, another catches **cold**

one-day
a one-day **wonder**

one-horse
a one-**horse** race

a one-**horse** town

one-man
a one-man **band**

one-track
have a one-track **mind**

one-way
a one-way **ticket**
one-woman
a one-woman **band**
onions
know your **onions**
open
be **wide** open
blow something **wide** open
the **floodgates** open
keep your **eyes** open
lay yourself **wide** open
leave yourself **wide** open
open and shut
an open **book**
open old **wounds**
open **season**
open someone's **eyes**
open the **floodgates**
open your **eyes**
push at an open **door**
opposite
opposite sides of the same **coin**
oranges
apples and oranges
order
in **apple-pie** order
the **order** of the day
the **pecking** order
put your **house** in order
a tall **order**
orders
marching **orders**
under **starter's** orders
organ
the **organ** grinder's monkey
OTT
OTT: see **top**
over
over the **hill**
over the **hump**
over the **moon**
over the **top**
overdrive
go into **overdrive**
over-egg
over-egg the **pudding**
overplay
overplay your **hand**
overshoot
overshoot the **mark**

overstep
overstep the **mark**
overturn
overturn the **applecart**
owl
a **night** owl
own
hold your **own**
off your own **bat**
on your own **hook**
an own **goal**
under your own **steam**
ox
strong as an ox
oyster
the **world** is your oyster
p
mind your **p's** and q's
pace
at a **snail's** pace
can't stand the **pace**
set the **pace**
paces
put someone through their **paces**
pack
ahead of the **pack**
the **joker** in the pack
pack a **punch**
packed
packed like **sardines**
packing
send someone packing
paddle
paddle your own **canoe**
up the **creek** without a paddle
paddock
kangaroos in your top paddock
page
on the same **page**
turn the **page**
paid
put **paid** to something
pain
a **pain** in the neck
pains
growing **pains**
paint
fresh as paint
paint someone into a **corner**
paint the **town** red

painted
not as **black** as you are painted
painting
no **oil** painting
pair
a safe pair of **hands**
show a clean pair of **heels**
pale
beyond the **pale**
palm
grease someone's **palm**
have someone eating out of the palm of your **hand**
in the palm of your **hand**
pan
flash in the pan
out of the **frying pan** into the fire
pancake
flat as a pancake
Pandora
a **Pandora's** box
pants
catch someone with their **pants** down
fly by the **seat** of your pants
keep your pants on: see **shirt**
wear the pants
paper
can't fight your way out of a **paper** bag
a clean **sheet** of paper
light the blue **touch** paper
light the **touch** paper
not worth the **paper** it's written on
on **paper**
paper over the **cracks**
a paper **pusher**
a **paper** tiger
a **paper** trail
papers
walking **papers**
par
par for the course
parade
rain on someone's **parade**

paradise
  live in a **fool**'s paradise

parapet
  keep your **head** below
    the parapet
  put your **head** above
    the parapet

parcel
  part and parcel

parker
  a nosey **parker**

parrot
  parrot fashion
  sick as a parrot

part
  look the **part**
  part and parcel
  part of the **furniture**
  take something in good
    part

parted
  a **fool** and his money
    are soon parted

party
  bring something to the
    party
  the **life** and soul of the
    party
  the **life** of the party

pass
  give someone the **flick**
    pass
  pass **muster**
  pass the **baton**
  pass the **buck**
  pass the **hat**
  pass the **hat** around
  sell the **pass**

passage
  a **bird** of passage

past
  first past the **post**
  past your sell-by **date**
  wouldn't put it **past**
    someone

pasture
  put someone out to
    pasture

pastures
  fresh **pastures**
  greener **pastures**
  pastures new

pat
  a **pat** on the back
  pat someone on the back

  stand **pat**

patch
  not a **patch** on someone

path
  beat a path to
    someone's **door**
  break a new **path**
  lead someone down the
    garden path
  lead someone up the
    garden path
  off the beaten path: see
    track

path-breaking
  path-breaking

Paul
  rob **Peter** to pay Paul

pave
  pave the **way**

paved
  the road to **hell** is
    paved with good
    intentions

pay
  he who pays the **piper**
    calls the tune
  hit **pay dirt**
  if you pay **peanuts**,
    you get monkeys
  pay **lip** service to
    something
  pay over the **odds**
  pay someone back in
    their own **coin**
  pay through the **nose**
    for something
  rob **Peter** to pay Paul
  strike **pay dirt**
  there'll be **hell** to pay
  there'll be merry **hell**
    to pay

peanuts
  if you pay **peanuts**,
    you get monkeys

pearls
  cast **pearls** before
    swine
  pearls of wisdom

peas
  like two **peas** in a pod

pebble
  not the only **pebble** on
    the beach

pecker
  keep your **pecker** up

pecking
  the **pecking** order

pedestal
  knock someone off
    their **pedestal**
  put someone on a
    pedestal

peel
  slip on a **banana** peel

peeled
  keep your **eyes** peeled

peg
  a square **peg** in a
    round hole
  take someone down a
    peg or two

pegged
  have someone **pegged**

pen
  a **pen** pusher

pencil
  have **lead** in your pencil
  a pencil **pusher**
  put **lead** in your pencil

pennies
  not have two pennies
    to **rub** together
  pinch **pennies**

penn'orth
  your two **penn'orth**

penny
  in for a **penny**, in for a
    pound
  the **penny** drops
  ten a **penny**
  turn up like a bad
    penny
  two a **penny**

penny-wise
  penny-wise and
    pound-foolish

perch
  fall off the **perch**
  fall off your **perch**
  knock you off your
    perch

petard
  hoist by your own
    petard

Peter
  rob **Peter** to pay Paul

phrase
  to coin a **phrase**

pick
  have a **bone** to pick

with someone
pick **nits**
pick someone's **brains**
pick up **steam**
pick up the **baton**
pick up the **pieces**
pick up your **marbles**
   and go home
picnic
   be no **picnic**
   one sandwich **short** of
      a picnic
picture
   get the **picture**
   in the **picture**
   keep someone in the
      picture
   out of the **picture**
   put someone in the
      picture
pie
   American as apple pie
   easy as pie
   eat humble **pie**
   have a **finger** in every
      pie
   have a **finger** in the pie
   nice as pie
   pie in the sky
   sweet as pie
piece
   all of a **piece**
   give someone a piece of
      your **mind**
   a **piece** of cake
   a **piece** of piss
   say your **piece**
   the **villain** of the piece
pieces
   go to **pieces**
   pick up the **pieces**
   shot to **pieces**
pig
   happy as a pig in muck
   like a greased **pig**
   make a **pig**'s ear of
      something
   a **pig** in a poke
   sick as a pig
   squeal like a stuck **pig**
pigeon
   be someone's **pigeon**
pigeons
   put the **cat** among the
      pigeons

piggy
   the **piggy** in the middle
pigs
   pigs might fly
pike
   come down the **pike**
pikestaff
   plain as a pikestaff
pill
   a bitter **pill** to swallow
   sugar-coat the **pill**
   sugar the **pill**
   swallow a bitter **pill**
   sweeten the **pill**
pillar
   from **pillar** to post
   a pillar of strength: see
      tower
   pillar to post
pilot
   on automatic **pilot**
pin
   pin back your **ears**
   pin someone's **ears** back
pinch
   at a **pinch**
   feel the **pinch**
   in a **pinch**
   pinch **pennies**
   take something with a
      pinch of **salt**
pink
   in the **pink**
   tickled **pink**
pins
   for two **pins**
   on **pins** and needles
pint
   a **quart** into a pint pot
pip
   pip someone at the **post**
pipe
   put that in your **pipe**
      and smoke it
pipeline
   in the **pipeline**
piper
   he who pays the **piper**
      calls the tune
piss
   a **piece** of piss
   take the **piss**
pitch
   make a **pitch**
   queer someone's **pitch**

place
   between a **rock** and a
      hard place
   a **place** in the sun
   put someone in their
      place
   your **heart** is in the
      right place
places
   go **places**
plague
   avoid something like
      the **plague**
plain
   plain as a pikestaff
   plain as day
   plain as the nose on
      your face
   plain **sailing**
plan
   a **game** plan
plank
   walk the **plank**
planks
   thick as two planks
   thick as two short
      planks
plant
   plant the **seeds** of
      something
plate
   hand someone
      something on a **plate**
   have a lot on your **plate**
   have enough on your
      plate
   have your **plate** full
   step up to the **plate**
platter
   on a **platter**
   on a silver **platter**
play
   child's play
   not play with a full
      deck
   play a straight **bat**
   play **ball**
   play both **ends** against
      the middle
   play **ducks** and drakes
      with someone
   play **fast** and loose
   play for **time**
   play **gooseberry**
   play **hardball**

play **hell**
play **hell** with
something
play into someone's
hands
play it by **ear**
play merry **hell**
play merry **hell** with
something
play **possum**
play second **fiddle**
play someone at their
own **game**
play the **field**
play the **game**
play to the **gallery**
play with a loaded **deck**
play with a stacked
deck
play with **fire**
play your **ace**
play your cards close
to the **vest**
play your cards close
to your **chest**
play your **cards** right
play your **trump** card
the **state** of play
when the **cat's** away,
the mice will play

playing
a level **playing field**
level the **playing field**

pleased
pleased as **punch**

plot
the **plot** thickens

plough
plough a lonely **furrow**

ploughshares
beat **swords** into
ploughshares

plowshares: see
ploughshares

plug
pull the **plug** on
something

plum
a **plum** in your mouth

plumb
plumb the **depths**

plunge
take the **plunge**

poacher
poacher turned

gamekeeper

pocket
burn a **hole** in your
pocket
dig deep into your
pocket
dip into your **pocket**
in someone's **pocket**
out of **pocket**

pockets
line your **pockets**
live in each other's
pockets

pod
like two **peas** in a pod

point
boiling **point**
not to put too fine a
point on it
point the **finger** at
someone
a sticking **point**

points
brownie points
score **points**

poison
one man's **meat** is
another man's poison

poisoned
a poisoned **chalice**

poke
a **pig** in a poke
poke your **nose** into
something

pole
the greasy **pole**
pole position
wouldn't touch
something with a
barge **pole**
wouldn't touch
something with a
ten-foot **pole**

poles
poles apart

polish
spit and polish

pond
a big **fish** in a small
pond

pony
a **dog** and pony show

poor
poor as a church mouse

pop
pop your **clogs**

port
a **port** in a storm

position
pole position

possum
play **possum**

post
deaf as a post
first past the **post**
from **pillar** to post
pillar to post
pip someone at the **post**

posted
keep someone **posted**

pot
be **pot luck**
go to **pot**
in the **melting pot**
keep the **pot** boiling
the **pot** calling the
kettle black
a pot of **gold**
the pot of gold at the
end of the **rainbow**
a **quart** into a pint pot
take **pot luck**
a watched **pot** never
boils

potato
a **couch** potato
drop something like a
hot **potato**
a hot **potato**

potatoes
small **potatoes**

pottage
a mess of **pottage**

pound
in for a **penny**, in for a
pound
your **pound** of flesh

pound-foolish
penny-wise and
pound-foolish

pour
it never rains but it
pours: see **rain**
pour cold **water** on
something
pour **oil** on troubled
waters

powder
keep your **powder** dry
sit on a **powder keg**

power
all **power** to your elbow

the **power** behind the
throne
practice: see practise
practise
practise what you
preach
praise
damn with faint **praise**
praises
sing the **praises** of
someone
prawn
come the raw **prawn**
prayer
not have a **prayer**
on a **wing** and a prayer
preach
practise what you
preach
pregnant
you can't be half
pregnant
press
a full-court **press**
press the right **button**
pretty
pretty is as pretty does:
see **handsome**
a pretty **kettle** of fish
sit **pretty**
prick
prick the **bubble**
prick up your **ears**
pricks
kick against the **pricks**
pride
swallow your **pride**
prime
prime the **pump**
print
the fine **print**
a **licence** to print
money
the small **print**
prisoners
take no **prisoners**
problems
teething problems
production
make a **production** of
something
profile
keep a low **profile**
promise
promise the **earth**

proof
the **proof** of the
pudding is in the
eating
prove
the **exception** that
proves the rule
public
air your **dirty** laundry
in public
do your **dirty** washing
in public
wash your **dirty** linen
in public
pudding
over-egg the **pudding**
the **proof** of the
pudding is in the
eating
pull
pull the other one
pull the other one, it's
got bells on it
pulling
like pulling **teeth**
pump
prime the **pump**
punch
pack a **punch**
pleased as **punch**
punches
not pull your **punches**
pull no **punches**
roll with the **punches**
pup
sell someone a **pup**
purse
hold the **purse** strings
loosen the **purse** strings
tighten the **purse**
strings
you can't make a **silk**
purse out of a sow's
ear
push
get the **push**
if **push** comes to shove
push at an open **door**
push the **boat** out
push the **envelope**
push up the **daisies**
when **push** comes to
shove
pusher
a paper **pusher**

a pencil **pusher**
a pen **pusher**
putty
putty in your hands
q
mind your **p's** and q's
QT
on the **QT**
quart
a **quart** into a pint pot
quarterback
a Monday morning
quarterback
queer
in Queer **Street**
queer someone's
pitch
question
the 64,000 **dollar**
question
beg the **question**
quick
cut someone to the
quick
quick off the **mark**
quits
call it **quits**
quote
quote, end quote
quote, unquote
rabbit
like a rabbit caught in
the **headlights**
pull a rabbit out of the
hat
race
a one-**horse** race
the **rat** race
rack
on the **rack**
put someone on the
rack
rack and ruin
rack your **brains**
rag
lose your **rag**
a red rag to a **bull**
ragged
run someone **ragged**
rags
rags to riches
riches to **rags**
rails
jump the **rails**
off the **rails**

on the **rails**
rain
 it never rains but it
  pours: see **rain**
 rain on someone's
  parade
 right as rain
 take a **rain** check
rainbow
 at the end of the
  rainbow
 the pot of gold at the
  end of the **rainbow**
rainbows
 chase **rainbows**
raining
 it's raining **cats** and
  dogs
rainy
 save for a rainy **day**
raise
 not raise a **finger**
 raise **Cain**
 raise **eyebrows**
 raise its **head**
 raise someone's
  hackles
 raise the **ante**
 raise the **roof**
rake
 rake over the ashes: see
  coals
 rake over the **coals**
 rake someone over the
  coals
 thin as a rake
ram
 ram something down
  someone's **throat**
ranch
 bet the **ranch**
rank
 break rank: see **ranks**
 pull **rank**
ranks
 break **ranks**
 close **ranks**
ransom
 hold someone to
  ransom
 a king's **ransom**
rap
 rap someone on the
  knuckles
 take the **rap**

rare
 rare as **hen**'s teeth
 a rare **bird**
rat
 like a rat leaving a
  sinking **ship**
 the **rat** race
 smell a **rat**
rate
 at a **rate** of knots
rattle
 rattle someone's **cage**
 rattle your **sabre**
raw
 come the raw **prawn**
 get a raw **deal**
 strike a raw **nerve**
ray
 a **ray** of sunshine
reach
 reach for the moon: see
  stars
 reach for the sky: see
  stars
 reach for the **stars**
 reach **rock** bottom
read
 read between the **lines**
 read someone's **lips**
 read the **riot** act
 read the **runes**
ready
 rough and ready
real
 the real **McCoy**
reap
 as you sow, so shall
  you **reap**
 reap the harvest
 reap the whirlwind
 sow the wind and **reap**
  the whirlwind
 you **reap** what you sow
rear
 rear its **head**
 rear its ugly **head**
rearguard
 fight a **rearguard** action
reason
 without **rhyme** or
  reason
recharge
 recharge your **batteries**
reckoning
 the **day** of reckoning

record
 off the **record**
 a **track** record
red
 bleed red **ink**
 in the **red**
 out of the **red**
 paint the **town** red
 red as a beet
 red as a beetroot
 a red **flag**
 a red flag before a **bull**
 a red **herring**
 red in **tooth** and claw
 a **red** letter day
 a red rag to a **bull**
 red **tape**
 roll out the red **carpet**
 see **red**
red-handed
 catch someone
  red-handed
reed
 a broken **reed**
reign
 a **reign** of terror
rein
 give someone free **rein**
 hold someone on a tight
  rein
 keep a tight **rein** on
  someone
reinvent
 reinvent the **wheel**
reopen
 reopen old **wounds**
reply
 a **dusty** reply
rest
 a **cut** above the rest
 not rest on your **laurels**
 rest on your **oars**
revolving
 the revolving **door**
rhyme
 without **rhyme** or
  reason
rich
 rich as Croesus
 strike it **rich**
riches
 rags to riches
 riches to **rags**
ride
 a free **ride**

go along for the **ride**
ride **herd** on someone
ride **high**
ride high in the **saddle**
ride out the **storm**
ride **roughshod** over
    someone
ride the **crest** of the
    wave
ride two **horses** at the
    same time
take someone for a **ride**
riding
be riding for a **fall**
right
along the right **lines**
give your right **arm**
in your right **mind**
left and right
left, right, and centre
make the right **noises**
on the right **lines**
on the right **track**
play your **cards** right
press the right **button**
right as rain
the right **hand** doesn't
    know what the left
    hand is doing
right off the **bat**
right on the **button**
right on the **money**
right up your **alley**
right up your **street**
start off on the right
    foot
your **heart** is in the
    right place
right-hand
your **right**-hand man
your **right**-hand
    woman
rights
bang to **rights**
dead to **rights**
Riley
live the **life** of Riley
ring
alarm **bells** ring
the **brass** ring
ring a **bell**
ring off the **hook**
ring someone's **bell**
ring the **changes**
throw your cap into the

ring: see **hat**
throw your **hat** into the
    ring
warning **bells** ring
ringer
a dead **ringer** for
    someone
rings
run **rings** round
    someone
ringside
a **ringside** seat
a **ringside** view
riot
read the **riot** act
run **riot**
rise
get a **rise** out of
    someone
rise to the **bait**
someone's **hackles** rise
take the **rise** out of
    someone
risk
risk your **neck**
river
sell someone down the
    river
road
down the **road**
the **end** of the road
get the **show** on the
    road
hit the **road**
the road to **hell** is
    paved with good
    intentions
take the high **road**
take the low **road**
rob
rob **Peter** to pay Paul
rob the **cradle**
robbery
daylight **robbery**
highway **robbery**
Robinson
before you could **say**
    Jack Robinson
rock
at **rock** bottom
between a **rock** and a
    hard place
hit **rock** bottom
reach **rock** bottom
rock the **boat**

rock you back on your
    heels
rocker
off your **rocker**
rocket
not **rocket** science
a **rocket** scientist
rocks
on the **rocks**
rod
make a **rod** for your
    own back
roll
heads roll
on a **roll**
roll in the **aisles**
roll out the red **carpet**
roll with the **punches**
rolling
a rolling **stone**
a rolling **stone** gathers
    no moss
set the **ball** rolling
Romans
when in **Rome**, do as
    the Romans do
Rome
fiddle while **Rome**
    burns
Rome was not built in
    a day
when in **Rome**
when in **Rome**, do as
    the Romans do
roof
a **cat** on a hot tin roof
go through the **roof**
hit the **roof**
lift the **roof**
raise the **roof**
rooftops
shout something from
    the **rooftops**
room
elbow room
no room to swing a **cat**
not give someone
    house room
a smoke-filled **room**
roost
the chickens come
    home to **roost**
come home to **roost**
rule the **roost**
root
the love of money is the

root of all evil
money is the **root** of all
evil
root and branch
take **root**

roots
put down **roots**

rope
at the end of your **rope**
give someone enough
rope
give someone enough
rope to hang
themselves
money for old rope

ropes
know the **ropes**
learn the **ropes**
on the **ropes**
show someone the **ropes**

rose-colored: see
rose-coloured

rose-coloured
rose-coloured glasses:
see **rose-tinted**

roses
come up smelling of
roses
everything is coming
up **roses**
not a bed of **roses**
not all **roses**

rose-tinted
rose-tinted spectacles

rotten
a rotten **apple**

rough
cut up **rough**
a **diamond** in the rough
give someone the rough
side of your **tongue**
rough and ready
rough and tumble
a rough **diamond**
rough **edges**
take the **rough** with
the smooth

roughshod
ride **roughshod** over
someone

roulette
Russian **roulette**

round
get your **tongue** round
something

round the **bend**
round the **houses**
round the **twist**
run **rings** round
someone
a square **peg** in a
round hole

roundabouts
swings and
roundabouts
what you lose on the
swings you gain on
the roundabouts

row
get your **ducks** in a row
a hard **row** to hoe
not worth a row of
beans
skid row
a tough **row** to hoe

rub
not have two nickels to
rub together
not have two pennies
to **rub** together
rub **elbows** with
someone
the **rub** of the green
rub **salt** into the wound
rub **shoulders** with
someone
rub someone's **nose** in it
rub someone's **nose** in
the dirt
rub someone the wrong
way
rub someone up the
wrong **way**
rub your **hands**

Rubicon
cross the **Rubicon**

ruffle
ruffle someone's
feathers

ruffled
smooth ruffled **feathers**

rug
pull the **rug** from under
you
pull the **rug** from under
your feet
snug as a bug in a rug
sweep something under
the rug

ruin
rack and ruin

rule
divide and rule
the **exception** that
proves the rule
a **rule** of thumb
rule the **roost**

run
cut and run
a dummy **run**
give someone a **run** for
their money
hit a **home** run
make your **blood** run
cold
run around in **circles**
run a tight **ship**
run before you can
walk
run out of **gas**
run out of **steam**
run **rings** round
someone
run **riot**
run someone into the
ground
run someone **ragged**
run someone to **earth**
run someone to **ground**
run something into the
ground
run something up the
flagpole
run the **gauntlet**
run the **show**
run to **seed**
run with the **hare** and
hunt with the hounds
still **waters** run deep
take the **ball** and run
with it

runaround
give someone the
runaround

runes
read the **runes**

running
hit the **ground** running
in the **running**
out of the **running**
a running **battle**
up and running

run-of-the-mill
run-of-the-**mill**

rush
fools rush in

fools rush in where
  angels fear to tread
get the **bum**'s rush
a **rush** of blood
a **rush** of blood to the
  head
Russian
  Russian **roulette**
saber: see **sabre**
sabre
  rattle your **sabre**
sabre-rattling
  sabre-rattling
sack
  hit the sack
sacred
  a sacred **cow**
sacrificed
  sacrificed on the **altar**
  of something
saddle
  in the **saddle**
  ride high in the **saddle**
safe
  safe as houses
  safe **hands**
  a safe pair of **hands**
sail
  sail close to the **wind**
  sail under false **colours**
  take the **wind** out of
  someone's sail
sailing
  clear **sailing**
  plain **sailing**
  smooth **sailing**
sails
  take the **wind** out of
  someone's sails
  trim your **sails**
salad
  your **salad** days
salesman
  a **snake** oil salesman
saloon
  drinking in the last
  chance **saloon**
  the last chance **saloon**
salt
  rub **salt** into the wound
  the **salt** of the earth
  take something with a
  grain of **salt**
  take something with a
  pinch of **salt**

  worth their **salt**
sand
  build something on
  sand
  bury your **head** in the
  sand
sandboy
  happy as a sandboy
sands
  shifting **sands**
sandwich
  the filling in the
  sandwich
  the meat in the
  sandwich
  one sandwich **short** of
  a picnic
sardines
  packed like **sardines**
sauce
  what's **sauce** for the
  goose is sauce for the
  gander
save
  save **face**
  save for a rainy **day**
  save someone's **bacon**
  save your **skin**
  a **stitch** in time saves
  nine
saved
  saved by the **bell**
saving
  a saving **grace**
sawdust
  spit and sawdust
say
  before you could **say**
  Jack Robinson
  before you could **say**
  knife
  say your **piece**
  wouldn't say boo to a
  goose
scales
  the **scales** fall from
  your eyes
  tip the scales
scare
  scare the living
  daylights out of
  someone
scene
  set the **scene**
scenes
  behind the **scenes**

scent
  scent **blood**
  throw someone off the
  scent
school
  the old **school**
  the old **school** tie
  the **school** of hard
  knocks
science
  blind someone with
  science
  not **rocket** science
scientist
  a **rocket** scientist
score
  know the **score**
  score **points**
  settle an old **score**
  settle a **score**
scorned
  hell hath no fury like a
  woman scorned
scrape
  bow and scrape
  scrape the **barrel**
  scrape the bottom of the
  barrel
scratch
  from **scratch**
  not up to **scratch**
  scratch the **surface**
  scratch your **head**
  you scratch my **back**
  and I'll scratch yours
scream
  scream bloody **murder**
  scream blue **murder**
screw
  have a **screw** loose
  tighten the **screw** on
  someone
  turn the **screw** on
  someone
screwed
  have your **head**
  screwed on
screws
  put the **screws** on
  someone
Scylla
  between **Scylla** and
  Charybdis
sea
  all at **sea**

at **sea**

between the **devil** and the deep blue sea

a **sea** change

there are other **fish** in the sea

there are plenty more **fish** in the sea

seal

seal someone's **fate**

sealed

signed and sealed

signed, sealed, and delivered

seams

burst at the **seams**

come apart at the **seams**

fall apart at the **seams**

search

search **high** and low for something

season

open **season**

seat

fly by the **seat** of your pants

in the **catbird** seat

in the driver's **seat**

in the driving **seat**

in the hot **seat**

on the **edge** of your seat

a **ringside** seat

take a back **seat**

second

get to second **base**

play second **fiddle**

a second **bite** at the cherry

a second **wind**

security

a **security** blanket

see

not see beyond your **nose**

not see someone for **dust**

not see the forest for the **trees**

not see the wood for the **trees**

see **eye** to eye with someone

see **red**

see someone in their

true **colours**

see the **light**

see which way the **cat** jumps

suck it and see

seed

eat your **seed** corn

go to **seed**

run to **seed**

seed corn

seeds

plant the **seeds** of something

sow the **seeds** of something

seen

haven't seen **hide** nor hair of someone

have seen better **days**

wouldn't be seen **dead**

seize

seize the **day**

self

a **shadow** of your former self

sell

sell like **hot cakes**

sell like hotcakes: see **hot cakes**

sell someone a **bill** of goods

sell someone a **pup**

sell someone down the **river**

sell someone **short**

sell the **pass**

sell yourself **short**

sell your **soul**

sell-by

past your sell-by **date**

send

send someone packing

send someone to **Coventry**

send someone to the **showers**

separate

separate the grain from the **chaff**

separate the **men** from the boys

separate the **sheep** from the goats

separate the wheat from the **chaff**

serve

not serve two **masters**

service

pay **lip** service to something

set

not set in **stone**

not set the **world** on fire

set out your **stall**

set the **ball** rolling

set the **heather** on fire

set the **pace**

set the **scene**

set the **stage** for something

set the **wheels** in motion

set you back on your **heels**

set your **cap** at someone

set your **face** against something

set your **sights** on something

set your **teeth** on edge

settle

the **dust** settles

settle an old **score**

settle a **score**

sevens

at **sixes** and sevens

seventh

in seventh **heaven**

shade

put someone in the **shade**

shades

shades of

shadow

afraid of your own **shadow**

a **shadow** of your former self

shake

more things than you can shake a **stick** at

shake the **dust** of somewhere from your feet

shakers

the **movers** and shakers

shakes

in two **shakes**

in two **shakes** of a lamb's tail

no great **shakes**
shape
  knock something into **shape**
  lick something into **shape**
  shape up or ship out
  whip something into **shape**
share
  the **lion**'s share
sharp
  the sharp **end**
shave
  a close **shave**
shed
  shed **crocodile** tears
sheep
  the black **sheep**
  the black **sheep** of the family
  like sheep to the slaughter: see **lambs**
  make **sheep**'s eyes
  might as well be hanged for a **sheep** as a lamb
  separate the **sheep** from the goats
  a sheep in **wolf**'s clothing
  sort out the **sheep** from the goats
  a **wolf** in sheep's clothing
sheet
  a clean **sheet**
  a clean **sheet** of paper
  sing from the same hymn sheet
  sing from the same song sheet
  white as a sheet
sheets
  three **sheets** to the wind
shelf
  on the **shelf**
  shelf life
shell
  come out of your **shell**
  go into your **shell**
  a **shell** game
shifting
  shifting **sands**
shine
  make **hay** while the

sun shines
  take a **shine** to someone
  take the **shine** off something
shining
  a **knight** in shining armour
ship
  abandon a sinking **ship**
  abandon **ship**
  don't spoil the **ship** for a ha'porth of tar
  jump **ship**
  like a rat leaving a sinking **ship**
  run a tight **ship**
  shape up or ship out
  a sinking **ship**
  when your **ship** comes in
shirt
  a **hair** shirt
  keep your **shirt** on
  lose your **shirt**
  put your **shirt** on something
  a **stuffed shirt**
shit
  the **shit** hits the fan
  up shit **creek**
shoe
  drop the other **shoe**
  if the **shoe** fits
  the shoe is on the other **foot**
shoe-in: see **shoo-in**
shoes
  dead men's **shoes**
  fill someone's **shoes**
  in someone's **shoes**
  lick someone's shoes: see **boots**
  step into someone's **shoes**
shoestring
  on a **shoestring**
shoo-in
  be a **shoo-in**
shoot
  shoot a **line**
  shoot **daggers** at someone
  shoot down in **flames**
  shoot for the same **target**

shoot from the **hip**
  shoot the **breeze**
  shoot the **messenger**
  shoot your **bolt**
  shoot your **mouth** off
  shoot yourself in the **foot**
  a **turkey** shoot
shooting
  like shooting **fish** in a barrel
  the whole shooting **match**
shop
  all over the **shop**
  a **bull** in a china shop
  close up **shop**
  like a child in a sweet shop: see **candy**
  shop talk
  shut up **shop**
  a talking **shop**
  a talk **shop**
  talk **shop**
shopping
  a **shopping** list
short
  by the **short** and curlies
  by the short **hairs**
  draw the short **straw**
  get the short end of the **stick**
  have a short **fuse**
  on a short **fuse**
  on a short **leash**
  one sandwich **short** of a picnic
  sell someone **short**
  sell yourself **short**
  several cards **short** of a full deck
  short **shrift**
  thick as two short planks
  to cut a long **story** short
  to make a long **story** short
shot
  be **shot** of something
  by a long **shot**
  get **shot** of something
  give something your best **shot**
  a long **shot**
  one **shot** in your locker

a **shot** across someone's bows
a **shot** in the arm
a shot in the **dark**
shot to **pieces**
a warning **shot**
a warning **shot** across someone's bows

shots
call the **shots**

shoulder
a **chip** on your shoulder
cry on someone's **shoulder**
give someone the cold **shoulder**
put your **shoulder** to the wheel
a **shoulder** to cry on
shoulder to shoulder
straight from the **shoulder**

shoulders
carry the **weight** of the world on your shoulders
rub **shoulders** with someone

shout
shout something from the **rooftops**

shove
if **push** comes to shove
when **push** comes to shove

show
a **dog** and pony show
get the **show** on the road
run the **show**
show a clean pair of **heels**
show someone the **ropes**
show your **hand**
show your **teeth**
show your true **colours**
steal the **show**
stop the **show**

showers
send someone to the **showers**
a trip to the **showers**

shrift
short **shrift**

shrinking
no shrinking **violet**

shuffle
lost in the **shuffle**

shut
open and shut
shut up **shop**
with your **eyes** shut

shy
once **bitten**, twice shy

sick
sick as a dog
sick as a parrot
sick as a pig
sick to the back **teeth**

side
from the wrong side of the **tracks**
get out of **bed** the wrong side
give someone the rough side of your **tongue**
the **grass** is always greener on the other side of the fence
know which side your **bread** is buttered
laugh on the other side of your **face**
laugh out of the other side of your **mouth**
let the **side** down
look on the bright **side**
the other side of the **coin**
sunny **side** up
a **thorn** in your side

sides
opposite sides of the same **coin**
speak out of both sides of your **mouth**
two sides of the same **coin**

sieve
a brain like a **sieve**

sight
out of **sight**, out of mind
a **sight** for sore eyes

sights
have something in your **sights**
set your **sights** on something

sign
sign someone's **death** warrant
sign your own **death** warrant

signals
smoke signals

signed
signed and sealed
signed, sealed, and delivered

silk
you can't make a **silk** purse out of a sow's ear

silver
born with a **silver** spoon in your mouth
every cloud has a **silver** lining
on a silver **platter**
a **silver** lining

simple
simple as falling off a **log**

sing
it isn't over until the fat **lady** sings
sing a different tune
sing for your **supper**
sing from the same hymn sheet
sing from the same song sheet
sing the **praises** of someone
sing the same song
sing the same tune

singing
all-singing, all-dancing

sink
sink or swim
sink your **teeth** into something

sinker
hook, line, and sinker

sinking
abandon a sinking **ship**
like a rat leaving a sinking **ship**
a sinking **ship**

sit
sit on a **powder keg**
sit on the **fence**
sit on your **hands**
sit **pretty**

sitting
a sitting **duck**

six
hit someone for **six**
knock someone for **six**
six of one and half a
dozen of the other

sixes
at **sixes** and sevens

size
cut someone down to
size
try something on for
size

skate
skate on thin **ice**

skates
get your **skates** on

skeleton
the skeleton at the **feast**
a **skeleton** in the closet
a **skeleton** in the
cupboard

skid
skid row

skids
on the **skids**
put the **skids** under
something

skin
by the **skin** of your
teeth
get under someone's
skin
get under your **skin**
it's no **skin** off my nose
jump out of your **skin**
make your **skin** crawl
save your **skin**
skin and bone
skin and bones
slip on a **banana** skin
there's more than one
way to skin a **cat**
a thick **skin**
a thin **skin**

skinned
keep your **eyes** skinned

skip
a **hop** and a skip
a **hop**, skip, and a jump

skittles
not all **beer** and skittles

skunk
drunk as a skunk

sky
out of a clear blue **sky**

pie in the sky
reach for the sky: see
stars
the **sky**'s the limit

sky-high
blow something
sky-high

slack
cut someone some **slack**
take up the **slack**

slap
a **slap** in the face
a **slap** on the wrist

slate
a clean **slate**
on the **slate**
wipe the **slate** clean

slaughter
like **lambs** to the
slaughter
like sheep to the
slaughter: see **lambs**

sledgehammer
a sledgehammer to
crack a **nut**

sleep
not get a **wink** of sleep
not sleep a **wink**

sleeping
let sleeping **dogs** lie
a sleeping dog: see **dogs**

sleeve
have a card up your
sleeve
have an ace up your
sleeve
have something up
your **sleeve**
laugh up your **sleeve**
wear your **heart** on
your sleeve

sliced
the best thing since
sliced **bread**

sling
sling **mud**
sling your **hook**

slings
slings and arrows

slip
a **slip** of the tongue
slip on a **banana** peel
slip on a **banana** skin
slip through the **cracks**
slip through the **net**

there is many a **slip**
twixt cup and lip

slippery
slippery as an eel
a slippery **slope**

slope
a slippery **slope**

slow
the slow **lane**
slow off the **mark**

small
a big **fish** in a small
pond
it's a small **world**
small **beer**
small **potatoes**
the small **print**
small **world**

smart
a smart **alec**
a smart aleck: see **alec**
a smart **cookie**
the smart **money**

smell
smell a **rat**
wake up and smell the
coffee

smelling
come up smelling of
roses

smile
smile from **ear** to ear

smoke
blow **smoke**
blow **smoke** in
someone's eyes
blow **smoke** in
someone's face
go up in **smoke**
put that in your **pipe**
and smoke it
smoke and mirrors
smoke signals
there's no **smoke**
without fire
where there's **smoke**
there's fire

smoke-filled
a smoke-filled **room**

smoking
a smoking **gun**

smooth
smooth ruffled **feathers**
smooth **sailing**
take the **rough** with
the smooth

snail
at a **snail**'s pace

snake
a **snake** in the grass
snake oil
a **snake** oil salesman

snap
snap someone's **head** off

sneeze
when one person
sneezes, another
catches **cold**

snook
cock a **snook** at
someone

snow
a **snow** job
white as snow

snug
snug as a bug in a rug

sober
sober as a judge

sock
put a **sock** in it

socks
knock the **socks** off
someone
knock your **socks** off
pull your **socks** up
work your **socks** off

soft
have a soft **spot** for
someone
a soft **touch**

song
for a **song**
make a **song** and dance
about something
on **song**
sing from the same
song sheet
sing the same song

soonest
least said, soonest
mended

sore
like a **bear** with a sore
head
a **sight** for sore eyes
stick out like a sore
thumb

sorrows
drown your **sorrows**

sort
sort out the **men** from
the boys
sort out the **sheep** from
the goats

soul
bare your **soul**
keep **body** and soul
together
the **life** and soul of the
party
sell your **soul**

sound
empty **vessels** make
the most sound
sound as a bell
sound the death **knell**

soup
in the **soup**

sour
sour **grapes**

sow
as you sow, so shall
you **reap**
sow the **seeds** of
something
sow the wind and **reap**
the whirlwind
sow your wild **oats**
you can't make a **silk**
purse out of a sow's
ear
you **reap** what you sow

spade
call a **spade** a spade

Spain
castles in Spain

span
spick and span

spanner
throw a **spanner** in the
works

spark
a bright **spark**

sparks
sparks fly
strike **sparks** off each
other

speak
actions speak louder
than words
speak of the **devil**
speak out of both sides
of your **mouth**
speak **volumes**
speak with forked
tongue

spectacles
rose-tinted spectacles

spectre
the spectre at the **feast**

speed
bring someone up to
speed
bring something up to
speed

spell
spell **curtains**

spic: see **spick**

spice
variety is the spice of
life

spick
spick and span

spike
spike someone's **guns**

spill
spill the **beans**
spill your **guts**

spilled
it's no use crying over
spilled **milk**

spin
in a flat **spin**
in a **spin**
spin your **wheels**

spit
the dead **spit**
the **spit** and image
spit and polish
spit and sawdust
spit in someone's **eye**
spit in the **wind**
spit out the **dummy**
spit the **dummy**

spite
cut off your **nose** to
spite your face

spitting
the spitting image: see
spit

splash
make a **splash**

split
split **hairs**

spoil
a bad **apple** spoils the
barrel
don't spoil the **ship** for
a ha'porth of tar
too many **cooks** spoil
the broth

spoke
put a **spoke** in someone's wheel

sponge
throw in the sponge: see **towel**

spoon
born with a **silver** spoon in your mouth
the wooden **spoon**

spot
have a soft **spot** for someone
hit the **spot**
on the **spot**

spots
knock **spots** off something
a **leopard** does not change its spots

spout
up the **spout**

sprat
a **sprat** to catch a mackerel

spread
spread like **wildfire**
spread yourself too **thin**
spread your **wings**

spring
no **spring** chicken

spur
on the **spur** of the moment

spurs
earn your **spurs**
win your **spurs**

square
back at **square** one
back to **square** one
fair and square
from **square** one
on the **square**
a square **meal**
a square **peg** in a round hole
square the **circle**

squeaky
squeaky **clean**

squeal
squeal like a stuck **pig**

squib
a damp **squib**

stab
a stab in the **dark**

stab someone in the **back**

stable
close the stable **door** after the horse has bolted

stack
blow your **stack**
stack the cards
stack the deck

stacked
play with a stacked **deck**

stage
centre stage
set the **stage** for something

stake
go to the **stake**

stalking
a stalking **horse**

stall
set out your **stall**

stamping
stamping **ground**

stand
can't stand the **pace**
if you can't stand the **heat**, get out of the kitchen
make your **hair** stand on end
not have a **leg** to stand on
stand on your own **feet**
stand on your own two **feet**
stand out like a sore **thumb**
stand **pat**
stand something on its **head**
stand the **test** of time
stand up and be counted

standard
the **standard** bearer

star
hitch your **wagon** to a star

stars
reach for the **stars**
stars in your eyes

start
start a **hare**

start off on the right **foot**

starter
under **starter's** orders

starting
off the starting **blocks**

starts
in **fits** and starts

state
the **state** of play

steady
a steady **hand** on the tiller

steal
steal a **march**
steal someone's **clothes**
steal someone's **thunder**
steal the **show**

steam
blow off **steam**
full **steam** ahead
have steam coming out of your **ears**
a **head** of steam
let off **steam**
pick up **steam**
run out of **steam**
under your own **steam**

steer
a **bum** steer
steer **clear**
steer someone **clear** of something

step
in lock step: see **lockstep**
step into someone's **boots**
step into someone's **shoes**
step on someone's **toes**
step out of **line**
step up to the **plate**

stew
in a **stew**
let someone **stew**
let someone **stew** in their own juice

stick
carrot and stick
carry a big **stick**
get hold of the wrong end of the **stick**
get the short end of the **stick**

get the wrong end of the **stick**
in a cleft **stick**
let the cobbler stick to his **last**
more things than you can shake a **stick** at
mud sticks
stick out like a sore **thumb**
a **stick** to beat someone with
stick to your **guns**
stick to your **knitting**
stick to your **last**
stick your **head** in a noose
stick your **neck** out
stick your **nose** into something
thin as a stick
wield a big **stick**

sticking
a sticking **point**

stick-in-the-mud
a stick-in-the-**mud**

sticky
bat on a sticky **wicket**
on a sticky **wicket**

stiff
stiff as a board
a stiff upper **lip**

still
the **jury** is still out
still **waters** run deep

sting
a **sting** in the tail
take the **sting** out of something

stir
stir up a **hornet**'s nest

stitch
a **stitch** in time
a **stitch** in time saves nine

stock
lock, stock, and barrel

stomach
butterflies in your stomach

stomping
stomping **ground**

stone
kill two **birds** with one stone
leave no **stone** unturned

like getting **blood** out of a stone
not set in **stone**
a rolling **stone**
a rolling **stone** gathers no moss
a **stone**'s throw

stones
people who live in **glass** houses shouldn't throw stones

stony
fall on stony **ground**

stools
caught between two **stools**
fall between two **stools**

stop
the **buck** stops here
pull out all the **stops**
stop in your **tracks**
stop someone in their **tracks**
stop something dead in its **tracks**
stop something in its **tracks**
stop the **show**

storage
into cold **storage**

store
give away the **store**
like a kid in a **candy** store

stories
tall stories

storm
the calm before the **storm**
the **eye** of the storm
the lull before the **storm**
a **port** in a storm
ride out the **storm**
a **storm** in a teacup
take somewhere by **storm**
weather the **storm**

story
a **cock** and bull story
to cut a long **story** short
to make a long **story** short

straight
the **home** straight
keep a straight **face**

play a straight **bat**
the **straight** and narrow
a straight **arrow**
straight as a die
straight from the **shoulder**

strain
strain at a **gnat**
strain at a **gnat** and swallow a camel
strain at the **leash**

straw
draw the short **straw**
a drowning man will clutch at a straw: see **straws**
the final **straw**
the last **straw**
the last **straw** that breaks the camel's back
make **bricks** without straw
a man of **straw**
a **straw** man
the **straw** that breaks the camel's back

straws
clutch at **straws**
grasp at **straws**
straws in the wind

streak
talk a blue **streak**

stream
on **stream**

street
in Queer **Street**
just up your **street**
the man in the **street**
right up your **street**

streets
streets ahead

strength
a pillar of strength: see **tower**
a **tower** of strength

stretch
at full **stretch**
the **home** stretch

stride
get into your **stride**
hit your **stride**
put someone off their **stride**
take something in **stride**

take something in your
stride
strike
lightning does not
strike twice
strike a **blow** against
something
strike a **blow** for
something
strike a raw **nerve**
strike **gold**
strike **home**
strike it **rich**
strike **lucky**
strike **oil**
strike **pay dirt**
strike **sparks** off each
other
strike while the **iron** is
hot
strikes
three **strikes** against
someone
two **strikes** against
someone
string
another **string** to your
bow
have someone on a
string
strings
apron strings
hold the **purse** strings
loosen the **purse** strings
many strings to your
bow: see **string**
pull **strings**
pull the **strings**
tighten the **purse**
strings
with no **strings** attached
without **strings**
with **strings**
strip
tear a **strip** off someone
tear someone off a **strip**
stroke
put someone off their
stroke
strokes
broad brush **strokes**
broad **strokes**
different **strokes** for
different folks

strong
strong as a bull
strong as a horse
strong as an ox
strut
strut your **stuff**
stubborn
stubborn as a mule
stuck
squeal like a stuck **pig**
stuff
strut your **stuff**
stuffed
a stuffed **shirt**
stuffing
knock the **stuffing** out
of someone
stumbling
a stumbling **block**
stump
on the **stump**
style
cramp someone's **style**
suck
suck it and see
teach your
grandmother to
suck eggs
sucker
give a sucker an even
break
sugar
sugar the **pill**
sugar-coat
sugar-coat the **pill**
suit
follow **suit**
suit someone down to
the **ground**
your long **suit**
suits
the men in grey **suits**
the men in **suits**
sully
sully your **hands**
summer
an Indian **summer**
one **swallow** doesn't
make a summer
sun
make **hay** while the
sun shines
a **place** in the sun
Sundays
a **month** of Sundays

sunny
sunny **side** up
sunshine
a **ray** of sunshine
supper
sing for your **supper**
sure
sure as eggs
sure as eggs is eggs
surface
scratch the **surface**
swallow
a bitter **pill** to swallow
one **swallow** doesn't
make a summer
strain at a **gnat** and
swallow a camel
swallow a bitter **pill**
swallow your **pride**
swear
swear **blind**
swear **up** and down
sweat
blood, sweat, and tears
by the **sweat** of your
brow
sweat **blood**
sweep
make a clean **sweep**
a new **broom** sweeps
clean
sweep something under
the **carpet**
sweep something under
the **rug**
sweep the **board**
sweet
cop it **sweet**
like a child in a sweet
shop: see **candy**
sweet as pie
a sweet **tooth**
sweeten
sweeten the **pill**
swim
sink or swim
swim against the **tide**
swim with the **tide**
swine
cast **pearls** before
swine
swing
get into the **swing** of
something
go with a **swing**

in full **swing**
no room to swing a **cat**
swing in the **wind**
swing the **lead**

swinging
come out swinging

swings
swings and roundabouts
what you lose on the **swings** you gain on the roundabouts

Swiss
more holes than **Swiss cheese**

sword
a double-edged **sword**
the **Sword** of Damocles
a two-edged **sword**

swords
beat **swords** into ploughshares
cross **swords**
turn **swords** into ploughshares

system
get something out of your **system**

systems
all **systems** go

t
dot the **i**'s and cross the **t**'s
to a **T**: see **tee**

table
drink someone under the **table**
get your **feet** under the table
lay your **cards** on the table
on the **table**
under the **table**

tables
turn the **tables**

tabs
keep **tabs** on someone

tacks
get down to **brass tacks**

tail
cannot make **head** or tail of something
chase your own **tail**
in two **shakes** of a lamb's tail

on your **tail**
a **sting** in the tail
the **tail** wags the dog
turn **tail**
with your **tail** between your legs
with your **tail** up

tale
a **cock** and bull tale
an old **wives'** tale

tales
dead men tell no **tales**
tall tales

talk
money talks
shop talk
talk a blue **streak**
talk **nineteen** to the dozen
talk of the **devil**
talk out of both sides of your **mouth**
talk over someone's **head**
a talk **shop**
talk **shop**
talk the hind **leg** off a donkey
talk through your **hat**
talk **turkey**
talk under **water**

talking
a talking **shop**

tall
a tall **order**
tall stories
tall tales

tangent
go off at a **tangent**
go off on a **tangent**

tangled
a tangled **web**

tango
it takes two to **tango**

tap
on **tap**

tape
red **tape**

taped
have got something **taped**

tar
don't spoil the **ship** for a ha'porth of tar
tar someone with the

same **brush**

target
shoot for the same **target**

taste
give someone a taste of their own **medicine**
leave a bad **taste** in your mouth
taste **blood**

tea
not for all the **tea** in China
not your **cup** of tea

teach
teach your **grandmother** to suck eggs
you can't teach an old **dog** new tricks

teacup
a **storm** in a teacup

teapot
a **tempest** in a teapot

tear
tear a **strip** off someone
tear someone off a **strip**
tear your **hair** out

tears
blood, sweat, and tears
shed **crocodile** tears

tee
to a **tee**

teeth
armed to the **teeth**
by the **skin** of your teeth
cut your **teeth**
fed up to the back **teeth**
get the **bit** between your teeth
get your **teeth** into something
gnashing of **teeth**
gnash your **teeth**
grind your **teeth**
grit your **teeth**
have **teeth**
lie through your **teeth**
like pulling **teeth**
rare as **hen's** teeth
set your **teeth** on edge
show your **teeth**
sick to the back **teeth**
sink your **teeth** into something

wailing and gnashing
of **teeth**

weeping and gnashing
of **teeth**

would give your **eye**
teeth for something

teething
teething problems
teething troubles

telegraph
the **bush** telegraph

tell
dead men tell no **tales**
tell someone where to
get off

tempest
a **tempest** in a teapot

ten
ten a **penny**

ten-foot
wouldn't touch
something with a
ten-foot **pole**

tenterhooks
on **tenterhooks**

territory
go with the **territory**

terror
a **reign** of terror

test
the **acid** test
a **litmus** test
stand the **test** of time
test the **water**
test the waters: see
water

tether
at the end of your
tether

thick
in the **thick** of it
in the **thick** of
something
lay it on **thick**
thick as mince
thick as thieves
thick as two planks
thick as two short
planks
thick on the **ground**
a thick **skin**
through **thick** and thin

thicken
the **plot** thickens

thicker
blood is thicker than
water

thick-skinned
thick-skinned: see **skin**

thieves
thick as thieves

thin
into thin **air**
out of thin **air**
skate on thin **ice**
spread yourself too **thin**
thin as a rake
thin as a stick
the thin end of the
wedge
thin on the **ground**
a thin **skin**
through **thick** and thin

thing
the best thing since
sliced **bread**
there's no such thing
as a free **lunch**

things
more things than you
can shake a **stick** at

thinking
put your thinking **cap**
on

thin-skinned
thin-skinned: see **skin**

third
a third **wheel**

thorn
a **thorn** in your flesh
a **thorn** in your side

thought
food for thought

thread
hang by a **thread**

three
three **sheets** to the wind
three **strikes** against
someone

three-ring
a three-ring **circus**

throat
bring a **lump** to your
throat
cut your own **throat**
a **frog** in your throat
grab someone by the
throat
jump down someone's
throat

a **lump** in your throat
ram something down
someone's **throat**
take someone by the
throat

throats
at each other's **throats**

throne
the **power** behind the
throne

throttle
at full **throttle**
in full **throttle**

throw
people who live in
glass houses
shouldn't throw stones
a **stone**'s throw
throw a monkey
wrench into the
works
throw a **spanner** in the
works
throw a wobbler: see
wobbly
throw a **wobbly**
throw a **wrench** into
the works
throw **caution** to the
wind
throw down the
gauntlet
throw good **money**
after bad
throw in the sponge:
see **towel**
throw in the **towel**
throw in your **hand**
throw in your **lot** with
someone
throw **mud**
throw someone a **curve**
throw someone a **curve**
ball
throw someone for a
loop
throw someone off the
scent
throw someone to the
dogs
throw someone to the
lions
throw someone to the
wolves
throw the **baby** out

with the bath water
throw the **book** at
someone
throw your cap into the
ring: see **hat**
throw your **hat** into the
ring
throw your **weight**
about
throw your **weight**
around
throw your **weight**
behind something

thrown
be thrown into your **lap**

thrust
the **cut** and thrust

thumb
have a green **thumb**
a **rule** of thumb
stand out like a sore
thumb
stick out like a sore
thumb
thumb your **nose** at
someone
under someone's **thumb**

thumbs
all fingers and **thumbs**
all **thumbs**
the **thumbs** down
the **thumbs** up
twiddle your **thumbs**

thump
thump the **tub**

thunder
blood and thunder
steal someone's
thunder

ticket
a **dream** ticket
a **meal** ticket
a one-way **ticket**

tickled
tickled **pink**

tide
swim against the **tide**
swim with the **tide**

tie
the old **school** tie
tie someone in **knots**
tie the **knot**
tie yourself in **knots**

tied
fit to be tied

your **hands** are tied

tiger
a **paper** tiger

tight
hold someone on a tight
rein
keep a tight **rein** on
someone
on a tight **leash**
run a tight **ship**

tighten
tighten the **purse**
strings
tighten the **screw** on
someone
tighten your **belt**

tightrope
walk a **tightrope**

tiles
on the **tiles**

till
have your fingers in
the **till**
have your hand in the
till

tiller
a steady **hand** on the
tiller

tilt
tilt at **windmills**

time
big **time**
the big **time**
have a **whale** of a time
hit the big **time**
in the **nick** of time
live on borrowed **time**
mark **time**
play for **time**
ride two **horses** at the
same time
stand the **test** of time
a **stitch** in time
a **stitch** in time saves
nine
time on your hands

tin
a **cat** on a hot tin roof
have a **tin** ear for
something
a little **tin** god
put the tin **lid** on
something
a **tin** god

tinker
not give a **tinker's** cuss

not give a **tinker's**
damn

tip
on the **tip** of your
tongue
the **tip** of the iceberg
tip someone the **wink**
tip the **balance**
tip the scales

tod
on your **tod**

today
jam today

toe
a **toe** in the water
toe the **line**
toe to toe

toes
keep you on your **toes**
make your **toes** curl
step on someone's **toes**
tread on someone's **toes**
turn up your **toes**

toffee
can't do something for
toffee

told
a little **bird** told me

Tom
every **Tom**, Dick, and
Harry

tomorrow
jam tomorrow

ton
come down on someone
like a **ton** of bricks
like a **ton** of bricks

tongs
go at it **hammer** and
tongs
go at someone
hammer and tongs

tongue
bite your **tongue**
find your **tongue**
get your **tongue** round
something
give someone the rough
edge of your **tongue**
give someone the rough
side of your **tongue**
hold your **tongue**
on the **tip** of your
tongue
a **slip** of the tongue

speak with forked **tongue**
tongue in cheek
tongues
tongues are wagging
toot
toot your own **horn**
tooth
an **eye** for an eye, a tooth for a tooth
fight **tooth** and claw
fight **tooth** and nail
long in the **tooth**
red in **tooth** and claw
a sweet **tooth**
top
blow your **top**
kangaroos in your top paddock
off the top of your **head**
on top of the **world**
over the **top**
the top **drawer**
the top of the **heap**
the top of the **tree**
torch
carry a **torch** for someone
carry the **torch**
toss
argue the **toss**
not give a **toss**
toss-up
be a **toss-up**
touch
the common **touch**
an easy **touch**
kick something into **touch**
light the blue **touch paper**
light the **touch paper**
a soft **touch**
touch all the **bases**
touch and go
touch a **nerve**
touch **base**
touch **wood**
touch your **forelock**
wouldn't touch something with a barge **pole**
wouldn't touch something with a ten-foot **pole**

tough
tough as nails
tough as old boots
a tough **cookie**
a tough **nut**
a tough **nut** to crack
a tough **row** to hoe
towel
throw in the **towel**
tower
an **ivory** tower
a **tower** of strength
town
go to **town**
a one-**horse** town
the only **game** in town
paint the **town** red
traces
kick over the **traces**
track
the fast **track**
have the inside **track**
off the beaten **track**
on the right **track**
on the wrong **track**
a **track** record
tracks
cover your **tracks**
from the wrong side of the **tracks**
make **tracks**
stop in your **tracks**
stop someone in their **tracks**
stop something dead in its **tracks**
stop something in its **tracks**
trades
a **jack** of all trades
a **jack** of all trades and a master of none
trail
blaze a **trail**
a **paper** trail
trail your **coat**
train
a **gravy** train
trap
fall into the **trap**
tread
fools rush in where angels fear to tread
tread on someone's **toes**
tread **water**

treat
a **Dutch** treat
treat someone with **kid** gloves
tree
bark up the wrong **tree**
out of your **tree**
the top of the **tree**
up a **gum** tree
trees
not grow on **trees**
not see the forest for the **trees**
not see the wood for the **trees**
trial
a **trial** balloon
trick
do the **trick**
every **trick** in the book
not miss a **trick**
the oldest **trick** in the book
tricks
someone's **bag** of tricks
up to your old **tricks**
up to your **tricks**
you can't teach an old **dog** new tricks
trim
in fighting **trim**
trim your **sails**
trip
a trip to the **showers**
Trojan
a Trojan **horse**
trolley
off your **trolley**
troubled
fish in troubled **waters**
pour **oil** on troubled waters
troubles
teething troubles
trousers
all **mouth** and no trousers
all **mouth** and trousers
catch someone with their trousers down: see **pants**
wear the trousers
trowel
lay it on with a **trowel**

truck
  have no **truck** with
    something
true
  see someone in their
    true **colours**
  show your true **colours**
trump
  play your **trump** card
  a **trump** card
trumpet
  blow your own **trumpet**
trumps
  come up **trumps**
  turn up **trumps**
truth
  the **gospel** truth
try
  nice try but no **cigar**
  try something on for
    size
  try your **wings**
trying
  like trying to nail
    Jell-O to the wall
tub
  thump the **tub**
tub-thumping
  tub-thumping
tuck
  nip and tuck
tucker
  your best **bib** and
    tucker
tug
  tug at the **heartstrings**
  tug your **forelock**
tumble
  rough and tumble
tune
  call the **tune**
  change your **tune**
  dance to someone's
    tune
  he who pays the **piper**
    calls the tune
  march to a different
    tune
  sing a different tune
  sing the same tune
tunnel
  the **light** at the end of
    the tunnel
  tunnel vision
turkey
  talk **turkey**

  a **turkey** shoot
turkeys
  like **turkeys** voting for
    Christmas
turn
  at every **turn**
  not turn a **hair**
  turn a blind **eye** to
    something
  turn a deaf **ear** to
    something
  turn **heads**
  turn in your **grave**
  turn on a **dime**
  turn over a new **leaf**
  turn over in your **grave**
  turn something on its
    head
  turn **swords** into
    ploughshares
  turn **tail**
  turn the **corner**
  turn the other **cheek**
  turn the **page**
  turn the **screw** on
    someone
  turn the **tables**
  turn **turtle**
  turn up like a bad
    penny
  turn up **trumps**
  turn up your **nose** at
    something
  turn up your **toes**
  the **worm** turns
turned
  poacher turned
    gamekeeper
turning
  the **wheels** are turning
turnip
  like getting **blood** out
    of a turnip
turn-up
  a **turn-up**
  a **turn-up** for the books
turtle
  turn **turtle**
twain
  never the **twain** shall
    meet
twice
  lightning does not
    strike twice
  once **bitten**, twice shy

twiddle
  twiddle your **thumbs**
twist
  get your **knickers** in a
    twist
  round the **twist**
  twist in the **wind**
  twist someone around
    your little **finger**
  twist someone's **arm**
  twist the **knife**
twixt
  there is many a **slip**
    twixt cup and lip
two
  a **bird** in the hand is
    worth two in the bush
  caught between two
    stools
  cut two **ways**
  fall between two **stools**
  for two **pins**
  in two **minds**
  in two **shakes**
  in two **shakes** of a
    lamb's tail
  it takes two to **tango**
  kill two **birds** with one
    stone
  the lesser of two **evils**
  like two **peas** in a pod
  not give two hoots: see
    hoot
  not have two nickels to
    rub together
  not have two pennies
    to **rub** together
  not serve two **masters**
  of two **minds**
  put **two** and two
    together
  ride two **horses** at the
    same time
  stand on your own two
    feet
  take someone down a
    peg or two
  thick as two planks
  thick as two short
    planks
  two a **penny**
  two bites of the cherry:
    see **bite**
  two left **feet**
  two sides of the same
    coin

two **strikes** against
 someone
your two **cents'** worth
your two **penn'orth**
two-edged
 a two-edged **sword**
ugly
 rear its ugly **head**
umbilical
 cut the umbilical **cord**
uncle
 Bob's your uncle
unglued
 come **unglued**
unquote
 quote, unquote
unstuck
 come **unstuck**
unturned
 leave no **stone** unturned
upper
 a stiff upper **lip**
 the upper **hand**
uppers
 down on your **uppers**
 on your **uppers**
upset
 upset the **applecart**
upstairs
 kick someone **upstairs**
use
 it's no use crying over
  spilled **milk**
 no use to man or **beast**
vacuum
 in a **vacuum**
vain
 take someone's **name**
  in vain
value
 at **face** value
variety
 variety is the spice of
  life
veil
 draw a **veil** over
  something
velvet
 an **iron** fist in a velvet
  glove
verse
 chapter and verse
vessels
 empty **vessels** make
  the most noise

empty **vessels** make
 the most sound
vest
 play your cards close
  to the **vest**
vicious
 a vicious **circle**
view
 a bird's-eye **view**
 a **ringside** view
 a worm's eye **view**
villain
 the **villain** of the piece
vine
 die on the **vine**
 wither on the **vine**
violet
 no shrinking **violet**
vision
 tunnel vision
voice
 a lone voice in the
  wilderness
 a voice crying in the
  wilderness
volumes
 speak **volumes**
vote
 vote with your **feet**
voting
 like **turkeys** voting for
  Christmas
wag
 the **tail** wags the dog
wagging
 tongues are wagging
wagon
 fall off the **wagon**
 hitch your **wagon** to a
  star
 hitch your **wagon** to
  someone
 on the **wagon**
wagons
 circle the **wagons**
 pull your **wagons** in a
  circle
wailing
 wailing and gnashing
  of **teeth**
wait
 wait on someone **hand**
  and foot
waiting
 a waiting **game**

wake
 in something's **wake**
 in the **wake** of
  something
 wake up and smell the
  coffee
wake-up
 a **wake-up** call
walk
 run before you can
  walk
 walk a **knife**-edge
 walk a **tightrope**
 walk into the **lion**'s den
 walk on **air**
 walk on eggs: see
  eggshells
 walk on **eggshells**
 walk the **plank**
walking
 walking **papers**
wall
 bang your head against
  a brick **wall**
 bang your head against
  a **wall**
 come up against a brick
  wall
 drive someone up the
  wall
 a **fly** on the wall
 go to the **wall**
 the handwriting is on
  the **wall**
 have your **back** to the
  wall
 hit the **wall**
 like trying to nail
  Jell-O to the wall
 nail someone to the **wall**
 the writing is on the
  wall
walls
 climb the **walls**
 walls have ears
war
 all's **fair** in love and
  war
 lose the **battle**, win the
  war
 a war of **nerves**
 a **war** of words
 win the **battle**, lose the
  war
warm
 warm the **cockles** of
  your heart

warmed
like **death** warmed over
like **death** warmed up

warning
warning **bells** ring
a warning **shot**
a warning **shot** across
someone's bows

warpath
on the **warpath**

warrant
sign someone's **death**
warrant
sign your own **death**
warrant

wars
in the **wars**

warts
warts and all

wash
come out in the **wash**
wash your **dirty** linen
in public
wash your **hands** of
something

washing
do your **dirty** washing
in public

watch
on someone's **watch**
watch someone like a
hawk

watched
a watched **pot** never
boils

water
blood is thicker than
water
blow something out of
the **water**
come **hell** or high water
dead in the water
a **fish** out of water
in deep **water**
in hot **water**
keep your **head** above
water
like **water** off a duck's
back
make your **mouth**
water
milk and water
not hold **water**
of the first **water**
oil and water

pour cold **water** on
something
take to something like
a **duck** to water
talk under **water**
test the **water**
throw the **baby** out
with the bath water
a **toe** in the water
tread **water**
water over the dam
water under the bridge
you can lead a **horse** to
water but you can't
make him drink

waterfront
cover the **waterfront**

Waterloo
meet your **Waterloo**

waters
cast your **bread** upon
the waters
fish in troubled **waters**
muddy the **waters**
pour **oil** on troubled
waters
still **waters** run deep
test the waters: see
water

wave
catch the **wave**
on the **crest** of a wave
ride the **crest** of the
wave

wavelength
on the same
wavelength

waves
make **waves**

wax
the whole **ball** of wax

way
be way off **beam**
can't fight your way
out of a **paper** bag
pave the **way**
rub someone the wrong
way
rub someone up the
wrong **way**
see which way the **cat**
jumps
that's the way the
cookie crumbles
there's more than one

way to skin a **cat**
which way the **wind** is
blowing

ways
cut both **ways**
cut two **ways**
mend your **ways**

wayside
fall by the **wayside**

weak
a weak **link**
a weak **link** in the chain

wear
wear the pants
wear the trousers
wear your **heart** on
your sleeve

weather
keep a **weather** eye on
something
make heavy **weather**
of something
under the **weather**
weather the **storm**

web
a tangled **web**

wedge
drive a **wedge** between
people
the thin end of the
wedge

weeping
weeping and gnashing
of **teeth**

weight
carry the **weight** of the
world on your
shoulders
a dead **weight**
pull your **weight**
throw your **weight**
about
throw your **weight**
around
throw your **weight**
behind something
worth your **weight** in
gold

west
go **west**

wet
get your **feet** wet
wet behind the **ears**
a wet **blanket**
wet your **whistle**

whale
have a **whale** of a time
wheat
separate the wheat from the **chaff**
wheel
a big **wheel**
break a **butterfly** on a wheel
a fifth **wheel**
put a **spoke** in someone's wheel
put your **shoulder** to the wheel
reinvent the **wheel**
a third **wheel**
the wheel has come full **circle**
wheels
grease the **wheels**
oil the **wheels**
set the **wheels** in motion
spin your **wheels**
the **wheels** are turning
wheels within wheels
wherefores
the **whys** and wherefores
whet
whet someone's **appetite**
whimper
not with a **bang** but a whimper
whip
crack the **whip**
a fair crack of the **whip**
have the **whip** hand
whip something into **shape**
whipping
a whipping **boy**
whirl
give something a **whirl**
whirlwind
reap the whirlwind
sow the wind and **reap** the whirlwind
whisker
by a **whisker**
within a **whisker** of something
whiskers
the **cat's** whiskers

whistle
blow the **whistle** on someone
wet your **whistle**
whistle **Dixie**
whistle for something
whistle in the **dark**
whistle in the **wind**
whistles
bells and whistles
white
black and white
bleed someone white
in **black** and white
white as a ghost
white as a sheet
white as snow
a white **elephant**
a white **lie**
whiter than **white**
whiter
whiter than **white**
whole
go the whole **hog**
go whole **hog**
the whole **ball** of wax
the whole **caboodle**
whole **cloth**
the whole kit and **caboodle**
the whole nine **yards**
the whole shooting **match**
the whole **works**
whys
the **whys** and wherefores
wick
get on someone's **wick**
wicket
bat on a sticky **wicket**
on a sticky **wicket**
wide
be **wide** open
blow something **wide** open
cast a wide **net**
give someone a wide **berth**
into the wide blue **yonder**
lay yourself **wide** open
leave yourself **wide** open
wide of the **mark**

wider
cast the **net** wider
wield
wield a big **stick**
wig
flip your wig
wild
go **hog** wild
into the wild blue **yonder**
sow your wild **oats**
a wild **card**
a wild **goose** chase
wild **horses**
wilderness
in the **wilderness**
a lone voice in the **wilderness**
a voice crying in the **wilderness**
wildfire
spread like **wildfire**
willies
give you the **willies**
win
lose the **battle**, win the war
win **hands** down
win the **battle**, lose the war
win your **spurs**
wind
blow in the **wind**
get the **wind** up
get **wind** of something
how the **wind** is blowing
in the **wind**
it's an ill **wind**
it's an ill **wind** that blows nobody any good
put the **wind** up someone
sail close to the **wind**
a second **wind**
sow the wind and **reap** the whirlwind
spit in the **wind**
straws in the wind
swing in the **wind**
take the **wind** out of someone's sails
three **sheets** to the wind
throw **caution** to the wind

twist in the **wind**
which way the **wind** is blowing
whistle in the **wind**
windmills
tilt at **windmills**
window
go out of the **window**
go out the **window**
wing
on a **wing** and a prayer
take someone under your **wing**
under the **wing** of someone
wings
clip someone's **wings**
in the **wings**
spread your **wings**
try your **wings**
wink
a **nod** and a wink
not get a **wink** of sleep
not sleep a **wink**
a **nudge** and a wink
tip someone the **wink**
winks
forty **winks**
wink-wink
nudge-nudge, wink-wink
wipe
wipe the **floor** with someone
wipe the **slate** clean
wire
down to the **wire**
a live **wire**
under the **wire**
wires
get your wires **crossed**
wisdom
pearls of wisdom
wither
wither on the **vine**
wives
an old **wives'** tale
wobbler
throw a wobbler: see **wobbly**
wobbly
throw a **wobbly**
wolf
cry **wolf**

keep the **wolf** from the door
a lone **wolf**
a sheep in **wolf**'s clothing
a **wolf** in sheep's clothing
wolves
throw someone to the **wolves**
woman
hell hath no fury like a woman scorned
your **right**-hand woman
wonder
a nine-day **wonder**
a one-day **wonder**
wood
babes in the wood
dead **wood**
knock on **wood**
knock **wood**
not see the wood for the **trees**
touch **wood**
wooden
a wooden **nickel**
the wooden **spoon**
woods
out of the **woods**
your **neck** of the woods
woodwork
come out of the **woodwork**
wool
pull the **wool** over someone's eyes
word
a dirty **word**
get a **word** in edgeways
get a **word** in edgewise
someone's **word** is law
a **word** in someone's ear
words
actions speak louder than words
eat your **words**
famous last **words**
not mince your **words**
put **words** into someone's mouth
take the **words** out of someone's mouth
a **war** of words

work
do someone's dirty **work**
do the **donkey** work
have your **work** cut out
work your **fingers** to the bone
work your **socks** off
works
in the **works**
throw a monkey **wrench** into the works
throw a **spanner** in the works
throw a **wrench** into the works
the whole **works**
the **works**
world
carry the **weight** of the world on your shoulders
dead to the **world**
it's a small **world**
not long for this **world**
not set the **world** on fire
on top of the **world**
out of this **world**
small **world**
the **world** is your oyster
worm
the early **bird** catches the worm
a **worm**'s eye view
the **worm** turns
worms
a bag of **worms**
a can of **worms**
worse
your **bark** is worse than your bite
worth
a **bird** in the hand is worth two in the bush
the **game** is not worth the **candle**
not worth a row of **beans**
not worth the **candle**
not worth the **paper** it's written on
worth their **salt**
worth your **weight** in gold

your two **cents'** worth
wound
  rub **salt** into the wound
wounds
  lick your **wounds**
  open old **wounds**
  reopen old **wounds**
wrap
  wrap someone around
    your little **finger**
  wrap yourself in the
    flag
wraps
  keep something under
    wraps
  take the **wraps** off
    something
  the **wraps** come off
wrench
  throw a monkey
    wrench into the
    works
  throw a **wrench** into
    the works
wring
  wring your **hands**

wringer
  go through the **wringer**
wrist
  a **slap** on the wrist
write
  nothing to write **home**
    about
  something to write
    home about
writing
  the writing is on the
    wall
written
  not worth the **paper**
    it's written on
wrong
  back the wrong **horse**
  bark up the wrong **tree**
  caught on the wrong
    foot
  from the wrong side of
    the **tracks**
  get hold of the wrong
    end of the **stick**
  get off on the wrong
    foot

get out of **bed** the
  wrong side
get the wrong end of
  the **stick**
not put a **foot** wrong
on the wrong **track**
rub someone the wrong
  way
rub someone up the
  wrong **way**
yank
  yank someone's **chain**
yards
  the whole nine **yards**
year
  since the year **dot**
years
  donkey's years
yonder
  into the wide blue
    yonder
  into the wild blue
    yonder
young
  young **blood**
zero-sum
  a **zero-sum** game